PENGUIN  CLASSICS

THOMAS AQUINAS: SELECTED WRITINGS

ST THOMAS AQUINAS was born around 1225 at Roccasecca near Aquino, to the nobleman Landulf of Aquino. Educated by Benedictine monks at Monte Cassino and then at the University of Naples, it was during his time at university, around 1244, that he joined the Dominican monastic order. This decision so shocked the other members of his noble family that they kidnapped him and held him against his will for a year. Despite this, he remained committed to the religious life and, once he was free, Aquinas went to Cologne to study under St Albert the Great. In 1256 he took the degree of Master in Theology, and then embarked on a life of teaching, preaching and writing, living and working in France and Italy. He died from an illness at the abbey of Fossanuova while on his way to attend a meeting of the general council at Lyon in 1274. Thomas Aquinas was formally canonized in 1323.

Aquinas' religious writing has had a significant influence on both theological and philosophical thought through the centuries. His two great works are *Summa contra Gentiles* (1259–64), a treatise on God and his creation, and *Summa theologica* (1266–73), a massive, though unfinished, work, designed as a complete systematic exposition of theology.

RALPH MCINERNY is the Michael P. Grace Professor of Medieval Philosophy at the University of Notre Dame, Indiana. He is a fellow of the Pontifical Academy of Saint Thomas Aquinas and has published several works on the thought of Thomas, most recently *Aquinas and Analogy* (1996) and *Ethica Thomistica* (1997).

THOMAS AQUINAS

Selected Writings

Edited and translated with an introduction and notes by
RALPH MCINERNY

PENGUIN BOOKS

PENGUIN BOOKS

Published by the Penguin Group
Penguin Books Ltd, 80 Strand, London WC2R 0RL, England
Penguin Putnam Inc., 375 Hudson Street, New York, New York 10014, USA
Penguin Books Australia Ltd, 250 Camberwell Road, Camberwell, Victoria 3124, Australia
Penguin Books Canada Ltd, 10 Alcorn Avenue, Toronto, Ontario, Canada M4V 3B2
Penguin Books India (P) Ltd, 11 Community Centre, Panchsheel Park, New Delhi – 110 017, India
Penguin Books (NZ) Ltd, Cnr Rosedale and Airborne Roads, Albany, Auckland, New Zealand
Penguin Books (South Africa) (Pty) Ltd, 24 Sturdee Avenue, Rosebank 2196, South Africa

Penguin Books Ltd, Registered Offices: 80 Strand, London WC2R 0RL, England

www.penguin.com

This translation first published 1998

030

Set in 9.25/11.5 pt Monotype Sabon
Typeset by Rowland Phototypesetting Ltd, Bury St Edmunds, Suffolk
Printed in England by Clays Ltd, St Ives plc

ISBN-13: 978-0-14-043632-7

www.greenpenguin.co.uk

Contents

Introduction

Shortly after Thomas Aquinas died in the Cistercian abbey at Fossanova on 7 March 1274, a message came from the theology faculty at the University of Paris asking that the body of the saintly theologian be sent to Paris for burial and veneration. Although that request was not granted, the body did eventually come to rest in France.

Thomas was buried for the first time before the high altar of the church of the Cistercian abbey in which he had died after a funeral Mass attended by members of his family as well as by fellow Dominicans and other non-Cistercians. Because the subprior at Fossanova was cured of blindness when he touched Thomas's body and soon other miracles occurred, the Cistercians began to fear that the remains would be stolen and taken off to a Dominican resting place. As a result of this fear, the body was disinterred and reinterred at Fossanova several times during the next two years. Jealous of their treasure, the monks took macabre precautions. They 'exhumed the corpse of Brother Thomas from its resting place, cut off the head and placed it in a hiding place in a corner of the chapel'. The idea was that, even if the corpse were taken, the head would be theirs. His sister was given a hand, a finger of which was to describe a grisly trajectory of its own. This story of reverent mutilations is a long one. By the time the canonization process began in 1319 the corpse had been reduced to bones from which the flesh had been removed by boiling. In 1368, the bones were then removed to the Dominican monastery at Toulouse where they remained until the French Revolution. They were then removed to the church of St Sernin in the same city. In 1974, the seventh centenary of the death of Thomas, his remains were returned to the Dominican church in Toulouse, where they have rested to this day.

The fate of Thomas's literary corpus, while not so lurid, has been similarly interesting, as is usually the case with authors who lived before the advent of printing. Manuscripts were copied and recopied and handed on. Some of the manuscripts that Thomas wrote in his own illegible hand have come down to us, as well as many of those written by the secretary-companions assigned to him. Over the years since the invention of printing several editions of his *opera omnia* have appeared, but oddly, when we consider his importance for scholars, the critical edition launched by Leo XIII more than a century ago is still incomplete. It may not be precisely analogous to his body's long trek to Toulouse – thought is more difficult to dismember – but it does sometimes seem that critical editions of a host of lesser medievals will sit upon the shelf before Thomas finds penultimate rest in the literary equivalent of St Sernin. For all that, there is no problem in discovering what Thomas taught, and why. Even the where and when can usually be determined.

THOMAS IN HIS TIME

The life of Thomas is easily told, although of course nearly every element of the account is subject to at least mild disagreement, including the year of his birth. Most likely this took place in 1225 at Roccasecca, in the family castle, where Thomas passed the first five years of his life before being sent, as an oblate, to the great Benedictine monastery of Monte Cassino, some twenty kilometres away. Here Thomas began the study that would characterize his life. His formal education began with a solid grounding in the liberal arts – first the trivium of grammar, rhetoric and dialectic, and then the quadrivium of arithmetic, geometry, music and astronomy. Later Thomas would be at pains to show the compatibility of the liberal arts tradition with the order of learning the philosophical sciences that could be gleaned from Aristotle.

In 1239 Thomas entered the university that Frederick II had founded in Naples. It was here that Thomas first encountered members of the Order of Preachers, the mendicant followers of St Dominic. The young man was attracted to the Dominicans and in April 1244 he took the habit of the order. This decision did not please his family and Thomas was subjected to a year of detention and inept dissuasion, but eventually he was allowed to go north with his new confrères to Paris. Here he continued his studies and met the formidable Dominican, Albert the Great. Three years later, when Albert was sent to Cologne to set up a Dominican House of Studies, he took Thomas with him.

Among many other things, Albert was remarkable for his knowledge of Aristotle. Indeed, he wrote a vast paraphrase of the Aristotelian corpus and a commentary on the *Nicomachean Ethics* while Thomas studied with him in Cologne. Thomas was given the task of preparing the text of the commentary for the stationer, his first literary effort, unless we accept the authenticity of several logical works said to have been composed when he was enduring domestic detention. It should be noted that Thomas had already been introduced to the new Aristotelian learning at Naples under the tutelage of Peter of Ireland. The indefatigable translator Michael Scot was a protégé of Frederick, and translations from the Greek and Arabic went on apace. Already in his late teens, Thomas was reading the natural writings of Aristotle. (Of course the traditional liberal arts curriculum included some logical works of Aristotle.) He clearly preferred the close commentaries of Averroes to the paraphrases of Avicenna. This openness to Greek and Arabic thought was reinforced by Albert during the years in Cologne, and by the time Thomas returned to Paris in 1252 to continue his theological studies, he had an excellent understanding of Aristotle. Moreover, Albert also gave the young friar a thorough grounding in Neoplatonism.

Some maintain that Thomas already functioned as *cursor biblicus* while at Cologne and date his commentary on Isaiah from this period. In Paris, from 1252 to 1256, Thomas was a 'Bachelor of the Sentences' – namely a student of the *Sentences* of Peter Lombard, a twelfth-century bishop of Paris who had sought to summarize in four books the wealth of Christian wisdom. Once the fledgling theologian had exhibited his prowess in explicating both the Old and New Testaments, he turned to Lombard's summary. This is why we find among the works of all the great, and little, medieval theologians a commentary on the *Sentences*.

In the spring of 1256 Thomas was credentialled as a master of theology. For the next three years, as regent master, he occupied one of the two Dominican chairs of theology. But it was not until 1257, that Thomas and his Franciscan counterpart, Bonaventure, were actually accepted by the other masters. This was accomplished by an intervention of the Pope. The mendicants were in bad odour at the University of Paris for a number of reasons, but not least among them would have been the Dominican refusal to join the other masters when they went on strike and removed to Angers and Toulouse in 1229, staying away for two years. During his first regency, Thomas would address the charges and accusations of a theological nature that were brought against the mendicants.

From 1259 until 1268, for ten years, Thomas was in Italy, teaching in various houses of his order. He may have spent some time in his home priory of Naples, it is certain that he was in Orvieto and Viterbo with the papal curia. Towards the end of the decade, from 1265 to 1268, he was regent master in the Dominican House of Studies at Santa Sabina in Rome. This Italian period was among the most fecund of Thomas's life.

When he left Paris, he had already written much, having polished up his commentary on Peter Lombard and produced the *Disputed Question on Truth* as well as some *Quodlibetal Questions*. Two of his better known philosophical works, *On Being and Essence* and *On the Principles of Nature*, actually antedate his first regency at Paris. The unfinished exposition of Boethius's *On the Trinity* dates from the first regency. And there were other works, not least the *Against Those Impugning Religion and the Cult of God*, a response to critics of the mendicant orders. All that prior productivity being acknowledged, the Italian decade was none the less astonishingly productive. Thomas finished the *Summa contra Gentiles*, commented on Job, composed the *Golden Chain*, a composite Patristic commentary on the four Gospels, began the *Summa theologiae* and *Compendium theologiae* as well as the *Disputed Question on the Power of God*. And in Rome, before returning to Paris, he wrote the first of his commentaries on Aristotle, that on the *De anima*.

When Thomas returned to Paris in 1268 for a second stint as regent master he came into a maelstrom created by the so-called Latin Averroists in the arts faculty and the reaction to their excesses on the part of theologians, many of them Franciscans. From 1268 to 1272 Thomas produced many theological works – continuing the *Summa theologiae*, composing the *Disputed Question on Evil* and holding many disputes that became *Quodlibetal Questions*. But this period is of special interest to the philosopher because during it, despite his pressing magisterial tasks as regent master of theology, Thomas commented on eleven other Aristotelian works, although not all of them are complete. One need only consider such polemical works of the same period as *On the Eternity of the World* and *On There Being only One Intellect* to find the reason for this unusual moonlighting production on the part of a regent master of theology. The Latin Averroists adopted as they thought from Aristotle a number of positions which conflicted with the Christian faith; moreover they seemed insouciant about the logical position this put them in. If it is true that the world has always been as Aristotle claimed, then the Christian belief that the world and time had a beginning cannot be true – and vice versa. To their opponents, and Thomas was the most effective, the Latin Averroists seemed to be saying that contradictories can be simultaneously true. This assault on reason was bad enough, but more alarming still, they were suggesting that God proposes for our belief as true something we can know to be false.

Some theologians reacted to this by calling into question the value of studying Aristotle at all, let alone using him in doing theology. Discussion of the 'errors of Aristotle' occupied theologians. This reaction amounted to an acceptance of the claim that Aristotle's doctrine, on significant points – the major 'errors' had to do with personal immortality, the eternity of the world and providence – is incompatible with Christianity. The Latin Averroists themselves were taken to concede this but they did not find it sufficient reason to reject Aristotle. Thomas's mediating view was that the Latin Averroists were wrong on Aristotle who, when properly understood, is an unequivocal boon for the human mind as well as a powerful complement of the faith. The close reading of the Aristotelian text that we find in Thomas's commentaries is an effort to display what the Stagyrite really teaches and the arguments which establish that teaching as true. The commentaries are in many respects at variance with the influential Arabic interpreters of Aristotle, namely Averroes and Avicenna. We will come back to the importance of these commentaries for determining the best way to characterize Thomas as a philosopher.

In 1270, shortly after Thomas's return to Paris, there was a condemnation of the kind of Aristotelianism represented by the Latin Averroists. And it was to become clear that there were theologians who considered the teaching of Thomas Aquinas to be as heterodox as that of the Latin Averroists, but it was not until 1277, three years after the death of Thomas, with the Parisian condemnation of 219 propositions, that teachings of Thomas are found among the proscribed propositions. Clearly Thomas's understanding of Aristotle was not standard fare either in the faculty of arts or in the faculty of theology.

In 1272, Thomas returned to Italy as regent master at Naples. He continued work on Part 3 of the *Summa theologiae*, composed some biblical commentaries, and preached in his native tongue, on one occasion explaining the *Ave Maria*. In 1274, while *en route* to the Council that had been called at Lyons, he fell ill and on 7 March, at Fossanova, died.

WHAT THOMAS TAUGHT

From at least 1248, Thomas devoted himself to the study of theology. Once he had become a master, he held teaching positions in theology for the rest of his life. Of course so many of the major medieval figures were theologians that it has seemed to some that nothing significant in philosophy proper went on during the Middle Ages. This charge has been made by Bertrand Russell, Will Durant and Emile Brehier, among others, and annoying as many have found this, important issues are raised by the judgement, some having to do with latter-day assumptions, others with the medieval master's self-understanding.

The twentieth-century professional philosopher is apt to think of his discipline as not only different from theology but as immune to any of the assumptions of that benighted discipline. The theologian is in thrall to religious beliefs, whereas the philosopher starts with an unadorned mind, at square one, and follows the argument whither it goeth, obedient only to the exigencies of reason – that is, of pure reason. This charming myth has captured the imagination of many philosophers, despite the fact that it cannot account for why they raise the questions they do, in the order they do, and with the quite palpable professional passion that they do.

Such a thinker's charge against the Christian philosopher is of course just, or can be restated so as to make it just. One who accepts Christian revelation as true will no doubt be influenced by that fact as he goes about his philosophical work. Let us call this an antecedent influence on, and the continuing ambience of, his thinking. Those who profess to be shocked by this seem to imagine a philosopher who has no antecedent convictions and no cultural ambience within which he does his professional work. Perhaps this would be possible for pure reason in East Prussia or a disembodied spirit but it is manifestly impossible for any flesh and blood human thinker. Doubtless this is why modern philosophers wearied themselves in the task of finding a method with which to disencumber themselves of all antecedent beliefs. It may seem to amount only to a Johnsonian kick but Kierkegaard's *Johannes Climacus: or De omnibus dubitandum est* is the best purgative for this ailment.

Recognition of the inescapable existential setting of any human activity, including thinking, may seem to relativize all philosophical positions, as if each can be reduced back into its existential antecedents. But these antecedents are manifestly different in the case of the non-believer and believer. Does this mean that what each of them says is thought to be true only because it jibes with the antecedent assumptions of his inquiry? Are truth and falsity to mean only 'true within the assumptions of Christian belief' or 'true within the assumptions of, say, reductive materialism'? That such unexamined if workaday relativism explains a good deal of the failure to communicate between philosophers has been observed by many, not least by Alasdaire MacIntyre. If such relativism were absolute, so to say, philosophical agreement, or disagreement, would be explained by features extrinsic to what is being said.

The way out of utter relativism is to maintain that, whatever one's antecedent existential assumptions, a philosophical position must obey criteria which are public and intrinsically independent of one's motives for philosophizing. Lord Russell set out to show that free love is morally acceptable; he was looking for arguments on behalf of that amorous position. But if his arguments are convincing only to those who share his antecedent dispositions, they may be called rationalizations and not philosophy. So too a Christian sets out to show that God can be known to exist from the world around us, prodded, let us say, by Romans 1.19. But his arguments have to hold in the public philosophical forum and be cogent to those without as well as with faith.

It seemed well to begin with this problem, the problem of Christian Philosophy, because it is often confused with what Thomas meant by theology. There are two kinds of truth about God, Thomas observes. First, truths which can be known by anyone employing his natural capacity to think about the world around us; second, truths which God has revealed about himself and which are accepted as true on the basis of a gratuitously granted disposition of mind called faith. The whole aim of philosophy, as it was begun by the Greeks, is to achieve wisdom; wisdom is knowledge of the first principles and causes; but the first principles and causes are divine. Philosophy by definition strives towards knowledge of the divine, and if it is successful, ends as theology. Truths about God do not begin where philosophy ends; they are the telos of the whole philosophical enterprise. On this basis, Thomas distinguished two kinds of theology, one philosophical, the other Christian theology. On what basis? There are two kinds of truth about God.

In the *Summa contra Gentiles* 1.3 Thomas writes: 'For there are some truths about God which quite exceed the capacity of human reason, for example, that God is three and one, but there are others to which even natural reason can attain, for example, that God exists and that he is one, and others like them, which in fact philosophers have demonstratively proved about God, led on by the light of natural reason.' This distinction between the theology of the philosophers and that of believers provides the basis for a general distinction between philosophy and theology.

Philosophy takes as its starting point knowledge that is in the public domain, which any human mind is in principle capable of knowing. A philosophical position, no matter how sophisticated, is characterized by the implicit promissory note that it can be shown to follow from what we and everyone else already know. Indeed, if this cannot be done, it is the philosopher who loses. In the Aristotelian methodology, it is assumed that latent in ordinary thinking there are certain truths of a necessary kind. Sometimes these are of breathtaking scope, such as, 'It is impossible for something to be and not to be at the same time and in the same respect,' and, 'Two things equal to a third are equal to one another.' These are such that they immediately claim our allegiance once we know what is being said. They are judgements known to be true of themselves, as opposed to being known in dependence on other truths. Acquired knowledge is such that a judgement is seen to be true because of its connection with other judgements already taken to be true. This is the nature of discourse, the Greek term for which is *syllogismos*. *Scientia*, knowledge in the strict sense, is discourse whose conclusion shares in the necessity of the premises from which it follows. That is, not only does it necessarily follow from them – that would be a feature of any successful discursive reasoning or syllogism – but what follows is necessary, that is, it could not be otherwise. Thus science is demonstrative reasoning or apodictic discourse.

This ideal of knowledge is variously attained. Mathematics was taken to exemplify it in an obvious way and the ideal of science thus seems to be simply a suite of demonstrations. Most subject matters do not permit this, needless to say, although Thomas, like Aristotle, thought that there were constitutive demonstrations in our knowledge of nature that permitted us to speak of natural science, even though most of the reasoning in the science falls short of being demonstrative, that is, necessary. Besides mathematics and natural science, there is a theoretical science that Aristotle called theology or first philosophy, and that came to be called metaphysics. If natural science has being as subject to change as its subject and mathematics has quantified being as its subject, metaphysics was assigned being as such, or being as being, as its subject. It is in this culminating intellectual effort that the philosopher achieved some knowledge of God. This is what made it wisdom, according to Aristotle, and that is the goal of philosophizing.[1]

Thus when Thomas speaks of two kinds of truth about God, he is comparing the culminating achievement of philosophy as he found it in Aristotle with the starting point of Christian reflection on revelation. A believer who holds, as Thomas did, that the pagan philosopher Aristotle achieved such truths as that God exists and is one and the like, will then of course notice that such truths are included in revelation, implicitly or explicitly. That is, some truths about God which are in principle knowable – Aristotle knew them – have none the less been proposed for our belief

1. *Book of Causes*, Prologue.

or revealed. Of course Scripture is characterized by those other truths about God – the Trinity, the Incarnation, and the like. Thomas called truths of the first kind, as they figure in revelation, 'preambles of faith', and truths of the second kind, 'mysteries of faith'. He derives a very important result from the fact that some truths about God that are knowable have been included in revelation. If some of the truths about God that have been revealed can come to be known (the preambles), then it is surely reasonable to accept other truths about God found in revelation that cannot be comprehended or understood in this life (the mysteries). This is not a proof of the truth of the mysteries of faith, but rather an argument on behalf of accepting those mysteries as true.

This comparison of philosophy and of 'the science of Sacred Scripture' is not merely adventitious. The discourse that is found in the theological writings of Thomas is unintelligible without acknowledging the influence of Aristotle. The very first question asked in the *Summa theologiae* is, 'What need is there for any science other than the philosophical ones?' This question only makes sense to a reader already acquainted with philosophy. Moreover, the questions that are posed at the outset of sacred science are only meaningful against the background of Aristotelian methodology. To ask what the subject of a science is, what its principles are, how it should make truths about its subject known – these questions only begin to be formulated by the theologians of the thirteenth century. If one looks at the theological work on which they all commented, the *Sentences* of Peter Lombard, he will find no comparable discussions. Peter follows St Augustine's *On Christian Doctrine* in saying that all the things considered in his four volumes are either divine things or signs of them – *res et signum*. This is a far cry from Aristotelian methodology.

The suggestion that a knowledge of the philosophical sciences is presupposed by Christian theology is not merely a pedagogical aside. It points us to the very heart of Thomas's thought. From his earliest theological writings he is employing what he clearly regards as the achievements of Aristotelian philosophy in his reflection on the mysteries of Christian faith. His knowledge of Aristotle, we have noted, would have begun at Monte Cassino, been deepened at Naples and, under the tutelage of Albert the Great, become a comprehensive command of the Philosopher. Impressed as we can be by his grasp of Aristotle when he returns to Paris from Cologne and writes *On Being and Essence* and *On the Principles of Nature* and comments on Peter Lombard, that knowledge grows over the course of his career. When, in the final phase of his academic life, at Rome in 1268 and then during the second regency at Paris and continuing when he returned to Naples, Thomas produces his amazing book by book, chapter by chapter, line by line, word by word, analyses of the Aristotelian corpus, we are getting the fruit of a lifetime's meditation on the works of the magnificent Macedonian who became simply the Philosopher. For others, this may have been merely a conventional sobriquet; for Thomas it was the literal truth.

It will be well to say a few things about some of the key Aristotelian doctrines that define Thomas's thinking.

'All our intellectual knowledge takes its rise from the senses.' This fundamental Aristotelian assumption pervades Thomas's intellectual work, both philosophical and theological. The commensurate object of human thinking is the nature of sensible reality. That is, what anyone can be taken to know are the things around us that we see and touch and smell and hear. Our ideas are in the first instance ideas of them. Since we name things as we know them, our language will reveal this priority of the sensible, the palpable, the visible. The trajectory of human knowing is a movement from what is obvious to us, though hardly most real, to knowledge of the more real but less obvious to us. Things most obvious to us are not obviously the most important things there are. The order of our learning does not match the order of things, as Aristotle took Plato to be saying. It is not subsisting Ideas or ideal Forms with which our mind is most at home, but rather with what we can grasp of the things we see and touch and hear. Knowledge of these sensible things can lead on to knowledge of the less obvious in the sensible world and even beyond the sensible world, but the order of our learning, like the priorities of our language which express our knowing, will reveal the primacy of the sensible.

'Whatever comes about as a result of a change is a composite of stuff and form.' It is scarcely an accident that one of the first philosophical works we have from Thomas's pen – and indeed one of the few purely philosophical works he wrote – is devoted to an exposition of the composition of natural things, that is, of things that have come to be as the result of a change. Written while he was yet a student, *On the Principles of Nature* cannot be read simply as an account of what Aristotle taught. The opusculum is clearly a laying out of what its author regards as the truth of the matter. The least we can say about the end result of a change is that something which did not have a certain characteristic has come to have that characteristic. When Agatha went to Miami she was not tanned, but look at her now. Some subject which was not-P is now P. A lump of clay that previously did not have the shape of my mother-in-law, after minimal manipulation now does. Shapes and forms are ways of discriminating things, of classifying them. The term 'shape', *forma*, comes to be used to talk of temperature and texture and even place, such as Agatha's being in Miami.

This progression and extension of terminology already exhibits a movement from the more to the less obvious. If the subject or matter of such forms as shape and temperature and weight and place is substance – a lump of clay, my mother-in-law, Agatha – the question arises as to how we can speak of substances themselves coming to be. Not just coming to be such-and-such, that is, white or light or over there, but coming to be *tout court*. What could be the subject of the becoming of the subject? We come to know it by an analogy, Aristotle said.

If there are substances, and if substances come to be, and if coming into being involves a subject or matter as well as a form, then we will seek the subject and form of substantial becoming on an analogy with the subject and form of accidental or incidental becoming. In substantial change, the subject cannot be itself a substance, since then the change would be an incidental one; that is, a change in which the subject acquires a form that does not account for its being a substance so much as a tanned, tired and impecunious substance. In the change whereby a substance comes to be a substance, the form must be of a kind that makes a substance to be a substance, not a form that makes an already existing substance to be such-and-such: in Florida, tanned, up to no good.

This pressing on to the principles of substantial becoming from reflections on the way things change colour and place and size and temperature is already a rich lesson in the development of philosophical terminology as Thomas learned it from Aristotle. And like his mentor, Thomas will use this same vocabulary to talk of sensing and imagining and thinking itself, and indeed to speak of the principle of life in living things. The soul is a substantial form. Ultimately, and by a vast stretch of imagination and understanding, he will be able to speak of separated forms. That is, forms of the kind with which Plato blithely began are the hard-won achievements of prolonged philosophical analyses for the Aristotelian. Along the way, thinking about thinking becomes an analysis on the model of physical becoming. Coming to know will thus be spoken of as acquiring a form, but whether in sensing or imagining or understanding, the form will be more unlike than like its physical counterpart, though sufficiently alike to form a pedagogical bridge.

These central tenets concerning progress in knowledge and the mirroring progress in language sank deeply into the mind of St Thomas Aquinas.

His Aristotelianism is not a patina over something more basic, or a terminology to express what he knows on some other basis. In learning from Aristotle Thomas does not of course think of himself as conforming his mind to another's, but rather as conforming his mind to the ways things are, aided in the task by his great precursor, the Philosopher.

Seen from this philosophical perspective, the mysteries of the Christian faith take on an awesome character, unimaginably exceeding the range of human reason. None the less, as the distinction of preambles and mysteries in revealed truths makes clear, Thomas sees philosophy as the necessary instrument for a meditation on faith that exemplifies the Anselmian motto: *fides quaerens intellectum*. Faith is the acceptance as true of what the mind cannot comprehend in this life; theology is the inevitable effort to diminish the strangeness by putting what is believed into juxtaposition with what is known. Theology comes to mimic the methodology of the philosophical sciences, but this never results in knowledge in the usual sense, that is, philosophical knowledge. The starting points of theology are not truths in the public domain, but truths that God has revealed which can only be accepted on his say-so. The theologian will defend those truths against attack, he will undertake to show that nothing we know is in conflict with them, and he will draw out the implications of what has been explicitly revealed, thereby contributing to the development of doctrine of which Cardinal Newman and then Vatican II have spoken. Theology in this sense is not addressed to just anyone; it can be a vehicle of truth only for one who accepts its starting points, and that acceptance has a name, faith.

Thomas's Aristotelianism is obvious in his insistence that God reveals himself to us through images and likenesses. Scripture is figurative and metaphorical, which is a concession to what is easily grasped by the human mind. The creator makes himself known through his creation first of all, and then through the Book, those inspired writings that come to us from the Chosen People. In Christ himself, there is the ultimate concession to our mode of knowing: God becomes man, he walks among us and speaks to us and shows us the way to salvation. And he speaks in parables and stories so that we can be led on from the obvious to the mystery beyond. The sacraments of the Church are also seen as making the spiritual palpable: outward signs of inward grace, in the phrase.

When Thomas undertook his commentaries on Aristotle, he was in part continuing a practice of his mentor Albert. If Thomas's commentary on Aristotle's *On the Soul* does date from 1268 when he was teaching at Santa Sabina in Rome, it could not have been prompted by the controversies raging in Paris. But when Thomas did go back to Paris, his Aristotelian commentaries multiplied and this at a time when he was busy about the many tasks of the regent master of theology. Doubtless the spur was what the so-called Latin Averroists were making of Aristotle. Thomas had long expressed discontent with the commentaries of the Commentator and now he called Averroes the distorter rather than the expositor of Aristotle. These commentaries cannot in any way be seen as a cynical or well-intentioned effort to tailor the Aristotelian text to alien demands, shaping it so that it conformed with Christian doctrine, baptizing Aristotle. It is simply libel to say that Thomas twisted Aristotle for polemical reasons, whether the twisting is taken to be conscious or unconscious. No one who reads *On Whether There Is but One Intellect*, a polemical work of this period, can have any doubt about what Thomas as commentator is doing. The task proceeds on two levels, guided by two overriding questions. First, what does Aristotle actually say? Second, is it true or false? The first question cannot be terminal for Thomas, but it *is* the first question. In this massively impressive effort, Thomas is every bit as much the defender of Aristotle against misreading as he is a defender of the Christian faith.

SKETCH OF THE HISTORY OF THOMISM

The history of Thomism may be said to begin with the condemnation of 1277 already mentioned, and it begins under a cloud. The thought of Aristotle, which had been represented for centuries in Christian education by only a few of his logical writings, begins to be better known in its full scope in the twelfth century when Latin translations of hitherto unknown treatises are made. These translations are sometimes made directly from the Greek but sometimes represent a filtering through intermediate languages. For example, we have a description of the joint work of Christians, Muslims and Jews in Toledo, which involved the translation of the Arabic Aristotle into vernacular Spanish and then into English. As often as not, these latter translations were accompanied by the commentaries of the eponymous commentator Averroes. Avicenna rethought Aristotle at some remove from the text, and he too was translated. Works of medicine and mathematics and astronomy seemed to crowd out the authors whose authority had characterized an education in the liberal arts. The university system, which begins with the thirteenth century – we can date the founding of Paris as 1200 – provided the arena in which the adjustment had to be made to the flood of new literature arriving in Latin translation. The central intellectual feature of Thomas's time is precisely the question of the relation between Aristotle and Christianity.

Of course this is a variation on a theme present from the beginning of Christianity, as Paul's sermon at Athens attests: How does the truth revealed by and in Christ relate to truths already known by the natural efforts of non-believers and believers? In the fledgling university, the natural outgrowth of the monastic and cathedral schools, the attitude towards the new learning was ambivalent. Committees were appointed to study the matter. It was forbidden to read Aristotle – that is, to lecture on him in the classroom – but such prohibitions appear to have had little effect. Eventually, with the bumptious arrival of the so-called Latin Averroists, notably Siger of Brabant, at the end of the third quarter of the thirteenth century, hostility towards Aristotle comes to characterize theologians. Thomas Aquinas sought to find a way between the light-headedness of some masters of arts and his wary fellow theologians. None the less, in 1270 a set of dangerous propositions was condemned.

Roger Marston, who was there, said this of the 1270 condemnation of the unicity of form: 'This opinion was solemnly excommunicated as contrary to the assertion and teaching of the saints, and especially of Augustine and Anselm.' Thus we will find the ensuing struggle described as one for and against Augustinianism. We have mentioned the way the lines were drawn when Thomas returned to Paris in 1269. There was effective agreement between the youthful masters of arts, on the one hand, and theologians, principally Franciscans, on the other, to the effect that the teachings of Aristotle conflicted with Christian faith. The artists were willing to waive that, apparently, and sought to follow Aristotle while they did philosophy and to recite the creed with other Christians at Mass. For Thomas, this amounted to the claim that contradictories could be simultaneously true. He rightly rejected Latin Averroism as embodying such nonsense, and impiety. Clearly the only room for manoeuvre here was to ask whether or not Aristotle was being understood properly.

The 219 propositions contained in the condemnation of 1277, three years after the death of Thomas – the result of a committee appointed by Stephen Tempier, bishop of Paris – gave pause to some friends and enemies of Thomas. Giles of Rome, Godfrey of Fontaines and Henry of Ghent, who had been a member of the commission, expressed surprise at some of the propositions that were taken to be heterodox. The aged Albert the Great returned to Paris to defend his late pupil against the implication of unsound doctrine. Among the 219 condemned propositions, 34 and 77, dealing with the unity of the world, 27, 82, 96 and 191, on the individuation of material and immaterial substances, and 69, 218, 219 on the localization of separated substances, are taken to be aimed at Thomas. But the ante was soon to be raised.

William de la Mare, an English Franciscan, published between 1277 and 1279 a *Correctorium fratri Thomae* in which he undertook to show the questionable positions one can find simply by perusing the beginning of Thomas Aquinas's commentary on the *Sentences* alone. At least four Dominican responses to this attack were published, called appropriately *Correctoria Corruptorii* – correctives of the distortions of Thomas's teaching. These are known by their opening words or *incipits*. Thus the response known as the *Quare*, once thought to be by Giles of Rome, but now attributed to the English Dominican Richard Kampwell (or sometimes to Thomas Sutton), deals with all of the 118 points of dispute raised by de la Mare. Not only is it the most complete reply, but it contains the text of de la Mare. Another response, the *Sciendum*, deals with all the points but without including the text being refuted. The *Circa* is a response attributed to Jean Quidort of Paris, which deals with only the first sixty charges; yet another response, *Quaestiones*, confronts only the first thirty-one charges.

The first and most permanent effect of this controversy, which amounted to a split among the mendicants, was to solidify Dominican identification with the teaching of Thomas and to give Franciscans the character of non-Thomists, if not anti-Thomists. That the initial attack came from an English Franciscan – perhaps inspired by John Peckham, who had been close to Bonaventure in Paris and returned to England as Archbishop of Canterbury – and that the Dominican responses too were largely from Englishmen is a feature of the history of Thomism not without interest. The anti-Thomist tradition among the Franciscans would be continued by John Duns Scotus and William of Ockham.

Sometime around 1286 or 1287, Rambert of Primadizzi, a Dominican of Bologna, published his *Apologeticum veritatis contra Corruptorium*, which takes on not only William de la Mare but such other Franciscan adversaries as Matthew of Acquasparta, Richard Middleton, Henry of Ghent and Giles of Rome. Giles, because of his defence of Thomas's distinction between *esse* and *essentia*, was often thought to be a Thomist but clearly was not. A text of his edited in 1934, called *Egidius contra Thomam*, cites seventy-three alleged errors of Thomas that Giles based on the exposition of Book 1 of the *Sentences* alone. Giles is also known for his *Errores Philosophorum*, in which he contests fourteen positions he attributes to Aristotle. Godfrey of Fontaines, on the other hand, while rejecting the real distinction, defends many Thomistic doctrines.

It should not be thought, however, that Thomas was immediately and universally adopted as intellectual champion by his Dominican confrères. There were anti-Thomist Dominicans, like Durandus de S. Porciano, who was following in the footsteps of his equally anti-Thomist teacher, James of Metz; the reaction to such deviance can be said to have played the unintended role of consolidating Thomas's position within the Order. Durandus's opponent within the Order was Herve Nedellec. Their quarrel continued until 1317 when Durandus was made bishop of Limoux and, in the following year, Herve was elected master general of the Dominicans.

If the foes of Thomas sought discrepancies between his teaching and Christian orthodoxy, Dominicans took up the task of reconciling conflicting statements of Thomas himself. And before the thirteenth century was over, there were already compilations meant to show that Thomas had taught *melius*, better, in dealing with a question at different times, a passage in the *Summa* preferred to its parallel in the *Scriptum* on the *Sentences*.[1] Such concordances multiplied and reached their epitome in the magnificent *Tabula Aurea* of Peter of Bergamo, an index which to this day remains one of the most useful companions to the study of Aquinas.

Jean-Pierre Torrell, O.P., points out that there were also Dominicans indifferent to Thomas; for example, Ulrich of Strasbourg who had studied under Albert at the same time as Thomas.

It is remarkable that Dante places in the same circle of heaven Thomas Aquinas, Bonaventure and Siger of Brabant. *The Divine Comedy* takes place in Holy Week of 1300 and Dante not only anticipates the canonizations of Bonaventure and Thomas, but may be the only one who regarded Siger as their intellectual and spiritual equal. How did Dante come by his knowledge of the events that link these three? (Bonaventure's principal function in the *Comedy* is to praise Dominic, and Thomas in turn praises Francis, but also plays a dominant role in the circle of the sun.) When Dante set about the plan of study that he tells us of at the end of *La Vita Nuova*, he is thought to have frequented both the Franciscan and Dominican houses of study in Florence; his Dominican teacher was one Remigio dei Girolami, who had studied under Thomas Aquinas during

---

1. See R. A. Gauthier, O.P., 'Les "Articuli in quibus frater Thomas melius in Summa quam in Scriptis" ', *Recherches de théologie ancienne et médiévale* (1952), pp. 271–326.

the saint's second Parisian regency. The prominence of Thomas in the *Paradiso* doubtless did as much as anything else to secure his place as the leading thinker of the thirteenth century.

Capreolus, the so-called *princeps Thomistarum*, entitled his chief work *Defences of the Theology of Saint Thomas Aquinas*, which gives us, according to Cornelio Fabro, a good sense of the Thomistic school of the fifteenth century. Capreolus died in 1444. Peter Nigri, a Hungarian who wrote a summary of Thomistic doctrine, *Clypeus thomisticus*, died in 1492, and Peter of Bergamo produced in the sixteenth century a *Tabula Aurea* which is the first index of Thomas's writings and to this day an indispensable tool for the student of Thomas. In the sixteenth century, in Dominican houses of study, the *Summa theologiae* replaces Lombard's *Sentences*, and there begins the long tradition of commentaries on the theological *summae* of Thomas. There is the great commentator on the *Summa contra Gentiles*, Sylvester of Ferrara, to be followed by Cardinal Thomas de Vio Cajetan, eventual master general of the Dominicans, who had been the papal envoy to Luther, and whose commentary on the *Summa theologiae* is contained, to the consternation of Etienne Gilson, in the Leonine edition of that work. Banez and John of St Thomas give testimony to the extraordinary authority Cajetan acquired as an interpreter of Thomas.

It is thanks to the Belgian, Peter Crockaert, the teacher of Francisco de Vitoria, the eventual glory of Salamanca, that in the sixteenth century the *Summa theologiae* came to replace the *Sentences* of Lombard as the work to be commented on by fledgling Dominican theologians. With Banez and Francisco de Vitoria, the centre of gravity of Thomism shifts to the Iberian peninsula. Vitoria (1483–1546) is praised, and sometimes chided, as a source of modern theories of rights. He is the hero of an interesting little book called *A Spaniard at the UN*.[1]

THE THOMISTIC REVIVAL

It is said that when Gioacchino Pecci was elected Pope in 1878 at the age of sixty-eight, the electors were determined not to have a reign as long as that of his predecessor, Pius IX, who had occupied the See of Peter for thirty-two years. As if to prove that God has a sense of humour, Leo

1. Ramon Hernandez, *Un Español en la ONU*, Biblioteca de Autores Cristianos, Madrid, 1977.

was to reign for twenty-six years. Pio Nono was a liberal who became conservative as a result of disturbing political developments, not least the loss of the papal states. But it is unfair to narrow his concerns to political ones; his misgivings about the times were far ranging. On 8 December 1864 he published the famous *Syllabus of the Principal Errors of Our Epoch*.[1] There are eighty in all and the first eighteen deal with pantheism, naturalism and rationalism. Errors 19 through to 55 deal with the Church and its relation to civil government, but many of the items are quite doctrinal. Indeed, Cardinal Newman's brief against Liberalism appended to his *Apologia pro vita sua* is not unlike the *Syllabus* both in target and in tone. Be that as it may, the document makes it clear that the pontiff did not think things were going well in the modern world. Nowadays, in the wake of 'the failure of the Enlightenment project', this censorious attitude will not surprise. Prominent among the errors condemned by Pius IX were those which saw an inevitable conflict between religion and science, to the detriment of the former. It is this perennial theme of the relation between faith and reason that Leo XIII takes up in his encyclical of 4 August 1879, *Aeterni Patris*. This document officially launched the modern Thomistic revival.

Etienne Gilson succinctly states the aim of the encyclical: '*Aeterni Patris* prescribes that Christian philosophy, as contained in the works of Thomas Aquinas, should be taught in schools in conformity with the teaching of the Church.'[2] Pius IX had discerned a fatal discrepancy between dominant intellectual trends and the teaching of the Church. Leo proposes that a true philosophy, and thus one in accord with both reality and revelation, can be found in Thomas Aquinas.

Leo begins by speaking of the teaching office of the Church, particularly of the popes, and then makes an indictment every bit as sweeping as that of his predecessor. 'The supreme pastors of the Church have always thought it their duty to advance, by every means in their power, science truly so called, and at the same time to provide with special care that all studies should accord with the Catholic faith, especially philosophy . . .' (n. 1) What is the source of the evils that afflict the modern world? '. . . false conclusions concerning divine and human things, which originated in

---

1. See *I Documenti Sociali della Chiesa, da Pio IX a Giovanni Paolo II (1864–1982)*, ed. Raimundo Spiazzi, O.P., Massimo, Milan, 1983. The *Syllabus* is found on pp. 11–22. See *Catholic Dossier*, vol. 2, no. 1, devoted to modernism.
2. See his introductory remarks to the encyclical in the English translation of Jacques Maritain's *Le docteur angélique: St Thomas Aquinas*, Meridian, New York, 1958, pp. 179–81.

the schools of philosophy, have now crept into all the orders of the State, and have been accepted by the common consent of the masses.' (n. 2)

If the trouble stems from false philosophy, it can only be countered by true philosophy. In a series of discussions that may remind the reader of Newman in *The Idea of a University*, Leo speaks first of what the faith has to gain from philosophy and then of what philosophy has to gain from association with the faith. It is not until halfway through the encyclical that Leo, after having sketched the intellectual activities of believers from the Fathers on, dwelling of course on Augustine, mentions Thomas Aquinas. 'Among the Scholastic Doctors, the chief and master of all, towers Thomas Aquinas, who, as Cajetan observes, because "he most venerated the ancient doctors of the Church, in a certain way seems to have inherited the intellect of all".' (n. 17) Thomas's teaching accordingly is seen as the epitome of Christian philosophy; he is regarded as the best of a kind, not as unique. This championing of Thomas is not meant to be detrimental to his great predecessors, contemporaries and successors.

Leo was as concerned with the condition of Christian schooling as he was with the errors in the wider culture. There were antecedents of this turning to Thomas as a way to confront the philosophical errors of the day, but there is little doubt that by the early nineteenth century Thomas had all but disappeared from the Roman schools.[1]

From this starting point in 1879, the Thomistic revival – which turned into a resurgence of Catholic interest in the Middle Ages that was destined to spill over into the academy at large – fanned out over Europe and the Americas. Chairs of Thomistic studies were founded, as that at Louvain which had the future Cardinal Mercier as its first occupant; societies were formed, journals founded, critical editions begun. The critical edition of the works of Thomas which is called the Leonine after its patron Leo XIII was inaugurated: it remains unfinished to this day, although the work continues. It is ironic that medieval authors other than Thomas fared better in the hands of their critical editors. Introductions, summaries, simplifications, explanations and developments of the thought of Thomas

1. Thus Newman, in Rome in 1846, was assured that Aristotle was out of favour and so was Thomas Aquinas. When Newman asked his interlocutor what philosophy they did adopt, 'He said *none*. "Odds and ends – whatever seems to them best . . . *Facts* are the great thing, and nothing else." ' See Marvin R. O'Connell, *Critics on Trial: An Introduction to the Catholic Modernist Crisis*, The Catholic University of America Press, Washington, D.C., 1994, pp. 27–8. See the same author's *The Oxford Conspirators*, Macmillan, New York, 1969.

Aquinas proliferated. If the first impact was fittingly felt in seminaries and ecclesiastical colleges, the Thomistic revival would count among its leaders such laymen as Jacques Maritain, Etienne Gilson and Charles DeKoninck. In North America, thanks largely to the Jesuit colleges and universities scattered across the continent, and to the University of Notre Dame beloved of Chesterton, young men and women took on Thomism as part of the intellectual patrimony of their faith.

The success of the Thomistic revival – and it continued unchecked until the opening of Vatican II in 1962 – was far from a triumph of uniformity of thought. From early on it could be said of Thomists what Dr Johnson said of the Irish: They are an honest race; they never speak well of one another. To the time-honoured *odium theologicum* was added an *odium philosophicum*, with Catholic philosophers sometimes seeing one another as a greater menace than the philosophies the revival had been meant to counter. There were, in short, types of Thomism.

Although it would be possible to see the variety of responses to Thomas in terms of the centres which produced generations of scholars – the Angelicum and Gregorianum in Rome, Louvain and the Saulchoir in Belgium, Toulouse in France, Salamanca in Spain, and, in the new world, Toronto, Laval and the Catholic University of America, it is more convenient to view the matter abstractly (and also somewhat chronologically). It is the differing estimates of the role of Aristotle in the philosophy of Thomas Aquinas that produces the most interesting varieties of Thomism.

ARISTOTLE AND AQUINAS

That St Thomas Aquinas was influenced by Aristotle and that the saint's philosophy and theology are characterized by the assimilation of Aristotle are commonplaces there would seem to be no need to repeat. Reformers deplored this pervasive influence of Aristotle almost as much as Thomas's own contemporaries had, but no one contested that *ubi Thomas, ibi Aristoteles est*. Nor would it enter anyone's mind today to deny this manifest case of intellectual filiation and discipleship. Rather it is the nature and character of the connection that have become the subject of changing estimation.

Not so very long ago, there was a hyphenated entity much heard of, Aristotelico-Thomistic philosophy. Tracing the gradual disappearance of that phrase would tell much about the changing estimate of Thomas's intellectual relation to Aristotle. Those like Gredt who composed an influential handbook of Aristotelico-Thomistic philosophy often seemed to assume that 'Aristotelian' and 'Thomistic' were simple synonyms as applied to philosophy. It is a nice question whether, during this period, Aristotle was much read independently of Thomas's comments on and uses of the great pagan's ideas; a case could be made that often things peculiar to Thomas were blithely attributed to Aristotle. Among the causes explaining the phrase's falling into disuse are two major ones.

The more important, within Thomistic walls, was the increasing insistence on the non-Aristotelian elements in the Thomistic synthesis. The work of Little and Geiger and Fabro drew attention to the influence of Platonism and Neoplatonism on Thomas, and the test case was participation. Although Aristotle, in criticizing Plato, had dismissed participation as an empty metaphor, and Thomas in commenting on the dismissal had not demurred, none the less the notion of participation pervades the work of Thomas.

Plato had posited ideal entities as the only adequate objects of knowledge worthy of the name. To *know* something is to possess a truth which is unaffected by change and time. But whence come such eternal truths? Let us say that you, as the result of years of study, have become the acknowledged expert on the earwig. (Of course you will want to speak of the many species of earwigs, but bear with me.) You have produced the definitive work on earwigs dedicated to friends, Romans and countrymen. Comes now a perky nephew who asks where the earwigs are of which you wrote so authoritatively. Have you kept them? You smile indulgently and then grow a little sad. The moment has arrived when the old must tell grim truths to the young. You tell the child that all the earwigs with whom you spent the best years of your life are long since gone to that bourne from which no earwig returns. All dead? All dead. Then what is your book about, dead earwigs? You explain that your subject is not this or that earwig, but *the* earwig. And where is he? Plato would not want to say that you know the set of existing earwigs, or the set of no longer existing earwigs, nor of course the set of not yet existing earwigs. Your book is of timeless value. But what is its subject if not all those individual earwigs with such a precarious hold on existence?

The nature of earwig. The ideal of earwig. That which it is to be an earwig. As for this earwig and that, they are and are what they are with reference to the ideal timeless earwig which is neither of them. It is this relation that Plato called participation. Aristotle thought it was based on a mistake – and Plato showed misgivings of his own in the *Parmenides*. As has been mentioned, Thomas accepts Aristotle's rejection of participation. And yet participation pervades the work of Thomas.

Almost from the beginning of the *Summa theologiae*, participation occurs and not as a marginal matter but central to the plan of the work just as it is definitive of the being of creatures. What kind of Aristotelian is this, one might ask, who so enthusiastically embraces the key idea of his mentor's chosen philosophical foil? And look at the sympathy with which he comments on Pseudo-Dionysius and Proclus, in the *Book of Causes*. When students of Thomas confronted this, they felt that important features, perhaps the central feature, of Thomas's thought, had been obscured by talk of Aristotelico-Thomism. Indeed, there were not lacking those who seemed to be pushing for its replacement by Platonico-Thomism.

So that was one thing. The growing sense that Aristotle had been oversold as the mentor of Thomas and that in the process essential elements of Thomism had been overlooked.

A second unsettling factor was the revolution in Aristotelian studies brought about by the introduction and then the wholesale pursuit of the genetic or evolutionary approach to the career and writings of Aristotle. If Aristotle became a critic of Plato, the question arose as to when Plato's pupil turned from the master's approach and devised the empirical, naturalistic approach associated with the name of Aristotle. The publication of the fragments of Aristotle's lost works in the mid-nineteenth century did not convince even their editor of the authenticity of the fragments. Why not? Because their outlook was so manifestly Platonic. But others did not see in this an impediment to accepting the fragments as authentic. All one needed to do was assign them to that part of Aristotle's life when he was a Platonist. After all, the Macedonian lived in the Academy nearly two decades until the death of Plato. Take him to be Plato's most precocious disciple. He began writing while still a member of the Academy, while still in agreement with Plato on Ideas, the nature of man, and so on. With age came creativity and intellectual autonomy so that when he left the Academy to found the Lyceum his lectures became the treatises that have come down to us – the treatises that since the first century have been taken to be the quintessential Aristotle. In them we find the anti-Platonist into which Aristotle eventually developed.

What Werner Jaeger did was to locate the development from Platonist to non- or anti-Platonist in the treatises themselves, first in the *Metaphysics*, then in all the others. There followed a flood of alternative and competing and mutually incompatible accounts of Aristotle's development but any of them alone and all taken together decisively shook a reader's confidence that, when picking up the *Metaphysics*, he was confronting a literary whole. But what then to make of Thomas's commentaries on Aristotle, which insist on the inner order of the treatises, not just generally, but in the finest detail, the *Metaphysics* emphatically among them?

The situation was somewhat analogous to that which confronted Thomists in the matter of their master's interpretation of Boethius. Pierre Duhem, a formidable scholar, had claimed that the *diversum est esse et id quod est* axiom of *On the Hebdomads* was nothing else than a distinction familiar from Themistius as well as Aristotle – one they expressed in terms of an infinitive preceded by a definite article and a substantive term in the dative: *to einai anthropo* – whereby the nature and the individual whose nature it is are distinguished. But Thomas clearly reads Boethius as speaking of a distinction between that which exists and its existing. What to do? One would have expected Thomists to take a close look at Duhem's argument and see if it was decisive. Not a bit of it. Almost without quibble Thomists accepted the claim that Boethius had meant something quite different from what St Thomas had said he meant.[1] And was not the same sort of creative reading going on in the commentaries on Aristotle? Rather than dismiss the commentaries or excuse Thomas for his ineptitude, Thomists began to devise exotic theories of what a commentary is and ended by praising rather than blaming Thomas for misinterpreting texts.

For these and other reasons the notion became widespread that the relation between Thomas and Aristotle was a far cry from that suggested by the old phrase Aristotelico-Thomistic. To be sure, we find many references to Aristotle in Thomas, we find the invocation of doctrines, the quoting of phrases. Confronted with these, we should not consult Aristotle for guidance on what Thomas is saying. Far better to see what Thomas means, how he is using the doctrines or language of Aristotle for his own purposes. It is almost as if Aristotle were a language Thomas used to make independent points of his own. And the notion grew that this was somehow one of those medieval practices we oddly find so odd: attributing to authors things they have not said.

It cannot be ignored that some Thomists began to reveal an anti-Aristotelian animus and seemed intent on dissociating Thomas entirely from Aristotle. The idea seemed to be that often Aristotle had meant the direct opposite of what Thomas said he meant and thus appeal to Aristotle

1. See Ralph McInerny, *Boethius and Aquinas*, The Catholic University of America Press, Washington, D.C., 1990, pp. 163–98.

was not only unhelpful, on the above assumption about the nature of commentary, but positively dangerous.[1] Gilson warned his readers that, for Aristotle, whatever exists necessarily exists and therefore cannot be created. How could an uncreated world become part of an account of reality that took the world to be radically contingent, caused all the way down, made not simply to be this or that, to alter, but to be in the first place? Aristotle thus became an absurd element in Thomism.

An oddity of this period was that the commentaries of Thomas on Aristotle continued to be consulted for the light they shed on the text. Aristotelian studies themselves evolved beyond the evolutionary approach and in several ways. Sometimes philosophers, noting the chaos reigning among philologists, said, in effect, let's just read the *Metaphysics* and the other treatises and see what happens (for example, D. J. Allan,[2] Marjorie Grene[3]). They didn't so much refute the philologist as ignore him. But there were those who confronted the claims of such as Werner Jaeger head on and argued that what Jaeger wanted to conclude did not follow from his premisses. Finally Giovanni Reale produced a magisterial interpretation of the *Metaphysics* as a unitary work[4] and buttressed this in his Italian translation of, and comments on, the *Metaphysics*.

Aristotle began to be read again, as he had been for centuries, as the author of a number of treatises, each of which was assumed to be more or less a literary whole – one had to take into account their origin as lectures, of course – and thus as ordered internally as well as to one another. Of course this did not produce uniform interpretations of Aristotle. Disputes of a small and great kind continued to rage, but the manner of their resolution is once more that of the great tradition of Aristotelian interpretation, from the Greek commentators, through Boethius and the medieval commentators, to the Renaissance and modern students of Aristotle up to 1912. It was not part of such discourse to resolve a difficulty of interpretation by imagining a phrase interpolated from elsewhere and gumming up the works. There was more likelihood of talk of inconsistency

1. For example, Mark D. Jordan, 'Thomas Aquinas's Disclaimers in the Aristotelian Commentaries', in *Philosophy and the God of Abraham: Essays in Memory of James A. Weisheipl, OP*, ed. James R. Long, Pontifical Institute of Mediaeval Studies, Toronto, 1991, pp. 99–112. For a refutation, see the Appendix to the doctoral dissertation of Christopher Kaczor, *Proportionalism*, University of Notre Dame, 1996, pp. 295–330.
2. D. J. Allan, *The Philosophy of Aristotle*, London, OUP, 1957.
3. Marjorie Grene, *A Portrait of Aristotle*, Chicago, University of Chicago Press, 1963.
4. Giovanni Reale, *The Concept of First Philosophy and the Unity of the Metaphysics of Aristotle*, tr. by John R. Catan, Albany, State University of New York Press, 1980.

than development. How reconcile the statements about substance in the *Categories* and in the *Metaphysics*? Maybe they can't be reconciled but it was not necessary to see the one as an advance over, or backsliding from, the other.

Quite recently Bertrand Dumoulin[1] has reopened the evolutionary approach in a book that can scarcely be ignored. Moreover, he provides us with the criteria of interpretation relevant to his enterprise. But he presents a far more unified *Metaphysics* than anyone in the Jaegerian heyday; moreover, he invokes the commentary of Thomas Aquinas without apology as casting precious light on the text.

A second subsidiary source of difficulty had to do with the accessibility of Aristotle to St Thomas Aquinas. There is only the flimsiest evidence to suggest that Thomas himself knew Greek and it must be assumed that he was wholly dependent on Latin translations of the treatises. Thanks to the progress of the *Aristoteles Latinus*, we can compare in critical editions the various Latin translations Thomas had at his disposal and the internal evidence of the commentaries as to the ones he used.

The assumption of the following selections is that the philosophy of Thomas Aquinas is fundamentally Aristotelian. Thomists who felt that this committed him to a naive realism that had been discredited by the critical turn devised a transcendental Thomism meant to gain Thomas credence with contemporary philosophers. The textual bases for this interpretation are slender and in any case its chief aim is to fashion what is conceived of as a more defensible philosophy than the one friend and foe alike find in Thomas; for these reasons it does not provide a good basis for a selection of texts.

Perhaps the most prominent interpretation of Thomas Aquinas in recent years is existential Thomism. Earlier we mentioned a number of scholars who maintained that there is no counterpart in Aristotle to Thomas Aquinas's talk of *esse* or the *actus essendi*. But the role of *esse* is taken to be central to Thomas and thus productive of a radical difference between him and Aristotle. The saying that Thomas's metaphysics was radically different from that of Aristotle became commonplace. As it happens, no one has ever succeeded in showing, in methodological terms accepted by Thomas Aquinas, in what this formal or radical difference consists. It is far more defensible to say that the science of metaphysics

---

1. Bertrand Dumoulin, *Analyse génétique de la métaphysique d'Aristote*, Paris, Les Belles Lettres, 1986.

formulated by Aristotle, with being as being as its subject, is formally the same metaphysics that Thomas develops. That development notably takes the form of finding an Aristotelian place for doctrines which are Neoplatonic in origin. The regulative role that Aristotle plays in Thomas's commentaries on the *Book of Causes* and *On the Divine Names* makes this clear.

Is this a reversion to Aristotelico-Thomism in the pejorative sense? Not at all. Rather it is an insistence on the methodological continuity between the Aristotelian base and the subsequent developments in Thomas's philosophy.

My first reaction when I was asked to prepare this volume was that there was no need for it. There are several extremely good collections of Thomas's writings available. In making an analysis of these in order to prove my point, I found myself thinking of another, and as it increasingly seemed to me, a better way of setting out the thought of Thomas. The idea grew on me that a collection that followed the chronology of Thomas's career had much to commend it. The following collection is guided by these two notions. A reader may be surprised at this, given the insistence on the role of Aristotle in the thought of Thomas. After all, the commentaries on Aristotle come late in Thomas's career, beginning in 1268, and come to an end, with his writing generally, in 1273. A moment's thought indicates that this is not a problem. Thomas's close study of Aristotle does not begin with the commentaries, it reaches its culmination in them. From his earliest writings we find him handling the thought of Aristotle with confidence. Misgivings about Averroes and Avicenna are there almost from the beginning. And we find among his earliest writings Thomas's presentation of key philosophical doctrines that are set forth as both Aristotelian and true.

There is an old maxim, passed on by Pico della Mirandola: *Sine Thoma, Aristoteles mutus esset*: without Thomas, Aristotle would be silent. The phrase is a signal tribute to the commentaries. But the reverse of the claim is also true, and true throughout Thomas's career: *Sine Aristotele, Thomas non esset*.

Chronology

1259–68	Thomas in Italy[1]
1263	William of Moerbeke, fellow Dominican, translates Aristotle directly from Greek
1264	Thomas composes the liturgy for the feast of Corpus Christi
1266–70	Averroist controversy at Paris
1268–72	Thomas regent master at Paris for second time
1270	Condemnation of Latin Averroism
1272	Thomas named regent master at Naples
1273	On 6 December Thomas stops writing
1274	On way to Council of Lyons in February Thomas falls ill, is taken to Fossanova where he dies on 7 March
	Letter from the faculty of arts to the master general of the Dominicans
1276	*Roman de la Rose*
1277	Condemnation at Paris of 219 propositions; Thomas comes under posthumous cloud
	At Oxford, Robert Kilwardby, Archbishop of Canterbury and Dominican, condemns propositions of Thomistic inspiration
1284	John Peckham, Archbishop of Canterbury and Franciscan, who had been resident in Paris during Thomas's second regency, confirms condemnations of his predecessor
1321	Thomas canonized by Pope John XXII at Avignon
1325	Revocation of Paris condemnation
1527	Thomas proclaimed Doctor of the Church

1. The chronology of Thomas's Italian sojourn is still contested. The following, in its main lines, is accepted: Thomas returned to Naples (1259–61); then was named lecturer at Orvieto where he seems to have been from 1261–5; from 1265–9 he was regent master at Santa Sabina in Rome. Some put Thomas at Viterbo – where he certainly was at some time during this Italian period – from 1267–8.

A Note on the Texts

The following selections follow the chronological order of their composition, an approach that was decided on after the undoubted attractions of various alternatives had been explored. The aim has been to give as comprehensive a portrait of the thought of Thomas Aquinas as possible. While emphasis is on Aquinas as philosopher, it is essential to see how he distinguished philosophical from theological inquiry. Because of his conception of theology, a good deal of philosophy is either imported into theological works or developed there in order to be put to theological purpose. This is why selections meant to convey his philosophical positions are sometimes drawn from theological writings. Explicitly theological selections are meant to illustrate Thomas's employment of philosophical reasoning in pondering the mysteries of the faith.

No one can fail to be struck by the amount of attention Thomas devoted to understanding and explaining the thought of others. In the case of his biblical commentaries, the motivation is obvious. Similarly, his exposition of the *Sentences* of Peter Lombard. But commentaries on two works of Boethius serve as a kind of bridge into the interpretation of Aristotle. Chronologically, commentaries on Aristotle fall to the last periods of Thomas's academic career. But Aristotle is present from the beginning as *On Being and Essence* and *The Principles of Nature*, early works, illustrate. Such short works could be included in their entirety, but given the extent of expositions and commentaries, selection had to be made of sections that are fairly self-standing. So too with such a disputed question as that on truth: it was possible to present entire sub-questions. Mere snippets have been avoided and the ideal of this series – to translate complete works – has been the ideal striven for but, for reasons just mentioned, not always reachable as such.

The inner divisions of the texts follow those of the editions from which the translations were made. In the case of the Aristotelian commentaries, the convention of the original Leonine editions is adhered to – that is, division into lessons – rather than the more recent Leonine practice of dividing them by the chapter divisions of the work being explained. I

have also retained paragraph numbers in the commentaries on Aristotle,
in order that nearly a century of scholarship can be easily related to the
text.

PART ONE
STUDENT (1245–56)

Student of the liberal arts at Monte Cassino, student at the University of Naples in the faculty of arts, student at Paris, at Cologne and then at Paris again – Thomas Aquinas served a long apprenticeship before he became a master of theology in his early thirties. He was twenty-seven when he returned from Cologne to Paris as a Bachelor of the Sentences. The task of giving a superficial or cursive commentary on the Bible that was part of the apprenticeship of the aspiring theologian seems to have been fulfilled while Thomas was at Cologne.

Lodged in the Dominican Convent of St Jacques, Thomas lived the life of a mendicant friar, bound by the three great vows of poverty, chastity and obedience, and he was now a priest as well. It is easy for us to think of him as the dominant figure at the University of Paris. We have already recounted the story of the faculty of theology requesting that the body of Thomas be returned to Paris so that he might be permanently venerated by his fellow masters. But this posthumous collegiality should not obscure the fact that from the outset Thomas and his fellow friars would have felt a little less than welcome.

There was an animus against mendicant masters. It was one thing for the new religious orders to want their men to profit from a Parisian theological education, after which they could return to their Dominican and Franciscan houses of study and teach there. And there is no doubt that the frequent turnover in the two Dominican chairs in theology was a feature of the effort to credential as many friars as possible for teaching roles within the order. The secular masters, understandably perhaps, felt that their turf was being invaded by friars who came to stay.

There were at the time some dozen masters in the faculty of theology at Paris. Of these, three were held by the mendicants, the Franciscans had one, the Dominicans two. The canons of the cathedral of Notre Dame also held chairs, so the secular masters understandably felt their position to be precarious. When to this is added the great popularity and success of the non-secular masters, and the memory of the fact that when the whole university went on strike in 1229, the Dominicans remained in place and continued to teach, all the ingredients for a feud are present. A disciple of Joachim of Fiore, in promulgating his master's view that mankind had entered into a new age, a third age, the age of the Holy Spirit, which had been preceded by the Age of the Son and the Age of the Father, suggested that Antichrist might be identified with the mendicants. The Convent of St Jacques, where Thomas lived and taught, was the site of demonstrations and protests.

The campaign against the mendicants reached rhetorical excesses that must seem overdrawn to us. William of St Amour, as if to prove that names are not destiny, became a rabid foe of the mendicants, who were, he was convinced, the Antichrist himself. Among the early writings of Thomas at Paris are those defending his vocation and the practices of his order. When he completed his apprenticeship and had become a master of theology, teaching at St Jacques, he was refused admittance into the corporation of masters. Bonaventure, who became master at the same time, was similarly excluded. When a year later, at the command of the Pope, they were admitted, only Thomas functioned as a regent master. Bonaventure had been elected master general of the Franciscan order, would eventually be named a cardinal and, in 1274, at the Council of Lyons that Thomas failed to reach, Bonaventure died.

In this part will be found two of the inaugural sermons Thomas delivered at the extended academic ceremony that marked the successful completion of his theological apprenticeship. Two works that antedate that occasion are also found here, one that summarizes Aristotelian hylomorphic theory, the other on being and essence that might have been written when Thomas was at the very height of his powers. These little works were said to have been composed by Thomas for his fellow students. Throughout his life, Thomas responded to requests for help on one difficult question or another. It is plausible that he would have written these opuscula on request. That Thomas was early recognized as an intellectual phenomenon is supported by a number of stories.

The *Scriptum* or commentary on the *Sentences* of Peter Lombard grew out of the teaching tasks Thomas performed prior to being named master. But the commentary was polished and prepared for publication during Thomas's first regency. None the less, it seems fitting to include an important section of it here.

1. The Inaugural Sermons
(1256)

The following texts mark milestones in Thomas's academic career, although there is lack of agreement as to when the first sermon was preached. Some date it from 1252 when Thomas came back to Paris to resume his studies. Others place both of them in 1256 when Thomas became a master of theology. These sermons have been known to modern readers only since 1912, when they were discovered at the Santa Maria Novella among the writings of Remigio dei Girolami. It will be remembered that this friar had studied under Thomas in Paris and in turn may have taught Dante. The reader will marvel at the deft manipulation of texts, with Scripture being used to comment on itself. An alternative title of the master of theology was magister in sacra pagina – *master of the sacred text. The new master exhibits his prowess in these sermons.*

COMMENDATION OF AND DIVISION OF SACRED SCRIPTURE

This is the book of the commandments of God, and the law that is for ever. All that keep it shall come to life: but they that have forsaken it, to death.

Baruch 4.1

According to Augustine in *On Christian Doctrine* 4.12, one skilled in speech should so speak as to teach, to delight and to change; that is, to teach the ignorant, to delight the bored and to change the lazy. The speech of Sacred Scripture does these three things in the fullest manner. For it firmly teaches with its eternal truth. Psalm 118.89: 'Thy word, O Lord, stands firm for ever as heaven.' And it sweetly delights with its pleasantness. Psalm 118.103: 'How sweet are thy words to my mouth!' And it efficaciously changes with its authority. Jeremiah 23.29: 'Are not my words as a fire, saith the Lord?'

Therefore in the text above Sacred Scripture is commended for three things. First, for the authority with which it changes: 'This is the book

of the commandments of God.' Second, for the eternal truth with which
it instructs, when it says, 'and the law that is for ever'. Third, for the
usefulness with which it entices, when it says, 'All that keep it shall come
to life.'

The authority of this Scripture is shown in three things. First, its origin,
because God is its origin. Hence it says, 'the commandments of God'.
Baruch 3.37: 'He found out all the way of knowledge.' Hebrews 2.3: 'For
it was first announced by the Lord and was confirmed unto us.' Such an
author is infallibly to be believed, both on account of the condition of
his nature, because he is truth; John 14.4: 'I am the way and the truth
and the life.' And on account of his fullness of knowledge; Romans 11.33:
'Oh, the depth of the riches of the wisdom and of the knowledge of God!'
And also on account of the power of the words; Hebrews 4.12: 'For the
word of God is living and efficient and keener than any two-edged sword.'

Second, it is shown to be efficacious by the necessity with which it is
imposed. Mark 16.16: 'He who does not believe shall be condemned.'
The truth of Sacred Scripture is proposed in the manner of a precept,
hence the text says, 'the commandments of God'. These commandments
direct the intellect through faith: 'You believe in God, believe also in me',
John 14.1; inform the affections with love: 'This is my commandment,
that you love one another', John 15.12; and induce to action: 'Do this
and you shall live', Luke 10.28.

Third, it is shown to be efficacious by the uniformity of its sayings,
because all who teach the sacred doctrine teach the same thing.
1 Corinthians 15.11: 'Whether then it is I or they, so we preach, and so
you have believed.' And this is necessary because they all had one teacher.
Matthew 23.8: 'Your teacher is one.' And they had one spirit, 'Have we
not walked in the same spirit?' and one love from above, 'Now the
multitude of believers were of one heart and one soul' (Acts 4.32).
Therefore, as a sign of the uniformity of doctrine, it says significantly,
'This is the book.'

The truth of this teaching of Scripture is immutable and eternal, hence
the words, 'and the law that is for ever'. Luke 21.33: 'Heaven and earth
will pass away but my words shall not pass away.' This law will endure
for ever because of three things: First, because of the power of the lawgiver.
Isaiah 14.27: 'For the Lord of hosts hath decreed, and who can disannul
it.' Second, on account of his immutability. Malachi 3.6: 'For I am the
Lord and I change not'; Numbers 23.19: 'God is not a man, that he should
lie: nor like the son of man, that he should be changed.' Third, because
of the truth of the law. Psalm 118.86: 'All thy commandments are faithful.'

Proverbs 12.19: 'The lip of truth shall be steadfast for ever.' 3 Ezra 4.38: 'Truth remains and gathers strength eternally.'

The usefulness of this Scripture is the greatest: 'I am the Lord thy God that teach thee profitable things.' Hence our text continues: 'All that keep it shall come to life.' Which indeed is threefold: First it is the life of grace, to which Sacred Scripture disposes. John 6.64: 'The words that I have spoken to you are spirit and life.' For through this life the spirit lives in God. Galatians 2.20: 'It is now no longer I that live, but Christ lives in me.' Second is the life of justice consisting in works, to which Sacred Scripture directs. Psalm 118.93: 'Thy decrees I will never forget, for by them thou hast given me life.' Third is the life of glory which Sacred Scripture promises and to which it leads. John 6.69: 'Lord, to whom shall we go? Thou hast words of everlasting life.' John 20.31: 'But these are written that you may believe that Jesus is the Christ, the Son of God, and that believing you may have life in his name.'

The Division of Sacred Scripture

Sacred Scripture leads to this life in two ways, by commanding and by helping. Commanding through the mandates which it proposes, which belong to the Old Testament. Ecclesiasticus 24.33: 'Moses commanded a law in the precepts of justice.' Helping, through the gift of grace which the lawgiver dispenses, which pertains to the New Testament. Both of these are touched on in John 1.17: 'For the Law was given through Moses; grace and truth came through Jesus Christ.'

Hence the whole of Sacred Scripture is divided into two principal parts, the Old and New Testaments, which are mentioned in Matthew 13.52: 'So then every Scribe instructed in the kingdom of heaven is like a householder who brings forth from his storeroom things new and old.' And Song of Songs 7.13: 'In our gates are all fruits, the new and the old, my beloved, I have kept for thee.'

The Old Testament is divided according to the teaching of the commandments, for the commandment is of two kinds, the binding and the warning. The binding is the command of a king who can punish transgressors. Proverbs 20.2: 'As the roaring of a lion, so also is the dread of a king.' But a warning is the precept of a father who must teach. Ecclesiasticus 7.25: 'Hast thou children? Instruct them.' The precept of a king is of two kinds, one which establishes the laws, another which induces to observance of the law, which is customarily done through his heralds and ambassadors. Thus it is that three kinds of command are distinguished, that of the king, that of the herald and that of the father. On this basis the Old Testament is subdivided into three parts, according to Jerome in his prologue to the Book of Kings.

The first part is contained in the law which is proposed by the king himself. Isaiah 33.22: 'For the Lord is our judge, the Lord is our lawgiver, the Lord is our King.'

The second is contained in the Prophets who were, as it were, ambassadors and heralds of God, speaking to the people in the person of God, and urging them to observance of the law. Aggeus 1.13: 'And Aggeus, the messenger of the Lord, as one of the messengers of the Lord, spoke.'

The third is contained in the works of hagiographers, writers who were inspired by the Holy Spirit and spoke as for themselves and not for God. Hence they are called saintly writers because they were writers of the sacred, *agios* meaning 'sacred', and *graphia* meaning 'scripture'. Thus the precepts found in them are paternal. As is evident in Proverbs 6.20: 'My son, keep the commandments of thy father.'

Jerome mentions a fourth kind of book, namely, the apocryphal, so called from *apo*, that is, 'especially', and *cryphon*, that is, 'obscure', because there is doubt about their contents and authors. The Catholic Church includes among the books of Sacred Scripture some whose teachings are not doubted, but whose authors are. Not that the authors are unknown, but because these men were not of known authority. Hence they do not have force from the authority of the authors but rather from their reception by the Church. Because there is the same manner of speaking in them and in the hagiographical works, they are for now counted among them.

The first part, which contains the law, is divided into two parts, insofar as there are two kinds of law, public and private.

A private law is imposed for the observance of one person or one family. Such law is contained in Genesis, as is evident from the first precept given to man, 'But of the tree of knowledge of good and evil, thou shalt not eat' (2.17), and to Noah, 'Saving that flesh with blood you shall not eat' (9.4), and to Abraham, 'And again God said to Abraham: And thou therefore shalt keep my covenant, and thy seed after thee in their generations' (17.9).

The public law is that which is given to the people. For the divine law was given to the Jewish people through a mediator, because it was not fitting that the people should receive it immediately from God. Deuteronomy 5.5: 'I was the mediator and stood between the Lord and you and at that time to show you his words.' Galatians 3.19: 'What then was the Law? It was enacted on account of transgressors, being delivered by angels through a mediator.' Thus a twofold level is found in legislation. First, when the law comes from the Lord to the mediator, and this pertains to three books, Exodus, Leviticus and Numbers. Hence we frequently read in them, 'God spoke to Moses.' Second, when the law is given to the people by the mediator, and this pertains to Deuteronomy, as is evident from its very beginning, 'These are the words which Moses spoke to all Israel.'

These three books are distinguished by the three things in which a people should be ordered. First, precepts bearing on equity of judgement, and this is found in Exodus. Second, in sacraments with respect to the establishment of worship, and this in Leviticus. And third, in offices, with respect to the administration of the community, and this in Numbers.

The second part, which is the prophets, is subdivided insofar as a herald ought to do two things. He should manifest the beneficence of the king, so that men will be inclined to obey, and he should declare the edict of the law.

There is a threefold divine beneficence that the prophets expose to the people. First, the effect of heredity, and this in Joshua, of which Ecclesiasticus 46.1 says, 'Valiant in war was Joshua.' Second, the destruction of armies, and this in the book of Judges, of whose destruction Psalm 82.10 says, 'Do to them as to Madian, as to Sisara.' Third, the exultation of the people, which is twofold, namely the private exaltation of one person, and this in Ruth, and a public which is of the whole people, and this in Kings, which benefice God grants to them. Ezekiel 16.13: 'And thou wast adorned with gold and silver.' For these books, according to Jerome, are placed in the rank of prophets.

In other books which are commonly said to be of the prophets, the prophets posed divine edicts for the observance of the law. And this is said, first, in general, in the major prophets who were sent to the whole people and called for the observance of the whole law; second, in particular, and this in the minor prophets, different ones of whom were sent for different reasons to special tribes, as Osee to the ten tribes of Joel, Jonah to the Ninevites, and so with the rest.

The major prophets differ according to the different ways the prophets sought to lead the people to observance of the law, namely, cajoling by the promise of benefits, frightening with the threat of punishment, arguing by condemnation of sins. Although each of these is found in every prophet, Isaiah chiefly cajoles, as is said in Ecclesiasticus 48.27: 'With a great spirit he saw the things that are come to pass at last, and comforted the mourners in Sion.' Jeremiah chiefly warns, hence Jeremiah 38.4: 'He weakened the hands of the men of war that remain in this city.' But Ezekiel argues and scolds. Ezekiel 16.3: 'Thy father was an Amorrhite and thy mother a Cethite.'

They can be distinguished in another way, insofar as Isaiah chiefly foretells the mystery of the Incarnation, which is why he is read during the time of Advent by the Church, and Jeremiah the mystery of the Passion, hence he is read in Passiontide, and Ezekiel the mystery of the Resurrection, hence his book finishes with the raising of the bones and the repair of the temple. Daniel, however, is included among the prophets insofar as he predicted future events in a prophetic spirit; although he did not speak to the people in the person of the Lord, he dealt with the divinity of Christ. Thus the four prophets answer to the four evangelists, and also to the call to judgement.

The third part, which contains the hagiographic and the apocryphal books, is subdivided according to the two ways fathers instruct their sons in virtue, namely, by word and deed, since in morals examples are no less important than words. Some teach by deed alone, some by word alone, some by word and deed.

By deed, however, in two ways. One, instructing about the future by warning, and this in Joshua, whom Jerome places among the hagiographs. For although one is a prophet because of the gift of prophecy, this is not his office, because he was not sent by God to prophesy to the people. Hence what is said in Wisdom 8.8 can be applied to the prophet: 'She knoweth signs and wonders before they are done.' In another way, speaking of past events as examples of virtue. There are four principal virtues, namely justice, which serves the common good, an example of which is given in Parapelomenon, in which the condition of a whole people who were governed with justice is described. The second is temperance, an example of which is given in Judith, which is why Jerome says, 'Take Judith as an example of the chaste widow.' Judith 15.11: 'For thou hast done manfully, and thy heart has been strengthened, because thou hast loved chastity.' Third is fortitude, which has two attributes. To attack, and an example of this is found in the Book of Maccabees; and to endure, and an example of this is found in Tobit 2.12: 'Now this trial the Lord therefore permitted to happen to him, that an example might be given to posterity of his patience.' The fourth is prudence, by which dangers are avoided, and an example of this is given in Ezra. For in that book we are shown how Ezra and Nehemiah and other princes prudently guarded against the plots of enemies wishing to impede the building of the temple and the city. It also pertains to prudence wisely to repel the violent, and an example of this is given in Esther, where it is shown how Mardocheus and Esther handled the deceptions of the most powerful Aman.

The hagiographical and apocryphal books which instruct by word, are divided insofar as words work in a twofold way to instruct, in one way, by asking for the gift of wisdom. Wisdom 7.7: 'Wherefore I have wished, and understanding was given me, and I called upon God, and the spirit of wisdom came upon me.' This is how the psalter instructs, speaking to God in prayer. In another way, by teaching wisdom, and this in two ways according to the twofold work of wisdom, one of which is to expose the liar, and Job who drove out errors by way of disputation exhibits this. Job 13.3–4: 'But yet I will speak to the Almighty and I desire to reason with God, having first shown that you are forgers of lies and maintainers of perverse opinions.' The other work is not to lie about what it knows, and thus we are instructed in a twofold way, because either wisdom is commended to us, and this in the book of Wisdom, or the precepts of wisdom are proposed, and this in the three books of Solomon, which indeed differ according to the three grades of virtue that Plotinus, in *Enneads* 1.1.2.2–7, distinguishes, since the precepts of wisdom ought to concern only the acts of virtue. In the first grade, according to him, are political virtues, whereby a man moderately uses the things of this world and lives among men, and this in the Proverbs. In the second grade are the purgative virtues, whereby a man regards the world with contempt, and this in Ecclesiastes, which aims at contempt of the world, as is clear from Jerome's prologue. In the third grade are the virtues of the purged soul, whereby a man, wholly cleansed of worldly cares, delights in the contemplation of wisdom alone, and this is found in the Song of Songs. In the fourth grade are the exemplar virtues existing in God, concerning which precepts of wisdom are not given but are rather derived from them.

In word and in deed Ecclesiasticus instructs. Hence the precepts of wisdom in praise of fathers close his book, as is clear in Chapter 44 and after.

The New Testament, which is ordered to eternal life not only through precepts but also through the gifts of grace, is divided into three parts. In the first the origin of grace is treated, in the Gospels. In the second, the power of grace, and this in the epistles of Paul, hence he begins in the power of the Gospel, in Romans 1.16 saying, 'For I am not ashamed of the Gospel, for it is the power of God unto salvation to everyone who believes.' In the third, the execution of the aforesaid virtues is treated, and this in the rest of the books of the New Testament.

Christ is the origin of grace. John 1.16-17: 'And of his fullness we have all received, grace for grace. For the Law was given through Moses: grace and truth came through Jesus Christ.' In Christ a twofold nature is to be considered, a divine, and the Gospel of John is chiefly concerned with this, hence he begins, 'In the beginning was the Word and the Word was with God, and the Word was God.' And a human, and the other Gospels treat chiefly of this, and they are distinguished according to the threefold dignity that belongs to the man Christ. With respect to his royal honour, Matthew speaks. Hence in the beginning of his Gospel he shows that Christ descended from kings and was adored by the Magi kings. With respect to his prophetic honour, Mark speaks, hence he begins with the preaching of the Gospel. With respect to his priestly dignity, Luke speaks, and he begins with the temple and the priesthood and ends his Gospel in the temple, and frequently returns to the temple, as the Gloss says about Luke 2.46: 'And they found him sitting in the temple in the midst of the teachers.'

In another way, Matthew might be said to speak of Christ chiefly with respect to the mystery of the Incarnation, and thus he is depicted in the figure of a man. Luke, with respect to the mystery of the Passion, and therefore he is depicted as a bull, which is an animal to be immolated. Mark, with respect to the victory of the Resurrection, and thus he is depicted as a lion. But John, who soars to the heights of his divinity, is depicted as an eagle.

[The part dealing with the power of grace as exemplified in the epistles of Paul is missing from the text.]

The execution of the power of grace is shown in the progress of the Church, in which there are three things to consider. First, the beginning of the Church, and this is treated in the Acts of the Apostles, hence Jerome says, in his preface to the Pentateuch, that 'The Acts of the Apostles seem to give the bare history of the birth and to clothe the infant Church.' Second, the progress of the Church, and to this is ordered the apostolic instruction of the canonical epistles. Third, the end of the Church, with which the whole content of Scripture concludes in the Apocalypse, with the spouse in the abode of Jesus Christ sharing the life of glory, to which Jesus Christ himself conducts, and may he be blessed for ever and ever. Amen.

ON THE COMMENDATION OF SACRED SCRIPTURE

Thou waterest the hills from thy upper rooms, the earth is sated with the fruit of thy works.

Psalm 103.13

Preface

The King and Lord of the heavens set down this law from all eternity that the gifts of his Providence should come to the lower through intermediaries. Hence Dionysius in the *Celestial Hierarchy* 5 says, 'It is the most sacred law of the divinity that things in the middle should be led to his most divine light by first things.'

This is found to be a law not only in spiritual things but also in corporeal. Hence Augustine in *On the Trinity* 3.4: 'Therefore, as the more crass and least are ruled in a given order by more subtle bodies, so all bodies are ruled by the rational spirit of life.' Therefore, in the psalm the Lord proposed this law observed in the communication of spiritual wisdom in a metaphor of bodily things: 'Watering the mountains . . .' It is plain to the senses that from the highest clouds rain flows forth by which the mountains and rivers are refreshed and send themselves forth so that the satiated earth can bear fruit. Similarly, from the heights of divine wisdom the minds of the learned, represented by the mountains, are watered, by whose ministry the light of divine wisdom reached to the minds of those who listen.

There are then four things to be considered in the chosen text: the *height* of spiritual doctrine; the *dignity* of those who teach it; the *condition* of the listeners; and the *order* of communicating.

I

Its height is expressed by the words, 'from thy upper rooms'. The Gloss has, 'from thy treasure houses on high'. The height of sacred doctrine comes from three things.

First, its origin: for this is the wisdom that is described as being from on high. James 3.15 and Ecclesiasticus 1.5: 'The word of God on high is the fountain of wisdom.'

Second, because of the subtlety of its matter, Ecclesiasticus 24.7: 'I dwelt in the highest places, and my throne is in a pillar of a cloud.' There are some heights of divine wisdom to which all come, though imperfectly, because, as Damascene says in *On Orthodox Faith* 1.1, 'knowledge of the existing God is naturally inserted in all'. In this respect, it is said in Job 36.25, 'All men see him: every one beholdeth afar off.' Other things are higher and only the wit of the wise achieves them. Romans 1.19: 'What is known about God is manifest to them.' Some are so high that they completely transcend human reason, of which it is said in Job 28.21, 'It is hid from the eyes of all living,' and Psalm 17.12, 'He put on darkness as his covering.' But this has been made known by the Holy Spirit, 'Now we have received not the spirit of this world, but the Spirit that is from God,' instructing holy teachers who passed it on in the text of Sacred Scripture; and these are the highest, in which this wisdom is said to dwell.

Third, from the sublimity of the end, for it has the highest end, namely, life eternal. John 20.31: 'But these are written that you may believe that Jesus is the Christ, the Son of God, and that believing you may have life in his name.' Colossians 3.1-2, 'Therefore, if you have risen with Christ, seek the things that are above, where Christ is seated at the right hand of God. Mind the things that are above, not the things of earth.'

2

Because of the height of this doctrine, there is required dignity in those who teach it, which is why they are symbolized by mountains when it is said, 'from thy upper rooms', and this for three reasons.

First, because of the height of mountains. For they are elevated above the earth and neighbours of the sky. Thus the holy teachers by despising earthly things cleave to heavenly things alone. Philippians 3.20: 'But our citizenship is in heaven from which also we eagerly await a Saviour, Our Lord Jesus Christ.' Hence of the teacher of teachers, Christ, it is said in Isaiah 2.2, 'And in the last days the mountain of the house of the Lord shall be prepared on the top of the mountain . . . and all nations shall flow unto it.'

Second, because of its splendour. For the mountains are illumined by beams. Similarly the sacred teachers of minds first receive the splendour. Like mountains the teachers are illumined by the first beams of divine wisdom. Psalm 75.5: 'Thou hast come, shining with light, powerful, from the everlasting hills. The foolish of heart have been despoiled,' that is, by the teachers who participate in eternity. Philippians 2.15: 'You shine like stars in the world.'

Third, because of the protection of the mountains, for the land is defended from the enemy by mountains. So too the doctors of the Church must in defence of the faith stand against errors. The sons of Israel do not put their trust in lance or bow, but the mountains defend them. Ezekiel 13.5: 'You have not gone up to face the enemy, nor have you set up a wall for the house of Israel to stand in battle in the day of the Lord.'

Therefore all the teachers of Sacred Scripture should give high thanks to their eminence of life, that they might be worthy to preach efficaciously, because as Gregory says in *On Pastoral Care*, 'The preaching of those whose life is despised will also be despised.' Ecclesiastes 12.11: 'The words of the wise are as goads, and as nails deeply fastened in, which by the counsels of masters are given from one shepherd.' For the heart cannot be stimulated or stirred to fear of God unless it is fixed in highness of life.

They should be enlightened, that they might fittingly teach by reading. Ephesians 3.8–9: 'Yes, to me, the very least of all the saints, there was given this grace, to announce among the Gentiles the good tidings of the unfathomable riches of Christ, and to enlighten all men as to what is the dispensation of the mystery which has been hidden from eternity in God.'

Armed, that they might refute errors in disputation. Luke 21.15: 'For I myself will give you utterance and wisdom, which all your adversaries will not be able to resist.'

Of these three offices, namely, to preach, to lecture and to dispute, it is said in Titus 1.9, 'that he may be able both to exhort in sound doctrine and to confute opponents'.

3

Third, the condition of those who hear, which are presented in the symbol of earth: 'the earth is sated'. This is because the earth is lowest. Proverbs 25.3: 'The heaven above, and the earth beneath.' Again, it is stable and firm. Ecclesiastes 1.4: 'One generation passeth away, and another generation cometh, but the earth standeth for ever.' Again, it is fruitful. Genesis 1.11: 'Let the earth bring forth the green herb, and such as may seed, and the fruit tree yielding fruit after its kind.'

Similarly, they should be low as the earth in humility. Proverbs 11.2: 'Where humility is, there also is wisdom.' Again, firm with the sense of rectitude; Ephesians 4.14: 'That we may be now no longer children, tossed to and fro and carried about by every wind of doctrine.' And fruitful, as the precepts of wisdom bear fruit in them, Luke 8.15: 'Having heard the word, hold it fast and bear fruit in patience.'

Therefore humility is required of them with respect to the learning that comes from listening, Ecclesiasticus 6.34: 'If thou wilt incline thy ear, thou shalt receive instruction: and if thou love to hear, thou shalt be wise.' Rectitude of the senses with respect to the judgement of what is heard; Job 12.11: 'Doth not the ear discern words?' But fruitfulness in discovery, by which from a few things heard, the good listener pronounces many things; Proverbs 9.9: 'Give an occasion to a wise man, and wisdom shall be added to him.'

4

The order of its coming about is touched on here with respect to three things, namely, the order of communicating, the amount, and the quality of the gift received.

First with respect to the order of communicating, because not everything that is contained in divine wisdom can be grasped by the minds of the teachers. Hence he does not say from the highest mountains, but from the upper; Job 26.14: 'Lo, these things are said in part.' Similarly, not everything that the teachers grasp is passed on to the hearers; 1 Corinthians 12.4: '. . . and heard secret words that a man may not repeat'. Hence he does not say, passing on to earth the fruits of the mountains, but 'the earth is sated with the fruit of thy works'. This is what Gregory, in the *Morals* on Job 26 says in explaining Job 26.8, 'He bindeth up the waters in his clouds, so that they break not out and fall down together': 'For the teacher should not preach to the simple as much as he knows, because he himself is unable to know how many divine mysteries there are.'

Second, the order with respect to the mode of having is touched upon, because God has wisdom naturally. Hence his 'upper rooms' are what is natural to him; Job 12.13: 'With him is wisdom and strength; he hath counsel and understanding.' But teachers share in wisdom abundantly. Hence they are said to be watered from on high. Ecclesiasticus 24.42: 'I said I will water my garden of plants, and I will water abundantly the fruits of my meadow.' But listeners sufficiently participate in it, and the satiety of the earth signifies this; Psalm 16.15: 'I shall be satisfied with the sight of thee.'

Third, with respect to the power of communicating, because God communicates wisdom by his own power. Hence by himself he is said to water the mountains. But the teachers do not communicate wisdom except as ministers. Hence the fruits of the mountains are not attributed to them but to the divine works, 'By the fruit of thy works'. 1 Corinthians 3.4–5: 'What then is Paul' and later, 'His minister in whom you believe'.

But 2 Corinthians 2.16: '. . . who is worthy of this . . .' For God requires innocent ministers; Psalm 100.6: 'He that walks in the unsullied way, he shall serve me.' Understanding; Proverbs 14.35: 'A wise servant is acceptable to the king.' Fervour; Psalm 103.4: 'Thou makest the winds thy messengers, and the blazing fire thy ministers.' Again, obedience; Psalm 102.21: 'Ye ministers of his who do his will'.

But although no one by himself, of himself, is sufficient for such a ministry, he can hope to have this sufficiency from God; 2 Corinthians 3.5: 'Not that we are sufficient of ourselves to think anything, as from ourselves, but our sufficiency is from God.' He must ask it of God; James 1.5: 'But if any of you is wanting in wisdom, let him ask it of God, who gives abundantly to all men, and does not reproach; and it will be given to him.'

Let us pray that Christ will grant it to us. Amen.

2. *On the Principles of Nature*
(1252–6)

This oeuvre de jeunesse *covers a great deal of Aristotle's natural philosophy, at least in its initial steps. Doubtless its intended reader came away from it with a mind more furnished than it had been before. What the work lacks is dialectical subtlety. In a way significantly different from most of his writing, Thomas does not here stress how one arrives at the position of Aristotle that he is laying out for his reader. We do not have a lively sense of the questions to which these are answers, and although a reader would be able to respond catechetically to questions about Aristotelian hylomorphism it is doubtful that he would be able to defend the answers. This is noteworthy because it is so uncharacteristic of Thomas's style, philosophical or theological. Perhaps the dialectical atmosphere of Paris had not yet put its stamp upon him.*

I

Note that sometimes a thing can be although it is not, whereas sometimes a thing simply is. That which can be is said to be potentially; that which already is is said to be actually. But existence is twofold, namely essential or substantial existence: for example, when a man is, this is to be simply speaking; but there is also accidental being, as when a man is white, and this is to be only in a secondary sense.

Something can be in potency to either kind of existence, as sperm and menstrual blood are potentially man, and a man is potentially white. Both that which is potentially a substantial being and that which is potentially some accidental being can be called matter, as sperm is the matter of man and man is the matter of whiteness, but they differ in this that the matter which is in potency to substantial being is called the *matter from which*, and that which is in potency to accidental being is called the *matter in which*.

Again, properly speaking, what is in potency to accidental being is called a subject, while what is in potency to substantial being is properly called matter. A sign that what is in potency to accidental being is called a subject is the fact that accidents are said to be in a subject, whereas substantial form is not said to be in a subject. Matter differs from subject in that the subject does not receive existence from that which advenes to it, but has complete existence in itself, as man does not receive existence from whiteness. Matter however has existence from that which advenes to it; of itself it has incomplete existence. Thus, simply speaking, form gives existence to matter, but the subject [gives it] to accident. Sometimes, however, these terms are used interchangeably, matter for subject, and vice versa.

Just as anything that is in potency can be called matter, so anything from which something has existence, whatever kind of being it is, whether substantial or accidental, can be called form: man when he is potentially white comes to be actually white through whiteness, and sperm when it is potentially man becomes man actually through the soul. And because form causes a thing to be in act, form is said to be act, but substantial form causes actual substantial existence, and what causes actual accidental existence is called accidental form.

Because generation is motion towards form, two kinds of generation respond to two kinds of form. Generation, simply speaking, involves substantial form; and generation in a secondary sense involves accidental form. For when substantial form is introduced, something is said to come to be simply speaking; but when accidental form is introduced, we do not say that something comes to be simply but becomes this. When a man becomes white, we do not say that a man comes to be or is generated, but we say he comes to be white. Two kinds of corruption answer to these two kinds of generation, namely, absolute corruption and corruption in a secondary sense. Generation and corruption simply speaking are only in the genus of substance, but generation and corruption in a secondary sense are in the other genera.

Generation is a kind of mutation from non-being or non-existence to existence or being, and conversely corruption is a change from existence to non-existence. However, generation does not come about from just any non-existence, but from the non-being which is potentially being, as the idol comes to be from a bronze which is potentially, although not actually, the idol.

Three things are required if there is to be generation: being in potency, which is matter, and not-being-in-act, which is privation; and that through which it becomes actual, namely form. When the idol comes to be from bronze, the bronze which is potentially the form of the idol is matter, whereas to be unshaped or indisposed is called privation; the shape by which it is called an idol is form, although not substantial form, because bronze has actual existence before the arrival of form or figure, and its existence does not depend on that shape which is an accidental form. All artificial forms are accidental, for art only operates on that which is already constituted and exists complete by nature.

2

There are three principles of nature: matter, form and privation. Of these one, namely form, is that *towards which* generation is aimed, while the other two are on the side of that *from which* generation is. Hence matter and privation are the same in subject but differ in account, for it is the same bronze that is unshaped before the coming of form, but in one account it is bronze and in another unshaped. Hence privation is not said to be a *per se* principle but *per accidens*, because it coincides with matter. Similarly we say 'The doctor builds' is *per accidens*, since it is not as a doctor that he builds, but as a builder, and it just happens that the same man is both physician and builder.

But accidents are of two kinds: namely necessary, which is inseparable from the thing, as risible is a necessary accident or property of man; and non-necessary, which is separable, as white from man. Hence although privation is an accidental principle, it does not follow that it is not necessary for generation, because matter is never denuded of privation: for insofar as it is under one form, it is in privation of another, and conversely – as in fire there is a privation of air, and in air the privation of fire.

Notice too that although generation is from non-being, we say not that negation is a principle but that privation is, because negation is not determined to a subject: 'does not see' can be said even of non-beings, as in 'The chimera does not see', as well as of beings that by nature have no sight, like rocks. But privation of a form is found only in a subject that by nature has that form, just as only things that see by nature are called blind.

Because generation does not come to be from non-being absolutely, but from a negation in some subject, and not in just any subject but in a determinate one – for it is not from just any non-fire that fire comes to be, but from a non-fire that is such that it can come to be the form of fire – therefore privation is said to be a principle. But it differs from the others in that they are principles not only of coming to be but also of being: in order for an idol to come to be there must be bronze, and its ultimate shape must be that of the idol; moreover, once it is an idol, these two must continue to be as its constituents. Privation, however, is a principle only of becoming and not of being: in order for an idol to come to be, it is necessary that the idol not already exist, because if it already were it would not come to be, since what comes to be does not exist save successively, as in time and motion. But that because of which it is now an idol, is not the privation of idol, because affirmation and negation are not simultaneous, nor are privation and possession.

Again, privation is a *per accidens* principle, as was set forth above, but the other two are *per se* principles.

From what has been said, it is therefore evident that matter differs from form and privation in definition. For matter is that in which form and privation are understood to be, as shaped and unshaped in bronze. Sometimes indeed matter is understood as in privation and sometimes not, as bronze when it is the matter of the idol does not imply privation, because by 'bronze' we do not mean the unshaped and unconstructed, whereas flour when it is the matter of bread implies the privation of the form of bread, because by 'flour' I mean something that lacks the form of bread. Matter or subject endures in generation, but not the privation or the composite of matter and privation; it is of course matter which does not imply privation that endures, privation is transient.

But notice that sometimes matter itself is composed with form: bronze is the matter of the idol, but is itself composed of matter and form. Therefore bronze is not called prime matter, because it itself has matter. Matter understood as without any form and privation, but subject to form and privation, is called prime matter, because prior to it there is no other matter, and it is also called Hyle. Because every definition and every cognition is through form, prime matter cannot be known or defined in itself, but only by comparison, as when it is said that prime matter is to all forms and privations as bronze is to the shape of idol and the lack of it, and it is called absolutely first. Something can also be called prime matter with respect to a given genus, as water is the matter of liquids, but not prime matter absolutely, because it is composed of matter and form and thus has a prior matter.

Neither prime matter nor form, it should be understood, is either generated or corrupted, because every generation is to something from something, and the *from-which* of generation is matter, and the *to-which* form. If matter or form were generated, therefore, there would be matter of the matter and form of the form and so on to infinity. Thus generation, properly speaking, is only of the composite.

Prime matter is said to be numerically the same in all, but numerically the same is said in two ways. First, that which has numerically one determinate form, like Socrates; prime matter is not said to be numerically one in this way, since it has no form. Second, something is also said to be numerically one because it is without the dispositions that make things differ numerically. This is the way that prime matter is said to be numerically one, because it is understood without any of the dispositions from which numerical difference arises.

And notice too that matter does not include any form or privation in its nature, any more than bronze includes in its notion either shaped or unshaped, although prime matter is never devoid of form and privation, for sometimes it is under one form, sometimes under another. Prime matter can never exist just as itself because, since it does not include form in its notion, it cannot actually be. A thing is actual thanks to form, but prime matter exists only potentially, which is why nothing actual can be said to be prime matter.

3

From what has been said, it is clear that there are three principles of nature, matter, form and privation, but these are not sufficient for generation. What is in potency cannot bring itself to actuality, as the bronze which is potentially an idol does not make itself to be an idol, but needs an agent to bring the form of the idol from potentiality to act. The form does not bring itself from potency to act: I mean the form of what is generated, which we call the term of generation, for the form is only in that which has come to be, but while it is being made it is in becoming, that is while the thing comes to be. Therefore besides matter and form there must be a principle which acts, and this is called the effecting or moving agent or that whence motion begins.

Because, as Aristotle says in *Metaphysics* 2, whatever acts acts only by intending something, there must be a fourth thing, namely, that which is intended by the agent, and this is called the end. Every agent, both natural and voluntary, acts for the sake of an end, though it does not follow that every agent knows the end or deliberates about it. Only those things whose actions are not determined, but are open to an outcome and its opposite, as in the case of voluntary agents, need to know the end. They must know the end by which they determine their acts. But the actions of natural agents are determined, so it is not necessary to choose the things which are for the end.

Avicenna gives the example of a zither player who does not need to deliberate about each striking of the chords since the movements are determined for him, otherwise there would be delay between strikings and disharmony would result. Since the voluntary agent, not the natural agent, deliberates, it can be argued that if a voluntary agent sometimes acts without deliberation then *a fortiori* the natural agent can act for an end without deliberation. This intending is nothing other than the natural inclination to something.

It is clear from what has been said that there are four causes, namely the material, the efficient, the formal and the final. However, although principle and cause are interchangeable, as is said in *Metaphysics* 5, Aristotle in the *Physics* posits four causes and three principles. By cause he means both extrinsic and intrinsic accounts: the material and the formal are said to be intrinsic to the thing because they are constitutive parts, whereas the efficient and final are called extrinsic because they are outside the thing. Aristotle calls only intrinsic causes principles here. Privation is not listed among the causes, however, because it is an accidental principle, as has been said. When we say four causes, this should be understood to mean four *per se* causes. Accidental causes are reduced to these, since whatever is incidental is piggy-back on that which is essential.

Although Aristotle means intrinsic causes by principles in *Physics* 1, still, as is said in *Metaphysics* 11, the term 'principle' is properly used of extrinsic causes, 'elements' of causes which are parts of the thing – namely intrinsic causes – and 'cause' of both. Sometimes, however, they are used interchangeably, for any cause can be called a principle and any principle a cause. But cause seems to add something to principle as commonly used, because what is first, whether or not any further being follows on it, can be called a principle, as the artisan is called the principle of the knife, but when something is moved from black to white, the black is said to be the principle of that motion, and generally that from which a motion begins is called a principle, but blackness is not that from whose existence the existence of what comes later, that is, whiteness, comes. But cause is said only of that prior thing from which the later being follows; hence a cause is defined as that from whose being another follows. That from which motion first begins to be cannot be called a cause *per se*, though it is called a principle. On this account privation is numbered among principles but not among causes, because privation is that from which generation begins, but it can also be called a cause *per accidens*, insofar as it is coincident with matter, as was set forth above.

Only those causes of which the thing is composed are properly called elements, but again this is so not just of any material, but only of that which is first in the composition – a man's limbs are not his elements, because they are composed of other things, but we call earth and water elements because they are not composed of other bodies, rather natural bodies are first composed of them. Thus Aristotle in *Metaphysics* 5 (1014a26–27) says that 'the element is that of which things are first composed, and remains in them and is indivisible into things different in kind'.

The meaning of the first part of the sentence, 'that of which things are first composed,' is clear from what we have said. The second, 'and remains in them', is meant to distinguish elements from that matter which is completely corrupted through generation. As bread is the matter of blood but blood only comes to be when bread ceases to be, so bread does not remain in the blood, whereas elements must in some way remain and are not corrupted, as is said in *On Generation*.[1] The third part, 'is indivisible into things different in kind', is meant to distinguish elements from those things which have parts diverse in form, like hand, whose parts are flesh and bones, which are specifically different. But the element does not have parts of different species: every part of water is water. For the being of the element does not require that it be quantitatively indivisible; it suffices that it is not divisible into parts of different kinds. If it is not so divisible, it is called an element, as letters are the elements of words. It is clear then that in some ways principle is found in more things than cause, and cause in more than element, which is what the Commentator says in *Metaphysics* 5.

4

Having seen that there are four kinds of cause, we should note that a thing can have a plurality of causes, for example, both bronze and the artisan are causes of the idol, but the artisan as the efficient cause and bronze as the material. Nor is it impossible that the same thing should be the cause of contraries, as the pilot is the cause of the safety of the ship and of its sinking, the one by his presence, the other by his absence.

1. Aristotle, 327b29–31.

Note too that it is possible for the same thing to be cause and caused with respect to the same, though differently: as taking a walk is the cause of health as efficient cause, but health is the cause of taking a walk, as its end, for one sometimes takes a walk for the sake of health. So too body is the matter of soul, but soul is the form of body. The efficient cause is said to be so with respect to the end, since the end can only actually be attained by the activity of an agent, but the end is said to be the cause of the agent that acts only with the intention of achieving the end. Hence, the efficient is the cause that the end is – that health might be – but it does not make the end to be end – that is, it does not cause the end to be final: just as the physician causes health actually to be, but he does not make health to be an end. For the end is the cause of that which is efficient, that is, the cause that the efficient is efficient – health doesn't cause the physician to be a physician: I mean the health that comes to be as the result of the physician's activity – but it causes the physician to act. The end, consequently, is the cause of efficient causality and makes the efficient cause efficient; similarly it makes matter to be matter and form to be form, since matter receives form thanks to the end, and form only perfects matter because of the end. That is why the end is called the cause of causes: it is the cause of the causality of the other causes.

Matter is said to be the cause of form insofar as form exists only in matter, and similarly form is the cause of matter in that matter has actual being only through form: matter and form are correlatives, as is said in *Physics* 2. They are to the composite as parts to whole and simple to complex.

Because every cause as cause is naturally prior to what it causes, it should be noted that 'prior' is said in two ways according to Aristotle, in *On the Generation of Animals*,[1] and because of this both cause and effect can be said to be prior and posterior to the same thing. One thing is said to be prior to another in generation and time, on the one hand, and in substance and perfection, on the other. Since then nature's operation is from imperfect to perfect and from incomplete to complete, the imperfect is prior to the perfect with respect to generation and time, but the perfect is prior from the point of view of completion. Thus it can be said that man is prior to boy in substance and completion, but the boy is before the man in generation and in time.

Although in generable things the imperfect is prior to the perfect and potency prior to act, given the fact that a thing first exists imperfectly

1. Aristotle, 742a19–22.

and potentially and then perfectly and actually, simply speaking the actual and perfect are prior, because what brings the potential to actuality is actual and what perfects the imperfect is the perfect. For matter is prior to form in generation and time, as that to which something comes is prior to what comes, but form is prior to matter in perfection, because matter is only completed through form. Similarly, the agent is prior to the end in generation and time, since it is from the agent that the motion to the end comes about, but the end is prior to the efficient cause in substance and completion, since the action of the efficient cause is completed only by the end. These two causes, then, the material and the efficient, are prior with respect to generation, but the formal and the final causes are prior with respect to perfection.

It should be noted that there are two kinds of necessity: absolute and conditional. Absolute necessity arises from causes prior in the way of generation, namely matter and the agent, just as the necessity of death comes from matter's disposition to join with contraries. This necessity is called absolute because it has no impediment: and it is also called the necessity of matter. Conditional necessity arises from causes posterior in generation, namely form and end, as we say that conception is necessary if a man is to be generated. This is conditional because for this woman to conceive is not absolutely necessary, but under a condition: if a child is going to be born. This is called the necessity of end.

Three of the causes – namely, form, end and agent – can coincide in one thing, as is clear in the generation of fire: fire generates fire, so fire, insofar as it generates, is the agent; it is also the form, insofar as it makes what was potential to be actual; and it is the end, insofar as it is intended by the agent and the activities of the agent terminate in it.

But end is of two kinds, namely the end of generation and the end of the thing generated, as is clear in the making of a knife: the form of the knife is the end of generation, but cutting, which is the work of the knife, is the end of the thing generated, namely, the knife. It is the end of generation not of the generated that coincides with the two other causes in the manner explained – namely, when generation comes from something specifically the same, as man generates man, and olive generates olive.

Notice that end and form can be numerically the same, since the end of generation is the form of the generated. The efficient cause is not numerically but only specifically the same: it is impossible that the maker and the made be numerically identical, though they can be of the same species. When a man generates a man, the generator and generated are numerically diverse but specifically the same. Matter does not coincide with the others because matter, by the fact that it is potential being, has the note of the imperfect; whereas the other causes, since they are in act, have the note of the perfect, and the perfect and imperfect cannot be identical.

5

Having seen that there are four causes, efficient, material, formal and final, we should note that each of these causes can be divided into many modes. For a cause can be called prior or posterior; for example, when art and the physician are given as causes of health, art is a prior and physician a posterior cause, and so too with the formal and other causes. Note that we ought always to take the question back to the first cause. When it is asked, 'Why is he healthy?', the reply should be, 'Because the physician cured him,' and to 'Why did the physician cure?' 'Because he had the art of curing.'

Notice that proximate cause is the same as posterior, and remote cause the same as prior, hence these two modes of cause, prior and posterior and proximate and remote, come to the same. It should be observed that it is always the more universal cause that is called remote and the more specific proximate, as we say that the form of man is his proximate definition, namely mortal rational animal, but that animal is more remote, and substance remoter still. All higher forms are forms of the inferior. Similarly the proximate matter of the idol is bronze, but the remote is metal, and still more remote is body.

Some causes are *per se* and others accidental. A *per se* cause is a cause of the thing as such, as the builder is the cause of the house and wood is the cause of the stool. The accidental cause is that which attaches to the *per se* cause, as when we say, 'The grammarian builds.' The grammarian is said to be the accidental or incidental cause of the building insofar as the builder happens to be a grammarian. And so too with the other causes.

Again, some causes are simple, others complex. A cause is said to be simple when only the *per se* cause is assigned or only the accidental cause, as when we say that the builder is the cause of the house or that the physician is the cause of the house. It is complex when we give them both together and say, 'The physician builder is the cause of the house.' According to Avicenna, a cause which is without the addition of anything else can also be called simple, as bronze is the cause of idol since without the addition of any other matter bronze is the matter of the idol; so too when we say that the physician cures or that fire warms. When it is necessary for several things to come together for there to be a cause then it is complex, as when several men, not just one, are necessary to sail the ship, or when many bricks, not one, are the matter of the house.

Again, some causes are *actual*, others *potential*. The actual cause causes the actual thing, as the builder when he builds, or bronze when the idol is made of it; the potential cause is that which, although it does not actually cause the thing, can do so, as the builder when he is not building. And it should be noted that, as regards actual causes, the cause and the caused must exist simultaneously, so that if the one is, the other is: for if one is an actual builder, it is necessary that one build, and if actual building takes place, there must be an actual builder. But this is not necessary with causes that are only potential.

Notice that the universal cause is referred to the universal effect and the singular cause to the singular effect: as we say that the builder is the cause of the house, and that this builder is the cause of this house.

6

Speaking of intrinsic principles, namely matter and form, it should be noticed that the similarity or difference of principles is based on the similarity or difference of what follows from them. For some are numerically the same, as Socrates and 'this man', point to Socrates; others are numerically distinct but specifically the same, like Socrates and Plato, who though they are alike in the human species none the less differ numerically. Others are specifically different but generically the same, as man and ass agree in the genus animal; others are generically different and the same only according to analogy, like substance and quantity, which do not agree in any genus but are alike only according to analogy: for they agree only in being, and being is not a genus, because it is not predicated univocally but analogically.

To understand this it must be understood that something is predicated of many in three ways: univocally, equivocally and analogically. That which is predicated according to the same name and the same account – that is, definition – is predicated univocally, as animal of man and ass, for both are called animal and both are animate sensible substance, which is the definition of animal. When the same term is predicated of several things according to different meanings it is predicated equivocally, as dog of the barking beast and of a celestial body, which agree in name only and not in definition or meaning: that which is signified by the name is the definition, as is said in *Metaphysics* 4. Something is predicated analogically when it is predicated of many things whose accounts differ but are attributed to one and the same thing, as when healthy is said of the body of an animal, of urine and of a potion: it does not signify the same thing in all of them, for it is said of urine as the sign of health, of the body as the subject of health, and of the potion as the cause of health. But all these definitions refer to one end, namely to health.

Some things which agree according to analogy, namely in a proportion or comparison or agreement, are attributed to one end, as is clear from the foregoing example, but sometimes to one agent, as medical is said of one who acts through the art and of one who acts without the art, like an old wife, and also of the instruments, but by attribution to one agent, which is the art of medicine; and sometimes, things which agree insofar as they can be attributed to one subject, as being is said of substance, quality and quantity and the other categories, though it is not with wholly the same account that being is said of substance and quantity and the others, but the rest are called beings because they are attributed to substance, which is the subject of the others. Being is said first of substance and secondarily of the others; therefore being is not the genus of substance and quantity, because no genus is predicated of its species according as prior and posterior. Being is predicated analogically. That is what was meant when we said that substance and quantity differ generically but are the same by analogy.

With things that are numerically the same, their form and matter are also numerically the same, as with Tullius and Cicero; of things specifically the same but numerically diverse, the form and matter are not numerically, but specifically, the same, as with Socrates and Plato. And similarly of those things generically the same, their principles too are generically the same, as body and soul are specifically different in ass and horse, but generically the same. Similarly when things agree only according to analogy, their principles too are the same only according to analogy or proportion. For matter and form and privation, or potency and act, are principles of substance and of the other genera, but they agree only according to a proportion: as the matter of substance is to substance in the account of matter, so is the matter of quantity to quantity. Just as substance is the cause of the others, so the principles of substance are the principles of all the others.

3. On Being and Essence
(1252–6)

*This little treatise, whose composition is thought to be contemporary
with the preceding, is an indisputable proof of the genius of its author.
Here some of the most vexing questions of metaphysics are handled with
an ease and authority that amazes. An original work? Thomas saw himself
as an inheritor and continuer of a tradition, but his mastery of that
tradition enables him to see what others had not seen, or seen as clearly
as he.*

*The immediate scope of this treatise is the nature of the things that
are, but it also brilliantly provides a statement of a common doctrine
underlying the metaphysical efforts of Greeks and Arabs, Christians
and Jews, Aristotelians and Neoplatonists – a doctrine that Thomas
fundamentally saw as the teaching of Aristotle.*

*This is a philosophical work which, on philosophical grounds, assumes
that the realm of being is not limited to the things before our eyes. To
ask about being, then, and what it is to be a being, and of the difference
between 'whatness' and existence, is to open questions that move from
the things of this world to God and to that great realm of beings between,
what the Neoplatonists called 'Intelligences'. Thomas calls them that here
too, no doubt a quite deliberate choice on the part of a man who came
to be called the Angelic Doctor, not least because of his insatiable interest
in those choirs and kinds of 'separated substances' the Christian calls the
angels.*

PROLOGUE

Because a small error at the outset ends by being great, according to the
Philosopher in *On the Heavens* 1,[1] and because being and essence are
what intellect first conceives, as Avicenna says in the beginning of his
Metaphysics, therefore, lest ignorance of them give occasion for error,

1. Aristotle, 271b8–13.

and in order to lay open the difficulty concerning them, it should be said what 'essence' and 'being' mean, how they are found in different things, and how they are related to logical intentions, namely, genus, species and difference.

We ought to derive knowledge of simple things from composite things, and come to the primary from the secondary. Since learning most fittingly comes about when we begin with easier matters, we should move from the meaning of 'being' to the meaning of 'essence'.

CHAPTER I
ON THE MEANINGS OF 'BEING' AND 'ESSENCE'

Notice therefore that, as the Philosopher says in *Metaphysics* 5,[1] being as such is said in two ways: first as it is divided into the ten genera, and second as meaning the truth of propositions. These differ because anything can be called being in the second sense if an affirmative proposition can be formed of it, even if it posits nothing in reality: thus privations and negations are called beings, as when we say that affirmation is opposed to negation, and that blindness exists in the eye. But in the first sense only that which posits something in reality can be called being; therefore, blindness and the like are not beings in this sense of the term.

The term essence does not apply to being in the second sense, for some things are called beings which have no essence, as is obvious in the case of privations; but essence does apply to being taken in the first sense. Hence the Commentator[2] says that being in the first sense signifies the essence of the thing. And because, as has been said, being in this sense is divided into ten genera, essence must mean something common to all natures thanks to which beings are placed in the different genera and species, such that humanity is man's essence, and similarly with other things.

Since that by which a thing is constituted in its proper genus or species is what is signified by the definition expressing what the thing is, it can be seen why philosophers changed the name essence to the name *whatness*, and this is what the Philosopher frequently calls *that-which-it-was-to-be* – namely, that through which a thing is some thing. It is also called *form*, insofar as form signifies the certainty of anything whatsoever, as Avicenna

1. Aristotle, 1017a22–35.
2. Averroes. See Glossary.

says in book 2 of his *Metaphysics*. And it is signified by yet another name, *nature*, taking nature in the first of the four senses that Boethius gives the term in his *On the Two Natures [of Christ]* – namely, anything the intellect can in any way grasp is called a nature because a thing is only intelligible through its definition and essence. The Philosopher too says in *Metaphysics* 5[1] that every substance is a nature. However, the term nature taken in this sense seems to signify the essence of a thing insofar as it is ordered to the thing's proper activity, and nothing is without a proper activity. The name quiddity however is taken from what is signified by the definition. *But essence means that through which and in which the thing has existence.*

Just as being is said absolutely of substances, but only in a secondary, qualified sense of accidental qualities, the same too is true of essence. Some substances are simple and others complex. Essence is found in both, although more truly and nobly in the simple, which are the causes of the complex – at least the first simple substance, God, is. But because the essences of such substances are largely hidden from us, we must begin with the essences of complex substances, so that we might fittingly learn from more accessible concepts.

CHAPTER 2
ESSENCE IN COMPOSITE SUBSTANCES

In complex substances there are form and matter, as in man there are soul and body. Neither of these alone can be called essence. Plainly, matter alone is not essence, because a thing is knowable and also placed in a species and genus through its essence, but matter is neither a principle of knowledge nor that according to which something is characterized as to genus and species: *that* has to be what makes the thing actual. Nor can form alone be called the essence of complex substance, though some have sought to maintain this. It is clear from what has been said that the definition of a thing signifies its essence, but the definition of natural substance contains both form and matter, otherwise natural and mathematical definitions would not differ. Nor can it be said that matter enters into the definition of the natural substance as something added to its essence, or as outside its essence – that mode of definition is peculiar to

1. Aristotle, 1014b36.

the accidental, which, having no complete essence, requires that its subject, which is outside its genus, be put into its definition. Clearly essence comprises both matter and form.

Nor can it be said that essence signifies some relation between matter and form, or something superadded to them, since this would necessarily be an accidental quality extraneous to the thing, and the thing could not be known by means of it, as it is by its essence. It is through form, which is the act of matter, that matter is made an actual being and made to be a kind of thing. Therefore, whatever more is added, does not make matter actually to be simply speaking, but only actually to be such-and-such, which is what accidental qualities do: whiteness makes something to be actually white. That is why when such a form is acquired, a thing is not said to be generated simply speaking but only in a certain respect.

We are left, then, with this, that the word essence in the case of complex substances signifies what is composed of matter and form. This agrees with Boethius in his commentary on the *Categories*, where he says that *ousia* signifies the complex: *ousia* means for the Greeks what essence means for us, as he himself points out in *On the Two Natures*. Avicenna too says that the quiddity of complex substance is the very composition of form and matter. And the Commentator also says, with reference to *Metaphysics* 7. 'The nature had by the species of generable things is something in between, that is, composed of matter and form.'

This stands to reason, since the existence of the compound substance is not of form alone nor of matter alone but of the composed thing itself; and the essence is that according to which a thing is said to exist. Necessarily then the essence whereby a thing is denominated a being cannot be form alone, nor matter alone, but is both, even though in a way only form is the cause of such existence. We see that other things constituted from several principles are not denominated from one of the principles alone but from that which comprises both. This is clear in tastes, because sweetness is caused by the heat which digests the moist, but something is not denominated sweet from heat but from taste which comprises the hot and the humid.

It might perhaps seem to follow from the fact that matter is the principle of individuation that essence cannot be defined universally, since it contains matter as well as form – particular matter, that is, not universal – and essence is what the definition signifies. But note that it is not matter understood in just any way that is the principle of individuation, but only designated matter: and I call designated matter that which is considered under determinate dimensions. Matter in this sense is not put into the definition of man as man but would be put into the definition of Socrates if Socrates had an essence. Non-designated matter is included in the definition of man, for it is not *this* bone and *this* flesh that are put into the definition of man, but bone and flesh as such which are the non-designated matter of man.

It is evident that the essence of man differs from the essence of Socrates only as the designated differs from the non-designated. Hence the Commentator says on *Metaphysics* 7, 'Socrates is nothing else than animality and rationality, which are his quiddity.' So too the essence of genus differs from that of species according to the designated and non-designated, though there is a different mode of designation than in the previous case, because the designation of the individual with reference to species is by matter with determinate dimensions, whereas the designation of species with respect to genus is by the constitutive difference taken from the form of the thing. The determination or designation in the species with reference to genus is not by way of something existing only in the essence of the species and not in the essence of the genus; indeed, whatever is in the species is also in the genus in an undetermined way. For if animal were not the whole that is man, but only its part, it would not be predicated of it, since no integral part is predicated of its whole. To see why this is so, consider that the difference between body as a part of animal and body as a genus is that body as a genus cannot be an integral part.

This term *body* has many meanings. In the genus of substance, body means that which has a nature such that three dimensions can be designated in it. Those three designated dimensions are body as it falls in the genus of quantity. For something that already has one perfection can receive another, as is evident in man who in addition to sensitive nature has intellectual nature. Similarly too, over and above the perfection of having a nature in which three dimensions can be designated, another perfection can be added, such as life and the like. The term body, then, can signify a thing whose form permits three dimensions to be designated in it but with precision, such that no further perfection follows from that form. If something were added, it would be outside the meaning of body in this sense. In this sense, body is an integral and material part of animal and soul is not included in its meaning but supervenes on it and from the two, body and soul, the animal is constituted as from its parts.

The term body can also be taken to signify something whose form permits three dimensions to be designated in it, whatever form that might be and whether or not any further perfection can come from it. In this sense, body is the genus of animal, because nothing should be understood in animal which is not implicitly contained in its genus body. For the soul is not a form other than the form thanks to which three dimensions can be designated in the thing. Therefore when it was said that 'body is that which has such a form that three dimensions can be designated in it', whatever form it has is understood, whether soul, or rock, or whatever. The animal's form is implicitly contained in the form of body, insofar as body is its genus.

This is also the way animal relates to man. For if animal meant only something whose perfection enables it to sense and be moved by an internal principle, prescinding from other perfections, then whatever other perfection supervened would relate to animal as a co-part and not as implicitly contained in the notion of animal. Animal would not be a genus. As a genus it signifies something from whose form sense and motion can flow, whatever that form might be, whether it is sensible soul alone or both sensible and rational.

Thus genus signifies indeterminately everything that is in the species and not just matter alone. Difference signifies the whole and not form alone and the definition too signifies the whole species – but differently. For genus signifies the whole by determining what is material in the thing without the determination of its proper form; genus is taken from the matter although it is not matter. This is clear because body means that which has a perfection such that three dimensions can be designated in it, which perfection is related materially to any further perfection. Difference on the other hand is a denomination drawn from the determined form without any determinate matter being mentioned. Take the case of a thing being called animate, namely, that which has a soul; this does not tell us whether it is a body or something else. Hence Avicenna says that genus is not understood in difference as part of its essence, but only as being outside essence, as the subject is in the understanding of properties. Therefore the genus is not predicated as such of difference, the Philosopher says in *Metaphysics* 3 and *Topics* 4, but in the way that a subject is predicated of its property. The definition or species comprises both, namely the determinate matter that the genus term signifies and the determinate form that the difference term signifies.

From this it is clear why genus, species and difference relate proportionally to matter, form and the natural compound, although they are not the same as them, because the genus is not matter, but drawn from matter as signifying the whole, nor difference form, but drawn from form as signifying the whole. That is why we say that man is rational animal, and not from animal and from rational as we say he is from soul and body: for man is said to be from soul and body as a third thing constituted from two things neither of which he is, for a man is not soul nor is he body. But if man is said in some way to be constituted of animal and rational, it will not be as a third thing constituted of two things, but as a third concept composed of two concepts. For animal is conceived without the determination of any special form and expresses the nature of the thing by means of that which is material with respect to its ultimate perfection. The concept of the difference 'rational' consists in the determination of special form: from these two concepts is constituted the concept of species or definition. Therefore just as the constituents of a thing are not predicated of it, neither are the constituent concepts predicated of the complex concept, for we do not say that the definition is the genus or the difference.

However although genus signifies the whole essence of species, it is not necessary that there be the same essence of different species of the same genus. The unity of genus stems from this very indetermination or indifference. But what is signified by genus is not numerically the same in the different species, in which something else supervenes – namely, the difference which determines it; in much the same way numerically one form determines matter. But because genus signifies some form – though not determinately this one or that – it is the same form that difference determinately expresses and that the genus indeterminately signifies. As the Commentator says in *Metaphysics* 11, prime matter is called one by the removal of all forms, but genus is called one by the comprehensive universality of the form signified. Thus it is clear that the addition of difference removes the indetermination that was the cause of the unity of genus and there come into view species essentially different.

We have said that the nature of species is undetermined with respect to the individual just as genus is undetermined with respect to its species. When the genus is predicated of species it implies in its signification, though indistinctly, everything that is determinately in the species. So too species as predicated of the individual signifies all that is essential in the individual, though indistinctly. In this way the essence of species is signified by the name man, and man is predicated of Socrates. However if the nature of species were signified as prescinding from designated matter, which is the principle of individuation, then it is to take it as a part and it is signified by the name humanity; humanity signifies that whereby man is man. Designated matter is not that thanks to which man is man, and thus is not among the things whereby man is man. Clearly then, designated matter is excluded from or prescinded from in its signification. It is because the part is not predicated of the whole that humanity is not predicated of man or of Socrates. Avicenna says that the quiddity of the composed thing is not the compound of which it is the quiddity, although the quiddity itself is composed: humanity, though it is complex, is not man. Indeed, it must be received in something which is designated matter.

Because, as has been said, the designation of species with respect to genus is through form, and the designation of the individual with respect to species is through matter, it is necessary that the name signifying that whence the nature of genus is taken, prescinding from the determinate form perfecting species, signify a material part of the whole, as body is a material part of man; but the name signifying that whence the nature of species is drawn, prescinding from designated matter, signifies a formal part. Humanity therefore is signified as a form and is called the form of the whole, not as superadded to the essential parts, namely form and matter, in the way the form of house is superadded to its integral parts, but rather as the form which is the whole, namely a form comprising matter as well, although with precision from those things by which matter is designated.

Clearly then the terms 'man' and 'humanity' signify the essence of man, though differently, as has been said. 'Man' signifies it as a whole because it does not prescind from the designation of matter but implicitly and indistinctly contains it, much as the genus is said to contain the difference, which is why the term man is predicated of individuals. But 'humanity' signifies the essence as a part, because it contains in its signification only what is proper to man as man, and prescinds from every other designation: which is why it is not predicated of individual men. Because of this, the term 'essence' is sometimes predicated of a thing, as when we say that Socrates is a certain essence, but sometimes this is denied, as when we say that the essence of Socrates is not Socrates.

CHAPTER 3
ESSENCE AND UNIVERSALITY

Having examined what the word essence means in complex substances, we go on to ask how it relates to the notions of genus and species and difference. Because that to which the notions of genus and species and difference belong is predicated of this designated singular, it is impossible that the notion of universal – namely of genus or of species – should belong to the essence as it is signified in the manner of a part, for example, humanity or animality. That is why Avicenna said that rationality is not the difference but the principle of the difference; for the same reason, humanity is not the species nor animality the genus. Nor can it be said that the notion of genus or species belongs to essence because it is something existing apart from singulars, as the Platonists held. If that were so genus and species could not be predicated of the individual; for we cannot say that Socrates is something separated from himself or that such a separated thing would contribute to knowledge of this singular thing. It remains that the notion of genus or species belongs to essence insofar as it is signified in the manner of a whole, as by 'man' or 'animal', which implicitly and indistinctly contain everything that is in the individual.

The nature or essence so taken can be considered in two ways. In the most absolute and proper consideration of it: nothing is true of the essence except what belongs to it as such; whatever else might be attributed to it would be a false attribution. For example, 'rational' and 'animal' and the other qualities which fall under his definition belong to man insofar as he is man. White and black and such qualities, which are not part of the concept of humanity, do not belong to man as man. Can a nature so considered be called one or many? Neither, because both are outside the understanding of humanity, yet both can attach to it. For if plurality were of the very understanding of a nature, it could never be one, yet it is one in Socrates. Similarly if unity were of its notion, then it would be one and the same in Socrates and Plato, nor could it be multiplied in many individuals. In another way the essence can be considered as it exists in this or that, and thus something can be predicated of it *per accidens* by reason of that in which it is, as when man is said to be white because Socrates is white, although this does not belong to man insofar as he is man.

This nature can exist in two ways, however: in one way in singulars and in another way in the soul, and in both cases accidental qualities befall the nature. In singulars it has multiple existence because of the different singulars. None of this pertains to the nature itself in its first or absolute consideration. For it is false to say that it pertains to the essence of man as such to exist in this singular, for then it would never exist outside this singular; similarly if it pertained to man as man *not* to exist in this singular, it would never be in him. But it is true to say that man, although not just as man, is such that it is in this singular or that, or in the soul. Therefore the nature of man absolutely considered clearly abstracts from any sort of existence, but in such a way that it does not prescind from either of them. The nature considered absolutely is what is predicated of all individuals.

It cannot, however, be said that the notion of universality belongs to the nature so taken. Unity and community are of the very meaning of the universal and neither of these belongs to human nature as it is considered absolutely. For if universality were included in the understanding of man, then in whatever individual the nature were found, universality would be found. This is of course false, because there is no universality in Socrates: whatever is in him is individuated. Similarly it cannot be said that the notion of genus or species belongs to human nature as it exists in individuals. Human nature is not found in individuals as a unit common to all, which the meaning of universal requires. It follows that the notion of species belongs to human nature as it exists in the intellect.

Human nature itself exists in the intellect as abstracted from all individuating characteristics; therefore it has a uniform notion in all individuals outside the soul, because it is equally the similitude of all and conducive to the knowledge of each insofar as they are men. Because the nature has such a relation to all individuals, the intellect fashions the notion of species and attributes it to the nature. Hence the Commentator says at the beginning of the *De anima* that 'it is intellect that causes universality in things'; and Avicenna says the same in his *Metaphysics*. And although this nature as understood has the notion of universality as it compares to things outside the soul, because it is the similitude of all, none the less insofar as it exists in this intellect or that it is a particular understood species. From this appears the defect of the Commentator in *De anima* 3, who wants to conclude from the universality of the form understood to the unity of the faculty of understanding in all men. But the universality of the form is not its existence in the intellect but only insofar as it refers to things as their likeness. If there were one statue representing many men, it is clear that the image or likeness of the statue has a singular and proper existence as it is in this matter, but it has the notion of community insofar as it is common to many things represented.

It pertains to human nature according to its absolute consideration to be predicated of Socrates, although the notion of species does not belong to it according to its absolute consideration but is one of the accidents that befall it as it exists in intellect. Hence species is not predicated of Socrates, as if we said, 'Socrates is a species.' This would necessarily happen if the notion of species belonged to man as it exists in Socrates, or according to its absolute consideration: whatever belongs to man as man is predicated of Socrates insofar as he is a man.

To be predicated belongs to genus as such, since it is part of its definition. For predication is something completed by the action of intellect composing and dividing, having as its basis in reality the unity of those things of which one is said of another. Hence the notion of predicability can be included in the notion of this intention which is the genus, which likewise is completed through the act of the intellect. Nevertheless that to which the intellect attributes the intention of predicability, joining it with another, is not itself the intention of genus, but rather that to which the intellect attributes the intention of genus, for example, to what is signified by the word animal.

Thus it is clear how essence or nature relates to the notion of species. The notion of species is not among the things which belong to the nature according to its absolute consideration, nor is it among the accidents which follow on the existence it has outside the soul, like whiteness and blackness; rather, it is among the accidents which follow on it according to the existence it has in intellect. It is in this way too that the notions of genus and difference belong to it.

CHAPTER 4
ESSENCE IN SEPARATED SUBSTANCES

It remains to be seen now how essence is found in separated substances – namely, in the soul, in intelligences and in the first cause. However, although everyone concedes the simplicity of the first cause, some seek to introduce the composition of form and matter into intelligences and in the soul. The author of this position seems to have been Avicebron, in his *Fountain of Life*. But this position conflicts with the common sayings of the philosophers, since they say that such substances are separated from matter and prove them to be without any matter. The most powerful demonstration of this is found in the faculty of understanding. For it is apparent that forms are actually intelligible only insofar as they are separated from matter and its conditions, and they are made actually intelligible by the power of the understanding substance insofar as they are received in it and are acted upon by it. Therefore every understanding substance must be wholly immune from matter. It has neither a material part nor is it like the material forms impressed in matter.

No one can say that intelligibility is impeded by corporeal matter alone. For if that were the case, since matter is called corporeal only insofar as it is subject to a corporeal form, it would follow that matter has the characteristic of impeding intelligibility from the corporeal form. But this cannot be, because the corporeal form itself is actually intelligible, like other forms, insofar as it is abstracted from matter. Hence in no way is there composition of matter and form in the soul or in the intelligence in such wise that essence in them would be understood as it is in corporeal substances.

But there is a composition of form and existence, hence in the comment on Proposition 9 of the *Book of Causes* we read that intelligence has form and existence: form meaning there the quiddity itself or the simple nature.

How this is so is easily seen. Things which are so related that one is the cause of the existence of the other are such that the cause can exist without the other, and not vice versa. But such is the relation of matter and form that form gives existence to matter; therefore it is impossible for matter to be without some form, but it is not impossible for there to be some form without matter, since form as form does not have dependence on matter. But if there are forms that can exist only in matter, this is true of them insofar as they are distant from the first principle which is first and pure act. Those forms which are closest to the first principle, accordingly, are forms as such, subsisting without matter. The entire genus of form does not require matter, as has been said; the forms which do not are called intelligences and it is not necessary that the essences or quiddities of these substances be anything other than form itself.

The essences of complex and simple substances differ in that the essence of the complex is not form alone but is composed of form and matter, whereas the essence of simple substance is form alone. Two other differences flow from this. One is that the essence of complex substance can be signified either as a whole or as a part, which befalls it on account of the designation of matter, as has been said. Therefore it is not in just any way that the essence of the complex thing is predicated of it, for it cannot be said that man is his quiddity. But the essence of the simple thing, which is its form, can be signified only as a whole, since there is nothing apart from form that might be the recipient of form; that is why the essence of the simple substance can be predicated of it. Avicenna said that 'the quiddity of the simple is the simple thing itself' because there is nothing else receiving it.

The second difference is that the essence of complex things, because it is received in designated matter, is multiplied according to its division. Hence it happens that some things are specifically the same and numerically different. But the essence of the simple is not received in matter, so there cannot be any multiplication of it. Nor in such substances do we find many individuals of the same species. There are as many species as there are individuals, as Avicenna expressly says.

Although they are forms alone without matter, such substances are not utterly simple nor pure act. They have a tinge of potentiality, which is clear from this – that whatever does not enter into the understanding of an essence or quiddity comes to it from without and is composed with the essence. No essence can be understood without the things that are parts of the essence. But every essence or quiddity can be understood without its existence being understood: for I can understand what a man or phoenix is and yet not know whether they exist in reality. Therefore, it is clear that to exist is other than the essence or quiddity. Unless of course there is something whose quiddity is its very existence. Such a thing is first and one, because it is impossible for there to be a multiplication of anything except by the addition of some difference, as the nature of genus is multiplied into species; either because form is received in diverse matters, as the nature of species is multiplied in diverse individuals, or because one is absolute and the other received in something, as if there were some separated heat it would be other than a non-separated heat by its very separation. If, however, there is given a thing which is existence alone, subsisting existence itself, this existence would not receive the addition of a difference, since it would not then be existence alone but existence along with some form. Much less would it receive the addition of matter, since then it would not be subsistent but material. Consequently, a thing which is its own existence can only be one, and it must be said that in every other thing its existence is one thing and its quiddity or nature or form other. In intelligences existence must be outside form, and that is why it is said that an intelligence is form and existence.

Whatever belongs to a thing is either caused by the principles of its nature, for example, risible in man; or comes to it from some extrinsic principle, as light to air from the influence of the sun. Existence cannot be caused by the form or quiddity of a thing – I mean as an efficient cause – because in this way a thing would be a cause of itself and produce itself in existence, which is impossible. Therefore it is necessary that each thing whose existence is other than its nature has its existence from another. And because whatever is from another is reduced to what is *per se* as to its first cause, there must be some thing which is the cause of the being of all things by the fact that it is existence alone, otherwise there would be an infinite regress in causes, since everything which is not existence alone has a cause of its existence, as has been said. It is evident then that an intelligence is form and existence, and that it has existence from the first being who is existence alone, and that this is the first cause, God.

If each thing which receives something from another is in potency to it, and what is received in it is its act, the quiddity or form that is the intelligence is in potency to the existence it receives from God, and that received existence is in the mode of an act. Thus potency and act are found in intelligences, but not form and matter except equivocally. To suffer, to receive, to be a subject, and all such qualities as are found in things by reason of matter, belong equivocally to intellectual substances and corporeal substances, as the Commentator says in *De anima* 3. And because the quiddity of intelligence is the intelligence itself, its quiddity or essence is identical with it and the existence it received from God is that whereby it subsists among the things that are. Because of this some say that such substances are composed of *that whereby* and *that which*, or, as Boethius says, from *what is* and *existence*.

Since potency and act are found in intelligences, it is possible to find a multitude of intelligences, as it would not be if there were no potency in them. Hence the Commentator says in *De anima* 3 that if the nature of the possible intellect were unknown, we would be unable to find a multitude in separated substances. Therefore the intelligences differ from one another on the basis of grade of potency and act, such that the higher intelligence, which is closer to the First Being, has more act and less potency, and so on accordingly with the others.

The human soul is the lowest level of intellectual substance and its possible intellect relates to intelligible forms as prime matter – which is the bottom of the scale of sensible being – relates to sensible forms, as the Commentator says in *De anima* 3. The Philosopher compares it to a tablet on which nothing has been written. Because it has more of potency than other intellectual substances, making it close to material things that they might be drawn to participate in its existence. The composition of soul and body results in one existent composite, although that existence as it pertains to soul does not depend on body. Therefore, after the soul come other forms which have more of potency and are closer to matter and which cannot exist apart from matter. Among them there are rank and order extending to the first forms of the elements which are closest to matter; hence the only operation they have follows on the demand of active and passive qualities and of other things which dispose matter for form.

CHAPTER 5
DIFFERENT BEINGS, DIFFERENT ESSENCES

In the light of the above it is clear how essence is found in different things. Essence relates to substance in three ways. First there is the one who is God, whose essence is his very existence. Indeed, because his essence is not different from his existence, some philosophers maintain that God has no quiddity or essence. It follows from this that he is not in a genus, because whatever is in a genus must have a quiddity different from its existence, since the quiddity or nature of the genus and species do not differ in their definitions in the things whose genera and species they are, although they have diverse existence in each.

Though we say that God is existence alone, we ought not to fall into the error of those who say that God is that universal existence whereby each thing formally is. A characteristic of the existence of God is that nothing can be added to it, hence it is distinct from every other existence by its own purity. That is why in the comment on Proposition 9 of the *Book of Causes* it is said that the individuation of the first cause, which is existence alone, is through its pure goodness. Common existence, however, is understood as neither including nor excluding addition since that would rule out the possibility of understanding it as in a being which is something besides existence.

Similarly too, although He is existence alone, He does not lack any other perfections and worthy properties. Indeed, He has all the perfections which are in all genera, thanks to which He is called simply perfect, as both the Philosopher and the Commentator say in *Metaphysics* 5, but He has them in a more excellent way than other things: in Him they are one, in others diverse. This is because all these perfections belong to Him according to His simple existence. If something through one quality could perform the activities of all qualities, it would have all qualities in its one quality. That is how God has all perfections in His existence.

In a second way, essence is found in created intelligences whose essence and existence differ, though their essence is without matter. Hence their existence is not absolute, but received, therefore finite and limited to the capacity of the receiving nature. Their nature or quiddity is absolute, not being received in any matter. Hence it is said in the *Book of Causes* that intelligences are infinite with reference to things below and finite with reference to what is above, for they are finite with respect to their existence, which they receive from above, but they are not limited downward because their forms are not limited to the capacity of any matter receiving them. As has been said, a plurality of individuals of one species is not found in such substances, except in the case of the human soul, and this because of the body with which it is united. And though its individuation depends on body opportunely by way of its beginning, since it only comes to be individuated in the body of which it is the act, it does not follow that its individuation perishes when body is subtracted. Its absolute existence is individuated by being made the form of this body, but that existence remains individuated for ever. Therefore Avicenna says that the individuation and multiplication of souls depend on body with respect to its beginning but not with respect to its end.

Because quiddity is not the same as existence in these substances, they can be placed in a category and genus and species and difference are found in them, although their proper differences are hidden from us. The essential differences of sensible things are also hidden from us, so they are signified through accidental differences which take their rise from the essential, as a cause is signified by its effect; for example, when biped is given as man's difference. The proper accidents of immaterial substances are unknown to us so we cannot signify their differences either by essential or accidental differences.

Note too that genus and difference cannot be taken in the same way in these two kinds of substances, because in sensible substance genus is taken from that which is material in the thing and difference from that which is formal in it. Hence Avicenna says at the beginning of his *On the Soul* that in things composed of matter and form 'their simple difference is constituted from it', that is, from the form. Form itself is not the difference, but the principle of the difference, as he says in his *Metaphysics*. Such a difference is called the simple difference because it is taken from that which is part of the thing's quiddity, namely its form. However, since immaterial substances are simple quiddities, in them the difference cannot be taken from a part of, but only from the whole of, quiddity. Therefore, at the beginning of *On the Soul*, Avicenna says that 'only things composed of matter and form have a simple difference'.

So too in them the genus is drawn from the whole essence, but in a different way. For one separated substance is like another in immateriality, but they differ from one another in grade of perfection according to distance from potentiality and closeness to pure act. In them genus is drawn from what follows on their being immaterial, such as intellectuality or the like, whereas difference is drawn from that which follows on grade of perfection, which however is unknown to us. Nor need these differences be accidental because they are according to greater or lesser perfection, which do not diversify species: the grade of perfection in receiving the same form does not diversify species – the more or less white share in the same nature of whiteness – but the diverse grades of perfection in these participated forms or natures diversify species, as nature proceeds through grades from plant to animal through things which are intermediate between plant and animal, according to the Philosopher in *On the History of Animals* 8.1. Again, it is not necessary that the distinction between intellectual substances always be through two true differences, since this cannot happen with anything, as the Philosopher says in *On the Parts of Animals* 1.2.

In a third way essence is found in substances composed of matter and form, in which existence is received and limited because they receive existence from another and furthermore their nature or quiddity is received in designated matter. Therefore they are finite both upward and downward, and in them there can be a multiplication of individuals of the same species because of the division of designated matter. How essence relates to logical intentions in them has already been discussed.

CHAPTER 6
ESSENCE AND ACCIDENTS

Having discussed how it is found in all the kinds of substance, it remains to be seen how essence is found in accidents. Because, as has been said, essence is that which is signified by the definition, accidents will have essence in the same way that they can be defined. But they have an incomplete definition, because they can be defined only by putting their subject into the definition. This is so because they do not exist themselves apart from the subject. But just as substantial existence results from form and matter when they are composed, so accidental existence results when the accident advenes to the subject. Neither substantial form nor matter has a complete essence, because in the definition of substantial form that of which it is the form must be put, and thus its definition is by way of an addition of something outside it, as is the case with the definition of accidental form. For example, the natural philosopher who considers soul only insofar as it is a form of physical body puts body in the definition of soul.

Substantial form and accidental form differ. Substantial form does not have absolute existence in itself apart from the thing that it informs, nor does the matter to which it advenes. This is why from the conjunction of the two an existence in which a thing subsists in itself results, and something *per se* one is brought about as well as a certain essence. Hence form, although considered in itself it does not have the complete notion of the essence, is none the less part of the complete essence.

That to which the accident advenes is a being complete in itself, already subsisting in its own existence, and this existence naturally precedes the accident that comes to it. Therefore the supervenient accident – the conjunction of itself with that to which it advenes – is not the cause of the existence in which the thing subsists and by which the thing is of itself a being. Rather, it causes a secondary existence without which the subsistent thing can be understood to exist, as the first can be understood without the second. Thus, what is brought about by the composition of accident and subject is accidentally rather than *per se* one. Thus the accident neither has the notion of a complete essence nor is it a part of a complete essence, but it is essence in a certain respect just as it is a being in a certain respect.

Because what is especially and most truly in any genus is the cause of the other things in that genus – fire, which is the limit of heat, is the cause of heat in warm things, as is said in *Metaphysics* 2 – so substance, which is first in the genus of being as especially and most truly having essence, must be the cause of accidents, which secondarily and as it were in a certain respect participate in the notion of being. Which occurs variously. For since the parts of substance are matter and form, some accidents chiefly follow on form and others on matter. There is a form whose existence does not depend on matter, namely, the intellectual soul; but matter exists only through form. Hence in the accidents which follow on form there are some that do not share in matter, for example thinking, which is not by means of a bodily organ, as the Philosopher proves in *On the Soul* 3, and others that do share in matter, for example sensing. But there is no accident following on matter that does not share in matter.

A certain diversity is found among the accidents which follow on matter. For some accidents follow on matter according to an ordering they have to a special form, such as masculine and feminine in animals, a diversity reducible to matter, as is said in *Metaphysics* 10. Hence, the form of animal being taken away, such accidents remain only equivocally. Others follow on matter according to an ordering to a general form, and these remain when the special form is taken away, as black pigment is in the Ethiopian from a mixture of elements and not by reason of soul, and therefore after death it remains.

Because a thing is individuated by matter and placed in a genus or species because of its form, the accidents which follow on matter are accidents of the individual, according to which members of the same species differ among themselves. The accidents which follow on form are properties of either genus or species and thus are found in everything which shares in the nature of the genus or species, as risible follows on man's form, since laughter is occasioned by some awareness in man's soul.

It should also be noted that accidents in full actuality are sometimes caused by the essential principles, like the heat in fire which is always hot, but sometimes only in aptitude such that they are completed by an external agent, as the diaphaneity of air is completed by the external luminous body. In the latter, the aptitude is an inseparable accident, but the completion that comes from a principle outside the essence of the thing, or which does not enter into the constitution of the thing, is separable, for example to be moved and the like.

It should further be noted that genus, difference and species are understood in accidents differently than they are in substances. From the coming together of substantial form and matter something in itself one results which is properly placed in the category of substance. In substances concrete names which signify the composite are properly said to be in a species or genus, for example, man or animal. Neither form nor matter is in a category in this way, save by way of reduction, as principles are said to be in a genus. Nothing in itself one comes to be from accident and subject; hence from their conjunction no nature results to which the intention of genus or species could be attributed. Hence accidental terms expressed concretely, like white or musical, are not put into a category as species or genera except by reduction, but only as abstractly expressed, like whiteness and music. And since accidents are not composed of matter and form, in them genus cannot be taken from matter or difference from form as they are in composed substances. Genus must first be taken from their very mode of being, insofar as being is said diversely, according to prior and posterior, of the ten genera of category. Thus the definition of quantity is that it is the measure of substance and quality that it is a disposition of substance, and so with the rest, according to the Philosopher in *Metaphysics* 9.

Differences in them are taken from the diversity of principles from which they are caused. And because properties are caused by the proper principles of the subject, the subject is put in their definition in the place of difference, if they are abstractly defined – which is how they are properly in a genus – for example, snubness is defined as the curvature of the nose. It is otherwise when they are defined as concretely expressed, for then the subject is put into the definition as the genus, because they would then be defined after the manner of composed substances in which the notion of genus is drawn from matter, for example we say that snub is a curved nose. It is similar when one accident is the principle of another, as action and passion and quantity are principles of relation, and thus it is with reference to these that the Philosopher subdivides relation in *Metaphysics* 5. However, because the proper principles of accidents are not always manifest, sometimes we take the differences of accidents from their effects, such as dispersion or concentration produces differences of colour, insofar as there is an abundance or paucity of light, from which the different species of colour are caused.

Thus it is clear how essence is found in substance and accident and in complex and simple substance, and how in all these the intentions of universality are logically found – except the First, in whom there is full simplicity and to whom neither the notion of genus and species nor consequently definition belongs because of His simplicity. And that is the end and completion of this discourse. Amen.

4. The Nature of Theology. Commentary on Sentences 1, Prologue (1252–4)

The twelfth century was one of cultural consolidation. The Glossa Ordinaria, *a great compendium of biblical criticism drawn from the Christian tradition of scriptural interpretation, is a case in point. Theologians were seeking to understand the nature of their discipline with a greater clarity. In the course of the century the works of Anselm, Peter Abelard, the Victorine school and particularly the work of Hugh of St Victor were examples of this quest. But the* Sentences *of Peter Lombard, a theologian who was to become bishop of Paris, would cast the longest historical shadow. Taking his cue from St Augustine, Peter Lombard presents the whole range of Christian doctrine, from the Trinity to the sacraments, from the Incarnation to moral goodness and badness. His* Sentences *became the set work during the following century on which the fledgeling theologian had to win his spurs. The Bachelor of the* Sentences *explained and expanded on Lombard's work, expanding the concept of commentary and interpretation in doing so.*

Thomas's commentary or scriptum *on the* Sentences *first gives the text of Lombard and then a* divisio textus, *basically an outline of the contents of the passage with an emphasis on its inner order. That being done, questions suggested by the text were taken up. Often these went far beyond the* Sentences. *Perhaps no discussion can better underscore the progress in theology from the twelfth to the thirteenth centuries than the passage making up this chapter. At the outset of his commentary, Thomas sensibly asks what the book is about. His discussion brings the work of Peter Lombard into the vastly different ambience of the thirteenth century. And it is a crisp and clear discussion of the distinction between philosophy and theology. Peter Lombard could not have engaged in such a discussion in the way that Thomas does. For the student of Thomas, apart from its intrinsic interest, this text maps out the intellectual terrain of Thomas's teaching.*

PROLOGUE

'I, wisdom, have poured out rivers. I, like a brook out of a river of mighty water: I, like a channel of a river, and like an aqueduct, came out of paradise. I said: I will water my garden of plants and I will water abundantly the fruits of my meadow.'   Ecclesiasticus 24.40–42

Among the many opinions coming from different sources as to what true wisdom might be, the Apostle gives one that is singularly firm and true when he says, 'Christ, the power of God and wisdom of God, has become for us God-given wisdom' (1 Corinthians 1.24, 30). This does not mean that only the Son is wisdom, since Father, Son and Holy Spirit are one wisdom, just as they are one essence. Rather, wisdom especially belongs to the Son because the works of wisdom in many ways agree with what is proper to the Son. Through the wisdom of God the hidden things of God are made manifest and the works of creatures are produced, and not only produced, but restored and perfected. I mean that perfection whereby a thing is called perfect when it has attained its proper end.

That *the manifestation of divine things* pertains to the wisdom of God is clear from the fact that God himself fully and perfectly knows himself by his wisdom. Hence, if we know anything of him it must be derived from him, because every imperfect thing takes its origin from the perfect. So it is said, 'And who shall know thy thought, except thou give wisdom and send thy Holy Spirit from above?' (Wisdom 9.17). This manifestation is effected specially by the Son: he himself is the Word of the Father, as is said at the beginning of John, and manifesting the Father and the whole Trinity in speech belongs to him. Hence we read in Matthew 11.27, 'Nor does anyone know the Father except the Son, and him to whom the Son chooses to reveal him'; and in John 1.18, 'No one has at any time seen God. The only begotten Son, who is in the bosom of the Father, he has revealed him.' It is rightly said of the person of the Son therefore, 'I, wisdom, have poured out rivers.' I take these rivers to be an eternal procession whereby the Son proceeds from the Father and the Holy Spirit from both in an ineffable manner. These rivers were once hidden and in some way confused with the likenesses of creatures, even in the enigmas of Scripture, so that scarcely any of the wise believed the mystery of the Trinity. The Son of God came and poured forth rivers, making known the name of the Trinity. Matthew 28.20: 'Go, therefore, and make disciples of all nations, baptizing them in the name of the Father, and of the Son, and of the Holy Spirit.' And Job 28.11: 'The depths also of rivers he hath searched: and hidden things he hath brought to light.' This touches on the matter of Book One.

The second thing that pertains to the wisdom of God is *the production of creatures*. He not only has speculative but also operative wisdom – like that of the artisan to his works – concerning created things. Thus Psalm 103.24: 'Thou hast made all things with wisdom.' And Wisdom itself says in Proverbs 8.30: 'I was with him, forming all things.' This attribute is especially found in the Son insofar as he is the image of the invisible God, in whose likeness all things are formed: 'He is the image of the invisible God, the first-born of every creature, for in him were created all things' (Colossians 1.15); 'All things were made through him' (John 1.3). Rightly then does the person of the Son say, 'I, like a brook out of a river of mighty water,' in which is noted both the order and mode of creation.

Order, because as a brook is derived from a river, so the temporal procession of creatures [derives] from the eternal procession of persons. Hence in Psalm 148.5 is said, 'He commanded and they were made.' The Word gave birth to what was in him in order that it might be, according to Augustine in the Supplement of his *Literal Commentary on Genesis* 1.2. It is always what is first that is the cause of what is after, according to Aristotle in *Metaphysics* 2; hence the first procession is the cause and reason of every subsequent procession.

The mode is signified in two respects: on the part of the one creating, who, although he completes all things, is measured by nothing else, which is conveyed by calling him mighty. And, on the part of the creature, because just as the brook proceeds beyond the bed of the river, so the creature proceeds from God beyond the unity of essence, in which as in a river bed the flow of the persons is contained. And in this the matter of the Second Book is made known.

The third thing that pertains to the wisdom of God is *the restoration of his works*. A thing should be repaired by the one who made it; hence it is fitting that those things which were made through wisdom, through wisdom should be repaired; hence in Wisdom 9.19 it is said, 'For by wisdom they were healed, whatsoever hath pleased thee, O Lord, from the beginning.' This restoration is especially accomplished by the Son, insofar as he has been made man and, by the restored state of man, in a certain way restores all things which were made for man. Hence in Colossians 1.20: 'Through him he should reconcile to himself all things, whether on the earth or in the heavens.' Rightly then from the person of the Son is it said, 'I like the channel of a river and like an aqueduct came out of paradise.' This paradise is the glory of God the Father, from which he came forth into the valley of our misery, not because he set it aside, but because he hid it. 'I came forth from God and have come into the world.' Concerning this coming forth two things are made known, namely, its mode and its fruit. The channel of a river is swiftest, hence it designates the mode whereby, as out of an impetus of love, Christ completed the mystery of our redemption. Hence Isaiah 59.19: 'He shall come as a violent stream which the spirit of the Lord driveth on.' Its fruit is designated when it is said 'like an aqueduct', for just as an aqueduct is produced from one source which it distributes in order to make the earth fruitful, so from Christ flow diverse kinds of grace for nourishing the Church, as is said in Ephesians 4.11: 'And he himself gave some men as apostles, and some as prophets, others again as evangelists, and others as pastors and teachers, in order to perfect the saints for a work of ministry, for building up the body of Christ.' This touches the matter of Book Three, in the first part of which the mysteries of our redemption are treated, and in the second the graces gathered for us by Christ.

The fourth thing that pertains to the wisdom of God is *perfection*, whereby a thing is conserved in its end. Take away the end, and only vanity remains, which wisdom cannot suffer to abide with her; hence it is said, in Wisdom 8.1, that wisdom 'reacheth from end to end mightily and ordereth all things sweetly'. A thing is ordered when it is stabilized in its end, which it naturally desires. This especially pertains to the Son, who, since he is the true and natural Son of God, leads us to the glory of our paternal inheritance. Hence Hebrews 2.10: 'For it became him for whom are all things and through whom are all things, who had brought many sons into glory.' Hence it is rightly said, 'I said, I will water my garden of plants.'

The attainment of the end requires preparation, by which whatever is not appropriate to the end is removed; thus Christ too, in order that he might lead us to the end of eternal glory, prepared the medicine of the sacraments, by which the wound of sin is wiped away. Two things are to be noted in the foregoing words, namely, preparation, which is through the sacraments, and leading into glory.

Preparation is made known by 'I will water my garden of plants.' The garden is the Church, of which the Song of Songs 4.12 says, 'My sister, my spouse, is a garden enclosed,' in which there are diverse plants according to the diverse order of the saints, all of them planted by the hand of the Omnipotent. This garden is watered by Christ with the streams of the sacraments, which flowed from his side. Hence in commendation of the beauty of the Church it is said in Numbers 24.5, 'How beautiful are thy tabernacles, O Jacob, and thy tents, O Israel!' and a little later, in verse 6, 'as watered gardens near the rivers'. Therefore the ministers of the Church who dispense the sacraments are called waterers: 'I have planted, Apollo watered' (1 Corinthians 3.6).

Induction into glory is made known in what follows: 'I will water abundantly the fruits of my meadow.' Christ's fruits are the faithful of the Church, which by his labour he brought forth like a mother, of which Isaiah 66.9: 'Shall not I that make others to bring forth children myself bring forth, saith the Lord?' The fruits of this bringing forth are the saints who are in glory, of which fruit the Song of Songs 5.1: 'Let my beloved come into his garden and eat the fruit of his apple trees.' He waters them from the abundance of his own fruition, of which abundance Psalm 35.9: 'They are filled with the bounteousness of thy house.' It is called bounteousness because it exceeds every measure of reason and desire. Isaiah 64.4: 'The eye hath not seen, O God, besides thee, what things thou hast prepared for them that wait for thee.' This touches the matter of Book Four, in the first part of which sacraments are treated, and in the second the glory of resurrection.

The aim of the *Sentences* is clear from what has been said.

QUESTION I

In order to make evident the sacred doctrine which is treated in this book, five things must be examined: (1) its necessity; (2) supposing it necessary, whether it is one science or many; (3) if one, whether it is practical or speculative; and if speculative, whether it is wisdom, knowledge or understanding; (4) its subject; (5) its mode.

Article 1: Is another doctrine beyond the natural disciplines necessary for men?

We proceed to the first question thus:

1. It seems that no doctrine beyond the natural disciplines is necessary for man. For as Dionysius says in the Letter to Polycarp, 'Philosophy is the knowledge of the things that exist.' And he observes, making an induction from each of them, that every kind of existing thing is treated in philosophy – of Creator and creature, of the works of nature as well as our works. But any doctrine must be of existing things, since there is no science of non-being. Therefore, there should be no doctrine beside the natural disciplines.

2. Again, every doctrine is for the sake of perfection, either of understanding, as with the speculative intellect, or with respect to an effect issuing in a work, as with the practical intellect. But both are accomplished by philosophy, because intellect is perfected by the demonstrative sciences, and the affections by the moral sciences. Therefore no other doctrine is necessary.

3. Moreover, whatever can be known from the principles of reason by the natural intellect is either treated in, or can be discovered by, the principles of philosophy. But the knowledge that can be achieved by natural intellect suffices for the perfection of man. Therefore, no other science than the philosophical is necessary.

In proof of the middle: That which can achieve its perfection by itself is more noble than that which cannot. But other animals and insensible creatures achieve their ends by purely natural means, though not without God, who works in all things. Therefore man, since he is nobler than they, can acquire knowledge sufficient for his perfection through natural intellect.

ON THE CONTRARY:
Hebrews 11.6: 'Without faith it is impossible to please God.' But it is of the highest necessity to please God. Therefore, since philosophy is incapable of attaining what is of faith, a doctrine which proceeds from the principles of faith is necessary.

Again, an effect which is not proportionate to its cause, leads only imperfectly to knowledge of the cause. All creatures are such an effect with respect to the creator, from whom they are infinitely distant. Therefore, they imperfectly lead to knowledge of him. Since philosophy proceeds from notions derived from creatures, it is insufficient to make God known. Therefore, there must be another higher science, which proceeds from revelation, and makes up for the defect of philosophy.

SOLUTION:

For light on this it should be known that all right-thinking men make contemplation of God the end of human life. But there are two kinds of contemplation. The one is through creatures and is imperfect, for the reason already given. Aristotle locates happiness in this kind of contemplation (*Ethics* 10) – it is a happiness 'on the way', of this life. To it is ordered the whole of philosophical knowledge which proceeds from concepts of creatures. The other is the contemplation of God whereby he is seen immediately in his essence. This is perfect and will be had in the Fatherland and is possible to man on the supposition of faith. Hence it is necessary that the things which are for the sake of the end be proportioned to the end, since a man while on the way is led by the hand to that contemplation, not through knowledge drawn from creatures, but rather as immediately inspired by the divine light. This is the doctrine of theology.

From this we can draw two conclusions. One, that this science as the principal one commands all the others; second, that it uses for its own sake all other sciences which are its vassals, as is evident in all ordered arts, where the end of one comes under the end of another. For example, pharmacy, which is the art of preparing remedies, is ordered to the end of medicine, which is health. Thus the physician orders the pharmacist and uses the medicines made by him for his own end. So too, since the end of philosophy in its entirety is below the end of theology, and ordered to it, theology ought to order the other sciences and use what is taught in them.

Ad 1. It should be said that although philosophy treats of existing things according to concepts derived from creatures, there must be another science which considers existing things according to notions received by the inspiration of the divine light.

Ad 2. From this the solution to the second objection is clear. Philosophy suffices for the perfection of intellect by natural knowledge, and of the affections by means of acquired virtue. But there must be another science through which intellect is perfected in the order of infused knowledge, and the affections by gratuitous love.

Ad 3. It should be said that in those things which acquire an equal goodness for their end, the argument set forth, namely, this is more noble than that which cannot achieve its end by itself. But that which acquires perfect goodness by many aids and activities is more noble than that which acquires an imperfect goodness through fewer means, or by itself, as the Philosopher says in *On the Heavens* 12. Thus is man, who is made to participate in divine glory itself, compared to other creatures.

Article 2: Should there be only one doctrine beyond the natural sciences?

We proceed to the second question thus:

1. It seems that there are several sciences and not just one beyond the natural sciences. Whatever a man can learn by concepts drawn from creatures, he can also learn by divine notions. But there are several sciences which employ creaturely concepts, differing in kind and in species, such as moral, natural, etc. Therefore sciences proceeding from divine notions ought to be many.

2. Again, each science is concerned with one kind of thing, as the Philosopher says in *Posterior Analytics* 1. But God and creature, both treated in divine doctrine, cannot be reduced to one genus, neither univocally nor analogically. Therefore divine science is not one. Proof of the middle. Whatever agree in genus whether univocally or analogically, share something the same, whether according to prior and posterior – as substance and accident share in the notion of being – or equally, as horse and cow share in the notion of animal. But God and creature do not share in anything that would be prior to and simpler than both. Therefore they are in no way reduced to one genus.

3. Again, the things we do, like acts of virtue, and the things nature does, are not contained in the same science, for the one pertains to moral, the other to natural science. But divine science deals with the things we do, treating virtues and precepts, and it also deals with things which are not our works, like angels and other creatures. It seems, then, that it is not one science.

ON THE CONTRARY:

Whatever agree in one notion can belong to the same science. Hence all things, insofar as they come together in the notion of being, pertain to metaphysics. But divine science treats things under a divine formality which embraces them all: all things are from him and for him. Therefore, although one, it can treat diverse things.

Moreover, things that belong to diverse sciences are treated in different books. But Sacred Scripture mixes everything, sometimes treating of morals, sometimes of the creator, sometimes of creatures, as is evident in practically all its books. Therefore the science is not diversified on this basis.

SOLUTION:

I reply that on this question it should be noted that knowledge is higher to the degree that it is more unified and extends to more things. Hence, God's intellect, which is highest, has distinct knowledge of all things through something one, which is God himself. So too, since this science is highest and derives its efficacy from the light of divine inspiration itself and, while remaining one and undivided, considers diverse things, and not just universally, like metaphysics, which considers all things insofar as they are beings, without descending to proper knowledge of moral matters or of natural things. Since the notion of being is diversified in diverse things metaphysics is insufficient for specific knowledge of them. But the divine light, remaining one in itself, is efficacious to make them manifest, as Dionysius says at the beginning of the *Celestial Hierarchy*.

Ad 1. The divine light, from the certitude of which this science proceeds, is efficacious in making manifest the many things which are treated in the different sciences of philosophy which proceed from conceptions of these things to knowledge. Therefore there is no need for this science to be divided.

Ad 2. The creator and creature are reduced to one, not by a community of univocation, but of analogy. This is of two kinds. Either it arises from this that things share in something in greater or lesser degrees, as potency and act – and substance and accident – share the notion of being. Or it arises from this that one thing receives its being and definition from another, and such is the analogy of creature to creator: the creature exists only to the degree that it descends from the primary being, and it is called being only because it imitates the first being. Thus it is with wisdom and all the other things which are said of the creature.

Ad 3. The things we do and the things nature does, taken in their proper notions, do not fall to the same science. However, one science having its certitude from the divine light, which is efficacious for knowledge of both, can consider both.

It might also be said that the virtues the theologian considers are not our work, but that God effects them in us without us, as Augustine says in *On Free Will*, 2.19.

Article 3: Is it practical or speculative?

We proceed to the third question:

1. This science seems to be practical. The end of the practical is some work, as the Philosopher says in *Metaphysics* 2. But this doctrine, which is of faith, is ordered chiefly to acting well: 'Faith without works is dead'; James 2.26 and, 'The good is understood by all doing it.' Psalm 90.10. [This is a mistaken reference.] Therefore, it seems to be practical.

ON THE CONTRARY:

In the preface to the *Metaphysics* the Philosopher says that the noblest of sciences is sought for its own sake. Practical sciences are not sought for their own sake, but for the sake of a work. Therefore, since this is the most noble among sciences, it will not be practical.

Moreover, practical science is concerned only with what is of our doing. But this doctrine includes angels and other creatures which are not works of ours. Therefore, it is not speculative but practical.

Sub-question 1: Is it a science?

It is further asked whether it is a science, and the answer seems to be no:

1. No science is concerned with the particular, according to the Philosopher in the *Posterior Analytics*. But Sacred Scripture tells of the doings of particular men, like Abraham, Isaac, etc. Therefore, it is not a science.

2. Moreover, every science proceeds from principles known of themselves which are obvious to all. But this science begins with believable things, which are not granted by all. Therefore, it is not a science.

3. Moreover, in every science a habit is acquired through the arguments set forth. But no habit is acquired in this science, because faith, on which the whole doctrine depends, is an infused, not an acquired, habit. Therefore it is not a science.

ON THE CONTRARY:
Augustine in *On the Trinity* 14 says that theology is the science of the things that pertain to man's salvation. So it is a science.

Sub-question 2: Is it wisdom?

It is further asked whether it is wisdom, and it seems that it isn't. Because, as the Philosopher says at the beginning of the *Metaphysics*, the wise man is most certain of the causes; but in this science no one is most certain because faith, on which this doctrine depends, is beneath science and above opinion. Therefore it is not wisdom.

ON THE CONTRARY:
1 Corinthians 2.6: 'Wisdom, however, we speak among those who are mature.' Since he is teaching this doctrine and speaking of it there, it seems that it is wisdom.

SOLUTION 1:
I reply that it must be said that this science, though one, is none the less perfect and sufficient for every human perfection, because of the efficacy of the divine light, something clear from the foregoing. Hence it perfects man both in right action and with respect to contemplation of the truth. Thus it is in some respects practical and in other respects speculative. But since every science ought to be thought of in terms of its end, and the ultimate end of this science is the contemplation of the First Truth 'in the Fatherland' of heaven, it is chiefly speculative. And since there are three speculative habits, according to the Philosopher in *Ethics* 6.7, namely wisdom, science and understanding, and we call something wisdom insofar as it considers the highest causes and is as it were the head and principle and commander of all sciences, this is more to be called wisdom than is metaphysics, since it considers the highest causes in the mode of those causes, because it is received from divine inspiration. Metaphysics, on the other hand, considers the highest causes through concepts drawn from creatures.

This science also has more claim to be called divine than has metaphysics because it is divine both as to its subject and to the mode of receiving, whereas metaphysics is called divine because of its subject alone. Wisdom, as the Philosopher says in *Ethics* 6.8, considers both conclusions and principles, therefore wisdom is both science and understanding, since science is of conclusions and understanding of principles.

Ad 1. It is not a work that is the ultimate end intended in this science, but rather contemplation of First Truth in the Fatherland, to which we come after having been purified by good works, as is said in Matthew 5.8, 'Blessed are the pure of heart.' Therefore, it is chiefly speculative rather than practical.

We concede the other two objections.

SOLUTION 2:

To the further question it should be said that this doctrine is a science, as has been said. To the objection about particulars, the response is that it is not about particulars as particulars, but only insofar as they are examples of things to be done, a practice followed in moral science as well because actions are particular and about particulars, which is why what pertains to morals is best exemplified by particular examples. Or it could be said that in science there are two things to consider, namely certitude, since not just any knowledge is called science, but only certain knowledge, and second that it is the term of learning, since everything in a science is ordered to knowing. From these it follows that science has two characteristics. From the first, that it is concerned with the necessary: contingent things cannot generate certitude. From the second, that it follows from principles. This varies from science to science, because higher sciences are from self-evident principles, for example, geometry, which has principles like, 'Equals taken from equals leave equals.' Lower sciences, which are subalternated to the higher, do not proceed from self-evident principles, but presuppose conclusions proved in the higher sciences and use them as principles though in truth they are not self-evident, but are proved in the higher science from self-evident principles. Thus perspective, which is concerned with the visual line, is subalternated to geometry from which it presupposes truths proved of the line as line. From them, as it were from principles, it proves conclusions about the line insofar as it is visual. But a science can be higher than another in two ways, either by reason of its subject, as geometry which is about magnitude is higher than perspective which is about visual magnitude, or by reason of its mode of knowing, and thus theology is below the knowledge that is God's. For we imperfectly know what he knows perfectly, and just as a science subalternated to a higher presupposes certain things and proceeds from these as from principles, so theology presupposes the articles of faith which are proved infallibly in God's knowledge, believes them and through them proceeds to prove what follows from the articles. Thus theology is as it were a science subalternated to the divine science from which it receives its principles.

Ad 1. This science has the articles of faith for its first principles which through the infused light of faith are known in themselves by the one having faith, much as principles are naturally instilled in us by the light of the agent intellect. Nor is it to be wondered at that they are not known to those who do not have the light of faith, since not even naturally instilled principles would be instilled in us without the light of the agent intellect. It is from such principles, not disdaining common principles, that this science proceeds; it has no way of proving them, save to defend them against naysayers, but then no scientist *proves* his principles.

Ad 2. It should be said that whereas the habit of first principles is not acquired by the other sciences but is had by nature, the habit of conclusions deduced from the first principles is acquired. So too in this doctrine the habit of faith, which is like the habit of principles, is not acquired, but the habit of those things which are deduced from them and which contribute to its defence.

We concede the third.

SOLUTION 3:
To the further question, whether it is wisdom, it should be answered that it is wisdom in the most proper sense, as has been said. To the objection that no one is most certain about this doctrine, we say it is false. The believer more firmly assents to the things that are of faith than to the first principles of reason. The statement that faith is below science is not true of infused faith, but of acquired faith, which is opinion fortified by argument. The habit of these principles, namely, of the articles, is called faith and not understanding because these principles are above reason and human reason is unable to grasp them perfectly. There results a kind of defective knowledge, but not from any defect of certitude in the things known, but from a defect in the knower. Reason led by faith grows in such a way that it more fully comprehends what is believed and thus in a way understands them. Hence Isaiah 7.9 says in one version, 'Unless you believe, you will not understand.'

Article 4: Is God the subject of this science?

We proceed to the fourth article thus:

1. It seems that God is the subject of this science. For a science should be entitled and named from its subject. But this science is called theology, that is, talk about God. Therefore, it seems that God is its subject.

ON THE CONTRARY: Boethius in *On the Trinity* 2 says that a simple form cannot be a subject. But such is God. Therefore he cannot be a subject.

2. Again, following Hugh of St Victor, it seems that its subject is the works of redemption, for he says in *On the Sacraments* 1.1.2 that 'the works of the first condition are the matter of other sciences, but the works of restoration are the matter of theology'. Therefore . . .

ON THE CONTRARY: Whatever is treated in a science must be contained in its subject. But theology considers the works of creation, as is evident in Genesis 1. It seems then that the works of restoration cannot be its subject.

3. Again, it seems that reality and sign are its subject for that on which the whole intention of the science bears is its subject. But the whole intention of theology bears on reality and sign, as the Master of the Sentences says at the beginning of Distinction 1. Therefore, reality and sign are the subject.

ON THE CONTRARY: Sciences differ from one another by the definitions of their subjects, since each science must have its proper subject. But other sciences too consider reality and sign. Therefore they are not the proper subject of this science.

SOLUTION:

I reply that the subject is compared to the science in at least three ways.

The first is that whatever falls to a science must be contained under its subject. Those considering this condition posit reality and sign as the subject of this science, some indeed the whole Christ, that is, head and members, because whatever is treated in this science can be reduced to this.

The second comparison is that what is chiefly sought in a science is knowledge of the subject. Hence since this science is chiefly ordered to knowledge of God, some posit God as its subject.

The third comparison is that a science is distinguished from all others by its subject, since sciences are divided somewhat as are things, as is said in *On the Soul* 3.8 and thus some posit the believable as the subject of this science. It is the fact that it proceeds from the inspiration of faith that distinguishes this science from all others. And some opt for the works of restoration, since the whole science aims at achieving the effect of restoration.

If we want a subject which would include all of these, we can say that *divine being as knowable through inspiration is the subject of this science.* Whatever is considered in this science is either God or things which are from God or ordered to God as such. So too the physician considers symptoms and causes and many other things insofar as they are healthy, that is, are in some way related to health. Thus to the degree that something more nearly approaches the true nature of divinity it deserves prior consideration in this science.

Ad 1. It should be said that God is not the subject save in the sense of what is chiefly intended, in the light of whom everything else in the science is considered. To the objection that a simple form cannot be a subject, we reply that this is true of an accident which none the less can be the subject of a predicate in a proposition, and any such thing can be the subject of a science so long as a predicate can be proved of it.

Ad 2. The works of restoration are not properly the subject of this science save in the sense that whatever is taught in this science is in some way ordered to our restoration.

Ad 3. Reality and sign, understood generally, are not the subject of this science, but only insofar as they are divine.

Article 5: Is its mode of proceeding artful?

To the fifth article we proceed thus:

1. The most noble science should have the most noble mode. But insofar as its mode is more artful it is more noble. Therefore, since this science is the most noble, its mode ought to be most artful.

2. Moreover, the mode of a science ought to be proportioned to the science. But this science is pre-eminently one, as has been proved, therefore its mode ought to be especially one. But the opposite seems true, since sometimes it proceeds by warning, sometimes by commanding, sometimes in other ways.

3. Widely differing sciences ought not to share the same mode. But poetry, which contains the least truth, is far different from this science

which is most true. Therefore, since the former proceeds by way of metaphorical locutions, the mode of this science should be different.

4. Moreover, Ambrose in *On Sacred Power* 1 says to Gratian, 'Away with arguments where faith is sought.' But faith is especially sought in sacred science. Therefore its mode should in no way be argumentative.

ON THE CONTRARY:

1 Peter 3.15 says, 'Be ready always with an answer to everyone who asks a reason for the hope that is in you.' But this could not be done without arguments. Therefore, it ought sometimes to use arguments.

The same is found in Titus 1.9: 'That he may be able both to exhort in sound doctrine and to confute opponents.'

SOLUTION:

I respond that it should be said that the mode of any science should be sought by considering its matter, as Boethius says in *On the Trinity* 1, and the Philosopher in *Ethics* 1. The principles of this science are received through revelation, therefore the mode of receiving these principles ought to be revelatory on the part of the one infusing, as in the visions of the prophets, and prayerful on the part of the recipient, as is evident in the Psalms. But because, apart from the infused light, the habit of faith is distinguished by determinate beliefs by the teaching of the preacher according to what is said in Romans 10.14 – 'And how are they to believe him whom they have not heard?' – just as the understanding of principles naturally instilled is determined by the sensibles received, so the truth of the preacher is confirmed by miracles, as is said in Mark 16.20: 'But they went forth and preached everywhere, while the Lord worked with them and confirmed the preaching by the signs that followed.' The mode of this science must also be narrative of signs which are done for the confirmation of faith. And because these principles are not proportionate to human reason in this life, which is accustomed to receive them from sensible things, it was necessary to prepare for knowledge of them by likenesses of sensible things. That is why the mode of this science must be metaphorical, or symbolic, or parabolic.

In Sacred Scripture the procedure from these principles leads to three things, namely, the *destruction of error*, which cannot be done without arguments, which is why the mode of this science is sometimes argumentative, both through authorities and also through natural reasons and similitudes. It also leads to *moral instruction*, which is why its mode must be preceptive, as in law, warning and promising, as in the prophets, and narrative of examples, as in the historical books. Thirdly, it leads to the *contemplation of truth* in the questions of Sacred Scripture; for this reason its mode must also be argumentative, which is characteristic of the Fathers and of this book which, as it were, brings them all together.

This enables us to see the reason for the fourfold way of interpreting Sacred Scripture, since insofar as the truth of faith is received there is the *historical sense*. Insofar as from this it proceeds to moral instruction, there is the *moral sense*. Insofar as it proceeds to contemplating the truth of things on the way, there is the *allegorical sense*, and of the things in the Fatherland, the *anagogical sense*. Only the literal sense is used for the destruction of error, since the other senses are through similitudes and there cannot be argumentation by means of terms expressive of similitudes. That is why Dionysius says in the Letter to Titus that symbolic theology is not argumentative.

Ad 1. A mode is called artful when it befits the matter; hence a mode which is artful in geometry is not so in ethics. Thus the mode of this science is most artful because it is most in conformity with its matter.

Ad 2. Although this science is one, it is none the less of many things and avails for many things, which is why its manner must be diversified, as is already clear.

Ad 3. Poetic knowledge is of things which on account of a defect of truth cannot be grasped by reason and that is why reason must be seduced by certain likenesses; theology, however, concerns things which are above reason. The symbolic mode is common to them both, therefore, because neither is proportioned to reason.

Ad 4. Away with arguments that would prove the articles of the faith indeed, but arguments must be used for the defence of the faith and for the discovery of truth in questions dependent on the principles of faith. This is what the Apostle too does: 1 Corinthians 15.16, 'For if the dead do not rise, neither is Christ risen.'

Book 2
Distinction 17

THE CREATION OF MAN
QUESTION I

Here two things are asked: first of his creation with respect to soul, second of his formation with respect to body.

Three things are asked under the first heading: whether the human soul is of the divine essence; if not, whether it is created from some matter; whether the soul is created outside the body.

Article 1: Is the human soul of the divine essence?

The first question is taken up thus:

1. It seems that the soul is of the divine essence, from what is said in Genesis 2.7: 'He breathed the breath of life into his face.' But what someone breathes, he sends forth from himself as a breath. Therefore the soul is of the essence of God.

2. Moreover, it is said in Acts 17.28, 'For we are of the race of God.' But this does not belong to man except with respect to his soul which distinguishes him from other sensible things. Therefore it seems that the soul belongs to the same genus as the divine nature.

3. Moreover, since a natural operation follows on nature, things that agree in operation must also agree in nature or essence. But the rational soul agrees with God in the operation of intellect, as the Philosopher says in *Ethics* 10.8. Therefore he shares a nature with him.

4. Moreover, whatever is understood is understood through a likeness or identity, since the intellect in act must be what is actually understood, and that can only happen if they are either the same in essence, as God understands himself, or because the similitude of the thing understood is received in the one understanding as its perfection. But our intellect understands both God and prime matter, and either through similitude or through identity. But it cannot be through a similitude abstracted from them, because nothing can be abstracted from what is most simple. Therefore it is necessary that our mind understands them by way of identity; and thus God, prime matter and the intellectual soul are the same in essence.

5. Moreover, things which in no wise differ are completely the same. But the intellect, prime matter and God in no way differ. Therefore, they are completely the same. Proof of the middle with respect to its second part: the first part being obvious. Things that differ, differ in something; but whatever differs from another in some way is composed of the difference and something else. Therefore since the three foregoing are completely simple, it seems that they in no way differ.

6. Moreover, whatever is participated in by a thing's existence is of the essence of that thing. But as Dionysius says in *On the Divine Names* 4, it is by participation in the divine goodness that the soul and all other things are and are good. It seems therefore that the divine goodness is of the essence of soul and of everything else. But the divine goodness is his essence. Therefore the divine essence is itself either the essence of the soul or something of its essence.

ON THE CONTRARY:

That which in itself is act alone cannot be of another species or kind of being. But the divine essence is pure act in which no potency is found. Therefore it is not possible for it to be transformed into the nature of the soul or of anything else, or to receive any addition.

Moreover, no privation is found in that which is pure act, because privation is of something a thing is meant to have but does not yet have or no longer has. But many defects and privations are found in the soul, such as ignorance, malice and the like. Therefore, the soul is not of the divine essence.

SOLUTION:

I answer that it should be said that it was the error of some of the ancient philosophers to hold that God was of the essence of all things, for they held that all things are simply one being and differ only perhaps for sensation or thought, as Parmenides taught; and a modern like David of Dinant agrees with these ancient philosophers, for he divided things into three sorts, bodies, souls and eternal separate substances. And the first indivisible from which bodies are constituted he called *hyle*; the first indivisible from which souls are constituted he called *nous* or mind; the first indivisible in eternal substances he called God; and these three are one and the same, from which it also follows that all things are one in essence – which both conflicts with sensation and has been sufficiently disproved by philosophers.

Others less confused said that God is not indeed the essence of all things, but only of intellectual substances, taking into account the similarity of operation and dignity of intellect and its immateriality. This could have its origin in the opinion of Anaxagoras, who held that intellect moves all things and has some basis in the authority of Genesis 1, which has been badly understood. This opinion contradicts both the faith and the teaching of philosophers who recognized intellectual substances of diverse orders and placed the human intellect last among intellectual substances, the first being the divine intellect, and that the divine intellect is in every way changeless faith holds and reason demonstrates. The human soul is some way variable, as with respect to virtue or vice and knowledge or ignorance.

Of all these errors and others like them one seems to be the first and basic: when it is disproved no probability remains in any of them. For many of the ancients wanted to draw their judgements about natural things from the intentions of intellect, such that whatever is found to share in some concept they thought to share in one thing. Thus arose the error of Parmenides and Melissus who, seeing that being is predicated of all things, spoke of being as of some one thing, arguing that being is one and not many, as their arguments as related in *Physics* 1 show. From this also followed the opinion of Pythagoras and Plato, who maintained that mathematicals and intelligibles are the principles of sensible things, since number is found in the former and latter and what share a number are one in essence. Similarly because Plato and Socrates are man, there is one man as an essence predicated of all. Many of the arguments of Avicebron in the book the *Fountain of Life* follow from this; he always seeks a unity of matter from an equal community of predication. From this too arises the opinion that there is one essence of genus which exists in all species – really and not just in understanding. But this is a very shaky foundation, for it does not follow, just because this one is a man and that one a man, that there must be numerically one humanity of both, any more than there is numerically the same whiteness in two white things. But this one is like that in that it has humanity, as the other does, and the intellect grasping humanity, not as belonging to this individual, but just as human-ity, forms an intention common to all. No more is it necessary that, because there is an intellectual nature in the soul and in God, that there is essentially the same intellectuality of both or that it be thanks to some one essence that both are called being.

Ad 1. It should be said that just as Augustine remarks in the *Literal Commentary on Genesis* 7, authority does not force us to say that the soul is of the substance of God. First, because that which a man by breathing emits, is of the exterior air, which by breathing he disturbs and is not of his substance. Second, because even if it were of the substance of the breather, it would in no way be of the substance of the soul, even if it were held to be of the substance of the body. God relates to the whole universe as its governor, as soul relates to body; from which it does not follow that the soul of man is of the substance of God. Third, because the soul is above the body in such a way that breath comes only from body; but God is above the whole of nature and was not constrained to make the soul of bodily elements; rather he creates it from nothing thanks to the immensity of his power. Hence he is said to be breath figuratively, as if he made a breath. Isaiah 57.16: 'And breathings I will make.'

Ad 2. It should be replied that we are said to be of the race of God with respect to the soul, not because the soul is of the divine essence but because it shares in the intellectual nature which is also in God; according to which it is also said to be in the image of God.

Ad 3. It should be said that since soul does not have numerically the same operation God has, but something similar to it, it does not follow that it has the same nature, but only a similar one: nor can a unity of essence be concluded from such a similitude, as has been said.

Ad 4. It should be said that the created intellect understands God not through an identity of nature, but through union with it, which is *either* through some similitude not indeed abstracted from him but infused by God in the intellect – Avicenna in *On Intelligence* 4.2 calls this kind of understanding 'through impression', saying that understanding comes about in us by the impressions things make on us; *or* by union with the essence itself of uncreated light, as it will be in heaven. Prime matter is knowable not by some species received from it but by analogy with form, as is said in *Physics* 1; and thus it is one of those things which because of their defect cannot be perfectly understood, as Boethius says in *On the Two Natures*.

Ad 5. It should be said that, according to the Philosopher in *Metaphysics* 10, to be diverse and to be different are not the same, because what differs refers to something else, such that each different thing, properly speaking, differs from another; but the diverse are so called absolutely, and it is not necessary that they be diverse in something, but in themselves, for if it were necessary that all diverse things differed in something, there would be an infinite regress. To avoid that we must come to some first simple things which are diverse in themselves, as is evident in differing things which are distinguished by certain species. If the different is taken strictly, according to the foregoing account, then the first proposition would be false, because some diverse things would not differ. The same is opposed, not to the different, but to the diverse. If, however, the different is taken broadly to include the diverse and the different, then the proposition is true, but the middle is false, as is clear from the foregoing.

Ad 6. It should be replied that creatures are not said to participate in the divine goodness as a part of their essence, but because they are constituted in being by a similitude of the divine goodness, according to which they do not imitate the divine goodness perfectly, but partially.

Article 2: Is the human soul constituted of some matter?

We proceed to the second question thus:

1. It seems that the soul is constituted of some matter, for every definite thing in nature is composed of matter, as is clear from *On the Soul* 2. But the rational soul is such a thing, because it is capable of existing in itself without the body, numerically distinct from another soul of the same species. Therefore . . .

2. Moreover, wherever the properties of matter are found, there matter is found, since the properties of a thing cannot be separated from that thing. But certain properties of matter are found in the soul, such as to be a subject, to receive, to suffer, and the like. Therefore it seems that it is composed of matter.

3. Moreover, according to the Philosopher in *Metaphysics* 2, matter must be imagined in the thing moved. The mutability of the soul is shown from this that it is deformed by vices and fallacies, but is formed by virtues and by the doctrine of truth, according to Augustine in the *Literal Commentary on Genesis* 7.6. Therefore, there is matter in the soul.

4. Moreover, according to the Philosopher in *Metaphysics* 8, the action of any agent terminates in a composite. But the action of God creating terminates in the soul which it brings into existence. Therefore it is composed of form and matter.

5. Moreover, nothing lives of itself except God. But the soul not only vivifies body but itself lives. Therefore it does not live of itself, but by something of itself. But everything in which there is the principle of life receives life, and is composed of matter and form. Therefore . . .

6. Moreover, in every created thing there is a difference between what is done and that whereby it is done, because only the first agent acts through his essence, but other things by partaking of something added to their essence. But the soul has its proper operations and thus it is

something operating through those operations. Therefore it is not that by which it operates and thus does not seem to be a simple form, but rather something having matter, because form is the principle whereby the operation is produced.

ON THE CONTRARY:

To the degree that something is near to the first and simple one, it is more one and simple, as is said in the *Book of Causes*, Propositions 17 and 31. But among natural forms the soul is nearer to God. Therefore, since other forms are simple, the soul must be even more so.

Moreover, there is not a substantial form of the substantial form, just as there is no quality of quality. But each thing that has matter also has a substantial form which gives being to the matter. Since the soul is substantial form, it seems that it is not composed of matter.

Moreover, Augustine in the *Literal Commentary on Genesis* 7.6, arguing by an enumeration of its kinds, shows that the soul is not made from matter. For it cannot be that it was made of rational spiritual matter. Because if the spiritual nature from which it came to be was happy it could not be changed into something worse, because matter, since it is formed by God, is formed for the better. If on the other hand it were miserable, some fault would have to be at the root of this, which is against what the Apostle says in Romans 9.12 – 'in order that the selective purpose of God might stand, depending not on deeds, but on him who calls . . .' If it were neither happy nor miserable, then it would not yet have the use of reason, as happens in childhood, and thus it would be idle. Similarly, not from irrational spiritual matter, for this would be close to the opinion of those who hold that souls pass from body to body and, worse yet, since that position does not hold that the soul of a beast passes into a man, but only the reverse. Similarly it cannot be of corporeal matter, since soul and flesh do not come to be from the same. Moreover, when the soul understands something, it removes itself from all corporeal things, which could not come about if it were of the nature of body. From all of which one can fashion this argument: according to Augustine everything which has matter has come to be from matter, even though matter did not precede it in time. If then the soul cannot be said to come from matter, as has been proved, the soul has no matter.

SOLUTION:

I answer that it should be said that, though some say otherwise, it seems to me that neither in the soul nor in any spiritual substances can there be matter in any way, but they are simple forms and natures. Apart from other reasons showing that this is impossible for angels, as was argued above (Distinction 4), there is a special reason why matter is absent from the notion of soul. For since soul is the form of body, it is necessary that it be the form of body according to its whole essence or according to part of its essence. If according to its whole essence, it is impossible that a part of its essence be matter, because that which in itself is pure potency cannot be the form or act of anything; but every potency in the genus of substance is pure potency, because it is the unmediated subject of substantial form and of generation, as is said in *On Generation and Corruption* 1. If however it is the form of body according to a part of its substance, through which it is in act, and not according to the other part which is its matter, two absurdities follow. The one is that numerically one act is the form of diverse matters, namely of corporeal and of spiritual matter of which the essence of the soul is constituted. The other is that there is one perfective act of potencies in different genera; for the same account cannot be given of corporeal and spiritual matter. Moreover, it is only that which is the act of a living body that we call soul. For a similar reason Avicenna shows, in his *Metaphysics* 9.4, intelligences are simple. We do not deny that in some sense the rational soul has some composition, namely of what it is and for it to be, as was shown above of angels (Distinction 3) and in Book One of the soul itself. This mode of composition is not found in other forms because they cannot subsist in their own existence, but are always components; in this the soul falls short of the divine simplicity. But all this was more fully explained in Book One, Distinction 8.

Ad 1. It should be replied that something can be said to be a definite thing in nature [*hoc aliquid*] for two reasons. Either because it exists as subsisting in a nature, and in this way the rational soul is a definite something. But from this it does not follow that it is composed of matter: for this is accidental to a subsistent thing, namely that it be composed of matter. In another way it can be called a definite something because some part of its essence is individuated, and thus the soul is not a definite something, for the principle of individuation of souls is taken from body and yet even after separation from body they remain individuated and distinct. (Book 1, Distinction 8) This is how the Philosopher understands 'a definite something' in *On the Soul* 2, when he expressly denies that the soul is a definite something.

Ad 2. It should be said that to suffer and receive and the like are said of the soul and of material things equivocally, as is evident from the Philosopher in *On the Soul* 3 and the Commentator on that text. Hence it is not necessary that matter be found in the soul, but it suffices that there be some potentiality in it and what that might be has already been discussed in Distinction 3.

Ad 3. It should be said that matter of the same kind is not required in all motion. Matter in potency to existence is not required for local motion but only a thing that is potential with respect to place. So too in the variation from vice to virtue or the reverse there is not required matter in potency to existence as part of the essence of the thing changed, but only matter in potency to virtue, and this is the very substance of the soul.

Ad 4. It should be said that the Philosopher is speaking of the natural agent which works from matter, as his arguments make clear, and he goes on to show that in every becoming there must be three things, namely that from which something comes to be, and that in which it terminates, and the agent, and from this he concludes that there is no coming into being of forms save incidentally. But we do not concede these principles in the case of the divine action through which he creates the soul; therefore it is not necessary that the soul or any other spiritual substance created by God be composed of matter. Even according to Avicenna, in *Metaphysics* 9.1, the divine agent does not act by way of motion and thus require matter. The Commentator even says that action is said equivocally of the action whereby God acts and of natural action.

Ad 5. It should be said that, according to the Philosopher in *On the Soul* 2, to live is nothing other than for the living thing to be; hence just as the rational soul is but is not that whereby it is, so too it lives but is not that whereby it lives. But just as that by which it formally exists is not some form which is part of its essence, but its very existence, so that whereby it formally lives, is not some form which is part of its essence, but its very living. But that where it is and lives is effectively God who infuses existence and life into all things – in composite things by the mediation of the form which is a part of their essence; in simple substances through their whole essence. God neither is nor lives from some efficient principle, but he is identical with his existence and his living, and the human soul falls short of the perfection of divine life in both ways.

Ad 6. It should be said that there are two ways in which that whereby the soul operates differs from it. For the soul acts by means of the one who infuses into it existence, living, and acting, namely God, who works all in all, and he clearly differs from the soul. It also operates by its natural power, which is the principle of its operation, namely by sense or intellect, which are not its essence, but powers flowing from the essence. In neither way does God act in virtue of something other than himself, because acting is something he has of himself and he is one with his power. But the soul is not said to operate through something which is not itself but a part of its essence, as natural bodies operate through the form which is part of their essence, but rather through the mediation of some power as an instrument, as fire by means of heat.

QUESTION 2

Third, it is asked whether the soul is created outside the body, and two questions arise here: whether there is one soul or intellect for all men, as it were a separated substance influencing all bodies; and if there are several, whether they are created in the body or outside it.

Article 1: Is the intellective soul or intellect one in all men?

We proceed to the first question thus:

1. It seems that the rational soul or intellect is numerically one in all. For no form is multiplied in existence according to the division of matter, unless it be a material form. But the intellect, as is proved in *On the Soul* 3, is not a material form, since it is not the act of some body, which is proved from the very activity whereby it knows all material forms, which could not be if it had one of them in its nature or were determined to it by the body whose act it would be, just as the seeing power would not know all colours if the pupil which is its organ had a determinate colour. Therefore the intellect does not become many because of the division of matter, and thus it remains one in all individuals of the human species, which are distinguished only by matter.

2. Moreover, it is impossible that a principle be more material than what issues from it, because the principle should be simpler. But, as all concede, there are some powers of the rational soul which are not acts of the body, nor attached to organs, and have as their root the very essence of the soul. Therefore it seems that the rational soul is not united in its very essence to body as its act, from which it seems to follow that the rational soul is not distinguished according to the division of matter.

3. Moreover, whatever is received in something is received according

to the mode of the receiver and not its own mode, as is said by Dionysius in *On the Divine Names* 4 and the *Book of Causes* Proposition 20. Therefore if the intellect were individuated according to the division of body, such that it be different in different bodies, it would be necessary that the intellectual forms received in it be also individuated, from which two absurdities seem to follow. One, since no particular is understood in act, but in potency, the species of such things will not be intelligible in act, but will need to be understood through other species, and so on to infinity. Two, forms will be received in the same way by prime matter and the possible intellect, because in both cases they are received as *these*, and not as forms simply speaking, and so, just as prime matter does not know the forms it receives, neither it seems would the possible intellect.

4. Moreover, when things are distinct from one another there must be something diverse in the nature of both. But since the intellect is none of the things that are before understanding them, it seems that nothing differentiating can be found in it apart from the diversity of the species of things understood. Therefore the intellect of this man does not differ from another's in essence, but through concepts alone.

5. Moreover, in all immaterial substances existing in themselves, numerical diversity amounts to diversity of species, because if they enjoy their absolute subsistent existence, they cannot be distinguished essentially by something which is outside their essence, to which they relate as bodily forms relate to matter. In the essence of the latter there is no diversity of form which brings about a diversity of species. But this is not to say that the intellects of different men are specifically different because of the diversity of their forms. Therefore since the rational soul is a substance subsisting in itself – otherwise it would not remain after the body – and is immaterial, it seems that it does not differ numerically in diverse men.

ON THE CONTRARY:

It is impossible that there be numerically one form of many individuals. But the rational soul is the form of a man; for if a man exists thanks to the substance of the sensitive or nutritive soul, there could not be found in him that whereby he is greater than the animals, which is absurd. Therefore it is impossible that there be one rational soul of all.

Moreover, it is impossible to find a difference in second existence in things which do not differ in primary existence, because the diversity and contrariety of secondary perfection is incompatible with a unity of first perfection, since then contraries would be in the same subject. But we find ultimate perfection following on second existence to be diverse and contrary in diverse men, some of whom are stupid and others wise, some vicious and others virtuous. Therefore it is necessary that first perfection, namely soul, with respect to primary existence, varies in diverse individuals.

Moreover, the soul is the form and mover of body. But in the heavenly bodies, so philosophers say, different movers are assigned to different bodies. Therefore it seems far more to be the case that in diverse men there should be diverse souls.

SOLUTION:

I answer that it should be said that there are several opinions of the philosophers concerning the unity and diversity of the rational soul, even setting aside those who hold that the intellect is one in the whole of intellectual nature, or who say that intellect is identical with the divine essence. In order to understand the diversity, we must note that three kinds of intellect are distinguished by the philosophers, namely, possible intellect, agent intellect and habitual intellect. The *possible intellect* is said to be that which is in potency to receive all understood forms, as the eye is in potency to receive all colours; the *agent intellect* is that which makes what is intelligible in potency to be actually understood, much as light makes colours which are potentially visible to be visible in act; they speak of *habitual* or *formal intellect* when the possible intellect is already perfected by an intelligible species such that it can operate: for no passive power has operation unless it is perfected by the species of its object, just as sight does not see before it receives the species of colour.

That being said, it should be known that in this practically all philosophers agree with Aristotle in *On the Soul* 3 that the agent and possible intellect differ in substance, and that the agent intellect is a kind of separate substance and the last among separate intelligences, and is related to the possible intellect with which we understand much as the higher intelligences are to the souls of the spheres. But this cannot be sustained according to the faith. For if, as Anselm proves in *Why God Became Man* 1.5, God did not choose to effect the reparation of man through an angel, lest the equality of man and angel in glory be taken away by the fact that the angel was the cause of man's salvation; similarly, if our soul were held to depend in its natural operation on some intelligence or angel, it could not reasonably be maintained that the soul is equal to the angel in future glory, because the ultimate perfection of any substance lies in the completion of its operation, and thus the foregoing philosophers held that man's happiness consisted of being united with an agent intelligence.

Some Catholic teachers, correcting this view but partly accepting it, held that it is sufficiently probable that God himself is the agent intellect, since by union with him our soul is made happy, and this is confirmed by John 1.9: 'He was the true light which illumined every man coming into this world.'

There was also great diversity among the philosophers who followed Aristotle on the nature of possible intellect. For some said that the possible intellect is different in different men; others said it was one and the same in all. Among those who held the former, however, there are three opinions. For some held that the possible intellect is nothing other than the preparation in human nature to receive the impression of the agent intellect, and this is a bodily power following on the complexion of human nature, and this was the opinion of Alexander. But this cannot be maintained even according to the intention of Aristotle in *On the Soul* 3 who says that the possible intellect is receptive of intelligible species. A preparation is not receptive but preparative, and what is prepared by this preparation is the body or a power in the body, so that which receives intelligible forms would have to be a body or a power of body, which the Philosopher rejects. Moreover, it would follow that the possible intellect is not a knowing power. For no power caused by the commingling of elements is cognitive, since then the quality of the elements would produce an effect beyond their kind, which is impossible.

So others said that the possible intellect is nothing other than the imaginative power, whose nature is such that in it are the forms which were actually understood: this is the opinion of Avempace. But this too is impossible, because according to the Philosopher in *On the Soul* 3, the phantasms which are in the imaginative power are to the human intellect as colours are to sight, so the phantasms must move the possible intellect as colour moves sight; hence the aptitude to understand which is in the possible intellect is similar to the aptitude that is in the potential receiver to be actually receiving. But the aptitude which is in the imaginative power is like the aptitude of the potential agent to be an actual agent, and it is impossible for the same thing to move and be moved or to be both agent and patient. Therefore, it is impossible that the imaginative power be the possible intellect. Moreover, it would also follow that the power receiving intelligibles in act would be using a bodily organ, since the imaginative power has a determinate organ.

Notice that according to these opinions, the possible intellect is generated when the body is and corrupts when the body corrupts: and since the only intellect which would be different in different men would be the possible intellect, if the agent intellect is one, it would follow that what remains of intellect after the death of men would be numerically one, namely, the agent intellect. This is completely heretical, because the reward for merits after death would be taken away.

The third opinion is that of Avicenna in *On the Soul* 7, who holds that the possible intellect is numerically different in different men, rooted in the essence of the rational soul, and is not a bodily power that would begin and end with the body. Hence, with respect to possible intellect, his opinion is in accord with the Catholic faith, although he errs along with the others on agent intellect, as has been said.

There are two views held by those who maintain that the possible intellect is one for all. One is that of Themistius and Theophrastus, as the Commentator relates in commenting on *On the Soul* 3. For they say that the habitual intellect – the third sense – is one in all and eternal and is composed as it were of the agent and possible intellects, in such a way that the agent intellect is as its form, and through the connection of the possible intellect the agent intellect too connects with us, such that the agent intellect is the substance of speculative intellect, which is also called habitual intellect, through which we understand. As a sign of this, they mention that the action of the intellect which is in our power pertains to habitual intellect. Since then it lies within our power to abstract species from phantasms, it is necessary that the agent intellect be the habitual intellect as its form. And on behalf of this position they take what they wish to understand as Aristotle's demonstration, namely that the possible intellect is one in all: because it is not a *this something* [*hoc aliquid*] nor a power of body, and consequently is eternal. And they also say that the agent intellect is similarly eternal, and that it is impossible for the effect to be generable and corruptible if the agent and recipient are eternal. Hence they maintained that the species understood are eternal, and therefore it is not the case that the intellect sometimes understands and sometimes does not. Through this they concluded that new intelligible species that previously were not come to be, but by the conjunction of the agent intellect with the possible, they are continued in us through its agency.

But this is disproved by the Commentator, because it would follow that the forms of natural things which are understood exist eternally without matter outside the soul, with the result that such species would not be in the possible intellect as its form, because they give the agent intellect as the form of the possible intellect. It would also follow, since man's ultimate perfection lies in knowledge had habitually, and primarily in possible intellect, that a man would not differ from another man either according to ultimate perfection or according to first, and thus there would be one existence and one operation of all men, which is impossible.

Therefore the Commentator took another path, holding that both possible and agent intellect are eternal and numerically one in all men, but intelligible species are not eternal; and he held that the agent intellect does not relate to the possible intellect as its form, but as the artisan to matter, and that the species abstracted from phantasms are the forms of the possible intellect, from both of which the intellect comes into possession of knowledge [in habitu].

This position was devised to avoid all the impossibilities which befell Themistius. For first he shows that if the agent intellect is eternal, and the receiver, namely the possible intellect, is eternal, it is not necessary that the forms, that is, the intelligible species, be eternal. For just as the visible species has a dual subject, one in which it has a spiritual existence, namely sight, and another in which it has a material existence, namely the coloured body, so too the intelligible species has a dual subject: one in which it enjoys a material existence, namely those phantasms which are in the imagination, and in this regard the species are not eternal; another in which it enjoys an immaterial existence, namely the possible intellect, and with respect to this subject they are not generable and corruptible.

But this response seems to come to nothing. For just as it is not numerically the same colour that is in the wall and in the eye, so it is not numerically the same species which is in the imagination and in the possible intellect. So it still remains that the species which is in the possible intellect has only one subject and that which is in the imagination and is generable and corruptible is numerically different. Unless perhaps it be said that they are simply eternal, but not with respect to him in whom there are no eternal phantasms, but their similitudes are in the possible intellect. But since no phantasms are eternal, it would still follow that the species which are eternally in the possible intellect were not abstracted from any phantasms: and this is contrary to the words and the intention of the Philosopher.

Secondly he strove to show that it does not follow from this position that there is one operation of all men according to which all are equally acting. For he says that the species understood relate to the possible intellect as form does to matter, in such a way that from them there is brought about one complete thing, whose connection with us is through that which is formal in the said connection, namely the understood species, one of whose subjects is said to be the phantasm which is in us and related to possible intellect. Hence since there are diverse phantasms in diverse men, the possible intellect is connected with diverse men by diverse connections, and thus men are diverse in existence, for one knows what another ignores, because there is an understood species according to which it is linked with the one and not with the other, although there are some understood intentions, such as the first conceptions of intellect of which the possible intellect is never denuded and according to which it is linked with all men, existing from eternity, as he says. Hence he concludes that as for intellect in us, in a way it is corruptible, and in a way it is not, since corruption occurs on the side of that whence phantasms are multiplied, but on the side of the possible intellect there is incorrupt-ibility. Hence it also follows that after the corruption of the body no diversity of souls remains.

That this argument is frivolous can be shown in many ways. First, because, as has been said, the species which is the form of the possible intellect is not numerically the same in the phantasm and in the subject but is its similitude; whence it follows that intellect is in no way conjoined to us, and thus we do not understand thanks to it. Second, because the conjunction of intellect with the understood species comes about through the operation of intellect pertaining to its second perfection, it is impossible that by means of such a conjunction a man receive his first perfection and substantial existence. And thus, since from such a conjunction is one having intellect, as they say, man would not be located in a determinate species through this that he has intellect. The means, namely the under-stood species, is conjoined with both of the extremes, namely the imaginat-ive power and possible intellect, as an accident to a subject, which is contrary to the Philosopher in *Metaphysics* 8, where he says that the soul is not united with the body by any mediator, not even the mediation of knowledge, as Licophron had suggested and into whose position this position seems to reduce.

Third, because operation does not arise from the object but from the power: it is not the visible that sees but sight. If therefore the intellect is not conjoined with us except insofar as the understood species in some way has a subject in us, it would follow that this man, namely Socrates, does not understand, but that the separated intellect understands what he imagines – and many other absurdities not difficult to come up with.

Therefore, setting aside the foregoing errors, I say with Avicenna, *On the Soul* 5.7, that the possible intellect indeed begins to exist with the body, but it does not cease with the body, and it is diverse in diverse men, and is multiplied according to the division of matter in diverse individuals, just like other substantial forms; I further add that the agent intellect is diverse in diverse men, for it does not seem probable that the rational soul lacks the principle whereby it can bring about its natural operation, but that is what would follow if one agent intellect is posited, whether it is called God or an intelligence. Nor do I say that these two, namely the agent intellect and possible intellect, are one power diversely named according to diverse operations, because whenever operations are reduced to contrary principles, it is impossible to reduce them to the same power, which is why memory is distinguished from the sense, because the receiving of the species of sensible things, which pertains to sense, and the retention which pertains to memory, are reduced to contrary principles even in bodies, namely the wet and the dry. Since then to receive the understood species, which is the task of possible intellect, and to make them actually intelligible, which is the task of agent intellect, cannot agree in the same respect, but to receive belongs to something insofar as it is in potency, and to make belongs to something insofar as it is in act – thus it is impossible for the agent and possible intellects not to be diverse powers. How they can be rooted in one substance is difficult to see, however, since it does not seem that one substance can be in potency with respect to all intelligible forms, as possible intellect is, and to be in act with respect to them all, as agent intellect is, since otherwise it could not make all forms intelligible, for nothing acts save insofar as it is in act.

However, it should be understood that it is not absurd that there be two things such that each is in potency with respect to the other though not in the same sense; as fire is potentially cold, which water actually is, and water is potentially warm which fire actually is. So it is that they act and are acted upon by one another. I say that sensible things relate similarly to the intellective soul: for the sensible thing is potentially intelligible and actually has a distinct nature; in the soul there is the actual intellectual light; but the determinant of knowledge with respect to this or that nature is in potency; just as the pupil is in potency with respect to this or that colour. The soul has a power, namely agent intellect, through which it makes sensible species to be actually intelligible, and it has a power through which it is in potency such that it can be brought into the act of determinate knowledge by the species of the intelligible thing made intelligible in act; and this power is called the possible intellect. All our understanding follows from the operation of these two powers, both of principles and of conclusions. Thus what some say seems false, namely, that the agent intellect is the habit of principles.

*

Ad 1. It should be said that it is not denied that intellect is a material form, since it gives existence to matter as a substantial form, with respect to its first being. Therefore on the division of matter, which causes diverse individuals, the multiplication of intellects also follows, that is of intellective souls. But it is called immaterial with respect to its second act, which is operation; because understanding is not brought about by the mediation of any bodily organ, and this happens because no operation proceeds from the essence of the soul except by way of some power or potency. Since it has some powers which are not the acts of any organs of the body, it is necessary that some operations of the soul do not take place by means of the body.

Ad 2. It should be said that whenever one of two joined things is more powerful than the other and draws the other to itself, it has some power other than that of subjecting the other to itself, as is clear in the flame; because fire, mastering the vapour with which it is brought in contact, has the power of illumining, over and beyond the action of igniting the vapour by warming. Since then in the conjunction of form and matter the form is found to be dominant, insofar as the form is more noble and dominates matter the more, to that degree it can have a power beyond the condition of the matter. Hence some mixed bodies, over and above the powers of their active and passive qualities, which derive from their matter, have other powers which follow on their species, as the magnet which attracts iron. This is found even more in plants, as is evident in the growth which is terminated through the power of the soul, which cannot be by the power of fire, as is said in *On the Soul* 2; and this is found even more so in animals, because to sense is entirely beyond the power of the qualities of the elements but most perfectly in the rational soul, which is the most noble of forms, which is why it has some powers in which the body in no way shares, and some in which it does share.

Ad 3. It should be said that according to Avicenna in that place the understood species can be considered in two ways: either according to the existence it has in intellect, and thus it enjoys a singular existence, or as the similitude of an understood thing, by which it leads us to knowledge of it. In the latter way, it has universality, because it is not the likeness of this thing as this, but according to the nature in which it is specifically like other things. It is not necessary that every singular be only potentially intelligible, as is clear from the separated substances, but those which are individuated by matter, as bodily forms are. But these species or concepts are individuated by the individuation of intellects, hence they do not lose their being intelligible in act. Just as I understand myself to understand, although my understanding is a singular operation. It is also self-evident that the second absurdity does not follow, because the mode of individuation through intellect is different from that through prime matter.

Ad 4. It should be said that the Commentator also says in commenting on *On the Soul* 3 that what is receptive of these things need not be deprived of any determinate nature, but that it is denuded of the nature of the things received, as the pupil is of the nature of colours; therefore the possible intellect must have a determinate nature. But before understanding, which is through the reception of species, it does not have in its nature anything of what it receives from sensible things; and that is what is meant by saying that it is none of those things which are . . . etc.

Ad 5. It should be said that although the soul does not have matter as a part of itself as something from which it is, it has matter insofar as it is its perfection, and by the division of which it too is numerically though not specifically multiplied. It is otherwise in those immaterial substances which do not have any matter of which they are the form, because in them there can be no material multiplication, but only formal, which brings about diversity of species.

5. The Work of the Six Days of Creation. Commentary on Sentences 2.2, d. 12 (1252–4)

The creation story in Genesis was a frequent topic of discussion in the Middle Ages and it was carried on under the influence of the succession of commentaries Augustine wrote on the opening book of the Bible. This lengthy tradition – the summing up of which was a purpose of Peter Lombard – was enriched by the introduction of the natural philosophy of Aristotle and of the rudiments of the history of ancient philosophy that was gleaned from his text. In this discussion of the six days of creation, Thomas orchestrates a host of sources. Possession of the text of Aristotle provided an understanding of matter that, while it was quite different from the seminal reasons of Augustine, enabled one to say that everything had been present from the beginning, in the potentiality of matter. Still, Thomas, after some wavering between alternatives, maintains that all natural species, indeed all the kinds of things, were present from the creation, fully constituted. Precious indications of the amount of 'give' the theologian had with respect to the text of the Scriptures are to be found here. Selection 16 will add to the discussion of the role of the angels in the act of creation.

THOMAS'S OUTLINE OF THE TEXT OF PETER LOMBARD

In the preceding part the master discussed purely spiritual nature; in this part he discusses corporeal nature, insofar as it pertains to the consideration of the theologian, namely insofar as it was instituted by God in the works of the six days. The discussion is divided into three parts. First, he discusses the institution of corporeal nature with respect to the work of creation; second, with respect to the work of distinction, in Distinction 13; third, with respect to the work of adorning it, in Distinction 15. The first is subdivided into two: first he discusses the work of creation in itself and then with respect to other works.

And the first is subdivided into two parts, in the first of which he sets down different opinions on the work of creation; in the second he pursues what was proposed in one of them: 'According to this tradition, therefore, we will inquire into the order and mode of creation and the formation of things.' The first is subdivided into two points: first, he states his intention and touches on the diversity of opinions; second, he explains them: 'Some of the holy fathers . . . seem to have written as adversaries . . .' We will inquire into the order and mode of the creation and formation of things according to this tradition. Here he inquires into the work of creation following one of the opinions mentioned, and does two things: first, he manifests the creation of matter first created with respect to the name it is given in Scripture; second, with respect to its condition, 'Before we treat of that there are two things we must discuss.'

The first is subdivided into two: first he clarifies the proposal, then he excludes a doubt: 'Attend to what Augustine says there, shadows are not something.' Before we treat this there are two things that must be discussed. He shows here the condition of the first created matter, first with respect to form, second with respect to place: 'There remains to explain what he proposed in the second place, an inquiry in an orderly fashion into the disposition whereby it is perfected.' He treats of the work of creation here by comparing it with other works, and he does two things: first, he posits the universality of the work, second he distinguishes among the divine works: 'In four ways . . . God acts.'

THOMAS'S DISCUSSION OF THE SUBJECT MATTER

There are five questions to be asked: (1) whether there is one matter for all corporeal things; (2) whether all bodies are created at the same time in their distinct species; (3) if they receive their specification simultaneously, how are the days mentioned at the outset of Genesis to be understood; (4) if they are not simultaneously distinct, of what kind was that unformed matter; (5) on the number of the four coevals.

Article 1: Is there one matter for all corporeal things?

It seems that there is.

1. Things whose form is of the same nature have a common matter because the proper act comes to be in the proper potency, as the Philosopher says. But the form of corporeity has one account in all bodies. It

seems therefore that there is the same matter of inferior and superior bodies.

2. Moreover, in the text it is said that from the first unformed created matter all bodies are formed in their distinct species by the work of distinction and adornment. Therefore there is the same matter in all bodies.

3. Moreover, things which are resolved back into one and the same first subject, whether by intellect or actually, have the same matter. But all bodies are such; therefore etc. Proof of the middle: that in which the ultimate resolution comes to rest is simple matter without any form; but as long as there is some form in matter, it can be further resolved. But in matter which is without form, there is no diversity, because the principle of the distinction of matter is on the side of form. Therefore all bodies are resolved back into one ultimate thing.

4. Moreover, in *Physics* 1 the Philosopher posits only one prime matter and since in that book he is treating of the mobile generally, it seems that there is one matter of all mobile bodies.

5. Moreover, according to the Philosopher in *Metaphysics* 2 matter must be imagined in the moved thing. Therefore things that share in some motion seem to agree in matter. But change of place is common to higher and lower bodies. Therefore matter is as well.

ON THE CONTRARY:

Things that have the same potency have the same matter, because just as form is act, so matter is potency. But there is not the same potency in higher and lower bodies because, according to the Philosopher, in lower bodies there is a potentiality to exist whereas higher bodies are only in potency to place. It seems therefore there is not one and the same matter of them.

Moreover, that which cannot be separated from a thing will be found wherever that thing is found. But the prime matter that is in lower things is never separated from privation of form, because whenever it is under one form there is conjoined with it the privation of another form; but privation conjoined with matter brings about corporeality. It seems therefore that the prime matter of lower bodies is not found in heavenly bodies which are naturally incorruptible.

RESPONSE:

It should be said that philosophers are of two minds on this matter and each side has its following. For Avicenna seems to hold that there is one matter in all bodies, basing his argument on the notion of corporeity which since it has the same definition ought to involve the same matter. Averroes rejects this position at the beginning of his commentary on *On the Heavens* and in many other places because, since matter as such is in potency to all forms, it cannot be subject to many at once, and thus when it is under one it remains in potency to the others. But no passive potency is found in nature to which some active potency which can actualize it does not answer, otherwise such a potency would be frustrated. Hence there is no natural active potency which could effect another form in the substance of the heavens, since this has no contrary, as the motion natural to it indicates. There is no contrary of its circular motion, as is said in *On the Heavens* 1, so the prime matter of lower bodies is not found in it. Nor can it be said that the whole potency of matter as it is under the form of heavens is fulfilled and no potency to further form remains in it, for potency is fulfilled only by the acquisition of form to which it was in potency. Hence, since prime matter considered in itself is in potency to all natural forms, its potency could only be completed by the acquisition of every form. For one form received in matter, no matter how noble and perfect it be, takes away the potency to a less noble form, for matter existing under the form of fire remains in potency to the form of earth. Hence although the form of the heavens is most noble, none the less if it were received in prime matter it will not fulfil every potency of it unless at the same time all other forms were received by matter, which is impossible. Moreover, if it were proposed that the form of the heavens because of its perfection completes the whole potency of matter, it would still be necessary that matter standing under the form of an element should be in potency to the form of the heavens and would be brought to actuality by the action of the celestial power; and thus the heaven would be generable and corruptible, and that is why he wants to deny that the same matter belongs to higher and lower bodies. This position seems more probable and more consonant with what Aristotle says.

Nor do I say, as some do, that they agree in matter, if it is taken for the first fundament, which is neither white nor black, as is said in *Metaphysics* 1, but they differ in matter insofar as matter is determined by motion. The diversity of motion is a sign of the diversity of matter, not its cause, because motion is the act of something existing in potency. Hence wherever there is found essentially the same matter there will be found a potency with respect to the same motion, insofar as matter is in potency to many.

*

Ad 1. It should be said that corporeity according to the logical intention is found univocally in all bodies, but considered as it exists it cannot receive the same account in the corruptible and incorruptible thing because they are not in potency to existence in the same way: one can be or not be and the other not, and this is why Aristotle says in *Metaphysics* 10 that there is nothing common to the corruptible and incorruptible except the name and that is how Averroes in the same place resolves the question.

Ad 2. It should be said that just as it is only after things are complete that they are called one world or one universe, so too insofar as they are unformed because of the lack of some perfection, they are called one unformed matter, although not by continuity, as if all things were numerically one matter.

Ad 3. It should be said that according to Avicenna we should seek a difference only between acts which share the same potency, for species, which share the potency of the same genus, are distinguished by specific differences, but differences which are not of the same genus, such that genus is part of their essence, are distinguished of themselves. No more are the most general genera distinguished by any differences but by themselves. So too compounds which agree in matter are distinguished by different forms, but different matters are distinguished by themselves according to an analogy to different acts, insofar as there is a different concept of possibility in them.

Ad 4. It should be said that the Philosopher in the books of the *Physics* has not yet proved the fifth essence that he demonstrates at the outset of *On the Heavens*. Therefore he determines nothing of what is proper to that essence in the books of the *Physics*, for which reason he repeats the treatise on the infinite, as Averroes points out in commenting on Aristotle.

Ad 5. It should be said that, as is said in *On Generation and Corruption* 1, matter is immediately the subject of generation and corruption, but of other motions according to prior and posterior such that the more change there is the greater perfection does the motion presuppose. Thus there is unity of matter only in things which share in the three motions, growth, decrease and alteration, insofar as growth and decrease are not without generation and corruption which are also the terms of alteration. But change of place, as is proved in *Physics* 8, is most perfect because nothing within the thing changes, hence the subject of this motion is a being complete in its first existence and in all its internal properties. Such a motion belongs to the celestial body, and therefore its matter is like the perfected substance in lower things, as Averroes says in *On the Substance of the Orb*. So there remains community only according to analogy.

Article 2: Are all things created simultaneously, distinct in their species?

It seems that they are.

1. It is said in Ecclesiasticus 18.1, 'He that liveth for ever created all things together.'

2. Moreover, there is more distance between the spiritual and corporeal creature than between two corporeal creatures. But spiritual and corporeal things are held to have been made at the same time. Therefore much more so must all corporeal things.

3. Moreover, as is said in Deuteronomy 32.4, 'The works of God are perfect,' nor can any reason be given why their perfection should be deferred in time, something a creature cannot achieve by itself nor from any one other than God. Therefore since species are distinguished by their specific perfections, it seems that from the beginning all things are created distinct in species.

4. Moreover, the work of creation manifests the divine power. But the power of an agent shows less when its effect is completed successively than when it is produced immediately in its perfection. Therefore it seems that all things are distinct from the beginning.

5. Moreover, it is clear that God produced the whole work of one day in one moment. Therefore it seems ridiculous to say that he stopped acting for a whole day until the beginning of the next, as if he were exhausted. Therefore it seems that creatures are not distinguished by the succession of days, but from the beginning of creation.

6. Moreover, the parts of the universe are mutually dependent and the lower are especially dependent on the higher. But where things depend on one another, one is not found without the other. Therefore it seems unfitting to say that first there was water and earth and afterwards the stars were made.

ON THE CONTRARY:
Augustine says that the authority of Scripture at the beginning of Genesis is greater than the most perspicacious human genius. But there it is written that different creatures came to be over the course of six days. Therefore it seems necessary to maintain this.

Moreover, nature imitates the activity of the creator, but in natural activity there is a process from the imperfect to the perfect. Therefore it seems that this should be so also in the work of creation. Therefore it seems that all things are not distinct from the very beginning of creation.

RESPONSE:
It should be said that what pertains to faith is distinguished in two ways, for some are as such of the substance of faith, such that God is three and one, and the like, about which no one may licitly think otherwise. Hence the Apostle in Galatians 1.8, 'But even if we or an angel from heaven should preach a gospel to you other than that which we have preached to you, let him be anathema!' Other things are only incidental to faith insofar as they are treated in Scripture, which faith holds to be promulgated under the dictation of the Holy Spirit, but which can be ignored by those who are not held to know scripture, such as many of the historical works. On such matters even the saints disagree, explaining scripture in different ways. Thus with respect to the beginning of the world something pertains to the substance of faith, namely that the world began to be by creation, and all the saints agree in this.

But how and in what order this was done pertains to faith only incidentally insofar as it is treated in scripture, the truth of which the saints save in the different explanations they offer. For Augustine holds that at the very beginning of creation there were some things specifically distinct in their proper nature, such as the elements, celestial bodies and spiritual substances, but others existed in seminal notions alone, such as animals, plants and men, all of which were produced in their proper nature in that work that God governs after it was constituted in the work of the six days. Of this work we read in John 5.17, 'My Father works even until now, and I work.' With respect to the distinction of things we ought to attend to the order of nature and doctrine, not to the order of time.

As to nature, just as sound precedes song in nature, though not in time, so things which are naturally prior are mentioned first, as earth before animals, and water before fish, and so with other things. But in the order of teaching, as is evident in those teaching geometry, although the parts of the figure make up the figure without any order of time, still the geometer teaches the constitution as coming to be by the extension of line from line. And this was the example of Plato, as we are told at the beginning of On the Heavens. So too Moses, instructing an uncultivated people on the creation of the world, divides into parts what was done simultaneously.

Ambrose, however, and other saints hold the order of time is saved in

the distinction of things. This is the more common opinion and superficially seems more consonant with the text, but the first is more reasonable
and better protects Sacred Scripture from the derision of infidels, which
Augustine teaches in his literal interpretation of Genesis is especially to
be considered, and so scripture must be explained in such a way that the
infidel cannot mock, and this opinion is more pleasing to me. However,
the arguments sustaining both will be responded to.

Ad 1. It should be said that, according to Gregory, all things are said to
be created together in the substance of matter not in specific form, or
even in its likeness, such as the rational soul, which is like the angels and
is not produced from matter.

Ad 2. It should be said that all corporeal things share in matter, whether
it be one or several, and because matter does not precede the compound,
therefore in order that the order of time might respond to the order of
nature, corporeal matter is first made and then distinguished by forms. But
corporeal nature is not produced from the spiritual either as from matter
or as from efficient cause, and therefore the argument does not work.

Ad 3. It should be said that just as the creature does not have existence
of itself neither does it have perfection, and therefore in order to show
both, God wills that the creature does not exist at first and afterwards
does, and similarly it was first imperfect and afterwards perfect.

Ad 4. It should be said that not only power should be shown in creation,
but also the order of wisdom, such that the things which are prior in
nature are first created.

Ad 5. It should be said that in order to show the diverse natures of
distinct things, God willed that one day should answer to each distinction
of things, not out of any necessity or weariness of the agent.

Ad 6. It should be said that a thing does not have the same nature as
once perfected and in its coming to be, and thus although the nature of
the completed world requires that all essential parts of the universe exist
simultaneously it can be otherwise in the making of the world, just as in
the perfected man the heart cannot be without the other parts, and yet
in the formation of the embryo the heart is generated before all the other
members.

Ad 7. It should be said that the authority of Sacred Scripture is not
derogated when it is differently explained, the faith being saved, because
the Holy Spirit made it fruitful with a greater truth than any man can
discover.

Ad 8. It should be said that it is due to the imperfection of nature that it comes from the imperfect to perfection, since without doubt it would give the ultimate perfection of which it is capable, saving, however, the condition of the work. Therefore it is not necessary that in this the divine work be similar to the operation of the creature.

Article 3: Does Augustine's interpretation retain the distinction of the days?

It seems that it does not.

1. Day signifies a certain time; but in the formation of things, according to Augustine, there was no succession of time. Therefore he does not retain the distinction of days.

2. Since day implies a kind of illumination, it is necessary that day be understood according to the illumination of some corporeal or intellectual light. But not corporeal light, because this would cause a day only by several revolutions which would be completed in a succession of times. Nor by intellectual light, because a created intellectual light does not flow by way of irradiation to the creation of things; but the notion of day required some irradiation; therefore it seems that these days are not properly assigned.

3. Moreover, spiritual illumination does not have different parts, but different parts are assigned to a day, namely morning and evening. Therefore it seems that those days cannot be understood according to the illumination of spiritual light.

4. If it should be said that the morning of the day is according to the knowledge of things in the Word and evening according to the knowledge of things in their proper nature, on the contrary: a thing is said to be known by that which receives its likeness. But the angels do not have knowledge through likenesses drawn from things but in species flowing into their minds from the Word. Therefore they know created things only in the Word and not in their proper nature, and thus they have only morning, not evening knowledge.

5. Moreover, wherever a thing is, there it can be known; but the created thing has a threefold existence, in the Word, in the angelic mind, and in its proper nature. Augustine indicates this in his literal exposition of Genesis by saying that the existence of things comes to be in the Word, it was made in the mind of the angel and it acts in its proper nature. Therefore three parts of the day should be recognized.

6. Moreover, a day in the usual sense has morning and evening and

midday as well. Therefore, just as we talk of morning and evening knowledge, we should speak of noontime knowledge.

7. Moreover, all days should be uniform. But the first days had no morning, because the morning of the first day did not follow on night, but ended in it, whereas the seventh day is held to have a morning in which the sixth day ends, but not an evening. Therefore morning and evening ought not both to be assigned to the other days.

8. Moreover, one comes from evening to morning only by way of night. But no mention is made of night. Therefore the order of the days is insufficiently treated.

RESPONSE:

It should be said that, according to Augustine, those six days are one day, six by the distinctions of things, according to which they are numbered, presented at the same time; just as there is one Word whereby all things are made, namely the Son of God, although we frequently read, 'God said.' And just as those works are saved in all things subsequently propagated by the activity of nature, so those six days remain in the whole subsequent time. We must see how this can be. The angelic intellectual nature is light, and if it is properly light, its illumination must be called a day. The angelic nature at the beginning of the establishment of things receives knowledge of them and thus in a certain way the light of its intellect is presented to created things insofar as they are known; hence the knowledge of things themselves is called a day, and according to the different kinds of things known and their order the days are distinguished and ordered; as in the first day is understood the formation of the spiritual creature by conversion to the Word; in the second day the formation of the bodily creature with respect to the higher part, which is called the firmament; in the third with respect to the lower part, namely earth, water and things in the vicinity of air; in the fourth, the higher part, the furnished firmament; in the fifth, the lower with respect to the earth. But since God is the fullness of light and the darkness is not in him (1 John 1.5) the knowledge of God himself in himself is the fullness of light, but because the creature is from nothing, has the darkness of possibility and imperfection, therefore the knowledge by which the creature is known, is mixed with darkness.

But they can be known in two ways: either in the Word, as they issue forth from the divine art, and their knowledge is called morning, because just as morning is the end of darkness and the beginning of light, so the creation also takes the beginning of light from the Word after first not having been. It is also known as existing in its proper nature, and such knowledge is called evening because evening is the end of light and tends towards night, so also the creature subsisting in itself is the termination of the operation of the Word, as made by the Word, and of itself defective and tending towards darkness unless it is sustained in the Word.

Nevertheless this knowledge is called day because just as in comparison to the knowledge of the Word it is shadowy, so it is light in comparison with ignorance, which is wholly darkness, just as the present life of the just is said to be misty with respect to future glory, which, however, is light in comparison to the life of sin, and thus there is a certain circulation between morning and evening, according to which the angel knowing himself in his own nature, takes this knowledge back to the Word as to its end, in which he takes knowledge of subsequent work in its beginning, and thus this sort of morning is the end of the preceding day and the beginning of the following.

This exposition is subtle and congruous so long as light and day are said properly and not metaphorically in spiritual things, as Augustine says in the literal commentary on Genesis; otherwise it would be a mystical and not a literal interpretation. But because it is denied by many, we, sustaining with Augustine that all things are created immediately distinct in species, can say that days are taken according to the illustration of bodily light. Such that the order of the days is taken according to the order and distinction of things in which bodily light shines forth, for just as the angels receive knowledge of all natural creatures, so too the light flows into all bodily things, as Dionysius says, but differently received in different things, according to the diversity of the recipients.

Therefore just as Augustine distinguishes six days according to the presentation of spiritual light, which is said to be made on the first day, by the six kinds of things, so according to the presentation of bodily light the six kinds of things can in a certain way be distinguished into six days without the distinction of time. And because the period of each bodily thing is prefigured according to the influence of light between two terms, since each bodily power is finite, therefore those terms beyond which the power of the thing does not extend are called morning and evening.

Ad 1. It should be said that day is also a part of time and the effect of light. Therefore the distinction of the first days is not drawn from the side of time, but from the side of light, insofar as different things are declared by light either with respect to angelic knowledge, or with respect to the influence of bodily light on different things.

Ad 2. It should be said that light can be understood both as bodily and as spiritual. If it is understood as bodily, the day will be distinguished according to the different things illuminated, and not according to the time of illumination; however if it is understood as spiritual, it is not by the influence of light on things to be created, but by the brightness of the light for knowing things.

Ad 3. It should be said that the parts of the day according to spiritual light are not according to the different things known, but according to the different modes of knowledge of the same things, and just as the days are not successive, because the angel intuits the different kinds of thing simultaneously in the Word, so the parts of the day are not one because he sees creatures all together in the Word and in their proper nature.

Ad 4. It should be said that the evening knowledge of things in their proper nature is not so called because they take the species through which they know from the things themselves, but because they receive certain species from creation, they know the things as they subsist in their proper nature.

Ad 5. It should be said that the species of things first exist in the divine art which is the Word, which existence is signified when we read, 'God spoke, and it comes to be.' That is, he generates the Word in which it was that they come to be. They have a second existence in the angelic intelligence which is signified by when it is said, 'It was done,' through the influence of the Word. They have a third existence in things, which is meant when it is said, 'He makes.' Therefore this threefold distinction is not posited in the production of spiritual light nor in the formation of man which is also intellectual. Thus the angel has a threefold knowledge of things, namely, insofar as they are in the Word, insofar as they are in his mind, and insofar as they are in their proper nature. Although he never knows things in their proper nature except by the species he has in himself; but the knowledge whereby he knows them in himself differs from the knowledge whereby he knows them in their own nature; for the intellect can be turned back to the species it has in itself in two ways: either by considering it as it is a thing in the intellect, and thus it knows of it that it is intelligible or universal or something of the sort, or as it is a likeness of a thing and then the consideration of the intellect does not come to rest in the species but through the species passes to the thing whose likeness it is, just as the eye sees the stone through the species that is in the pupil, and the stony image which can be considered insofar as it is some thing or as a likeness of the thing. Thus it is evident that the two knowledges differ, but both are evening knowledge, because the intellect of the angel is itself a creature, and a defect tending towards darkness insofar as it exists in itself.

Ad 6. It should be said that noonday knowledge cannot be knowledge of the creature in which the darkness of defectibility is mixed, but knowledge of God himself, which is complete light, and therefore noonday is not mentioned among the works of creation.

Ad 7. It should be said that in the first day, according to Augustine, the formation of intellectual nature itself is narrated, knowledge of which naturally follows on its existence in its proper nature. Therefore it does not have morning knowledge of itself, but only evening knowledge. Similarly the seventh day pertains to the rest of God in himself from all the works which he did for his own sake, and this rest involves no defect, and because of this evening is not mentioned in that day.

Ad 8. It should be said that if the angel, by knowledge taken from creatures, did not refer it to the praise of the creator but dwelled in the creature itself, night would come to be in him, for this would be to enjoy the creature perversely and this is not fitting to the blessed angels, who are signified by light, and therefore in the sixth of those days night is not mentioned. Or it can be said according to another path that morning and evening are mentioned because they are the beginnings of day and night. But there the institution of the principles of nature is shown, from which all things are propagated, and therefore the extremes are given and the intermediates set aside.

Article 4: Was prime matter unformed?

It seems that it was.

1. For matter was common to all the elements, because from it all were made. But the elements agree only in unformed matter. Therefore prime matter was wholly unformed.

2. Moreover, Augustine says in the *Confessions*, speaking to God, 'Lord you have taught your servant that before you did these things it was not anything, neither form, nor colour, etc.' But it was not wholly nothing, because it was something unformed. Therefore prime matter wholly lacked form.

3. Moreover, if that matter had some form, it would be either the form of a mixed body or of a simple body; but not of a mixed body, because then the mixed would be prior to simple bodies, which would be consonant with the position of Anaxagoras. Therefore it would have had the form

of a simple body and then we would return to the position of the ancient naturalists who posited one element of everything, whether fire, or water, or air.

4. If it be said that it had none of these forms but another, on the contrary: everything that is generated is generated out of its contrary. But the elements were made from prime matter existing under a bodily form. Therefore it is necessary that it have contrariety with the elements which are made from it. But the contrariety of the first bodies cannot extend beyond the number of four, as is proved in *On Generation and Corruption* 2. Therefore, matter had to be under the form of one of the four elements, if it was under some bodily form; and thus it would be only one of the first elements. But the Philosopher disproves this. Therefore it must be that that matter was in every way unformed.

ON THE CONTRARY:

1. All existence is from form. Therefore if prime matter existed before the distinction of things, it is necessary that it had some form.

2. Moreover, as natural body is to the different shapes, so prime matter is to substantial forms. But it is impossible for there to be a body without any shape. Therefore it is impossible for matter to be without any form.

RESPONSE:

It should be said that prime matter is said in two ways: either such that indicates the first order of nature, or such that it implies the order of time. Insofar as it indicates the order of nature, prime matter is that into which all natural bodies are ultimately reduced and must be without any form. Every subject that has a form is analysable into form and the subject of form. Therefore, because all knowledge is through form, prime matter is knowable, as the Philosopher says in *Physics* 1, according to analogy alone, insofar as we say that prime matter is that which is to all bodies as wood is to bed. And although prime matter so taken does not have any form as part of its essence, it is never separated from all form, as Avicenna proves in his *Metaphysics*. Indeed when it loses one form, it acquires another, insofar as the corruption of one is the generation of the other. Therefore prime matter so taken cannot be for any duration prior to the bodies formed from it. In another way of understanding prime implies the order of time, namely that which in duration preceded the ordered disposition of the parts of the world as we now see it, according to those who hold that the world did not always exist and that all things were not distinct from the beginning of creation. Understanding prime matter in this way, it has to have some form. On this point the ancient philosophers were divided, for some held that the whole of it was under form, saying that there is one prime matter of all the elements, or something between them and from this all are generated by density and rareness.

Others held that it was under many forms, not ordered among themselves but mixed in a kind of confusion which was reduced to order and distinction by the act of creation which they explained differently, as the Philosopher tells us. But this is not relevant here. All these positions are sufficiently refuted by Aristotle. Moderns too are divided according to these two paths. For some hold the whole of prime matter is created under one form, but lest they seem to fall into the error of the ancients they say that the one form is not one of the four elements, but something which is in process towards them, as imperfect to perfect, just as the form of the embryo is related to the complete animal.

But this cannot be said of the elements because, according to the Commentator, the first thing had by matter is the form of the element. Hence there is no form intermediate between prime matter and the form of the element although there are many intermediates between prime matter and the form of animal, one succeeding the other by intermediate generations and corruptions until it comes to ultimate perfection, as Avicenna says. Moreover, once natural principles are instituted, it would be necessary then to recognize another form before the form of the element in the natural generation of elements, which is nonsense. Unless perhaps it were said according to the sense of *The Fountain of Life* that there is one first form, and that first a common bodily form would be produced in prime matter and afterwards the special distinct forms. But Avicenna disproves this position because every substantial form gives an existence complete in the genus of substance. But whatever comes after things had been actually constituted is an accident, for it is in a subject which is called a being complete in itself. Hence it would be necessary that all natural forms are accidents and thus would be revived the ancient error that generation is the same as alteration. That is why he holds that it is by essentially one form that fire is fire and a body and a substance. Therefore, taking the path of the other saints who held there to be a succession in the works of the six days, it seems to me that we must say that prime matter was created under several substantial forms and that all the substantial forms of the essential parts of the world were produced at the beginning of creation. And Sacred Scripture shows this by mentioning the heaven and earth and water in the beginning. The Master says the same, holding that in unformed matter this earthly element consists in a mean, and that rarer waters were in the form of clouds over the deep. But I say that the active and passive powers were not yet in the beginning conferred on the parts of the world, thanks to which they are said afterwards to be distinguished and ordered. That this is possible is clear, if we wish to hold the position of Avicenna who taught that the elements remained in the mixed body according to their substantial forms with respect to their primary existence, but transmuted with respect to their secondary, namely with respect to active and passive qualities: for there a mixture is the union of mixable alternates. Hence it is possible that matter be under one substantial form without having active and passive qualities in its perfection, and thus since first existence naturally preceded second, the order of nature was expressed as an order of time, since things first came to be in first existence before they were perfected in second.

Ad 1. It should be said that the prime matter which is numerically one in all elements as a part of their essences is in every way unformed as considered in its essence, but cannot precede the elements in duration. Hence the matter which precedes in duration was bodily, not one with the unity of essence, but by the likeness of formlessness with respect to secondary forms.

Ad 2. It should be said that since Augustine is not giving the order of duration but of nature alone, it must be said according to him that prime matter is wholly unformed; which cannot be according to the position of the other saints.

Ad 3. It should be said that it did not have one form but several, not indeed the forms of mixed bodies, because these follow on the active and passive powers of the principles of the world, of which they are essentially composed.

Ad 4. The reply is evident from the foregoing.

Article 5: Are the four coevals properly assigned?

It seems that they are not.

1. It seems that the four coevals, namely, the empyreal heavens, the angelic nature, the matter of the four elements, and time, are improperly enumerated. For place follows the generation of things, just like time. But there is no mention of place among the first created things. Therefore time should not be mentioned.

2. Moreover, time is an accident. But no mention is made of the other

accidents, which are understood as created with their subjects. Therefore it seems that time ought not to be mentioned.

3. Moreover, time is the measure of the motion of the first movable. But the first movable, namely the firmament, was made on the second day. Therefore time did not exist at the beginning of creation.

4. Moreover, there is not the same matter of the higher and lower bodies. Therefore it seems that there should be six, namely, the celestial empyrium, the matter of the firmament, the matter of the four elements, etc.

5. Moreover, in each of the six days it is said, 'God said and it came to be,' in order that it be shown that the work of that day was made through the Word. Since therefore the unformed matter was made by the Word, it seems that it ought not to be said of its creation, 'God said and heaven and earth came to be.'

RESPONSE:

This should be dealt with last. The whole creation with respect to its unformed existence was first instituted by the work of creation, hence it is the things that cannot be led to one unformed principle, which is matter, that are enumerated in the work of creation. For substance and accident are not reduced to the same matter because matter is not a part of the accident; therefore they do not agree in any matter-from-which. But the accident can in a way be said to agree with substance in the matter-in-which, insofar as the accident is in substance; therefore that accident which is denominating as measuring from outside is numbered with substance, namely time. Similarly spiritual and bodily substance are not reduced to one matter, since the spiritual lacks matter; and thus they are numbered with the angels. Similarly there is not the same matter of celestial and lower bodies, and therefore the heaven and the matter of the four elements are enumerated. That is why the four are mentioned in the work of creation.

Ad 1. It should be said that place is the surface of the locating body, and therefore the creation of place is understood with the creation of bodily nature.

Ad 2. It should be said that some accidents denominate that in which they are, like whiteness; and these are understood to be created in the creation of their subjects, if they are things which follow on the first existence, like figure and quantity and the like. However they also denominate that in which they do not inhere as in a subject, like place. For place is not of the containing body in which it is as in a subject, but of the contained body, and time is the measure of all motions, although first of that in which it is as in a subject, namely the motion of the first mobile, by which all others are measured, as is said in *Metaphysics* 10. But there is not the same reason with respect to time and place, because place is not essentially the same as the surface of the locating body, and time is not numerically the same as any accident founded in substance. Moreover place has its whole perfection in the thing; but the notion of time is in some way completed by the action of the soul of the one numbering; hence it has more the note of the extrinsic than place does; therefore it rather than place or any other accident is enumerated among the first created things. I think this is chiefly done to remove the ancient error of the philosophers, who held time to be eternal, except for Plato, as is said in *Physics* 8.

Ad 3. It should be said that the motion of the heavens begins the second day, but not all things are simultaneously created, hence it cannot be understood of time which is the number of the motion of the prime mobile; but it is necessary that either *aevum* is signified by time, as some say, or time is taken broadly for the number of some succession, such that time is said to be first created and measures the creation of things, whereby after not being, they issue forth in being.

Ad 4. It should be said that the firmament according to some is of the nature of lower bodies, and thus its matter is understood in the matter of four elements; and thus only the empyrean heaven will be of another nature, and the fifth essence. But if we call the firmament the fifth essence, then by heaven is understood the empyreal heaven, and the crystalline and sidereal heavens; but with respect to the unformed nature of these two, for the empyreal heaven immediately has its ultimate perfection in its creation.

Ad 5. It should be said that word, properly speaking, implies the notion of the exemplar form of creatures, because the word is art, as Augustine says; and therefore in the sixth of the days, where the formation of the creature is narrated, the word is properly mentioned; but where the formation of matter is narrated, the Son is shown to be a cause as principle and not as Word. Hence diversely the causality of the whole trinity is shown differently by each. In the creation of unformed matter the Father is designated by the name of God who created, the Son by the name of principle, the Holy Spirit by his proper name, when he is called the spirit of the Lord. But in the formation of things the Father is signified as speaking, the Son as Word, the Holy Spirit as benignity, whereby what has been made is approved. By the same love whereby God willed that the creature should come to be, it pleases him that it should remain.

THOMAS'S EXPLANATION OF THE TEXT OF PETER LOMBARD

'As Augustine says in *Against the Manicheans*, "What Moses calls by the name of earth, because earth among all the elements of the world is the least beautiful."' It should be known that according to Augustine, who does not introduce the order of time into the distinction of things, prime matter must be understood as wholly unformed, as was said, and thus it will be called by the name of water or earth by reason of similitude, as it is called earth on account of the lack of form. For earth has the least form of all the elements since it is the grossest element, but water, because of its receptibility to forms, because the wet is receptive and terminable. But it is called the abyss because it is incidentally evil, as is said in *Physics* I, for abyss is formed from *a*, 'without', and *byssus*, which is the genus of the brightest line, that is, without light, and this is incidental to matter because of privation.

Or it is called abyss, as without basis, of some great depth and of the deepest waters, according to Augustine. So too prime matter is called abyss insofar as it is deprived of form through which it receives substantive existence. But according to other saints we can say that according to the text it was under the substantial form of earth or water.

'But earth was inane and vacuous.' If by unformed matter earth is understood then the receptibility of matter must be explained in some way similar to the receptibility of place, insofar as different forms succeed one another in the same matter, as different bodies succeed one another in one place. For which reason Plato says that place and matter are the same, as is said in *Physics* 4. Therefore what is said of place is said by way of similarity of matter; matter is said to be inane and vacuous, according to its lack of form: empty insofar as form fulfils the capacity of matter; inane, insofar as form is the end towards which the appetite of matter tends. But if earth is taken for the still unformed element, it is called vacuous and inane in the text because of its lack of mixed bodies of which it is the place and to which as to an end they are ordered.

'Or of air obscured by quality.' It should be known that every privation, with respect to that which is signified by the word, is non-being; but something must be presupposed, because privation is a negation in a subject apt to have it, as is said in *Metaphysics* 4 – hence the subject is presupposed and its potentiality to the reception of the form of which it is deprived – therefore since darkness is opposed to light by way of privation, it can be understood in three ways. It can be understood as the very deprived subject, which is obscure air, and thus it is clear that darkness is something and a creature. Second, it can be taken for the very power of air by which it is receptive of light, which is diaphaneity, insofar as it is not perfected by light, and thus darkness can be called an obscure quality of air, which is something created. In a third way, it is taken properly for that which is signified by the word, and thus privation is non-being, and in this way, speaking *per se*, it cannot be said to be created by God, but only incidentally, insofar as he makes the opaque nature, darkness arising from its blocking the luminous body. So one who closes the window is said to cause darkness in the house.

'First in the Word, disposing all things.' This seems to be false, because nothing that comes to be in the Word is made, and thus God does nothing in the Word. To which it should be said that according to some Alcuin spoke improperly and should be understood thus: that is done in the Word, that is, generates the Word, which is the art of all the things done by him. They say this because they do not distinguish between acting and making, which differ a lot, because to make is properly an act passing to the external matter; hence the Philosopher in *Ethics* 6 says artificial things are makable; and thus God does not make anything from eternity. But activity is called an act of the thing, even if it does not pass into the external, as understanding is an activity of intellect and can be without motion; hence the Philosopher says in *Ethics* 7 that God takes enjoyment from one simple operation, but in this way God acts eternally in the Word, as the artisan fashions the forms of artificial things.

PART TWO
MASTER AT PARIS (1256–9)

After completing his lengthy apprenticeship and being named master, Thomas was not immediately welcomed into the professorial ranks at the University of Paris. Indeed, it took a papal intervention to counter the reluctance of the secular masters to his elevation. Among the reasons for this resistance was a reluctance to recognize the new mendicant orders in general and the appropriateness of their members becoming masters of theology in particular. Thomas could not be expected to remain silent when the very legitimacy of his religious vocation was called into question. It would be possible, if somewhat distorting, to make his response to the attacks on his Order the centrepiece of his first stint as a regent master in Paris. Polemical skills that will remain quiescent until the flare-up of Latin Averroism ten years later are vibrantly on display.

The principal opponent of the mendicants was William of St Amour, who had set down his condemnations in a *Treatise on the Perils of the Last Days*. Casting the followers of St Francis and St Dominic in the role of Antichrist is a rhetorical excess that would seem to discredit the discrediter, but Thomas took this attack with great seriousness, responding to it in detail in *Against Those Impugning Religion and the Cult of God*, thought to have been written in 1256. In it Thomas defended the new Orders and justified the teaching mission of the mendicants and their roving commission as preachers and confessors. An irony of this is that Thomas was unaware when he wrote this response that William's work had already been condemned.

What was Thomas's day like as a regent master resident in the Dominican convent on the Rue St Jacques? His day began with Mass – the saying of his own and the hearing of another. It was still very early in the day when Thomas gave his lecture. His was followed by that of the bachelor apprenticed to him. The afternoon was given to disputation, and to this we owe the series of disputed questions brought together under the portmanteau title *On Truth*.

Disputation, along with lecturing and preaching, made up the threefold task of the master. Lecturing was the *lectio*, the reading and explication of a book of Scripture or the *Sentences* of Lombard. Here the indispensable task of assimilating a tradition was observed. One must grasp the authors (*auctores*) who were authorities (*auctoritates*) in one's discipline. The scholar was engaged in a communal enterprise that antedated him and would continue when he was no more. T. S. Eliot's 'Tradition and the Individual Talent' discusses the delicate dialectic that the poet must engage in between the old and the new, the poetic tradition and his contribution to it. *Mutatis mutandis*, the essay can be taken to describe the task of the medieval scholar.

Mastering texts might seem to threaten a backward-looking attitude, a nostalgia for a lost golden age, but for two things. First, the concept of a commentary developed, so that room was made for an independent discussion of themes raised by an authoritative text – after the scholar had shown that he understood the text as such. Furthermore, there was the second magisterial task, namely, to dispute. In a dispute the master offered to defend a given resolution of a question. But this was prefaced by a search for the best arguments in favour of the opposite answer. With those before him, the master would redirect the discussion by first appealing to an authority that favoured his proposed answer – *sed contra est*. Then he would develop arguments on behalf of his proposed resolution of the question. Finally, since the value of a solution can best be seen in its ability to handle initially attractive objections, the master took up the counter-arguments one by one.

The disputed questions that have come down to us are not transcripts of the lively occasions that filled the afternoons at St Jacques. But they are directly and essentially connected to them. As made available for copying, they retained the living language of thought, the conversation of the soul that Plato spoke of which requires more than one voice, recognizes a plurality of plausible answers to a question and then defends an answer against its worthy competitors. Thomas found this method so congenial that he adapted it for use in his masterpiece, the *Summa theologiae*.

Appropriately, then, the readings selected for this part rely heavily on the *Disputed Question on Truth*. But the selections begin with two commentaries on Boethius, commentaries of two significantly different kinds, which are of fundamental importance in grasping the mind of Aquinas.

6. Theology, Faith and Reason. On Boethius On the Trinity, 1–2 (1257)

Although the writings of Boethius had been commented on frequently in previous centuries, Thomas Aquinas was the only one to do so in the thirteenth century. He commented on two of the so-called theological tractates of the Catholic scholar who had been brutally executed by Theodoric the Ostrogoth emperor in 524 at Pavia. Prior to his death, Boethius wrote the deathless Consolation of Philosophy, the most copied book after the Bible in the Middle Ages. Thomas's commentaries give no indication that he was aware of earlier commentaries on Boethius and it may well have been through his mentor Albert the Great that his interest in Boethius began.

On the Trinity and On the Hebdomads are the two tractates on which Thomas commented, and the first is incomplete, breaking off in the middle of Boethius's second chapter at a point which caused scholars to rue the fact that he did not continue. Both commentaries are placed roughly in the year 1257, therefore during Thomas's first regency. Were they public courses? Were the courses available only to residents of the Dominican convent of St Jacques? They seem to have been written for Thomas's own edification, and thus establish a precedent of enormous importance. Later, burdened with his magisterial duties, he would none the less find time to comment on a dozen works of Aristotle.

The Boethian commentaries are good examples of the two kinds of commentary Thomas wrote. His commentary on the Sentences consists of a close analysis of the text (divisio textus) followed by questions suggested by the text but often only remotely related to it. The commentary of On the Trinity is like that, except that the relation between the expositio and the quaestiones is closer. Each expositio is followed by two questions comprising four articles apiece. There are six in all. Questions five and six have exerted an enormous influence on Thomistic interpretation, because the text in Thomas's own hand exhibits a series of drafts of a crucial discussion until he hit upon the tack he wished to take. The first two questions discuss matters of supreme importance, and they are included here.

The Exposition of Boethius's *On the Trinity*

QUESTION I
ON KNOWLEDGE OF THE DIVINE

A twofold question occurs. The first concerns knowledge of divine things, the second the manifestation of them, and four things need to be asked about the first: (1) whether the human mind needs a new illumination of divine light for knowledge of the truth; (2) whether it can come to knowledge of God; (3) whether God is the first thing known by the mind; (4) whether it is sufficient unto itself to come to knowledge of the divine trinity.

Article 1: Does the human mind need a new illumination of divine light for knowledge of the truth?

The first question asks if the human mind needs a new illumination of divine light in order to know any truth.

And it seems that it does. Knowing the truth

1. In 2 Corinthians 3.5 it is stated: 'Not that we are sufficient of ourselves to think anything . . .' But the perception of truth takes place through knowledge. Therefore the human mind cannot know any truth unless it is illustrated anew by God.

2. Moreover, it is easier to learn the truth from another than to look for it on one's own. Hence those who know things on their own are preferred to those who can learn from others (*Ethics* 1.2). But a man cannot learn from others unless his mind is inwardly taught by God, as Augustine says in *On the Teacher* and Gregory in his *Homilies on the Gospel* 30.3. Therefore no one can discover truth on his own unless his mind is illumined anew by God.

3. Moreover, as the bodily eye is to seeing bodies, so is the intellect to knowing intelligible things, as is clear from *On the Soul* 3.4. But the bodily eye can see bodies only by means of the supervenient illumination of the material sun. No more then can the human intellect know truth unless it is illumined by the light of the invisible sun which is God.

4. Moreover, acts are said to be in us if we have within us the sufficient principles for their exercise. But knowledge of the truth is not in us, since there are many who labour to know the truth yet are unable

to do so. Therefore we do not have within us principles sufficient for knowing the truth. In order to know it, then, we must be helped from without.

dependent on God

5. Moreover, the operation of the human mind is more dependent on divine light than the operation of lower sensible creatures. Although the latter have forms which are the principles of natural operations, yet they cannot bring off their own operations unless they are helped by the supervenient light of the sun and the stars. (*On the Soul* 3.4) Hence Denis, in *On the Divine Names* 4, says that the light of the sun 'contributes to the generation of visible things and moves them to life, nourishes and increases them'. Therefore neither does the natural light, which is, as it were, its form, suffice for the human mind to know truth, unless another light, namely the divine, supervenes. The same conclusion follows.

6. Moreover, whenever causes are ordered *per se* and not *per accidens* an effect does not proceed from the second cause without the operation of the first cause, as is clear from the *Book of Causes* 1. But the human mind is subordinated to uncreated light essentially and not accidentally. Therefore the operation of mind, which is its proper effect, namely, knowledge of the truth, cannot proceed from it without the operation of the first uncreated light, which operation would seem to be nothing other than illumination. The same conclusion follows.

7. Moreover, as the will is to willing well, so is the intellect to understanding correctly. But the will cannot will well unless it be aided by divine grace, as Augustine says (*Against Two Pelagian Epistles* 1.3). Therefore, neither can the intellect understand the truth unless it is illumined by the divine light.

connection to Augustine

8. Moreover, that for which our natural powers suffice is ascribed to our powers irreprehensibly, like running and building. But it is reprehensible of one to ascribe his knowledge of truth to his own ability, according to Ecclesiasticus 51.23: 'To him that giveth me wisdom will I give glory.' Therefore our powers do not suffice for knowing truth. The same conclusion follows.

ON THE CONTRARY:

1. The human mind is divinely illumined by a natural light, according to Psalm 4.7: 'The light of thy countenance is sealed upon us, O Lord.' If therefore this light, which is created, does not suffice for knowing truth, but requires a new illumination, by parity of reasoning the superadded light would not suffice but would need another light, and so on to infinity,

a process which could never be finished, with the result that it would be impossible to know any truth. We should stay with the first light, therefore. That is, the human mind by its natural light, without any other superadded, can know the truth.

2. Moreover, just as the actually visible suffices to move sight, so the actually intelligible suffices to move the intellect, if it is proportioned to it. But our mind has within it the ability to make something actually intelligible, namely, the agent intellect, and this intelligible is proportioned to it. Therefore the mind does not need some new illumination in order to know the truth.

3. Moreover, as bodily light is to bodily vision, so is the intellectual light to the vision of intellect. But any bodily light, no matter how slight, causes something bodily to be seen, if only itself. Therefore, the intellectual light too, which is connatural to mind, suffices for knowing some truth.

4. Moreover, all artefacts depend on some knowledge of truth, since knowledge is the principle of them. But there are some artefacts which are products of free will as such, according to Augustine, such as building a house and the like. Therefore the human mind without any new divine illumination suffices to know some truth.

RESPONSE:

It should be said that the difference between active and passive powers is this, that the passive powers cannot actually perform their proper operations unless they are moved by the active: sense cannot sense unless it is moved by the sensible. But the active powers can operate without being moved, as is evident in the powers of the vegetative soul.

In the realm of intellect there are two powers, an active, namely agent intellect, and a passive, possible intellect. Some indeed held that only the possible intellect is a power of the soul, whereas the agent intellect is a kind of separated substance. This is the opinion of Avicenna, a consequence of which is that the human soul cannot actually engage in its proper operation, which is knowledge of the truth, unless it is illumined by an outside light, namely of that separated substance which he calls the agent intellect.

But the words of the Philosopher in *On the Soul* 3.5 seem rather to mean that the agent intellect is a power of the soul, something in harmony as well with the authority of Sacred Scripture which professes that we are signed with an intelligible light (Psalm 4.7), with which the Philosopher's agent intellect agrees. Thus he posits in the soul with respect to intelligible activity, which is knowledge of truth, both a passive and an active power. Hence just as other active natural powers conjoined with passive powers suffice for natural operations, so the soul having within a passive and active power suffices for the perception of truth.

However, since any created active power is finite, its sufficiency is limited to determinate effects. Hence it cannot achieve other effects unless a new power is added. There are some intelligible truths to which the efficacy of the agent extends, such as the principles which a man naturally knows and the things which are deduced from them, and for knowledge of these no new intelligible light is required, but the naturally inborn light suffices. But there are things to which these principles do not extend, such as what pertains to faith and exceeds the capacity of reason, future contingents, and the like. The human mind cannot know these unless it is illumined by a new light superadded to the natural.

Although the addition of a new divine light is not needed for knowledge of those things to which natural reason extends, divine activity is needed. Over and above the operation whereby God institutes the natures of things, giving each thing its form and proper powers, thanks to which it can exercise its operations, He also brings about in things the works of his providence, directing and moving the powers of all things to their proper operations. The created universe is subject to divine governance much as instruments are to the governance of the artisan and natural qualities to the nutritive powers of soul, as is said in *On the Soul* 2.4. Thus just as from natural heat the work of digestion follows according to the rule which the digestive power imposes on heat, and all the powers of bodies below act insofar as they are moved and directed by the powers of the celestial bodies, so all created active powers operate insofar as they are moved and directed by the creator. Therefore in any knowledge of truth the human mind stands in need of divine operation, but in knowing natural things it does not require a new light, but only its own motion and direction, although in other things it needs a new illumination. It is because Boethius speaks of these things in the text that he says in the preface of *On the Trinity*, 'I have very long pondered this question, so far as the divine light has deemed it fitting for the spark of my intelligence to do so.'

Ad 1. It should be said that although we are not sufficient of ourselves to know anything without divine operation, it is not necessary that in all our knowledge a new light is infused in us.

Ad 2. It should be said that on this basis God teaches us within with respect to the naturally known, as the natural light causes in us and directs it to the truth, in other things, however, by infusing a new light as well.

Ad 3. It should be said that the illumination of the material sun does not bring about in the bodily eye some light connatural to it, through which it can make things actually visible, as does happen in our mind by the illustration of the uncreated sun. Therefore the eye always needs an exterior light, but mind does not.

Ad 4. It should be said that where intelligible light is pure as in the angels it makes manifest without difficulty all naturally known things, which is why there is in them knowledge of all natural things. In us however the natural light is obscured because of its conjunction with body and bodily powers, and impeded so that it cannot freely know even naturally knowable truth, according to Wisdom 9.15: 'For the corruptible body is a load upon the soul . . .' Thence it is that it is not wholly in our power to know truth, namely, because of impediments. But anyone has it more or less in his power, insofar as the intelligible is purer in him.

Ad 5. It should be said that bodies here below, although they need to be moved by heavenly bodies in order to act, do not, however, need to receive new forms to effect their proper operations. Similarly it is not necessary that the human mind, which is moved by God to know naturally known things, be infused by a new light.

Ad 6. It should be said that, as Augustine remarks in his literal commentary on Genesis 8.12, as air is illumined by the present light, which were it absent would immediately be darkened, so is it with the mind illumined by God. Therefore God always causes even the natural light in the soul, not different lights, but the same, since he is cause not only of its becoming but of its being. In this way God continuously operates in the mind, when he causes in it the natural light and directs it, and thus mind is not moved to its proper act without the operation of the first cause.

Ad 7. It should be said that will can never will well without the divine impulse, but it can will well without the infusion of divine grace, though not meritoriously. Similarly intellect cannot know any truth without divine movement, but it can without the infusion of a new light, although not those things which exceed natural knowledge.

Ad 8. It should be said that by the very fact that God by conserving in us the natural light causes and directs it to seeing, it is manifest that the grasp of truth ought to be especially ascribed to him, just as artistic activity is attributed to the artist rather than to his chisel.

Article 2: Can the human mind attain knowledge of God?

We raise the second question thus: Can God be known by us?
And it seems that he cannot be.

1. That which remains unknown to us at the highest level of our knowledge is in no way knowable by us. But God, in the most perfect level of our knowledge, is attained only as unknown, as Denis says in the *Mystical Theology* 1. So God is in no way knowable by us.

2. Moreover, whatever is known is known through some form. But, as Augustine says, God escapes every form of our intellect. Therefore he is in no way knowable by us.

3. Moreover, there must be some proportion between the knower and knowable, as between its object and any power. But there can be no proportion between our intellect and God, any more than there can be between the finite and infinite. Therefore, there is no way the intellect can know God.

4. Moreover, since potency and act are found in the same genus, for example, those which divide every genus of being, no potency has a correlative act outside its genus, as sense cannot know intelligible substance. But God is beyond any genus. Therefore he can in no way be known by an intellect which is in a given genus. But that is the case with our intellect. Therefore, etc.

5. Moreover, take away what is first and all things that follow on it are taken away. But the quiddity of a thing is the primary intelligible, which is why that which a thing is is said to be the proper object of intellect (*On the Soul* 3.6), and the *what* is said to be the means of demonstrating whether a thing is and all the other conditions of a thing. But we cannot know of God what he is, as Damascene says in *On the Orthodox Faith* 1.2. Therefore we can know nothing of him.

ON THE CONTRARY:

1. There is what is said in Romans 1.20: 'Men can from the things that are made come to knowledge of the invisible things of God.'

2. Moreover, there is Jeremiah 9.24: 'But let him that glorieth glory in this, that he understandeth and knoweth me . . .' But this would be vainglory if we were not able to know him. Therefore, we can know God.

3. Moreover, only what is known can be loved, as is clear from Augustine in *On the Trinity* 10.1. But we are commanded to love

God. Therefore, we can know him, since we are not ordered to do the impossible.

Knowing // loving

RESPONSE:

It should be said that something can be known in two ways. In one way, through its own form, as the eye sees the stone through the image of stone. In another way, through the form of something similar to it, as the cause is known by its likeness to the effect and man by the form of his image. And something seems to be known through its own form in two ways. In one way, through the form which is the thing itself, as God knows himself through his essence and so too the angel knows himself. In another way, through a form which derives from it, whether it is abstracted from it, and then the form is more immaterial than the thing, as the form of stone is abstracted from stone, or is impressed on the one understanding by it, as when the thing is simpler than the similitude through which it is known, as Avicenna says that we understand intelligences through their impressions in us. Because in this life our intellect has a determinate relation to forms which are abstracted from the senses, since they are compared to phantasms as sight is to colours (*On the Soul* 3.7), it cannot know God in this life through the form which is his essence – that is the way he is known by the blessed in heaven.

Whatever likeness might be impressed on the human intellect would not suffice to make his essence known since it infinitely exceeds any created form; that is why God is not accessible by the intellect through created forms, as Augustine says. Nor can God be known by us in this life through purely intelligible forms which might be some likeness of him because of our intellect's connaturality with phantasms, as has been said. For effects are of two kinds. There are some which are equal to the power of their cause, and through such effects the power of the cause can be fully known, and consequently its quiddity; other effects are deficient in the aforesaid equality, and neither the power nor consequently the essence of the cause can be known through them, but only that the cause exists. Knowledge of the effect is a principle of knowing of the cause that it exists and functions as the quiddity of the cause does when it is known through its form. Every effect is related to God in this way. Therefore in this life we can only attain knowledge that he exists.

One of those who know of a thing that it is can do so more perfectly than another, because a thing is more perfectly known from its effect to the degree that the relation of the effect to the cause is manifested by the effect. Now this relation in the effect which does not attain to equality with its cause is based on three things, namely, on the progression of the effect from the cause, insofar as it approaches the likeness of its cause, and insofar as it falls short of it. Thus the human mind approaches knowledge of God in three ways, though it never attains to knowledge of what he is, but only that he is. First, insofar as his effectiveness in producing things is more perfectly known. Second, insofar as he is known as cause of more noble effects, which since they bear some likeness to him better display his eminence. Third, in this that he is known to be more and more distant from all those things which appear in his effects. Hence Dionysius says in *On the Divine Names* 7 that he is known as the cause, the excess and negation of all things.

In the pursuit of this knowledge the human mind is especially helped when its natural light is strengthened by a new illumination, such as the light of faith and the gifts of wisdom and understanding through which the mind is said to be raised above itself in contemplation insofar as it knows God to be everything that it naturally comprehends. But because it does not suffice to penetrate to seeing his essence, he himself is said to be in some way reflected by that excellent light, and that is what is meant by Gregory in his gloss on Genesis 32.30, 'I have seen God face to face,' when he says, 'The sight of the soul when it turns to God vibrates with the trembling of his immensity.'

Ad 1. We are said to know God as unknown at the term of our knowing in the sense that the mind is seen especially to progress in knowledge when it knows his essence to be above anything that can be grasped in this life and thus, although what he is remains unknown, we know that he exists.

Ad 2. It should be said that because God escapes every form of the intellect it is clear that what he is cannot be known, but only that he exists, as has been said.

Ad 3. It should be said that proportion is nothing else than the relation of two things to one another insofar as they agree or differ in terms of some conformity. This conformity can be understood in two ways. In one way, in that they agree in some genus of quantity or quality, like the relation of surface to surface or number to number, insofar as one exceeds or is equal to the other, or even of heat to heat. In this way there can in no wise be a proportion between God and creature, since they do not agree in any genus. This conformity can be taken in a second way insofar as they agree in some order, and in this way the proportion of matter and form and of maker and made and other such things is understood.

This kind of proportion obtains between the knowing power and the knowable, since the knowable is the act of the knowing power. The proportion of creature to God is like that of caused to cause and of knower to knowable, but because of the infinite excess of creator over creature there is no proportion of creature to creator as if the creature received his influx according to its complete power, nor that it knows him perfectly, as he knows himself perfectly.

Ad 4. It should be said that understanding and the understandable are in the same genus in the way that potency and act are. Although God is not contained in the genus of intelligible things, God is as it were comprehended under the genus, as participating in the nature of the genus, because he pertains to this genus as its principle. His effects are not outside the genus of intelligible things and that is why in this life he can be known through his effects and in heaven through his essence. Moreover, he seems to be called intelligible by negation rather than affirmation. Something is intelligible insofar as it is immune to or abstracted from matter. Negations are verified in matters divine although affirmations are indecipherable, as Dionysius says in the *Celestial Hierarchy* 2.

Ad 5. It should be said that when a thing is not known through its own form but through its effect, the form of the effect takes the place of the form of the thing: it is from the effect itself that the cause is known to exist.

Article 3: Is God the first thing known by the mind?

The third question is this:
   Is God the first thing known by the mind?
   And it seems that he is.

1. That through which all other things are known and through which we judge what we know of all other things is what is first known by us, as light is known by the eye before the things which are seen in the light, and principles before conclusions by intellect. But all things are known in the first truth and by it we judge of all things, as Augustine says in *On the Trinity* 9.7 and in *On True Religion* 31. Therefore the first truth, namely God, is that which is first known by us.

2. Moreover, when there are many ordered causes, the first cause flows into the caused before the secondary cause and stops last, as is said in the *Book of the Causes* 1. But since human science is caused by things, the knowable or intelligible is the cause of understanding in the human mind. Therefore the first intelligible flows into it first. But the influx of

the intelligible into intellect, as such, takes place in order that it might understand. Therefore God, who is the first of intelligible things, is the first understood by our intellect.

3. Moreover, in every instance of knowledge in which those things which are prior and more simple are first known, that which is first and most simple is known first. But in human knowledge it seems that the things which first occur are prior and more simple, because being is that which the intellect first knows, as Avicenna says; but existence is first among created things. Therefore God, who is absolutely first and most simple, comes first to human knowledge.

4. Moreover, the end which is the last thing attained is first in intention. But God is the ultimate end of the human will to which all other ends are ordered. Therefore, he is the first in intention. But this can only be insofar as he is known. Therefore, that which the human mind must first know is God.

5. Moreover, that which has no need of any preceding activity in order that it might be the activity of something is first in the activity of that agent before that which needs some other activity; for example, wood already planed falls to the activity of one making a bench before wood not yet planed. But sensible things need to be abstracted from matter by the agent intellect before they are understood by the possible intellect. But God himself is most separate from matter. Therefore he is understood by possible intellect before sensible things.

6. Moreover, things known naturally and which cannot be understood not to be are first in our knowledge. But the knowledge of God existing is naturally imparted to us, as Damascene says. God cannot be thought not to be, as Anselm says in *Proslogion* 3. Therefore, God is the first thing known by us.

ON THE CONTRARY:

[1] According to the Philosopher all our knowledge takes its rise from the senses. Therefore, God is not the first but the last known.

[2] According to the Philosopher those things which are naturally posterior are first for us, and what in nature is less known is especially known by us. But creatures are posterior to and less known than God himself. Therefore God is known only last by us.

[3] Moreover, that which is promised as the ultimate reward is not the first, preceding all merits. But knowledge of God is promised us as the ultimate reward of all knowledge and action. Therefore, God is not first known by us.

RESPONSE:

It should be said that some taught that the first thing known by the human mind even in this life is God himself who is the first truth and that through whom all other things are known. But this appears to be false: to know God in his essence is man's beatitude and it would thus follow that every man is happy. Moreover, since all the things said of the divine essence are one, no one would be mistaken about the things which are said of God, which experience shows is evidently false. Again, those things which are first in the intellect's knowledge must be most certain, hence the intellect would be certain it knows these things, which is patently untrue in the case in point. And this position is repugnant to the authority of Scripture which tells us in Exodus 33.20: 'For man shall not see me and live.'

Hence others said that the divine essence is not the first thing we know in this life, but rather the influence of its light, and in that sense God is the first thing known by us. But this cannot be maintained either, since the first light that flows divinely into the mind is the natural light whereby the intellectual power is constituted. But this light is not the first thing known by the mind – neither the knowledge of what it is, since much inquiry is needed to learn what the intellect is, nor the knowledge whereby its existence is known, since we only perceive that we have an intellect insofar as we perceive ourselves to understand, as is clear from the Philosopher in *Nicomachean Ethics* 9.9. But no one understands himself to understand except insofar as he understands something intelligible. From which it is clear that knowledge of some intelligible thing precedes the knowledge whereby anyone knows himself to understand and consequently the knowledge whereby someone knows that he has an intellect. Thus the influence of the natural intelligible light cannot be the first thing known by us and much less any other influx of light.

Therefore it must be said that the first thing known by man can be understood in two ways: either according to the order of the different powers or according to the object of a single power. In the first way, since all our intellect's knowledge derives from sense – what is knowable by the senses is known by us before what is knowable by intellect, that is, the singular or sensible is known before the intelligible.

Or, in another way, insofar as its proper object is the first thing knowable to any power. Since in the human intellect there is an active and passive power, the object of the passive power, that is, the object of the possible intellect, will be that which is made actual by the active power, or agent intellect, since a passive power should answer to its proper active power. But the agent intellect does not make separate forms intelligible since they are intelligible of themselves, but rather forms, which it abstracts from phantasms. It is such things, then, which our intellect first understands.

And among these those are prior which first occur to the abstracting intellect. But these are what include many things, either in the manner of a universal whole or in the manner of an integral whole. Therefore, the most universal is first known by the intellect, and composites before their components, for example, the defined is known before the parts of the definition. And insofar as there is a kind of imitation of intellect in the senses, which themselves in a way receive what has been abstracted from matter, in sense too the more common singulars are known first, as this body before this animal. It is thus evident that God and the other separate substances can in no way be the first things understood, but they are understood from other things, as is said in Romans 1.20: 'From the things that are made . . .'

Ad 1. It should be said that from those words of Augustine and other similar remarks it should not be thought that uncreated truth is the proximate principle whereby we know and judge, but that we know and judge through a light imparted to us which is his similitude. Nor does this light have any efficacy save from the first light, just as in demonstrations secondary principles are only made certain on the strength of the first. But that imparted light need not be what is first known by us, since we do not know other things in it as if it were the means through which we know the knowable, but it is that which makes other things to be knowable. Hence it is not necessary that it be known otherwise than in those knowable things, any more than light is what is first seen by the eye except in the colour illumined.

Ad 2. It should be said that it is not the case in all ordered causes that the influence of one reaches to the ultimate effect. Hence it is not necessary that the primary intelligible influence our intellect in this way in order that it might understand, but it confers on it the power to understand. Or it might be said that although God is absolutely first in the order of intelligible things, he is not first in the order of things intelligible by us.

Ad 3. It should be said that, although those things which are first in the genus of things that the intellect abstracts from phantasms are first known by us, such as being and one, it is not necessary that the things which are absolutely first, which are not contained in the formality – *ratio* – of its proper object, should be first known by us.

Ad 4. It should be said that, although God is the ultimate end attained and the first intended by natural appetite, he need not be first in the knowledge of the human mind which is ordered to the end, but in the knowledge of the one ordering, as is the case with others that tend to their ultimate end by natural appetite. He is known from the beginning and intended in a general way insofar as the mind desires to be good and to live well, which it will only achieve when it has God.

Ad 5. It should be said that although separate substances do not need abstraction in order that they might be understood, they are not, however, intelligible through the light of the agent intellect, and that is why they are not first known by our intellect. It is only what is made intelligible in this way that is the object of intellect, as the visible is the object of sight thanks to bodily light.

Ad 6. 'That God exists,' it should be said, taken as such, is known by itself [per se notum] because his essence is his existence – this is how Anselm speaks – but not for us who do not see his essence. Knowledge of him is said to be innate in us because through principles which are innate in us we can easily perceive that God exists.

Article 4: Is the human mind sufficient of itself to reach knowledge of the divine Trinity?

The fourth question is opened thus:

It seems that the mind suffices for itself to come to knowledge of the divine Trinity by natural argument.

1. Whatever belongs to being as being is especially to be found in the first being. But trinity belongs to being as being, since it is found in all beings insofar as all things have mode, species and order, as Augustine says in *On the Nature of the Good* 3. Therefore it can be known by natural reason that there is a trinity in God.

2. Moreover, no perfection should be absent from God. But three is the number of any thing's perfection, as is said in *On the Heavens* 1.1. Therefore trinity should be attributed to God, with the same conclusion as before.

3. Moreover, every inequality is reduced to a prior equality, as multitude to unity. But between God and the first created being there is inequality. There must precede, then, some equality, which since it must involve many, is some plurality in the divine.

4. Moreover, every equivocal is reduced to the univocal. But the pro-

cession of the creature from God is equivocal. We must posit prior to this, then, a univocal procession, whereby God proceeds from God, from which the trinity of persons arises.

5. Moreover, there can be no joyful possession of any good without sharing. But in God there is from eternity the most joyful sharing of the good. Therefore, he has an eternal sharing, which can only be of the divine persons, because no creature is eternal. We must therefore recognize in the godhead a plurality of persons.

6. Moreover, it can be known by natural reason that God is intelligent. But from the fact that he is intelligent it follows that he conceives a word, since this is common to every understanding thing. Therefore it can be known by natural reason that there is the generation of the Son and by the same argument a procession of love.

7. Moreover, Richard of St Victor says in *On the Trinity* 1.4, 'I believe without a doubt, since for the explanation of some things, which necessarily are, there are not only probable but also necessary arguments.' But that God is one and triune is necessary, because it is eternal. Therefore, there must be necessary arguments for it. From which the same conclusion follows.

8. Moreover, Platonists had knowledge of God only through reason. They recognized at least two persons, namely God the Father and the mind engendered by him, which contains the ideas of all things, which is what we say of the Son. Therefore, the plurality of persons can be known by natural reason.

9. Moreover, the Philosopher says in *On the Heavens* 1.1, 'For through this number we apply ourselves to magnify God the creator.' And thus the same as before.

10. Moreover, in this life we can in no way know of God what he is, but only that he exists. However, in a way we know that God is three and one, namely, through faith. Therefore this does not pertain to the question *What he is*, but rather to *That he is*. But we can know that God is through natural reason. Therefore it can also be known by natural reason that God is three and one.

ON THE CONTRARY:

[1] Faith is the substance of things to be hoped for, as is clear from Hebrews 11.1. But that God is three and one is an article of faith. Therefore reason does not suffice for seeing that this is so.

[2] Moreover, every natural argument takes its efficacy from naturally known first principles. But that God is three and one cannot be deduced

from naturally known principles, which are drawn from sense, since in sensible things nothing similar is to be found, for example, that there be three supposits of one essence. Therefore that God is three and one cannot be known by reason.

[3] Moreover, Ambrose says in *On Faith* 1.10, 'It is impossible for me to know the secret of this generation; my mind fails; and not only my voice but even those of the angels fall silent.' Therefore, natural reason does not suffice for knowing the divine generation and, consequently, the trinity of persons.

RESPONSE:

It must be said that God's being three and one is only believed and can in no way be demonstratively proved, though some arguments of a non-necessary kind and of little probability except to the believer can be fashioned. This is evident from the fact that we know God in this life only from his effects, as is evident from the foregoing. Therefore, we can know of God from natural reason only what is perceived of him from the relation of effects to him, such as those which indicate his causality and eminence above what is caused and which remove from him the imperfect characteristics of effects. The trinity of persons cannot be perceived from the divine causality itself, since causality is common to the whole trinity. No more can it be said by way of removal. Hence in no way can it be proved that God is three and one.

Ad 1. It should be said that those things which are plural in creatures are really one in God. Therefore, although some trinity is found in any created being, it cannot be necessarily concluded from this that there is some three in God, except in our way of thinking, and such plurality does not suffice for the distinction of persons.

Ad 2. It should be said that the perfection of three is found in God even according to the unity of essence – not that his essence is numbered, but because it virtually contains every perfection of number, as Boethius says in *On Arithmetic* 2.8.

Ad 3. It should be said that, even removing the distinction of persons, there is equality in divine things, insofar as his power is equal to his wisdom. Or it might be said that there are two things to consider in equality, namely the plurality of individuals, between which a relation obtains, and the unity of quantity which is the meaning of equality. Therefore, the reduction of inequality to equality does not come about by reason of the plurality of individuals, but by reason of the cause, because just as unity is the cause of equality, so inequality is the cause of plurality. Therefore the cause of equality must be prior to the cause of inequality, not that there must be some equal things prior to any unequal things. Otherwise it would be necessary for there to be in the order of numbers something before unity and duality, which are unequals, or to find plurality in unity itself.

Ad 4. It should be said that although every equivocal is reduced to the univocal, it does not follow that equivocal generation is reduced to univocal generation, but to a generator that is in itself univocal. In natural things, we see that equivocal generations are prior to the univocal because equivocal causes exercise causality on the whole species whereas univocal causes do not, but only on one individual, which is why they are, as it were, instruments of equivocal causes, as inferior bodies are of celestial bodies.

Ad 5. It should be said that the reason a man cannot have a joyful life without sharing is that he is not of himself sufficient for all things. For this reason, animals which have of themselves everything they need do not require a shared life, but are solitary. God, however, is especially self-sufficient. Hence, even if the distinction of persons were taken away, there would still remain the greatest joy.

Ad 6. It should be said that in God the knower and the known are the same. That is why it does not follow from the fact that there is understanding in God that there must be in him some really distinct concept, as there is in us. But the trinity of persons requires a real distinction.

Ad 7. It should be said that the meaning of those words is apparent from what follows them: '. . . although it happens to escape our effort'. Therefore, all things necessary in themselves are either knowable in themselves or in other things, but it is not necessary that they should be thus known by us. Hence we cannot find, thanks to our efforts, a necessary argument to prove all necessary things.

Ad 8. It should be said that the position of the Platonists establishes nothing concerning the truth of the matter under discussion. For the Platonists did not claim that mind would be of the same essence with God the Father, but that it would be some other separate substance proceeding from it, and the third they posited was the soul of the world, as is clear in Macrobius. And because they called all separate substances gods, they called these three gods, as Augustine points out in *The City of God* 10.29. It is because they did not posit anything like the Holy Spirit as well as Father and Son – for the soul of the word is not a link between the other two, according to them, as the Holy Spirit is of Father and Son – that they are said to have failed in the third sign, namely in knowledge of the third person. Or it might be said, and commonly is, that they knew the two persons with respect to what is appropriated to them, power and wisdom, but not what is proper to them. Goodness, which is appropriated to the Holy Spirit, looks especially to effects that they did not know.

Ad 9. It should be said that Aristotle did not mean to say that God should be esteemed as three and one, but that he was honoured by three days of sacrifice and prayer by the ancients because of the perfection of the number three.

Ad 10. It should be replied that whatever is said of God is one with his simple essence, but that the things that are one in him are many in our intellect, which is why our intellect can apprehend one without another. That is why in this life we can know of none of them what it is but only that it is, and it happens that one of these [attributes] can be known to be without knowing another; for example, one might know that God is wise yet not know that he is omnipotent. In much the same way we can know by natural reason that God is, but not that he is three and one.

QUESTION 2
ON THE MANIFESTATION OF DIVINE KNOWLEDGE

We pass on to the question of the manifestation of divine knowledge, about which four things are asked: (1) whether it is licit to treat of it by way of an investigation; (2) whether there can be any science of the divine; (3) whether in the science of faith which is from God it is licit to use philosophical arguments and authority; (4) whether things divine should be hidden behind obscure neologisms.

Article 1: Is it licit to treat the divine by way of investigation?

We open the question thus: It seems that it is not licit to investigate the divine by way of argumentation.

1. Ecclesiasticus 3.22: 'Seek not the things that are too high for thee, and search not into things above thy ability.' But things divine especially are above man, particularly those which are of faith. Therefore it is not licit to scrutinize such things.

2. Moreover, punishment is only meted out for faults. But, as is said in Proverbs 25.27, 'A searcher of majesty shall be overwhelmed by glory.' Therefore to look into the things pertaining to the divine majesty is illicit.

3. Moreover, Ambrose says, 'Away with arguments where faith is sought.' But in divine matters, especially the trinity, faith is particularly needed. Therefore in this area it is not permitted to investigate the truth through arguments.

4. Moreover, Ambrose says, speaking of the divine generation, 'It is not licit to scrutinize the highest mysteries; it is licit to know what comes to be but it is not licit to discuss how.' By the same token, nothing pertaining to the trinity is licitly investigated by way of argument.

5. Moreover, as Gregory says in his Easter homily, 'faith for which human reason seeks proof has no merit.' But it is evil to get rid of the merit of faith. Therefore, it is not licit to scrutinize what is of faith by way of arguments.

6. Moreover, all honour is owed to God. But secrets are honoured by silence. That is why Denis says at the end of the *Celestial Hierarchy*, 'Honouring the secret that is above us with silence.' And this agrees with Psalm 64.2, according to the translation of Jerome, 'To thee, God, praise in silence,' that is, silence itself is your praise. Therefore we should engage in quiet inquiry into the divine.

7. Moreover, nothing is endlessly moved, as the Philosopher says in *On the Heavens* 1.7, because every motion is the pursuit of an end, which is not found in the endless. But God is infinitely distant from us. Since inquiry is a kind of movement of reason towards what is sought, it seems that divine things ought not to be asked about.

ON THE CONTRARY:

[1] There is what is said in 1 Peter 3.15: 'Be ready always with an answer to everyone who asks a reason for the hope that is in you.' But this cannot be unless what is of faith is inquired into by way of argument. Therefore the inquiry into the things of faith by way of argument is necessary.

[2] Moreover, as is said in Titus 1.9, of a bishop it is required 'that he may be able both to exhort in sound doctrine and to confute opponents'. But those contradicting the faith can be refuted only by arguments. Therefore, in matters of faith arguments must be used.

[3] Moreover, Augustine says in *On the Trinity* 1.2.4, 'With the help of our God we will undertake what they seek, an argument that the trinity is one God.' Therefore a man may inquire into the trinity by way of arguments.

[4] Moreover, Augustine says in *Against Felicianus*, 'Not improperly you discern these two, since setting forth argument you do not omit testimonies. I agree that he will follow what you prove' – namely that I might employ both argument and authority. And thus the same as before.

RESPONSE:
It should be said that since man's perfection consists in union with God, a man must direct everything in him, insofar as possible, to divine things, such that the intellect is free for contemplation and reason free for inquiry into divine things, according to Psalm 72.28: 'But it is good for me to be near God . . .' That is why the Philosopher in *Ethics* 10.7 rejects those who say that man ought not to intrude himself into matters divine, but stay with the human, saying, 'But we must not follow those who advise us, being men, to think of human things, and, being mortal, of mortal things, but must, so far as we can, make ourselves immortal, and strain every nerve to live in accordance with the best thing in us.'[1]

One errs in three ways in this matter. First, out of presumption, as when one so scrutinizes these things as if perfectly to comprehend them, the kind of presumption Job addresses (11.7): 'Peradventure thou wilt comprehend the steps of God, and wilt find out the Almighty perfectly?' And Hilary says, 'Do not plunge into the secret silence of that unthinkable nativity, nor intrude yourself, presuming to comprehend the most intelligible things, but understand that they are incomprehensible.' Second, the error that in matters of faith reason precedes faith not faith reason, such that one wants to believe only what reason can discover, when it should be the reverse. Hence Hilary: 'Begin by believing.' Namely, seek, 'pursue, persist.' Third, pushing oneself beyond the way in which one is capable of scrutiny into divine things; as Romans 12.3 says: 'Let no one rate himself more than he ought, but let him rate himself according to moderation, and according as God has apportioned to each one the measure of faith.' All ought not to pursue the same amount: something can exceed the measure of one but not that of another.

Ad 1. It should be said that those things are said to be above man which exceed his capacity, not what are naturally more worthy; as to what is more worthy, a man is made perfect insofar as he turns to them in his own way. But if someone exceeds his mode even in the consideration of

1. Aristotle, 1177b31–4.

lesser things, he easily falls into error. Thus the Gloss there says, 'Heretics are made in two ways, namely when in the consideration of creator or of creatures they fall into error and depart from the truth.'

Ad 2. It should be said that to search through – *perscrutari* – is to search even to the end. It is illicit and presumptuous when one searches divine things as if to arrive at the goal of comprehension.

Ad 3. It should be said that where faith is sought those arguments should be eschewed which oppose faith and try to precede it, not those which follow it in a fitting manner.

Ad 4. It should be said that although it is illicit to scrutinize the highest mysteries in such a way that one has the intention of comprehending them, which is clear from what follows, 'It is licit to know that he was born, but not to discuss how he was born.' He discusses the mode of nativity who seeks to know the very essence of that birth, since in divine things we can know only that they are, not what they are.

Ad 5. It should be said that there are two kinds of human argument. One is demonstrative, forcing the assent of intellect, and argument of this kind cannot be had of the objects of faith, but they can be had to refute those who assert that faith is impossible. For although the objects of faith cannot be demonstrated, neither can they be demonstratively disproved. If this kind of argument could be put forward to prove the objects of faith there would be no merit, since assent to them would not be voluntary, but necessary. Persuasive argument taken from things similar to what is of faith is not in conflict with the concept of faith, since it does not make them evident, since there is no resolution into the first principles grasped by intellect. Nor does it take away the merit of faith, because it does not force intellect to assent and thus assent remains voluntary.

Ad 6. It should be said that God is honoured by silence, not because nothing is said or asked about him, but because we understand whatever is said or asked to fall short of comprehension of him. Hence it is said in Ecclesiasticus 43.32: 'Glorify the Lord as much as ever you can: for he will yet far exceed, and his magnificence is wonderful.'

Ad 7. It should be said that since God surpasses every creature infinitely, no creature is moved to God in such a way as to be equal to him whether by receiving from him or by knowing him: that which is infinitely distant from the creature cannot be the term of the creature's movement. But every creature is so moved as to be made more and more like God insofar as it can be. That is why the human mind should always be seeking to know God more and more according to its manner. As Hilary says, 'He who piously seeks the infinite, though he will never reach it, ever advances.'

Article 2: Can there be a science of divine things?

We open the question thus: It seems that there can be no science of the things which fall under faith.

1. Wisdom is distinguished from science. But wisdom is concerned with divine things. Therefore, science is not.

2. Moreover, as is said in *Posterior Analytics* 1.1,[1] of its subject every science presupposes what it is. But we cannot in any way know what God is, as Damascene says in *On Faith* 1.4. Therefore there can be no science of God.

3. Moreover, every science considers the parts and passions of its subject. But God who is a simple form has no parts to be distinguished, nor can he be the subject of properties. Therefore there can be no science of God.

4. Moreover, in every science argument precedes assent: a demonstration in the sciences causes assent to the knowable. But in matters of faith the opposite must obtain, namely that the assent of faith precedes argument, as has been said.[2] Therefore there can be no science of God.

5. Moreover, every science proceeds from self-evident principles 'accepted by anyone who hears them,' as Boethius says, or from principles which are held on faith. But the articles of faith, which are first principles of faith, are not of that kind since they are neither self-evident nor can they be demonstratively resolved into self-evident principles, as has been said.[3] Therefore there can be no science of divine things held on faith.

6. Moreover, faith is of things not seen. But science is concerned with the seen, because the things treated in science are brought to light by science. Therefore there can be no science of the divine things held on faith.

7. Moreover, understanding is at the origin of every science, because from the understanding of principles one proceeds to knowledge of conclusions. But in matters of faith understanding is not the beginning but the end, because, as is said in Isaiah, 'Unless you believe, you shall not understand.' Therefore there can be no science of the divine things which are of faith.

---

1. Aristotle, 71a13.
2. Article 1.
3. q. 2, art. 1, ad 5.

ON THE CONTRARY:

[1] There is what Augustine says in *On the Trinity* 12.1.3: 'I assign to this science only that whereby wholesome faith which leads to true happiness is engendered, defended and strengthened.' Therefore there is a science of the things of faith.

[2] Moreover, the same is seen in what is said in Wisdom 10.10: 'He gives them the science of the saints,' which can only be understood as that which distinguishes the saints from the impious, namely, the science of faith.

[3] Moreover, speaking of the knowledge of believers, the Apostle says in 1 Corinthians 8.7, 'There is not science of everything,' and thus the same as before.

RESPONSE:

It should be said that since it is the definition of science that from some known things other things are necessarily concluded, and this comes about with divine things, obviously there can be a science of the divine. But knowledge of divine things can be taken in two ways. In one way, from our side, and thus only created things, knowledge of which we take from the senses, are knowable to us. In another way, from the nature of these things, and thus they are of themselves the most intelligible, and though they cannot be known by us in our manner of knowing, they are none the less known by God and the blessed according to his mode.

On this basis, there are two kinds of science of the divine. One according to our mode, which uses the principles of sensible things to make the divine known, and so it was that philosophers developed a science of the divine, calling divine science first philosophy. Another following the mode of divine things themselves, which grasps divine things in themselves, which indeed is impossible in this life, but some share in and likeness to divine knowledge comes about in us in this life insofar as through infused faith we adhere to first truth for its own sake.

Thus God, in knowing himself, knows other things according to his way of knowing, that is, by simple intuition, not discursively, so we, adhering to the first truth thanks to what we have grasped through faith come to knowledge of other things in our way, discursively, from principles to conclusions. In this science what we hold on faith are for us as it were principles and other things are conclusions. From this it is clear that this is higher than the other divine science taught by the philosophers, since it proceeds from higher principles.

*

Ad 1. It should be said that wisdom is not distinguished from science as something is distinguished from its opposite but because it adds to science. For wisdom, as the Philosopher says in *Nicomachean Ethics* 6.7,[1] is the head of all the sciences, governing all the others insofar as it is of the highest principles, for which reason it is also called, at the beginning of the *Metaphysics*,[2] the 'goddess of the sciences', all the more so because it is not only of the highest but from the highest. It is the mark of the wise to order; therefore that highest science which rules and governs all others is called wisdom, much as in the mechanical arts they are called wise who command others, namely, the master builders. The name of science is reserved for the lower. In this way, science is distinguished from wisdom as a property is distinguished from a definition.

Ad 2. It should be replied, as was said above, that when causes are known through their effects, knowledge of the effects takes the place of knowledge of the essence of the cause, a requirement in those sciences which are of things which can be known in themselves. Thus, in order for us to have a science of divine things, it is not necessary that knowledge of essence be presupposed. Or it might be said that the fact that we know of him what he is not plays the role in divine science of knowledge of what he is, because just as a thing is distinguished from others by what it is, so too can it be by knowledge of what it is not.

Ad 3. It should be said that by 'parts of the subject of a science' is to be understood not only subjective and integral parts, but all those things knowledge of which is needed for knowledge of the subject, though all such things are treated in the science only insofar as they are related to the subject. Whatever can be proved of something are called its properties [*passiones*], whether negations or relations to other things. Many such things can be proved of God from principles naturally known as well as from the principles of faith.

Ad 4. It should be said that in any science some things function as principles and others as conclusions. The argument set forth in science precedes assent to the conclusions, but follows assent to the principles, since it proceeds from them. In this science, the articles of faith do not play the role of conclusions but rather of principles which are defended against those impugning them, just as the Philosopher in *Metaphysics* 4 refutes those denying principles. They are also clarified through certain

1. Aristotle, 1141a18-20.
2. q. 1, art. 2, ad 5.

similitudes, much as principles known naturally are through induction but are not proved by demonstrative argument.

Ad 5. It should be said that even in some humanly devised sciences there are some principles which are not known to all, but must be accepted from higher sciences. In subalternated sciences certain things from higher sciences are supposed and believed which are known to be self-evident only in the higher sciences. The articles of faith, which are the principles of this science, relate to divine knowledge in this way, because what is self-evident in the science God has of himself are presupposed in our science and believed by us as pointed out by his messengers, as the physician believes the natural scientist that there are four elements.

Ad 6. It should be said that what is seen in science proceeds from principles which are seen, since the science does not make the principles to be seen, but, the principles being seen, it makes the conclusions to be seen. In this way the science of which we speak does not make those things which are of faith to be seen, but from these makes other things to be seen in the way that certitude of the first is had.

Ad 7. It should be said that the first, though not always the proximate, principle of any science is understanding: sometimes faith is the proximate principle of a science. This is clear in subalternated sciences whose conclusions proceed as from their *proximate* principle from the belief in what is presupposed from the higher science, but as from the understanding in the higher science, where certain knowledge of these believed things is had, as from their *first* principle. Similarly the proximate principle of this science is faith, but its first principle is the divine understanding, in which we believe, but the end of faith is that we might come to understand what we believed, much as one knowing the inferior science might learn the higher and then things he had hitherto only believed would become understood and known.

Article 3: Is it licit in the science of faith that is concerned with God to use philosophical arguments and authorities?

We open the question thus: It seems that in matters of faith it is not licit to use philosophical arguments.

1. 1 Corinthians 1.17: 'For Christ did not send me to baptize, but to preach the gospel, not with wisdom of words . . .' which the Gloss explains as 'with the doctrine of philosophers'. And on verse 20, 'Where is the disputant of this world?' the Gloss says, 'The disputant is one who probes

the secrets of nature and God does not receive such among his preachers.' And later, on 2.4, 'And my speech and my preaching were not in the persuasive words of wisdom,' the Gloss says, 'Although my words were persuasive, this was not through human wisdom as with the words of pseudo-apostles.' From all of which it is seen that it is not licit to use philosophical arguments in matters of faith.

2. Moreover, on Isaiah 15.1, 'Because in the night Ar of Moab is laid waste,' the Gloss says, 'Ar, that is the adversary, namely worldly knowledge which is an adversary of God.' Therefore we should not use worldly science in those things which concern God.

3. Moreover, Ambrose says, 'The sacrament of the faith is free of philosophical arguments.' Therefore where faith is concerned, philosophical arguments and sayings ought not to be used.

4. Moreover, Jerome in his Letter to the virgin Eusthochius tells how in a vision he was assailed by divine judgement for having read the works of Cicero, and those standing by pleaded that lenience be granted youth and no punishment should be exacted for having sometimes read the books of the gentiles. Then imploring the name of God, he cried out, 'Lord, if I ever had secular books and read them I denied you.' If then it is not permitted to read and study them, much less is it licit to use them in divine treatises.

5. Moreover, worldly wisdom is frequently signified in Scripture by water and divine wisdom by wine. In Isaiah 1.22 inn-keepers who mix water with wine are censured. Therefore teachers who mix philosophical texts with sacred doctrine are to be censured.

6. Moreover, as Jerome says in the Gloss on Osee 2, 'We ought not to have even words in common with the gentiles.' But heretics use philosophical texts for the corruption of the faith, as is said in the Gloss on Proverbs 7.16 and Isaiah 15.5. Therefore Catholics ought not to use them in their treatises.

7. Moreover, just as every science has proper principles, so too does sacred doctrine, namely, articles of faith. It is not proper procedure in the other sciences to assume the principles of another science, but each must proceed from its own principles, according to the Philosopher in *Posterior Analytics* 1.7. Therefore it is not proper procedure in divine science to use the teachings of the philosophers.

8. Moreover, if someone's teaching is repudiated on a given point, his authority to confirm something is weakened; hence Augustine says that if we should concede that there is something false in Sacred Scripture its authority to confirm the faith would be destroyed. But sacred doctrine

repudiates the teaching of philosophers on many points, because they are found to be mistaken about many things. Their authority, therefore, is not efficacious for confirming anything.

ON THE CONTRARY:

[1] The Apostle in Titus 1.12 uses a verse of the poet Epimenides, saying, 'Cretans, always liars, evil beasts, lazy gluttons,' and in 1 Corinthians 15.33, the words of Menander, 'evil companionships corrupt good morals,' and to the Athenians he uses the words of Aratus, 'For we are also his offspring,' as is told in Acts 17.28. Therefore it is licit for other teachers of Sacred Scripture to use philosophical arguments.

[2] Moreover, Jerome in his Letter to Magnus, orator of the city of Rome, having listed a number of teachers of Sacred Scripture, like Basil, Gregory and some others, adds, 'All of whom so filled their books with the teachings of philosophers and their views that you don't know which to marvel at more, their worldly erudition or their knowledge of the scriptures.' Which they would not have done if it were not licit and useful to do it.

[3] Moreover, Jerome in his Letter to Pammachius on the dormition of Pauline, 'Therefore, it is fruitful for one to use worldly wisdom.'

[4] Moreover, Augustine says in *On the Trinity* 2.1, 'I will not be slow to ask after the substance of God whether through the Scriptures or through creatures.' But knowledge of creatures is set forth in philosophy. Therefore it is not improper if one uses philosophical arguments in sacred doctrine.

[5] Moreover, Augustine in *On Christian Doctrine* 40 writes, 'If those who are called philosophers happen to have said anything true or suitable to our faith, not only should they not be feared, but such things must be taken as from unjust possessors and put to our use.' And thus the same as before.

[6] Moreover, on Daniel 1.8, ' But Daniel purposed in his heart that he would not be defiled with the king's table,' the Gloss says, 'If anyone unskilled in mathematics should write against mathematicians or one inexpert in philosophy against philosophers, who would not find it laughable?' But sometimes the teacher of Holy Scripture must contest the philosophers. Therefore he must make use of philosophy.

RESPONSE:

It should be said that the gifts of grace are so added to nature that they do not destroy it, but rather perfect it; so too the light of faith, which is infused in us by grace, does not destroy the light of natural reason divinely placed within us. And although the natural light of the human mind is insufficient to manifest the things made manifest by faith, still it is impossible that those things which have been divinely taught us through faith should be contrary to what has been placed in us by nature. For one of them would have to be false, but since both come to us from God, God would have to be the author of falsity, which is impossible. Rather, since some imitation of the perfect is found in the imperfect, in things that are known by natural reason there are likenesses to the things taught by faith.

Sacred doctrine is based on the light of faith just as philosophy is based on the light of natural reason. Hence it is impossible that what pertains to philosophy should be contrary to what is of faith, though they fall short of it. For they contain certain similitudes and preambles to faith, much as nature is a preamble to grace. If something contrary to the faith should be found in philosophy, this is not philosophy, but rather an abuse of philosophy because of defective reasoning. Therefore it is possible to refute such an error making use of philosophical principles either by showing it is in every way impossible or by showing that it is not necessary. For just as the things of faith cannot be demonstratively proved, so what is contrary to them cannot be demonstrated to be false, but it can be shown that they are not necessary.

We can then use philosophy in sacred doctrine in three ways. First, to demonstrate those things which are preambles of faith, which it is necessary for faith to know, such as the things proven of God by natural arguments, namely, that God exists, that God is one, and the like, or whatever of God or creature is proved in philosophy that faith presupposes. Second, to make known the things of faith by means of certain similitudes, as Augustine in *On the Trinity* uses many similitudes taken from philosophical doctrines to manifest the trinity. Third, to resist what is said against the faith either by showing it to be false or by showing it not to be necessary. *false or not necessary*

But one can err in two ways in using philosophy in sacred doctrine. One way is to use things contrary to faith, which is not philosophy, but its corruption or abuse; Origen did this. Another way is this, that the things of faith are reduced to the measure of philosophy, such that someone wishes to believe only what can be established in philosophy. It is rather the reverse that should be done, philosophy reduced to the measure of the faith, following the Apostle in 2 Corinthians 10.5: 'Bringing your mind into captivity to the obedience of Christ.'

*

Ad 1. From everything that has been said, it is clear that the teaching of philosophers ought not to be used as the principal thing, as if the truth of faith is believed on its account, but this does not disturb the fact that sacred doctors can employ it as secondary. That is why, on 'I will destroy the wisdom of the wise,'[1] the Gloss says, 'Let it not then be said that the understanding of truth is disapproved by God, but rather the prudence of those who rely on their erudition.' In order that the whole of faith not be attributed to human power and wisdom but to God, God willed that the primitive teaching of the apostles should be in weakness and simplicity, to which afterwards, however, worldly power and wisdom being added, he shows through the victory of faith that the world is subject to God both in power and in wisdom.

Ad 2. It should be said that worldly wisdom is said to be contrary to God as to its abuse, in the way heretics abuse it, not as to its truth.

Ad 3. It should be said that the sacrament of faith is said to be free of philosophical arguments insofar as it cannot be confined with the bounds of philosophy, as was said.

Ad 4. It should be said that Jerome was so enamoured of the books of the gentiles that he contemned, in a way, Sacred Scripture; hence he himself says in the same place, 'If when I returned to myself I began to read the prophets, the uncultivated style repelled me.' And that this is reprehensible no one would doubt.

Ad 5. It should be said that argument ought not to be fashioned of metaphors, as the Master says in *Sentences* 3, Distinction 11, and Denis says in the Letter to Titus. Symbolic theology is not argumentative, especially since it is not the exposition of any author. It can be said however that it is not called a mixing when one of the two passes into the power of the other, but when both are altered in their nature. Hence those who employ philosophical texts in sacred doctrine, putting it to the service of the faith, do not mingle water with wine, but change water into wine.

Ad 6. It should be said that Jerome speaks of those words fashioned by heretics adapted to their errors. But philosophical disciplines are not like that, indeed it is only their abuse that leads to error, so there is no reason to avoid them.

Ad 7. It should be said that sciences which are ordered to one another are such that one can use the principles of the other, as subsequent sciences use the principles of prior sciences, whether they be superior or inferior.

1. 1 Corinthians 1.19.

Hence metaphysics, which is superior to all, uses what has been proved in the other sciences. Similarly theology, since all other sciences are, as it were, its servants and preambles in the order of discovery, although they are beneath it in dignity, can use the principles of all the other sciences.

Ad 8. It should be said that insofar as sacred doctrine uses philosophical texts for its own sake, it does not accept them on the authority of those writing them, but because of the arguments for what is said; hence it takes things well said and repudiates others. But when it uses them to refute others, it uses them insofar as they have authority for those being refuted, because the testimony of adversaries is efficacious.

Article 4: Should divine things be veiled and hidden with obscure words?

We open the question thus: It seems that in the science of the faith divine things ought not to be hidden by obscure language.

1. Because, as is said in Proverbs 14.6, 'The learning of the wise is easy.' Therefore it ought to be proposed without obscurity of language.

2. Moreover, Ecclesiasticus 4.28, 'Hide not thy wisdom in her beauty,' and Proverbs 11.26, 'He that hideth corn' – that is, according to the Gloss, preaching – 'shall be cursed among the people.' Therefore the words of Sacred Scripture ought not to be hidden.

3. Moreover, there is Matthew 10.27, 'What I tell you in darkness' – that is, according to the Gloss, in mystery – 'speak it in the light' – namely, as the Gloss says, openly. Therefore the obscure things of faith are rather to be disclosed than hidden by difficult words.

4. Moreover, teachers of the faith are obliged to both the wise and the simple, as is clear from Romans 1.14. Therefore they ought to speak in such a way that they can be understood by both the great and the small, that is, without obscurity of language.

5. Moreover, Wisdom 7.13: 'Which I have learned without guile, and communicate without envy.' But he who hides them does not communicate them. Therefore he seems guilty of jealousy.

6. Moreover, Augustine says in *On Christian Doctrine* 4.8, 'Commentators on Sacred Scripture ought not to speak as if they propose themselves to be interpreted, but in all their remarks first and chiefly that they might be understood, speaking so clearly that he who does not understand is very slow.'

ON THE CONTRARY:

[1] There is what is said in Matthew 7.6, 'Do not give to dogs what is holy, neither cast your pearls before swine,' on which the Gloss says, 'Hidden things are sought more avidly, and the concealed seems more venerable, and things long sought are cherished the more.' Since therefore it is fitting that the sacred writings be looked into with the highest veneration, it seems that they ought not to be broadcast, but passed on obscurely.

[2] Moreover, Denis says in the *Ecclesiastical Hierarchy* 1.5, 'Do not tell others of the sacred praise unless like you they are godlike.' By sacred praise he intends to embrace all the sacred writings, which you are to pass on only to those similar to yourselves. But if they were set forth in obvious language, they would be open to all. Therefore the secrets of faith are to be veiled in obscure language.

[3] Moreover, relevant here is what is said in Luke 8.10: 'To you' – that is, to the perfect – 'it is given to know the mystery of the kingdom of God,' that is, understanding of the scriptures, as is clear from the Gloss on 'but to the rest in parables'. Therefore it must be hidden from the multitude by a certain obscurity of language.

RESPONSE:

It should be said that the words of the teacher ought to be so fashioned that they help not harm the hearer. There are some things which when heard harm nobody, such as all those things everyone is held to know; and these are not to be hidden but manifestly set forth to all. There are other things, however, which when set forth openly harm hearers; this happens in two ways. In one way, if the secrets of faith are disclosed to infidels who abhor the faith. For with them they come into derision and for this reason the Lord says in Matthew 7.6, 'Do not give to dogs what is holy,' and Denis in the *Celestial Hierarchy* 2, 'Concealing what is holy from the unclean multitude I have kept it intact.' Second, when subtle matters are proposed to the unlearned, who cannot perfectly comprehend the matter, they are led into error. Hence the Apostle says in 1 Corinthians 3.1 ff., 'And I, brethren, could not speak to you as to spiritual men but only as carnal, as to little ones in Christ, I fed you with milk, not with solid food.' And on this in Exodus 21.33, 'If a man open a pit . . .', the Gloss of Gregory says: 'He who understands in sacred writ things so high, protects with silence the sublime meaning from those incapable of grasping it, lest by scandal he should harm the simple believer or impede the non-believer who would believe.' These things then should be kept hidden from those they might harm.

But a distinction in speaking can be made, such that what is made manifest to the wise apart is left unsaid in public. Thus Augustine says in *On Christian Doctrine* 4.1.9.23, 'There are some things the full force of which is not understood, or scarcely understood, however much and often or how eloquently they are spoken, and such things ought never or only rarely out of some urgent need to be proclaimed to a popular audience.' This distinction cannot be observed in writing, because books once written can come into the hands of anyone, and therefore they should be couched in obscurity of language, such that they are clear to the wise who can understand them and are hidden from the simple who cannot grasp their meaning. No harm is done by this, because those who understand, read, and those who do not understand, are not forced to read. Hence Augustine says in the same work, 'In works written in such a way that they hold the attention of those who understand them and do no harm to those who do not read them. Is not this the point of discourse that true things, although they be difficult to understand, lead us on to the understanding of others?'

Ad 1. It should be said that the text is not relevant, for its meaning is not that the teaching of the prudent is actively easy, that is, that they easily teach, but passively, because they are easily taught, as is clear from the Gloss.

Ad 2. It should be said that those authorities speak of one who hides what should be made manifest, hence Ecclesiasticus 4.28 is preceded by, 'And refrain not to speak in the time of salvation.' But this does not exclude that those things which ought to be hidden should be concealed in obscurity of language.

Ad 3. It should be said that the teaching of Christ is to be plainly and publicly preached, such that to each is made plain what is important for him to know, not, however, that what it is not necessary to know should be made public.

Ad 4. It should be said that the teachers of sacred doctrine are not so obliged to the wise and simple that they must propose the same to both, but that to both they propose what is appropriate to each.

Ad 5. It should be said that it is not out of jealousy that subtle things should be hidden from the multitude, but rather the discretion due them, as has been said.

Ad 6. It should be said that Augustine is talking of commentators who speak to the people, not of those who commit something to writing, as is clear from what follows.

7. How are Things Good? Exposition of On the Hebdomads of Boethius (1257)

The following little work may seem to turn simply on the logical problem of predication. The great divide between predicates, for Thomas as for Aristotle, is between those that are predicated in quid *and those that are predicated in* quale *– the difference, in short, between those that tell us what the thing is, what pertains to its nature or essence, and those that attribute incidental properties, relations, location, etc. to a substance. In one of his shorter works, St Anselm wondered whether calling someone a grammarian amounted to a predicate of the first or second type. Boethius's question can seem to be like that. When I say of someone that he is good – say the Samaritan – I seem to be doing something very much like saying, 'The Samaritan is a grammarian.' He had to exist in order to acquire this skill and he would go on being who he is if all his knowledge of grammar suddenly deserted him. But when he is said to be a man, on the other hand, the predicate informs us of the kind of thing he is. He could not be without that predicate and go on being a man.*

Boethius's problem arises from the fact that he is thinking of the difference between calling God good and calling a creature good. A man might be called morally good in terms of characteristics he at first did not have – virtues – and which he could lose and still go on being the same person, though no longer one we would care to live with. But Boethius has another sense of 'good' in mind; not an incidental predicate, but one pointing to what the thing is. Whatever is, is good just as it is one. To lose goodness in this sense would be to cease to be. So it looks to be a substantial rather than an incidental predicate. But what then of 'God is good'?

Boethius sets up a neat dilemma. If good can be predicated either incidentally or substantially, there are reasons why we would want to deny that the predicate in 'Socrates is good' is either. After all, God is goodness and Socrates only has it. This is the basis for the distinction between saying something essentially and saying something by way of participation of a subject. But, as you will see, this creates problems of its own.

Thomas's commentary turns a fairly opaque piece into a relatively easy argument.

EXPOSITION OF *ON THE HEBDOMADS* OF BOETHIUS

I

You ask me to state and explain somewhat more clearly that obscure question in my *Hebdomads* concerning the manner in which substances can be good in virtue of existence without being absolute goods. You urge that this demonstration is necessary because the method of this kind of treatise is not clear to all. I can bear witness with what eagerness you have already attacked the subject. But I confess I like to expound my *Hebdomads* to myself, and would rather bury my speculations in my own memory than share them with any of those pert and frivolous persons who will not tolerate an argument unless it is made amusing. Wherefore do not you take objection to the obscurity that waits on brevity; for obscurity is the sure treasure house of secret doctrine and has the further advantage that it speaks a language understood only of those who deserve to understand. I have therefore followed the example of the mathematical and cognate sciences and laid down terms and rules according to which I shall develop all that follows.

A common conception of the soul is a statement accepted as soon as one hears it. These are of two kinds. One is common to all men, for example were you to say, 'Equals taken from equals leave equals,' no one hearing this would deny it. The other is of the learned alone, though it arises from the first, for example 'Incorporeal things are in no place,' etc., to which the learned but not the crowd assent.   Boethius, *On the Hebdomads*[1]

Boethius writes a book for us on his thoughts, called *On the Hebdomads*, that is, on the publications, because the Greek word means to publish. Boethius does two things in this book. First, he writes a preface, second he gets on with the body of the work: *For a thing to be and what it is differ.*

In the first part, he states his intention, next he tells us how he will proceed there, 'You urge that . . .', and third he speaks of the order of procedure, 'I have therefore followed . . .'

1. The text of *On the Hebdomads* is taken from J. P. Migne, *Patrologiae Cursus Completus*, vol. 64, Paris, Migne, 1882, 1311–14.

He dedicates the book to John, a deacon of the Roman church, who had asked him to discuss certain matters from his *Hebdomads*, that is, publications, to clarify a difficult question so that an apparent contradiction might be resolved. For it is said that created substances, insofar as they exist, are good, yet created substances are not substantial goods, for this is said to be peculiar to God. What pertains to a thing insofar as it exists, belongs to it substantially. Therefore, if created substances, insofar as they exist, are good, it seems to follow that they are substantial goods.

When he says, *You urge that . . .*, he shows the way he wishes to speak here, not plainly, but obscurely. He does three things, first, says that he means to speak obscurely, second, he mentions that this is his customary manner, *But I confess . . .*, and third he shows that this manner ought to be accepted, *Wherefore do not you . . .*

First, he says that the one for whom he writes asked him to treat these matters in such a way that what is here written will not be understood by those who are not as attached to them as he. And of him Boethius testifies that he had embraced these matters eagerly before, that is, by profoundly understanding and fervently desiring.

He goes on to say that this manner is customary with him, remarking that it is his wont to comment, that is to compose and excogitate these *Hebdomads* or editions or conceptions, which he preserves, turning them over in memory.

When he writes, *Wherefore do not you . . .*, he concludes from the foregoing that he ought gratefully to receive this obscure speech, that is, the one who requested it; and that is why he says, *do not you . . .* namely because you did it, lest the journey of our descriptions should be open to all. Nor should you be adverse, that is contrary, to the obscurities of brevity, that is to the obscurity of the present book, which is linked to its brevity. By the fact that some things are briefly said, they become more obscure, but obscurity since it faithfully guards the secret, has this utility that he speaks only with the worthy, that is with the understanding and serious who are worthy to be admitted to the secrets of wisdom.

Then when he says, *I have therefore followed the example of the mathematical*, he shows the order of proceeding, that is, from things which are known of themselves, and he does two things, first, he states the order of proceeding, second, he makes known the things from which he intends to proceed: *A common conception of the soul.*

He says that he intends first to propose some self-evidently known principles which he calls terms or rules – terms, because in such principles the resolution of any demonstration comes to an end; rules, because by them one is directed to knowledge of the conclusions that follow. From such principles he intends to conclude and make known everything which is later to be treated, in the manner of geometry and the other demonstrative sciences, which are for that reason called disciplines because by them knowledge is acquired by learners from the demonstration that the teacher puts forward.

Then when he says *the common conception of the soul*, he makes known the self-evident principles, first by definition, second by division, there, *These are of two kinds*.

With respect to the first point it should be considered that such principles, which are terms because they are rules of demonstrations, are called common conceptions of the soul: *A common conception of the soul is a statement accepted as soon as one hears it*, that is, that anyone immediately approves when he hears it. For other propositions which are demonstrated by these are not immediately approved by the listener, but must become known through others. But there should not be an infinite regress so we must come to some that are known immediately of themselves. Hence they are called common conceptions of the soul and commonly fall within the conception of any intellect. The reason for this is that the predicate enters into the account of the subject, such that, once the subject is named and understood as to what it is, immediately it is manifest that the predicate is in it.

Then when he says, *These are of two kinds*, he divides the foregoing principles, saying that there are two kinds of common conceptions of the soul. For some conceptions of the soul are common to all men, for example, if equals be taken from equals equals remain. Another conception of the soul is common only to the learned and is derived from the first conceptions of the soul which are common to all men. For example, incorporeal things are not in place, which is not accepted by the unlearned, but only by the wise.

The reason for this distinction is this, since the common conception of the soul, or self-evident principle, is a proposition whose predicate enters into the account of the subject, if what is meant by subject and predicate is within the ken of all, such a proposition will be self-evident to all: for example what is equal is known to all, and so too what it is to take away, and therefore the foregoing proposition is self-evident to all. And so too, every whole is greater than its part, and other like propositions. But only the intellect of the wise rises to the understanding of the incorporeal thing, for the intellect of the mass of men does not transcend imagination, which is only of corporeal things, and therefore what is proper to bodies, for example to be circumscriptively in place, the intellect of the wise at once removes from incorporeal things, which the unlearned cannot do.

2

1. To be and that which is are different.

a. For to be itself is not yet, but that which is, having received a form of being, is and subsists.

b. That which is can participate in something, but to be itself in no wise participates in anything. Participation comes about when something already is, and something is when it receives existence.

c. That which is can have something outside what it is, but to be itself has nothing outside itself mixed with it.

2. To be such and such and to be something as that which is, differ.

a. The former signifies accident, the latter, substance.

b. That which is participates in existence in order to be and participates in another to be such and such.

c. That which is participates in that which is existence in order to be, and is in order to participate in something else.

3. In every composite, to be is one thing, and the thing that is, another.

4. In every simple thing, its existence and that which is are the same.

5. All difference is discord, but likeness is to be desired.

What desires another is itself shown to be naturally like what it desires.

What we have set forth suffices. The wise interpreter with his own reasons can adapt each of them to arguments.   Boethius, *On the Hebdomads*

Boethius said above that he would proceed in this order that having set forth certain terms and rules, he would go on from them to further matters, and so according to the order stated, he begins first to set down some rules or some conceptions of the wise, and second he begins to argue from them: *but a question of this kind . . .*

As has already been said, those propositions are most known which use terms everyone understands. But the things that occur to any intellect are the most common that are: being, one and good. Therefore, Boethius first states some conceptions pertaining to being; second, some pertaining to one, from which the notions of simple and complex are taken: paragraph 3. Third, he states some conceptions pertaining to the good: paragraph 5.

With respect to being, to be itself is considered something common and indeterminate, which is determined in two ways, first on the part of the subject, which has existence, and another way on the part of the predicate, as when we say of man, or of anything, not that it simply is, but that it is such and such, for example white or black. First therefore he states conceptions which are taken from the comparison of that which is simply to be to that which is to be such and such: paragraph 5.

The first point he subdivides into two: first he states the difference between that which is existence and that which is; second he manifests this difference: *For to be itself is not yet . . .* (paragraph 1a)

First he says that to be and that which is are different. This difference is not now to be referred to things, of which he does not yet speak, but to the notions or intentions themselves. For we mean one thing when we say *to be* and another when we say *that which is*, just as we signify one thing by *to run* and another by *runner*. For *to run* and *to be* are signified in the abstract, like *whiteness*, but *what is*, that is *being* and *runner*, are signified in the concrete, like white.

When he says, *For to be itself . . .*, he manifests this difference in three ways, of which the first is this: to be itself is not signified as if it were the subject of being, any more than to run signifies the subject of running. Just as we cannot say that to run itself runs, so we cannot say that to be itself is, and just as that which is is signified as the subject of being, so that which runs is signified as the subject of running. Therefore, just as we can say of him who runs, or the runner, that he runs, insofar as he is the subject of running and participates in it, so we can say that being, or that which is, is. That is what he means when he says, *to be itself is not yet*, because to be is not attributed to it as to a subject of being; but that which is, having received a form of being, that is, by receiving the very act of being, is and consists, that is, subsists in itself. For being is only said properly and as such of substance, of which it is to subsist. Accidents are not called being as if they were beings, but insofar as something is their subject, as will be said later.

He states the second difference in paragraph 1b: *That which is can participate.* This difference is based on the notion of participation. To participate is as it were to take a part, and therefore when something receives in a particular way what pertains to another, it is generally said to participate in it, as man is said to participate in animal, because he does not have the notion of animal according to its full extension; for the same reason, Socrates participates in man. So too the subject participates in its accident, and matter in form, because the substantial or accidental form, which of its own notion is common, is determined to this or that subject, and similarly the effect is said to participate in its cause, especially when it is not equal to the power of its cause, for example when we say that air participates in the light of the sun because it does not receive it with the brightness the sun has.

Setting aside this third kind of participating, it is impossible that to be itself should participate in anything according to either of the first two modes. For it cannot participate in anything in the way in which matter or a subject participates in form or accident, because, as has been said, to be itself is signified as something abstract. No more can it participate in something in the way that the particular participates in the universal, even though some things abstractly stated can participate in something, as whiteness in colour. But to be itself is most common: it is indeed participated in by others, but does not itself participate in anything else. But that which is, or being, although most common is said concretely, and therefore it participates in to be itself, not in the way that the more common is participated in by the less common, but it participates in to be itself in the way the concrete participates in the abstract.

This is what he means by *that which is* – that is, being – *can participate in something; but to be itself in no way participates in anything* (paragraph 1b). And in this way he proves what was said above, namely that *to be itself is not yet* (paragraph 1a). Clearly what is not cannot participate in anything. Consequently, participation belongs to that which already is. Something is because it receives to be itself, as has been said; so it remains that that which is can participate in something, but to be itself cannot participate in anything.

He states the third difference in paragraph 1c, *that which is*, and this difference is based on the admixture of something extraneous. On this point, consider that with respect to anything abstractly considered, it is true that it does not have in itself anything extraneous, that is, anything that would be outside its essence, for example humanity or whiteness and anything else so said. The reason is that humanity is signified as *that whereby* something is a man, and whiteness as *that whereby* something is white. Nothing is a man, formally speaking, except by that which pertains to the definition of man, and similarly a thing is white formally only because of what pertains to the definition of white. Therefore, such abstractly stated things cannot have anything alien in themselves. It is otherwise with things stated concretely.

For 'man' signifies that which has humanity, and 'white' that which has whiteness. But just because a man has humanity or whiteness does not prevent him from having something else which does not pertain to the definitions of these – except of course what is contrary to them. Therefore man and the white thing can have something besides humanity and whiteness. This is the reason that whiteness and humanity are signified in the manner of a part and are not predicated of the concrete, any more than the part is of its whole. Therefore, as has been said, because to be itself is signified as abstract and that which is as concrete, what is here said is true, *that which is can have something besides that which it is* (paragraph 1c), that is, outside its essence, but to be itself can have nothing mixed with it outside its own essence.

Then when in paragraph 2 he says *To be such and such and to be something*, he states conceptions which are based on the comparison of what it is to be simply and what it is to be such and such. First he states their difference, second, in paragraph 2a he assigns the differences: *The former signifies accident.*

With respect to the first, note that because that which is can have something outside its own essence, a twofold existence must be recognized in it. For since form is the principle of being, it is necessary that according as it has some form it will be said to have being in some way. Therefore, if the form is not outside the essence of the one having it, but constitutes his essence, by the fact that he has such a form he will be said to have existence simply, like a man because he has a rational soul. But if the form be such that it is extraneous to the essence of the one having it, because of this form it will not be said to be simply, but to be such and such, as thanks to whiteness a man is said to be white. That is what he means by *to be such and such, which is not to be simply, differs from something as that in which it is, which is the proper subject of existence* (paragraph 2).

When he says, *The former signifies accident* (paragraph 2a), he states three differences between the foregoing.

Of which the first is that *there*, that is, where it is said of a thing that it is such and such, and not that it is simply, an accident is signified, because the form that causes such being is outside the essence of the thing, but *here* when something is said to be in that which is signified as substance, namely because the form causing being constitutes the essence of the thing.

He states the second difference in paragraph 2b, *That which is participates in existence*, where he means that in order for something to be simply a subject, it participates in to be itself, but in order to be such and such, it must participate in something else; as a man in order to be white participates not only in substantial existence, but also in whiteness.

He states the third difference in paragraph 2c, *That which is particip-ates*, which indeed is based on the order of both and is derived from what has gone before. The difference is that something must first be understood as simply being, and afterwards as being such and such; but when once it is, that is, by participation in to be itself, there remains for it to participate in something else, that is, in order to be such and such.

Then when he said, *In every composite* (paragraph 3), he states concep-tions having to do with the complex and simple, which pertain to the notion of one. It should be noted that what was said already about the difference between to be itself and that which is, is based on their meanings or intentions. Here he shows how it is applied to things, and first he shows this in complex things, second in simple, in paragraph 4: *In every simple thing . . .*

First it must be noted that, just as to be and what is differ in simple things according to intentions, so they *really* differ in complex things. This is indeed manifest from what has gone before. For it was said above that to be itself neither participates in anything, such that its notion would be constituted of many, nor does it have anything extraneous mixed with it, such that there might be in it a composition with accident. To be itself is not complex. Therefore, the complex thing is not its own existence. That is what he means by *In every composite, to be is one thing, and the thing that is is another* (paragraph 3) – namely that which has participated in to be itself.

When he says, *In every simple thing* (paragraph 4), he shows how it is with the simple, in which to be itself and that which is must be really one and the same. For if to be itself were really other than that which is, it would not be simple, but composed. But note that although to be simple means to lack composition, nothing prevents something from being simple in a certain respect, because it lacks a kind of composition, which is not simple in every way. Thus fire and water are called simple bodies, insofar as they lack the composition of contraries that is found in mixed bodies, but each of them is composed both of quantitative parts and of form and matter. Therefore, if there should be found forms apart from matter, each of them is simple in that it lacks matter, and consequently quantity, which is a disposition of matter, none the less, because each form is determinative of to be itself, none of them is its own existence, but is something having existence.

For example, if we should adopt the opinion of Plato and posit an immaterial form to subsist which is an idea and notion of material men, and another form which is the idea and notion of horses, clearly the immaterial subsisting form, since it something determined to a species, is not common existence itself, but participates in it. In this respect it does not matter whether we posit immaterial forms of a higher rank than the notions of these sensible things, as Aristotle wishes: each of them, insofar as it is distinct from the others, is a special form participating in existence itself. Thus none of them is truly simple.

That will be truly simple which does not participate in existence as something inhering in it but is *subsistent existence*. But this can only be one. Because if existence itself has nothing added to itself besides existence, as has been said, it is impossible that that which is its own existence be multiplied by something diversifying it; and because it has nothing outside itself mixed with it, the consequence is that it is susceptible of no accident. This one simple and sublime being is God himself.

When he says, *All difference* . . . (paragraph 5), he states two conceptions pertaining to appetite from which good is defined; for the good is said to be what all things desire.

Here then is the first conception: all difference is discord, and similarity is to be desired. Concerning which, note that the discordant clashes with desire, so discord is said to be what is repugnant to desire. The different as such is repugnant to desire; the reason is that the like augments and perfects what is like it and everything desires its own growth and perfection, and therefore the like, as such, is desirable to anything and, by parity of reasoning, the diverse is repugnant to desire insofar as it diminishes and impedes perfection.

Therefore he says that all difference is discord, that is, discordant with desire, but likeness is to be desired. It happens accidentally that an appetite abhors the like and desires the different or contrary. As has been said, each thing first of all and as such desires its own perfection, which is the good of anything, and is always proportioned to what is perfectible of it, and so far forth has similarity to it. Other exterior things are desired or avoided insofar as they contribute to proper perfection, in which something sometimes fails either by defect or excess.

The proper perfection of anything consists of a kind of commensuration, as the perfection of the human body consists in commensurated heat which, when it fails, something hot is desired by which heat can be augmented, and if it is excessive it seeks the contrary, namely the cold, to reduce its temperature, in which consists the perfection conformed to nature. Thus one potter might resent another insofar as he takes away from him a desired perfection, namely profit.

He states the second conception in paragraph 5, *What desires another . . .*, which is derived from the foregoing. For if likeness is as such to be desired, that which desires another is shown naturally to be of the same sort as the thing it wants, because it has a natural inclination to what it desires. This natural inclination sometimes follows the essence of the thing, as the heavy desires to be down according to the notion of its essential nature, but sometimes it follows on the nature of some supervenient form, as when someone with an acquired habit desires that which is agreeable to him because of that habit.

Finally he adds an epilogue, *What we have set forth suffices*, namely what has been said is sufficient for the thesis, and one who wisely interprets these axioms can adapt each of them to arguments, applying them to appropriate conclusions, as will be clear in what follows.

3

Now the problem is this. Things which are, are good. For all the learned are agreed that every existing thing tends to good and everything tends to its like. Therefore things which tend to good are good. We must, however, inquire how they are good – by participation or by substance.

If by participation, they are in no wise good in themselves; for a thing which is white by participation in whiteness is not white in itself by virtue of what it is. So with all other qualities. If then they are good by participation, they are not good in themselves; therefore they do not tend to good. But we have agreed that they do. Therefore they are good not by participation but by substance.

But those things whose substance is good are substantially good. But the fact that they are is due to existence. Therefore their existence is good. Existence therefore is a good of all things. But if existence is good the things that are, are good just insofar as they are. For them to be and to be good is the same. They are substantial goods since they do not participate in goodness. But if their existence is good, there is no doubt that, as substantial goods, they are like the First Good. Indeed, they will be the First Good since nothing other is like it. From which it follows that they are God, an impious assertion. Therefore they cannot be substantial goods, their existence is not good, and they are not good because they exist.

But neither do they participate in goodness. Therefore, they in no way tend to the good and in no way are good.   Boethius, *On the Hebdomads*

Having set down certain principles which are necessary for the discussion of the question before us, he goes on now to the question and does three things. First, he proposes the question; second, he advances a solution to it, in Chapter 4; third, he sets aside some objections to the solution, in Chapter 5.

Next he does two things: first, he sets down what the question presupposes; second, what in the question generates doubt: *We must, however, inquire how they are good.*

He says that the way for us to approach the question is to presuppose that all the things that are are good. To prove this, he advances an argument based on what he has earlier set down, and it is this: Everything tends towards its like. He set down above that what desires another thereby shows itself to be naturally like the thing that it desires.

But whatever is, tends to the good. This invokes the second common conception of the learned, for at the outset of the *Ethics* the Philosopher says that the wise declare the good to be that which all things desire. For good is the proper object of the will, as sound is the proper object of hearing, and just as sound is perceived by any hearer, so good must be that towards which every appetite tends. Thus, since everything has some appetite, intellectual, sensitive, or natural, it follows that every thing desires the good. And thus he concludes, *Every thing is good*, something our question presupposes.

When he says, *We must inquire how they are good*, he shows the doubt the question raises, and on this point he does three things: first, he states the question; second, he argues against one aspect of the question, *If by participation . . .*; third, he goes on to exclude the first supposition, *therefore they are not good because they exist . . .*

First he says that, supposing that all things are good, the way of it must be looked into, namely, how they are good. Something can be predicated of a thing in two ways, in one way, substantially, in another way, by participation. Hence the question arises whether beings are good in essence or by participation. To understand the question, it should be noted that the question presupposes that to be in essence and to be by participation are opposed. And in one of the modes of participation distinguished earlier this is manifestly true, that is, according to the mode whereby the subject participates in an accident, or matter in form.

For an accident is outside the nature of the subject and form is outside the very substance of matter. But in another mode of participation, that whereby the species participates in the genus, this is also true, according to the opinion of Plato who posited that the idea of animal is different from the idea of the biped man. But according to the view of Aristotle, who held that man truly is what animal is, the essence of animal not existing apart from the difference of man, nothing prevents what is said by participation from being predicated substantially. But Boethius here speaks in terms of the participation whereby subject participates in accident, and then what is predicated substantially can be the opposite of what is predicated participatively, as is clear from the examples he subsequently introduces.

When he says, *If by participation . . .*, he argues against both sides of the suggestion, and first against this, that things are good by participation, and second against the claim that they are good by their own substance: *But those things whose substance is good . . .*

First he says that if all things are good by participation, it follows that they are in no way good in themselves. And this indeed is true if 'in themselves' is taken to mean 'is in the definition of that of which it is said', as man is animal of himself, since what enters into a thing's definition pertains to its essence; and thus is not said of it by way of participation as we are now using that term. If it were taken in another way, namely insofar as the subject enters into the definition of the predicate, then what is said here would be false. For the proper accident is in this way in its subject *per se*, and yet is predicated of it participatively.

Therefore, since Boethius here understands participation in the way the subject participates in an accident, and *per se* or of itself that which is put into the definition of the subject, it necessarily follows that if things are good by participation, they are not good of themselves. He manifests this with an example: that which is white by participation, is not white of itself, that is, in that which it is, which pertains to the first mode of speaking *per se*, and it is the same with other qualities. If therefore all beings were good by participation, it follows that all are not good *per se*, that is, in their substance. From this it follows that the substances of beings do not tend to the good, the opposite of which was conceded earlier, namely that all things tend to the good. It seems therefore that beings are not good by participation but through their substance.

When he says, *But things whose substance . . .*, he objects to the other side in this way. Those things whose substance is good must be good in that which they are: for those things pertain to the substance of a thing which come together in order for it to exist. But that things are they owe to existence. For it was said above that something is when it receives existence. It follows therefore that the very existence of things which are good according to their substance is good. Therefore, if all things were good in their substance, it would follow that the existence itself of all things is good. And, since the premises from which he is arguing are convertible, he proceeds conversely. For it follows conversely that if the existence of all things is good, then the things that are, insofar as they are, are good, and it is the same for a thing to exist and to be good. Therefore it follows that they are substantial goods from the fact that they are good, and not by participation in goodness. He goes on to show that something absurd follows from this. If the very existence of all things is good, and from this it follows that they are substantial goods, the consequence is that they are like the First Good, which is substantial good and for which to exist and to be good are the same.

From which it further follows that all things *are* the First Good itself, because nothing apart from it is like it, that is with respect to the mode of goodness. Nothing else outside the first good is good in the same way as it, which alone is the First Good. Other things are said to be like it insofar as they are secondary goods derived from the first and principal good. If therefore all things are the first good itself, since that first good is nothing other than God, it would follow that all beings are God, to say which is sinful. Thus it follows that what has gone before is false and all things are not substantial goods nor is their very existence good, since from that it followed that all things are God. It would further follow that all things are not good insofar as they are.

When he says, *but neither do they participate . . .,* he goes on to remove the first supposition, and says that, if to this, that beings are not substantially good, be added the other conclusion arrived at above, namely that all beings are not good by participation, since from that it followed that they would not then tend to the good, as was said above, it seems possible to conclude finally that there is no way in which beings are good – which is contrary to what was set down earlier.

4

This problem admits of the following solution. There are many things which can be separated by a mental process which cannot be separated in fact. No one, for instance, can actually separate a triangle or other mathematical figure from the underlying matter; but mentally one can consider a triangle and its properties apart from matter.

Let us, therefore, abstract mentally for a moment the presence of the First Good, whose existence is admitted by the universal consensus of the learned and unlearned and can be deduced from the religious beliefs of savage races.

The First Good having been thus for a moment abstracted, let us postulate as good all things that are, and let us consider how they could possibly be good if they did not derive from the First Good. This process leads me to perceive that their goodness and their existence are two different things. For let me suppose that one and the same substance is good, white, heavy, and round. Then it must be admitted that its substance, roundness, colour, and goodness are all different things. For if each of these qualities were the same as its substance, weight would be the same thing as colour or goodness, and goodness would be the same thing as colour; which is contrary to nature. For them to be, then, differs from their being such-and-such, and they would be good but their very existence would not be good. Therefore, if they were in any way to exist, they would neither be goods nor from the good, they would not be the same as the good, and for them to be and to be good would differ.

But if they were nothing else but good substances, and were neither heavy nor coloured, and possessed neither spatial dimension nor quality, beyond that of goodness, they (or rather it) would seem to be not things but a principle of things. For there is one thing alone that is by nature good to the exclusion of every other quality.

But since they are not simple, they could not even exist at all unless that which is the one sole good willed them to be. They are called good simply because their existence derived from the will of the Good. For the First Good is essentially good in virtue of his existence. Secondary goods are good in their turn because they derive from the good whose very existence is good. The existence of all things derives from the First Good, of whom it is rightly said that for him to be is to be good. Therefore their existence is good. But for them to be and to be good would not be the same if they did not derive from the First Good.   Boethius, *On the Hebdomads*

Boethius here provides a solution to the foregoing question and to the arguments brought forward, in three steps. First, he settles the truth of the question; then he answers an objection, and finally he raises some objections to his resolution, and answers them.

On the first point, he does three things: first, he sets down a certain supposition; second, he shows what follows from that supposition with regard to the goodness of things: *The First Good having been thus for a moment removed* . . .; third, he shows what the truth of the matter is about the goodness of things, no supposition being made: *But since they are not simple* . . .

He subdivides the first into two: first he sets down something that is necessary in order to show that such a supposition can be made; second, he introduces the supposition: *Let us therefore abstract . . .*

First he says that there are many things which cannot be actually separated but which can be separated in the soul by thought; the reason for this is that things exist in one way in the soul and in another in matter. Therefore, it can be that something, given the mode of existence it has in matter, is inseparably joined to it, yet insofar as it is in the soul, it is not inseparably joined to it, because the notion of the one is distinct from the notion of the other. He gives the example of triangle and other mathematical entities which cannot actually be separated from sensible matter, yet the mathematician, abstracting in his mind from sensible matter, considers the triangle and its properties, because the notion of triangle does not depend on sensible matter.

When he says, *Let us, therefore, abstract . . .*, he states the supposition he has in mind, namely that by a mental consideration we remove for now the presence of the first good from other things, which is possible in the order of things as knowable by us. Even though in the natural order of knowing God is the first known, for us his sensible effects are first known. So nothing prevents that the effects of the highest good should fall to our consideration without our considering the First Good. Thus we will remove the First from the consideration of the mind, though it is wholly obvious to us that he exists, for it can be known from the common opinion of all, both the learned and unlearned, and even from the religions of barbarous peoples, that nothing would be if God did not exist.

When he says, *The First Good having been thus for a moment abstracted . . .*, he shows what follows for the goodness of things on this supposition; and he does two things: first, he states his intention; second, he proves something that it presupposes: *But if there were nothing else but good . . .*

He says first that, taking away the first good with our intellect, we hold that other things are good because from the goodness of the effects we come to knowledge of the First Good. Therefore, we shall consider how they could be good if they did not proceed from the First Good. This supposition being made, it seems that in them goodness would be one thing and their existence another. For if one and the same substance were taken to be good, white, heavy and round, it would follow that its substance was one thing, and roundness another, colour another, goodness another.

The goodness of a thing is its virtue, by which it produces good activity.

For virtue is what makes the one having it good and makes his work good, as is evident from the Philosopher in *Ethics* 2.6. That these things are other than the substance of the thing, he proves as follows. If each of the foregoing were the same as the substance of the thing, it would follow that all of them are the same as one another: that is, heaviness would be the same as colour, and as good, and as white, and as roundness, because whatever are the same as some third thing are the same as one another. But the nature of things does not allow all things to be the same. Therefore it remains that, the aforementioned supposition being made, it is one thing for a thing to be and another for it to be something, that is, good or white or whatever such thing it is called. Thus, the foregoing supposition being made, things would indeed be good, but their existence would not be good. Therefore, if in some way they were not from the First Good and yet were in themselves good, it would follow that their being such and their being good would not be the same but for them to be would be one thing and for them to be good another.

When he says, *But if they were nothing else but good . . .*, he proves what he has supposed, namely, that the foregoing supposition being made, for them to be good would be one thing and for them simply to be or to be in any other way would be different. Because, if there were nothing else about them save that they are good, and they were not heavy or coloured or distinct by some dimension of space, as all bodies are, but only this one quality of being good, they would no longer seem to be created things but would rather be the first principle of things himself. Consequently it would follow that we could not speak in the plural of all these things that seem to be the principle of things: but only in the singular could they be the first principle of things. It would be as if all good things were absolutely one, because only one thing and no other could be good in such a manner. But this is patently false. And it is also false that created things, setting aside the First Good, are nothing other than what it is to be good.

When he says, *But since they are not simple . . .*, he shows what should be thought of the goodness of things in truth, and he says that created things do not have utter simplicity such that there could be nothing in them except the essence of goodness, nor could they even be among the things that are unless God, who alone is what is, namely insofar as he is the essence of goodness, willed them to be. It follows that it is because the existence of things flows from the will of him who is essentially good that created things are said to be good. For the First Good, namely God, is good just insofar as he is because he is essentially goodness itself, but the secondary or created good is good because it flows from the First Good. That is why the existence itself of things is good and any created thing, insofar as it exists, is good. Thus created things are only good insofar as they exist because their existence derives from the highest good.

Therefore his solution comes to this: the existence of the First Good is good according to its proper notion, because the nature and essence of the First Good is nothing other than goodness. The existence of the secondary good is indeed good, though not according to the proper notion of its essence – its essence is not goodness itself, but humanity or something else like it – but its existence is good because of its relation to the First Good, which is its cause, to which it is compared as to its first principle and ultimate end. It is in this way that something is called healthy because it is ordered to the end of health, as something is called medical with reference to the effective principle of the art of medicine.

According to what has been set down, it should be noticed that there is a twofold goodness in created goods. One, insofar as they are called good by relation to the First Good, and on this basis their existence and whatever is in them from the First Good, is good. But there is another goodness in them taken absolutely, insofar as each is said to be good because it is perfect in existence and activity. This perfection does not belong to created goods according to their essential existence, but because of something superadded, which is called their virtue, as was said above. According to this, to exist itself is good, but the First Good has every manner of perfection in his existence, and therefore his existence is as such and absolutely good.

5

Thereby the problem is solved. For though things be good through the fact that they exist, they are not like the First Good, since their existence is not in every way good. Things can only exist insofar as their existence derives from the First Existence, that is, Good. For them to exist is good but not in the manner of that from which they derive. He is in every way good insofar as he exists, and is nothing other than goodness. The secondary good, if it did not derive from him, might be good but not insofar as it exists. It might perhaps participate in the good, but if its existence did not derive from the Good, it could not be good.

Therefore, the First Good having been abstracted from them by the mind and thought, although they might be good, would not be good in virtue of their own existence. Since they could only actually exist insofar as that which is truly good produces them, their existence is good, but it is not like the substantial good from which they derive. And unless they derive from it, although they might be good, they could not be good insofar as they exist because they would be apart from Good and not derived from the Good which is the First Good in whom existence itself and goodness itself and good existence itself are one.

But isn't it also the case that white things are white because they flow from God's will that they be white? Not at all. To be is one thing and to be white another, not least because he who made them is good indeed, but certainly not white. It is in accordance with the will of the Good that they should be good through the fact that they exist, but it is not in accordance with the will of one who is not white that a thing have a property thanks to which it should be white insofar as it exists: they do not derive from the will of one who is white. And so they are white simply because one who is not white willed them to be white and they are good insofar as they exist because one who is good willed them to be.

Does it follow that all things are just because one who is just willed them to be? Not so, for good refers to essence, justice to action. In him to be and to act are the same and to be and to be just are one, but in us to exist and to act differ: we are not simple beings. For us, goodness is not the same thing as justice, but being is the same for us all. We are all good, but we are not all just.

Finally, good is something general, to be just is something special, but things can be in the same genus and in different species. That is why some are just, some are not, but everything is good.　　　　　Boethius, *On the Hebdomads*

After he has established the truth about the foregoing question, here he solves an objection with the upshot that created goods are goods insofar as they are similar to the first good. He does two things: first, he solves the objection; second, he summarizes what has been said: *Therefore, if the First Good having been abstracted . . .*

First he says that from the foregoing it is obvious that the question has been answered. Things are not similar to the First Good in this that they are good in that which they are, since the existence of created things is not absolutely good, in the way they have it, but only according to a relation to the First Good. But since the existence of created things can only be derived from the First Good, it is for that reason that their existence is good. But it is not similar to the goodness of the First Good, because he is absolutely good in the way in which he is, since in him there is nothing other than the essence of goodness. This is so because in him there is no perfection by way of addition, but in his simple existence he has every form of perfection, as has been said. But perhaps the created good too can be considered good in itself, even if the impossible supposition be made that it does not proceed from the First Good, that is, but by a goodness which belongs to it absolutely. But it would not be good in that which it is, since then it would be good by participation in the superadded good. But its very existence would not be good unless it is derived from the good, by relation to which the existence of creatures is good.

When he says, *Therefore the First Good having been abstracted . . .*, he gathers together what has been said, observing that if the First Good is removed by the mind from things, all other things, if they be given, would not be good nor could they be good from the fact that they exist. But since they can only actually be insofar as they are produced by the First Good, who is truly good, their existence is at once good. However, existence flowing from the first good is not like the first insofar as he is substantially good, and they, though they are good, would not be good insofar as they exist if they had not flowed from it, since the First Good is his own existence and his existence is his substance, and good itself, because he is the essence of goodness, and his existence is good because for him to be and what is do not differ.

When he says, *But isn't it the case that white things . . .*, he raises two objections against what has been said, the second of which begins at, *Does it follow that all things . . .*

He raises this first objection: It has been said that all things are good insofar as they exist because they proceeded from the will of the First Good that they be good. But would not all white things, insofar as they exist, be white because they proceeded from the will of God that they be white? He replies that this is scarcely relevant because in white things to be simply, which belongs to them because of their essential principles, is one thing and that thanks to which they are white is another. The reason for this difference between white and good is that God who created good things and white things is good but he is not white.

Therefore, that they be good followed on the will of the First Good, insofar as he willed them to be good and good insofar as they are because produced by the good; the existence of created things has the note of the good from the fact that it is from the good, as has been said, but this property does not follow on the will of God that what is created, insofar as it exists, be white, the reason being that they do not flow from the will of white, as goods flow from the will of the good. We cannot say that their existence is white insofar as they are from the first white. Therefore, it is manifest that because God, who is not white, willed that some things be white, it can only be said of them that they are white, though not insofar as they exist. Because God who is good willed all things to be good, they are good insofar as they are, because their existence has the note of the good on account of this, that it is from the Good.

When he says, *Does it follow that all things are just . . .*, he raises a second objection. Someone might say all things are good because he who is good willed them to be good, but by the same reason they ought to be just, because he who is just willed them to be. He replies that this does not follow for two reasons. First, because good signifies a certain nature or essence. For it has been said that God is the very essence of goodness, and everything according to the perfection of its proper nature is called good. But one is called just with reference to an act, as with every other virtue. But in God to be and to act are the same; hence in him to be good and to be just are the same. But in us to be and to act are not the same since we fall off from the simplicity of God, so that to be good and to be just are not the same, whereas existence belongs to us all insofar as we are. Therefore goodness too belongs to us all. But the act which is characterized by justice does not belong to all, nor in those who have it is it the same as their existence. It follows that not everything is just insofar as it exists.

He gives another argument. For the good is something general, and justice is a certain species of it, as are the other virtues. But in God is found every notion of goodness, and therefore he is not only good but just. But not all species of goodness are found in all, but different kinds in different kinds. So it is not necessary that the species which is justice should derive to all beings though goodness is. Hence some beings are just while others have another species of goodness, yet all are good insofar as they are derived from the First Good.

This completes our exposition of this book. Blessed be God for ever. Amen.

8. *The Meanings of Truth.* Disputed Question on Truth, *1* (1256–9)

Of the three great tasks of the master of theology – legere, disputare, praedicare (to lecture, to dispute and to preach) – perhaps the most distinctive of the medieval university was the disputation. There were two kinds of question that formed the basis of these public events: the quodlibetal question – literally, 'what-you-will' – in which the master did not set the scene as to what would be discussed. Here ingenuity and self-assertion, and the other vices of the intellectual, soon made themselves known, and triumph rather than truth was sometimes the goal. In less than a century, the quodlibetal questions came to involve only graduate students, as we might say, and the masters stayed away. The disputed question was a meatier occasion. The master posted a thesis he intended to defend and on the appointed day the whole university – or at least the relevant faculty – gathered, ready to test the mettle of the master. A first go at responding to difficulties posed to the thesis was the task of the assistant – this was part of his apprenticeship – but the magisterial response came, appropriately, from the master. He was obliged, within a set period of time after the public event, to present to the university stationer his final shaping of the question in written form so that others could obtain copies.

Although the written product is far from being a transcript of the public disputation, its literary form bears the impress of its origin. A question, a proposed answer and then difficulties to that answer. The master must not only respond to those objections but develop arguments on behalf of his own position. This was the genre Thomas adapted to his Summa theologiae. *The so-called* Disputed Question on Truth *of Thomas that has come down to us is a collection of some twenty-nine such disputations. What they certainly have in common is the time and place of their production: Paris, during the three years of Thomas's first stint as a regent master, 1256–9. It is possible to see clusters and groupings among them, but each one stands by itself. What follows is the first and titular disputation of the collection.*

QUESTION ONE: ON TRUTH

The question comprises six articles: (1) what is truth? (2) whether truth is found chiefly in intellect or in things; (3) whether truth is in the intellect only when it composes or divides; (4) whether there is only one truth whereby all things are true; (5) whether there is any truth apart from the first truth which is eternal; (6) whether created truth is immutable.

Article 1: What is truth?

It seems that the true is in every way the same as being.

1. Augustine in *Soliloquies* says that 'the true is that which is'. But that which is, is nothing else but being. Therefore 'true' signifies in every way the same thing as 'being'.

2. It has been said that they are the same according to supposits, but differ in notion [*ratio*]. In retort, the notion of anything is what is signified by its definition; but that which Augustine assigns as the definition of the true, having rejected other definitions, is that which is. Therefore since that which is fits both the true and being, it seems that they are the same in notion.

3. Moreover, things which differ in notion are such that one of them can be understood without the other; that is why Boethius, *On the Hebdomads*, says that God can be understood to be if the mind separates from him for the nonce his goodness. Being, however, can in no way be understood if true be separated from it because by the true is understood that which is. Therefore the true and being do not differ in notion.

4. Moreover, if the true is not the same as being it must be a disposition of it; but this it cannot be, for it is not a disposition that completely destroys, as if it followed that 'It is true, therefore it is not being,' as it does follow that 'He is a dead man, therefore he is not a man.' Similarly, it is not a diminishing disposition, otherwise it would not follow that 'It is true, therefore it is,' any more than it follows that 'He has white teeth therefore he is white.' Similarly it is not a contracting or specifying disposition because then it would not be converted with being. Therefore the true and being are in every way the same.

5. Moreover, things which have the same disposition are the same; but there is the same disposition for true and being; therefore they are the same. For it is said in *Metaphysics* 2.1 [993b30] that 'As each thing is in

respect of being, so is it in respect of truth.' Therefore true and being are in every way the same.

6. Moreover, whatever are not the same must differ in some way; but the true and being in no way differ, because they do not differ in essence since every being is true through its essence, nor do they differ by any other differences because then they would have to belong to a common genus. Therefore they are in every way the same.

7. Again, if they are not in every way the same, true must add something to being; but it doesn't since it is found in even more things than being is. This is evident from *Metaphysics* 4.16 [1011b25] where the Philosopher says that we define the true thus: 'to say of what is that it is or of what is not that it is not.' Thus true includes being and non-being. Therefore the true does not add anything to being and appears to be in every way the same as being.

ON THE CONTRARY:

[1] 'The useless repetition of the same thing is frivolous'; accordingly, if the true were the same as being, it would be frivolous to speak of true being, and it isn't. Therefore they are not the same.

[2] Again, being and good convert; but true does not convert with good, for something is true that is not good, such as that someone fornicates; therefore, since true and good do not convert, they are not the same.

[3] Moreover, according to Boethius in *On the Hebdomads,* 'to be and that which is are diverse' in every creature; but the true signifies the being [*esse*] of the thing, therefore in created things to be true is different from what is [*quod est*]. But that which is is the same as being; therefore the true is different from being in creatures.

[4] Moreover, things related as prior and posterior must be diverse; but true and being are so related because as is said in the *Book of Causes,* 'The first of created things is being [*esse*],' and the commentator on that same work says that all other things signify some form of coming to being and thus are posterior to being; therefore true and being are diverse.

[5] Moreover, things said commonly of cause and effect are in the cause more than in the effect and *a fortiori* more in God than in creatures. But these four things, being, one, true and good are appropriated to God: being pertains to essence, one to the person of the Father, true to the person of the Son and good to the person of the Holy Spirit. But the divine persons are distinguished not only in notion but really, hence they

are not predicated of one another. *A fortiori* then these four ought to be more than notionally different in creatures.

RESPONSE:
It should be said that just as in demonstrable matters a reduction must be made to principles the intellect knows *per se*, so too in investigating what anything is, otherwise there would be an infinite regress and all science and knowledge of things would perish. That which the intellect first conceives as most known and in which all other concepts are resolved is being, as Avicenna says at the beginning of his *Metaphysics*. Hence all other conceptions of the intellect are formed by adding to being. But nothing can be added to being as if it were extraneous to it in the way that difference is added to a genus or accident to subject, because every nature is essentially being, and thus the Philosopher proves in *Metaphysics* 3.8 [998b22] that being cannot be a genus. But things are said to add to being insofar as they express a mode of being that the term being does not express, and this happens in two ways. In one way such that what is expressed is a special mode of being, for there are different grades of being insofar as different modes of being are grasped. The different genera of being are based on these modes. Substance does not add some difference to being which would designate some nature superadded to being; rather a certain special mode of being is expressed by the term substance, namely, *per se* being, and so it is with the other genera.

In another way, such that what is expressed is a general mode following on every being, mode can be taken in two ways: first, insofar as it follows on any being as such, second, insofar as it follows on one being in its relation to another. The first mode is subdivided into two, because it expresses something of being either affirmatively or negatively. But the only thing that can be absolutely affirmed of every being is its essence according to which it is said to be. That, according to Avicenna at the beginning of his *Metaphysics*, is the meaning of the term *thing* which differs from being insofar as the term being is taken from the act of existing [*essendi*] whereas the term *thing* expresses the quiddity or essence of the being. The negation that is absolutely consequent on every being is indivision, and this the term *one* expresses: one is nothing other than undivided being.

If however the mode of being is taken in the second sense, namely, insofar as one thing is ordered to another, this can be understood in two ways. First, according to the division of one thing from another; and the term 'something' [*aliquid*] expresses this, for something means, as it were, 'another what' [aliud quid]; hence just as a being is called one insofar as it is undivided in itself so it is called something insofar as it is divided from others. Second, according to one being's harmony together with another, and this can only be if there is something whose nature it is to be in harmony with every being – and that is the soul, which 'in a certain way is all things', as is said in On the Soul 3. In soul there is the appetitive power and the cognitive power: the harmony of being with appetite is expressed by the term 'good', which is why at the beginning of the Ethics it is said that 'the good is that which all seek'. The term 'true' expresses the harmony of being with intellect.

All knowledge is perfected by the assimilation of the knower to the thing known, such that assimilation is said to be the cause of knowledge, as sight insofar as it is disposed by the species of colour knows colour. For the first comparison of being to intellect is insofar as being is in accord with intellect, which accord is called the adequation of intellect and being, and in this the perfect notion of the true consists. What the true adds to being, accordingly, is the conformity or adequation of thing and intellect, on which conformity, as has been said, knowledge of the thing follows. Thus, a thing's being is presupposed by the notion of truth but knowledge is a certain effect of truth. On this basis, truth or true can be defined in three ways.

In one way according to that which precedes the notion of truth and is that in which the true is grounded; thus Augustine defines it in Soliloquies, 'The true is that which is,' and Avicenna in his Metaphysics, 'The truth of any thing is a property of its existence which is established in it,' and some define it thus, 'The true is the indivision of existence and what is.'

In another way truth is defined according to that in which the notion of true is formally perfected, and thus Isaac says, 'Truth is the adequation of thing and intellect,' and Anselm in On Truth writes, 'Truth is rectitude perceptible to mind alone' – by this rectitude is meant a certain adequation – and the Philosopher says in Metaphysics 4.16 [1011b25] that we define the true as 'to say that what is is and that what is not is not.'

In a third way truth is defined according to an effect consequent on it, as Hilary says: 'The true is declarative and manifestive'; and Augustine writes in On True Religion: 'Truth is that whereby what a thing is is shown'; and in the same book: 'Truth is that according to which we judge of interior things.'

*

Ad 1. It should be said that Augustine defines truth insofar as it has a foundation in reality and not insofar as the notion of true is completed in the adequation of thing and intellect. Or it could be said that when the true is defined as that which is, the word 'is' is not taken to signify the act of existing but is a sign of the composing intellect, that is, it signifies the affirmation of a proposition. Thus to say that the true is that which is is understood as saying of something that it is. Then the definition of Augustine comes to the same thing as that of the Philosopher cited above.

Ad 2. The solution of this is evident from the foregoing.

Ad 3. It should be said that for something to be understood without another can be taken in two ways. In one way, when something is understood without something else, and thus things which differ in notion [ratione] are such that one can be understood without the other. That something is understood without another can be understood in a second way as understanding that the other does not exist, and in this way being cannot be understood without the true, because being cannot be understood without being in accord with or adequate to intellect. It is not necessary, however, that whoever understands the notion of being understands the notion of true, any more than it is necessary that whoever understands being understands the agent intellect, although without agent intellect nothing can be understood.

Ad 4. It should be said that the true is a disposition of being, not as adding some nature or as expressing some special mode of being, but something that is found generally in every being yet is not expressed by the term being. Hence it need not be a destroying or diminishing or partially contracting disposition.

Ad 5. It should be said that disposition is not taken there as it is in the genus of quality, but insofar as it implies a certain order. For since things that cause other things to exist are beings in a higher sense, and that which is the cause of truth is maximally true, the Philosopher concludes that a thing's rank in being is the same as its rank in truth, such that where we find the highest being there we also find the true in the highest sense. This is not so because being and true are the same in notion, but because something has being to that degree that it is fashioned to be adequate to intellect, and thus the notion of true follows the notion of being.

Ad 6. It should be said that true and being differ in notion because there is something in the notion of true that is not in the notion of being, not because something is in the notion of being that is not in the notion of true. Hence they do not differ by essence nor are they distinguished from one another by opposed differences.

Ad 7. It should be said that the true is not in more than being; for being in a certain sense is said of non-being insofar as non-being is grasped by the intellect, hence in *Metaphysics* 4.1 [1003b5] the Philosopher says that negation and the privation of being are called being in one sense of the term, and Avicenna too at the beginning of his *Metaphysics* says that an enunciation can only be formulated of being because that of which a proposition is formulated must be apprehended by intellect. From which it is clear that whatever is true is in some way being.

Ad [1]. To the first contrary argument that was advanced it should be said that it is not frivolous to say, 'true being', because something is expressed by the term true that is not expressed by the term being, but not because they really differ.

Ad [2]. It should be said that although for this man to fornicate is evil, anything insofar as it has being is fashioned to be conformed to intellect and the notion of true follows on that. Thus it is evident that the true neither exceeds nor is exceeded by being.

Ad [3]. It should be replied that when it is said that 'to be and what is are diverse', the act of existing is distinguished from that to which the act belongs; the term being is taken from the act of existing, not from that to which the act belongs, and therefore the argument does not follow.

Ad [4]. It should be said that the true is posterior to being insofar as the notion of the true differs from the notion of being in the way stated above.

Ad [5]. It should be said that that argument is deficient in three things: first, because although the divine persons are distinguished really, what is appropriated to the persons does not differ really but only in notion; second, because although the persons are really distinguished from one another, they are not really distinguished from the essence, hence neither is true, which is appropriated to the person of the Son, really different from being, which is taken from the essence; third, because although being, one, true and good are more unified in God rather than in created things, none the less it does not follow from the fact that they are distinguished in God that they should also be distinguished really in created things. This happens when things which given their notions are not one in reality, such as wisdom and power, although they are really one in God, are really distinct in creatures. But being, one, true and good, given their notions, are such that they are one thing, hence wherever they are found, they are really one, although there is a more perfect unified thing when they are united in God than when they are united in creatures.

Article 2: Is truth primarily in intellect rather than in things?

It seems not.

1. For the true, as has been said, is converted with being; but being is chiefly found in things rather than in the soul; and so it must be with the true.

2. Moreover, the thing is in the soul not through its essence but through its likeness [species], as the Philosopher says in On the Soul 3.13. Therefore if truth were found chiefly in the soul, it would not be the essence of the thing but its likeness or species, and the true would be a likeness of being existing outside the mind. But the species of the thing existing in the soul is not predicated of the thing which is outside the soul, nor is it convertible with it, for to be converted is to be predicated of one another; thus the true would not convert with being, which is false.

3. Moreover, whatever is in something is appropriate to that in which it is; therefore if truth were principally in the soul, the judgement of truth would be according to the appraisal of the soul, and we would be back in the error of the ancient philosophers who said that whatever one thought in his mind is true, so two contradictories are true simultaneously, which is absurd.

4. Moreover, if truth is chiefly in intellect, something pertaining to intellect would have to be put into the definition of truth. But in the Soliloquies, Augustine rejects such a definition as, 'The true is that which is as it seems,' because then what is not seen would not be true, which is clearly false of stones hidden in the bowels of the earth. Similarly he reproves and rejects this suggestion, 'The true is whatever is as it appears to a knower, if he can and wishes to know it,' because then there would only be truth when a knower could and wished to know it. Other definitions in which something of intellect is put are open to the same criticism. Therefore truth is not chiefly in intellect.

ON THE CONTRARY:

[1] The Philosopher in Metaphysics 4.4: says 'The true and the false are not in things but in the mind.'

[2] Moreover, 'truth is the adequation of thing and intellect,' but this

adequation can only be in the intellect; therefore, truth too is only in the intellect.

SOLUTION:
It should be said that in things which are said of many according to prior and posterior, it is not necessary that what is first called by the common name be the cause of the others; rather it is that in which the notion of the common predicate is found complete. For example, healthy is first predicated of the animal in which the perfect notion of health is first found, even though medicine is called healthy insofar as it is a cause of health. Therefore, since the true is said of many according to prior and posterior, it must be said first of that in which the complete notion of truth is first found. The complement of any motion or operation is in its term. But the movement of the cognitive power is terminated in the soul – for the known is in the knower in the mode of the knower – whereas appetitive movement terminates in things. Hence it is that the Philosopher in *On the Soul* 3.15 [433a14] speaks of a kind of circle in the acts of the soul, insofar as the thing which is outside the soul moves the intellect and the thing understood moves appetite which aims to reach the thing from which the motion began. Because good, as was said, indicates the order of being to appetite, the true indicates its order to intellect. Hence the Philosopher says in *Metaphysics* 6.4 [1027b26] that good and evil are in things, but the true and false are in the mind. The thing is called true only insofar as it is adequated to intellect. So the true is primarily in intellect and secondarily in things.

It should be noted that things relate to practical intellect differently than they do to the speculative, for the practical intellect causes things, and thus is the measure of the things that come about because of it, but speculative intellect, because it receives from things, is in some way moved by those things, and thus they measure it. From this it is clear that natural things, from which our intellect derives knowledge, measure our intellect, as is said in *Metaphysics* 10.2 [1053a31], but they are measured by the divine intellect in which all things exist, just as all artifacts are in the intellect of the artist. Thus, the divine intellect measures but is not measured, the natural thing is measured and measures, but our intellect is measured by and does not measure natural things, but only artificial things. The natural thing, placed between two intellects, is called true because of adequation to both. It is called true according to its adequation to the divine intellect insofar as it fulfils that to which it is ordered by the divine intellect, as is clear from Anselm in *On Truth* and from

Augustine in *On True Religion* and from Avicenna in the definition mentioned, namely: 'The truth of anything is the property of its existence which is established in it.' The thing is called true according to its adequation to human intellect insofar as it is fashioned to give a true account of itself, just as, as on the other hand, those things are called false which 'are so made as to seem what they are not or as they are not', as is said in *Metaphysics* 5.29 [1029b21]. The truth is in things in the first sense before the second, because its comparison to the divine intellect is prior to its comparison to the human intellect. Hence, even if the human intellect did not exist, things could still be called true in relation to the divine intellect. But if both intellects were absent and, impossible hypothesis, the things remained, no notion of truth would remain.

Ad 1. The response to the first, then, is that, as is clear from what has been explained, the true is said first of the true intellect and secondarily of the thing adequated to it, and in both senses it is converted with being, but diversely, because insofar as it is said of things it converts with being through predication – for every being is adequated to the divine intellect and can adequate itself to the human intellect, and conversely. If, however, it is understood as it is said of intellect, then it converts with the being outside the mind, not through predication but by way of consequence, because some being must answer to every true understanding, and conversely.

Ad 2. The solution of the second is clear from this.

Ad 3. It should be said that that which is in something follows on it only when it is caused by its principles. Hence light, which is caused in air by something extrinsic, namely the sun, follows the motion of the sun rather than air. Similarly truth, which is caused in the mind by things, does not follow the appraisal of the soul but the existence of things, 'since insofar as the thing is or is not, speech is true or false', and similarly in intellect.

Ad 4. It should be said that Augustine is speaking of the vision of the human intellect, on which the truth of the thing does not depend: there are many things which our intellect does not know. But there is nothing that the divine intellect does not actually know and that the human intellect does not know potentially, since the agent intellect is called 'that whose role is to make everything', and the possible intellect 'that in which all things come to be'. Hence it being actually seen by the divine intellect can be placed in the definition of the true thing, but not by human intellect, save in potency, as is clear from the foregoing.

Article 3: Is truth only in the intellect composing and dividing?

It seems not.

1. For the true is signified according to some comparison of being and intellect, but the first comparison of intellect to things is insofar as it forms the quiddities of things in conceiving their definitions; therefore it is in this operation of intellect that the true is first and chiefly found.

2. Moreover, 'the true is the adequation of things and intellect'; but just as the intellect composing and dividing can be adequate to things, so too the intellect understanding the quiddities of things; therefore truth is not only in the intellect composing and dividing.

ON THE CONTRARY:

[1] There is what is said in *Metaphysics* 6.4 [1027b23]: 'The true and false are not in things but in the mind; while with regard to simple things and essences falsity and truth do not exist even in thought.'

[2] Moreover, in *On the Soul* 3.6 [430a26]: 'The thinking of indivisibles is found in those cases where falsehood is impossible.'

RESPONSE:

It should be said that just as the true is first in intellect and secondarily in things, so too it is first found in the act of intellect composing and dividing rather than in the act of intellect forming the quiddities of things.

The notion of the true consists in the adequation of thing and intellect. A thing is not adequated with itself – it is distinct things that are equal: hence the notion of truth is first found in intellect when it first begins to have something proper to itself that the thing outside the soul does not have, yet something corresponding to it between which an adequation can be expected.

The intellect forming the quiddity of things has only the likeness of the thing existing outside the soul, as sense does when it receives the sensible species. But when it begins to judge the thing apprehended, then that judgement of intellect is something proper to it not found outside in things, and when it is adequated to that which is outside in the thing, it is called a true judgement.

The intellect judges the thing apprehended when it says that it is or is not, which is the intellect composing and dividing. Hence the Philosopher also says in *Metaphysics* 6.4 [1024b17] that 'composition and division are in the intellect and not in things'. And thence it is that truth is first found in composition and division of intellect. Secondarily, however, and later the true is said to be in the intellect forming definitions; thus a definition is called true or false, by reason of a true or false composition, as when the definition is wrongly attributed to something; for example if the definition of circle were attributed to triangle, or even when the parts of a definition form an oxymoron and cannot possibly fit together, for example if something were called insensible animal. The implied composition, that something could be an animal and lack senses, is false. The definition is only called true or false with reference to composition, much as a thing is called true with reference to the intellect.

From what has been said it is evident that 'true' is first said of the composition and division of the intellect; second, of the definitions of things, insofar as some composition is implied by them; third, of things insofar as they are adequated to the divine intellect, or such that they can be adequated to the human intellect; fourth, of man insofar as he can choose what he says, the true or the false, or who creates a true or false impression of himself or of others by what he says or does.

The spoken is said to be true in the same way as the thoughts that it expresses.

Ad 1. It should be said that, although the formation of the quiddity is the first operation of the intellect, the intellect does not have anything of its own that it might adequate to the thing because of it; so there is not truth there in the proper sense.

The response to the rest is clear.

Article 4: Is there a single truth whereby all things are true?

It seems not.

1. For Anselm says in *On Truth* that just as time is to temporal things so is truth to true things; but there is a single time for all temporal things; therefore truth must be so related to true things that there is only one truth.

2. But it will be said that truth is said in two ways: first, such that it is the same as the entity of the thing, as Augustine defines it in *Soliloquies*, 'The true is that which is,' and on this basis there must be as many truths as there are essences of things; second, insofar as it expresses itself in intellect, as Hilary defines it, 'The true is declarative of being,' and in this sense, since something can be manifested to intellect only through the

power of the first divine truth, all truths are in a certain way one insofar as they activate the intellect, just as all colours are one in the way in which they activate sight, namely by reason of one light. However, time is numerically one for all temporal things; if then truth is to true things as time is to temporal things, it would be necessary for there to be numerically one truth for all true things, and it would not suffice that all truths are alike in the way they move us or with respect to one exemplar.

3. Moreover, Anselm in *On Truth* argues in this way: if there are several truths for several true things, truths would have to vary according to the varieties of true things; but truths do not vary according to the variations of true things, because, if true or correct things were destroyed, the truth and rectitude according to which they are true or correct would remain; therefore there is only one truth. He proves the minor by this that, when the sign is destroyed, the correctness of signification still would remain, because it is correct when it signifies that which the sign signifies; for the same reason, if any true or right thing were destroyed, its correctness or truth would remain.

4. Moreover, in created things there is nothing which is its truth, as the truth of man is not man nor the truth of flesh flesh; but every created thing is true and since no created thing is truth, therefore any truth is uncreated and thus there is only one truth.

5. Moreover, the only thing greater than the human mind is God, according to Augustine; but truth, as Augustine proves in *Soliloquies*, is greater than the human mind. It could not be said to be less, for then it would be for the human mind to decide concerning truth, which is false – it does not judge it but according to it, as a judge does not judge the law but in accordance with it, as is said in *On True Religion*. Similarly, the human mind cannot be said to be equal to it, because the soul judges all things in accordance with truth; it does not judge all things in accordance with itself. Therefore, only God is truth and there is only one truth.

6. Moreover, Augustine proves in the *Eighty-three Questions* that truth is not perceived by bodily sense in this way: only the mutable is perceived by the senses; but truth is immutable; therefore it is not perceived by the senses. It could similarly be argued that every created thing is mutable, but truth is not mutable, therefore it is not a creature. So it is something uncreated and there is only one truth.

7. Moreover, in the same place Augustine argues for the same conclusion in this way: 'Everything sensible has something similar to the false that cannot be distinguished from it, for, to make a long story short, everything

we perceive with the body, even when it is not present to the senses, is perceived by us through images as if still present, as in dreams or anger.' But truth does not have something similar to the false; therefore truth is not perceived by the senses. Similarly, it could be argued, every created thing has something similar to the false insofar as it has some defect; therefore no created thing is truth, and thus there is only one truth.

ON THE CONTRARY:

[1] Augustine in *On True Religion* says, 'As similarity is the form of similar things, so truth is the form of true things'; but of many similar things there are many likenesses; therefore, there are many truths of the many true things.

[2] Moreover, just as every created truth derives from uncreated truth as from its exemplar and has its truth from it, so every intelligible light derives from the first uncreated light as from its exemplar and takes its power of manifesting from it; we say, however, that there are many intelligible lights, as is clear in Dionysius; therefore it seems that in a similar way it must be conceded that there are simply many truths.

[3] Moreover, although colours have the ability to activate sight from the power of light, it is none the less said without qualification that there are many different colours, nor can they be said to be one save in a manner of speaking; therefore, although all created truths express themselves to the intellect by the power of the first truth, it does not follow from this that there is but one truth – save in a manner of speaking.

[4] Moreover, just as created truth can only manifest itself to intellect by the power of uncreated truth, so no power of the creature can do anything except in virtue of uncreated power; but we would in no way say that there is only one power of all the things having power. Neither should we say, therefore, that in some way there is one truth of all true things.

[5] Moreover, God relates to things as a threefold cause – namely efficient, exemplar and final – such that by appropriation the entity of things is referred to God as efficient cause, their truth to God as exemplar cause, their goodness to God as final cause, although each of these can be properly effects of any mode of causality. But we do not thereby say that there is one goodness for all good things or one entity for all beings; therefore neither should we say that there is one truth for all true things.

[6] Moreover, although there is one uncreated truth in which all created truths are exemplified, they are not exemplified in the same way. Although it relates to all in the same way, all do not relate to it in the same way,

as is said in the *Book of Causes*. Necessary and contingent things differently exemplify in truth itself. But a different way of imitating the divine exemplar brings about a diversity in created things. Therefore absolutely speaking there are many created truths.

[7] Moreover, 'Truth is the adequation of thing and intellect.' But there cannot be the same adequation in specifically different things; therefore, since true things are specifically different, there cannot be one truth of all true things.

[8] Moreover, Augustine, in *On the Trinity* 12.15, says, 'It must be believed that the nature of the human mind is so connected to intelligible things that it is in a light of the same kind as itself that it knows whatever it knows.' But the light in which the soul knows all things is truth; therefore truth is of the same kind as the soul itself, so the truth must be a created thing: hence in diverse creatures there are diverse truths.

RESPONSE:

It should be said, and it is evident from what has been explained, that truth is found properly in the human and divine intellects, as health is found in the animal; but truth is found in other things in relation to intellect, as health is said of other things insofar as they are causative or conservative of the health of the animal. Truth is found first and properly in the divine intellect, secondarily and properly in the human intellect, secondarily and improperly in things, because only in relation to one of the other two truths. The truth of the divine intellect is only one, from which many truths are derived by the human intellect, 'as from a man's face there are many likenesses in a mirror', as the Gloss says on Psalm 11.2. 'Truths are diminished by the sons of men.' The truths which are in things are as many as the entities of things.

The truth said of things in comparison to the human intellect is in a certain way accidental to them because, on the supposition that the human intellect never was or ever could be, things in their essences would still remain. Truth said of things in relation to the divine intellect is inseparable from them since they can subsist only when the divine intellect produces them in existence. In things, therefore, truth said in relation to divine intellect is prior to that said in relation to the human intellect, since things relate to the divine intellect as to a cause, but to the human intellect as to an effect insofar as the intellect takes knowledge from things. Therefore a thing is said to be true chiefly with reference to the truth of the divine intellect rather than to the truth of the human intellect. So if truth is taken properly as that by which all things are principally said to be true, then all things are true by one truth, namely, the truth of the divine intellect, as Anselm says of truth in *On Truth*. If, however, truth is taken properly as that by which things are secondarily said to be true, then there are many truths in many true things, and there are even many truths of one true thing existing in several minds. However, if truth is taken improperly, as when all things are said to be true, then there are as many truths as there are true things, but there is only one truth of each true thing. When they are called true either from the truth that is in the divine intellect or the truth in the human intellect, this is similar to the way in which food is named healthy from the health that is in the animal, not from an inherent form. But when the thing is called true from the truth that is in it, which is nothing other than entity as adequate to intellect or as adequating intellect, then it is denominated from an inherent form, as food is called healthy from its own quality.

Ad 1. It should be said that time is to temporal things as a measure to the measured; hence it is clear that Anselm speaks of that truth which is the measure of all true things, and this is only numerically one, as time is one, which is the conclusion of the second argument. However the truth which is in the human intellect or in things themselves is not compared to things as an extrinsic and common measure to the measured, but either as the measured to the measure, as it is of the truth of the human intellect, and thus it must vary according to the variety of things; or as an intrinsic measure, as it is of the truth which is in the things themselves, and these measures too ought to be multiplied according to the plurality of the measured, as there are diverse dimensions of diverse bodies.

Ad 2. We concede the second.

Ad 3. It should be said that the truth which remains when things are destroyed is the truth of the divine intellect, and this is absolutely one in number. The truth which is in things or in the soul, however, varies according to the variety of things.

Ad 4. It should be responded that when it is said that 'nothing is its own truth', things which have complete being in nature are understood, just as when it is said that 'nothing is its own existence'. Yet the existence of the thing is created, and in the same way the truth of the thing is something created.

Ad 5. It should be said that truth according to which the soul judges of all things is the first truth; for just as from the truth of the divine intellect innate species of things flow into the angelic intellect thanks to which it knows all things, so from the truth of the divine intellect as from an exemplar the truth of first principles by which we judge all things comes into our intellect. And since we cannot judge by it except insofar as it is a similitude of first truth, we are said to judge all things according to the first truth.

Ad 6. It should be said that that immutable truth is the first truth, and this is neither perceived by the senses nor something created.

Ad 7. It should be said that this created truth does not have anything like the false, although every creature has something similar to the false insofar as it is deficient; but the truth is not taken from that part of the created thing which is deficient, but it is insofar as it recedes from defect that it is conformed to first truth.

Ad [1] To the first of the arguments adduced to the contrary it should be said that similarity is properly found in both similar things; truth however, since it is a certain agreement of intellect and thing, is not properly found in both, but only in intellect. Hence, since there is one intellect, namely the divine, in conformity with which all things are and are said to be true, all true things must be true with reference to one truth, although in several like things there are diverse likenesses.

Ad [2] It should be said that although the intelligible light is exemplified by the divine light, light is said properly of created intelligible lights; truth, however, is not properly said of things modelled by the divine intellect and that is why we do not speak of one light as we speak of one truth.

Ad [3] The same should be said about colours, because they too are properly called visible, although they are only seen because of light.

Ad [4] and [5] The same response should be made to the fourth concerning power, and the fifth concerning entity.

Ad [6] It should be said that, although they are defective examples of divine truth, this does not prevent things from being true by one truth, not many, properly speaking, because that which is imperfectly received in modelled things is not properly called truth as is the truth of the exemplar.

Ad [7] It should be said that although things which are diverse in species are not adequate to the divine intellect by one adequation on the part of the things themselves, the divine intellect, to which all things are adequate, is one, and on its part there is one adequation with respect to all things, although all things are not adequate to it in the same way. Therefore, in the manner mentioned, there is one truth of all things.

Ad [8] It should be said that Augustine speaks of the truth which the divine mind models in our mind in the way in which a likeness of the face is caused in a mirror, and truths of this kind effected in our mind by the first truth are many, as has been said. Or it might be said that the first truth is in a way of the genus of mind, taking genus in a broad sense, insofar as all intelligible or incorporeal things are said to be of one kind, in the way employed by Acts 17.28: 'For we are also his offspring.'

Article 5: Is any truth other than first truth eternal?

It seems not.

1. For Anselm, speaking of the truth of statements in the *Monologion*, says 'Whether or not truth is thought to have a beginning or end, truth cannot be confined by any beginning or end'; but every truth is understood either to have a beginning or end or not to have a beginning or end; therefore no truth is confined by beginning or end, but this is to be eternal. Therefore, every truth is eternal.

2. Moreover, whatever continues in being when its being is destroyed is eternal, because whether it is held to be or not to be it follows that it is, and at any time it must be said of anything that it either is or is not. But on the destruction of truth the being of truth follows, for if truth does not exist it is not true that truth does not exist, and nothing can be true save by the truth. Therefore the truth is eternal.

3. Moreover, if the truth of statements is not eternal, a time must be assigned when it is not; but then this statement would be true, 'There is no truth of statements.' Therefore the truth of statements must be given, which is contrary to what is claimed. Therefore it cannot be claimed that the truth of statements is not eternal.

4. Moreover, the Philosopher proves that matter is eternal in *Physics* 1.15 – though this is false – because it remains after its corruption and is prior to its generation from the fact that if it corrupts it corrupts into something and if it is generated it is generated from something. But that from which something is generated and into which it corrupts is matter. Similarly, if truth could either corrupt or be generated, it would follow that it was prior to its generation and after its corruption, because if it is generated it is changed from not being to being and if it is corrupted it is changed from being to not being, but when it is not it is true that there is no truth, which of course cannot be if truth does not exist. Therefore truth is eternal.

5. Moreover, whatever cannot be thought not to be is eternal, because whatever can not be can be thought not to be. But even the truth of statements cannot be thought not to be, because the only way intellect can think anything is as true. Therefore the truth of statements is eternal.

6. Moreover, that which is to be always was future and that which is past will always be past. But this proposition about the future is true because something will be and the proposition about the past is true because something is past. Therefore, the truth of the proposition about the future always was and the truth of the proposition about the past will always be so. Therefore, not only the first truth is eternal, but many others as well.

7. Moreover, Augustine says in *On Free Will* that 'nothing is more eternal than the definition of circle or that two and three are five'; but the truth of these is created. Therefore, some truth other than the first truth is eternal.

8. Moreover, the truth of a statement does not require that someone actually utter it; it suffices that there be that about which a statement can be made; but before the word was there was something to speak of, even apart from God; therefore, before the world came to be there was the truth of statements. But what existed prior to the world is eternal; therefore the truth of statements is eternal. The middle is proved thus: the world was made from nothing, that is, after nothing; therefore before the world was its not being was; but a true statement is made not only of what is but also of what is not: just as the statement that something is is true, so is the statement that something is not, as is clear from *On Interpretation* 9. Therefore before the world was there was that about which a true statement could be made.

9. Moreover, whatever is known is true while it is known; but God knew all enunciable things from all eternity; therefore the truth of statements is from all eternity, and thus many truths are eternal.

10. But it will be objected that from this it does not follow that they are true in themselves but only in the divine mind. On the contrary, something is said to be true as it is known and all things are known by God from all eternity not only insofar as they are in his mind but also insofar as they are existing in their proper natures: Ecclesiasticus 23.29: 'For all things were known to the Lord God before they were created, so also after they were perfected he beholdeth all things.' And thus he does not know things differently after they have been made than as he knew them from all eternity. Therefore, from all eternity there were many truths, not only in the divine intellect, but in themselves.

11. Moreover, something is said to be absolutely insofar as it is complete; but the notion of truth is completed in intellect; if then from all eternity there were several true things in the divine intellect, it must be conceded absolutely that there are many eternal truths.

12. Moreover, Wisdom 1.15 says, 'For justice is perpetual and immortal.' But truth is a part of justice, as Cicero says in the *Rhetoric* 2.53; therefore it is perpetual and immortal.

13. Moreover, universals are perpetual and incorruptible; but the true especially is universal since it is convertible with being; therefore truth is perpetual and incorruptible.

14. But it will be said that it is not as such but only in a manner of speaking that the universal does not corrupt. On the contrary, something should be denominated from what belongs to it as such rather than from what is accidental to it; if then truth as such is perpetual and incorruptible it can only corrupt or be generated accidentally, and it must be conceded that truth speaking universally is eternal.

15. Moreover, God was prior to the world from all eternity; therefore the relation of priority was eternally in God; but if one of relatives is given, the other must also be; therefore the posteriority of the world to God is from all eternity. Therefore, from all eternity there was something other than God to which truth in some way pertains, and thus the same conclusion as before.

16. But it will be objected that the relation of priority and posteriority is not something in things but only in the mind. On the contrary, as Boethius says at the end of the *Consolation of Philosophy* [5. pr 6]. God is naturally prior to the world even if the world always were; therefore the relation of priority is a relation in things and not simply in the mind.

17. Moreover, the truth of signification is correctness of signification; but from all eternity it was correct that something is signified; therefore the truth of signification was from eternity.

18. Moreover, it was eternally true that the Father generated the Son and that the Holy Spirit proceeds from them both. But these are several truths; therefore there are several truths from all eternity.

19. But it will be objected that these are true because of one truth. So it does not follow that there are many truths from all eternity. On the contrary, for the Father to be is not the same thing as generating the Son, and for the Son to be is not the same thing as the breathing forth of the Holy Spirit; but from the fact that the Father is the Father, this is true, 'The Father generates the Son,' or 'The Father is the Father,' and from the fact that the Son is the Son it is true that 'The Son is generated by

the Father.' Therefore, propositions of this sort are not true by one truth.

20. Moreover, although man and capable of laughter are convertible, the truth of the following propositions is not the same: 'Man is man,' and 'Man is capable of laughter,' for the reason that it is not the same property that is predicated by the terms 'man' and 'capable of laughter'; similarly the name Father and the name Son do not signify the same property. Therefore there is not the same truth in the two propositions.

21. But it will be said that these propositions are not from all eternity. On the contrary, whenever there is an intellect that could enunciate an enunciation is possible; but from all eternity there was the divine intellect understanding the Father to be the Father and the Son to be the Son and therefore enunciating them, since according to Anselm, in the highest spirit to understand and to speak are the same; therefore the foregoing enunciations are from all eternity.

ON THE CONTRARY:

[1] Nothing created is eternal, but every truth other than the first is created. Therefore only the first truth is eternal.

[2] Moreover, being and true convert, but only one being is eternal. Therefore only one truth is eternal.

RESPONSE:

It should be said that as was replied earlier truth implies an adequation and commensuration, and thus something is called true as it is called commensurated. A body is measured both by an intrinsic measure, such as line, surface or depth, and an extrinsic measure, as the placed is measured by place and motion by time and cloth by the yard. So also something can be called true in two ways: in one way from inherent truth and in another way by extrinsic truth as all things are denominated true from the first truth. Because truth which is in the mind is measured by the things themselves, it follows that not only the truth of the thing but also the truth of intellect or statements which signify what is understood is denominated from the first truth. For this adequation or commensuration of intellect and thing it is not required that both of the terms be actual, for our intellect can now be adequate to things which will be but are not now, otherwise this would not be true, 'The Antichrist will be born.' Hence this is denominated true from the truth which is intellect alone, even when the thing itself is not. Similarly too the divine intellect can be adequate from eternity with things which were not from eternity but come to be in time, and thus it is that temporal things can be denominated true from eternal truth. If therefore we take the truth of created true things inherent in them, which we find both in things and in the created intellect, neither the truth of the things nor of statements is eternal, since the things themselves or the understandings whereby these truths inhere are not from eternity. If however we take the truth of created true things as they are all denominated true by the extrinsic measure which is the first truth, then the truth of them all, both of things and of statements and of understandings, is eternal. It is the eternity of truth of this kind that Augustine pursues in the *Soliloquies* and Anselm in the *Monologion*. And so in *On Truth*, Anselm says, 'You can understand how in my *Monologion* I proved the highest truth not to have a beginning or end through the truth of speech.'

The first truth which relates to all can only be one. For in our intellect truth is diversified only in two ways: first, because of the diversity of the things thought, about which intellect has diverse thoughts, on which follow diverse truths in the mind; second, from diverse ways of understanding: Socrates's running is one thing, but mind, which by combining or separating understands time as well, as is said in *On the Soul* 3.11, differently understands Socrates's running as present, past or future, and according to these forms diverse conceptions in which diverse truths are found. Neither of these modes of diversity can be found in divine knowledge: he does not have diverse thoughts of diverse things but knows them all in a single knowing, because he knows them all in one, namely, in his essence – 'not dispersing his thought in each', as Dionysius says in *On the Divine Names* 7. Similarly his knowledge does not involve any time, since it is measured by eternity which abstracts from all time while containing all time. It follows then that there are not many truths from all eternity.

Ad 1. It should be said that, as Anselm interprets himself in *On Truth*, the truth of enunciations is not enclosed by a beginning and end, 'not because speech was without a beginning, but because it could not be thought that speech might be and its truth be absent', and the statement in question was that whereby something about the future is truly signified. From which it is apparent that he did not wish to construe the inherent truth of the created thing or speech to be without beginning and end, but rather the first truth by which as an extrinsic measure the enunciation is called true.

Ad 2. It should be said that we find two things outside the mind, namely, the thing itself and the negations and privations of the thing, which do not relate to intellect in the same way. The thing itself because of the form it has from the divine intellect is adequate as artefact to art, and in virtue of this same form is fashioned to be adequate to our intellect insofar as it causes knowledge of itself by means of its similitude received in the soul. But the non-being considered outside the mind does not have something whereby it might be equated to the divine intellect or knowledge of it be caused in our intellect; insofar as it is equated to any intellect this is not due to non-being but to intellect itself which receives in itself the notion of non-being. The thing which is something positive outside the mind has in itself something whereby it can be called true, but non-being does not so that whatever truth is attributed to it is due to intellect. Therefore when it is said that 'it is true that truth is not', since the truth there signified is of non-being, it has being only in intellect; hence on the destruction of the truth which is in the thing there follows only the truth which is in intellect, and it is clear that one cannot conclude from this that the truth which is in intellect is eternal. It must indeed be in an eternal intellect, and this is the first truth; hence from the argument is shown that only the first truth is eternal.

Ad 3 and 4. This provides the solution to both the third and fourth objections.

Ad 5. It should be said that it cannot be thought that there is absolutely no truth, although it is thinkable that there is no created truth, just as it is thinkable that no creature exists: for the intellect can think of itself as not being and not understanding, though it never thinks without being or thinking. For it is not necessary that what intellect understands it understands itself to understand, because it does not always reflect upon itself. So it is not inappropriate if it thinks that the created truth without which it cannot think is not.

Ad 6. It should be said that the future as future does not exist, and similarly the past as such; hence it is the same with the truth of future and past as with the truth of non-being, from which only the eternity of the first truth can be concluded, as was said above.

Ad 7. It should be said that the saying of Augustine should be understood as meaning that those things are eternal insofar as they are in the divine mind, or eternal is to be taken as perpetual.

Ad 8. It should be said that although a true statement can be of either being or non-being, it is not the case that being and non-being relate to truth in the same way, as is evident from the foregoing, from which the solution to the objection is also clear.

Ad 9. It should be said that God knows many enunciables from all eternity but he knows them all in one knowing; hence from all eternity there is only the one truth through which divine knowledge of many things in future time was true.

Ad 10. It should be said, as is evident from the foregoing, that the intellect is not only adequate with those things which are actual but even with things that are not, especially the divine intellect for which nothing is past or future. Hence, although things were not from all eternity in their proper natures, the divine intellect was adequate to things future in time in their proper nature, and therefore it has true knowledge of things from all eternity even in their proper nature, although the truths of things were not from all eternity.

Ad 11. It should be said that, although the notion of truth is completed in intellect, the notion of the thing is not completed in intellect. Hence, although it is conceded absolutely that the truth of all things was from all eternity because they were in the divine intellect, it cannot be conceded simply that true things were from all eternity because they were in the divine intellect.

Ad 12. It should be said that that is understood of divine justice, or, if it is understood of human justice, then it is called perpetual in the way natural things are called perpetual, as we say that fire always moves upward because of the inclination of nature, unless it is impeded. And because virtue, as Cicero says, is 'a habit in the manner of nature and consonant with reason', insofar as from the nature of virtue there is an unfailing inclination to its act although it is sometimes impeded. Therefore, at the beginning of the Digest of Canon Law too, it is said that 'justice is the constant and perpetual will always to give each his due'. However, the truth of which we are speaking is not a part of justice, but the truth that is in those making judgement.

Ad 13. It should be said that the statement that the universal is perpetual and incorruptible is explained by Avicenna in two ways: in one way insofar as it is called perpetual and incorruptible by reason of particulars, which never begin or end according to those holding the eternity of the world – for according to philosophers the purpose of generation is to achieve perpetuity in the species which cannot be achieved in the individual. In another way insofar as perpetual means what is not corrupted as such but only incidentally because of the corruption of the individual.

Ad 14. It should be said that something is attributed to a subject in two ways: in one way positively, as being borne upward is attributed to fire, and a thing is denominated *per se* from such a thing rather than from some accident: for we say that it belongs to fire to be borne upward and to be of the number of things which are borne upward rather than to things which are borne downward, although sometimes accidentally fire is borne downward, as in fired iron. Sometimes something is attributed to a thing *per se* by way of remotion, namely insofar as there are removed from it things which are such as to bring about the opposite disposition. Hence if something belongs to something accidentally, that contrary disposition is stated simply, as unity is attributed *per se* to prime matter not by the union of a form but by removal of diversifying forms, hence, when distinguishing forms come to matter, it is rather said to be absolutely many matters rather than one. And so it is in the proposal: for the universal is not called incorruptible as if it had some form of incorruption but because material conditions, which are the cause of corruption in individuals, do not belong to it as such. Hence the universal existing in particular things is said simply to corrupt in this or in that.

Ad 15. It should be said that, although the other genera as such posit something in the real order – quantity just as quantity expresses something – only relation is such that it does not posit something in the real order, because it does not express something but to-something. That is why there are some relations which posit nothing in reality but are only in the mind, and this comes about in four ways, as can be inferred from remarks of the Philosopher and Avicenna. First, when a thing is referred to itself, as when it is said, 'a thing is the same as itself', for if this relation posited something in the real order, added to that which is said to be the same, there would be an infinite regress in relations, because the relation by which a thing would be called the same would be the same as itself and so on to infinity.

Second, when the relation itself refers to something. For it cannot be said that paternity refers to its own subject by some other mediating relation, because that mediating relation would require another mediating relation, and so to infinity. Hence the relation between paternity and its subject is not a real relation but of reason alone.

Third, when one of related terms depends on the other but not vice versa, as knowledge depends on the knowable, but not the reverse; hence the relation of knowledge to the known is a real relation, but not that of the known to knower, which is of reason alone.

Fourth, when being is compared to non-being, as when we say that we are prior to those who will come after us; otherwise the same thing would have an infinity of relations, if generations should extend indefinitely into the future.

From the last too it appears that the relation of priority posits nothing in reality, but is in the intellect alone; both because God does not depend upon creatures, and because such a priority implies a comparison of being to non-being. Thus it would not follow from this that there is some other eternal truth, apart from the divine intellect, which alone is eternal, and is First Truth.

Ad 16. It should be said that, although God is naturally prior to all creatures, it does not follow that this relation is one of nature. But because that which is said to be prior and that which is posterior are understood by a consideration of nature, as the knowable is said to be naturally prior to knowledge, although the relation of the knowable to knowledge is not a real one.

Ad 17. It should be said that the remark, 'If signification did not exist it is correct that something is signified' is true in the order of things existing in the divine intellect, just as, the chest not existing, it is right that the chest has a hinge, according to the ordering of art in the artisan. So this is no basis for claiming that there is an eternal truth other than First Truth.

Ad 18. It should be said that the notion of truth is founded on being. Although three persons or properties are posited in the divine, it cannot be held that there is more than one existence there, because existence is said only of God essentially, and all of these statements – for the Father to be or to generate, for the Son to be and to be generated – insofar as they refer to the thing, there is but one truth which is the First and eternal Truth.

Ad 19. It should be said that, although the Father is Father by one thing and the Son Son by another, namely paternity and filiation, yet that whereby the Father is and that whereby the Son is is the same, because both exist by the divine essence which is one. The notion of truth is not founded on the notion of paternity and of filiation as such, but on the notion of being; but paternity and filiation are one essence, and thus there is the same truth of both.

Ad 20. It should be said that the property signified by 'man' and by the word 'risible' are not essentially one, nor do they have one existence, as is the case with paternity and filiation, so there is no parallel.

Ad 21. It should be said that the divine intellect knows things no matter how diverse in a unique cognition, even those which have different truths. So much the more it knows with a single knowledge what is understood of the persons. Hence even of all these there is only one truth.

Article 6: Is created truth immutable?

It seems that it is.

1. Anselm in *On Truth* says, 'I see that by this argument it is proved that truth remains immobile'; the argument referred to concerned the truth of signification as is clear from its premisses; therefore the truth of statements is immutable, and for the same reason the truth of the things they signify.

2. Moreover, if the truth of a statement is changed, it would especially change when the thing changed; but the truth of a proposition survives the changing of the thing; therefore the truth of the enunciation is immutable. Proof of the middle: according to Anselm truth is a certain correctness insofar as something fulfils that which it means in the divine mind. But the proposition, 'Socrates sits,' is taken in the divine mind as it signifies Socrates's sitting, which it means even if Socrates is not sitting. Therefore, even if Socrates is not sitting, truth remains in it, and the truth of the quoted proposition is not changed even if the thing is changed.

3. Moreover, if truth changes this can only be because the things in which truth is have changed, just as forms are said to change only insofar as their subjects change; but truth is not changed when true things change, because true things having been destroyed, truth remains, as Augustine and Anselm prove. Therefore truth is entirely immutable.

4. Moreover, the truth of the thing is the cause of the truth of the proposition, 'Because the thing is or is not, speech is true or false,' but the truth of the thing is immutable; and so then is the truth of the proposition. Proof of the middle: Anselm in *On Truth* proves that the truth of the enunciation remains immobile insofar as it fulfils what is in the divine mind; similarly any thing fulfils what is in the divine mind in order that it might have it. Therefore the truth of any thing is immutable.

5. Moreover, that which always remains after every change is completed never changes; for in alteration of colours we do not say that the surface is changed, because it remains whatever change of colour occurs; but truth remains in the thing whatever change of the thing occurs; therefore truth is immutable.

6. Moreover, where there is the same cause there is the same effect; but the same thing is the cause of the truth of these three propositions: Socrates will sit, sat and sits, namely, Socrates's sitting; therefore their truth is the same. But if one of the three is true, it is necessary that one

190 MASTER AT PARIS (1256-9)

of the other two is always true: for if it is sometimes true that Socrates sits, it always was and always will be true that Socrates sat or Socrates will sit; therefore the one truth of the three propositions is always the same, and so it is immutable. And so by the same reasoning is any other truth.

ON THE CONTRARY:

Causes being changed, effects are changed, but the things which are the cause of the truth of the proposition change. Therefore the truth of propositions changes.

RESPONSE:

It should be said that something is said to change in two ways: in one way because it is the subject of change, as we say that the body is mutable, and in this sense no form is mutable, which is why it is said that 'the form remains in its invariable essence'. Hence, since truth is signified in the manner of a form, the present question is not whether truth is mutable in this way. In another way something is said to be changed because it itself comes to be changed, as we say that whiteness is changed because the body is altered because of it. It is in this sense that we ask whether truth is mutable.

For purposes of clarification it should be noted that that in terms of which there is a change is sometimes said to be changed and sometimes not: for when it is inherent in that which is moved with reference to it, then it itself is said to be changed, as whiteness or quantity are said to be changed when something is changed with respect to them, because they themselves succeed one another in the subject because of this change; however, when that with reference to which there is change is extrinsic, it is not moved by the change, but remains immobile, as place is not said to be moved when something changes place. Hence it is said in *Physics* 4.4 that 'place is the immobile term of the container', because local motion is not a succession of places in one placed thing but rather of many things placed in one place. But there is a twofold change of inherent forms which are said to change: general forms are said to change otherwise than do special forms. For the special form does not remain the same either in being or in understanding after the change, as whiteness does not remain after the alteration takes place; but the general form after the change remains the same in notion though not in being: after the change from white to black, colour remains according to the common notion of colour, though not the same species of colour.

It was said above that a thing is denominated true from the first truth as from an extrinsic measure, but from inherent truth as from an intrinsic measure. Hence created things vary in their participation in the first truth, although the first truth according to which they are called true in no way changes. This is what Augustine says in *On Free Will* 2.12: 'Our minds see sometimes less sometimes more of truth itself, but it remains in itself neither increasing nor decreasing.' If however we take the truth inherent in things, then truth is said to change insofar as some things are changed according to truth.

Hence, as was said earlier, truth is found in creatures in two ways, in the things themselves and in the intellect. For the truth of action is contained under the truth of the thing and the truth of the enunciation under the truth of intellect which it signifies. The thing is said to be true in comparison to the divine and to the human intellect. If therefore the truth of the thing is understood according to its order to the divine intellect, then indeed the truth of the mutable thing changes, not into falsity, but into another truth, for truth is the most general form since the true and being are convertible. Hence, just as the thing remains being after no matter what change, although it has existence through different forms, so the true always remains but by another truth, because, whatever form or privation it acquires through change, through it it is conformed to the divine intellect which knows it whatever its disposition is. If the truth of the thing is taken with respect to human intellect or conversely, then sometimes there is a change from truth to falsity, sometimes a change from one truth to another.

Since 'truth is the adequation of thing and intellect', and if from equals equals be taken equals remain, although not the same equality, it is necessary that, when intellect and thing are changed in the same way, truth remains but a different one, for example if Socrates is seated it is understood that Socrates sits and after he is no longer seated he is understood not to sit. But if something be taken from one of equals but not from the other, or unequal portions be taken from both, inequality necessarily results, which is to falsity as equality is to truth. So it is that, given a true understanding, the thing is changed but not the understanding, or conversely either both are changed but not in the same way, falsity results, and thus there will be a change from truth to falsity. For example, if Socrates being white he is understood to be white, the understanding is true; if, however, later he is understood to be black, although Socrates remains white, or conversely Socrates becomes black and is still understood to be white, or having changed to pallor is understood to be red, there will be falsity in the intellect. Thus it is clear how truth changes and how truth does not change.

Ad 1. It should be said Anselm speaks there of first truth insofar as all things are said to be true by it as by an extrinsic measure.

Ad 2. It should be said that, because intellect reflects on itself and understands itself as it does other things, as is said in *On the Soul* 3.9, what pertains to intellect, insofar as it pertains to the definition of truth, can be understood in two ways: in one way, insofar as they are certain things, and thus truth is said of them in the same way it is of other things, such namely that, just as a thing is called true because it fulfils what is in the divine mind by retaining its nature, so the enunciation is called true by retaining its nature which is dispensed to it in the divine mind, nor can it be taken from it so long as the enunciation remains; in another way insofar as it is compared to the things understood, and thus the enunciation is called true when it is adequate to the thing, and such truth changes, as has been said.

Ad 3. It should be said that the truth which remains when true things are destroyed is the first truth, which also does not change when things are changed.

Ad 4. It should be said that while the thing remains there can be no change of it according to its essentials, just as it is essential to the enunciation that it signifies that which it was instituted to signify: hence it does not follow that the truth of the thing is in no way mutable, but that it is immutable with respect to the essentials of the thing, the thing remaining – with respect to which, however, change happens through the corruption of the thing. But with respect to accidentals change can happen even though the thing remains; and thus with respect to accidentals there can be a change in the truth of the thing.

Ad 5. It should be said that any change having occurred, truth remains but not the same one, as is evident from the foregoing.

Ad 6. It should be said that the identity of truth depends not only on the identity of the thing but on the identity of understanding, just as the identity of the effect depends on the identity of the agent and patient; however, although it is the same thing that is signified by the three propositions, there is not the same understanding of them because in the composition of the understanding time enters. Hence according to the variation of time there are diverse understandings.

9. *On the Teacher.* Disputed Question on Truth, 11 (1256–9)

The dominant figure throughout the Middle Ages was Augustine of Hippo. If anyone was an auctor *it was he, and his* auctoritas *in matters of Christian doctrine was unquestioned. He did not of course have the authority of Sacred Scripture and deferential criticism of the great doctor of the Church was not inappropriate. Thomas Aquinas himself took exception to a number of Augustinian tenets, something we would of course expect when we think of Augustine as the champion of Plato and Thomas as a convinced Aristotelian. Plato and Aristotle are in disagreement, therefore their followers must be in disagreement. This is a very superficial way to compare Thomas and Augustine.*

What continues to astonish students of Thomas is the way in which his thought transcends in a principled way seemingly irreconcilable positions. Disagreement presupposes agreement. Thomas was not one to be content with a plurality of views based on a variety of starting points. While conscious of, indeed insistent on, the clash in the middle distance, he sought to go beyond it in a way that sought a common ground. This is nowhere more evident than in the conflict between theories of knowledge. Historians of medieval philosophy have found it possible to range thinkers under the competing banners of Abstraction and Illumination, the former Aristotelian, the latter Platonic/Augustinian. St Augustine's position is conveniently set forth in his On the Teacher, *a dialogue between him and his natural son Adeodatus, conducted when Augustine was in retreat at Cassiciacum preparing at last for baptism. It is one of the most engaging works of the great saint.*

The eleventh of the twenty-nine questions making up Thomas Aquinas's Disputed Question on Truth *bears the same title as Augustine's dialogue. It is an important and self-contained work, but Thomas's principal interlocutor is Augustine. You will notice how deftly Thomas arrives at a reconciliation of the Augustinian and Aristotelian accounts.*

ON THE TEACHER

Article 1: Can a man teach and be called a master or God alone?

It seems that only God can teach and be called a teacher.

1. Matthew 23.8 says, 'You have but one master,' and earlier, 'Do not be called Rabbi,' on which the Gloss comments, 'Lest you attribute to men divine honour or usurp what is God's.' Therefore, to be a master and to teach seem to belong to God alone.

2. Moreover, if a man teaches it is only through signs, because if he seems also to teach something through the things themselves, as for example by walking when asked what walking is, this does not suffice for teaching, unless some sign be added, as Augustine proves in *On the Teacher* 1.3. The reason is that there are many aspects of a single thing and it is unclear which is relevant when it is pointed at, whether its substance or some accident of it. But we cannot come to knowledge of things through signs, because knowledge of things is more powerful than knowledge of signs, since knowledge of signs is ordered to knowledge of things as to its end, and the effect cannot be more potent than its cause. Thus no one can pass on knowledge of things to another and thus he cannot teach him.

3. Moreover, if signs of certain things be proposed by one man to another, either the one to whom they are proposed knows the things of which they are the signs or he doesn't. If he knows them, he is not taught concerning the things. If he does not know them but is ignorant of the things, the meanings of the signs cannot be known by him. For if someone does not know the thing that is a stone, he cannot know what is meant by the word 'stone'. Not knowing the meaning of the signs, he cannot learn anything through the signs. Therefore if all a man does in teaching is to propose signs, it seems that one man cannot be taught by another man.

4. Moreover, teaching is nothing other than causing knowledge in another in some way. But the subject of knowledge is intellect, and the sensible signs by which alone a man seems to teach do not reach to the intellective part but remain in the sensitive part. Therefore, a man cannot be taught by a man.

5. Moreover, if science is caused in one man by another, either the knowledge was in the learner or it was not. If it was not in him and is caused in the man by another, the latter created knowledge in the former,

which is impossible. If it was in him, either it was in him in complete actuality, and thus is not caused, because what is does not come to be, or it was in him as a kind of rational seed [*ratio seminalis*], but rational seeds cannot be brought to actuality by any created power, but are inserted in nature by God alone, as Augustine says in the literal commentary on Genesis. It remains then that one man cannot be taught by another.

6. Moreover, science is a kind of accident, but an accident cannot pass from its subject. Therefore, since teaching seems to be the transfer of the master's knowledge to the student, one man cannot be taught by another.

7. Moreover, on the remark in Romans 10.17, 'Faith comes from hearing,' the Gloss says, 'Although God teaches within, an outward herald proclaims. But science is caused in the interior of the mind and not outside in the senses.' Therefore, a man is taught by God alone, not by another man.

8. Moreover, Augustine says in *On the Teacher*, 'God alone has a chair in the heavens and on it he teaches truth; a man is so related to that chair as the farmer to the tree, which he does not make but cultivates.' Therefore, no man can be called a teacher of science, but rather disposes for science.

9. Moreover, if man were a true teacher, he would have to teach truth. But whoever teaches truth, illumines the mind, since truth is the light of the mind. Therefore, a man would illumine the mind if he taught. But this is false, since it is God who illumines every man coming into this world (John 1.9). Therefore, one man cannot truly teach another.

10. Moreover, if one man teaches another, he would have to bring someone who knows potentially to the state of actually knowing, so that his knowledge is brought from potency to act. But what is brought from potency to act is necessarily changed. Therefore, science or wisdom will be changed, which is in conflict with Augustine in *Eighty-three Questions*, where he says that when wisdom comes to man, it is the man who changes, not wisdom.

11. Moreover, science seems to be nothing else than the inscription of things in the soul, since science is said to be the assimilation of the knower to the known. But a man cannot inscribe in another's soul the likenesses of things, for then he would work within him, but that belongs to God alone. Therefore, one man cannot teach another.

12. Moreover, Boethius says in the *Consolation of Philosophy* 5.5 that through teaching the mind of man is summoned to know, but one who summons the intellect to know does not cause it to know, any more than he who summons another to bodily seeing causes him to see. Therefore,

one man does not cause another to know, and thus is not properly said to teach him.

13. Moreover, certainty of knowledge is required for science, otherwise it is not science, but opinion or belief, as Augustine says in *On the Teacher*. But one man cannot cause certainty in another through the sensible signs that he proposes, for what is in the senses is always oblique to what is in intellect, whereas certainty rather comes about through something direct. Therefore, one man cannot teach another.

14. Moreover, an intelligible light and species are required for science, but neither can be caused in a man by another man, because then a man would have to create something, since such simple forms seem to be produced only through creation. Therefore, a man cannot cause science in another, and thus cannot teach.

15. Moreover, only God can form the mind of man, as Augustine says in *On Free Will* 1.17. But science is a kind of form of mind. Therefore God alone causes science in the soul.

16. Moreover, ignorance like guilt is in the mind, but only God purges the mind of guilt. Isaiah 43.25: 'I am, I am he that blots out thy iniquities for my own sake: and I will not remember thy sins.' Therefore, God alone purges the mind of ignorance, and thus he alone teaches.

17. Moreover, since science is certain knowledge, one receives science from another through whose speech he is made certain. But one is not made certain because he hears a man speaking, otherwise whatever is said to him by a man would hold as certain for him. He is only made certain by hearing the truth speak within, which he consults concerning what he hears a man say in order that he might become certain. Therefore, a man does not teach, but truth speaks within and that is God.

18. Moreover, no one learns, through the speech of another, things which he would have been able to respond if asked before the speech. But the pupil, before the master speaks to him, would if asked respond concerning the things the master proposes. For he is only taught by the master when he knows that things are as the master proposes. Therefore, one man is not taught by another's speaking.

ON THE CONTRARY:

1. There is what is said in 2 Timothy 1.11: '. . . of which I have been appointed a preacher . . . and a teacher of the Gentiles.' Therefore a man can be, and be called, a teacher.

2. Moreover, see 2 Timothy 3.14: 'But do thou continue in the things thou hast learned, and that have been entrusted to thee,' and the Gloss

on this passage: 'From me, as from a true teacher.' Thus, concluding as before.

3. Moreover, Matthew 23.8 and 9 both say that your master is one and your father is one. But the fact that God is the father of all does not prevent a man too from truly being called a father. So this too excludes the claim that a man cannot truly be called a master.

4. Moreover, on Romans 10.15, 'How beautiful are the feet of those who preach,' the Gloss says, 'These are the feet that illumine the Church,' speaking of the apostles. Since to illumine is the act of the teacher, it seems that teaching pertains to men.

5. Moreover, it is said in *Meteorology* 4 that anything is perfect when it can generate something like itself. But science is perfect knowledge. Therefore, a man who has science, can teach another.

6. Moreover, Augustine, in *Against the Manicheans* 2.4, says that earth, which before sin was watered by a spring, after sin needed rain descending from the clouds. So the human mind, which is signified by earth, was made fruitful by the spring of truth, but after sin needed the teaching of others, like rain descending from the clouds. Therefore, at least after sin, a man can be taught by another man.

RESPONSE:

It should be said that there is the same diversity of opinion in three matters, namely, in bringing forms into existence, in the acquisition of virtue and in the acquisition of knowledge.

For some said that all sensible forms are from an external agent which is a substance or a separate form which they called the giver of forms or agent intellect, and that all lesser natural agents only prepare matter for the reception of form. So too Avicenna says in his *Metaphysics* the cause of the worthy habit is not our action but action rather adapts to it and prevents the contrary, such that habit comes from a substance perfecting the souls of men, which is the agent intelligence or a substance similar to it.

Likewise they hold that science is effected in us only by a separate agent. Hence Avicenna said in *On Natural Things* 6, 4.2 that intelligible forms flow into our mind from the agent intelligence.

Others thought the opposite, namely that whatever is inserted in things has its cause not in an external agent but is only brought to light by the external action. For some held that all natural forms are actually latent in matter and that the natural agent does nothing other than to bring them from a hidden to a manifest condition.

Similarly some held that all the habits of virtue are implanted in us by nature and that actions make these habits emerge from obscurity just as rubbing removes rust from steel and reveals its brightness.

So too some said that knowledge of all things is created along with the soul and that through teaching and the external aids of teaching nothing else happens than that the soul is led to the remembrance or consideration of what it previously knew. Hence they say that learning is nothing but remembering.

But these opinions are without foundation. For the first opinion excludes proximate causes by attributing to first causes alone all effects coming about in inferior things, which derogates from the order of the universe, which consists of the order and connection of causes. The first cause out of the eminence of his goodness not only makes things to be but also to be causes.

The second opinion comes to the same absurdity. Since the removal of an impediment is only to cause accidentally, as is said in *Physics* 8, if inferior agents did nothing but make the hidden manifest by removing impediments whereby forms and the habits of virtue and the sciences were obscured, it would follow that all inferior agents are only agents accidentally.

Therefore, following the teaching of Aristotle, the middle way between these two extremes is to be held in all these matters. For natural forms do indeed pre-exist in matter, but not actually, as these said, but only potentially, from which they are brought into act by the proximate external agent, not only the first cause, as the other opinion would have it.

Similarly, according to this teaching in *Ethics* 6, the habits of the virtues before their perfection pre-exist in us in certain natural inclinations which are, as it were, the beginnings of virtue, but afterwards by the doing of works they are brought to their fitting completion.

And we ought to say the same about the acquisition of sciences: certain seeds of the sciences pre-exist in us, namely, the first conceptions of the intellect which are known right away by the light of the agent intellect through species abstracted from sensible things, whether these be complex, like axioms, or incomplex, like the notions of being and one and the like, which the intellect apprehends straightaway. Everything that follows is included in these universal principles as in certain seminal reasons. Therefore when the mind is led from this universal knowledge to the actual knowing of particulars, which it previously knew in the universal and as it were potentially, then someone is said to acquire science.

But it should be noted that in natural things something is said to pre-exist potentially in two ways. In one way, in complete active potency, namely, when an intrinsic principle is sufficient to bring about a perfect act, as is evident in healing, for from the natural power which is in him the sick person is brought to health.

In another way, in passive potency, namely, when the intrinsic principle does not suffice for bringing to actuality, as is clear when fire is made from air, for this could not come to be through any power existing in the air.

Therefore when something pre-exists in complete active potency, the extrinsic agent only acts by aiding the intrinsic agent and supplying it with the things by which it comes forth to actuality, as the physician in healing is the minister of nature which principally acts by aiding nature and providing medicine which nature uses as instruments in healing.

But when something pre-exists only in passive potency, then it is the extrinsic agent that principally leads from potency to act, as fire makes of air, which is potentially fire, actual fire.

Therefore, science pre-exists in the learner in active and not purely passive potency, otherwise a man could not acquire science on his own.

Therefore, just as there are two ways to be cured, one by the operation of nature alone, the other by nature as aided by medicine, so too there are two ways of acquiring science, one, when natural reason by itself comes to knowledge of the unknown, and this way is called *discovery*, another when someone outside aids natural reason, and this way is called *learning*.

In things that come about both by nature and by art, art acts in the same way and through the same means as nature. For just as nature restores health to one suffering a chill by heating, so too the physician, which is why art is said to imitate nature. It happens similarly in the acquisition of science, because the teacher leads another in the same way to knowledge of the unknown as one by discovery brings himself to knowledge of the unknown.

But the process of coming to knowledge of the unknown by discovery is to apply the common self-evident principles to determinate matters and then to proceed to particular conclusions, and from those to others. So one man is said to teach another following this same discourse of reason which natural reason executes, showing signs to another so that the natural reason of the pupil, through what is proposed, as through certain instruments, comes to knowledge of the unknown.

Therefore, just as the physician is said to cause health in the infirm by acting with nature, so too a man is said to cause science in another by the activity of his natural reason, and this is to teach. Hence one man is said to teach another and to be his master. And thus the Philosopher says in *Posterior Analytics* 1 that demonstration is a syllogism that causes one to know.

If however someone proposed to another what is not included in self-evident principles or is not shown to be included, he will not cause knowledge, but perhaps opinion or belief, though these two are also in a way caused by innate principles. From these self-evident principles, one considers that those things which necessarily follow are to be held as certain and what is contrary to them to be repudiated, whereas to others he can give or withhold assent.

The light of reason by which principles of this kind are known is placed in us by God, bringing about in us a kind of likeness of uncreated truth. Hence, since all human teaching is only efficacious because of the power of this light, it follows that it is God alone who teaches within and principally, just as nature principally and within heals. Nevertheless, man can be properly said both to heal and to teach in the way explained.

Ad 1. It should be said that because the Lord commanded his disciples not to be called masters, lest this be taken to be absolutely forbidden, the Gloss explains how this prohibition should be understood. We are forbidden to call a man master in this sense that we attribute to him the principal role in teaching, which belongs to God, as if placing our hope in the wisdom of men rather than in what we hear from a man, consulting the divine truth, which speaks in us through the impress of his likeness, thanks to which we can judge all things.

Ad 2. It should be said that knowledge of things is not effected in us by knowledge of signs, but through knowledge of other more certain things, namely principles, which are proposed to us through signs and are applied to what previously was absolutely unknown, although known by us in a certain respect, as has been said. For the knowledge of principles, not knowledge of signs, causes in us knowledge of conclusions.

Ad 3. It should be said that the things of which we are taught by means of signs we indeed know in one respect but do not know in another. If we are taught what a man is we must know something of him beforehand, such as the notion of animal or of substance or at least of being itself, which cannot be unknown to us, and likewise if we are taught some conclusion, we must previously know what the predicate and subject are as also the previously known principles through which the conclusion is taught. For all learning comes from previously existing knowledge, as is said at the beginning of the *Posterior Analytics*, so the argument does not work.

Ad 4. It should be said that from sensible signs, which are received in the sense power, the intellect receives intelligible intentions, which it uses for bringing about science in itself. Signs are not the proximate cause of science, but reason, moving discursively from principles to conclusions, as has been said.

Ad 5. It should be said science previously existed in the one taught, not in complete act, but as it were in seminal reasons, according to universal concepts, knowledge of which is naturally put in us, which are like seeds of all the knowledge that follows. However, although through a created power the seminal reasons are not actualized as if they were infused by some created power, none the less what is in them originally and virtually can be brought to actuality by the act of a created power.

Ad 6. It should be said that the teacher does not transfer knowledge into the learner, as if numerically the same knowledge which was in the master comes to be in the pupil, but because through teaching there comes to be in the pupil knowledge similar to that which is in the master, brought forth from potency to act, as has been said.

Ad 7. It should be said that just as the physician, although he acts externally – nature alone acting internally – is said to cause health, so a man is said to teach truth although he states it externally, God teaching within.

Ad 8. It should be said that Augustine in *On the Teacher* does not mean to deny that a man teaches from without when he proves that God alone teaches, because God alone teaches within.

Ad 9. It should be said that man can truly be called a true teacher and a teacher of the truth and enlightener of the mind, not as if he were infusing light to reason, but as it were aiding the light of reason to the perfection of science through what he externally proposes. It is in this sense that it is said in Ephesians 3.8–9, 'To me the least of all the saints is given this grace . . . to enlighten all men.'

Ad 10. It should be said that wisdom is twofold, created and uncreated, and both are said to be infused in man and by this infusion a man is changed for the better. But uncreated wisdom is in no way mutable, though created wisdom is mutable accidentally, not as such. For it can be considered in two ways. In one way, with respect to the eternal things with which it is concerned, and thus it is wholly immutable; in another way, according to the existence it has in the subject, and thus it is changed accidentally, when the subject is changed from having it potentially to having it actually. For the intelligible forms, in which wisdom consists, are both likenesses of things and forms perfecting the intellect.

Ad 11. It should be said that intelligible forms are inscribed in the learner and through them the knowledge acquired through teaching is constituted, immediately by the agent intellect, but mediately by him who teaches. For the teacher proposes signs of intelligible things from which the agent intellect receives intelligible intentions and inscribes them in the possible intellect. Hence the teacher's words being heard or seen in writing, are related to causing science in the intellect just as things outside the soul are, because the agent intellect receives intelligible intentions from both, although the words of the teacher are more closely related to causing science than sensible things existing outside the soul, insofar as they are signs of intelligible intentions.

Ad 12. It should be said that intellect and bodily sight are not wholly alike, for bodily sight is not a collating power, such that from some of its objects it goes on to others, but all its objects are visible to it as soon as it turns to them. One having sight is related to intuiting all visible things as one who has a habit is to considering the things he knows habitually, and thus the one seeing does not need to be incited by anything else in order to see, except insofar as his sight is directed by another to the visible, as by pointing or the like. The intellectual power, since it is collative, goes from some things to others, and thus is not related equally to all intelligible things to be considered. Some it sees straightaway because they are self-evident and in them are implicitly contained other things which it cannot understand save through the office of reason by explicating. In order to know such things, before it has the habit, it is not only in accidental potency but also in essential potency, for it needs a mover which actualizes it by way of teaching, as is said in *Physics* 8. He who already knows things habitually does not need this. Therefore the teacher stirs the intellect to knowing what he teaches, as an essential mover bringing actuality from potency. But the one showing something to bodily sight, stirs it like an accidental mover, as one having the habit of science can be stirred to consider something.

Ad 13. It should be said that all the certainty of science derives from the certainty of the principles, for conclusions are known with certainty when they are resolved into the principles. Something is known with certainty in the light of reason divinely inserted within, whereby God speaks in us; but not by the man teaching without, save insofar as he in teaching us resolves conclusions into principles. We would not receive the certainty of science if there was not in us the certainty of the principles into which the conclusions are resolved.

Ad 14. It should be said that the man teaching externally does not infuse the intelligible light, but is in some way the cause of the intelligible species, insofar as he proposes to us certain signs of intelligible intentions, which our intellect receives from the signs and stores in itself.

Ad 15. It should be replied that when it is said that only God can form the mind, this should be understood of its ultimate form, without which it would be regarded as unformed, however many other forms it has. But this is the form by which it is turned to the word and inheres in it, by which alone the rational nature is called formed, as is clear from Augustine in the literal commentary on Genesis.

Ad 16. It should be said that fault is in the affection, in which God alone can make an impression, as will be clear in the following article; but ignorance is in the intellect, on which a created power too can make an impression, as the agent intellect impresses intelligible species on the possible intellect, by the mediation of which, from sensible things and from the teaching of men, science is caused in our soul, as has been said.

Ad 17. It should be said that as has been remarked, the certainty of science is in God alone, who instils in us the light of reason, through which we know the principles from which the certainty of science derives; yet science is caused in us in some way by man as well, as has been said.

Ad 18. It should be said that the learner interrogated before the teacher speaks would respond about the principles through which he will be taught, but not about the conclusions which someone would teach him: hence he does not learn principles from the master, but only conclusions.

Article 2: Can someone be called his own teacher?

It seems not.

1. Because an action ought to be attributed to the principal cause rather than to the instrumental; but what functions as the principal cause of the science caused in us is the agent intellect. But the man who teaches outside is an instrumental cause proposing to the agent intellect instruments by which it can attain to science. Therefore, the agent intellect is more of a teacher than the man outside. If because of exterior speech, the one

speaking is said to be the master of him who hears, so much the more so should the one who hears be called his own teacher, because of the light of the agent intellect.

2. Someone learns only insofar as he arrives at certainty of knowledge; but certainty of knowledge comes about in us through principles naturally known in the light of the agent intellect. Therefore, it belongs chiefly to the agent intellect to teach, with the same conclusion as above.

3. Moreover, teaching belongs more properly to God than to man; hence Matthew 23.8: 'You have but one teacher.' But God teaches us insofar as he gives us the light of reason by which we can judge all things. Therefore, the act of teaching ought chiefly to be attributed to that light, with the same conclusion as before.

4. Moreover, to know something by way of discovery is more perfect than to learn from another, as is evident in *Ethics* 1.4. Therefore, if the term 'teacher' is taken from that mode of acquiring science whereby one learns from another, so that one is the teacher of the other, in a much fuller sense the term 'teacher' should be taken from the mode of receiving science by way of discovery, so that someone can be called his own teacher.

5. Moreover, just as someone is led to virtue by another or by himself, so one is led to knowledge both by discovering on his own and by learning from another. Those who come to the works of virtue without an external instructor or legislator are said to be a law unto themselves; Romans 2.14: 'Since gentiles who have not the law naturally do what is of the law, they are a law unto themselves.' Therefore, one who acquires knowledge by himself ought to be called his own teacher.

6. Moreover, the teacher is the cause of knowledge as the physician is of health, as has been said. But the physician heals himself. Therefore, one is able to teach himself.

ON THE CONTRARY:

1. The Philosopher says in *Physics* 8 that it is impossible that the one teaching learns, because the teacher must have knowledge where the learner does not. Therefore, no one can teach himself or be called his own teacher.

2. Moreover, master, like lord, implies a relation of being placed above. But relations of this kind cannot obtain between a thing and itself. No one is his own father, or lord. Therefore, no one can be called his own teacher.

RESPONSE:

It should be said that without any doubt one can, through the light of natural reason placed within him and without any external aid, come to knowledge of many unknown things, as is evident in all who acquired science by way of discovery. And thus in a certain way one can be the cause of his own knowing, but he cannot properly be called his own teacher or be said to teach himself.

For we find two kinds of agent principles in natural things, as the Philosopher makes clear in *Metaphysics* 8.

There is a kind of agent that has within itself everything that it causes in the effect, whether in the same manner, as with univocal agents, or in a more eminent way, as in equivocal agents. But there are some agents in which there exists only partially within them what they bring, as motion causes heat, and heat causes medicine, in which heat is found either actually or virtually, but heat is not the whole of health but a part of it. In the primary agents there is action in the fullest sense, but not in agents of the secondary sort, because a thing acts insofar as it is actual. Hence, since it is not actually or more than partially what is brought about in the effect, it is not a perfect agent.

But teaching implies the perfect act of knowing in the teacher or master; hence it is required that he who teaches or is a master should have the science he causes in another, explicitly and perfectly, as it is acquired in the learning through teaching.

When someone acquires knowledge by himself through an intrinsic principle, what is the agent cause of science does not possess the science to be acquired, save in part, namely with respect to the seminal reasons of science, which are common principles. Therefore, from such causality the name teacher or doctor cannot be derived, properly speaking.

Ad 1. It should be said of the agent intellect that, though in a certain respect it is a more principal cause than the man teaching outside, science does not completely exist beforehand in it, as in the teacher. Hence the argument does not work.

Ad 2. The answer is similar to the first.

Ad 3. It should be said that God explicitly knows all things that man is taught by him, so the notion of teacher can fittingly be attributed to him; not so the agent intellect, for the reason given.

Ad 4. It should be said that the manner of acquiring science through discovery is more perfect on the part of the one receiving science, insofar as he is shown to be more equipped to know, yet on the part of the one causing science teaching is more perfect. The one teaching, who explicitly knows the whole science, can lead us to science more expeditiously than anyone can be brought to it on his own because he foreknows the principles of the science in some generality.

Ad 5. It should be said that law functions in practical matters as principle does in speculative matters, but not as the master; hence it doesn't follow from the fact that one can be a law unto himself that he can be his own teacher.

Ad 6. It should be said that the physician heals insofar as he has health, not actually, but in the knowledge of art; but the master teaches insofar as he actually has science. Hence he who actually has health, in the sense that he has knowledge of it by art, can cause health in himself. But it is not possible that someone actually have the science and yet not have it and thus be able to be taught by himself.

Article 3: Can man be taught by an angel?

It seems that he cannot.

1. Because, if an angel taught it would be either inwardly or outwardly, but not inwardly because this is proper to God alone, as Augustine says, nor outwardly, as it seems, because to teach outwardly is to teach by means of sensible signs, as Augustine says in *On the Teacher*. Angels do not teach us with such signs, except perhaps apparent sensibles. Therefore, the angels do not teach us except perhaps as appearing to the senses, which is outside the common course and, as it were, a miracle.

2. If it be said that the angels teach us in a certain way outwardly, insofar as they make an impression on our imagination, on the contrary: species impressed on the imagination do not suffice for actual imagining, unless an intention be present, as is evident in Augustine, *On the Trinity*. But the angel cannot induce an intention in us, since intention is an act of will, on which God alone can act. Therefore, not even by acting on the imagination can the angel teach us since, by the medium of imagination, we cannot be taught unless we actually imagine something.

3. Moreover, if we were taught by the angels without a sensible appar-ition, this could only be if they illumined the intellect, which they cannot do, it seems, because they neither give the natural light, which God alone does, as created along with mind, or even the light of grace, which God alone infuses. Therefore angels cannot teach us without a visible apparition.

4. Moreover, whenever one is taught by another, it is necessary that the learner see the concept of the teacher, in order that there might be a process of the mind of the pupil towards knowledge, just as there is a process from knowledge in the mind of the teacher. But a man cannot see the concept of an angel, for he neither sees them in themselves, any more than he could those of another man, indeed far less, as more distant, nor in sensible signs except perhaps when they appear sensibly, of which it is not a question here. Therefore angels cannot otherwise teach us.

5. Moreover, it is the prerogative of him who illumines every man coming into this world to teach, as is evident from the Gloss on Matthew 23.8: 'You have but one master, Christ.' But this does not belong to the angel, but to uncreated light alone, as is clear from John 1.9.

6. Moreover, whoever teaches another leads him to the truth, and thus causes truth to be in his soul. But only God has causality over the truth, because truth is an intelligible light and a simple form, it does not come into existence successively, and thus can only be produced by creation. Therefore, since the angels are not creators, as Damascene says, it seems that they cannot teach.

7. Moreover, an unfailing illumination can only come from an unfailing light because, when the light is taken away, the subject is no longer illumined. But teaching requires some unfailing light, in that science is of the necessary which always is. Therefore, teaching can only proceed from an unfailing light. But angelic light is not of this kind, since their light would fail if it were not divinely preserved. Therefore, the angel cannot teach.

8. Moreover, it is said in John 1.38 that when two of John's disciples following Jesus were asked by him, 'What do you seek?', they responded, 'Rabbi' – which interpreted means Master – 'where dwellest thou?' The Gloss here says that by this word they show their faith, and another gloss says, 'He asked, not out of ignorance, but that they might merit in replying, and being asked what, suggesting a thing, they answered not to a thing, but to a person. It follows from all this that in their reply they confessed him to be a person and that by this confession, they showed their faith, and in this merited.' But the merit of faith consists in this that we confess Christ to be a divine person. Therefore, to be a teacher pertains only to the divine person.

9. Moreover, whoever teaches must manifest the truth. But truth, since it is an intelligible light, is more known to us than the angel is. Therefore, we are not taught by the angel, since the more known is not made manifest by the less.

10. Moreover, Augustine says in *On the Trinity* that our mind, without the interposition of any creature, is immediately formed by God. But the angel is a creature. Therefore he is not interposed between God and the human mind to inform it, as superior to mind but inferior to God. Thus a man cannot be taught by an angel.

11. Moreover, as our will can reach even to God, so our intellect can attain to the contemplation of his essence. But God himself immediately forms our will by the infusion of grace, no angel mediating. Therefore, he forms our intellect by teaching, without a mediator.

12. Moreover, all teaching is through some species; therefore if an angel taught man he would have to cause some species in him through which he knows. But this cannot be, save either by creating the species, which in no way belongs to an angel to do, as Damascene says, or by illumining the species which are in phantasms so that intelligible species might result in the human possible intellect. And this seems to lead to the error of those philosophers who held that the agent intellect, whose role it is to illumine the phantasms, is a separate substance. Thus the angel cannot teach.

13. Moreover, there is a greater distance between the intellect of the angel and man's intellect than between man's intellect and his imagination. But the imagination cannot receive what is in the intellect, since imagination can grasp only particular forms, which intellect does not contain. Therefore, much less is the human intellect capable of what is in the angelic mind. Thus man cannot be taught by an angel.

14. Moreover, the light by which something is illumined must be proportionate to what is illumined, as bodily light to colours. But the angelic light, since it is purely spiritual, is not proportioned to phantasms which are in a way corporeal, as contained in a bodily organ. Therefore, angels cannot teach us by illumining our phantasms, as was said.

15. Moreover, whatever is known is known either through its essence or by a likeness. But the knowledge by which things are known in their essence by the human mind cannot be caused by the angels, because then the powers and the other things contained within the soul could be acted upon by the angels when such things are known in their essence. Similarly, the knowledge whereby things are known through their likenesses cannot be caused by them, since the things to be known are closer to the likeness which is in the knower than the angel is. Therefore, the angel cannot in any way be cause of man's knowledge, which is to teach.

16. Moreover, though the farmer from without incites nature to natural effects, he is not called a creator, as is clear from Augustine in the literal

commentary on Genesis. Therefore, by parity of reasoning, neither can angels be called teachers and masters, although they exceed the intellect of man in knowing.

17. Moreover, since the angel is superior to man, if he teaches his teaching must excel human teaching. But this cannot be, for a man can teach about those things which have definite causes in nature. Other things, like future contingents, cannot be taught by angels since they are unknown by them by their natural knowledge, since only God has knowledge of such future events. Therefore angels cannot teach men.

ON THE CONTRARY:

1. Dionysius says in *On the Celestial Hierarchy* 4, 'I see that the divine mystery of Christ's humanity was first taught to the angels and then through the grace of knowledge descends to us.'

2. Moreover, what the inferior can do, the superior can do and more nobly, as is made evident by Dionysius in the *Celestial Hierarchy*; but the human order is inferior to the order of angels. Since therefore man can teach a man, much more so can an angel.

3. Moreover, the order of divine wisdom is found more perfectly in spiritual creatures than in corporeal; but it pertains to the order of inferior bodies that inferior bodies reach their perfection because of the activity of superior bodies. Therefore, inferior spirits, that is, the human, achieve the perfection of science by the causality of superior spirits, that is, the angels.

4. Moreover, whatever is in potency can be led to act by that which is actual, and what is less actual by that which is more perfectly actual. But the angelic intellect is more actual than the human intellect. Therefore, the human intellect can be led to the act of knowledge by the angelic intellect. Thus the angel can teach a man.

5. Moreover, Augustine says in *On the Good of Perseverance* that some receive the teaching of salvation immediately from God, some from an angel, some from men. Therefore the angel and man, and not God alone, teach.

6. Moreover, to light the house means both sending light, that is, the sun, and opening the shutters which obstruct the light. But although God alone infuses the light of truth into the mind, none the less the angel or man can remove an impediment to perceiving the light. Therefore not only God but angel and man too can teach.

RESPONSE:

It should be said that an angel can act on man in two ways.

In one way, according to our manner, as when he appears sensibly to man, either by assuming a body or in some other way, and instructs him with sensible speech. We are not now asking about angelic teaching in this manner, for in this way an angel teaches no differently than a man.

In another way the angel acts on us in his own manner, that is, invisibly, and the thrust of our question is to ask how a man can be taught by an angel in this way.

It should be known, therefore, that, since the angel is between man and God, according to the order of nature a middle mode of teaching belongs to him, inferior to God's, but superior to man's. But how this is so cannot be perceived without looking at how God and man teach.

To clarify this it should be known that the difference between intellect and bodily sight is this, that all its objects are equally available for knowledge by sensible sight, for sense is not a collating power, as if it must proceed from one of its objects to another. But all intelligibles are not equally close for knowing to the intellect, but some can be seen immediately whereas some are only seen through others already seen.

A man therefore receives knowledge of things unknown from two things, the intellectual light and the first self-evident conceptions which are to this light, which is the agent intellect, as instruments are to the artisan.

With respect to both, God is the cause of man's knowledge in the most excellent manner, because he both seals the soul itself with intellectual light and impresses on it knowledge of first principles which are as it were the seeds of the sciences, just as he impresses on natural things the seminal reasons for producing all their effects.

But man, because in the natural order he is the equal of other men in the species of intellectual light, can in no way be the cause of science existing in another man by causing or augmenting in him the light. But given that knowledge of the unknown is caused by self-evident principles, he can in a certain way be the cause that knowing exist in another, not as if he conferred on him knowledge of the principles, but by bringing into actuality what is implicitly and in a certain manner potentially contained in the principles through certain sensible signs shown to exterior sense, as was said above.

But the angel, because he naturally has an intellectual light more perfect than man's, in both ways can be cause of a man's knowing, in a manner inferior to God's, though superior to man's.

With regard to the light, although he cannot infuse intellectual light as God does, he can however strengthen the infused light for more perfect seeing. For whatever is imperfect in any genus, when it is linked to what is more perfect in that genus, has its power strengthened, something we see in bodies as well, for the located body is strengthened by the locating body, which relates to it as act to potency, as is said in *Physics* 4. With regard to the principles, the angel can also teach man, not indeed by conferring on him knowledge of these principles, as God does, nor by the deduction of conclusions from the principles by proposing sensible signs, as a man does, but by fashioning certain forms in the imagination which can be formed by the movement of the bodily organ, as is evident with the sleeping or mentally defective, who according to the diversity of vapours rising to the head have different phantasms. In this way, by mingling it with another species, it can come about that what the angels know is shown as conjoined with such images, as Augustine says in the *Literal Commentary on Genesis* 12.

Ad 1. It should be said that teaching invisibly, the angel teaches indeed inwardly by comparison with man's teaching, who proposes teaching to the exterior senses, but by comparison with the teaching of God, who acts within the mind, infusing light, the teaching of the angel is reputed outward.

Ad 2. It should be said that although the intention of the will cannot be forced, the intention of the sensitive part can be, as when someone is pierced he must be aware of the wound, and so it is with all other sensitive powers which use a bodily organ. And such an intention suffices for imagination.

Ad 3. It should be said that the angel infuses neither the light of grace nor the light of nature, but he strengthens the light of nature which is divinely infused, as has been said.

Ad 4. It should be said that just as there is a univocal agent in natural things that causes a form in the same manner that it has it, and an equivocal agent, which has it in a way other than he causes it, so too it is with teaching, because a man teaches a man as a univocal agent, and in this way passes on to another the knowledge as he himself has it, namely by deducing from causes to the caused. It is necessary therefore that the concepts of the teacher be made plain to the pupil through signs. But the angel teaches like an equivocal agent: for he knows in an intellectual manner what is manifested to man by way of reasoning. Hence man is not so taught by an angel that the concepts of the angel are made plain to him, but because knowledge is caused in man, according to his mode, of the things the angel knows in a far different mode.

Ad 5. It should be said that the Lord is speaking of that mode of teaching which belongs to God alone, as is clear from the Gloss on that text, and we do not ascribe this mode of teaching to the angel.

Ad 6. It should be said that he who teaches causes not truth, but knowledge of the truth, in the learner. The propositions which are taught are true before they are known because truth does not depend on our knowledge, but on the existence of things.

Ad 7. It should be said that although the science that we acquire through teaching is of indefectible things, none the less knowledge itself can fail. Hence it is not necessary that the illumination of doctrine be from an unfailing light, or if it is from an unfailing light as from a first principle, this does not wholly exclude a defectible created light, which can function as a mediating principle.

Ad 8. It should be said that among Christ's disciples it is known that some progressed to faith, such that first they venerated him as a wise man and teacher, and afterwards attended to him as to God teaching, hence the Gloss, a little later, says, 'Because Nathaniel knew that Christ though absent knew what he had done in that place, which is a sign of divinity, he confessed that he was not only a teacher, but the son of God.'

Ad 9. It should be said that the angel does not make the unknown truth manifest by this that he shows his own substance, but by proposing another truth that is more known, or by strengthening the light of intellect, so the argument does not work.

Ad 10. It should be said that Augustine's intention is not to deny that the angelic mind is of a more excellent nature than the human mind, but the angel is not midway between God and the human mind in such a way that the human mind in conjunction with the angel is formed in its ultimate form, as some held, so that the ultimate happiness of man consists in this that our intellect is conjoined to the intelligence, whose happiness in turn consists in this that he is conjoined to God.

Ad 11. It should be said that some of our powers are forced by subject and object, as the sensitive powers which are excited by the movement of their organ, and by the strength of the object. But the intellect is not forced on the part of the subject, since it does not use a bodily organ, though it is forced by the object, because by the efficaciousness of a demonstration one is forced to consent to the conclusion. But the will is forced neither as to subject nor by the object, but by its own incitement moves to this or that; hence only God who acts within can influence the will. But both man and angel can, in a certain way, act on intellect, by representing objects by which the intellect is forced.

Ad 12. It should be said that the angel neither creates the species in our mind nor immediately illumines phantasms, but by a continuation of his light with the light of our intellect, our intellect can more efficaciously illumine phantasms. However, if it also immediately illumines phantasms, from this it does not follow that the position of those philosophers is true, for although the intellect of the agent might illumine the phantasms, it can be said that this is not from him alone.

Ad 13. It should be said that imagination can receive what is in the human intellect though in another mode, and similarly the human intellect can grasp what is in the angelic intellect, in its own way. However, although the intellect of man has more in common with imagination as to subject, insofar as they are powers of the same soul, none the less it is more like the angelic intellect in kind, because both are immaterial powers.

Ad 14. It should be said that there is nothing to prevent the spiritual from being proportionate in this that it affects the corporeal, since nothing prevents the inferior from being acted on by the superior.

Ad 15. It should be said that the angel is not cause of the knowledge whereby a man knows things in their essence, but of that whereby it knows through likenesses. Not that the angel is closer to things than their likenesses, but because he causes likenesses of things in the mind, either by moving the imagination or by strengthening the light of intellect.

Ad 16. It should be said that to create signifies primary causality, which is found in God alone, but to make signifies causality in a common sense, and similarly to teach with reference to knowledge. Therefore only God is called creator, but God and angel and man can be called maker and teacher.

Ad 17. It should be said that even with respect to things that have determinate natural causes an angel can teach more than a man, since he knows more, and what he teaches he also teaches in a more noble manner. Hence the argument does not follow.

Article 4: Is teaching an act of the active or contemplative life?

It seems that it is an act of the contemplative.

1. The active life fails when the body does, as Gregory teaches in commenting on Ezekiel. But to teach does not fail with the body, because

the angels too, who lack body, teach, as has been said. Therefore it seems that teaching pertains to the contemplative life.

2. Moreover, as Gregory also says, the active life is first engaged in so that afterwards we might come to the contemplative. But teaching follows and does not precede contemplation. Therefore, to teach does not pertain to the active life.

3. Moreover, as Gregory says in the same place, since the active life is occupied with work it sees less, but it is necessary that one who teaches sees more than one who simply contemplates. Therefore teaching pertains rather to the contemplative than to the active.

4. Moreover, a thing is perfect in itself and passes on a like perfection to others for the same reason, just as through the same heat fire is hot and heats. But for one to be perfect in himself in the consideration of divine things pertains to the contemplative life. Therefore teaching too, which is the transmission of the same perfection to another, pertains to the contemplative life.

5. Moreover, the active life turns on temporal things, but teaching turns rather on the eternal, teaching about that which is more excellent and perfect. Therefore, teaching does not pertain to the active life, but to the contemplative.

ON THE CONTRARY:

1. In the same homily, Gregory says, 'The active life is to give bread to the hungry and to teach the word of wisdom to those who do not know it.'

2. Moreover, the works of mercy pertain to the active life, and teaching is numbered among spiritual alms. Therefore teaching is of the active life.

RESPONSE:

It should be said that the contemplative and active lives are distinguished from one another by end and by matter.

Temporal things, on which human acts bear, are the matter of the active life, whereas the matter of the contemplative is the notions of knowable things on which the contemplator dwells. This diversity of matter comes from the diversity of ends, just as in everything else the matter is determined according to the requirements of the end.

For the end of the contemplative life, as we now speak of it, is the seeing of truth; I mean uncreated truth to the degree possible for the one contemplating. Which in this life is imperfectly seen, but in the future life will be seen perfectly. Hence Gregory also says that the contemplative life begins here, that it might be perfected in the heavenly fatherland.

But the end of the active life is action, which is aimed at for its usefulness to neighbours.

We find a twofold matter in the act of teaching, a sign of which is that there is a double object conjoined to the act of teaching. One matter of it is the thing itself that is taught, another the one to whom the science is passed on. By reason of the first matter, the act of teaching pertains to the contemplative life, but by reason of the second to the active.

From the point of view of its end, teaching is seen to pertain to the active life alone, because its ultimate matter, in which it achieves the intended end, is the matter of the active life. Hence it pertains rather to the active than to the contemplative life, although it also in a certain way pertains to the contemplative, as is clear from what has been said.

Ad 1. It should be said that the active life in this respect fails with the body it is engaged in with labour and with which it supplies the infirmities of neighbours, in keeping with what Gregory says, that the active life is laborious, because it involves sweaty work, neither of which will obtain in the future life. Nevertheless, there is hierarchical action in the celestial spirits, as Dionysius says, and that action is of a higher mode than the active life of which we are treating. Hence the teaching there will also be far different from this teaching.

Ad 2. It should be said that Gregory in the same place writes that the well-ordered living is to move on to the contemplative from the active; but often the soul usefully applies to the active what is drawn from the contemplative, such that when the mind is kindled by the contemplative the active is more perfectly lived. It should be noted, however, that the active precedes the contemplative with respect to those acts in which it in no way is like the contemplative, but with respect to those acts which take their matter from the contemplative the active life must follow the contemplative.

Ad 3. It should be said that the vision of the teacher is the beginning of teaching, but the teaching itself consists rather in the transmission of knowledge of the things seen than in the vision of them. Hence the vision of the teacher pertains to the contemplative rather than to the active.

Ad 4. It should be said that that argument proves that the contemplative life is the principle of teaching; just as heat is not the heating but the principle of heating, so the contemplative life is found to be the principle of the active insofar as it directs it, just as conversely the active life disposes for the contemplative.

Ad 5. The solution is obvious from what has been said, because with respect to the first matter, teaching belongs to the contemplative, as has been said.

10. *On Conscience.* Disputed Question on Truth, *17* (1256–9)

Thomas's most haunting teaching on the matter of conscience is that, while a conscience always binds, it does not always excuse. So much for the exculpating trump of the appeal to conscience. After all, one's conscience may be badly formed and one may be culpable for that. This chapter consists of the seventeenth of the twenty-nine questions gathered into the Disputed Question on Truth. *It is preceded by a discussion of synderesis, which is to the precepts of natural law as intellect is to the first self-evident principles of reasoning. Each, that is, is the subjective hold on, or habit of, such principles. Conscience is introduced as the rational application to present contingent circumstances of the first principles of practical reason, viz. natural law. The disputed question below is the most extensive discussion of conscience in the writings of Thomas Aquinas. And it comes relatively early in his teaching life. This has led some to suggest that Thomas more or less discarded the notion in favour of an alternative and more Aristotelian analysis of moral reasoning – without, of course, any overt rejection of it. This is overstated but not without some basis. Later discussions are meagre. Conscience is the subject of Article 13 of Question 79 of Part 1 of the* Summa theologiae *– Article 12 is devoted to synderesis – and in the moral part of the* Summa, *conscience does not seem to occupy pride of place. It can of course be argued that in the supple, less complex and intentionally complete account of the* Summa, *we are better instructed on the relative importance of conscience in the full picture of human action. In any case, the text that follows is a unique and magnificent discussion of conscience. In reading Article 5, the reader might think of Newman's remark to the Duke of Norfolk that, if it came to it, he would toast first his conscience, then the Pope.*

QUESTION SEVENTEEN
ON CONSCIENCE

Article 1: The question is about conscience. And we ask first whether it is a power or habit or act.

1. It seems that it is a power, for Jerome says in his Gloss on Ezekiel 1.9, after he has made mention of synderesis, 'We see that sometimes this conscience is set aside,' from which it seems that conscience is the same as synderesis. But synderesis is in some way a power. Therefore conscience is too.

2. Moreover, only a power of the soul is a subject of vice; but conscience is subject to the stain of sin, as is clear from Titus 1.15, 'For both their mind and their conscience are defiled.' Therefore conscience is a power.

3. It will be said that the stain is not in conscience as in a subject. On the contrary, nothing numerically the same can be both stained and clean if it is not the subject of stain; but whatever changes from dirty to clean while remaining numerically the same thing is sometimes dirty and sometimes clean. Therefore, whatever changes from dirty to clean, or the reverse, is the subject of dirtiness and cleanliness. But conscience changes from filth to cleanliness. Hebrews 9.14: 'How much more will the blood of Christ, who through the Holy Spirit offered himself unblemished unto God, cleanse your conscience from dead works to serve the living God?' Therefore conscience is a power.

4. Moreover, conscience is said to be a dictate of reason, which dictate is nothing other than a judgement of reason; but reason's judgement pertains to free will [*arbitrium*], from which it is named; therefore free will and conscience appear to be the same; but free will is a power and so too must conscience be.

5. Moreover, Basil says that conscience is the natural seat of judgement [*iudicatorium*]; but synderesis is the natural seat of judgement, so conscience is the same as synderesis and since synderesis is in a way a power, so too is conscience.

6. Moreover, sin is only in will or reason; but sin is in conscience; therefore conscience is reason or will and, since reason and will are potencies, so too must conscience be.

7. Moreover, neither habit nor act is said to know, but conscience is said to know. Ecclesiastes 7.22: 'For thy conscience knoweth that thou

hast often spoken evil of others.' Therefore, conscience is neither a habit nor act and must be a power.

8. Moreover, Origen says that conscience is the 'rebuker of the spirit and a teacher resident in the soul whereby it is separated from evil things and adheres to the good'. But spirit names either a power of the soul or its very essence; therefore conscience names some power of the soul.

9. Moreover, conscience is either an act, a habit or a power. But it is not an act because an act does not always remain and is not in one sleeping who none the less is said to have a conscience. Nor is it a habit. Therefore, it is a power.

But that it is not a habit is shown thus:

1. No habit of reason is concerned with particulars; but conscience bears on particular acts; therefore, conscience is not a habit of reason or of any other power since conscience pertains to reason.

2. Moreover, in reason there are only speculative or practical habits; but conscience is not a speculative habit since it is ordered to action; nor is it an operative since it is neither art nor prudence – and these are the only ones the Philosopher in *Ethics* 6 places in the operative part. Therefore conscience is not a habit. That conscience is not art is obvious. That it isn't prudence is proved thus: prudence is right reason concerning things to be done, as is said in *Ethics* 6; but it can be concerned with singular possible deeds since these are infinite and reason cannot be of them. Again it would follow that prudence would be augmented, absolutely speaking, according to the consideration of more singular acts, which does not seem true. Conscience however does look to singular deeds. Therefore, conscience is not prudence.

3. But one says that conscience is a certain habit whereby the universal judgement of reason is applied to the particular deed. Against this: what can be brought about by one habit does not require two. But one having the universal habit can apply it to the singular through the mediation of the sensitive power alone, just as from the habit whereby one knows that every mule is sterile he may know that this mule is sterile when he perceives with the senses that it is a mule. Therefore no other habit is needed for the application of the universal judgement to the particular act.

4. Moreover, a habit is either natural or infused or acquired, but conscience is not a natural habit because such a habit is the same in everyone but all do not have the same conscience. Nor is it an infused habit which is always correct for conscience is sometimes incorrect. Nor is it an acquired habit because then children would not have a conscience

since a man acquires a habit as the result of many acts. Therefore conscience is not a habit, with the same result as before.

5. Moreover, according to the Philosopher a habit is acquired from many acts; but one has a conscience from one act; therefore conscience is not a habit.

6. Moreover, conscience is a punishment for the damned, as is said in the Gloss on 2 Corinthians 1.12; but a habit is rather a perfection than a penalty for the one having it; therefore conscience is not a habit.

ON THE CONTRARY:

It seems that conscience is a habit, for [1] conscience according to Damascene is 'the law of our intellect'; but the law of intellect is the habit of the universal principles of the law. Therefore conscience is a habit.

[2] Moreover, on 'When the Gentiles who have no law . . .' in Romans 2.14 the Gloss says, 'Although they had no written law they had, however, the natural law which everyone understands and by means of which everyone is conscious of what is good and evil'; from which is seen that natural law is that whereby each is conscious of himself and each is conscious of himself through conscience. Conscience, then, is natural law – the same conclusion as before.

[3] Moreover, science names the habit of the conclusion; but conscience is a kind of science; therefore it is a habit.

[4] Moreover, from the multiplication of acts a habit arises, but one acts frequently through conscience. Therefore from such acts a certain habit which can be called conscience is generated.

[5] Moreover, on 1 Timothy 1.5, 'Now the purpose of this charge is charity, from a pure heart and a good conscience and faith unfeigned,' the Gloss says 'good conscience, that is hope'. But hope is a certain habit, so too, then, is conscience.

[6] Moreover, that which is put into us by God seems to be an infused habit; but according to Damascene in *On Faith* 4 as tinder [*fomes*] is put in us by the demon so conscience is put in us by God. Therefore conscience is an infused habit.

[7] Moreover, according to the Philosopher in *Ethics* 2 everything in the soul is either a power or habit or passion; but conscience is not a passion because we neither merit nor the opposite by passions – 'we are neither praised nor blamed', as the Philosopher says. Nor again is it a power because a power cannot be laid aside as conscience can be. Therefore conscience is a habit.

ON THE CONTRARY:
It seems that conscience is an act, for [1] conscience is said to accuse or excuse; but one is accused or excused only insofar as he actually considers something; therefore conscience is a kind of act.

[2] Moreover, knowing which consists in a putting-together is actual knowing; but conscience names a science with a putting-together, for it is said to be a knowing-with [con-scire]. Therefore conscience is actually knowledge.

RESPONSE:
It should be said that some say that conscience is understood in three ways: for sometimes conscience is taken to mean the very thing known, as faith is sometimes taken to mean the thing believed; sometimes for the power whereby we know; sometimes for the habit; and by some it is sometimes taken for the act. The reason for this distinction seems to be that conscience is some act, and an act involves an object, power, habit and the act itself, and sometimes a name is used equivocally of these four, as 'understanding' sometimes signifies what is understood, sometimes the intellective power itself, sometimes indeed a habit, and sometimes the act. In namings of this sort we should follow linguistic usage because 'words are to be used as most people use them', as is said in Topics 2. It seems to be a matter of usage that conscience is sometimes taken for the thing known, as when it is said, 'I have my conscience,' that is, what is in my consciousness. The term cannot properly be attributed to the power or habit but only to the act, a meaning which is in harmony with all the things said of conscience.

Notice that the same word is used of act and power or habit only when some act is proper to the power or habit, as seeing is the proper act of the power of sight and knowing of the habit of science, and thus sight sometimes signifies the power and sometimes the act, and so too with knowing. If, however, there should be an act which belongs to several or even to all habits and powers, it is not customary to name any power or habit by its name, as is clear with the word 'use' which signifies the act of any habit. The act of any habit or power is the use of that whose act it is; hence this word 'use' signifies act and never power or habit. And so it seems to be with 'conscience'. The term conscience signifies the application of knowledge to something, hence to 'know with' [conscire] means, as it were, to know at the same time. But any science can be applied to something, so conscience cannot name any special habit or power, but it names the act which is the application of some habit or of some knowledge to a particular act.

Knowledge can be applied to an act in two ways: in one way insofar as we consider whether the act is or was; or, in another way, insofar as we ask whether the act is right or not.

According to the first kind of application we are said to have consciousness [*conscientiam*] of an act insofar as we know it to be an act that was done or not done, as is commonly meant when it is said that I have no conscience of this fact, that is, I do not or did not know whether the thing is or was done. It is in this sense that we should understand Genesis 43.22, 'We cannot tell who put it in our bags,' and Ecclesiastes 7.23, 'For thy conscience knoweth that thou hast often spoken evil of others.' In this way, conscience is said to testify to something, as in Romans 9.1, 'My conscience beareth me witness.'

According to the other way in which knowledge is applied to an act such that it is known whether it is right, there is a twofold path. One according as through the habit of science we are directed that we should or should not do something; another insofar as the act once done is examined by the habit of science as to whether it was right or not. This twofold path in actions is distinguished according to a twofold path that is found in theoretical matters, namely the way of discovering and the way of judging. For the way in which through knowledge we look into what ought to be done, as it were taking counsel, is like the discovery which starting from principles investigates conclusions. And the way in which we examine what has been done and discuss whether it is right is like the way of judgement which resolves conclusions into principles. We use the term conscience for both kinds of application. When knowledge is applied to an act in directing it, conscience is said to goad or persuade or bind; when knowledge is applied to an act in the manner of an examination of what has already been done, conscience is said to accuse or worry when what was done is found to be out of harmony with the knowledge by which it is examined, or to defend or excuse when what has been done is found to have taken place in conformity with the science.

It should be said, however, that in the first kind of application, when knowledge is applied to an act in order to know whether it was done, the application is a particular act of sensitive knowledge, of memory in which what was done is recorded, of the sense through which we perceive this particular act we are now doing. But in the second and third applications whereby we deliberate what ought to be done or examine what has been done, it is a habit of practical reason that is applied, namely the habit of synderesis and the habit of wisdom through which higher reason is perfected and the habit of science through which lower reason is perfected, whether all together or one alone should be applied. By these habits we examine what we have done and deliberate about what is to be done. Examination bears not only on what has been done but also on what is to be done, whereas deliberation concerns only things to be done.

Ad 1. It should be replied that when Jerome says, 'We see this conscience to be set aside,' he is not referring to synderesis itself, which he called the spark of conscience, but conscience as we spoke of it above. Or it could be said that the whole force of examining and deliberating with conscience depends on the judgement of synderesis, just as the whole truth of speculative reason depends on first principles, and therefore he calls conscience synderesis only insofar as it works from its force, especially when he wanted to express a failure of synderesis: it does not fail with respect to the universal but in the application of it to singulars. So synderesis does not itself fail but only in a certain way when conscience does. Therefore in explaining the failure of synderesis, he links it to conscience.

Ad 2. It should be said that a stain is not said to be in conscience as in a subject but as the known is in knowledge; for someone is said to have a stained conscience when he is conscious of some stain in himself.

Ad 3. It should be said that a stained conscience is said to be cleansed when someone who was first conscious of some sin in himself later knows that the sin has been cleansed away, and he is then said to have a clean conscience. Therefore it is the same conscience that before was unclean and after is clean, not indeed that the conscience is the subject of cleanness or uncleanness, but because both are known by the examining conscience. Nor is it numerically the same act whereby someone first knows himself to be unclean and later to be clean, but both are known from the same principles, as considerations which proceed from the same principles are called the same.

Ad 4. It should be said that the judgements of conscience and of free will in some ways differ and in some ways are similar. They are similar in that both bear on the particular act – it belongs to the judgement of conscience as examining – and in this the judgements of both differ from that of synderesis. But the judgement of conscience differs from that of free will because the judgement of conscience consists of pure knowledge, but the judgement of free will lies in the application of knowledge to the affections, which indeed is the judgement of choice. That is why it sometimes happens that the judgement of free will is perverted and not that of conscience. As when someone examines something imminently to be done and judges as if still speculating through principles that this is evil, for example, to fornicate with this woman. But when he begins to apply it to action, many circumstances of that act occur, for example the pleasure of fornication, from desire of which reason is bound and its dictate is not carried out in choice. In this way one errs in choosing and not in conscience; rather he acts against conscience and is said to do this with a bad conscience only insofar as what is done is not in accord with the judgement of knowledge. Evidently, then, conscience should not be said to be the same as free will.

Ad 5. It should be said that conscience is called the natural judging power insofar as every examination or deliberation of conscience depends on the natural judging power [*iudicatorium*], as was said above.

Ad 6. It should be said that sin is in reason and will as in a subject, in conscience in another way, as has been said.

Ad 7. It should be said that conscience is said to know something, not properly, but in that manner of speaking whereby that whereby we know is said to know.

Ad 8. It should be said that conscience is called spirit, that is the instinct of our spirit, insofar as reason is called spirit.

Ad 9. It should be said that conscience is neither a power nor a habit but an act, and, although the act of conscience is not permanent nor in one sleeping, this act remains in its root, and is in the habits applicable to the act.

We concede those arguments which prove that conscience is not a habit.

As to those which on the contrary object that it is a habit:

Ad 1. It should be said that conscience is called the law of our intellect because it is a judgement of reason deduced from natural law.

Ad 2. It should be said that one is said to be conscious of himself through natural law in the same manner of speaking that one is said to consider according to principles, but through conscience in that manner of speaking that one is said to consider by the very act of consideration.

Ad 3. It should be said that although science is a habit the application of science to something is not a habit but an act: and it is this that is meant by the word conscience.

Ad 4. It should be said that from acts no habit is generated of another kind than that from which the acts are elicited, but either some habit of the same kind, as from acts of infused charity an acquired habit of love is generated, or a pre-existing habit is strengthened, as in one who has the acquired habit of temperance that habit is strengthened by acts of temperance. Thus since the act of conscience proceeds from the habit of wisdom and science, no habit other than these is generated but they are perfected.

Ad 5. It should be said that when conscience is called hope it is a predication from its cause, insofar as a good conscience makes a man to be of good hope, as the Gloss explains.

Ad 6. It should be said that even those natural habits are in us by divine insertion [*immissio*], and therefore since conscience is an act proceeding from that natural habit that is synderesis, conscience is said to be of divine insertion, in the way in which all knowledge of the truth that is in us is said to be from God, by whom the knowledge of first principles has been placed in our nature.

Ad 7. It should be said that distinction of acts by the Philosopher is included in habit from the fact that he has proved that the habit is generated from acts and is the principle of similar acts. Thus conscience is neither passion nor power but an act which is reduced to a habit.

We concede the arguments which prove conscience to be an act.

Article 2: Can conscience err?

It seems that it cannot.

1. The natural judging power [*iudicatorium*] never errs, but conscience, according to Basil, is the natural judging power. Therefore it does not err.

2. Moreover, conscience adds something to science; that which it adds does not diminish the notion of knowledge; but science never errs because it is a habit thanks to which the true is always said, as is evident from *Ethics* 6. Therefore conscience cannot err.

3. Moreover, synderesis is the 'spark of conscience', as the Gloss on Ezekiel 1.9 says. Therefore conscience is compared to synderesis as fire to a spark, so what is true of synderesis is true of conscience. But synderesis does not err, and neither, then, does conscience.

4. Moreover, according to Damascene in *On Faith* 4, conscience is 'the law of our intellect'; but the law of our intellect is more certain than intellect itself; but 'intellect is always correct', as is said in *On the Soul* 3. Therefore even more so conscience is ever correct.

5. Moreover, reason in the part that touches synderesis does not err; but reason conjoined with synderesis makes conscience. Therefore conscience never errs.

6. Moreover, judgement rests on the word of witnesses; but in divine judgement conscience is as witness, as is clear from Romans 2.15, 'Their conscience bears witness to them . . .' Since then divine judgement cannot fail, it seems that conscience can never err.

7. Moreover, in all things it should be that the rule according to which others are measured should have unfailing rectitude; but the rule of human acts is conscience. Therefore it is necessary that conscience be always correct.

8. Moreover, hope is founded on conscience, as the Gloss says on 1 Timothy 1.5, 'from a pure heart and a good conscience . . .' But hope is most certain, as is said in Hebrews 6.18: 'We who have sought refuge in holding fast the hope before us. This hope we have, as a sure and firm anchor of the soul . . .' Therefore conscience has unfailing rectitude.

ON THE CONTRARY:

[1] There is what is said in John 16.2: 'Yes, the hour is coming for everyone who kills you to think that he is offering worship to God.' Therefore, conscience dictated to those who killed the apostles that they should kill them. But this was erroneous. Therefore conscience errs.

[2] Moreover, conscience means a kind of bringing together; but reason in bringing things together can be deceived. Therefore conscience can err.

RESPONSE:

It should be said that, as has been argued, conscience is nothing else than the application of science to some special act, in which application error can arise in two ways: in one way, because that which is applied contains an error in itself, in another way in this that it is not correctly applied. Just as in syllogizing fault comes about in two ways, either because one uses falsehoods, or because one does not reason correctly. That someone makes use of falsehoods can come about in one part but not in the other. It was said above that through conscience the knowledge of synderesis and of higher and lower reason is applied to the particular act under examination. Since the act is particular and the judgement of synderesis is universal, the judgement of synderesis can only be applied to the act if there is an assumption of some particular, which particular sometimes comes under higher reason and sometimes under lower reason. Thus conscience is perfected in a kind of particular syllogism. For example, if the judgement of synderesis states, 'Nothing prohibited by the law of God is to be done,' and from the knowledge of higher reason is taken, 'Sleeping with this woman would be against the law of God,' the application of conscience being made, the conclusion follows that 'Sleeping with this woman must be refrained from.'

In the universal judgement of synderesis error cannot occur, as is evident from the foregoing; but in the judgement of higher reason there can be an error as when one thinks God's law is against something, or for something, which it is not, like the heretics who believe an oath is prohibited by God, and in this way error can occur in conscience because of a falsehood that was in the higher part of reason. Similarly, error can come about in conscience from an error in the lower part of reason, as when someone errs in civil arguments about the just or unjust, the honourable or dishonourable. Conscience can also err when the application is not made in a correct manner, because just as in syllogizing in speculative matters it happens that the proper form of arguing is not maintained and from this falsehood shows up in the conclusion, so too can it happen in the syllogism required in things to be done, as has been said.

It should be known, however, that in some things conscience can never err, namely when the particular to which conscience is applied has a universal judgement about it in synderesis. For just as in speculative matters, no error occurs about particular conclusions that are assumed under universal principles in the same terms. No one could be deceived into thinking that *this* whole is greater than its part, nor could any conscience err in this that God ought not to be loved *by me* or that *some* evil ought to be done, because both in the syllogism about speculative things and about things to be done the major is self-evident as existing in a universal judgement, and the minor too in which the same thing is predicated of itself particularly, as when it is said: Every whole is greater than its part; this whole is a whole, therefore it is greater than its part.

Ad 1. It should be said that conscience is called the natural *iudicatorium* insofar as it is a certain conclusion deduced from the natural *iudicatorium*, in which error can occur, although not on account of an error of the natural *iudicatorium*, but on account of an error in the particular assumed, or on account of an improper mode of reasoning, as has been said.

Ad 2. It should be said that conscience adds to knowledge the application of knowledge to the particular act, and in this application there can be error even when there is no error in the knowledge. Or it should be said that when I say conscience I do not imply science taken only strictly, insofar as it is of truths alone, but science taken in a large sense for any knowledge, since whatever we know [*novimus*] in common usage we are said to have science of [*scire*].

Ad 3. It should be said that a spark is purer than fire and leaps above the whole fire, so synderesis is found to be that which is supreme in the judgement of conscience, so synderesis is metaphorically called the spark of conscience. But this does not entail that in all other respects synderesis is to conscience as spark is to fire. However, even in material fire something occurs in fire because of the addition of some alien matter which does not affect the spark by reason of its purity. So too an error can occur in conscience because of its mingling with particulars which are as alien matter to reason, which does not affect synderesis persisting in its purity.

Ad 4. It should be said that conscience is called the law of intellect because of that which it takes from synderesis, and error in it never occurs on this score but comes from elsewhere, as has been said.

Ad 5. It should be said that reason, thanks to being conjoined to synderesis, does not err. None the less, erring higher and lower reason can be applied to synderesis, as a false minor is added to a true major premiss.

Ad 6. It should be said that in judgement the words of witnesses rule when their testimony cannot be accused of falsity through certain manifest signs. In him in whom conscience errs, the testimony of conscience is proved false from the very dictate of synderesis, and thus the divine judgement is not ruled by the dictate of erring conscience but rather by the dictate of natural law.

Ad 7. It should be said that conscience is not the first rule of human acts, synderesis is; but conscience is a rule under a rule [*regula regulata*], so it is no surprise that error can occur in it.

Ad 8. It should be said that the hope that is based on right conscience has certainty, and this is graced hope; of the hope which is based on an erroneous conscience it is said, 'The hope of the impious will perish.'

Article 3: Third, it is asked whether conscience binds.

It seems that it does not.

1. Only a law binds with respect to things to be done; but man does not make a law for himself; therefore since conscience is an act of man, conscience does not bind.

2. Moreover, one is not bound by counsels; but conscience comes about by way of taking counsel, thus that conscience like counsel precedes choice; therefore conscience does not bind.

3. Moreover, one is only bound by a superior; but a man's conscience is not superior to the man himself; therefore man is not bound by his own conscience.

4. Moreover, it pertains to the same to bind and to loose; but conscience is insufficient to absolve a man; therefore it is insufficient to bind him.

ON THE CONTRARY:

[1] On Ecclesiastes 7.23, 'For thy conscience knoweth . . .' the Gloss says, 'by which judgement no one doing harm is absolved'; but the precept of the judge obliges. Therefore the dictate of conscience also obliges.

[2] Moreover, on Romans 14.23, 'Whatever is not of faith . . .' Origen takes the Apostle to say that I should say nothing, think nothing, do nothing save according to conscience. Therefore conscience binds.

RESPONSE:

It should be said without any doubt that conscience binds. In order to see the way in which it binds it should be noted that binding is transferred metaphorically from bodily to spiritual things. He who is bound is forced to stay in the place to which he is bound and his power to go elsewhere is removed; thus it is evident that binding has no place in things which are necessary in themselves – we don't say that fire is bound to be borne upward although it is necessary for it to be borne upward – but binding applies only to those necessary things on which necessity is imposed by another.

There are two kinds of necessity which can be imposed by another: one of force, when someone necessarily has to do something because of the action of the enforcer, since otherwise it would not properly be called force but inducement; another which is conditioned, namely on the supposition of some end, as a certain necessity is imposed on one when if he does not do such-and-such he will not receive a reward. The first kind of necessity, that of force, is not found in movements of the will but only in bodily things, because the will is naturally immune to force. But the second kind of necessity can be imposed on the will, such that one must choose this in order to attain a good or avoid an evil – to lack an evil is counted with having a good in such matters, as is clear from the Philosopher in *Ethics* 5.1. And just as the necessity of force is imposed on bodily things through some action, so too conditioned necessity is imposed on the will through some action. The act whereby the will is moved is the command of the king or governor, hence the Philosopher says in *Metaphysics* 5.1 that the king is a principle of motion through his command.

Such a command is to binding in voluntary matters – the kind of binding to which the will can be subject – as a bodily act is to binding bodily things with the necessity of force. The action of the bodily agent induces necessity in something only through the contact of that action with the thing acted on. And neither can the command of a king or lord bind anyone unless the command reaches the one commanded by it – and this is accomplished through knowledge. Thus no one is bound by a precept except through knowledge of the precept, and he who is incapable of knowledge of the precept is not bound by it, nor can anyone ignorant of the precept be said to be bound to act according to the precept except insofar as he is held to know the precept. If he neither knows it nor is held to know of it he is in no way bound by the precept. For just as in bodily things the bodily agent acts only through contact, so in spiritual matters the precept binds only through knowledge. Therefore just as it is the same force whereby touch acts and the power of the agent acts, nor can the latter act save through the former, so too it is the same power with which the precept binds and knowledge binds, since knowledge binds only through the power of the precept which can bind only through knowledge. Since conscience is nothing else than the application of knowledge to an act, it is clear that conscience is said to bind in virtue of the divine precept.

Ad 1. It should be said that man does not fashion a law for himself, but through the act of his knowledge whereby he knows the law fashioned by another he is bound to fulfil the law.

Ad 2. It should be said that counsel can mean two things: sometimes science is nothing other than the act of reason inquiring about things to be done, and counsel in this sense is to choice as the syllogism or question is to the conclusion, as is clear from the Philosopher in *Ethics* 3.8. So taken, counsel is not opposed to precept. In this sense we take counsel about the very things that are in the precept, and that is why one can be bound by counsel in this sense. In another sense, counsel means persuasion or inducement to do something which does not have coercive force. In this sense precepts are opposed to counsel's friendly exhortations. But conscience sometimes proceeds from counsel in this sense too, when knowledge of the counsel is applied to a particular act. But since conscience only binds due to the force of what it contains, the conscience that follows from counsel can bind only in the way counsel itself does, that is, one is not bound to fulfil it but is bound not to despise it.

Ad 3. It should be said that although a man is not superior to himself, that of which he has knowledge through the precept is higher, and in this way he is bound by his conscience.

Ad 4. It should be said that an erroneous conscience is insufficient to absolve when it sins from its own error, as when it errs about things it is held to know. If, however, it is an error about things one is not held to know, one is absolved by his conscience, as is evident in one who sins out of ignorance of fact, for example, lying with another's wife whom he thinks to be his own.

Article 4: Can an erroneous conscience bind?

It seems that it does not because:

1. As Augustine says, sin is any speech or deed or desire contrary to the law of God. Therefore nothing binds with the penalty of sin save the law of God; but an erroneous conscience is not according to the law of God, therefore it does not bind on penalty of sin.

2. Moreover, on Romans 13.1, 'Let everyone be subject to the higher authorities, for there exists no authority except from God,' the Gloss of Augustine says that one is not held to obey a lesser power against the command of a higher, as one is not held to obey the proconsul if he commands something contrary to the emperor. But conscience is inferior to God; therefore when conscience commands what is contrary to the precepts of God, the precept of such an erring conscience seems not to oblige.

3. Moreover, according to Ambrose sin is the transgression of the divine law and disobedience to heavenly mandates. Therefore, whoever deviates from obedience to divine law sins; but an erroneous conscience makes one deviate from obedience to the divine power as when one's conscience tells him he must do what is prohibited by divine law. Therefore an erroneous conscience when followed leads to sin rather than binds under penalty of sin if it is not observed.

4. Moreover, in law if someone is conscious that a wife comes to him who falls into a prohibited degree, and that conscience is probable, then he ought to follow it against the precept of the Church, even if the penalty be excommunication. If, however, it is not a probable conscience it does

not bind such that one must follow it, but one ought rather to obey the Church. But an erroneous conscience, particularly in the case of intrinsic evils, is in no way probable; therefore a conscience of this kind does not bind.

5. Moreover, God is more merciful than a temporal lord, but a temporal lord does not impute sin to a man for something done out of error; so much the less, then, would someone acting from an erroneous conscience be held sinful by God.

6. But one might say that an erroneous conscience binds in indifferent matters but not in those which are intrinsically evil. On the contrary, a conscience erring about intrinsically evil things would be said not to bind because the dictate of natural reason says the opposite; but so too natural reason dictates the opposite of an erroneous conscience erring in indifferent matters; so neither does it bind.

7. Moreover, an indifferent act can go either way, but what can go either way is not necessarily done or necessarily not done; therefore in indifferent matters one is not necessarily obligated by his conscience.

8. Moreover, if someone acts contrary to the law of God because of an erroneous conscience he is not excused from sin; if therefore one also sins by acting contrary to such an erring conscience, it would follow that whether or not he acts in accord with an erroneous conscience sin will result. Therefore he is in a dilemma such that he cannot avoid sin. But it seems impossible that someone sins because he cannot avoid it, according to Augustine; therefore it is impossible that such an erring conscience should bind.

9. Moreover, every sin falls into some category of sin; but if someone's conscience tells him to fornicate, abstaining from fornication cannot be put into any category of sin; therefore one acting contrary to such a conscience would not sin; therefore such a conscience does not bind.

ON THE CONTRARY:

[1] There is what is said in Romans 14.23, 'Whatever is not of faith is sin,' on which the Gloss says, 'That is, even what is good in itself can be a sin according to conscience.' But a conscience which prohibits that which is good in itself is an erroneous conscience. Therefore, such a conscience binds.

[2] Moreover, to observe what the [old] law requires after the time of revealed grace was not indifferent but intrinsically evil; hence it is said in Galatians 5.2, 'If you be circumcised, Christ will be of no advantage to you.' But a conscience saying that circumcision should be observed

obliged, hence in Galatians 5.3 is added, 'And I testify again to every man who has himself circumcised that he is bound to observe the whole Law.' Therefore an erroneous conscience binds even in intrinsically evil matters.

[3] Moreover, sin resides chiefly in the will. Whoever wills to transgress a divine precept has a bad will, and thus sins. But whoever believes something to be a precept and wills to transgress it, has the will not to serve the law; therefore he sins. One who has an erroneous conscience, whether about intrinsically evil matters or about whatever, believes that what is contrary to his conscience is contrary to the law of God. Therefore, if he wills to do it, he wills contrary to the will of God and thus sins. Thus a conscience in whatever way it be erroneous obliges on penalty of sin.

[4] Moreover, according to Damascene, conscience is the 'law of our intellect'. But to act against the law is a sin. Therefore in whatever way a conscience be erroneous, it binds.

RESPONSE:

It should be said that there are different opinions about this. For some say that a conscience may err either about intrinsic evils or about matters of indifference and that a conscience erring about intrinsic evil does not bind whereas it does bind in matters of indifference. But those who say this seem not to understand what it is for conscience to bind. That conscience binds means that when one does not follow it he incurs sin, not that one following it does the right thing. Otherwise counsel would be said to bind, since one following it acts rightly. But we say that counsels do not bind because if one sets them aside he does not sin; and we are said to be bound by precepts because we incur sin when we do not observe them. Therefore conscience is not said to oblige us to do something because to follow it is good but because not to follow entails sin. But it does not seem possible that anyone could evade sin if his conscience in whatever way it might err judges something to be the precept of God, whether it be a matter of intrinsic evil or matters of indifference, and decides to the contrary while he still has that conscience. Taken as such, he wills not to observe the law of God, and thus sins mortally. Therefore although such an erroneous conscience can be changed, none the less while it remains it is binding, and one transgressing it necessarily incurs sin. A correct and erroneous conscience binds differently, however: a correct one binds absolutely and as such, whereas an erroneous one does so accidentally and in a certain respect.

I say that the correct conscience binds absolutely because it binds absolutely in every event. For if someone had a conscience that adultery should be avoided, this conscience could not be changed without sin, because if he would change it he errs by that very fact and sins gravely. While it remains, it cannot be ignored in an action without sin, hence it binds absolutely and in every event. But an erroneous conscience binds only relatively speaking and under a condition: he whose conscience tells him he must fornicate is only obliged not to avoid fornication without sin under this condition: while this conscience endures. But this condition can be removed without sin, hence such a conscience does not oblige in every event, since something can happen, namely a change of conscience, after which one is no longer bound. What is the case only under a condition is said to be in a certain respect.

I say also that a correct conscience binds *per se*, but an erroneous accidentally. He who wills or loves something for the sake of something else, loves that for the sake of which he loves the first *per se*, and what he loves for the sake of another he loves accidentally. For example, he who loves wine for the sake of its sweetness, loves sweetness *per se* and wine accidentally. He who has an erroneous conscience, believing it to be correct – otherwise he would not err – adheres to the erroneous conscience on account of the rectitude he thinks it to have; he adheres then *per se* speaking to a correct conscience and to the erroneous as it were accidentally, insofar as the conscience he believes to be correct is erroneous. Thence it is that he is bound, properly speaking, by a correct conscience, and accidentally by the erroneous. This solution can be taken from the Philosopher's words in *Ethics* 7.9, where he asks practically the same question, namely whether it should be said that the incontinent is only one who withdraws from right reason or one who withdraws from false reason as well. He solves it by saying that the incontinent man withdraws *per se* from correct reason and accidentally from false – from the former simply speaking and from the latter in a certain respect, because what is *per se* is absolutely and what is accidental is in a certain respect.

Ad 1. It should be said therefore that although what an erroneous conscience dictates is not consonant with the law of God, it is taken by the one erring as the very law of God. Therefore *per se* if he violates it he violates the law of God, though not so accidentally.

Ad 2. It should be said that that argument works when there are distinct precepts of the superior and inferior and both arrive distinctly as such to the one obliged by the precept, which is not the case here because the dictate of conscience is the arrival of the precept of God to the one whose conscience it is, as is clear from the foregoing. It would be similar in the example proposed if the precept of the emperor could get to one only by the intermediary of the proconsul, and the proconsul would command what he does only as passing on the precept of the emperor. For then it would be the same thing to despise the precept of emperor and proconsul whether the proconsul told the truth or lied.

Ad 3. It should be said that an erroneous conscience erring about things which are intrinsically evil dictates what is contrary to the law of God, but says that what it dictates is the law of God; therefore one who transgresses this conscience is effectively a transgressor of the law of God, although in following this conscience and fulfilling it in deed he acts against the law of God and sins mortally, because in the very error there was sin since it came about through ignorance of that which he ought to know.

Ad 4. It should be said that when conscience is not probable it ought to be changed; but as long as it remains one sins mortally by acting against it. Hence by this it is not proven that an erroneous conscience does not bind while it remains but only that it does not bind simply speaking and in every event.

Ad 5. It should be said that from that argument it is not concluded that an erroneous conscience does not bind on penalty of sin if it is not fulfilled, but that if it is fulfilled it excuses from sin, hence it is not to the point. It concludes something true when the error itself is not a sin as for example when it is due to ignorance of fact. If, however, it is from ignorance of the law then it does not follow, because the very ignorance is a sin. Thus a secular judge does not excuse someone who pleads ignorance of a law which he ought to know.

Ad 6. It should be said that by natural reason one could arrive at the contrary of what the erroneous conscience dictates. Whether it be an error about indifferent or intrinsically evil acts, natural reason does not actually dictate the contrary; if it did conscience would not err.

Ad 7. It should be said that although an indifferent act as such can go either way, one who thinks it to fall under a precept makes it no longer indifferent on account of his judgement.

Ad 8. It should be said that he whose conscience tells him he ought to commit fornication is not in a dilemma simply speaking because he can do something which being done he would not fall into sin, namely, change his conscience. But he is in a dilemma in a certain respect, namely while the erroneous conscience remains; it is not absurd to say that, something being supposed, a man cannot avoid sin. For example, presupposing the intention of vainglory, he who is held to give alms cannot avoid sin, for if he gives with this intention, he sins, and if he does not give, he is a transgressor.

Ad 9. It should be said that when the erroneous conscience dictates that something ought to be done, it dictates it under some notion of good either as a work of justice or of temperance, and so on, and therefore the transgressor falls into the vice contrary to that virtue under which conscience dictates it; but if it dictates it under the aegis of a divine command or of some prelate one only incurs the sin of disobedience in transgressing conscience.

Article 5: In indifferent matters is conscience more binding than the command of a bishop?

It seems that it is less binding.

1. A religious subject vows obedience to his prelate, and he is held to keep his vow. Psalm 75.12: 'Make ye vows and pay them to the Lord your God.' It seems then that one is held to obey the command of the prelate rather than conscience.

2. Moreover, the prelate is always to be obeyed in things which are not against God. But matters of indifference are not against God. Therefore, in these he is held to obey the prelate, with the same result as in the previous case.

3. Moreover, the higher power is more to be obeyed than the lower, as the Gloss says on Romans 13.2. But the soul of the prelate is higher than that of the subject. Therefore the subject is more bound by the command of the prelate than by his own conscience.

4. Moreover, the subject ought not to judge the command of the prelate; rather the prelate judges the acts of the subject. But the subject would judge the command of the prelate if because of his own conscience he drew back from his command. Therefore, whatever conscience dictates in matters of indifference, he must go with the command of the prelate.

ON THE CONTRARY:
The spiritual bond is stronger than the corporeal, and is intrinsic rather than extrinsic. But conscience is an intrinsic spiritual bond and the prelate a corporeal and extrinsic one, as it seems, since every prelate acts by a

temporal dispensation. Hence with the coming of eternity it is dissolved, as the Gloss says on 1 Corinthians 15.24. Therefore it seems that conscience is to be obeyed rather than the prelate.

RESPONSE:
It should be said that the resolution of this question ought sufficiently to be seen from the foregoing.

For it was said above that conscience only binds because of the force of the divine command or because of the law of nature written within. Therefore, to compare the binding force of conscience and that of the command of the prelate is nothing other than to compare the binding force of the divine command and the command of the prelate. Hence, since the divine command binds against the command of the prelate, the binding force of conscience will be greater than the binding force of the prelate's command, and conscience will bind if the command of the prelate is contrary to it.

But this comes about differently depending on whether conscience is right or erroneous.

Correct conscience absolutely and perfectly obliges against the command of the prelate. Absolutely, because its obligation cannot be removed since such a conscience cannot be set aside without sin. Perfectly, because right conscience not only binds in this way that he who follows it incurs no sin, but also in that he is immune from sin no matter what command of the prelate be to the contrary.

Erroneous conscience binds against the command of the prelate in matters of indifference in a certain respect and imperfectly. In a certain respect, because it does not oblige in any event but only while it endures, for one can and ought to correct such a conscience. Imperfectly, because it binds insofar as he who follows it does not incur sin, but not in such a way that he avoids sin when the command of the prelate is to the contrary and obliges in that indifferent matter: in such a case he would sin, whether he acts, because he would act against his conscience, or whether he does not because he is disobedient to the prelate. He sins more if he does not do what his conscience dictates, while his [erroneous] conscience lasts, since it is more binding than the command of the prelate.

Ad 1. It should be said that he who vows obedience is held to obey in everything to which the good of obedience extends, nor can he be absolved from this obligation by an error of conscience, nor again can he be absolved from the binding force of conscience by this command: therefore he has two conflicting obligations. One of which, that of conscience, is greater, because more intense; the other is less and more dissolvable. The obligation to the prelate cannot be dissolved, as the erroneous conscience can be corrected.

Ad 2. It should be said that although that deed be indifferent in itself, it comes about that it is no longer indifferent by the dictate of conscience.

Ad 3. It should be said that although the prelate is superior to the subject, God, under the formality of whose command conscience is bound, is greater than the prelate.

Ad 4. It should be said that it is not for the subject to judge the command of the prelate, but to fulfil it. Everyone is bound to examine his acts in the light of the knowledge he has from God, whether natural, acquired or infused: every man ought to act according to reason.

PART THREE
ITALY (1259–68)

Thomas had been absent from Italy for some fourteen years when he returned in 1259, more likely than not first going to his home priory in Naples. I say more likely than not because historians are far from being of one mind on how Thomas spent the ten years before his return to Paris in 1269. If he did indeed return to Naples, he would have remained there until 1261 when he assumed the post of lecturer in the convent at Orvieto. It is thought that Thomas was associated with the papal court, which in those years was something of a movable feast, spending time in one town or another north of Rome. In Viterbo there is a pulpit on a street corner from which Thomas Aquinas allegedly preached during these years. From 1265 to 1268, Thomas was regent master at Santa Sabina in Rome.

But of course it is the works Thomas wrote during this period that most interest us. Before leaving Paris he conceived the idea of the *Summa contra Gentiles*, a work in four books, the first three of which were to be a defence of the faith on the basis of principles available to all, not only to adherents of other religions of the Book, but to non-believers as well. Only in Book 4 does Thomas claim to be mounting formally theological arguments, that is, arguments whose premisses are supernatural truths that God has chosen to reveal. The work was completed in 1265 and we have the bulk of the text in Thomas's own hand. But the text also indicates another factor in the literary production of Thomas, the help of secretaries. Increasingly, he would dictate to a Dominican *socius* assigned to him for this purpose. Reginald of Piperno thus makes his début in the career of Thomas, a faithful and devoted companion to the end. But there are other hands in evidence as well, indicating that Thomas had the help of more than one confrère in his writing.

Among the scriptural commentaries contemporary with the *Summa contra Gentiles*, mention must be made of that on Job. In the prologue Thomas tells us that he intends to produce a commentary on the literal meaning of the text, its moral meaning having been exhaustively treated by St Gregory the Great. Boleslaw Sobocinski, the logician, professed to be an admirer of this commentary because of its logical sophistication.

Increasingly, students of Thomas's biblical writings are recognizing the importance of his commentary on Job. Thomas also composed the extraordinary *Golden Chain* during this period, beginning it at Orvieto and completing it in Rome. Patristic sources are mined to produce a commentary on the four Gospels: it is one of the most self-effacing of Thomas's works. He is nowhere in it, yet of course presides over the selection and orchestration of the texts. This is a work that found its way into English because of the interest of John Henry Newman and his fellows in the Oxford Movement.

Thomas's three-year stay at Santa Sabina is notable for several reasons. First, the *Disputed Question on the Power of God*, from which we have selected the imposing Question 7 dealing with the divine simplicity and the reach of human language to speak of God. Second, in his final year in Rome, Thomas commented on Aristotle's *On the Soul*. This was the first of twelve commentaries on Aristotelian works he would compose during the next five years. Finally, it was in Rome that Thomas began the *Summa theologiae*, writing there the first part of that magisterial work.

As often as not, Thomas's teaching on proofs of God's existence is conveyed by a text in the Summa theologiae *in which he gives in crisp and succinct form five proofs, the famous* quinque viae. *This text has led many to assume that concentration on it alone suffices to understand and appraise the proof. Furthermore, those five ways of proving God's existence are preceded by a swift dismissal of the argument of St Anselm in his* Prologion. *The following selection contains both a more extended treatment of Anselm and a number of extremely sophisticated arguments drawn from Aristotle. Since Kant the kind of argument Anselm offered has been called an 'ontological argument', and the kind of proof that Thomas favours is called a 'cosmological argument': Thomas, in short, is no more impressed by Anselm's argument here than he would be in the later* Summa theologiae, *but he asks why it appeals so and has some interesting things to say in that regard. The two lengthy proofs from motion that Thomas lays out are, as he makes repeatedly clear, drawn from Aristotle. This is important because, complicated as these expositions are, they are at key points dependent on arguments that are mentioned but not formulated. The reader thus comes away with a dual conviction. Thomas, as a Christian believer, is insistent that God can be known to exist on the basis of natural reason. But it is also clear that he does not consider such proofs easy of attainment. His respect for Aristotle is palpable as he retains the proof of the* Physics. *From the perspective of the faith, the truths about God that the Philosopher achieves must look thin and meagre. None the less they attest to the reach of the human mind. The human mind fashions its concepts and forms propositions about the things of which we have sense experience. That our knowledge can extend beyond the sensible is far from being evident. The believer may be so accustomed to talk about God and of the way he exceeds and differs from the things around us that he is tempted to think that God is as available to us as the truth that there are things moving and being moved. That familiarity is the source of the appeal of the ontological argument, Thomas feels. It is not only in following the philosophical effort that Thomas sees how difficult it is. There are reasons within his faith to expect that this will be so. But there are also reasons to expect that it is possible to come to some knowledge of God from the things he has made, from his effects. The following texts represent the best Thomas ever wrote on the subject.*

SUMMA CONTRA GENTILES, BOOK I, CHAPTERS 9–14

9. On the manner and order of proceeding in this work.

From the foregoing it is evident that the wise man turns his intention to two kinds of truth in divine matters as well as to the destruction of the errors opposed to them. The one kind of truth pertains to the investigation of reason, whereas the other wholly exceeds the reach of reason. The twofold truth in divine things of which I speak is not on the side of God, who is one simple truth, but on the side of our knowledge, which is diversely related to divine things.

We ought therefore to proceed to showing the first kind of truth with demonstrative arguments by which the adversary can be convinced, but since such arguments cannot be had in the case of the second kind of truth, our intention ought not to be that the adversary should be convinced by such arguments, but rather that the arguments he has against the truth should be refuted, since natural reason cannot be contrary to the truth of faith, as has been shown. A singular way of convincing one's adversary of such truth is from the authority of Scripture divinely confirmed by miracles, for we can only believe what is above human reason if God reveals it. There are, however, some likely reasons that can be advanced for manifesting such truth for the exercise and solace of the faithful but not for convincing adversaries, because the insufficiency of such arguments would rather confirm them in error, since they might think that it is on the basis of such weak arguments that we assent to the truth of faith.

Proceeding in the manner proposed, we shall first try to manifest the truth that faith professes and reason investigates, setting forth demonstrative and probable arguments, some of which we have gathered from the books of philosophers and saints, so that the truth may be confirmed and the adversary convinced. Then, proceeding from the more to the less obvious, we shall go on to the manifestation of that truth which exceeds reason, answering the arguments of adversaries by probable arguments and authorities, as God provides them, declaring the truth of faith.

Turning, then, to the truths about God that reason can investigate, we shall consider first what belongs to God himself, second, his causing of creatures and, third, the way in which creatures are ordered to him as to their end.

With respect to what belongs to God in himself, let us first lay the necessary foundation for the whole enterprise by considering how God can be shown to exist, for unless this is established, there is nothing else to consider.

10. *On the opinion of those who say that the existence of God cannot be demonstrated because it is self-evident.*

The attempt to prove that God exists would perhaps seem superfluous to some, namely those who assert that it is self-evident that God exists, so much so that the contrary cannot be thought. In this case it cannot be demonstrated that God exists. Their position seems to follow from these considerations.

Those things are said to be self-evident which are known as soon as their terms are understood. For example, when it is known what a whole is and what a part is, it is immediately known that every whole is greater than its part. But to say that God exists is like that. For by the term 'God' we understand something than which nothing greater can be thought. This is formed in the mind of one who hears and understands the term 'God', and thus that God exists must be at least in his mind. But it cannot be in his mind alone, since what is in the mind and in reality is greater than that which is in the mind alone. But that nothing is greater than God is shown by the word itself. It follows then that God exists is self-evident, manifest from the very meaning of the term.

Again, it can be thought that there is something that cannot be thought not to exist. And this is manifestly greater than that which can be thought not to be. Thus, something could be thought to be greater than God, if he could be thought not to be, which is against the very meaning of the term. It follows that it is self-evident that God exists.

Again, those propositions are most known in which a thing is predicated of itself, such as, 'Man is man,' or of which the predicate enters into the definition of the subject, such as, 'Man is animal.' But in God, in a way beyond all other things, as will be shown below, his existence is his essence. It is as if the same answer were given to the questions 'What is he?' and 'Is he?' Therefore when it is said that God exists, either the predicate is the same as the subject or it is included in the definition of the subject. And thus to say that God exists is self-evident.

Moreover, things known naturally are known in themselves, for they are not known by an inquiry of reason. But that God exists is naturally known, since man's desire naturally tends to God as to his ultimate end, as will be shown below. Therefore it is self-evident that God exists.

Again, that by which all other things are known must be known of itself. But so it is with God, for just as the light of the sun is the principle of every visual perfection, so the divine light is the principle of all intelligible knowledge, since in him especially is to be found the first intelligible light. Therefore that God exists must be self-evident.

From this and similar considerations some thought that God's existence is so knowable of itself that its contrary cannot be thought.

11. The disproof of the foregoing opinion and the refutation of the arguments presented.

The foregoing opinion prospers. Partly because from the outset we are accustomed to hear God invoked and hear his name. Custom, especially that which dates from childhood, takes on the force of nature and as a result the things with which the mind has been imbued from childhood take such firm root that it is as if they were naturally known of themselves. Partly because what is self-evident as such and what is self-evident for us are not distinguished. Simply speaking, that God exists is self-evident since what God is is his existence. But because our mind cannot conceive what God is, he remains unknown to us. Similarly, it is simply self-evident that every whole is greater than its part, yet one who has not mentally grasped the notion of whole would not know it. Thus it happens that, with respect to things that are most knowable, our mind is as the eye of a nightbird towards the light of the sun, as is said in *Metaphysics* 2.

It is not necessary that God be known to exist immediately upon knowing that the name God means that than which nothing greater can be thought, since many of the ancients held that this world is God. Nor from the meanings of the name God that Damascene gives does anything of this kind follow. Even if everyone granted that the name God means that than which nothing greater can be thought, it is not necessary that that than which nothing greater can be thought should exist in reality. The thing and the meaning of the name must be given in the same way.

From the fact that the mind conceives what is meant by the name God, it follows only that God is in the intellect. It is not necessary that that than which nothing greater can be thought exist anywhere but in the intellect; it does not follow that in reality there exists that than which nothing greater can be thought. There is nothing absurd in denying that God exists. Nor is it absurd to hold that there can be something greater than whatever be given, in thought or reality, unless one already concedes that that than which nothing greater can be thought exists in reality.

Nor is it necessary, as the second argument proposes, that something greater than God can be thought if he can be thought not to exist. For he can be thought not to exist, not from any imperfection or uncertainty of his existence, since his existence is in itself most manifest, but because of the weakness of our intellect, which cannot intuit him in himself but can know him only from his effects and thus is led to knowledge of his existence by reasoning.

Thus the third argument too is refuted, for just as it is self-evident to us that the whole is greater than its part, so to those seeing the divine essence it is of itself most known that God exists because his essence is his existence. But because we cannot see his essence, we come to know of his existence from his effects and not in itself.

And the response to the fourth argument is also evident. For a man naturally knows God in the way he naturally desires him, but he naturally desires God insofar as he naturally desires happiness, which is a kind of likeness of the divine goodness. For this, it is not necessary that God himself be naturally known to men, but a likeness of him. For it is from his likeness, discovered in his effects, that we come to knowledge of God through reasoning.

The response to the fifth argument is also easily seen. For God is indeed that by which all things are known, not that other things are known only if he is known, as happens in the case of self-evident principles, but because all knowledge is caused in us by him.

12. On the opinion of those who say that God's existence cannot be demonstrated but can be held by faith alone.

There is another opinion, the contrary of the previous one, which would make useless the effort of those trying to prove that God exists. For they say that reason cannot discover that God exists, but this is accepted only by way of faith and revelation.

Some are prompted to say this because of the weakness of the arguments that others have proposed to prove that God exists.

This position can find false support in the sayings of some philosophers who show that in God essence and existence are identical, namely that what responds to the question 'What is it?' and to the question 'Is it?' are the same. But we cannot by way of reason come to know of God what he is. Therefore, we cannot by reason determine that he is.

Again, if according to the art of the philosopher one must take as a principle for showing that a thing is what the name signifies, and the notion signified by the name is a definition, according to the Philosopher in *Metaphysics* 4, there will be no way remaining to demonstrate that God exists, once knowledge of the divine essence or quiddity is removed.

Again, if the principles of demonstration have their origin in knowledge by sense, as is shown in the *Posterior Analytics*, what wholly exceeds every sense and sensible thing seems to be indemonstrable. But the existence of God is such. Therefore it is indemonstrable.

The falsity of this opinion is shown to us both by the art of demonstration which teaches that causes can be deduced from effects and from the order of the sciences themselves. For if there were no substance knowable beyond sensible substance, there would be no science beyond natural science, as is said in *Metaphysics* 4. Its falsity is also shown by the effort of philosophers who have tried to prove that God exists. Not to mention Romans 1.20, asserting with apostolic truth, 'His invisible attributes are clearly seen – his everlasting power also and divinity – being understood through the things that are made.'

Nor ought we to be moved by the fact that in God essence and existence are the same, as the first argument proposed. For this is understood of the existence whereby God subsists in himself, which is unknown to us as to how it is, as is his essence. But it is not understood of the existence that signifies the composition of intellect, for thus God's existence falls to demonstration when from demonstrative arguments our mind is led to form of God the proposition which expresses that God exists.

In arguments proving God's existence the divine essence or quiddity is not taken as a middle term, as the second argument proposed, but in place of quiddity the effect is used as middle, as happens in demonstrations of fact. From such an effect the meaning of the name God is drawn. For all the divine names are imposed either by the separation of God from his effects or by some relation of God to his effects.

From this it is clear as well that although God exceeds all sensibles and senses his effects, from which the demonstration is taken for proving that

God exists, are sensible. And thus the origin of our knowledge in sense holds even when what is known exceeds sense.

13. Arguments proving that God exists.

Having shown that it is not idle to try to prove that God exists, we go on now to set down the arguments by which both philosophers and Catholic doctors have proved that God exists.

First we will lay out the arguments by which Aristotle proves that God exists. He intends to prove this from the part of motion, and in two ways.

The first of which is this: Whatever is moved is moved by another. It is evident to sense that something is moved, for example, the sun. Therefore it is moved by some other mover. And either that mover is moved or not. If it is not moved, the thesis is proved that it is necessary to hold that there is something moving that is immobile. And this we call God. But if it is moved, it is then moved by some other mover. Either this goes on to infinity or we come to some immobile mover. But it cannot go on to infinity. Therefore we must hold that there is some immobile mover.

In this proof there are two propositions that must be proved, namely, that whatever is moved is moved by another and that in movers and moved things there cannot be an infinite regress.

The Philosopher proves the first of these in three ways. First, thus. If something moves itself, there must be within it a principle of its own motion, since otherwise it is manifestly moved by another. It is also necessary that it primarily be moved, namely that it be moved by reason of itself and not by reason of its part, as when an animal is moved by the motion of its foot, for then the whole would not be moved by itself but by its part, and one part by another. But it must also be divisible and have parts, since whatever is moved is divisible, as was proved in *Physics* 6. These things being supposed, he argues thus. What is held to be moved by itself is moved primarily. Thus when one part of it rests, it follows that the whole rests. For if when one part rests, another part of it should be moved, then the whole itself would not be what is primarily moved, but the part of it which is moved when the other rests. But nothing that rests when another rests is moved by itself, for that whose rest follows on the rest of another must be such that its motion follows on the motion of that other, and thus it is not moved by itself. Therefore that which was held to be moved by itself would not be moved by itself. Therefore it is necessary that whatever is moved is moved by another.

This argument is not impeded because someone might say that the part of that which is held to move itself cannot rest, and further that the rest or being moved of the part is only *per accidens*, as Avicenna craftily put it. The force of the arguments consists in this that if something moves itself primarily and as such and not by reason of the parts, it must be that its being moved does not depend on something. The being moved of this divisible, like its existence, depends on parts; and thus it cannot move itself primarily and *per se*. Therefore it is not required for the truth of the conclusion inferred that it be supposed that the part of the thing moving itself rest as if it were some absolute truth. But this conditional must be true: if the part should come to rest, the whole would come to rest. Which can of course be true even if the antecedent is impossible, just as this conditional is true: if man is an ass, he is irrational.

Second, he proves it by induction, thus: Whatever is moved incidentally is not moved by itself, for it is moved by the motion of another. Similarly neither is that which is moved by violence, as is obvious. Nor is that which is moved by nature, as moved of itself, like animals, which of course are moved by soul, nor what are moved by nature as the heavy and light, because they are moved by the one generating them and removing an impediment. But whatever is moved is moved either by itself or incidentally. If by itself, either by violence or by nature, and this is either moved from itself [*ex se*] like the animal, or is not moved from itself, like the heavy and light. Therefore whatever is moved is moved by another.

The third way he proves it is this. The same thing cannot be simultaneously actual and potential in the same respect. But whatever is moved is as such in potency, since motion is the act of something existing in potency just as such. But whatever moves is actual, as such, since nothing acts except insofar as it is actual. Therefore nothing is mover and moved with respect to the same motion. And thus nothing moves itself.

It should be known that Plato who held that every moving thing is moved understood the term motion more broadly than Aristotle. For Aristotle understood motion properly insofar as it is the act of something existing in potency just as such, and as such it is only in divisibles and bodies, as is proved in *Physics* 6. But according to Plato the thing moving itself is not a body, for he took motion to be any activity, such that to understand and think is a kind of being moved, a mode of speaking that Aristotle himself touches on in *On the Soul* 3. In this sense Plato said that the prime mover moves himself insofar as he understands himself and wills and loves himself. In some respects this is not in conflict with the arguments of Aristotle, for there is no difference between arriving at some first thing that moves itself, with Plato, and to come to a first that is in every way immobile, with Aristotle.

The other proposition, namely that in movers and moved things there is no infinite regress, he proves in three ways.

The first is this. If in movers and moved things we should proceed to infinity, it would be necessary that all such bodies be infinite, because whatever is moved is divisible body, as is proved in *Physics* 6. But every body that moves a moved thing is moved at the same time that it moves. Therefore all of these infinite bodies are moved at the same time that one of them is moved. But one of them, since it is finite, is moved in a finite time. Therefore all these infinite bodies are moved in a finite time. But this is impossible. Therefore it is impossible to proceed to infinity with movers and moved things.

That it is impossible for these infinites to be moved in a finite time he proves thus. Mover and moved must exist simultaneously, as he proves by induction in each of the species of motion. But bodies can exist together only by continuity and contiguity. Therefore since all the aforementioned movers and moved things are bodies, as has been proved, it is necessary that they are, as it were, one movable thing by continuity or contiguity. And thus one infinite thing would be moved in a finite time, which is impossible, as is proved in *Physics* 6.

The second argument is this. In ordered movers and moved things, one of which namely is moved by another in order, it must be the case that if you take away the first mover or if it ceases to move, none of the other things will move or be moved, because the first is the cause of moving in all the others. But if there were ordered movers and moved things to infinity, there would not be a first mover, but all would be as intermediate movers. Therefore none of them could be moved. And then nothing in the world would be moved.

The third proof comes to the same though by a changing of the order, beginning with the higher. That which moves instrumentally cannot move unless there be something that principally moves. But if there is an infinite regress in movers and moved things, all will be like instrumental movers, because they would be posited as moved movers, and nothing would be as the principal mover. Therefore nothing will be moved.

So go the proofs of both the propositions which are supposed in the first way of demonstration whereby Aristotle proves that there is a first unmoved mover.

The second way is this. If every mover is moved, his proposition is true either as such or only incidentally. If incidentally, then it is not necessary, for that which is incidentally true is not necessary. Therefore it is contingent that no mover is moved. But if the mover is not moved, it will not move, as the adversary says; therefore it is contingent that nothing is moved, for, if nothing moves, nothing is moved. But Aristotle takes this to be impossible, namely that at some time there should be no motion. Therefore the first is not contingent, because from a false contingent a false impossible does not follow. Thus this proposition, whatever moves is moved by another, is not incidentally true.

Again, if two things are incidentally linked in a third, and one of them is found without the other, it is probable that the latter can be found without the former. For example if white and musical are found in Socrates, and in Plato musical without white is found, it is probable that in someone else white can be found without musical. Therefore if moving and moved are linked in something incidentally, and being moved is found in something without this that it moves, it is probable that a mover can be found that is not moved. Nor can the instance of two, one of which depends on the other, be advanced against this, because they are linked *per se*, not incidentally.

But if the foregoing proposition is true *per se*, a similar impossibility or absurdity follows – because either it must be that the mover is moved by the same species of motion whereby it moves, or by another. If the same, then it will have to be that what alters is altered, and further that what heals is healed and that the teacher is taught and with respect to the same knowledge. But this is impossible, for it is necessary that the one teaching have knowledge and the learner not have it, and thus the same thing would be had and not had, which is impossible. But if it is moved by some other species of motion, such that the altering is moved locally, and the local mover is increased in size, and so on with the others, since the genera and species of motion are finite, this cannot go on to infinity. Thus there would be some first mover that is not moved by another. Unless perhaps someone should say that a turnaround takes place in such a way that, having completed all the genera and species of motion, we must go back to the first, and that which moves according to place is altered and the altering is increased, and that which causes increase would be moved according to place. But from this would follow the same as before, namely that that which moves according to some species of motion is moved according to the same species, although mediately, not immediately.

PROOF OF GOD'S EXISTENCE   253

We are left then with the necessity of holding that there is some first which is not moved by another outside it.

But because, given that there is a first mover that is not moved by anything external to it, it does not follow that it is in every way immobile, Aristotle continues, saying that this can be in either of two ways. First, such that the first is in every way immobile and, given that, the position is secured, namely that there is some first immobile mover. In another way, such that the first is moved by itself. This seems probable, because what is of itself is always prior to that which is because of another. So it is reasonable that in moved things the first is moved by itself and not by another.

But, given this, the same thing follows again, for it cannot be said that the whole is moved by the whole in the thing moving itself, because then the aforementioned absurdities would follow, namely that someone would at the same time teach and be taught, and similarly in the other motions, and again that something would be simultaneously in potency and in act, for the mover as such is in act, and what is moved is in potency. So it remains that one part of it alone is moved and the other moving. And thus the same thing as before follows, namely that something is an unmoved mover. It cannot be said that both parts are moved such that one is moved by the other, nor that one part moves itself as well as the other, nor that the whole moves the part, nor that the part moves the whole, because the previous absurdities would follow, namely that something is at the same time and with respect to the same motion mover and moved, and at the same time in potency and in act, and further that the whole would not be moving itself primarily but by reason of its part. So it follows that in that which moves itself, one part must be immobile and moving the other part.

But because in the things moving themselves that we know of, namely animals, the moving part – that is, the soul – although it is immobile of itself, still it is moved incidentally, he goes on to show that in the prime mover the part moving himself is not moved either as such or incidentally.

The things we know of that move themselves, namely animals, being corruptible, the moving part in them is moved incidentally. But corruptible self-movers must be reduced to some prime self-mover that is sempiternal. Therefore it is necessary that there be some mover of that which moves itself which is not moved, either *per se* or incidentally.

That it is necessary, on his view, that something moving itself be sempiternal is clear, for if motion is sempiternal, as he supposes, it is necessary that the generation of self-movers that are generable and corruptible should be perpetual. But the cause of this perpetuity cannot be one of the self-movers that is not always. Nor all at the same time. Both because they would be infinite, and because they would not all be at the same time. Therefore it remains that there must be some perpetual self-mover that causes the perpetuity of generation in the lower self-movers. And thus its mover is not moved either as such or incidentally.

Again, we see in self-movers that some begin to be moved afresh by some motion that is not caused by the animal itself, such as by digested food or a change of air, by which motion the thing moving itself is moved incidentally. From this it can be concluded that nothing moving itself is always moved if its mover is moved *per se* or incidentally. But the prime self-mover is always moved, otherwise his motion could not be sempiternal, since every other motion is caused by the prime self-mover. It remains then that the prime self-mover is moved by a mover that is not moved either as such or incidentally.

Nor is this argument threatened by the fact that movers of the lower orbs cause a sempiternal motion and yet are said to be moved incidentally, because they are said to be moved incidentally not by reason of themselves but by reason of their mobiles which follow the motion of the higher orb.

But because God is not a part of any self-mover, Aristotle pursues the matter further, in his *Metaphysics*, proceeding from this mover which is a part of the self-mover to another wholly separate, who is God. For since every self-mover is moved by desire, it is necessary that the mover that is part of a self-mover should be moved on account of some desirable. Which is superior to it in moving, for the desirer is in a certain way a moved mover, but the desirable is a mover wholly unmoved. Therefore it must be said that the separate prime mover is completely immobile and this is God.

Two things seem to weaken these arguments, of which the first is that they proceed on the supposition of the eternity of motion, which Catholics take to be false.

To this it must be said that the most efficacious way to prove that God exists is on the supposition of the eternity of the world since on that assumption it seems to be less obvious that God exists. For if the world and motion began as new, it is plain that there must be some cause which produces the world and motion, because whatever begins as new must take its origin from some cause, since nothing brings itself from potency to act or from not existing to existing.

The second difficulty is that the foregoing arguments presuppose that the first moved, namely the celestial body, is moved from itself, from which it follows that it is animate, and that is not conceded by all.

To this it should be said that if the first thing moved is not held to be moved from itself, it is necessary that it be immediately moved by the wholly immobile. Hence Aristotle introduces this conclusion under a disjunction: namely that we must either come to a separated first unmoved mover, or to something moving itself, from which again we come to a separate first unmoved mover.

The Philosopher proceeds in another way, in *Metaphysics* 2, to show that there cannot be an infinite regress in efficient causes, but we must come to one first cause, and this we call God. That way is this. In all ordered efficient causes, the first is the cause of the intermediate and the intermediate the cause of the last, whether there be one or many intermediates. The cause being removed, that of which it is the cause is removed. But if in efficient causes there is an infinite regress, none of the causes will be first. Therefore all the others are removed, since they are intermediates. But this is manifestly false. Therefore we must recognize that there is a first efficient cause that is God.

There is another argument that can be fashioned from the texts of Aristotle. For in *Metaphysics* 2 he shows that those things which are most true are also the greatest beings. But in *Metaphysics* 4 he shows that there is something most true, from the fact that we see that of two falsehoods one is more false than the other, hence it is necessary that one thing can be truer than another. But this is according to approximation to that which is simply and most true. From which it can be concluded further that there is something which is maximal being and this we call God.

Another argument to the same effect, put forward by Damascene, is drawn from the governance of things, which the Commentator also gestures towards in *Physics* 2, and it is this. It is impossible that contrary and dissonant things can harmonize in one order always or usually except by someone's governance, by which each and all are made to tend to a certain end. But in the world we see things of diverse natures harmonize in one order, not rarely and by chance, but always or for the most part. Therefore it is necessary that there be someone by whose providence the world is governed, and him we call God.

14. That the way of negation is necessary for knowledge of God.

Having shown that there is a first being that we call God, we must investigate his characteristics.

The way of remotion [or negation] is chiefly to be used in the consideration of the divine substance since the divine substance exceeds by its immensity every form that our intellect can attain, and thus we cannot apprehend it by knowing what it is. But we have knowledge of a sort of it by knowing what it is not. We come closer to knowledge of it insofar as we are able with our intellect to remove more things from it. We know anything more perfectly when we grasp more fully its differences from others, for each thing has its proper existence distinct from that of all other things. Hence in things whose definitions we know, we first place a thing in a genus, by which we know generally what it is, and afterwards add differences by which it is distinguished from other things, and thus complete knowledge of the substance of the thing is achieved.

But because in considering the divine substance we cannot grasp what it is as a genus nor its distinction from other things by affirmative differences, we must grasp it by negative differences. For just as a positive difference contracts a thing, we approach nearer to the complete designation of the thing insofar as more distinctions are made. So too when we say that God is not an accident, he is thereby distinguished from all accidents, and then if we add that he is not a body, we distinguish him also from some substances, and thus by such negations he is distinguished in an orderly way from everything that is other than himself. His substance will be properly thought of when it is known to be distinct from everything, but this will not be perfect knowledge, because what he is in himself will not be known.

Therefore in discussing God by way of remotion, we take as a principle that which is obvious from the foregoing, namely that God is in every way immobile. The authority of Sacred Scripture confirms this, for it is said in Malachi 3.6, 'For I am the Lord and I change not'; in James 1.17, 'With whom there is no change nor shadow of alteration'; and in Numbers 23.19, 'God is not a man, that he should lie: nor as the son of man, that he should be changed.'

Thomas began the Summa contra Gentiles *before leaving Paris for Italy in 1259, writing fifty-three chapters of Book 1. Once back in Italy, he revised those chapters and pressed on with the planned four books of the great summary of Christian doctrine. A good portion of the work in Thomas's hand has come down to us.*

A recurring question about this Summa *is what precisely is it – philosophy or theology? Thomas himself is quite clear on the matter. The first three books deal with truths accessible to unaided human reason, whereas Book 4 deals with truths of the faith which exceed the capacity of natural reason. The controversy continued none the less. If one's conception of philosophy is antiseptically modern, any mention of the faith and revelation will be considered irrelevant to the establishing of truths on the basis of premises available to all, believer and non-believer alike. To open those first three books is to enter a world very different from what philosophy has become. The pages are replete with references to Scripture. It is not surprising that some have felt that if this is philosophy, it is not philosophy in the sense the term has come to have in recent centuries.*

Very early on in Book 1, Thomas draws a distinction between truths of God that can be known by reason alone and truths about God that can only be held to be such on the basis of the gift of supernatural faith. Many of the matters discussed in the first three books amount to things Thomas and other believers hold to be true on the basis of faith. The study of Aristotle had led Thomas to see that some of the things that had been revealed and were to be found in Scripture had been established by argument in the works of pagan philosophers. In effect, the first three books of the Summa contra Gentiles *consist of philosophical arguments for these overlapping truths. Thomas's phrase for them was 'preambles of faith' (praeambula fidei). The arguments are meant to be cogent for non-believers as well as believers.*

The following chapters convey key concepts of Thomas's moral philosophy.

SUMMA CONTRA GENTILES, BOOK 3

Chapter 1

For the Lord is a great God, and a great King over all the gods: in his hand are the depths of the earth, and the heights of the mountains are his. The sea is his: for he made it, and the dry land which his hands formed.   Psalm 94.3–5

We have shown above that there is one first being possessing the full perfection of existence whom we call God and who from the abundance of his perfection grants being to all existing things. Thus not only is he the first of beings but the principle of all others. He grants existence to other things, not out of any necessity of nature, but of his free will, as is clear from the foregoing. The result is that he is the Lord of all the things he has made, for he rules over what is subject to his will. He has perfect dominion over the things produced by him, since in producing them he requires no external agent nor foundation of matter, since he is the cause of universal being.

Things which are voluntarily produced by an agent are each ordered to some end, for the good is the end and object of will, hence it is necessary that what proceeds from will is ordered to some end. But any thing attains its ultimate end through its action, which must be directed to the end by him who gives to things the principles through which they act.

Therefore it is necessary that God, who is completely perfect in himself and by his power grants existence to all beings, stand as the ruler of all beings and is directed by no one else. Nor is there anything outside his rule, since there is nothing that has not received existence from him. He is therefore perfect in ruling just as he is perfect in being and causing.

The effect of this rule is differently manifested in different things according to their different natures. There are some things produced by God that have intelligence and bear his likeness and represent his image. Hence they are not only directed but also direct their own actions to their proper end. And if by their own direction they are subject to divine rule, they are able to attain the ultimate end; but if by their own direction they depart from it, they are expelled. Things lacking intelligence do not direct themselves to the end but are directed by another. Some of these are incorruptible and neither in their natural being nor in their actions ever depart from the order to the end that has been set them, but are unfailingly subject to the first ruler: for example, celestial bodies whose motion is always uniform. Other such things are corruptible and can suffer defect in their nature – though this defect can be offset by something arising from it, as the corruption of one is the generation of another – and in their actions, which can deviate from the natural order, though this defect can be compensated for by a good arising from it. From which it is clear that these things do not depart from the order of the first ruler nor escape his power. These corruptible bodies, having been created by God, are perfectly subject to his power.

The Psalmist, therefore, filled with the Holy Spirit and pondering how he might show us the divine rule, first points out to us the perfection of the first ruler: perfection of nature, by calling him God; of power, by calling him the great Lord, as needing only his own power to produce his effect; of authority, by calling him the great King above all the gods, because, though many rule, all are subject to his dominion. Second, he describes for us the manner of his rule first with respect to intellectual beings which, by following his rule, achieve through Him their ultimate end, which is God himself: and therefore he says, because God will not forget his people. Then with respect to corruptible beings, because, even if from time to time they deviate in their proper activities, they are not removed from the power of the first ruler, so he says that the ends of the earth are in his hands. With respect to celestial bodies, which surpass the heights of the earth – that is, of corruptible bodies – and always abide by the right ordering of the first ruler, he says that the heights of the mountains are his. Third, he assigns the reason for this universal rule: it is necessary that the things God has made should be governed by him. And this is what he means when he says that the sea is his, etc.

Since in the first book we treated of the perfection of the divine nature and in the second of the perfection of his power, insofar as he is the maker and lord of all, it remains for us in this third book to treat of his perfect authority or dignity, insofar as he is the end and ruler of all things. This will be the order of procedure: first, to treat of him insofar as he is the end of all things; second, of his universal governance, insofar as he rules every creature; third, of his special governance, insofar as he rules creatures having intelligence.

Chapter 2: Every agent acts for an end.

It must first be shown that every agent, in acting, intends some end.

Of things which manifestly act for an end we say that that towards which they tend is their end, for the attainment of the end is the fulfilling of this and failure to fulfil it is to fall short of the end intended; for example a doctor acting to effect health and a man running towards a certain goal. In this respect, it doesn't matter whether what intends the end does so knowingly or not, for the target is the end both of the archer and of the arrow's flight. The bent of any agent tends to a definite thing: not just any sort of activity proceeds from an agent, whatever its kind, but heating from what is hot and cooling from what is cold. Thus activities are distinguished by the different kinds of agents. Sometimes an action terminates in a product, as construction in a house, healing in health; but sometimes not, as in the case of understanding and sensing. When an activity does end in a product, the bent of the agent tends by way of action to that product, but if it does not terminate in a product, the bent of the agent is to the activity itself, though in the former cases to a product by means of the activity.

Again, in all things acting for an end we call the ultimate end that beyond which the agent seeks nothing further, as the activity of the doctor extends to health and, when it is achieved, nothing further is striven for. But there is in any activity something beyond which the agent seeks nothing further; were this not so, actions would extend into infinity, which indeed is impossible, because, since the infinite cannot be traversed, the agent would not even begin to act, for nothing is moved towards that which it cannot attain. Therefore, every agent acts for an end.

Moreover, if the actions of an agent did proceed to infinity, either there is a product of such activities or not. If there is, its existence would be consequent upon an infinity of actions. But what requires an infinity of antecedents cannot be, for it is impossible for it to come to be, and what cannot possibly come into being it is impossible to do. That is why it is impossible for an agent to begin to do something which requires an infinity of actions. If on the other hand the actions have no product, their order either follows the order of the active powers, as when a man senses in order to imagine, imagines in order to understand, and understands in order to will; or it follows the order of objects, as when I consider body in order to consider soul, which I consider in order to consider a separate substance, which I consider in order to consider God. But it is impossible to proceed to infinity either in the order of active powers – any more than in the forms of things, as was shown in *Metaphysics* 2, and form is the principle of acting – or in the order of things, since there is a first being, as was proved earlier. It is impossible, therefore, for actions to proceed to infinity. There must then be something which, when had, brings the activity of the agent to rest. Therefore every agent acts for an end.

Again, in things which act for the sake of an end all the intermediates between the primary agent and the ultimate end are ends with respect to what is prior and active principles with respect to what follows. If then the effort of the agent is not directed to something definite, but actions, as has been suggested, proceed to infinity, active principles must be infinite in number. And this, as has been shown, is impossible. Therefore it is necessary that the striving of the agent be for something determinate.

Again, every agent acts either by nature or by intellect. But there is no doubt that things which act by intellect act for the sake of an end, for they act by preconceiving that which they pursue by their actions, acting on this preconception: this is what is meant by acting according to intellect. Now just as the whole likeness of the effect pre-exists in the intellect at which the knower aims by his actions, so in the natural agent there pre-exists the likeness of the natural effect by which the action is determined to an effect, for fire generates fire, and the olive an olive. Therefore, just as the intellectual agent tends to a determinate end by its action, so too does the natural agent. Therefore, every agent acts for the sake of an end.

Moreover, fault can only be found in things which are for the sake of an end, for fault is not imputed to something that fails to achieve what it is not aiming at. The doctor is at fault if he fails to cure, but not the builder or grammarian. But fault is to be found not only in things done according to art, as when the grammarian does not speak correctly, but also in things that occur by nature, as is evident when monsters are born. Therefore, both the natural agent and one who acts according to art and on purpose act for the sake of an end.

Again, if an agent were not to tend to some determinate effect, all effects would be indifferent to it. But something related indifferently to many does not do one of them rather than another, which is why in agents related equally to several, there can be no effect except insofar as it is brought about by something determined to one. Accordingly, it would be impossible [for the indifferent] to act. Therefore every agent tends to some determinate effect, which is called its end.

There are some actions which do not seem to be for the sake of an end, such as playful or contemplative activities and thoughtless deeds, such as scratching one's beard and the like. For this reason some have thought that something can be done though not for the sake of an end. With respect to contemplative activities, however, it should be noted that while they are not done for the sake of any further end, they are their own end. Playful activities are sometimes engaged in for their own sake, as when one plays for the sake of the pleasure to be had in the game, but sometimes for the sake of an end, as when we play in order to study better afterwards. Acts which are without thought are not intended but arise from imagination or a natural principle, as when an indisposition of the humours causes an itch which is the cause of scratching, which comes about without thought. But this is to tend towards an end, though one outside the order of intellect.

This excludes the error of the ancients who completely removed the final cause from things and held that everything comes about from the necessity of matter.

Chapter 3: Every agent acts for the sake of the good.

That every agent acts for the sake of an end is manifest from the fact that every agent tends to something determinate and what it determinately tends towards must be fitting for it, because it would tend towards it only because of some fittingness to itself. But what is fitting to something is its good. Therefore every agent acts for the sake of the good.

Moreover, the end is that in which the appetite of the agent or mover, as well as of what is moved, comes to rest. But it is the mark of the good that it terminates appetite: the good is that which all things seek. Every action and motion, therefore, is for the sake of the good.

Again, every action and motion seems ordered to existence in some way, either that it might be preserved in the species or individual, or that it might be newly acquired. But existence itself is good, which is why all things desire to exist. Therefore, every action and motion is for the sake of the good.

Moreover, every action and motion is for the sake of some perfection. For if the action is itself the end, it is manifestly the second perfection of the agent. If however the action is a changing of external matter, it is manifest that the mover intends to bring about some perfection in the thing moved, to which the movable too tends, if it is a natural motion.

But to be perfected is what we mean by being good. Therefore, every action and motion is for the sake of the good.

Again, every agent acts insofar as it is in act, but in acting it tends towards something similar to itself. Therefore, it tends towards some act, but act has the note of the good, for evil is found only in a potentiality falling short of act. Therefore every action is for the sake of the good.

Again, the intelligent agent acts for the sake of an end, determining itself to the end, but the natural agent, although it acts for an end, does not determine itself to the end, since it does not have the concept of end, but is moved to an end determined for it by another. The intelligent agent determines an end for itself only under the formality of the good, which is the object of will. Therefore, the natural agent neither moves nor acts for the sake of an end except insofar as it is good, since the end is determined for the natural agent by some appetite. Therefore, every agent acts for the sake of an end.

Again, to seek the good and to flee evil come to the same, just as to be moved from above and to move below receive the same account. But all things are seen to flee evil, for intelligent agents flee anything they apprehend as evil, and all natural agents, to the degree that they can, resist corruption, which is an evil for anything. Therefore all things act for the sake of the good.

Moreover, what any agent brings about outside its intention is said to come about by chance or fortune. But what we see come about in the works of nature is always or usually for the better, as in plants the leaves are designed to protect the fruit, and the parts of animals are designed for the safety of the animal. Now if this should come about apart from the intention of the natural agent, it would be by chance or fortune. But this is impossible, for things that happen always or usually are not chance or fortuitous events, but only what happens rarely, which is even more obvious in the case of intelligent agents. Therefore every agent in acting intends the good.

Again, whatever is moved is brought to the term of motion by the mover and agent. Therefore, mover and moved tend to the same. But what is moved, since it is in potency, tends to act, and thus to the perfect and good, and it is through motion that it passes from potency to act. Therefore, the mover and agent always intend the good when moving and acting.

That is why, when they defined the good, philosophers said that the good is what all things desire. And Dionysius, in *On the Divine Names* 4, says everything desires the good and the best.

Chapter 25: To know God is the end of every intellectual substance.

All creatures, even those lacking intelligence, are ordered to God as to their ultimate end, and they achieve this end insofar as they share some similarity with him. Intellectual creatures attain him in a more special manner, namely by understanding him through their proper activity. To understand God then must be the end of the intellectual creature.

For God is the ultimate end of every thing, as has been shown. Thus it is that a thing seeks to be united with God as to its ultimate end to the degree this is possible for it. But a thing is more intimately united with God insofar as it attains to his substance, which comes about when it knows something of the divine substance, which requires some likeness of him. Therefore the intellectual substance tends towards divine knowledge as to its ultimate end.

Moreover, the proper activity of anything is its end, for it is its second perfection, which is why something is called virtuous or good insofar as it performs its proper activity well. But understanding is the proper activity of the intellectual substance and is therefore its end, since the greatest perfection of that activity is the ultimate end, especially in those acts which like sensing and understanding are not ordered to effects. Since such activities are specified and differentiated by their objects, it follows that they are perfect to the degree that their objects are. Thus to understand the most perfect intelligible object, which is God, is the most perfect of acts of understanding. Therefore to know God by understanding is the ultimate end of the intellectual substance.

Someone might object that although the ultimate end of an intellectual substance consists in understanding the most intelligible object, what is most intelligible for this or that intellectual substance is not what is absolutely most intelligible; rather, the higher the intellectual substance, the higher will be what it can understand. The highest created intellectual substance might perhaps have as its highest object what is most intelligible simply, and its happiness would thus consist in understanding God, but the happiness of a lesser intellectual substance would consist in understanding a lesser object which would none the less be highest for it. It seems particularly true that the human intellect, because of its weakness, does not understand what is absolutely most intelligible, for it relates to the most intelligible as the eye of a night bird to the sun.

But clearly the end of any intellectual creature, even the least, is to understand God. For it was shown above that the ultimate end to which any creature tends is God. But the human intellect, although it is the least in the hierarchy of intellectual substances, is none the less above things lacking intellect. But since of more noble creatures there should not be a less noble end, to understand God is the end of human intellect too. Every intelligent thing attains its ultimate end by understanding it, as has been shown. Therefore it is by way of understanding that the human intellect attains to God as its ultimate end.

Moreover, just as things lacking intellect tend to God as their end by way of assimilation, so do intellectual substances by way of knowledge, as is clear from the foregoing. Although things lacking intellect tend towards a similitude with proximate agents, the intention of nature does not come to rest there, but has as end the assimilation with the highest good, as is clear from what has been said, although such things can attain this similitude only most imperfectly. Therefore, however little an intellect can grasp of divine knowledge, that little will be its ultimate end, rather than perfect knowledge of less intelligible things.

Moreover, a thing especially desires its ultimate end. But the human intellect desires and loves and takes more delight in knowledge of divine things, though it can grasp but a little of them, than in the perfect knowledge it has of lesser things. Therefore, to understand God in some way is man's ultimate end.

Again, anything tends to a divine similitude as to its proper end, and that by which anything is made most like to God is its ultimate end. The intellectual creature is especially assimilated to God because it is intellectual: this similitude sets it apart from other creatures and includes all other [similitudes]. With respect to this type of similitude, however, the greater similarity lies in actually rather than merely potentially or habitually understanding God, because God is always actually understanding, as was proved in Book 1. But our actually understanding is most similar to God's insofar as we understand God himself, for God in understanding himself understands all else, as was proved in Book 1. Therefore, to understand God is the ultimate end of every intellectual substance.

Again, what is lovable only for the sake of another is lovable for the sake of what is lovable in itself or there would be an infinite regress in natural appetite, and that cannot be since then the desire of nature would be frustrated, because an infinite series is inexhaustible. But all practical sciences and arts and powers are desirable only for the sake of something else, for their end is not to know but to do (or make). Speculative sciences are desirable for their own sake, for their end is knowing itself. Indeed there is no other human activity other than speculative thought that is not ordered to some further end, for even the playing of games, which doesn't seem to be done for the sake of an end, has an appropriate end, namely mental relaxation, since after play we seem mentally keener and more studious. If play were engaged in for its own sake, we would play always, which is inappropriate. Therefore all practical arts are ordered to the speculative and similarly all human activities to the intellect's speculation, as to their end. For the ultimate end of all ordered sciences and arts is found in that which orders and is architectonic with respect to them, just as the art of navigation, which pertains to the use of the ship, is architectonic and directive of shipbuilding. Just so first philosophy relates to the other speculative sciences, for all others depend on it, as it were, receiving their principles from it as well as help against those who deny the principles. But the whole of first philosophy is ordered to knowledge of God as to its ultimate end, which is why it is also called divine science. Therefore knowledge of God is the ultimate end of all human knowledge and activity.

Again, in all ordered agents and movers the end of the first agent and mover must be the ultimate end of all, as the end of the leader of the army is the end of all those serving under him. Of all the parts of man, the intellect is seen to be the higher mover, for intellect moves the appetite by proposing an object to it, and intellectual appetite, that is, will, moves the sensitive appetites, namely, the irascible and concupiscible, since we never obey concupiscence without a command of will; the sensitive appetites, the consent of will advening, then move the body. The end of intellect therefore is the end of all human activities, but the end and good of intellect is the true. Consequently, the ultimate end is the First Truth. Therefore the ultimate end of the whole man and of all his operations and desires, is to know the First Truth, which is God.

Furthermore, there is a natural desire in men to know the causes of what they see. Hence because of the wonder induced by what is seen, the causes of which are hidden, men first began to philosophize, and when they discovered the cause they were content. Nor did inquiry cease until they had come to the first cause. For we think ourselves to know perfectly when we know the first cause. Therefore man naturally desires to know the first cause as his ultimate end. But God is the first cause of all; therefore man's ultimate end is to know God.

Moreover, given any effect man naturally desires to know its cause. Now the human intellect knows universal being, and therefore desires to know its cause, which is God alone, as was proved in Book 2. Therefore it is not just the attainment of any ultimate end that assuages natural desire. For it is not knowledge of just any intelligible thing that suffices for human happiness, which is the ultimate end, but divine knowledge, which terminates natural desire as its ultimate end. Therefore, man's ultimate end is knowledge of God.

Moreover, a body which tends to its proper place by natural appetite, moves more vehemently and faster as it nears its end; hence Aristotle proves in *On the Heavens* 1 that straight natural motion cannot be infinite because it would not be moved more before than after; that which tends towards something more vehemently after than it did before, is not moved to infinity, but tends towards something determinate. We find this in the desire for knowing, for the more someone knows the more he wants to know. Therefore man's natural desire for knowing tends to some determinate end, and this can only be the most noble of knowable objects, which is God. Therefore divine knowledge is the ultimate end of man.

The ultimate end of man, as of any intellectual substance, is called felicity or happiness. For it is this that every intellectual substance desires as its ultimate end and for its own sake. Therefore it is the happiness and felicity of every intellectual substance to know God.

Thus we read in Matthew 5.8, 'Blessed are the clean of heart, for they shall see God,' and in John 17.3, 'This is life eternal, that they might know thee, the true God.'

Aristotle agrees with this judgement in the final book of the *Ethics*, where he says that man's happiness is speculative, that is, speculation bearing on the best speculable object.

Chapter 26: Does happiness consist in an act of will?

Because the intellectual substance attains God by his own activity and not only by knowing but also through the act of will, desiring and loving him and taking its delight in him, it might seem that the ultimate end, and the ultimate happiness of man, should lie not in knowing God, but rather in loving him or in some other act of will relating to him. Especially since the object of the will is the good, which has the note of end, whereas the true, which is the object of intellect, has the note of end only insofar as it is a good. Thus it seems that man does not attain the ultimate end through an act of intellect but rather through an act of will.

Moreover, the ultimate perfection of an activity is pleasure, which perfects an operation the way beauty does youth, as the Philosopher says in *Ethics* 10. Therefore, if the perfect operation is the ultimate end, it seems that the ultimate end lies rather in the operation of will than of intellect.

Again, pleasure seems always to be desired for itself and not for the sake of something else, for it is silly to ask someone why he wants to be pleased. But to be sought for its own sake is a mark of the ultimate end. Therefore the end seems to lie in the activity of will rather than in that of intellect.

Again, all especially agree in desire of the ultimate end, since it is natural, but more seek pleasure than knowledge. Therefore, the end seems to be pleasure rather than knowledge.

Moreover, will seems to be a higher power than intellect, for the will moves intellect to its act: intellect actually considers what it habitually knows when one wills it to. Therefore, the ultimate end, which is happiness, seems to consist in an act of will rather than an act of intellect.

This can be clearly shown to be impossible.

Since happiness is the proper good of the intellectual nature, it must come to an intellectual nature according to what is peculiar to it. But appetite is not peculiar to intellectual nature since it is in everything, though differently in different things. But this difference arises from the fact that things are differently related to knowledge. For things which completely lack knowledge have only a natural appetite, and things which have sense knowledge have sensitive appetite, which includes the irascible and concupiscible. And things that have intellectual knowledge also have an appetite proportional to it, namely the will. Therefore the will, insofar as it is an appetite, is not peculiar to intellectual nature. Happiness, then, and felicity are found substantially and principally in the act of intellect rather than the act of will.

Again, in all powers which are moved by their objects, the objects are naturally prior to the acts of those powers, just as the mover is naturally prior to the mobile thing's being moved. The will is a power of this kind, for the appetitible moves the will. Therefore, the object of will is naturally prior to its act and its first object precedes any of its acts. That is why the act of will cannot be the first thing willed. But that is just what the ultimate end or happiness is. Therefore it is impossible that happiness or felicity should lie in the act of will itself.

Moreover, in all powers which can reflect on their own acts, the act must first bear on some other object and only afterwards on its own act. For if intellect understands itself to understand, it must first be given that it understands some thing and then understands itself to understand: for the understanding that intellect understands is of some object. Thus, either we proceed to infinity or, if we come to some first thing understood, that cannot be understanding itself, but some intelligible thing. Similarly, the first thing willed cannot be the act itself of willing, but some good thing. But the first thing willed by an intellectual nature is happiness or felicity itself: it is for its sake that we will whatever we will. Therefore it is impossible for happiness to consist essentially in an act of will.

Moreover, the truth of anything's nature is according to the things which make up its substance, for a true man differs from a picture in the things which constitute the substance of a man. But true happiness does not differ from false happiness according to an act of the will, for the will is the same in desiring and loving and taking delight, whatever it be that is proposed to it as the highest good, whether true or false. Whether what is proposed as the highest good is true or false is determined by intellect. Therefore, happiness or felicity consists essentially in intellect rather than in an act of will.

Again, if some act of will were itself happiness this act would be desiring or loving or taking delight. But it is impossible that desire should be the ultimate end, for desire occurs when the will tends to what it does not yet have, which is contrary to the meaning of ultimate end. For good is not only loved when it is had but also when it is not, for it is by love that the not-had is sought by desire, and if love of what is already had is more perfect, this follows from the fact that the good loved is had. Therefore, having the good, which is the ultimate end, is different from loving, which before possession is imperfect though perfect after possession. No more can pleasure be the ultimate end. For it is the having of the good which causes pleasure, either when we are aware that we now have the good, or when we remember having had it or when we hope to have it in the future. Pleasure therefore is not the ultimate end. Indeed no act of will can itself be what happiness substantially is.

Again, if pleasure were the ultimate end, it would be sought for its own sake, which is false. For the pleasure desired is gauged on the basis of the object on which the pleasure follows; if the pleasure follows on good activities that ought to be desired it is good and desirable, but if on evils it is evil and to be avoided. So pleasure is good and desirable because of something else. Therefore, it is not the ultimate end or happiness.

Again, the right order of things agrees with the order of nature, for natural things are ordered to their ends without error. But in natural things, pleasure is for the sake of operation, and not the reverse. For we observe that nature attaches pleasure to those operations of animals which are clearly ordered to necessary ends, such as taking food, which is ordered to the preservation of the individual, and venereal pleasure, which is ordered to the preservation of the species. If pleasure did not accompany them, animals might abstain from these necessary matters. Therefore, it is impossible for pleasure to be the ultimate end.

Again, pleasure is nothing but the will's coming to rest in an agreeable good, just as desire is the inclination of will to attain some good. And just as a man is inclined through will to the end and rests in it, so natural bodies have natural inclinations to their proper ends and come to rest when those ends are attained. It is ridiculous to say that it is not the end of the heavy body to be in its proper place, but the repose of the inclination by which it tends to it. For if nature principally intended that its inclination should find repose, it would not give it, for it gives it in order that through it a body might tend to its proper place, which when attained, as an end, the repose of the inclination follows. Therefore the repose as such is not the end, but concomitant with the end. Nor can pleasure itself be the ultimate end, but it is a concomitant of it. So much the less can any act of will be happiness.

Moreover, if some exterior thing should be something's end, the activity by which it first attained that thing would also be called its ultimate end, as having money is said to be the end of those whose end is money, not the wanting of it. But God is the ultimate end of the intellectual substance and that operation whereby a man first attains God is said to be substantially his happiness or felicity. But this is understanding, because we cannot will what we do not know. Therefore the ultimate felicity of man lies substantially in knowing God with his intellect, not in an act of will.

The solution to the earlier objections is clear from what has now been said.

It is not necessary, because happiness is defined as the highest good, that it must substantially be an act of will, as the first argument maintained. Indeed, from the fact that it is its first object, it follows that it is not its act, as is clear from the foregoing.

Nor is it necessary that everything by which a thing is perfected should be its end, as the second argument assumes, for a thing's perfection is of two kinds: in one way, of a thing when it is constituted in a given species, in another way, of a thing already having a species, for example the perfection of something already a house is that for which a house is built, namely being lived in, for a house is only built for this purpose, and that is why to be lived in should be put in its definition for it to be complete.

The perfection with respect to the species of house is both what is required for it to be of that species, its substantial principles, and what serves to make it more fitting, such as the beauty of the house. But that which is the perfection of a thing as already constituted in a species is its end, as being lived in is of the house. Similarly, the proper activity of a thing, which is, as it were, its use, is its end. The perfection of a thing with regard to its species is not its end: rather it is their end for matter and form are for the sake of the species. For though form is the end of generation, it is not the end of the thing generated and having a species; in fact form is sought in order that the species might be complete. Similarly, what preserves a thing in its species, such as health and the nutritive power, though they perfect the animal, are not the end of the animal, but rather vice versa, like beauty of a man, strength of body, and the like, of which the Philosopher says in *Ethics* 1 that they serve happiness instrumentally. Pleasure, however, is the perfection of activity, not as if the activity were ordered to it according to its species, but it is ordered to other ends, as eating is ordered to the species of the thing for the preservation of the individual. It is similar to the perfection which is ordered to the species of the thing since because of pleasure we bend ourselves more attentively and properly to the activity in which we delight. Hence in *Ethics* 10 the Philosopher says that pleasure perfects activities as comeliness does youth, which indeed is for the sake of the one having youth, not the reverse.

The fact that men desire pleasure for its own sake and not because it is for the sake of something else is insufficient sign that pleasure is the ultimate end, as the third argument concludes. For pleasure, although it is not the ultimate end, is none the less a concomitant of the ultimate end, since pleasure follows on the attainment of the end.

There are not many who seek the pleasure to be found in knowing rather than knowledge itself, but many seek sensible pleasure rather than intellectual knowledge and the pleasure consequent upon it. For most men know external things, because of the fact that human knowledge takes its rise from sensible things.

The fifth argument which maintains that will is higher than intellect because it is its mover is manifestly false. It is intellect which as such and in the first place moves the will, for will, as such, is moved by its object, which is the good apprehended. The will moves intellect as it were accidentally, that is insofar as understanding itself is apprehended as a good, and thus it is desired by will, with the result that intellect actually understands. This is the reason that intellect precedes will, for will never desires to understand unless intellect first apprehends understanding as a good. Again, the will moves intellect actually to know in the way in which an agent is said to move; but intellect moves will in the way in which the end moves, since the known good is the end of will, but the agent is subsequent to the end in moving, for the agent moves only for the sake of the end. It is evident then that intellect is higher than will simply, but will is superior to intellect accidentally and in a certain respect.

Chapter 27: Human happiness does not lie in pleasure.

From the foregoing it is evident that it is impossible that human happiness should consist in bodily pleasures, the chief of which are found in food and sex.

For it was shown that according to the natural order pleasure is for the sake of activity and not conversely. Therefore, if activities were not the ultimate end, neither could the pleasures following on them be the ultimate end, nor those concomitant with the ultimate end. But the activities on which these pleasures follow are not the ultimate end, for they are ordered to certain obvious ends, eating to the preservation of the body and coition to the generation of a child. Therefore these pleasures are neither the ultimate end nor those concomitant with the ultimate end. Therefore the ultimate end should not be located in them.

Again, will is higher than sense appetite, for it moves it, as was said above. But happiness does not consist in an act of will, as has already been shown. Far less then will it be found in the aforementioned pleasures, which are in sense appetite.

Moreover, happiness is a good proper to man, for beasts cannot properly be called happy. But the pleasures in question are common to man and beast. Therefore, happiness is not to be sought in them.

Again, its ultimate end is the noblest among a thing's features, for it has the note of the best. But these pleasures do not belong to man according to what is most noble in him, which is intellect, but according to sense. Therefore happiness is not to be sought in such pleasures.

Moreover, man's highest perfection cannot lie in that which links him with lesser things, but rather in what links him to some higher thing, for the end is better than that which is for the sake of the end. But the pleasures in question consist in this that man is linked to things less than himself thanks to sense, namely to sensible things. Happiness, then, is not to be sought in such pleasures.

Moreover, what is good only insofar as it is moderated is not good of itself but receives goodness from the moderating. But the enjoyment of the aforementioned pleasures is only good for man as moderated, otherwise these pleasures would impede one another. Such pleasures, then, are not in themselves the good of man, but the highest good is that which is good of itself, and what is good in itself is better than that which is good through something else. Such pleasures, then, are not man's highest good, which is happiness.

Again, in things taken in themselves, more follows on more, if both what follows and what is followed be taken simply as such. For example, if what is hot heats, the hotter will heat more, and the hottest will heat the most. Therefore, if such pleasures were good of themselves, the maximal enjoyment of them would be best. But this is clearly false, since excess is accounted vice and is harmful to the body as well as an obstacle to other such pleasures. They cannot, therefore, be man's good as such, nor can human happiness consist of them.

Moreover, acts of virtue are praiseworthy because they are ordered to happiness. If then human happiness were to consist of such pleasures, acts of virtue would be praiseworthy by acceding to rather than abstaining from such pleasures. But this is false. For the act of temperance is especially praised for abstaining from pleasures, hence its name. Man's happiness, therefore, is not found in such pleasures.

Moreover, God is the ultimate end of everything, as is clear from the foregoing. That then should be accounted man's ultimate end by which he especially draws near to God. But by the pleasures in question a man is impeded from drawing closest to God, for that comes about through contemplation, which these pleasures especially impede, since they immerse a man in the sensible order, thereby drawing him away from intelligible things. It is not in bodily pleasures, therefore, that human happiness is to be sought.

The error of the Epicureans who held that happiness consists in sensual delights is thereby rejected. Solomon in Ecclesiastes 5.18, speaking in their name, says, 'This therefore hath seemed good to me, that a man should eat and drink and enjoy the fruit of his labour . . . and this is his portion.' And in Wisdom 2.9: 'Let us everywhere leave tokens of joy: for this is our portion and this is our lot.' The error of the Cerinthiani is also rejected: they held that in the ultimate happiness to be had after the resurrection there would be a thousand years of the reign of Christ according to carnal pleasure. That is why they are called Chiliasts or Millenarists. Also rejected are fables of Jews and Saracens that saw the reward of the just to lie in such pleasures. Happiness is the reward of virtue.

Chapter 28: Happiness does not consist of honours.

It is also clear from the foregoing that the highest good of man, or happiness, does not lie in honours.

Man's ultimate end and his happiness lie in his most perfect activity, as is clear from the above. A man's honour is not a matter of his own deed but of another's towards him, who shows him reverence. That is why happiness ought not to be sought in honours.

Again, that which is desirable for the sake of some other good is not the ultimate end. But such is honour, for no one is rightly honoured save for some good in him, which is why men seek honour as though wishing to receive acknowledgement of some good in them, and why they rejoice more if they are honoured by the great and wise. Man's happiness, therefore, is not to be sought in honours.

Moreover, one achieves happiness through virtue, and the acts of virtue are voluntary, since otherwise they would not be praiseworthy. Therefore it is necessary that happiness lie in some good that a man can voluntarily achieve. But it is not in a man's power that he be honoured: that lies with the one bestowing honour. Therefore, human happiness ought not to be sought in honours.

Again, a man is worthy of honour only because of the good that is in him. But the evil too can be honoured. Therefore it is better to become worthy of honour than to be honoured and honour is not man's highest good.

Moreover, the highest good is the perfect good which permits no alloy of evil. That in which there is no evil cannot be evil. Therefore there is no evil in the highest good. But a bad man can receive honour. Therefore honour is not man's highest good.

Chapter 29: Human happiness does not consist of glory.

From this it is clear that man's highest good cannot lie in glory either, which is the celebration of reputation.

Cicero says that glory is the constant praise of someone's reputation and Ambrose calls it full acknowledgement with praise. Men seek

THE HUMAN GOOD 275

the acknowledgement of praise and renown in order to be honoured by those to whom they become known. Glory, therefore, is sought for the sake of honour, so if honour is not the highest good, glory is even less so.

Again, goods are praiseworthy which show that one is ordered to the end, but what is ordered to the end has not yet reached the ultimate end. Therefore praise is not accorded to one who has already attained the ultimate end, but rather honour, as the Philosopher says in *Ethics* 1. Therefore, glory cannot be the highest good since it consists principally in praise.

Moreover, to know is nobler than to be known, for only the more noble of things know whereas the least are known. Therefore, man's highest good cannot be glory, which comes about when someone is known.

Again, one only desires to be known for good things and wants his evil to be hidden. To be known is good and desirable on account of the goods that are recognized in someone. These then are better. Therefore the highest good of man is not glory which consists in someone's being known.

Moreover, the highest good must be perfect since it assuages appetite; the knowledge of renown, in which human glory consists, is imperfect, for it is something full of uncertainties and error. Therefore such glory cannot be the highest good.

Again, that which is man's highest good must be the most stable of human things, for the enduring constancy of the good is naturally desired. But glory, which consists in renown, is most unstable, since nothing is more mutable than human opinion and praise. Such glory, therefore, is not the highest good of man.

Chapter 30: Human happiness does not lie in riches.

It follows that riches cannot be the highest good of man for riches are only sought for the sake of something else; they carry nothing of the good in themselves but only when we use them, either to sustain the body or for something like. What is the highest good, however, is desired for its own sake and not for the sake of something else. Therefore riches cannot be the highest good of man.

Again, the possession and saving of things whose chief benefit for man lies in their being dispersed cannot be the highest good of man. But riches benefit most when they are expended, for this is their use. Therefore, the possession of riches cannot be the highest good of man.

Further, the act of virtue is praiseworthy insofar as it brings happiness. The acts of liberality and munificence are praiseworthy rather because they deal with the expenditure of money than with its conservation: hence the derivation of their names. Therefore happiness does not consist in the possession of riches.

Again, that the possession of which is man's highest good must be better than man, but man is better than riches which are things ordered to man's use. The highest good of man, therefore, does not lie in riches.

Moreover, man's highest good is not subject to fortune, since the fortuitous comes about without the application of reason. But man must achieve his proper end through reason. But fortune plays a maximal role in the pursuit of wealth. Therefore human happiness does not lie in riches.

This becomes even more evident from the fact that riches are involuntarily lost, that they can bring evils which the highest good must lack, that they are unstable, and other like things which can be derived from our earlier arguments.

Chapter 31: Happiness does not consist in worldly power.

Similarly, worldly power cannot be man's highest good because in obtaining it too a great deal of luck is involved, it is unstable, it is not subject to a man's will, and many evils attend it – all of which are repugnant to the highest good, as is evident from what has gone before.

Again, a man is called good especially insofar as he attains the highest good. But he is called neither good nor bad because he has power, for nothing is good just because it can bring about good, nor bad just because it can bring about evils. And that is why the highest good cannot lie in the fact that one has power.

Again, all power is related to something else. But the highest good is not related to something else. Therefore, power is not man's highest good.

Moreover, that which can be used well or badly cannot be man's highest good, since what cannot be badly used is better. But power is something that can be used well or badly, for rational powers are open to opposites. Therefore human power is not man's highest good.

Moreover, if any power were the highest good, it would have to be the most perfect. But human power is most imperfect, for it is rooted in the wills and opinions of men in which there is the greatest inconstancy. And the greater the power is thought to be the more it depends on man, which contributes to its weakness, since what depends on many can be destroyed in many ways. Therefore worldly power is not man's highest good.

Man's happiness, therefore, does not consist in any external good, since all external goods, which are called goods of fortune, are contained among those discussed.

Chapter 32: Happiness does not consist in bodily goods.

Similar considerations will show that man's highest good does not lie in goods of the body, such as health, beauty and strength, for these too are common to the good and evil, are unstable and are not subject to will.

Moreover, the soul is better than the body, which only lives and has the aforementioned goods through the soul. Therefore since the good of the soul, such as understanding and the like, is better than the good of body, the good of body cannot be man's highest good.

Again, these goods are common to man and other animals, but felicity is man's proper good. Therefore man's felicity cannot lie in such goods.

Moreover, many animals excel men with respect to goods of the body, for some are swifter than man, some more robust, and so on with others. Therefore, if man's highest good were to lie in these, man would not be the best of animals, which is clearly false.

Chapter 33: Human happiness does not lie in the senses.

For much the same reasons it is apparent that man's highest good cannot lie in goods of the sensitive part, for these goods too are common to man and other animals.

Again, intellect is better than sense; therefore the good of intellect is better than the good of sense. Man's highest good, therefore, cannot lie in sense.

Again, the keenest sense pleasure lies in food and sex, in which the highest good would have to lie, if it were in sense. However, it does not lie in these, and therefore man's highest good is not in sense.

Moreover, the senses are loved for their usefulness and for the sake of knowledge. But the whole usefulness of sense is with respect to goods of body. But sense knowledge is ordered to intellectual, hence animals lacking intellect delight in sensing only with reference to its usefulness with respect to body, insofar as good and sex are consequent upon sense knowledge. Therefore, man's highest good, which is happiness, does not lie in the sensitive part.

Chapter 34: Man's happiness does not lie in acts of the moral virtues.

It seems that man's ultimate happiness does not lie in moral activities either.

Human happiness is not ordered to a further end if it is ultimate. But all moral activities are ordered to something else, which is evident from the chief among them. Acts of courage, which occur in warfare, are ordered to victory and peace, for it would be stupid to make war for its own sake. Similarly acts of justice are ordered to keeping the peace among men which comes about when everyone has what is his. Therefore human happiness does not consist in moral activity.

Again, moral virtues are for the sake of preserving the mean in inner passions and external things, but it could not be that the moderating of passions and of external goods is the ultimate end of human life. These passions and external things are ordered to something else, so it is not possible that the ultimate happiness of man should lie in acts of the moral virtues.

Moreover, since a man is a man because he possesses reason, it is necessary that his proper good, which is happiness, should be something proper to reason. But that which is intrinsic to reason is more proper to it than what it brings about in another. Therefore, since the good of moral virtue is something of reason established in other things, it could not be what is best for man as happiness is, which is rather some good situated in reason itself.

Again, it was shown above that the ultimate end of things is to be assimilated to God. Therefore, man's happiness will lie in that which most assimilates him to God. But this does not come about through the moral virtues, since such acts can only be attributed to God metaphorically, because God does not have passions or anything like them, which are the subject of moral virtues. Therefore, man's ultimate happiness, which is his ultimate end, does not consist in the moral acts.

Moreover, happiness is the proper good of man. Therefore his ultimate happiness must be sought in that good which is the most proper of all the human goods in contrast to the other animals, and the acts of moral virtues are not that, for some animals partake something of liberality or courage, but no animal partakes anything of intellectual activity. Therefore man's ultimate happiness is not in moral acts.

Chapter 35: Ultimate happiness does not lie in the act of prudence.

From this it is also clear that man's ultimate happiness does not lie in the act of prudence.

For the act of prudence deals only with moral virtues, and man's ultimate happiness does not lie in acts of moral virtues. Therefore, not in the act of prudence.

Again, man's ultimate happiness lies in his best activity, but the best activity of man, with respect to what is proper to him, relates to the most perfect objects. The activity of prudence does not bear on the most perfect objects of intellect or reason, for it deals with contingent things to be done, not necessary things. Therefore, man's ultimate happiness does not lie in its activity.

Moreover, what is ordered to another as its end is not man's ultimate happiness. But the act of prudence is ordered to another as to an end, both because all practical knowledge, which includes prudence, is ordered to activity, and also because prudence disposes a man to act well with regard to things to be chosen, as is clear in Aristotle, *Ethics* 6. Therefore, man's ultimate happiness does not lie in the act of prudence.

Again, irrational animals partake nothing of happiness, as Aristotle proves in *Ethics* 1, but they do partake something of prudence, as is clear from the same author in *Metaphysics* 1. Therefore, happiness does not consist in the activity of prudence.

Chapter 36: Happiness does not consist in artistic activity.

It is also clear that it cannot consist in artistic activity.

Because the knowledge of art is also practical and thus ordered to an end and cannot itself be the ultimate end.

Moreover, the artefact is the end of artistic activity, and it cannot be the ultimate end of human life, since we are rather the end of all artefacts, because all of them are made for the benefit of man. Therefore ultimate happiness cannot lie in artistic activity.

Chapter 37: Man's ultimate happiness lies in the contemplation of God.

If man's ultimate happiness does not lie in those external things which are called the goods of fortune, nor in goods of the body, nor in the goods of soul whether of the sensitive part or, in the intellectual part, in the acts of moral virtue, nor in any intellectual activities pertaining to action, namely, art and prudence, it remains that man's ultimate happiness lies in the contemplation of truth.

This is the only activity of man that is peculiar to him and is in no way shared by the other animals.

Nor is it ordered to anything else as its end, since contemplation of truth is sought for its own sake.

By this activity man is linked with higher things by way of similitude, since only this among human activities is found in God and the separated substances.

And by this activity he attains those higher things by knowing them in some manner.

And man is sufficient to himself with respect to this activity, needing for it little help from external things.

To this all other human activities are seen to be ordered as to their end. For the perfection of contemplation requires a sound body to which are ordered all the artefacts necessary for life. It requires as well freedom from the disturbance of the passions, something secured by the moral virtues and prudence, and from external disturbance, to which civil governance is ordered. So, rightly considered, all human functions seem to be at the service of those contemplating the truth.

It is not possible, however, that man's ultimate happiness should consist in the contemplation consequent on the understanding of principles, which is most imperfect because most universal, comprising the potential knowledge of all things; moreover, it is the beginning, not the end, of human study, granted to us by nature and not due to the pursuit of the truth. Nor could ultimate happiness be found in the sciences which have things below as their objects, since happiness must be located in that intellectual activity which bears on the most noble of intelligible things. It remains, then, that man's ultimate happiness consists in the contemplation of wisdom, which is the consideration of things divine.

Thus what was proved earlier by argument is also clear from induction, namely that man's ultimate happiness consists in the contemplation of God.

*Chapter 38: Human happiness does not consist in the
knowledge of God.*

There remains to ask in what kind of knowledge of God the ultimate happiness of the intellectual substance consists. For there is a common and confused knowledge of God which is had by all men, whether because it is self-evident that God exists, like the principles of demonstration, which seemed so to some as we pointed out in Book 1, or which seems rather to be true, because by natural reason man can come straightaway to some kind of knowledge of God. For when men see natural things occurring in an orderly fashion, and there is no order without someone ordering, they perceive, for the most part, that there is something ordering the things they see. But what it be, or of what kind, or whether there be but one ordering nature is not known straightaway from this common consideration. For just as when we see a man move and accomplish other works, we perceive that there is in him some cause of these activities which is not in other things, and we call this cause the soul, still we don't yet know what the soul is, whether it is a body, or how it brings about these activities.

It is not possible that this knowledge should be sufficient for happiness. For the activities of the happy person must be without defect, but this knowledge can have many errors mixed up in it, for some believed that the things of this world had nothing else ordering them than celestial bodies, so they called the celestial bodies gods. Some said the very elements from which these things are generated were gods, maintaining that the motion and other natural activities they manifest have no other cause of being than such things themselves, and other things are ordered by them. Some held that human acts are subject to no ordering other than the human, and they called the men who ordered others gods. This knowledge of God does not, then, suffice for happiness.

Moreover, happiness is the end of human acts, but human acts are not ordered to the foregoing knowledge as to their end; indeed it is had by all straightaway from the beginning. It is not in this knowledge of God, therefore, that happiness consists.

Again, no one seems blameworthy because he lacks happiness, rather those lacking it and striving for it are praised. But from the fact that one lacks the foregoing knowledge of God he appears especially blameworthy, for one would be accounted quite stupid if he did not perceive such manifest signs of God, just as someone who saw a man and did not grasp that he had a soul would be thought stupid. Thus the Psalmist says, 'The fool has said in his heart, there is no God.' Therefore it is not this knowledge of God that suffices for happiness.

Moreover, knowledge of what is common rather than proper to a thing is most imperfect, for example the knowledge of a man insofar as he moves, for by such knowledge he is known only potentially, since the proper is potentially contained in the common. But happiness is a perfect activity, and man's highest good must be according to what is actual, not what is potential, for it is insofar as potency is perfected by act that it has the mark of the good. Therefore, this kind of knowledge of God is not sufficient for happiness.

Chapter 39: Human happiness does not consist in the knowledge of God had through demonstration.

There is another kind of knowledge of God, higher than the former, which is had by way of demonstration by which we gain proper knowledge of him, for by demonstration many things are removed from him, by the denial of which his difference from others is understood. For demonstration shows God to be immobile, eternal, incorporeal, in every way simple, one, and the like, which we proved of God in Book 1. We arrive at proper knowledge of a thing not only through affirmations but also through negations, for just as it is proper to man to be a rational animal, so it is proper to him not to be inanimate or irrational. But there is this difference between these two modes of proper knowledge, that by affirmations we have proper knowledge of the thing, knowing that it is a thing and separate from others, whereas the proper knowledge of a thing achieved by negation tells us that the thing is distinct from others, but what it is remains unknown. Such is the proper knowledge of God that we have through demonstration and it is not sufficient for man's ultimate happiness.

Members of a species by and large attain the end of that species, for what comes about by nature does so either always or for the most part, but fails in a few cases because of some defect. But happiness is the end of the human species, since all men naturally desire it. Happiness therefore is a certain common good which all men can attain unless they are handicapped by some impediment. But only a few attain to knowledge of God by way of demonstration, because of the obstacles to this knowledge which we touched on at the beginning of Book 1.

THE HUMAN GOOD 283

Therefore, such knowledge of God is not what human happiness essentially is.

Again, it is the end of what is potential to be actual, as is clear from the foregoing. Happiness, however, which is the ultimate end, is an act which is not in potency to any further act. But the knowledge of God had by way of demonstration remains in potency with respect to knowing further what God is, or in a nobler manner, for those who come later strive to add to the knowledge of God that has been handed down to them from their predecessors. Such knowledge, then, is not ultimate human happiness.

Moreover, happiness excludes all misery, for no one can be at the same time miserable and happy. But deception and error are a large part of misery, for all naturally flee them. But many errors can be conjoined to the foregoing knowledge of God, which is clear in the case of many who knew some truths about God through demonstration but, following their opinions, fell into many errors where demonstration was wanting. If there were some who by way of demonstration discovered truth in divine matters with which no falsity was mixed because of their opinions, it is clear that they were very few, which is incompatible with happiness, which is the common end. Therefore, it is not in this knowledge that man's ultimate happiness lies.

Moreover, happiness consists in perfect activity, but certainty is required for the perfection of knowledge, which is why we are not said to know a thing unless we know that it is impossible to be otherwise, as is evident from *Posterior Analytics* 1. But the knowledge in question has much uncertainty, as is shown by the diversity of opinions concerning divine things which is learned by way of demonstration. Therefore, in such knowledge ultimate happiness does not lie.

Again, when the will attains the ultimate end, its desire is at rest. But the ultimate end of all human knowledge is happiness. That knowledge of God will be happiness essentially which, when it is had, knowledge of no other object will be desired. But the knowledge which philosophers can have through demonstration is not like that, because when it is had we yet desire to know other things, which are not yet known through this knowledge. Therefore, happiness does not lie in such knowledge of God.

Again, the end of anything existing in potency is to be made actual, and it tends to this through motion by which it is moved to the end. Anything that is in potency tends to become actual to the degree this is possible. For there is something existing in potency whose potentiality can be completely actuated, hence its end is to be made totally actual; for example, the heavy being found outside the centre is in potency to its proper place. But there is something whose complete potentiality cannot be reduced to act at one time, as is clear with prime matter: hence by motion it seeks successively to take on different forms which, because of their diversity, cannot simultaneously be in it. Our intellect, on the other hand, is in potency to all intelligible things, as was said in Book 2. But two intelligible objects can exist simultaneously in the possible intellect according to first act, which is knowledge, although perhaps not with respect to second act, which is their consideration. From which it is evident that the potency of the possible intellect can be simultaneously actualized. This is required for its ultimate end, which is happiness. But this does not come about by the knowledge of God gained by demonstration because, although it is had, we still do not know many things. That is why this knowledge of God is not sufficient for ultimate happiness.

Chapter 40: Human happiness does not consist in the knowledge of God which is by faith.

There is another knowledge of God, that by which men know him through faith, which in one respect is superior to the foregoing, exceeding the knowledge of God gained through demonstration by an eminence that demonstrating reason could never attain, as was said at the beginning of this work. But man's ultimate happiness cannot consist in this knowledge of God either.

Happiness is the perfect activity of intellect, as is clear from the foregoing. But in the knowledge of faith there is a most imperfect activity from the point of view of intellect although most perfect from the point of view of the object, because the intellect does not grasp that to which it gives assent. Therefore it is not in this knowledge of God either that man's ultimate happiness can be found.

Again, it was shown above that ultimate happiness does not lie principally in the act of will. But will plays the chief role in the knowledge of faith, for in faith intellect assents to things which are proposed because it wills, but it is not moved necessarily by the very evidence of the truth. Therefore man's ultimate happiness does not lie in this knowledge.

Again, he who believes gives his assent to what is proposed to him but which he does not see, hence faith is a knowledge more like hearing than

THE HUMAN GOOD 285

seeing. But no one would believe things proposed to him by another which he does not see unless he thought the other to have more perfect knowledge of what is not seen than he who does not see. Either this estimate of the believer is false or the one proposing does have more perfect knowledge of what is proposed. And if he only knew these things by hearing them from another, this could not go endlessly on, for then the assent of faith would be vain and without certainty, since there would not be anything first and certain in itself to lend certainty to the faith of believers. But it is not possible for the knowledge of faith to be false or vain, as is evident from what was said at the beginning of this work. But if it were false and vain, happiness could not consist in such knowledge. Therefore, there is a knowledge higher than that of faith, either because the man proposing faith immediately sees the truth, as we believe in Christ, or because he accepts it from the one seeing it immediately, as we believe the apostles and prophets. Therefore, since man's happiness consists in the highest knowledge of God, it is impossible that it should lie in the knowledge of faith.

Moreover, natural desire comes to rest in happiness, which is the ultimate end. But the knowledge of faith does not give rest to desire, but rather increases it, because everyone wants to see what he believes. Therefore, man's ultimate happiness lies in the knowledge of faith.

Moreover, knowledge of God is said to be the end insofar as it unites us with the ultimate end of things, namely God. But through the knowledge of faith the thing believed does not come to be perfectly present to the intellect, because faith is of absent not of present things. Hence the Apostle says in 2 Corinthians 5 that so long as we walk in faith, we are exiled from the Lord. Through faith God becomes present to affection since the believer voluntarily assents to God, as is said in Ephesians 3.17: through faith Christ dwells in our hearts. Therefore, it is not possible that ultimate human happiness should lie in the knowledge of faith.

Chapter 41: Can man in this life understand separate substance by means of the study and inquiry of speculative science?

There is yet another kind of knowledge of God that the intellectual substance can have, for it was said in Book 2 that the separate intellectual substance, in knowing its own essence, knows both what is above and below it according to the mode of its own substance. Which is particularly necessary if that which is above it is its cause, since the likeness of the cause must be discovered in effects. Hence, since God is the cause of all created intellectual substances, as is clear from the foregoing, it is necessary that separate intellectual substances, in knowing their own essence, should know God himself in the manner of a vision, for only something whose likeness exists in the intellect is known through knowledge of vision, just as the likeness of a thing seen bodily is in the sense of the one seeing. Therefore, any intellect that grasps separate substance, knowing of it what it is, sees God in a higher way than in any of the previous types of knowledge of him.

Therefore, since some held that man's ultimate happiness was had in this life because he knew separate substances, it must be asked whether man can in this life know separate substances, for this is doubtful. Our intellect, in its present state, understands nothing without a phantasm which relates to the possible intellect, whereby we understand, as colours do to sight, as is evident from what was said in Book 2. If, therefore, any of us could come to know separate substances by means of the intellectual knowledge which is through phantasms, it would be possible for someone in this life to understand those separate substances and he would share in the knowledge by which the separate substance, in understanding himself, understands God. But if through the intellectual knowledge that is gained through phantasms we can in no way come to understand separate substances, it would not be possible for man in his present state of life to acquire this kind of knowledge of God.

There is a division of opinion as to our ability to achieve knowledge of such substances by the knowledge that involves phantasms, however. Avempace held that we can through the pursuit of the speculative sciences come to an understanding of separate substances from the things we know through phantasms. For we can by the act of the intellect extract the quiddity of anything having a quiddity which is not identical to its quiddity. For our intellect is designed to know some quiddity insofar as it is a quiddity, since the proper object of intellect is that which is. If then the first thing known by the possible intellect is something having a quiddity, we can by the possible intellect abstract the quiddity of that quiddity, and since this cannot be infinitely prolonged, it must come to an end somewhere. Therefore, by way of analysis our intellect can come to know a quiddity that does not have a quiddity. But such is the quiddity of separate substance. Therefore our intellect can, from the knowledge of sensible things gained through phantasms, come to an understanding of separate substances.

He goes about showing the same thing by another similar argument.

For he says that the understanding of one thing, for example a horse, is multiplied in me and in you only by the multiplication of spiritual species, which are different in me and in you. Therefore it is necessary that an understanding which is not sustained by any such species should be the same in me and in you. But the quiddity of the thing known which our intellect is designed to abstract, as has been proved, does not have any spiritual and individual species, since the quiddity of the thing understood is the quiddity of the individual, neither spiritual nor corporeal, since the thing understood, as such, is universal. Therefore, our intellect is designed to understand a quiddity which is one in all. But such is the quiddity of separate substance. Therefore, our intellect is designed to know separate substance.

If these arguments be considered carefully they are seen to be frivolous. For if the thing understood were as such universal, the quiddity of the thing understood would have to be the quiddity of some universal, namely either of genus or of species. But the quiddity of the genus or species of these sensible things, of which we achieve intellectual knowledge through phantasms, comprises both matter and form. Therefore it is wholly unlike the quiddity of separate substance, which is simple and immaterial. Therefore it is not possible from the fact that the quiddity of the sensible thing is understood through phantasms that the quiddity of separate substance is understood.

Moreover, the form which cannot exist apart from some subject and that which can so exist are not forms in the same sense, even though both can be thought of without such a subject. Nor is there the same meaning of extension and of separate substance unless we posit separated extensions between species and sensible things, as some Platonists did. The quiddity of the genus and species of sensible things cannot exist separate from this individual matter, except perhaps if, following the Platonist, we hold the species of things to be separate, which is disproved by Aristotle. Therefore this quiddity is wholly unlike separate substances, which are in no way in matter. Therefore, separate substances cannot be understood just because these quiddities are understood.

Again, even if the quiddity of separate substance were granted to be the same as the quiddity of the genus or species of these sensible things, we could not say that it is of the same species unless we should say that the species of these sensible things were themselves separate substances, as the Platonists did. It remains that they are not of the same meaning except with respect to the definition of quiddity as quiddity. But this is a meaning common to species and substance. Therefore through these quiddities nothing could be understood of separate substances except the remote genus of them. But to know generically is not to know specifically, save in potency. Therefore, separate substances cannot be understood through an understanding of the quiddity of sensible things.

Moreover, there is a greater distance between separate and sensible substances than between one sensible substance and another. But to understand the quiddity of one sensible thing it does not suffice to know the quiddity of another, for one born blind in no way comes to know the quiddity of colour from the fact that he knows the quiddity of sound. Much less, therefore, from the fact that one understands the quiddity of sensible substance, is he able to understand the quiddity of separate substance.

Again, if we should hold that separate substances move the orbs by which motions the forms of sensible things are caused, this way of knowing separate substances from sensible things does not suffice to know their quiddity. For the cause is known from its effect either because of a similarity of effect to cause, or insofar as the effect shows the power of the cause. On the basis of similarity, however, one cannot know from the effect what the cause is unless it is a cause of the same species, but it is not in this way that separate substances are related to sensible things. On the basis of power, this is not possible except when the effect is equal to the cause, for then the whole power of the cause is known through the effect, and the power of a thing demonstrates its substance. But this cannot be said in the case in point, for the powers of separate substances exceed all the sensible effects which we comprehend with our intellect, as universal power exceeds a particular effect. Therefore, it is not possible that we can come to understand separate substances by understanding sensible things.

Again, all intelligible things that we come to know by inquiry and study pertain to one of the speculative sciences. Therefore, if from the fact that we understand the natures and quiddities of these sensible things we come to understand separate substances, this would occur in one of the speculative sciences. But we do not find this to be the case, for there is no speculative science which teaches what any separate substance is, but only that it is. Therefore, it is not possible from the fact that we understand the natures of sensible things that we can arrive at understanding of separate substances.

If it should be said that there could be such a speculative science, only it has not yet been discovered, this comes to nothing, for it is not possible to come to an understanding of such substances by means of any principles

known to us. For all the proper principles of any science depe
first indemonstrable and self-evident principles, knowledge of
take from sensible things, as is clear at the end of the *Posterior*
Sensible things do not sufficiently lead to knowledge of immaterial things,
as has been proved by the earlier arguments. Therefore it is not possible
for there to be a science through which such separate substances could
come to be understood.

13. *On the Divine Simplicity*. Disputed Question of the Power of God, 7 (1265–6)

The collection of disputed questions gathered together as On the Power of God *dates from 1265 to 1266, while Thomas was teaching in Rome and just prior to commencement of work on his masterpiece, the* Summa theologiae. *The disputed question on the simplicity of God deals with fundamental aspects of Thomas's teaching on the human capacity to know and to talk about God.*

Aristotle's insistence that it is only with great difficulty and prolonged effort that we can establish the existence of anything beyond the realm of sensible objects was one that Thomas took to heart, not least because it so obviously harmonized with what is found in Scripture. The connatural object of the human mind is the essence of sensible reality. Our language is fashioned primarily to talk about such things. If our study of sensible objects provides a basis for proving that there are beings which are not material and changeable, we do not devise a new vocabulary to speak of what might be called metaphysical beings. Rather, the language first used to speak of material objects is extended in meaning to encompass immaterial beings as well. This extension of meaning of familiar language provides an Ariadne's thread that enables us to return from the metaphysical stratosphere to the palpable objects of our sense experience. These remain our touchstone of certainty and the native habitat of our language.

A problem encountered in efforts to speak of the human soul and human thinking and willing as activities which are not physical changes is exacerbated when human language is employed to speak of God. Our knowledge of God is indirect, oblique, dependent on knowledge of sensible reality.

It may be thought that this difficulty disappears in the realm of faith when God reveals himself to us, in Scripture and in his divine son. For Thomas, revelation is merely a special case of the epistemological and terminological problem. God speaks to us in our language and mercifully observes what is for us the natural way of knowing.

The pattern of our efforts to know and talk about God is first to see

how unlike the things of our immediate experience he is. Negative ter~~
such as 'immobile' and 'timeless' and 'immaterial' are devised to express
this. And yet there are certain things we affirm of God: that he is good,
just, wise and loving. Of course these terms are learned in speaking about
good, just, wise and loving human beings. How can God and creature
share these terms?

This magnificent disputed question on the simplicity of God anticipates
discussions that will occupy Thomas in the Summa theologiae. *But here*
they receive a far more detailed and exhaustive treatment.

On the Power of God

QUESTION 7
ON THE SIMPLICITY OF GOD

This disputation addresses eleven questions: (1) whether God is simple;
(2) whether in God substance and essence are the same as existence; (3)
whether God is in a genus; (4) whether 'good', 'just' and 'wise' are
incidental predicates of God; (5) whether those names signify the divine
substance; (6) whether they are synonyms; (7) whether such names are
said of God and creatures univocally or equivocally; (8) whether a relation
exists between God and creatures; (9) whether relations between God
and creatures are relations in creatures; (10) whether God is really related
to creatures such that the relation is really in God; (11) whether temporal
relations are relations of reason in God.

Article 1: Is God simple?

It seems that he is not.

1. From one simple thing only one thing comes, for a thing causes
something the same as itself, according to the Philosopher. But a multitude
of things proceeds from God. Therefore, he is not simple.

2. Moreover, when the simple is attained it is attained as a whole. But
God is attained by the blessed since, as Augustine says, the greatest
happiness is for the mind to attain God. Therefore, if he were simple, he
would be attained as a whole by the blessed, but what is attained as a

whole is comprehended. Therefore God is comprehended by the blessed – which is impossible. Therefore, God is not simple.

3. Moreover, what is the same does not satisfy the characteristics of different causes, but God does, as is evident in *Metaphysics* 11. Therefore, there must be different things in him and he must accordingly be complex.

4. Moreover, wherever there is this plus that, there is composition; but in God there is this and that, namely, property and essence. Therefore, in God there is composition.

5. But it will be said that his property is the same as his essence. On the contrary: an affirmation and its negation are not verified of the same thing. But the divine essence is communicable to the three persons and incommunicability is a property. Therefore, property and essence are not the same.

6. Moreover, that of which different categories are predicated is complex. But substance and relation are predicated of God, as Boethius says. Therefore, God is complex.

7. Moreover, in any thing there is substance, power and activity, as Dionysius says, from which it seems that activity follows power and substance. But there is plurality in the divine activities. Therefore, multitude and composition are to be found in his substance.

8. Moreover, wherever many forms are found, there must be composition. But there are many forms in God because, as Averroes says, all forms are actually in the first mover just as all are potentially in prime matter. Therefore, there is composition in God.

9. Moreover, whatever comes to a thing after it is complete is accidental to it. But some things are said of God temporally, for example, that he is creator and lord. Therefore, they are accidental to him. But there is composition of an accident with its subject. Therefore, there is composition in God.

10. Moreover, wherever there are many things there is composition. But there are three persons in God, that is, three things, as Augustine says. Therefore, there is composition in God.

ON THE CONTRARY:

1. Hilary says, 'God is not made up of components in the human way, such that in him there is what is had and that which has.'

2. Moreover, Boethius says, 'That truly is one in which there is no number.' But wherever there is composition, there is number. Therefore, God is without composition and wholly simple.

RESPONSE:

It should be said that God must be held to be simple in every way. For now this can be proved by three arguments. Of which the first is this. It was shown in another disputation that all beings come from a first being, which we call God. However, in one and the same thing, which is at one time potential and at another time actual, potency is temporally prior to actuality even though by nature it is posterior. Absolutely speaking, act must be prior to potency, both in nature and in time, because every potential being is made actual by some actual being. Therefore, that being which makes all other beings actual and is himself from nothing else must be First Act without any mixture of potency. For if he were in any way potential, there would have to be a prior being through which he would become actual. In a complex thing of whatever kind of composition, potency is mingled with act. For in complex things, either one of the things of which it is composed is in potency to the other, like matter to form, subject to accident, genus to difference, or at the least all the parts are in potency to the whole. For the parts are as matter and the whole as form, as is evident from *Physics* 2. Thus no composite thing could be First Act. The first being that God is must be Pure Act, as has been shown. Therefore, since it is impossible that God be composed, he must be completely simple.

The second argument is this. Since composition is only of different things, these different things require some agent to unite them, because the different, as such, are not united. But for a composite to exist is for the things of which it is composed to be united. Therefore, since every composite thing must depend on some prior agent, the first being, who is God, from whom all things come, cannot be composite.

The third argument is this. The first being, who is God, must be most perfect and consequently the best, for the principles of things are not imperfect, as Pythagoras and Leucippus thought. The best is that in which no goodness is lacking; for example, the whitest is that in which nothing black is to be found. But this is impossible for any composite thing, since the good that results from the composition of parts, thanks to which the whole is good, is not in each of the parts. Hence the parts are not good with the goodness that is proper to the whole. Therefore, what is best is most simple and lacks all composition. This is the argument the Philosopher gives[1] and Hilary too when he says that because God is light he

1. *Metaphysics* 12.

is not affected by the obscure and because he is power there are no weaknesses in him.

Ad 1. It should be said that Aristotle does not mean that a multitude cannot proceed from one, for since the agent causes something similar to itself and the effect imperfectly represents its cause, that which is united in the cause must be multiplied in the effects, much as all generable forms are, as it were, in the sun, which as its effects are distinct. Thus it comes about that through one capacity a thing can bring about different effects, as fire by means of its heat can both liquefy and solidify, make soft and hard, burn and char. And through the power of reason a man can acquire different sciences and perform the works of different arts. How much more, then, can God through his simple power create many things. The Philosopher means that something that remains the same does not cause different things at different times if it acts with the necessity of nature, unless this happens accidentally because of the diversity of matter or of some other accident. But this is not relevant here.

Ad 2. It should be said that the whole God is attained by the mind of the blessed but not wholly, because the mode of the divine knowability infinitely exceeds the mode of created intellect. Thus the created intellect cannot understand God as perfectly as he is intelligible and accordingly cannot comprehend him.

Ad 3. It should be said that one and the same God has the character of different causes because as pure act he is an agent and the exemplar of all forms, and as pure goodness he is the end of everything.

Ad 4. It should be said that property and essence in the divine do not differ really but in understanding alone, for paternity itself is the divine essence, as will be made clear later.

Ad 5. It should be said that what is one in being and different in understanding can have contradictories predicated of it, as the Philosopher says; it is evident that a point which is really one can be understood differently as beginning and end, but insofar as it is the beginning it is not the end and vice versa. Hence, since essence and property are the same in reality and differ in understanding, there is nothing to prevent the same thing from being communicable and incommunicable.

Ad 6. It should be said that absolute and relative do not really differ in divine things, but only in understanding, as has been pointed out, and thus no composition comes from this.

Ad 7. It should be said that God's activity can be considered either on the part of the doer or of the done. If on the part of the doer, there is only one activity in God, which is his essence, for he does not do things by an action that would intervene between God and his willing, which is his very existence. But considered on the side of what is done, there are indeed different activities, since through his understanding there are diverse effects of the divine activity. But this does not introduce any composition in him.

Ad 8. It should be said that the form of the effect is found in one way in the natural agent and in another way in one who acts through art. For in that which acts by nature the form of the effect exists insofar as the agent assimilates its effect to its own nature, since every agent produces something like itself. This happens in two ways, for when the effect is perfectly like the agent, and equal to the power of the agent, the form is in the effect and cause according to the same account [ratio], as is evident in univocal agents, for example, when fire generates fire. But when the effect is not perfectly assimilated to the agent, and is not made equal to the power of the agent, then the form of the effect is not in the agent in the same sense, but in a more eminent way, as is clear in equivocal agents; for example, the sun generates fire.

In agents that work by art, forms of the effects pre-exist with the same account but not in the same way of existing, for in the effects they have material existence and in the mind of the artist intelligible existence. Something is said to be in the intellect both as that which is understood and as the species whereby it is understood, but the forms of art are in the mind of the artist as that by which something is understood. For it is because the artist conceives the form of the artefact that he produces it in matter. But the forms of things are in God in both ways, for although he acts through intellect, this is not without the action of nature. In lesser artefacts, art acts in virtue of extraneous nature, which it uses as an instrument, as the potter uses fire to make bricks. But the divine art does not use exterior nature in acting, but in virtue of its own nature causes its effect. Therefore the forms of things are in the divine nature as in an operative power, but not according to the same account, since no effect is equal to his power. Hence all forms which are multiplied in effects are as one in him, and thus no composition arises from this. Similarly, there are in his intellect many things understood through one and the same thing, namely his essence. But that many are understood through one does not introduce composition in the one understanding. Hence, from this it does not follow that there is composition in God.

Ad 9. It should be said that the relations which are said temporally of God are not really in him but only according to understanding. There is a real relation when one thing really depends upon another, whether absolutely or in a certain respect. Thus there is a real relation of knowledge to the thing known, but conversely only a relation in understanding, as is clear from the Philosopher. Therefore, since God does not depend on anything else, but rather all things depend on him, in other things there are real relations to God, but there can only be a relation of reason between him and things, because the intellect cannot understand a relation of this to that without understanding a relation of that to this.

Ad 10. It should be said that the plurality of persons introduces no composition in God. For the persons can be considered in two ways: first, as compared to essence with which they are really the same, and thus no composition results; second, as they are compared with one another, and then they are compared as distinct, not as made one. So no composition comes from this side either, since every composition is a union.

Article 2: Is substance or essence in God the same as existence?

It seems that it is not.

1. For Damascene says, in *On Orthodox Faith* 1, that God exists is indeed manifest to us, but *what* he is in substance and nature is incomprehensible and entirely unknown. But the same thing cannot be at once known and unknown. Therefore, God's existence and his substance or essence are not the same.

2. But it will be said that even God's existence is unknown to us as to what it is, just like his substance. On the contrary: whether a thing is and what it is are two different questions, one of which we know and the other of which we do not, as is plain from the authority quoted as well. Therefore, that which answers to the question whether God exists and that which answers to the question what he is are not the same; existence answers to whether he is, and substance or nature to what he is.

3. But it might be said that God's existence is known, not in itself, but in the likeness of the creature. On the contrary: in the creature are existence and substance or nature, and since God has both, he is like God in both, in that the agent causes something like himself. If therefore God's existence were known through the likeness of created existence, his substance would have to be known through the likeness of created substance, and then we would know of God not only that he is, but what he is.

4. Moreover, one thing is said to differ from another by its substance.

But that which is common to all provides no difference among them; hence the Philosopher says that being ought not to be put into the definition because the defined is not distinguished from anything else in that, since to be is common to all. But God is something distinct from all other things. Therefore, his existence is not his substance.

5. Moreover, only things whose existence is different are themselves different. But the existence of this thing is not different from the existence of that as existence, but rather insofar as it is in this or that nature. If then there should be some existence which is not in any nature other than existence, this will not be different from any other existence. Thus it follows that if the divine substance is his existence, he would be the existence common to anything.

6. Moreover, the being to which no addition is made is the being common to all. But if God were himself existence, he would be the being to which no addition is made, and therefore common, and then he would be predicated of everything and would be a God mixed with all things. Which is heretical and in disagreement with the Philosopher in the *Book of Causes* saying that the first cause rules all things without being confused with them.

7. Moreover, nothing is said of that which is wholly simple by way of concretion. But existence is such, for existence seems to relate to essence as white does to whiteness. Therefore, it is unfitting to say that the divine substance is existence.

8. Moreover, Boethius says that everything that is participates in that which is existence in order to be, and participates in something else in order to be something. But God exists. Therefore, besides his existence there is in him something else thanks to which he is something.

9. Moreover, what is most imperfect ought not to be attributed to God who is most perfect. But existence is most imperfect, like prime matter, for just as prime matter is determined by all forms, so existence, since it is most imperfect, has to be determined by all proper categories. Therefore, just as prime matter is not in God, so neither should existence be attributed to the divine substance.

10. Moreover, that which is signified in the manner of an effect does not belong to the first substance, which has no principle. But existence is such, for every being has existence according to the principles of its essence. Therefore, it is unfitting to say that the substance of God is existence itself.

11. Moreover, every proposition in which a thing is predicated of itself is self-evident. But if the substance of God were his own existence, subject

and predicate would be the same in 'God exists'. Therefore, it would be a self-evident proposition, which seems false, since it is demonstrable. Therefore, God's existence is not his substance.

ON THE CONTRARY:

1. Hilary says in *On the Trinity*: 'Existence is not an accident of God, but his subsistent truth.' But that which is subsistent is the substance of the thing. Therefore, God's existence is his substance.

2. Moreover, Rabbi Moses says that God is not being by essence, nor living by life, nor powerful by power, nor wise by wisdom. Therefore in God essence is not other than his existence.

3. Moreover, a thing is properly denominated from its quiddity, for the noun properly signifies substance and quiddity, as is said in *Metaphysics* 4. But this nominal phrase 'that which is' is of all names the most proper name of God, as is clear from Exodus 4. Therefore, since this name is imposed from that which is existence, it seems that God's existence is his substance.

RESPONSE:

It should be said that in God existence is not other than his substance. In evidence of which it should be considered that, since causes producing different effects have one effect in common besides the different ones, it is necessary that their common effect should be produced by the power of some higher cause whose proper effect it is. And this because, since the proper effect is produced by a cause according to its proper nature or form, different causes having different natures and forms must have different proper effects.

Hence, if they have some effect in common, it cannot be their proper effect, but that of something higher, in virtue of which they act. Just as it is evident that different compounds all heat, such as pepper and ginger and the like, although each has its proper effect different from those of the others. Hence the common effect has to be referred to a prior cause whose proper effect it is, namely fire. Similarly, in celestial motions, each planetary sphere has proper motions as well as a common one which must be proper to some higher sphere moving them all according to diurnal motion.

But all created causes have one common effect, which is existence, although each has its proper effect by which they differ from one another. For heat causes something to be warm, and the builder causes a house to be. Therefore they have in common the fact that they cause existence, but differ in that fire causes fire and the builder causes a house. There must therefore be some cause higher, by whose power all cause existence and of which existence is the proper effect. And this cause is God.

The proper effect of any cause proceeds from it according to a likeness to its nature. Therefore, that which is existence must be the substance or nature of God. On account of which it is said in the *Book of Causes* that the Intelligence gives existence only insofar as it is divine, and the first effect is existence and before it nothing else is created.

Ad 1. It should be said therefore that being and existence are said in two ways, as is evident from *Metaphysics* 5. For sometimes it signifies the essence of the thing, or the act of being; sometimes it signifies the truth of the proposition, even in things which do not have existence, as we say that blindness exists because it is true that a man is blind. When therefore Damascene says that the existence of God is manifest to us, he understands the existence of God in the second way and not the first. In the first way the existence of God is the same as his substance, and just as his substance is unknown to us, so is his existence. But in the second way we know that God exists, since we form this proposition in our intellect from his effects.

The solution to the second and third difficulties is clear from this.

Ad 4. It should be said that the divine existence which is his substance is not common existence but is an existence different from any other existence. Hence, by his existence God differs from every other being.

Ad 5. It should be replied that, as is said in the *Book of Causes*, the existence itself of God is distinguished and individuated from any other existence in this that it is subsistent existence, and does not advene to any nature that is other than this existence. All other existence, not being subsistent, must be individuated by the nature and substance which subsists in that existence. Of these it is true that the existence of this is other than the existence of that because it is of another nature. Just as if there were one heat existing of itself without a matter or subject, it would be distinguished from every other heat by that very fact, although the heat in this subject differs from the heat in that because of their subjects.

Ad 6. It should be said that the 'common being to which no addition is made' does not mean no addition can be made to it; but the divine existence is not common existence. Just because in the common animal the difference rational is not included, this does not mean that no addition to it can be made, for there is also the irrational animal, which is a species of animal.

Ad 7. It should be said that the mode of signifying in our talk of things follows on our mode of understanding, for speech signifies the conceptions of the intellect, as is said in *On Interpretation* 1. But our intellect understands existence in the way it is found in lower things, from which our knowledge begins and in which existence is not subsistent but inherent. Reason discovers that there is a subsistent existence and then, although what is called existence is signified in the manner of concretion, the intellect attributing existence to God transcends the mode of signifying, attributing to God *what it signifies*, but not *the mode of signifying* it.

Ad 8. It should be said that the saying of Boethius is to be understood of things to which existence belongs by participation, not by essence; that which is through its essence, if we attend to the import of speech, ought rather be called that which is existence than that which is.

Ad 9. It should be said that what I call existence is the most perfect of all things, which is clear because act is always more perfect than potency, and designated form is understood to be actual only when it is held to exist. For humanity or fieriness can be considered as existing in the potency of matter or in the power of the agent or even in the intellect, but that which has existence is made to be actually existent. It is thus clear that what I call existence is the actuality of all acts, and because of that is the perfection of all perfections. Nor should it be understood that something more formal could be added to that which I call existence, determining it, as act determines potency. This kind of existence is other in essence from that to which it is added and which determines it. Nothing extraneous can be added to it, since nothing other than non-being is extraneous to it, which can be neither form nor matter. Thus existence is not determined by another as potency is by act but rather as act is by potency. For in the definition of forms their proper matter is put in place of difference, as when we say the soul is the act of a physically organized body. In this way, this existence is distinguished from that, insofar as it is this nature's or that's, which is why Dionysius says that although living things are more noble than existent things, still to be is more noble than to live. For living things not only have life, but along with life they have existence.

Ad 10. It should be said that the order of ends follows the order of agents, such that the ultimate end answers to the first agent, and proportionately through the order other ends to other agents. For if the ruler of the city and the leader of the army and a single soldier be considered, it is clear that the ruler of the city is first in the order of agents at whose command the leader of the army marches to war, and under him is the soldier, who, at the command of the leader of the army, puts his hand to fighting. The end of the soldier is to slay the enemy, which is ordered to the victory of the army, which is the end of the leader, and this is further ordered to the good condition of the city or realm, which is the end of the ruler and king. Therefore, existence which is the proper effect and end of the activity of the first agent must hold the place of ultimate end. The end, though it is first in intention, is last in execution and is the effect of other causes. Therefore, created existence, which is the proper effect answering to the first agent, is caused by other principles, although what primarily causes existence is the first principle.

Ad 11. It should be said that a proposition can be of itself self-evident but yet not be such for this or that person. As when the predicate is of the definition of the subject yet the definition of the subject is unknown to someone. For someone ignorant of what a whole is the proposition stating that the whole is greater than its part would not be self-evident. For such propositions become self-evident when their terms are known, as is said in *Posterior Analytics* 1. But this proposition, 'God exists,' taken in itself is self-evident, because subject and predicate are the same. But it is not self-evident to us because we do not know what God is. So for us it requires demonstration, but not for those who see the essence of God.

Article 3: Is God in some genus?

It seems that he is.

1. For Damascene says that substance in matters divine signifies a species common to persons similar in species, and hypostasis points out the individual, namely Father, Son and Holy Spirit, Peter and Paul. So God is compared to Father, Son and Holy Spirit as species to individuals. But wherever species and individual are found, there genus is found, because the species is made up of genus and difference. Therefore it seems that God is in some genus.

2. Moreover, things that are in no way different are wholly the same. But God is not the same as other things. Therefore he differs from them in some way. But whatever differs from another, differs from it by some difference. Therefore, in God there is some difference, by which he differs from other things. It cannot be something accidental, because there is no accident in God, as Boethius says in *On the Trinity*. But every substantial difference divides some genus. Therefore, God is in a genus.

3. Moreover, things can be the same either in genus, or species or

number, as is said in *Topics* 1.4. Therefore, different as well, for if one of opposites is said in many ways, so is the other. Therefore, God is different from creature only numerically, or numerically and specifically; and so it follows that he agrees with the creature in kind and thus is in a genus. If he differed generically from the creature, he would have to be in some other genus than the creature, since diversity springs from multiplicity, and thus generic difference requires a plurality of genera. Therefore, however you look at it, God must be in a genus.

4. Moreover, to whatever the notion of the genus substance fits, is in a genus. But the notion answering to substance is that which exists of itself, which especially belongs to God. Therefore, God is in the genus of substance.

5. Moreover, whatever is defined must be in a genus. But God is defined, for he is said to be pure act. Therefore, God is in some genus.

6. Moreover, whatever is predicated of something expressing what it is, and extends to others as well, either relates to it as species or as genus. But everything predicated of God is meant to express what he is, for all the categories, when they become divine predicates, amount to substance, as Boethius says. But it is evident that these pertain not only to God but also to other things, and thus they are in more. Therefore, either they are compared to God as species to individual or as genus to species, and either way God must be in a genus.

7. Moreover, anything is measured by the least in its genus, as is said in *Metaphysics* 10. But, as the Commentator says at that place, that by which all substances are measured is God. Therefore, God is in the same genus as other substances.

ON THE CONTRARY:

1. Whatever is in a genus, adds something to the genus, and consequently is composite. But God is wholly simple. Therefore, he is not in a genus.

2. Moreover, whatever is in a genus can either be defined or included in some defined thing. Since God is infinite, he is not like that. Therefore, he is not in a genus.

RESPONSE:

It should be said that God is not in a genus, which for now can be shown by three arguments. First, because nothing is put in a genus because of its existence but by reason of its quiddity, which is clear from this that the existence of anything is proper to it and distinct from the existence of any other thing, but the notion of substance can be common. Because of this the Philosopher too says that being is not a genus. God, however, is his own existence. Hence, he cannot be in a genus.

The second argument is this. Although matter is not a genus, nor is form difference, yet the notion of genus is drawn from matter, and the notion of difference is drawn from form; for example, in man sensible nature is that from which the notion of animal is drawn, and is material with respect to reason, from which the difference rational is drawn. An animal is something that has a sensitive nature, the rational is what has reason, hence there must be a composition of matter and form or of act and potency in anything that is in a genus. This cannot be the case with God, who is pure act, as has been shown. It remains therefore that he cannot be in a genus.

The third argument is this. Since God is absolutely perfect, he comprehends in himself the perfections of all genera, for this is the meaning of the absolutely perfect, as is said in *Metaphysics* 5. Whatever is in a genus is determined by the things that are of that genus, and thus God cannot be in some genus, for then he would not be of an infinite essence, nor of absolute perfection, but his essence and perfection would be limited to the range of one limited genus.

From which it is further evident that God is not a species or an individual, nor does he have either difference or definition, for every definition is from genus and species, hence no demonstration can be made about him except through effects, since the middle of the demonstration of the reasoned fact is the definition.

Ad 1. It should be said that Damascene speaks by way of similarity and not properly, for God's name, which is God, has a similarity to species in this that it is predicated of numerically many distinct substantial things, but it cannot properly be called species because a species is not something numerically one and common to many but one only in reason; the numerically one divine substance is common to three persons, hence the Father and Son and Holy Spirit are one God, but Peter and Paul and Mark are not one man.

Ad 2. It should be said that the different and diverse differ, as the Philosopher says, for the diverse, absolutely speaking, is what is not the same, but the different relates to something, for one thing differs from another with respect to something. If, then, we understand the term 'different' properly, then this proposition is false: 'Existent things that in no way differ, are the same.' However, if the term 'different' is understood broadly, then it is true, and thus it can be conceded that God differs from others. But it does not follow that he differs by some difference, but that he differs from others by his substance: this must be said of first and simple things. For a man differs from an ass by the difference rational, but rational does not further differ from ass by some difference, since then there would be an infinite regress, but by itself.

Ad 3. It should be said that God is said to be diverse in genus from creatures, not as existing in a genus, but as existing wholly outside a genus.

Ad 4. It should be said that being-of-itself is not the definition of substance, as Avicenna says. For being cannot be the genus of anything, as the Philosopher proves, since nothing can be added to being which does not participate in it, but difference ought not to participate in the genus. If substance could have a definition, despite the fact that it is the most general genus, it would be this: a substance is something of whose very quiddity it is not to be in another. And then the definition of substance would not belong to God, who does not have a quiddity apart from his existence. Hence God is not in the genus of substance, but is above every substance.

Ad 5. It should be said that God cannot be defined, for the defined is comprehended by the intellect of the one defining. But God is incomprehensible by intellect; hence when God is said to be pure act, this is not his definition.

Ad 6. It should be said that it is required for the notion of genus that it be univocally predicated. But nothing can be univocally predicated of God and creatures, as will be evident below. Hence although those things which are said of God, are predicated of him substantially, nevertheless they are not predicated of him as a genus.

Ad 7. It should be said that although God does not pertain to the genus of substance as contained in a genus as the species or individual are contained in genus, he can be said to be in the genus of substance by reduction, as a principle, much as the point is in the genus of continuous quantity, and unity in the genus of number. In this way he is the measure of all substances, as unity is of numbers.

Article 4: Are good, wise, just and the like predicated of God as accidents?

It seems that they are.

1. Whatever is predicated of something not as signifying substance but what follows on nature signifies an accident. But Damascene says that

good and just and holy as said of God follow nature and do not signify substance itself. Therefore they predicate accidents of God.

2. But it will be said that Damascene speaks with respect to the mode of signifying. On the contrary. The mode of signifying follows the notion of genus and must be referred to the thing, for the genus predicate signifies the substance of the subject, since it is predicated of it as what it is. But the foregoing names signify in the manner of following on the nature by reason of the genus, for they are in the genus of quality, which in its proper signification relates to a subject, for quality is that by which things are signified as to how they are. Therefore this mode of signifying must refer to the thing, such that what is signified by the foregoing names are things following on the nature of that of which they are predicated, and consequently they are accidents.

3. But it might be said that these names are not predicated of God with respect to their genus, which is quality, for names imposed by us are not properly said of God. On the contrary: if the genus were removed from a thing, the species would be falsely predicated of it: what is not an animal is falsely called a man. If therefore the genus of the predicate, which is quality, is not predicated of God, it is not only improperly but falsely predicated of God, and thus it would be false to say that God is just or that God is holy, which is absurd. Therefore, it must be said that the foregoing names are predicated of God as accidents.

4. Moreover, the Philosopher says that what truly is – that is, substance – is accidental to nothing. Therefore, for the same reason what in itself is an accident is an accident wherever. But justice and wisdom and the like are of themselves accidents. Therefore, there are accidents in God.

5. Moreover, there is an exemplar in God of whatever is found in created things, for he is the exemplar form of all. But wisdom, justice and the like are accidents in created things. Therefore they are accidents in God.

6. Moreover, wherever there is quantity and quality, there is accident. But in God there seems to be quantity and quality, for there is similarity and equality in God, since we say that the Son is similar and equal to the Father. But quality is caused from the unit in quality as equality is from the one in quantity. Therefore, there are accidents in God.

7. Moreover, anything is measured by the first in its genus. But God is not only the measure of substances, but of all accidents, because he is the creator of substance and accident. Therefore, in God there is not only substance but also accident.

8. Moreover, that without which something can be understood is

accidentally predicated of it. Porphyry proves that there are some separable accidents because we can think of white crows and white Ethiopians. But God can be understood without good, as is evident in Boethius. Therefore, good signifies an accident in God, and the same goes for the others.

9. Moreover, two things are to be considered in the meaning of the name God: *that from which* it is imposed and *that on which* it is imposed. With respect to both, however, the word wisdom seems to signify an accident, for it is imposed from that which makes one wise, which seems to be the action of wisdom; and that from which it is imposed is some quality, and thus in God there is some accident.

ON THE CONTRARY:

1. Boethius says that God, since he is a simple form, cannot be a subject. But every accident is in a subject. Therefore, in God there cannot be any accident.

2. Moreover, every accident depends on something else, but there cannot be such dependence in God, because what depends on another must be caused. God, however, is the first cause, in no way caused. Therefore there cannot be an accident in God.

3. Moreover, Rabbi Moses says that names of this kind do not signify intentions added to the substance of God. But every accident signifies an intention added to the substance of its subject. Therefore the foregoing names do not signify an accident in God.

4. Moreover, an accident is something that comes and goes without the corruption of the subject. But this cannot be in God, since he is immutable, as is proved by the Philosopher. Therefore there can be no accident in God.

RESPONSE:

It should be said that without any doubt it must be held that in God there is no accident, which for the present can be shown by three arguments.

The first argument is this. Nothing extraneous is joined to any nature or essence or form, even though that which has the nature, form or essence can have something extraneous, for humanity receives only what is of the notion of humanity. This is clear from the fact that anything added to or subtracted from definitions signifying essence changes the definition, something clear in numbers too, as the Philosopher says.

But man, who has humanity, can have something which is not of the notion of humanity, such as whiteness and the like, which are not in humanity but in man. In every creature the difference between *that which has* and *what is had* obtains. For in composite creatures there is a twofold difference, since the supposit or individual itself has the nature of the species, as man has humanity and existence besides: for a man is neither his humanity nor his existence. So there can be an accident in man but not in humanity itself or in his existence.

In simple substances there is only one difference, namely, that of essence and existence. For in any angel, the supposit is its nature, for the quiddity of the simple is itself simple, as Avicenna says; but it is not its own existence. Hence, the quiddity subsists in its existence. In substances of this kind an intelligible accident can be found, but not a material one.

In God there is no difference between the haver and the had, or of participant and participated; indeed he is both his nature and his existence, and therefore nothing alien or accidental can be in him. Boethius seems to have hit upon this argument when he says, 'That which is can have something beyond what it itself is, but existence as such has nothing other than itself within it.'

The second argument is this. Since accident is extrinsic to the essence of the subject, and the diverse are only joined by some cause, it would be necessary, if there were an accident in God, that this be due to some cause. But it cannot be any extrinsic cause, because then it would follow that the extrinsic cause acts on God and would be prior to him, as mover to moved, and maker to made. For an accident is caused in a subject from without insofar as an external agent acts on the subject in which the accident is caused.

Similarly, it cannot be from an intrinsic cause, as is the case with proper accidents, which have their cause in the subject. For a subject cannot be the cause of an accident in the same way that it receives the accident, because no potency moves itself to act. So it is necessary that it be susceptible of the accident because of one thing and be the cause of the accident because of another. But then it would be composed, like things that receive accidents because of matter and cause accidents because of form. But it was shown above that God is not complex. Hence it is impossible for there to be any accident in him.

The third argument is this. The accident relates to its subject as act to potency, since it is a certain form of it. Hence since God is pure act without any admixture of potency, he cannot be the subject of accident. It is plain from what has gone before that in God there is no composition of matter and form nor of any substantial parts nor of genus and difference nor of subject and accident. It is evident then that the names mentioned do not predicate an accident of God.

Ad 1. It should be said that Damascene speaks of those names not with regard to *what* they predicate of God but with regard to *that from which* they are imposed to signify. For they are imposed by us from certain accidental forms found in creatures and he wishes to prove from this that the substance of God is not made known to us by such names.

Ad 2. It should be said that although quality is the genus of human happiness and wisdom and justice, it is not their genus as said of God, because quality, as such, is called being insofar as it in some way inheres in a subject. Wisdom and justice are not named from this, however, but rather from some perfection or act, hence they enter into talk about God by reason of the difference and not by reason of the genus. On account of this Augustine says that as much as we can we understand good without quality and great without quantity. Hence it is not necessary that the mode which follows on the nature be found in God.

Ad 3. It should be said that if good and just were univocally predicated of God, the predication would be false, the genus being removed. However, nothing is said of God and creature univocally, as will be shown below, so the argument does not follow.

Ad 4. It should be said that wisdom, which is an accident, is not in God, but another wisdom not univocally meant, and for this reason the argument has no force.

Ad 5. It should be said that examples do not always perfectly represent the exemplar. Hence sometimes what is in the exemplar is found only defectively and imperfectly in the example. This is especially so in the things which exemplify God who is an exemplar exceeding every creature in degree.

Ad 6. It should be said that likeness and equality are said of God not because there is quality and quantity in him, but because we predicate of God that which in us signifies quality and quantity, as when we call God great and wise and the like.

Ad 7. It should be said that accidents are called being only in relation to substance as first being. Hence accidents are not measured by some first that is an accident, but by the first one that is substance.

Ad 8. It should be said that anything without which a thing can be understood with respect to its essence has the note of accident, for we cannot understand what is of the substance of a thing while ignoring something that is of its substance, as if we could understand what a man is without understanding animal. We do not know God in his essence but think of him from his effects. So nothing prohibits our thinking of him from the effect of his being and not thinking of him from the effect of his goodness. For it is thus that Boethius speaks. However, it should be noticed that although we can in a way understand God without understanding his goodness, we cannot understand God by understanding that he is not good, any more than we could understand man by understanding him not to be animal, since this would remove the substance of God, which is goodness. The saints in heaven who see God in his essence, in seeing God, see his goodness.

Ad 9. It should be said that wisdom is verified of God with respect to that from which the name is imposed, and it is not imposed from this that it causes wisdom but from this that the things of wisdom are intellectually possessed. For knowledge as knowledge refers to the known, but insofar as it is an accident or form it refers to the knower. To possess the things of wisdom is accidental to man but not to God.

Article 5: Do the foregoing names signify the divine substance?

It seems they do not.

1. For Damascene says that each of the things said of God should not be taken to mean what he is in his substance, but rather to show that he is not some relation, or any of the things from which he is separate, or any of those things which follow on nature or activity. The existence which is substantially predicated of something signifies what its substance is. But the foregoing names are not predicated of God substantially as if signifying his substance.

2. Moreover, no name that signifies the substance of a thing can truly be negated of it. But Dionysius says that as to the divine, negations are true and affirmations incompact. Therefore, such names do not signify the divine substance.

3. Moreover, these names signify the procession of the divine goodness to things, as Dionysius puts it. But the goodness proceeding from God is not the divine substance itself. Therefore, such names do not signify the divine substance.

4. Moreover, Origen says that God is called wise because wisdom fulfils us. But this does not signify the divine substance, but its effect. Therefore, these names do not signify the divine substance.

5. Moreover, in the *Book of Causes* it is said that the first cause is not

named by the name of the first caused, which is intelligence. When, then, a cause is named with the name of its effect, this is not predication through essence but through causality. Therefore names said of God are not predicated of him substantially, but only causally.

6. Moreover, names signify conceptions of intellect, as is clear from the Philosopher. But we cannot understand the divine substance, for we do not know what God is, but only that he is, as Damascene says. Therefore we cannot name him with any name nor signify his substance.

7. Moreover, all things participate in the divine goodness, as is clear from Dionysius. But all things do not participate in his substance, but only the three persons. Therefore, divine goodness does not signify his substance.

8. Moreover, we can only know God from his likeness in the creature because, as the Apostle says, in Romans 1.20, 'The invisible things of God are understood from the things that are made.' But as we know him, so we name him. Therefore, we can only name him from the likeness of creatures. But when something is named from the likeness, the name is not predicated of it substantially but metaphorically. Thus it is clear that it is said of God secondarily, but primarily of that from which the likeness is taken. What signifies the substance of something is said first of it.

9. Moreover, according to the Philosopher, to signify substance is to signify this and nothing else. Therefore, if the name good signifies the divine substance, there will be nothing in the divine substance it does not signify, just as there is nothing in human substance that is not signified by 'man'. But good does not signify wisdom, and thus wisdom would not be the divine substance and, by parity of reasoning, none of the others. Therefore, it cannot be said that these names signify the divine substance.

10. Moreover, as quantity is the cause of equality and quality is the cause of similarity, so substance is of identity. If, therefore, all such names signified the substance of God, they would suggest identity rather than equality and similarity, and thus the creature would be said to be the same as God insofar as he imitates his wisdom or goodness, or any of the others, which is absurd.

11. Moreover, in God, who is the principle of all nature, there can be nothing contrary to nature. The Gloss on Romans, 'You are set against nature,' makes clear he can do nothing contrary to nature, but that accident should be substance is contrary to nature. Therefore, since wisdom, justice and the like are in themselves accidents, it cannot be that in God they should be substance.

12. Moreover, when God is called good, this is a complex statement.

But there would be no complexity if the goodness of God were his substance. Therefore, it does not seem that good signifies the divine substance, and for the same reason neither do the other names.

13. Moreover, Augustine says that God eludes every concept of our intellect and therefore cannot be included in intellect. But this would not be if these names signified the divine substance, because God would correspond to the concept of our intellect. Therefore names of this kind do not signify the divine substance.

14. Moreover, Dionysius says that the all good God is united to us when we know that in knowing we know nothing of him. But this would not be if what is conceived and signified were the divine substance. Therefore, the same conclusion as before.

ON THE CONTRARY:

1. Augustine says God is what it is to be brave and to be wise, and whatever you might say that signifies his substance. Therefore all such names signify the divine substance.

2. Moreover, Boethius says that when categories other than relation are used in divine predication, they all change into substance, much as 'just', although it seems to signify a quality, signifies substance, and similarly 'great' and others like them.

3. Moreover, whatever is said by way of participation is reduced to something said of itself and essentially. But the names mentioned are said of creatures by way of participation; therefore when they are taken back to God as to the first cause, they must be said of God essentially. And thus it follows that they signify his substance.

RESPONSE:

It should be said that some held that these names as said of God do not signify the divine substance, something Rabbi Moses most forcibly maintains. He says that such names should be understood of God in two ways: in one way, through the likeness of the effect, as God is called wise not because wisdom is something in him but because he accomplished his effects in the manner of the wise, that is, ordering each thing to its appropriate end, and similarly he is called living insofar as he acts in the manner of one having life, that is, acting of himself. In another way, by negation, such that when we say that God is living, we do not mean that life is in him, but we remove from God that mode of being whereby inanimate things exist. Similarly when we call God intelligent, we do not mean to signify that intellect is something in him, but we remove from

God that mode of being whereby brutes exist, and so on with the others.

But both these ways seem insufficient and unfitting. The first, for two reasons, of which one is that on this interpretation there would be no difference between saying that God is wise and God is angry or God is fire. He is called angry because he acts in the manner of an angry person when he punishes, for this is what angry men are wont to do. He is called fire because he acts in the manner of fire when he cleanses, which fire in its way does. But this conflicts with the view of the saints and prophets speaking of God, who affirm some things of God and deny others, affirming that he is alive, wise and the like, and denying that he is a body or subject to passion. But according to this opinion, all things could with equal reason be said of and denied of God, this no more than that.

The second argument is this. Since according to our faith we hold that creatures did not always exist, which he concedes, it would follow that we cannot say that anyone wise and good existed before creatures did. It is obvious that before creatures existed none of these effects was achieved, neither in the manner of the good nor of the wise. But this is completely repugnant to faith, unless perhaps he means to say that before creatures it was possible to speak of the wise, not because he acted wisely, but because it was possible for him to do so. But then it would follow that something existing in God is signified by it, that is, substance, because whatever is in God is substance.

The second way seems absurd for the same reason. For the name of any species takes away some mode that does not belong to God; in the name of any species is included the signification of the difference by which is excluded the other species that is divided against it. Just as in the name of lion is included the difference quadruped by which the lion differs from the bird. Therefore if predications were made of God only to remove something, as we say God is living – because he does not have existence in the manner of the inanimate, as he says – so we can say that God is a lion because he does not exist in the manner of a bird. Moreover, the intellect always bases a negative on some affirmation, and from this it is clear that every negative is proved through an affirmative; hence unless the human intellect knew something affirmatively of God it could deny nothing of God. But it would know nothing, if nothing it says of God is verified of him affirmatively.

Therefore, according to the opinion of Dionysius, it should be said that names of this kind signify the divine substance, though deficiently and imperfectly. This is clear because every agent acts insofar as it is in act, and consequently brings about something similar. It is necessary that the form of the thing made is in some way in the agent, but diversely, because when the effect is equal to the power of the agent, it is necessary that the form is in the maker and made according to the same notion, for then the maker and the made would belong to the same species, which happens with all univocals, for man generates man, and fire fire. But when the effect is not equal to the power of the agent, the form is not in the maker and made according to the same notion, but more eminently in the agent. Insofar as it is in the agent, the agent has the power of producing the effect. Hence if the whole power of the agent is not expressed by what is made, it follows that the mode by which the form is in the agent exceeds the mode by which it is in the effect. And we find this in all equivocal agents, as when the sun generates fire.

It is clear that no effect is equal to the power of the first agent who is God; otherwise only one effect would proceed from that one power. But when from one power we find many and various effects proceeding, we are shown that any of those effects falls short of the power of the agent. Therefore, no form of any divine effect is of the same notion in the effect as in God. None the less, it must be there in a higher mode, and thus it is that all forms which are distinct in different effects and divided from one another are united in him as in one common power, just as all forms produced in lower things by the power of the sun are in the sun according to its unique power, to which all things generated by the action of the sun are assimilated in their forms.

So too the perfections of created things are assimilated to God according to his unique and simple essence. But when our intellect receives knowledge from created things, it is informed by the likenesses of the perfections found in creatures, such as wisdom, virtue, goodness and the like. Hence just as created things by their perfections are made similar to God, though deficiently, so our intellect is informed by the species of these perfections.

Whenever the intellect is assimilated to a thing through its intelligible form, then what it conceives and speaks according to that intelligible species is verified of the thing to which it is made similar through the species. For knowledge is the intellect's assimilation to the thing known. What intellect, informed by the perfections of these species, thinks and says of God, must truly exist in God who answers to each of these species as that to which all are similar. If this kind of intelligible species in our intellect were made equal in similarity to the divine essence, it would comprehend him and this would be a perfect notion of God, as walking biped is a perfect notion of man.

But the species is not perfectly assimilated to the divine essence, as has been said; therefore, when the intellect attributes such names to God according to these conceptions, they signify the divine substance – not perfectly according as it is, but rather imperfectly as it is understood by us.

Therefore it should be said that each of these names signifies the divine substance, but imperfectly, not as comprehending it; and that is why the name *He Who Is* belongs especially to God, because it does not determine any form of God but signifies existence indeterminately. This is what Damascene means when he says that this name He Who Is signifies a boundless ocean of substance.

This solution is confirmed by the words of Dionysius, who says that because God precontains, simply and limitlessly, all existent things in himself, he is properly praised and named by diverse things. He says 'simply', because the perfections which are in creatures thanks to different forms, are attributed to God according to his simple essence; he says 'limitlessly' to show that no perfection found in creatures comprehends the divine essence such that the intellect could define God as that perfection is in him. This is also confirmed by what is said in *Metaphysics* 5, that the simply perfect is that which has in itself the perfections of all kinds, as the Commentator explains at that place.

Ad 1. It should be said that Damascene means that names of this kind do not signify what God is as comprehending and defining his substance; hence he adds that this name He Who Is, which indefinitely signifies the substance of God, is most properly attributed to God.

Ad 2. It should be replied that Dionysius says that negations of these names are true of God but does not assert that affirmations are false and incompact, but with respect to the thing signified they are truly attributed to God and in some way are in him, as has been shown; but with respect to the mode with which they signify they can be denied of God, for each of these names signifies some definite form, and thus they cannot be attributed to God, as has been said. Therefore, they can be absolutely denied of God since they do not belong to him in the mode signified, for the mode signified is according as they are in our intellect, as has been said; they belong to God in a more sublime mode, hence the affirmation is said to be not in every way fittingly conjoined because of the different mode. According to the teaching of Dionysius they are said in a threefold way of God, first *affirmatively*, as we say that 'God is wise'; which we must say because there is in him some likeness of the wisdom flowing from him. Because wisdom is not in God as we understand and name it, it can truly be *denied,* saying 'God is not wise.' Wisdom is not denied of God because he falls short of it, but because it is in him more *super-eminently* than it is said or understood, so we must say, 'God is super-wise.' And thus by this threefold manner of speaking according to which God is called wise, Dionysius conveys perfectly how these names are attributed to God.

Ad 3. It should be said that these names are said to signify the divine processions because they are first imposed to signify the processions as they are in creatures, and from their likenesses our intellect is led by the hand so that it can attribute them to God in a more eminent way.

Ad 4. It should be said that the word of Origen is not to be understood as meaning that when we say God is wise we mean to signify that God is the cause of wisdom, but that from the wisdom he causes our intellect is led to the point where it can attribute wisdom to him supereminently, as has been said.

Ad 5. It should be said that when God is said to be intelligent, he is named from his effect: because the name that signifies the substance of his effect cannot be attributed definitely to him according to the mode the name signifies; and thus this name although it belongs to him in a way, does not belong to him as his name, because what the name signifies is a definition; but it belongs to the effect as its name.

Ad 6. It should be said that this argument proves that God can not be named by a name defining his substance or comprehending it or equal to it: for in this way we do not know what God is.

Ad 7. It should be said that just as everything participates in the goodness of God – not numerically the same as he, but by similitude – so it participates in the existence of God. With this difference, however, that goodness implies the relation of some cause, for the good is diffusive of itself, but essence is signified in that in which it is, as at rest.

Ad 8. It should be said that in the effect there is found something in which it is like its cause and something in which it differs from its cause. It agrees with it either in matter or something like, as is evident in brick hardened by fire. Because the mud is heated by the fire, it is assimilated to fire, but because the heated is made heavy and hard it differs from fire, but it has this from the condition of matter. If, therefore, that in which the brick is made like the fire is said of fire, it would be properly said of it, and more eminently and first of all. For fire is hotter than the brick and again more eminently: because the brick is hot because heated but fire is naturally hot. But if we should predicate of fire that in which the brick differs from fire, this would be false; and a name having a condition of this kind in its concept could only be said metaphorically of fire. For it is false to call fire, the most subtle of bodies, gross although it can be called hard because of the violence of its action and its resistance to control. Similarly, in creatures there are things to be considered according to which they are made like God, which with respect to the thing signified imply no imperfection, like to be, to live, to understand, and so on. These are properly said of God, indeed more eminently and primarily of him than of creatures. There are other things in which creatures differ from God because of the fact that they are from nothing, such as potentiality, privation, motion and other like things, which are falsely said of God. Names that include such conditions in their concepts can be said of God only metaphorically, like lion, rock and the like, because they have matter in their definitions. Such names are said metaphorically of God because of a likeness of effect.

Ad 9. It should be said that this argument proceeds from the assumption that it signifies substance definitively or circumscriptively, but none of these names signifies the substance of God in this way, as has been said.

Ad 10. It should be said that although in God such perfections are the divine substance itself, in the creature they are not substantial perfections. Therefore with respect to them creatures are not said to be the same as God, but like him.

Ad 11. It should be said that it would be against nature if wisdom were in God according to its meaning as an accident, but this is not the case, as is evident from the foregoing. Nor is the authority invoked relevant: God does nothing against nature in himself because he does nothing in himself.

Ad 12. It should be said that the complexity of the remark when it is said that God is good does not refer to any composition in God, but to the composition that is in our intellect.

Ad 13. It should be said that God eludes the form of our intellect because he exceeds every form of our intellect, but not such that our intellect cannot be assimilated to God according to any intelligible form.

Ad 14. It should be said that from the fact that our intellect is not equal to the divine substance, the substance of God exceeds our intellect and thus is not known by us; what is ultimate in human knowledge of God is that one knows that he does not know God, because he knows that what God is exceeds everything that we can understand of him.

Article 6: Are these names synonyms?

It seems that they are.

1. Names are called synonyms which completely signify the same thing. But all these names said of God signify the same, because they signify the divine substance, which is in every way simple and one, as has been shown. Therefore all these names are synonyms.

2. Moreover, Damascene says that in the divine all things are one, except non-generation, generation and procession. But names signifying one are synonyms. Therefore, all these names as said of God, apart from those that signify the personal properties, are synonyms.

3. Moreover, things that are the same as one and the same thing are the same as one another. But wisdom in God is the same as his substance, and similarly will and power. Therefore, wisdom, power and will in God are wholly the same, and thus it follows that these names are synonyms.

4. It will be said that these names signify the same thing but according to different notions and therefore are not synonyms. On the contrary, a notion to which nothing in things responds is false and vain. But if the notions of these names are many and the thing is one, it seems that these notions are vain and false.

5. But it will be said that these notions are not vain, since something in God answers to them. On the contrary. Created things are made like God insofar as they proceed from an ideal likeness in him. But the plurality of ideas or of ideal notions is not taken according to their relation to creatures, for God himself according to his one essence is the idea of all things. Therefore, the notions of the names we say of God from the likeness of creatures have nothing answering to them on the side of the divine substance.

6. Moreover, that which is maximally one cannot be the root and basis of multiplicity; but the divine essence is maximally one. Therefore the notions of the foregoing names cannot be founded or rooted in the divine substance.

7. Moreover, the distinction of relations which are really in God causes the plurality of persons. Therefore, if something in God answered to the common notions of the attributes, there would also be a multitude of persons in God according to the multitude of attributes. Thus there would be more than three persons in God, which is heretical. So it seems that these names are completely synonymous.

ON THE CONTRARY:

1. The adding of synonym to synonym is frivolous, as if one were to say clothing and garment. Therefore, if these names were synonyms, it would be frivolous to say that God is good, God is wise – and that is false.

2. Moreover, whoever denies one synonym of a thing, denies the rest. But there were those who denied his power but not his knowledge or goodness. Therefore, these names are not synonyms.

3. Moreover, this is clear from the Commentator on *Metaphysics* 11 when he says that these names as said of God are not synonyms.

RESPONSE:

It should be said that all who understand are agreed that these names are not synonyms. This would be easy to maintain on the view of those for whom these names do not signify the divine substance, but only certain added essential intentions or modes of acting on effects or even negations of creatures.

But supposing that these names signify the divine substance, as has been shown above, then the question is seen to involve a great difficulty, because then one and the same simple thing, the divine substance, is signified by all these names.

But it should be noted that the signification of a name does not refer immediately to the thing, but through the mediation of understanding, for speech is the sign of passions of the soul and these concepts of intellect are likenesses of things, as is evident from the Philosopher at the beginning of *On Interpretation*.

Names can be prevented from being synonyms either on the side of the things signified or on the side of the notions understood through the names, for the signifying of which the names are instituted. Of the names said of God, synonymy cannot be prevented by the diversity of the things signified, given what has been established, but only by the notions of the names which follow the conception of the things understood.

Thus the Commentator on *Metaphysics* 11 says that there is multiplicity in God only because of a difference in understanding, not in being, which we say is one thing conceived in many ways. For the different concepts in our intellect cannot be such that nothing answers to them in reality, for our intellect attributes to God the things of which they are the concepts. Hence if there were nothing in God either as to himself or as to his effects that would answer to these concepts, the intellect would be false in attributing them, as would all propositions signifying such attributes, which is absurd.

There are some notions to which nothing in the thing understood answers, but the intellect does not attribute the things of which these are the concepts to things as they are in themselves, but only as they are understood; this is clear in the case of genus and species, and of other intellectual intentions, for there is nothing in the things outside the mind whose likeness the notion of genus or species might be. Yet the intellect is not false because it does not attribute the things of which these are the notions, namely genus and species, to things as they exist outside the intellect but only as they exist in the intellect. Insofar as the intellect reflects on itself, it understands things existing outside the mind and it also understands them to be understood. Thus, just as there is some conception or notion to which the thing outside the mind answers, so there is a conception or notion to which the thing understood answers as understood. For example, to the notion or concept of man a thing outside the mind answers, but to the notion or concept of genus or species only the thing as understood answers.

It is not possible that the meanings of the names said of God be like that, because then the intellect would attribute them to God not as he is in himself but as he is understood, which is patently false, for then the sense of 'God is good' would be that God is so understood, and not that this is what he is.

Therefore, some say that to the different notions of these names different connoted things answer, which are the different effects of God. They mean that when God is said to be good, his essence along with some connoted effect is signified, such that the sense would be that God is and causes goodness, so that the diversity of these notions would be caused by the diversity of effects.

But this does not seem appropriate, because, since the effect proceeds from the cause according to similitude, the cause must be understood to be such before the effects. God is not called wise because he causes wisdom, but because he is wise and therefore causes wisdom. Hence Augustine says that because God is, we are, and insofar as we are, we are good.

It would further follow from this that names of this kind would be said of creatures first rather than of the creator, as health is said of the healthy before it is said of medicine. If when we say that God is good, nothing other than that God is the cause of goodness were understood, by the same token it would follow that all names of divine effects can be predicated of him, as we might say that God is heaven because he causes the heaven.

Again, if this were said of actual causality, it is evidently false, because on that basis we could not say that God was from all eternity good or wise or any such thing since he was not from all eternity a cause in act.

And if it be understood of virtual causality – as if he were called good because he has the power of diffusing goodness – then we will have to say that the term 'good' signifies that power. But the power is a supereminent likeness of its effect, as is the power of any equivocal cause, so it would follow that the intellect conceiving goodness would be made like that which is in God and that which God is. Thus something in God answers to the notion and conception of goodness and that God exists.

Therefore it should be said that there is something in God answering to all these many and diverse notions of which all these conceptions of intellect are likenesses. It is clear that there can be only one specific likeness of a form which has the same notion as it, but there can be many imperfect likenesses which fail in perfectly representing the form. Since then, as is clear from the foregoing, the conceptions of perfections found in creatures are imperfect likenesses and not of the same notion as the divine essence, nothing prevents the one essence from answering to all these conceptions, as imperfectly represented by them. Thus all notions are indeed in our intellect as in a subject, but they are in God as in the verifying root of these conceptions. The conceptions that the intellect has of a thing would not be true unless that thing answered to them by way of similitude.

The cause of the diversity or multiplicity of names is from the side of our intellect, which cannot come to see the essence of God as it is, but sees it through many deficient likenesses which come about in creatures as in a glass. If it should see the essence itself, it would not need many names nor would it need many concepts. Because of this, the Word of God, which is a perfect conception of him, is only one. Thus it is said in Zacharias 14.9, 'In that day there shall be one Lord, and his name shall be one.' That is, when the very essence of God is seen and knowledge of God is not gathered from creatures.

Ad 1. It should be said, therefore, that although these names signify one thing, they do so via many notions, as has been argued, and because of these they are not synonyms.

Ad 2. It should be said that Damascene means that in God all things are one as to the thing, except for the personal properties which constitute the real distinction of persons, but this does not exclude that what is said of God should differ in notion.

Ad 3. The response is obvious: because just as goodness and wisdom are the same thing as the divine essence, so with respect to one another, but the notions of the name differ, as has been said.

Ad 4. It should be said that it is already clear from the foregoing that God is in every way one, yet these many conceptions or notions are not false, because to all of them one and the same thing answers which is imperfectly represented by them. They would be false if nothing answered to them.

Ad 5. It should be said that there is unity through and through on the side of God; multiplicity is from the side of creatures. Just as when God understands creatures there is one intelligible form with respect to his essence and many with respect to different creatures, so our intellect rising to God from the multiplicity of creatures has many species relating to one God.

Ad 6. It should be said that these notions are not founded in the divine essence as in a subject but as in the cause of truth, or as represented by all, which does not derogate from his simplicity.

Ad 7. It should be said that paternity and filiation are opposed to one another and therefore require a real distinction of supposits, but not goodness and wisdom.

Article 7: Are such names said of God and creatures univocally or equivocally?

The answer seems to be, univocally.

1. The measure and the measured share the same notion, but the divine goodness is the measure of the goodness in the creature, and his wisdom of all wisdom. Therefore, they are said univocally of God and creature.

2. Moreover, things are similar when they share a form, but the creature can be made similar to God, as is evident in Genesis 1.26: 'We will make man in our image and likeness.' Therefore there is some sharing of form between creature and God, but all things that communicate in form can have something predicated of them univocally. Therefore, something can be predicated univocally of God and creature.

3. Moreover, the greater and less do not cause specific diversity. But when the creature is called good and God is called good they seem to differ in that God is better than any creature. Therefore the goodness of God and of creature are not specifically diverse, and good is predicated univocally of God and creature.

4. Moreover, things in different genera cannot be compared, as the Philosopher proves, for the velocity of alteration and the velocity of local motion are not comparable. But between God and creature some comparison is made, for God is called the highest good and the creature is good. Therefore, God and creature are of one genus and something can be predicated univocally of them.

5. Moreover, a thing is only known through the species of one notion, for the whiteness that is in the wall would not be known through the species in the eye unless there were one notion of both. But God through his goodness knows all beings, and so too with the other attributes. Therefore, the goodness of God and creature are of one notion, and good is predicated univocally of God and creature.

6. Moreover, the house which is in the mind of the artisan and the house which is in matter are of one notion, but all creatures proceed from God as artefacts from artisan. Therefore the goodness which is in God is of one notion with the goodness that is in the creature, and thus the same conclusion as before.

7. Moreover, every equivocal agent is reduced to some univocal agent. Therefore, the first cause that God is must be univocal. But something can be predicated univocally of the univocal cause and its proper effect. Therefore, something can be predicated univocally of God and creature.

ON THE CONTRARY:

1. The Philosopher says that nothing but a name is common to the eternal and temporal. But God is eternal and creatures are temporal. Therefore, there can be nothing common to God and creatures but a name. Thus names are predicated purely equivocally of God and creatures.

2. Moreover, since genus is the first part of a definition, to take away the genus is to remove the notion signified by the name; hence if a name is imposed to signify that which inheres in another, it will be an equivocal one. But wisdom said of the creature is in the genus of quality. Therefore, since wisdom said of God is not a quality, as has been shown, it seems that this name 'wisdom' is equivocally predicated of God and creatures.

3. Moreover, where there is no similarity, there cannot be anything commonly predicated, except equivocally. But there is no similarity between God and creature, for we read in Isaiah 40.18, 'To whom then have you likened God?' Therefore, it seems that nothing can be predicated univocally of God and creatures.

4. But it will be said that although God cannot be called similar to the creature, the creature can be called similar to God. On the contrary, we

read in Psalm 82.2, 'God, who will be like unto thee?' as if to say, no one.

5. Moreover, nothing in the order of accident can be similar to substance; but wisdom in the creature is an accident whereas in God it is substance. Therefore, man cannot be likened to the divine wisdom through his wisdom.

6. Moreover, since in the creature to be is one thing and form or nature another, through form or nature nothing is made like that which is existence; but these names predicated of creatures signify some nature or form. But God is his existence. Therefore, the creature cannot be like God because these things are said of the creature, and thus the same as before.

7. Moreover, God differs from the creature more than number differs from whiteness. But it would be stupid to say that number is like whiteness, or vice versa. Therefore it is stupid to say that the creature is like God, and thus the same as before.

8. Moreover, when things are similar to one another, they agree in some one thing, and things which agree in one are transmutable among themselves. But God is in every way untransmutable. Therefore, there cannot be any similarity between God and creature.

RESPONSE:

It should be said that it is impossible for something to be predicated univocally of God and creature; this is clear because every effect of a univocal cause is equal to the power of the agent. But no creature, since it is finite, can be equal to the power of the first agent, who is infinite. Hence it is impossible that the creature should receive the likeness of God univocally.

Again, it is clear that, although the notion of the form existing in the cause and in the effect is one, yet the different mode of existing impedes univocal predication, for although the notion of the house which is in matter and the house which is in the mind of the artisan are the same – because the one is the reason for the other – still house is not predicated univocally of both because the species of the house in matter has material existence but it has immaterial existence in the mind of the artisan. Granting therefore, what is impossible, that goodness were of the same notion in God and creature, still good would not be predicated univocally of God since what in God exists immaterially and simply exists in the creature materially and multiplied. Moreover, being is not said univocally of substance and accident because substance is being as having existence of itself, and accident that for which to exist is to exist in something. From which it is clear that a diverse relation to existence impedes the univocal predication of being. God is related to existence differently than any creature, for he is his own existence, something that is true of no creature. Hence in no way can the creature be said univocally of God; and consequently none of the other predicates either, among which is First Being. When there is diversity in the first, diversity must be found in others; hence nothing is univocally predicated of substance and accident.

Some have said otherwise, however, holding that nothing is predicated analogically of God and creature, but purely equivocally. And Rabbi Moses was of this opinion, as is clear from what he says.

But this opinion cannot be true. In pure equivocals, which the Philosopher calls chance equivocals, nothing is said of one with reference to the other. But all the things said of God and creatures are said of God according to some relation to creatures, or vice versa, as is clear from all the opinions on the exposition of divine names. Hence it is impossible that it should be pure equivocation.

Again, all our knowledge of God is taken from creatures, so that if there were agreement in name alone, we would know nothing of God save some empty words with nothing to underwrite them.

It would also follow that all the demonstrations concerning God advanced by the philosophers would be sophistical. For example, if it were said that whatever is in potency is reduced to act by a being in act, and from this it were concluded that God is being in act, since all things are brought into existence by him, there would be a fallacy of equivocation. And so with all the others. Moreover, it is necessary that the effect be in some way like the cause; so nothing is predicated purely equivocally of effect and cause, but rather is predicated as healthy is predicated of medicine and animal.

On the other hand it must be said that nothing is predicated of God and creature univocally and that the things predicated commonly are not predicated purely equivocally, but analogically. There are two modes of this kind of predication, one in which something is predicated of two things with respect to a third, as being of quality and quantity with respect to substance, another in which something is predicated of two things because of the relation of one to the other, as being is said of substance and quantity.

In the first kind of predication there must be something prior to the two to which both have a relation, as substance with respect to quantity and quality, but not in the second, where it is necessary that one be prior to the other. Therefore, since nothing is prior to God but he is prior to creature, the second mode of analogy belongs to divine predication and not the first.

Ad 1. It should be said the argument proceeds from the measure which can be coequal to or commensurate with the measured; but God is not such a measure, since he infinitely exceeds everything measured by him.

Ad 2. It should be said that the likeness of creature to God falls short of the likeness of univocals in two things. First, because it is not participation in one form, as two things are hot by participating in one heat, for what is said of God and creature is predicated of God essentially and of creature by participation, such that this likeness of creature to God is understood as that of the heated to heat and not of one heated thing to another. Second, because the form participated in by the creature falls short of the notion of what God is, just as the heat of fire falls short of the notion of solar power, through which heat comes into being.

Ad 3. It should be said that the more and less can be considered and thus predicated in three ways. In one way, according to the quantity alone of the participated, as snow is said to be whiter than the wall because whiteness is more perfectly in snow than in the wall, yet of the same notion; so this difference of more and less does not cause diversity in species. In a second way, insofar as one is said by participation and the other through essence, as we say that goodness is better than the good. In a third way, insofar as it belongs in a more eminent way to one thing than to another, as heat to the sun rather than to fire. These two modes impede unity of species and univocal predication, and in this way something is predicated more and less of God and creature, as is evident from what has been said.

Ad 4. It should be said that when God is called the better or the highest good he is not compared to creatures as participating in a nature of the same genus with creatures, as species of the same genus do, but God is the principle of the genus.

Ad 5. It should be said that to the degree that an intelligible species is more eminently in something, to that degree there is more perfect knowledge of it; like the species of stone in the intellect rather than in the sense. Hence God can know things perfectly by his essence insofar as his essence is the supereminent, and not the equal, likeness of things.

Ad 6. It should be said that there is a twofold likeness between creature and God. One is of the creature to the divine intellect, and thus the form understood by God is of one notion with the thing understood, although it does not have the same mode of existing, because the form as understood is in the intellect alone, but the form of the creature is also in the thing. In another way insofar as the divine essence is a superexcellent likeness of all things and not of the same notion. From this kind of likeness but not the first, such terms as 'good' come to be commonly predicated of God and creatures. When God is called good the meaning is not that he understands the goodness of creatures, which is already clear from what has been said. Nor is house said univocally of the house which is in the mind of the artisan and the house in matter.

7. It should be said that the equivocal agent must be prior to the univocal agent because the univocal agent does not exercise causality over the whole species, otherwise he would be cause of itself, but only over an individual of the species. But the equivocal agent exercises causality over the whole species, so the first agent must be an equivocal cause.

As for the arguments advanced on the contrary:

Ad 1. It should be said that the Philosopher speaks of a natural and not a logical community. Things which have different modes of existing do not communicate in anything according to existence as considered by the natural philosopher, but they can communicate in some intention which the logician considers. Moreover, for the natural philosopher the elementary and celestial bodies are not of the same genus, whereas for the logician they are. Nevertheless the Philosopher does not mean to exclude analogical community, but only univocal, for he wishes to show that corruptible and incorruptible do not share a genus.

Ad 2. It should be said that although diversity of genus removes univocation it does not take away analogy, which is evident from the fact that healthy, as said of urine, is in the genus of sign, but as said of medicine it is in the genus of cause.

Ad 3. It should be said that there is no way in which God can be said to be similar to the creature, but only vice versa, because as Dionysius says we do not find in cause and effect a convertible similarity, but only co-ordinates, for a man is not said to be like his image, but vice versa, since the form on which similarity is based is in man before it is in his image. Therefore, we do not say God is like creatures, but vice versa.

Ad 4. It should be said that the statement, 'No creature is like God,' should be understood, as Dionysius explains in the same chapter, to mean that the effects have little of their cause and are incomparably inadequate to it. Which is not to be understood with respect to the quantity participated, but in the other two ways, as was said above.

Ad 5. It should be said that on the basis of an accident a thing cannot be similar to substance by the similarity that is based on a form of the same notion, but this does not preclude the similarity of effect and cause. For the first substance must be the cause of all accidents.

The same should be said in response to 6.

Ad 7. It should be said that whiteness is not in the genus of number nor is it the principle of the genus, and therefore there is no similarity to be expected of one to the other. God, however, is the principle of every genus and therefore all things are in some way like him.

Ad 8. It should be said that the argument is based on what communicates in genus or in matter, which is not the condition of God to creatures.

Article 8: Is there any relation between God and creature?

It seems there is not.

1. For relatives are simultaneous, according to the Philosopher, but the creature cannot be simultaneous with God, for God is in every way prior to the creature. Therefore, there can be no relation between creature and God.

2. Moreover, things between which a relation obtains must also be comparable to one another. But between God and creature there is no comparison, for things which are not of the same genus are not comparable, such as number and line. Therefore, there is no relation between God and creature.

3. Moreover, in whatever genus one relative is found, the other must also be found. But God is not in the same genus with the creature. Therefore, they cannot be said to be relative to one another.

4. Moreover, the creature cannot be opposite to the creator because a thing is not the cause of its opposite. But relatives are opposed to one another. Therefore, there can be no relation between creature and God.

5. Moreover, anything of which something new begins to be said can in some way be said to have come to be. Therefore it follows that if something is said of God relative to creature, God in some way came to be. Which is impossible, since he is immutable.

6. Moreover, whatever is predicated of something is predicated either as such or accidentally. But what implies a relation to creature is not predicated of God *per se*, because such predicates are predicated necessarily and always, and not accidentally. Therefore, in no way can such relatives be predicated of God.

ON THE CONTRARY:
Augustine says that the creator is said relatively to the creature, as lord to servant.

RESPONSE:
It should be said that relation differs from quantity and quality in this that quantity and quality are accidents abiding in a subject, whereas relation, as Boethius says, does not signify something abiding in a subject, but, as it were, in transit towards another. Hence the disciples of Gilbert de la Porre said that relations are not inherent, but assistant, which in a way is true as will be shown later.

Whatever is attributed to something as proceeding towards another is not a component of it, as action is not of the agent. Because of this the Philosopher proves in *Physics* 5 that there cannot be motion in the category of relation because without any change in that which is referred to another, the relation can cease solely because of a change in the other, as is evident in action, which is motion only metaphorically and improperly. We are said to change when from rest we begin to act, which would not be if relation or action signified something abiding in the subject.

From this it is clear that it is not against the notion of anything's simplicity that there be many relations between it and others, indeed the more simple the thing, the more relations attend it. For the more simple a thing is the less limited is its power and thus its causality can extend to more. That is why it is said in the *Book of Causes* that the more a power is unified, the more infinite it is than any multiplied power. Some relation must be understood between a principle and the things that derive from it, not only the relation of origin, according to which the effects arise from the principle, but also the relation of difference, because the effect must be distinguished from the cause, since nothing is cause of itself.

Therefore, it follows on the supreme simplicity of God that infinite relations exist between creatures and him, insofar as he produces creatures different from himself, but in some way like unto him.

Ad 1. It should be said that those relatives are simultaneous in nature which refer to one another for the same reason, such as father and son, lord and servant, double and half. But those relatives in which there is not the same basis of referring on both sides are not by nature simultaneous, but one is naturally prior to the other, as the Philosopher says of sense and the sensible as well as of knowledge and the knowable. Thus it is clear that there is no need for God and creature to be by nature simultaneous, since there is not the same basis for referring on each side. Nor is it necessary even in relatives which are by nature simultaneous that their subjects be naturally simultaneous, but only the relations.

Ad 2. It should be said that not all things related to one another are comparable to one another, but only those whose relation is based on quantity or quality, such that one can be called greater or better, or whiter or something like that. The differences of relations can be referred to one another even when of different genera, for those which are of different genera are different from one another. None the less, although God is not in the same genus as creature, as though contained in a genus, he is, however, in every genus as the principle of the genus, and on this basis there can be a relation between creature and God as between the caused and the cause.

Ad 3. It should be said that it is not necessary for the subjects of relations to be of the same genus, but only the relations themselves, as is evident from this that quantity is said to be different from quiddity. And yet, as has been said, there is not the same notion of God and creatures, as things which are in different genera are in no way co-ordinates of one another.

Ad 4. It should be said that the opposition in relations differs from other oppositions in two ways. First, is that in the others one is said to be opposed to the other insofar as it removes it, for negation removes affirmation, and they are opposed on this basis; the opposition of privation and habit and of contrariety includes the opposition of contradiction, as is said in *Metaphysics* 4. But this is not the case with relatives: son is not opposed to father as removing him, but because of the basis for the relation to him. And from this the second difference results, because in other opposites there is always the perfect and imperfect, which comes about by reason of the negation which is included in privation and the other contraries. But this is not required in relatives, indeed both can be considered perfect, as is especially evident in symmetrical – *aequiparantiae* – relations and in relatives of origin, like equal, similar, father and son. Therefore relation and not the other oppositions is attributed to God. By reason of the first difference, the opposition of relation can obtain between creature and God though not any other opposition – since God rather posits than takes away creatures – but there is a relation of creatures to God. By reason of the second difference there is in the divine persons themselves – in which nothing imperfect can exist – the opposition of relation and no other, as will appear later.

Ad 5. It should be said that since coming to be is properly to be changed, it is not found in relation save accidentally, that is, because the thing on which the relation follows has been changed. A body that is changed in quantity becomes equal, not that change as such aims at equality, but is accidentally related to it. But it is not necessary for something new to be said of a relation that some change come about in it, but it suffices that there be a change in one of the extremes, for the cause of the relation between two things is something inherent in both. Hence, from whatever side there be a change in that which caused the relation, the relation between the two is taken away. On this basis, because some change comes about in the creature, a relation in God is said to begin. Hence insofar as something new is said of God, he cannot be said to have changed, save metaphorically, because he is related to the likeness of the changed thing. And thus we say, 'O Lord, you are made a refuge for us.' (Psalm 89)

Ad 6. It should be said that when such relations begin to be said of God because of change in the creature, it is obvious that the reason they are said of God is on the side of the creature and they are said accidentally of God. Not that there is any accident in God, as Augustine pointed out, but because of something existing outside himself, which is accidentally compared to him. For the existence of God is not dependent on the creature any more than the existence of the builder is on the house. Hence, just as it is incidental to the [existence of] builder that the house exists, so is it with God and creature. A thing is said to relate accidentally to another, when it can exist without it.

Article 9: Are the relations between creatures and God really in creatures?

It seems that they are not.

1. For there are relations which involve nothing real on either side of the relation, as Avicenna says of the relations between being and non-being. But there is no relation whose extremes are more distant from one another than that between God and creature. Therefore this relation does not involve anything real on either side.

2. Moreover, anything on which an infinite regress follows must be rejected. But if the relation to God be something real in the creature, there will be an infinite regress, for that relation will be something created, if it is a thing, and then there will be another relation of it to God, by parity of reasoning, and so on to infinity. Therefore, we should not say that the relation to God is something real in the creature.

3. Moreover, a thing is related only to one definite thing: double is not with reference to just anything, but to half, and father to son, and so with the rest. Therefore, it is necessary that according to the difference of the things related, there are differences in the things to which they are related. But God is absolutely one being. Therefore, all creatures cannot be related to him by some real relation.

4. Moreover, a creature is referred to God insofar as he proceeds from him; but the creature proceeds from God according to his substance. Therefore, he is referred to God according to his substance and not according to some supervening relation.

5. Moreover, a relation is midway between the extremes of the relation. But nothing can really be between God and the creature which is immediately created by God. Therefore, the relation to God is not something in the creature.

6. Moreover, the Philosopher says that if all appearances were true, things would follow our opinions and sensations. But it is clear that all creatures follow the opinion or knowledge of the creator. Therefore, all creatures refer substantially to God and not by some inherent relation.

7. Moreover, there seems to be less of a relation between greatly distant things, but the distance between the creature and God is greater than that between one creature and another. But the relation of creature to creature is not some thing, as it seems, for since it is not substance, it must be an accident, and thus it is in the subject and cannot be removed without a change of the subject: the contrary of which was said above about relation. Therefore, the relation of creature to God is not some thing.

8. Moreover, just as created being is infinitely distant from non-being, so it is infinitely distant from God. But between created being and pure non-being there is no relation, as Avicenna says. Therefore, there is none between created and uncreated being.

ON THE CONTRARY:

1. Augustine says that what begins to be said of God temporally was not said of him before and manifestly is said of him relatively, not because of any accident in God, as if something happened to him, but plainly because of an accident in the relative to which God begins to be spoken. But an accident is something in the subject. Therefore, the relation to God is something in the creature.

2. Moreover, whatever is referred to something by its own change is really referred to it. But the creature is referred to God by its own change. Therefore, it is really referred to God.

RESPONSE:

It should be said that the relation to God is something in the creature. In evidence of which it should be noted that, as the Commentator says in *Metaphysics* 11, some thought relation to be a second intention because it is the weakest being of all the categories. The things first understood are outside the soul, and intellect bears on them as things to be understood; what is thought secondly are called intentions consequent on our mode of understanding, and these the intellect understands secondarily insofar as it reflects on itself, understanding itself to understand and the manner in which it understands.

It would follow from this position that relation is not among the things outside the mind, but only in the intellect, like the intentions of genus and species, and of second substances.

But this cannot be. Only what exists outside the mind is placed in any of the categories. But the being of reason is contrasted with being divided by the ten categories, as is clear from *Metaphysics* 5. If relation were not among the things outside the soul, it would not be included as one kind of category. Moreover, the perfection and good that are in things outside the soul are based not only on something absolutely inhering in things but also on the order of one thing to another, just as the good of the army consists in the order of the parts of an army. The Philosopher compares the order of the universe to this order.

Therefore it is necessary that in things themselves there be an order and this order is a kind of relation. Hence, there must be relations in things themselves according to which one is ordered to another. One thing is ordered to another either on the basis of quantity or of some active or passive power. Only on the basis of these two does something exist in one with respect to another extrinsic thing. For something is measured not only by intrinsic quantity but also by extrinsic. By active power a thing acts on another and by passive power is acted upon by another. By substance and quality, however, something is ordered only to itself, not to another, except incidentally; that is, insofar as quality – or substantial form or matter – have the note of active or passive power and insofar as some notion of quantity is considered in them: thus what is substantially one is the same, the qualitatively one is the similar, and number or multitude cause the dissimilar and diverse in the same; the dissimilar is taken to be the more or less so than another: for thus something is said to be whiter than another. On account of this, the Philosopher in *Metaphysics* 5, assigning the species of relation, holds that some are caused by quantity and some by action and passion.

Therefore, it is necessary that things ordered to something are really referred to it, and that the relation is something in them. But all creatures are ordered to God as to principle and end, for the order of the parts of the universe among themselves is from the order of the whole universe to God, just as the order between the parts of the army is for the sake of the order of the army to the leader, as is clear from *Metaphysics* 12. Hence it is necessary that creatures are really referred to God and that this relation is something in the creature.

Ad 1. It should be said that the fact that when there is a mutual relation of creatures that posits nothing in either of the extremes this is not because of the distance between them but rather because the relation is not based on any order among the things but on one which is in intellect alone. Which cannot be said of the order of creatures to God.

Ad 2. It should be said that these relations are not referred to another by some other relation but of themselves, because they are essentially relations. It is not the same with things that have absolute substance, hence it does not follow that there is an infinite regress.

Ad 3. It should be said that the Philosopher in the same place concludes that if all are referred to the best, that which is infinite in species must be the best, and thus nothing prevents what is infinite in species from being referred to an infinity of things. But God is such, since the perfection of his substance is restricted to no genus, as was said above. On account of this, nothing prevents an infinity of creatures from being referred to God.

Ad 4. It should be said that the creature is referred to God, according to his substance as the cause of the relation, but according to the relation formally, just as something is called similar according to quality causally, but according to similarity formally. For the creature is denominated similar from it.

Ad 5. It should be said that an intermediate cause is excluded when the creature is said to proceed from God immediately, but not a mediating real relation, which follows naturally on the production of the creature; just as equality follows the production of quantity indeterminately, so the real relation naturally follows on the production of created substance.

Ad 6. It should be said that creatures follow on God's knowledge as effect on cause, not as the proper notion of their being, as if a creature were nothing else than being known by God. This is the way those spoke who held that all appearances are true, and the thing to follow on opinion and sensation, such that for anything to be is for it to be sensed or thought by another.

Ad 7. It should be said that the relation that is nothing other than the order of one creature to another has one feature insofar as it is an accident and another insofar as it is a relation or order. For insofar as it is an accident, it is in a subject, but not insofar as it is a relation or order, but only because it is, as it were, passing into another and in a way taking up a position in the related thing. Thus relation is something inherent, though not insofar as it is a relation, just as action insofar as it is action is considered to be from the agent, but insofar as it is an accident it is considered as in the acting subject. So nothing prevents such an accident from ceasing to be without a change in that in which it is, because its nature is not perfected by the fact that it is in the subject but insofar as it tends to another. That being taken away, the notion of this accident is taken away as actual but it remains with respect to its cause, just as, matter being taken away, heating is taken away, although the cause of heating remains.

Ad 8. It should be said that created being is not ordered to non-being, although it has an order to uncreated being, so the similarity does not obtain.

Article 10: Is God really referred to the creature in such a way that this relation is something in God?

The answer seems to be yes.

1. The mover is really related to the moved, hence the Philosopher, in *Metaphysics* 5, identifies the relation of mover to moved as a species in the category of relation. But God is compared to the creature as mover to moved. Therefore, he is really related to the creature.

2. But it might be said that he moves creatures without any change in himself, and therefore is not really related to the thing moved. On the contrary, one of relative opposites does not cause the other to be called by the same name: for something is not double because it is half, nor is God Father because he is the Son. Therefore, if the mover is said relatively to the moved, the relation of moving is not in something because the relation of being moved is in it. Therefore, the fact that God is not moved does not prevent him being really related as mover to the moved.

3. Moreover, as a father gives existence to his son, so does the creator

give existence to the creature. But a father is really related to his son; therefore, the creator is really related to the creature.

4. Moreover, things which are properly and not metaphorically said of God place the thing signified in God. But among such names Dionysius puts 'Lord'. Therefore the thing signified by the name 'Lord' is really in God. But this is a relation to creature, therefore, etc.

5. Moreover, knowledge is really related to the knowable, as is evident in *Metaphysics* 5. But God is compared to created things as knower to known. Therefore, there is in God a relation to creatures.

6. Moreover, what is moved always has a real relation to the mover. But will is compared to the thing willed as mover to moved, for the desirable is an unmoved mover and appetite a moved mover, as is said in *Metaphysics* 12. Therefore, since God wills things to be, he seems to be really related to creatures.

7. Moreover, if God is not related to creatures, there seems to be no other reason for this than that he does not depend on creatures and because he exceeds creatures. But in a similar way celestial bodies do not depend on elementary bodies and exceed them disproportionately. Therefore, on this basis it would follow that there is no real relation of the higher bodies to the lower.

8. Moreover, every denomination is from form. But form is something inherent in the thing whose form it is. Since therefore God is named from relations to creatures, it seems that these relations are something in God.

9. Moreover, proportion is a real relation, for example double to half, but there seems to be a proportion of God to creature, since there must be a proportion between mover and moved. Therefore it seems that God is really related to the creature.

10. Moreover, since concepts are likenesses of things and words are signs of things, as the Philosopher says, these have one order for the learner and another for the teacher, for the teacher begins with things from which he receives knowledge in his intellect, of whose conceptions words are signs, but the learner begins with words by which he attains the conceptions in the teacher's intellect, and from them knowledge of things. It is necessary that what is said of the foregoing relations is first known by some teacher. Therefore, with him such relative names follow the conceptions of his intellect which are consequent on things. Therefore, it seems these relations are real.

11. Moreover, such relatives as are said of God temporally are either relatives according to existence or according to talk. If they are relatives according to talk, nothing real is posited in either extreme. But this is

false according to the foregoing, for they exist really in the creature related to God. So they must be relatives according to existence, and it seems therefore that they posit something real in both extremes.

12. Moreover, it is the nature of relatives that, when one is given, the other is given, and if one is taken away, so is the other. If, therefore, there is some real relation to God in the creature, there must be a real relation to creatures in God.

ON THE CONTRARY:

1. Augustine says in *On the Trinity* 5, that it is manifest that God is spoken of relatively because of an accident in the thing relative to which God begins to be talked of. Therefore, it seems that these relations are said of God, not because of something in himself, but according to something outside, and thus they posit nothing real in him.

2. Moreover, as the knowable is the measure of knowledge, so God is the measure of all things, as the Commentator says in *Metaphysics* 10. But the knowable is not related to knowledge by a relation which is really in it, but rather because of the relation of knowledge to it, as is clear from the Philosopher in *Metaphysics* 5. Therefore, it seems that God is not spoken of relatively to creatures because of some relation which is really in him.

3. Moreover, Dionysius says, 'We do not have conversion between causes and effects, for the effect is said to be like the cause, but not vice versa.' What is true of similarity seems true of other relations. Therefore it seems that no more do the other relations bring about a conversion from God to creature, such that, because the creature is really related to God, God is really related to creatures.

RESPONSE:

It should be replied that when God is said to be related to creatures the relation is not really in him. In evidence of which it should be noted that since a real relation consists in the order of one thing to another thing, as has been said, a mutual real relation is only found in things in which on both sides there is some notion of order of the one to the other, which is found in all relations based on quantity, for since the notion of quantity is abstracted from everything sensible, there is the same notion of quantity in all natural bodies. For the same reason that one thing having quantity is really related to the other, the reverse is true.

But a quantity taken absolutely has an order to another according to the notion of measure and measured, and according to the name of whole and part, and other such things that follow on quantity. But in relations which are founded on active and passive power there is not always the order of motion from both sides. For that which always has the note of patient and being moved, or caused, is ordered to agent or mover, since an effect is always perfected by its cause and depends on it, hence it is ordered to it as to its perfecter.

But agents or movers or even causes are sometimes ordered to patients, to the moved, to the caused, insofar as having brought about the effect or passion or moved, a certain good and perfection of the mover and agent results, as especially is evident in univocal agents which by acting bring about a likeness of their species, and to the degree possible preserve it in perpetuity.

The same is clear in all other things which are moved in moving or acting or causing, for by the motion itself they are ordered to producing effects, and similarly in all of them some good comes about in the cause from the effect. There are some things which are ordered to others, but not vice versa, because they are quite outside the genus of actions or powers which this order follows. As it is clear that knowledge relates to the knowable, because the one knowing, through an intelligible act, is ordered to the thing known which is outside the soul. The thing itself that is outside the soul is in no way touched by such an act, since the act of intellect does not pass out to change any external matter. Hence the thing itself outside the soul is completely outside the intelligible genus, and because of this the relation consequent on the act of intellect is not in it.

There is a similar argument concerning sense and the object of sense, for although the object of sense changes the organ of sense in its action, and because of this has a relation to it – as other natural agents to the things acted on by them – still the alteration of the organ does not bring about actual sensing, which is brought about by the act of the sense power, of which the sensible outside the soul is wholly incapable. Similarly man is related to a column as being to the right of it because of the power to move that is in him, according to which he can move to right or left, to front or rear, up or down. Therefore, such relations are real in the man or animal, but not in the thing that lacks this power. Similarly the coin is outside the activity through which the price comes to be, which is an agreement arrived at between men, and a man is outside the genus of the art-making activities through which his image is effected.

Therefore, a man does not have a real relation to his image, nor coin to price, but vice versa. God does not act through an intervening action which is understood as proceeding from God and terminating in the creature, but his action is his substance and whatever is in him is wholly outside the genus of created existence by which the creature is related to God. Nor does any good accrue to the creator from the production of the creature. Hence his action is supremely liberal, as Avicenna says. It is also clear that he is not moved to act, but without any change on his own part makes mutable things.

The result is that there is in him no real relation to the creature, although there is a relation of the creature to him, that of effect to cause. The Rabbi was multiply wrong when he tried to prove that there is no relation between God and creature because God, not being a body, has no relation to time or place. For he considered only the relation consequent on quantity, not that which follows on action and passion.

Ad 1. It should be said that the natural mover and agent move and act by means of action or motion which is between the mover and moved, the agent and the acted upon. Thus the agent as agent is not extraneous to the genus of the acted upon insofar as acted upon. Hence there is a real relation of both to the other, especially when that mediate action is the proper perfection of the agent. Consequently, that in which action terminates is its good. But this does not happen in God, as has been said, so there is no similarity.

Ad 2. It should be said that the fact that the mover is moved is not the reason why the relation of moving is really in it, but a sign. From this it appears that in a certain way it falls into the genus of the moved, from the fact that it is a moved mover, and it also appears that that to which it is moved is its good from the fact that it is ordered to it by its motion.

Ad 3. It should be said that the father gives existence of his own kind to his son, since he is a univocal agent, but it is not thus that God gives existence to the creature, so the similarity does not obtain.

Ad 4. It should be said that the word 'Lord' includes three things in its meaning, namely, the power of coercing subordinates, an order to the subordinate which follows this power, and being the term of the order of subordinates to the Lord, for in one relative the other is understood. This meaning of the word is saved in God with respect to the first and third, but not the second. Hence Ambrose says that this word 'Lord' is a name of power and Boethius says that dominion is the power whereby the servant is coerced.

Ad 5. It should be said that the knowledge of God compares to things differently than does ours, for it compares to them as cause and measure. Such things are according to the truth which God in his knowledge has ordered. But these things are the cause and measure of our knowledge. Hence just as our knowledge really refers to things, and not vice versa, so things really relate to God's knowledge, and not the reverse. Or it could be said that God understands other things in understanding himself, hence the relation of divine knowledge is not directly to things, but to the divine essence itself.

Ad 6. It should be said that the desirable which moves appetite is the end; those things which are for the sake of the end do not move appetite except by reason of the end. But the end of the divine will is not something other than the divine goodness. Hence it does not follow that other things are compared to the divine will as movers to moved.

Ad 7. It should be said that celestial bodies really relate to inferior bodies according to relations consequent on quantity, because there is the same notion of quantity in both, and also according to relations consequent on active and passive power, because they move as moved by a mediate action which is not their substance, since some good of theirs is had from this that they are causes of the lower bodies.

Ad 8. It should be said that that from which a thing is denominated is not always a natural form but it suffices that it be signified in the manner of form, grammatically speaking. For man is denominated from action and from clothing and other like things which are not really forms.

Ad 9. It should be said that if proportion be understood as some definite excess, there is no proportion of God to creature. But if proportion is understood as a relation alone, then there is one between creator and creature, in the creature really, but not in the creator.

Ad 10. It should be said that although the teacher begins with things, the conceptions of things are received in the mind of the teacher in a way different from the way they are in the nature of things, but what is received is received in the manner of the receiver, for it is evident that conceptions in the mind of the teacher exist immaterially, although they exist materially in nature.

Ad 11. It should be said that this distinction of relatives according to existence and according to speech has nothing to do with a relation's being real. For there are relations according to existence which are not real, like right and left in the column, and there are some relatives according to speech which imply real relations, as is evident in knowledge and sensing. Relatives are said to be according to existence when the names are imposed to signify the relations themselves, and they are said to be relatives according to speech when the names are imposed to signify the qualities or the like principally, on which relations follow. And this has nothing to do with relations being real or of reason alone.

To the last it should be said that although to posit one relative is to posit the other, it is not necessary that both be posited in the same way, but it suffices that one be posited according to reality and the other according to reason.

Article 11: Are these temporal relations in God according to reason?

It seems not.

1. A notion to which nothing corresponds is empty and vain, as Boethius says. But these relations are not really in God, as is clear from the foregoing. Therefore, the notion would be empty and vain if they were in God only according to reason.

2. Moreover, what is according to reason alone is only attributed to things insofar as they are in the intellect, like genus and species and order. But such temporal relations are not attributed to God only insofar as he is in our intellect, for thus it would be nothing to say that God is Lord since God is understood to pre-exist creatures, which appears false. Therefore, such relations are not in God according to reason.

3. Moreover, this word 'Lord' signifies a relation, since it is a relation according to existence. But God is not Lord according to reason alone. Therefore such relations are not in God according to reason alone.

4. Moreover, even if no created intellect existed, God would still be Lord and creator. But there cannot be any being of reason if no created intellect exists. Therefore Lord and creator and the like do not mean relations of reason alone.

5. Moreover, that which is only according to our reason was not from all eternity. But some relations of God to creature were from eternity, such as the relations implied by knowledge and predestination. Therefore, such relations are not in God according to reason only.

ON THE CONTRARY:

Names signify notions or concepts, as is said in the beginning of *On Interpretation*. But these names are clearly said relatively. Therefore, such relations must be according to reason.

RESPONSE:

It should be said that just as the real relation consists of an order of thing to thing, so the relation of reason consists in an order among things conceived, which can come about in two ways: in one way, insofar as this order is discovered by intellect and attributed to that which is said relatively, and relations of this kind are attributed to things understood insofar as they are understood, like the relation of genus and species, for reason discovers these relations in considering the order of that which is in the intellect to things which are outside it, or also the order of things understood to one another.

In another way, insofar as such relations follow on the mode of understanding, namely that intellect understands something as ordered to another, although intellect is not fashioned by intellect but rather it follows with necessity on the mode of understanding. Intellect does not attribute relations of this kind to that which is in the intellect, but to that which is in things.

And this indeed comes about insofar as some things which do not have an order in themselves are understood as ordered, although the intellect does not understand them to have the order, because this would be false. In order for things to have an order, it is necessary that both be beings and distinct (for there is no order between a thing and itself) and orderable to the other.

Sometimes, however, intellect takes two things as beings, of which one alone or neither is a being, as when it considers two future events, or one present and the other future, and understands the one as ordered to the other, saying one is prior to the other. Such relations are of reason alone, as following on the mode of understanding.

Sometimes it takes one as two, and understands it with some order, as when something is said to be the same as itself, and thus such a relation is of reason alone.

Sometimes it takes two as orderable to one another, between which no mediate order exists – indeed one of them essentially is order, as when a relation is said to be an accident of the subject. Hence this relation of reason to whatever other things is of reason alone.

Sometimes it takes something as ordered to another, insofar as it is the term of the ordering of the other to itself, although it is not itself ordered to the other, as when taking the knowable as the term of the order of knowing to it and thus with some order to knowledge: thus the word knowable signifies relatively, and it is a relation of reason alone. And similarly, our intellect attributes some relative names to God insofar as it takes God as the term of the relations of creatures to him, and such relations are of reason alone.

Ad 1. It should be said that something on the side of the thing answers to such relations, namely the relation of the creature to God. For just as the knowable is said relatively, not because it is related to knowledge, but because knowledge is related to it, as is said in *Metaphysics* 5, so God is said relatively because creatures are related to him.

Ad 2. It should be said that the argument proceeds from those relations of reason which are fashioned by reason and are attributed to things existing in the intellect. But these relations are not like that, but consequent on the mode of understanding.

Ad 3. It should be said that just as someone is really the same as himself and not just according to reason, although the relation is of reason alone, because of the fact that the cause of the relation is real, namely, the unity of the substance which intellect understands as a relation, so the power of coercing subordinates is in God really, which the intellect understands as an order to subordinates because of the order of subordinates to him. Because of this he is said to be really Lord, although the relation is of reason alone, and in the same way it is clear that he would be Lord even if no intellect existed.

From which the solution to the fourth is obvious.

Ad 5. It should be said that God's knowledge is not related to the creature first and as such, as was said before, but to the essence of the creator, through which God knows all things.

14. On Goodness and the Goodness of God.
Summa theologiae, 1, 5–6 (1268)

In our effort to talk about God, we look in effect for words or names common to God and creature, and then ask questions about how the meanings of such common terms must vary in order to permit the extension of the vocabulary of creatures to God. There are certain words whose meaning is as broad as that of being itself. These so-called transcendental properties of being have an ordered set of meanings which enable them to be used in each of the categories. It is just because they are not confined to one category that they are said to transcend categorical limitations.

The transcendentals are 'one', 'true', 'good' and 'beauty' and the claim comes down to this: whatever is, is one; whatever is, is true; whatever is, is good; whatever is, is beautiful. This entails that, like being, they are 'said in many ways', that is, as Thomas would put it, that they are analogical terms. The extension of such names to God may seem to involve the following simple argument:

Whatever is, is good.

God exists.

Therefore, God is good.

The following selection will make clear that the matter is a good deal more complicated than that. God is not just another being among the things that are.

In Chapter 6, we saw how painstakingly Thomas looks into the way in which terms like 'wise' and 'just' can be applied to God. The base for such terms is of course much less broad than it is for the transcendentals. Man as the image and likeness of God provides a privileged springboard to knowledge of the divine. But Thomas, having established God's simplicity in Question 3 of Part 1 of the Summa theologiae, *is initially concerned with the way in which God shares terms with anything*

*whatsoever. First he will discuss good in general; then he will speak of
the goodness of God.*

Summa theologiae, Part 1

QUESTION 5
ON GOODNESS IN GENERAL

We turn now to the good, and first to good in general, then to the goodness
of God. There are six things to be asked about the first: (1) whether good
and being are the same thing; (2) supposing that they differ only in
account, which account is first, that of good or of being? (3) supposing
being to be first, whether every being is good; (4) to what cause is the
notion of the good reduced? (5) whether the notion of good consists in
manner, species and order; (6) how good is divided into moral, useful
and pleasant.

Article 1: Do good and being differ in reality?

It seems that they do.

1. Boethius says in *On the Hebdomads* that it is one thing for things
to be good and another for them to exist. Therefore, good and being
really differ.

2. Moreover, nothing is informed by itself. But good is said of being
by way of informing it, as we are told in the *Book of Causes* 6. Therefore
good differs from being in reality.

3. Good is susceptible of more and less, but existence is not; therefore
good really differs from being.

ON THE CONTRARY:
Augustine says in *On Christian Doctrine* 1.32 that we are good because
we exist.

RESPONSE:
It should be said that good and being are the same in reality and differ
only in account. Which is clear from this: the notion of good consists in
this that something is desirable, which is why the Philosopher, in *Ethics*

1, says that the good is that which all things desire. But it is manifest that a thing is desirable insofar as it is perfected, for all things desire their own perfection. A thing is perfected to the degree that it is actual; clearly, then, a thing is good to the degree that it is being, for existence is the actuality of every thing, as is clear from the foregoing. So it is obvious that good and being are really the same, but good adds the note of desirable, which being does not.

Ad 1. It should be said that although good and being are really the same, because they differ in account a thing is not called a being simply speaking and good simply speaking in the same way. For since being means that something is properly actual, and act is related to potency, a thing will be called a being simply speaking insofar as it is first distinguishable from mere potency. But this is the substantial existence of the thing. Hence it is because of its substantial existence that a thing is said to be simply speaking. Through superadded acts something is said to be in a certain respect, as to be white means to be in a certain respect, for to be white does not replace being potential simply speaking, since it attaches to a thing already actually existing. But good expresses the note of the per- fected, which is desirable, and consequently it expresses the note of the complete. Hence that which is completely perfected is said to be good simply speaking. What does not have the complete perfection it is meant to have, although it has some perfection insofar as it is actual, is not called perfect simply speaking nor good simply speaking but only in a certain respect. Therefore, with respect to first existence, which is substantial, something is called being simply speaking and good in a certain respect, that is, insofar as it is, but according to the complete act something is called being in a certain respect and good simply speaking. Therefore, what Boethius said, that a thing is good is one thing and that it is another, should be understood in terms of being good and of being simply speaking, because something is being simply speaking by first act and good simply speaking by ultimate act. However, it is good in a certain respect because of first act and according to the ultimate act it is being in a certain respect.

Ad 2. It should be replied that good is said by way of informing, insofar as good simply speaking is meant, with reference to the ultimate act.

Ad 3. Similarly, in response to the third, it should be noted that good admits of more or less according to a supervenient act, such as knowledge or virtue.

Article 2: Is the notion of good prior to that of being?

It seems that it is.

1. The order in names is according to the order of the things signified by them. But Dionysius puts good before being among the names of God as is clear from *On the Divine Names* 3. Therefore the notion of good is before that of being.

2. Moreover, that which is prior in notion extends to more things, but good extends to more things than does being, because, as Dionysius says in *On the Divine Names* 5, the good extends to the existing and non-existing, whereas being extends to the existing alone. Therefore, good is prior in notion to being.

3. That which is more universal is prior in notion. But good seems to be more universal than being, because the good has the note of the appetitible. But for some non-being is desirable, for it is said of Judas in Matthew 26.24: 'It were better for that man if he had not been born.' Therefore, the good is prior in notion to being.

4. Moreover, not just existence is desirable, but also life and wisdom and many other things, and so it seems that existence is a particular desirable thing whereas good is universal. Therefore, good is absolutely prior in notion to being.

ON THE CONTRARY:

In the *Book of Causes* it is said that the first of all created things is existence.

RESPONSE:

It should be said that being is prior in notion to good, for the notion signified by the name is what the intellect conceives of the thing and signifies by means of the word; therefore, that is prior according to notion which is first conceived by intellect. But it is being that intellect knows first, because anything is knowable to the degree that it is actual, as is said in *Metaphysics* 9. Hence being is the proper object of intellect, and thus is the first intelligible, as sound is the first audible. Therefore, being is prior in notion to good.

Ad 1. It should be said that Dionysius discusses the divine names insofar as they imply causality in God, for we name God, as he says, from creatures, as the cause from effects. But good, since it has the note of the desirable, implies the relation of final cause, whose causality is first, because an agent only acts for the sake of the end, and the matter is moved to form by the agent, hence it is said that the end is the cause of causes. Thus, in causing, the good is prior to being, as end is to form, and for this reason, among the names signifying divine causality, good is placed before being.

Again, because according to the Platonists, who did not distinguish matter from privation, matter is non-being, the participation in good extends to more things than the participation of being. For prime matter participates in the good, since it desires it (nothing desires anything other than its like), but it does not participate in being, since they held it to be non-being. Therefore, Dionysius says that good extends to non-existing things.

Ad 2. Thus the solution to the second is obvious. If not, it should be said that good extends to existing and non-existing things according to causality and not according to predication, such that by non-existing we understand not simply that which wholly is not, but things which are potential and not actual, because the good has the note of end, in which not only the things that are actual rest, but to which also are moved those things which are not in act but only in potency. Being implies only the relation of formal cause, whether inherent or exemplar, whose causality extends only to things in act.

Ad 3. It should be said that not to be is not as such desirable, save incidentally, insofar as the taking away of some evil is desirable, which evil is taken away by non-being. But the taking away of evil is not desirable except insofar as some good is negated by the evil. Therefore that which is desirable in itself is existence and non-existence only incidentally, insofar as some existence is desired in which a man would not be deprived. Thus non-being is called good only incidentally as well.

Ad 4. It should be said that life and knowledge and the like are desired insofar as they are actual, hence in all of them some existence is desired. Thus only being is desirable and consequently nothing is good except being.

Article 3: Is every being good?

It seems not.

1. The good adds to being, as is clear from what has been said. But the things that add something to being, contract it, for example, substance, quantity, quality and other such things. Therefore, the good contracts being and not every being is good.

2. Moreover, no evil is good. Isaiah 5.20: 'Woe to you that call evil good, and good evil.' But some being is called evil. Therefore, not every being is good.

3. Moreover, good has the note of the desirable. But prime matter does not have the note of the desirable, but only of desiring. Therefore, prime matter does not have the note of the good. Therefore, not every being is good.

4. Moreover, the Philosopher says in *Metaphysics* 3.2 that there is no good in mathematicals. But mathematicals are kinds of being, otherwise there would be no science of them. Therefore, not every being is good.

ON THE CONTRARY:
Every being that is not God is a creature of God. 'For every creature of God is good,' as is said in 1 Timothy 4.4. Therefore, every being is good.

RESPONSE:
It should be said that every being, insofar as it is a being, is good. For every being, insofar as it is a being, is actual and in some way perfect, because every act is some sort of perfection. Therefore, the perfected has the note of the appetitible and good, as is clear from what has been said. It follows, therefore, that every being, as such, is good.

Ad 1. It should be said that substance, quantity and quality, and what is contained under them, contract being by applying being to some quiddity or nature. Good does not add to being in this way, but adds only the note of appetitible and perfection, which belongs to existence in whatever nature it is. Hence good does not contract being.

Ad 2. It should be said that no being is called evil insofar as it is being, but insofar as it lacks some existence, as a man is called evil insofar as he lacks some virtue, and the eye is called bad insofar as it lacks the sharpness of sight.

Ad 3. It should be said that prime matter, just as it is being only in potency, so it is good only in potency. Although, according to the Platonists, prime matter can be said to be non-being, because of the adjunct privation. But it participates in something of good, namely its order or aptitude to good. Therefore, it does not belong to it to be desirable, but that it should desire.

Ad 4. It should be said that mathematicals do not subsist separately in existence, because if they should subsist, there would be good in them, namely their own existence. But mathematicals are separate only in understanding, insofar as they are abstracted from motion and from matter, and thus they are abstracted from the note of end, which has the note of mover. There is nothing absurd in the fact that there should be no good or note of good in some being as it is thought, since the notion of being is prior to that of good, as was said above.

Article 4: Does good have the note of final cause?

It seems not.

1. As Dionysius says in *On the Divine Names* 4, the good is praised as beauty is. But beauty implies the note of formal cause. Therefore, good has the note of formal cause.

2. Moreover, the good is diffusive of its existence, as can be drawn from the words of Dionysius when he says that the good is that by which all things subsist and are. But to be diffusive implies the note of efficient cause. Therefore, good has the note of efficient cause.

3. Moreover, Augustine says in *On Christian Doctrine* 1.32 that because God is good, we exist. But we are from God as from an efficient cause. Therefore, the good implies the note of efficient cause.

ON THE CONTRARY:

The Philosopher says in *Physics* 2.3, 'The others are causes in the sense of the end or the good of the rest.' Therefore, the good has the note of final cause.

RESPONSE:

It should be said that since the good is that which all things desire, it has the note of end, for it is manifest that the good implies the note of end. However, the notion of good presupposes the notions of efficient cause and of formal cause. For we see that what is first in causing is the last caused, for fire first warms before it introduces the form of fire, since heat in fire follows on substantial form. But in causing, the good and end are found first, which move the efficient; second, the action of the efficient, moving to form; third, form advenes. So it must be the reverse in what is caused: first there is the form, through which the thing is being; second, there is in it its effective power, according to which it is perfected in being (for anything is perfect when it can make something like itself, as the Philosopher says in the *Meteorology* 4.3); third, the notion of the good follows, on which perfection in the thing is grounded.

Ad 1. It should be said therefore that the beautiful and good are indeed the same in subject, since they are founded on the same thing, namely, form, and because of this the good is praised as beauty is. But they differ in notion. For good properly looks to appetite, for the good is that which all things desire. And so it has the note of end, for appetite is like a movement towards the thing. But beauty looks to the cognitive power, for things are called beautiful which when seen please. Hence beauty consists of fitting proportion, for sense takes pleasure in things duly proportioned, as in things similar to itself; for sense is a kind of reason, as is every knowing power. And since knowledge comes about through assimilation, and similitude looks to form, the beautiful properly pertains to the notion of formal causality.

Ad 2. It should be said that the good is said to be diffusive of its being in the way in which the end is said to move.

Ad 3. It should be said that anyone having a will is called good insofar as he has a good will, because by means of the will we use all else in us. Hence a man who has a good intellect is not called good, but one who has a good will. Will looks to the end as its proper object, hence the remark, 'Because God is good, we are,' refers to the final cause.

Article 5: Does the notion of good consist of mode, species and order?

It seems not.

1. Good and being differ in notion, as has been said above, but mode, species and order seem to pertain to the notion of being because, as is said in Wisdom 11.21, 'But thou hast ordered all things in measure and number and weight.' To these three, species, mode and order are reduced, because, as Augustine says in the literal commentary on Genesis 4.3, 'Measure fashions the mode of each thing, and number gives every thing

its species, and weight draws a thing to rest and stability.' Therefore, the notion of good consists of mode, species and order.

2. Moreover, mode, species and order are certain goods. Therefore, if the notion of good consists of mode, species and order, mode must have mode, species and order, and similarly species and order. Therefore, it will go on to infinity.

3. Moreover, evil is the privation of mode, species and order. But evil does not totally remove the good. Therefore, the notion of good does not consist of mode, species and order.

4. Moreover, that of which the notion of good consists cannot be called evil. But we speak of an evil mode, an evil species, a bad order. Therefore, the notion of good cannot consist of mode, species and order.

5. Moreover, mode, species and order are caused by weight, number and measure, as can be inferred from the authority of Augustine. But not all good things have weight, number and measure, for Ambrose says in the *Hexameron* 9 that the nature of light is that it not be created in number or in weight or in measure. Therefore, the notion of good does not consist of mode, species and order.

ON THE CONTRARY:

Augustine says in *On the Nature of the Good* that these three, mode, species and order, are, as it were, certain general goods created by God in things, and thus, where these are great, there are great goods, where they are small, there are small goods, where they are not, there is no good. Which would not be the case if the notion of good did not consist of these. Therefore, the notion of good consists of mode, species and order.

RESPONSE:

It should be said that anything is called good insofar as it is perfect, for thus it is desirable, as was said above. But that is called perfect which is lacking nothing of the mode of its perfection. But since anything is that which it is through its form, and form presupposes some things and other things necessarily follow on it, in order for something to be perfect and good, it must have form and the things presupposed to it and the things consequent on it. Presupposed to form is the determination or commensuration of principles, whether material, or the things which effect it, which is what mode means. Hence it is said that measure preshapes mode. The form itself is meant by species, because a thing is constituted in its species by form. That is why number is said to supply species, because the definitions signifying the species are like numbers, as the Philosopher says in *Metaphysics* 7.3. For just as the species of number changes when a unit is added or subtracted, so in definitions when a difference is added or subtracted. The inclination to the end or to action or something like follows on form because a thing acts insofar as it is actual, and tends towards that which befits it according to its form. This pertains to weight and order. Hence the notion of good, insofar as it consists in perfection, also consists in mode, species and order.

Ad 1. It should be said that these three do not follow on being except insofar as it is perfect and thus is good.

Ad 2. It should be said that mode, species and order are called goods in the same way they are called beings, not because they are subsistent things, but because by them other things are both being and good. Hence it is not necessary that there be other things thanks to which these are good, for they are not called good as if they were formally good by other things, but because by them some things are formally called good; just as whiteness is not called being as if it were so *by* something, but because thanks to it something else is in a certain respect, namely white.

Ad 3. It should be said that any existence is according to some form, hence mode, species and order follow on any kind of being of the thing, as a man has species, mode and order insofar as he is a man, and similarly insofar as he is white, he has mode, species and order, and insofar as he is virtuous and knowing or anything else that is said of him. But evil negates some being, as blindness negates sight, hence it does not take away every mode, species and order, but only the mode, species and order that follow on being sighted.

Ad 4. It should be said that, as Augustine says in *On the Nature of the Good*, every mode, as mode, is good (and the same can be said of species and order), but a bad mode or bad species or bad order are so called either because they are less than they ought to be or because they are not proportioned to the things they ought to be proportioned to and are called bad because they are alien and incongruous.

Ad 5. It should be said that the nature of light is said to be without number, weight and measure, not simply speaking, but by comparison with bodily things, because the power of light extends to all bodily things, insofar as it is an active quality of the first altering body, namely the heavens.

Article 6: Is good fittingly distinguished into honourable, useful and pleasant?

It seems not.

1. The good, as the Philosopher says in *Ethics* 1.6, is divided into the ten categories. But honourable, useful and pleasant can be found in any category. Therefore good is not fittingly divided by these.

2. Moreover, the members of a division are opposites, but these three do not appear to be opposites, for some honourable things are pleasant, and nothing dishonourable is useful (but honourable and useful would have to be opposed if the members of the division were opposites), as Cicero also says in *On Offices*. Therefore, the foregoing division is inappropriate.

3. Moreover, where one thing is for the sake of another, then there is but one. But the useful is not good except insofar as it is pleasant and honourable. Therefore, the useful ought not to be divided against the pleasant and honourable.

ON THE CONTRARY:
Ambrose uses this division in his work *On Offices* 1.9.

RESPONSE:
It should be said that this division may seem to be proper to the human good. But if we take a more common and higher notion of good, this division will be seen to belong properly to the good as good. For something is good insofar as it is desirable and the term of the movement of appetite. The termination of this movement can be considered from the point of view of the movement of a natural body. But the motion of a natural body is terminated, simply, at the limit; and only in a certain respect at the midpoint through which it passes to the limit that terminates the motion. And it is called a term of motion insofar as it terminates some part of the motion. But that which is the ultimate term of the motion can be understood in two ways: either the thing itself towards which it tends, such as place or form; or rest in the thing. So then in the motion of appetite, that which is desirable as terminating the motion of appetite in a certain respect, as a middle through which it tends towards something further, is called useful. That which is desired as ultimate, totally terminating the motion of appetite, as something in which appetite tends essentially, is called the honourable, because that is called honourable which is desired

in itself. But that which terminates the motion of appetite as rest in the things desired is pleasure.

Ad 1. It should be said that good, insofar as it is the same in subject as being, is divided by the ten categories, but this division belongs to it according to its proper notion.

Ad 2. It should be said that this division is not through opposite things, but through opposite notions. Those things are properly called pleasant which have only that aspect of the notion of desirability that is pleasure, since sometimes the harmful and dishonourable are called useful, which are not desired in themselves but are desired only as leading to something else, like the taking of bitter medicine. Things are called honourable which are desired for themselves alone.

Ad 3. It should be said that good is not divided into these three as something univocal predicated equally of them, but as something analogous which is predicated first of one, and then of the others. It is first said of the honourable and secondarily of the pleasant, and thirdly of the useful.

QUESTION 6
ON THE GOODNESS OF GOD

We turn now to the goodness of God, about which four things are asked: (1) whether to be good belongs to God; (2) whether God is the highest good; (3) whether he alone is essentially good; (4) whether all things are good by the divine goodness.

Article 1: Does it belong to God to be good?

It seems not.

1. The notion of the good consists of mode, species and order. But these do not seem to belong to God, since God is immense and is not ordered to anything else. Therefore, it does not belong to God to be good.

2. Moreover, the good is that which all things desire, but all things do not desire God, because all things do not know him and nothing desires what it does not know. Therefore, it does not belong to God to be good.

ON THE CONTRARY:

Lamentations 3.25 says, 'The Lord is good to them that hope in him, to the soul that seeketh him.'

RESPONSE:

It should be said that the good especially belongs to God, for something is good insofar as it is desirable. But each thing desires its perfection, but the perfection and form of the effect are a kind of likeness of the agent, since every agent produces its like. Hence the agent itself is desirable and has the notion of good, for this is what is desired in it, that its likeness might be participated. Since therefore God is the first effective cause of all things, it is manifest that the notion of good and desirable belong to him. Hence Dionysius in *On the Divine Names* 4, attributes good to God as the first efficient cause, saying that God is called good as that by which all others subsist.

Ad 1. It should be said therefore that to have mode, species and order pertains to the notion of caused good. But good is in God as in a cause, hence it is for him to impose on others mode, species and order. Hence these three are in God as in their cause.

Ad 2. It should be said that all things, in seeking their proper perfections, seek God himself, insofar as the perfections of all things are certain likenesses of the divine existence, as is clear from what has been said. Of the things that seek God, some know him in himself, and this is proper to the rational creature; others know certain participations of his goodness, something that extends to sensible knowledge; some have natural desire without cognition, as inclined to their ends by a knowing superior.

Article 2: Is God the highest good?

It seems he is not.

1. The highest good adds something to good, otherwise it would belong to every good. But whatever is by way of addition to something, is composed. Therefore, the highest good is composed. But God is supremely simple, as has been shown. Therefore, God is not the highest good.

2. Moreover, the good is that which all things seek, as the Philosopher says. But there is nothing save God alone that all things seek, since he is the end of everything. Hence, nothing other than God is good. Which can also be seen from what is said in Matthew 19.17: 'One there is who

is good, and he is God.' But the highest is said in comparison with others, as the hottest in comparison with all hot things. Therefore, God cannot be called the highest good.

3. Moreover, the highest implies comparison. But things which are not of the same genus are not comparable, as sweetness is inappropriately called greater or less than the line. Therefore, since God is not in a genus with other goods, as is evident from the foregoing, it seems that God cannot be called the highest good with respect to them.

ON THE CONTRARY:

Augustine, in *On the Trinity* 1.2, says that the trinity of divine persons is the highest good that can be discerned by minds that have been cleansed.

RESPONSE:

It should be said that God is the highest good absolutely, not only in some genus or order of things. For as has been said, good is thus attributed to God insofar as all desired perfections flow from him as from their first cause. But they do not flow from him as from a univocal agent, as is clear from the above, but as from an agent who does not share with his effects the notion of a species or genus. The likeness of the univocal cause is found uniformly in the effects, but is more excellent in the equivocal cause, as heat exists in a more excellent mode in the sun than in fire. Therefore, when good is said of God as of the first non-univocal cause of all things, it must be in him in the most excellent mode. That is why he is called the highest good.

Ad 1. It should be said that the highest good adds to good, not something absolute, but only a relation. The relation by which something is said of God relatively to creatures is not really in God, but in the creature; it is in God as he is understood, just as the knowable is named relative to knowledge, not because the knowable refers to knowledge, but because knowledge refers to the knowable. Thus there need not be any composition in the highest good, but only that other things fall short of him.

Ad 2. It should be said that when good is said to be what all things desire, this should not be understood as if each good were desired by everything, but rather because whatever is desired has the notion of the good. When it is said that no one save God alone is good, this should be understood as essentially good, as will be said later.

Ad 3. It should be said that those things which are not in the same genus, if they are contained in different genera, are in no way comparable. God is said not to be in the same genus as other good things, not because he is in another genus, but because he is outside any genus but the principle of every genus. Thus he is compared to others by way of excess, and such a comparison implies the highest good.

Article 3: Is God alone essentially good?

It seems that he is not.

1. Just as one is convertible with being, so too is good, as was shown above. But every being is essentially one, as is clear from the Philosopher in *Metaphysics* 4.2. Therefore, every being is essentially good.

2. Moreover, if good is that which all things seek and existence itself is desired by all, the existence of each thing is its good. But each thing is essentially a being. Therefore, each thing is essentially good.

3. Moreover, everything is good by its own goodness. If then there is a thing which is not good in its own essence, it will have to be the case that its goodness is not its essence. Therefore that goodness, since it is some being, must be good, and if by some other goodness, again the goodness of that will be sought. Therefore, either we go on to infinity or we come to a goodness which is not good because of some other goodness. For that reason we should stop with the first. Therefore everything is good through its own essence.

ON THE CONTRARY:

Boethius says in *On the Hebdomads* that every thing other than God is good by participation and therefore not essentially.

RESPONSE:

It should be said that God alone is good through his essence. For anything is said to be good insofar as it is perfect. But there is a threefold perfection of the thing. First, insofar as it is constituted in its existence. Second, insofar as the accidents necessary for its perfect operation are added to it. Third, the perfection the thing has insofar as it reaches something else as its end. For example, the first perfection of fire consists in the existence it has thanks to its substantial form; its second perfection consists in heat, lightness and dryness, and the like; its third perfection is insofar as it rests in its own place.

No creature has this threefold perfection according to its essence, but

God alone, whose essence alone is his existence and to whom no accidents come since what belong to other things accidentally belong essentially to him, such as to be powerful, wise and the like, as is clear from what has been said. Nor is he ordered to anything else as his end, but he himself is the ultimate end of all things. Thus it is clear that God alone has every kind of perfection according to his essence. Therefore, God alone is essentially good.

Ad 1. It should be said that one does not imply the note of perfection, but of indivision alone, which belongs to each thing according to its essence. The essences of simple things are undivided both actually and potentially. But the essences of composite things are undivided only actually. Thus, each thing must be one in its essence, but not good, as has been shown.

Ad 2. It should be said that although any thing is good insofar as it has existence, still the essence of the created thing is not its existence, and therefore it does not follow that the created thing is good in its essence.

Ad 3. It should be said that the goodness of the created thing is not its very essence, but something superadded, either its existence, or some added perfection, or the order to the end. But the goodness superadded in this way is called good as it is called being: it is called being because it is something, not because something else is because of it. For that reason, it is called good because something is good because of it, not because it itself has some other goodness by which it is good.

Article 4: Are all things good by the divine goodness?

It seems that they are.

1. Augustine says in *On the Trinity* 8.3: 'Take this thing and that, take away this good and that, and see, if you can, the good; what you will see is God, not good by another good, but the good of every good.' But everything is good by its own good. Therefore, everything is good by the good that is God.

2. Moreover, Boethius says in *On the Hebdomads* that every thing is called good insofar as it is ordered to God, and by reason of the divine goodness. Therefore, all things are good by the divine goodness.

ON THE CONTRARY:

All things are good insofar as they exist. But a thing is called being, not by the divine existence, but from its proper existence. Therefore things are not called good by the divine goodness, but by their own.

RESPONSE:

It should be said that in things which imply a relation nothing prevents something from being extrinsically denominated, as something is denominated placed from place and measured from measure. But there is a diversity of opinion concerning things said absolutely. For Plato held that there are separated species of all things and that individuals are denominated from them, by participating in the separated species; for example, Socrates is called man with reference to the separate idea of man. And just as he posited a separate idea of man and of horse, which he called man itself and horse itself, so he posited separate ideas of being and of one which he called being itself and one itself, and it is by participation in them that each thing is called being and one. That which is good itself and one itself, he held to be the most high God, from whom all things are called good by way of participation. Although this opinion seems irrational insofar as it posited separate species of natural things, subsistent in themselves, as Aristotle proved again and again, still it is absolutely true that there is something one that is essentially good which we call God, as is clear from the foregoing. Aristotle agrees with this opinion. From the first, which is essentially being and good, each thing can be called good and being, insofar as it participates in him by way of some assimilation, although remotely and deficiently, as is clear from the above. Therefore, each thing is called good from the divine goodness as from the first exemplar, efficient and final principle of all goodness. Nevertheless, each thing is called good by a likeness of the divine goodness inherent in it, which is formally its own goodness denominating it. Thus there is one goodness of all things as well as many goodnesses.

Ad 1–2. The response to the objections is evident through this.

15. On Creation. Summa theologiae, 1, 44 (1268)

We may perhaps think of creation as a deliverance of religious revelation – 'In the beginning God created heaven and earth' – and not a philosophical topic. Thomas, characteristically, makes a distinction. If by creation we mean creation in time, Thomas will agree that, apart from the authority of Genesis, we could never be sure that the world and time had a beginning. The truth is certain for us on the basis of belief, not on the basis of any philosophical argument. If, on the other hand, we mean by creation that all things other than the First Being depend on him in order to exist, then creation is a philosophical topic.

Does this mean that any philosophers actually taught the doctrine of creation? That Thomas thought so is clear from Article 1 in this important selection. Question 44 of the first part of the Summa theologiae has often been invoked as proof that Thomas did not think that Aristotle's world is a created world. Article 2 describes a gradual progress towards a more sweeping account of the coming into being of the things of this world. The final step is made by those whose perspective was 'being as being' and whose quest was for the cause of being as such. Surprisingly, some have thought that Aristotle was being excluded from those whose focus was being as being. As has already been suggested, this interpretation does not agree with Article 1. The very phrase 'being as being' was coined by Aristotle to express the subject of that culminating science, one of whose names is theology.

Summa Theologiae, Part 1

QUESTION 44

Having considered the divine persons, we go on to discuss the procession of creatures from God. This will be a discussion in three parts: first the production of creatures will be considered, second their differences, third, their preservation and governance. Three things will be taken up under the first heading: the first cause of all being; how creatures proceed from the first cause; the principle of the duration of things. The first cause of all being involves four considerations: (1) whether God is the efficient cause of all beings; (2) whether prime matter is created by God, or is a coequal principle with him; (3) whether God is the exemplar cause of things or are there other exemplars beside him; (4) whether he is the final cause of things.

Article 1: Must every being be created by God?

It seems not.

1. Nothing prevents a thing's being without something that is not part of its definition, as a man without whiteness. But the relation of caused to cause does not seem to be of the definition of things because things can be understood without it. Therefore, they can be without it. So nothing prevents there being some things that are not created by God.

2. Moreover, a thing needs an efficient cause in order to be. Therefore, what cannot be has no need of an efficient cause. But nothing necessary can fail to be, because what necessarily is, cannot not be. Therefore, since there are many necessary things, it seems that not all beings are from God.

3. Moreover, when things have a cause, things can be demonstrated about them through that cause, but in mathematicals there is no demonstration through the agent cause, as is clear from the Philosopher in *Metaphysics* 3. Therefore, not everything is from God as an agent cause.

ON THE CONTRARY:

It is said in Romans 11.36, 'And through him and in him all things are.'

RESPONSE:

It should be said that we must affirm that whatever in any way exists is from God, for if something is found to be in a thing through participation, it must be caused in it by that which essentially is that something, as iron is heated by fire. It was shown above, however, when we treated of the divine simplicity, that God is subsistent existence itself, and it was also shown that subsistent existence must be unique, just as if there were a subsistent whiteness there could only be one, since whitenesses are multiplied by recipients. It follows therefore that nothing apart from God can be its own existence, but rather participates in existence. Therefore it is necessary that all the things that are diversified because of diverse participation in being, such that they are more or less perfect, are caused by the first being who is most perfect. Hence Plato said that it is necessary that all plurality be reduced to unity, and Aristotle says in *Metaphysics* 2 that that which is maximal being and truth is cause of every being and of every truth, just as that which is hottest is the cause of all heat.

Ad 1. It should be said that although the relation to its cause does not enter into the definition of the being that is caused, it none the less follows on what is of its nature, because from the fact that something is being through participation it follows that it is caused by another. Hence being of such a kind can only be if caused, just as a man incapable of laughter could not exist. It is because to be caused is not part of the account of being absolutely, that there is some uncaused being.

Ad 2. It should be said that some were moved by this argument to hold that what is necessary has no cause, as is said in *Physics* 8, but this shows itself to be manifestly false in the demonstrative sciences where necessary principles are the causes of necessary conclusions. Therefore Aristotle says in *Metaphysics* 5 that there are some necessary things which have a cause of their necessity. Therefore, it is not on account of this alone that an agent cause is needed, namely because the effect is capable of not being, but because the effect would not be if the cause were not. This conditional is true whether the antecedent and consequent are possible or impossible.

Ad 3. It should be said that mathematicals are abstract as understood but are not taken to exist as abstract. A thing has an agent cause in the way in which it has existence. Therefore, although mathematicals have an agent cause it is not according to a relation to agent cause that they come under the consideration of mathematics. Therefore in mathematical sciences nothing is demonstrated through agent cause.

Article 2: Is prime matter created by God?

It seems that it is not.

1. For whatever comes to be is composed of a subject and something else, as is said in *Physics* 1. But prime matter has no subject. Therefore prime matter cannot be made by God.

2. Moreover, action and passion are opposed to one another, but just as the first active principle is God, so the first passive principle is matter. Therefore, God and prime matter are two contrary principles opposed to one another, neither of which is from the other.

3. Moreover every agent causes something like itself and thus, since every agent acts insofar as it is actual, it follows that everything that is made is in some way actual. Therefore it is against the nature of prime matter that it should be made.

ON THE CONTRARY:

There is what Augustine says in Book 12 of the *Confessions*, 'Two things you made, Lord: one close to you, namely, the angel, the other close to nothing, namely, prime matter.'

RESPONSE:

It should be said that the ancient philosophers little by little and, as it were, haltingly entered into knowledge of the truth. In the beginning, being as it were more gross, they thought that sensible bodies were the only beings. And those who recognized motion in them, considered motion only with respect to accidents, as for example rarity and density, gathering and separating. And supposing the very substance of bodies to be uncreated, they assigned such causes of its accidental transformations as friendship, strife, intellect and the like.

Progressing further, they distinguished intellectually between substantial form and matter, which they held to be uncreated; and they perceived transformation to come about in bodies by essential forms. Of which transmutation some posited more universal causes, as the oblique circle (Aristotle), or Ideas (Plato).

But it should be considered that matter is restricted to a determinate species through form: much as the substance of any species is restricted to a determinate mode of existence through the accident advening to it, as man is restricted by white. Both therefore considered being in a particular way, either insofar as it is this being, or insofar as it is such a being. And thus they assigned particular agent causes of things.

Some extended themselves yet further to consider being as being, and considered the cause of things not only with respect to these or of such a kind, but as beings. That which is the cause of things insofar as they are being must be their cause not only insofar as they are of such kinds through accidental forms, nor insofar as they are these through substantial forms, but also according to everything that pertains in any way to their existence. And thus it is necessary to recognize prime matter too as created by the universal cause of being.

Ad 1. It should be said that the Philosopher in *Physics* 1 speaks of particular becoming, which is from form to form, whether accidental or substantial, but we are speaking now of things according to their emanation from the universal principle of being, from which emanation matter is not excluded, although it is excluded from the first kind of making.

Ad 2. It should be said that passion is an effect of action, hence it is reasonable that the first passive principle should be an effect of the first active principle, for every imperfect thing is caused by a perfect. But the first principle must be most perfect, as Aristotle says in *Metaphysics* 12.

3. It should be said that the argument does not show that prime matter is not created but only that it is not created without form, for although every created thing is actual, it is not pure act. Hence it is necessary that that which is on the side of potency should also be created, if the whole to which existence belongs is created.

Article 3: Is anything other than God the exemplar cause?

The answer seems to be yes.

1. The copy has a similarity to the exemplar, but creatures are far from divine similitude. Therefore God is not their exemplar cause.

2. Moreover, whatever is by way of participation is reduced to that which exists of itself, as the heated to fire, as has already been said. But whatever is found among sensible things is only through participation in a species, which is clear from this, that in no sensible thing do we find only what belongs to the definition of the species, but individuating principles are added to the principles of the species. Therefore, we must posit species existing of themselves, like man himself, horse itself, and the like. And these are called exemplars. Therefore the exemplars of things are apart from God.

3. Moreover, science and definition are of species as such, and not as they are in particulars, because there is no science or definition of the particular. Therefore there are some beings, which are beings or species apart from singulars, and they are called exemplars. Therefore, as before.

4. Moreover, the same thing is found in Dionysius, who says in *On the*

Divine Names 5 that to be as such is prior to life as such and also to wisdom as such.

ON THE CONTRARY:

The exemplar is the same as the Idea. But Ideas, according to what Augustine says in the *Eighty-three Questions*, are the principal forms which are contained in the divine intelligence. Therefore, the exemplars of things are not outside God.

RESPONSE:

It should be said that God is the first exemplar cause of all things. For evidence of which it should be noted that an exemplar is required for the production of a thing, as an effect follows on a determinate form, for the artisan produces a determinate form in matter, because of the exemplar he studies, whether that exemplar be something seen outside or is interiorly conceived by mind. It is manifest that things which come about naturally follow on determinate forms. But this determination of forms must be taken back as to a first principle to divine wisdom which thought up the order of the universe, which consists in the distinction of things. So it must be said that in the divine wisdom are the reasons of everything, which above we called Ideas, that is, exemplar forms existing in the divine mind. Although they are multiplied with respect to things, they are not really other than the divine essence, insofar as its likeness can be diversely participated by diverse things. Therefore God himself is the first exemplar of all things. Among created things, some can be called the exemplars of others, insofar as they are in the likeness of others, whether with respect to species, or according to the analogy of some imitation.

Ad 1. It should be said that although creatures do not attain to similarity with God's nature by a similitude of species, as a man generated is to the man generating, they attain similitude with him according to the representation of a notion understood by God, as the house which is in matter does to the house in the artisan's mind.

Ad 2. It should be said that it is of man's definition that he be in matter, so no man can be found apart from matter. Therefore, though this man is by participation in the species, he cannot be traced back to something existing as that species itself, but to something exceeding species, such as the separate substances are. And the same argument holds for other sensible things.

Ad 3. It should be said that although science and definition are of beings alone, it is not necessary that things should exist in the way they are understood. For we, thanks to the power of agent intellect, abstract universal species from particular conditions, but universals need not subsist apart from particulars as their exemplars.

Ad 4. It should be said that, as Dionysius writes in *On the Divine Names* 11, life itself and wisdom itself sometimes name God himself and sometimes the powers given to things – not, however, as subsisting things, as the ancients thought.

Article 4: Is God the final cause of all things?

It seems that he is not.

1. To act for the sake of an end seems to be proper to what is needful of the end. But God does not need anything. Therefore, it is not fitting that he should act for the sake of an end.

2. Moreover, the end of generation and the form of the generated and the agent are not numerically identical, as we read in *Physics* 2, because the end of generation is the form of the generated. But God is the first agent cause of all things; therefore he is not their final cause.

3. Moreover, all things seek the end. But not everything seeks God, because not everything knows him. Therefore God is not the end of all things.

4. Moreover, the final cause is the first of causes. Therefore, if God were the agent cause and the final cause, it would follow that in him the posterior would be the prior. Which is impossible.

ON THE CONTRARY:
There is what is said in Proverbs 16.4: 'The Lord hath made all things for himself.'

RESPONSE:
It should be said that every agent acts for the sake of an end, otherwise from its action neither this rather than that would follow, except by chance. The end of the thing acted on and of the agent is the same, as such, but with a qualification, for it is one and the same thing that the agent intends to confer and the thing acted upon intends to receive. There are some things which mutually act upon and are acted upon by one another; these are imperfect agents, and it is true of them that even in acting they intend to acquire something. But it is not fitting that the first

agent, who is just an agent, should act for the acquisition of some end, but he intends only to communicate his perfection, which is his goodness. And every creature intends to acquire its own perfection, which is a likeness of divine perfection and goodness. In this way, therefore, the divine goodness is the end of all things.

Ad 1. It should be said that to act out of need is proper to an imperfect agent which is fashioned to act and to be acted upon. But this is not the case with God. Therefore he alone is completely liberal because he does not act because of some utility, but only on account of his own goodness.

Ad 2. It should be said that the form of the thing generated is the end of generation only insofar as it is the likeness of the generating form, which intends to communicate its likeness. Otherwise the form of the generated would be more noble than the one generating, since the end is more noble than what is for the sake of the end.

Ad 3. It should be said that all things desire God as their end by seeking any kind of good whether by intellectual, sensible or natural appetite, which is without knowledge, because a thing has the note of the good and is desirable only insofar as it participates in the likeness of God.

Ad 4. It should be said that since God is the efficient, exemplar and final cause of everything and prime matter is from him, it follows that the first principle of everything is really only one. But nothing prevents there being considered in him things many according to reason, some of which are grasped by our intellect before others.

16. *On Angelic Knowledge.* Summa theologiae, *1, 54–8* (1268)

Thomas Aquinas is called the Angelic Doctor not only because of his legendary chastity but also because of his interest in those immaterial beings which are unimaginably more perfect than humans although infinitely inferior to God himself. The doctrine of the angels is both a philosophical and a theological doctrine. The Neoplatonic ontological cascade moved from the One through the realm of Intelligences to that of Souls. In Chapter 18 below will be found Thomas's ruminations on philosophical speculation about this intermediate rank of beings. Thomas finds a doctrine on angels (though not by that name) in both Plato and Aristotle. Indeed, he wrote a work, On Separated Substances, *that recounts the history of philosophical efforts to speak of the angels.*

In comparing Plato and Aristotle on this subject, Thomas commends Plato because of the enormous number of separated entities he recognizes, but he adds ruefully that the argument for their existence is fatally flawed. Aristotle, on the other hand, had sound reasons for positing separated substances between the Prime Mover and material entities, but unfortunately he limited their number severely to the cosmic roles they can play.

The theology of the angels is grounded in what Sacred Scripture has to say of them, and Thomas is indefatigable in finding clues to the angelic hierarchy in the books of the Bible. He sees the realm of the angels as, so to speak, exploding into choirs and ranks and roles. There is reason to think that he held that there are more angels than there are, or will be, human persons.

What Thomas can say of the angels is a projection from what he knows of human beings. There is no independent immediate access to such separated substances. But his doctrine on the angels plays an important and indispensable role in what he has to say of human cognition as well as of divine cognition. It was one of Jacques Maritain's shrewder observations that Descartes's account of human knowledge bears a strong resemblance to Thomas's theory of angelic cognition.

The following treatise from the Summa theologiae *provides a sense of Thomas's teaching on the angels.* ›

Summa theologiae, Part 1, Questions 54–8

QUESTION 54
ON THE KNOWLEDGE OF THE ANGELS

Having discussed the substance of the angel, we must go on to his knowledge, which is a four-part consideration. First, we must ask about the cognitive power of the angel; second, what pertains to his means of knowing; third, of the things known by him; and fourth, of the mode of his knowledge. The first of these involves five questions: (1) whether the understanding of the angel is identical with his substance; (2) whether his existence and his understanding are the same; (3) whether his substance is his knowing power; (4) whether the angel has an agent and possible intellect; (5) whether in the angel there is any knowing power other than intellect.

Article 1: Is the understanding of the angel identical with his substance?

It seems that it is.

1. The angel is much more sublime and simple than the agent intellect of our soul. But the substance of the agent intellect is its action, as is clear from Aristotle in *On the Soul* 3.5, as well as the Commentator. Much more so, then, must the substance of the angel be his action, that is, understanding.

2. Moreover, the Philosopher says in *Metaphysics* 12.11 that the action of the intellect is life. But since for a living thing to exist is for it to live, as is said in *On the Soul* 2.4, it seems that its essence is life. Therefore, the action of the intellect is the essence of the understanding angel.

3. Moreover, if the extremes are the same, the middle does not differ from them, since there is more distance from extreme to extreme than from extreme to the middle. But in the angel to understand and what is understood are the same, at least insofar as he understands his own essence. Therefore, understanding, which falls between the intellect and the thing understood, is the same as the substance of the understanding angel.

ON THE CONTRARY:

The substance of a thing differs from its action more than it does from its existence. But in no created thing is existence the same as its substance, for this is proper to God alone, as is clear from the foregoing. Therefore, neither angels nor any other creatures are such that their action is their substance.

RESPONSE:

It should be said that it is impossible that the action of the angel, or of any other creature, should be its substance. For action is properly the actuality of a power, as existence is the actuality of substance or essence. It is impossible, however, that something which is not pure act but has something of potentiality in it should be its own actuality, because actuality is opposed to potentiality. Only God is pure act, hence in God alone is his substance both his existence and his acting. Moreover, if the understanding of the angel were its substance, it would be necessary that the understanding of the angel were subsistent. But there can be only one subsistent intellect, just as any subsistent abstraction must be unique. Hence the substance of one angel would not be distinct from the substance of God, who is subsistent understanding, nor from the substance of another angel. Also, if this angel were its understanding, there could not be more and less perfect levels of understanding, since this is a result of different participations in understanding.

Ad 1. It should be responded that when it is said that the agent intellect is its action, this is not a predication by essence, but by concomitance, because when its substance is actual, immediately, taken in itself, action accompanies it. But this cannot be the case with possible intellect, which has actions only after having been actualized.

Ad 2. It should be said that in that sense of it life is not related to living as essence is to existence, but rather as the race is to running, one of which signifies the act abstractly and the other concretely. So it does not follow that if living is existing, then life is essence. Sometimes, however, life is taken for essence, following what Augustine says, in On the Trinity 8.8, that memory and intelligence and will are one essence, one life. But it is not taken in this sense by the Philosopher when he says that the action of intellect is life.

Ad 3. It should be said that the action which passes into something extrinsic, is really a mean between the agent and the subject receiving the action. But the action which remains in the agent is not really a middle between agent and object, save only in the way we speak, but really there results the union of the object with the agent. From the fact that what is understood becomes one with the one understanding, it follows that understanding is, as it were, an effect differing from both.

Article 2: Whether the understanding of the angel is the same as his existence.

It seems that it is.

1. For living things to be is for them to live, as is said in *On the Soul* 2.4. But understanding is a kind of living, as is said in the same place. Therefore, the understanding of the angel is its existence.

2. Moreover, as cause is to cause, so is effect to effect. But the form by which the angel is is the same as the form by which he understands, at least himself. Therefore, his understanding is the same as his existence.

ON THE CONTRARY:

The understanding of the angel is his motion, as is clear from Dionysius, *On the Divine Names* 4. But existence is not a motion. Therefore the existence of the angel is not his understanding.

RESPONSE:

It should be said that the action of the angel is not his existence, nor is the action of any creature. For there are two kinds of action, as is said in *Metaphysics* 8.8. There is an action which passes into something exterior, causing a reception in it, for example sawing and burning. There is another kind of action which is not transitive, but remains in the agent, such as sensing, understanding, willing. Nothing exterior is changed by action of this kind, but everything is done within the agent. Manifestly the first kind of action cannot be the existence of the agent, for its existence is signified as within it, but such action is an outflowing into what is acted upon by the agent.

Action in the second sense carries the note of infinity, either simply or in a certain respect. Simply, as in understanding, whose object is the true, and willing, whose object is the good, both of which are convertible with being, and thus understanding and willing, considered as such, relate to all things, and both are specified by their objects. Sensing is infinite in a certain respect, because it relates to all sensible things, just as sight does to all visible things. The existence of any creature is determined to one kind or species, since God's existence alone is absolutely infinite, comprehending everything in itself, as Dionysius says in *On the Divine Names* 4. Hence only the divine existence is his understanding and willing.

Ad 1. It should be said that living sometimes is taken for the very existence of the living thing, and sometimes for the activity of life – that by which it is shown that something is alive. It is in this sense that the Philosopher says that understanding is a kind of living, for he is there distinguishing the different levels of living things according to the different vital activities.

Ad 2. It should be said that the essence itself of the angel is the formal measure [*ratio*] of its whole existence, but not of its whole understanding, because it cannot understand everything through its own essence. Therefore, according to its proper definition, insofar as it is an essence of a certain kind, it is compared to the very existence of the angel. But it is compared to its understanding according to the universal notion of its object, namely the true or being. Thus it is clear that although it is the same form, it is not the principle of being and the principle of understanding under the same formality [*rationem*].

Article 3: Is the angel's intellectual power his essence?

It seems that it is not.

1. Mind and intellect name the intellectual power. But Dionysius in several places in his works calls the angels themselves intellects and minds. Therefore, the angel is its intellectual power.

2. Moreover, if the intellectual power of the angel is something outside its essence, it would have to be an accident, for we call what is outside the essence of a thing its accident. But a simple form cannot be a subject, as Boethius said in *On the Trinity* 2. Therefore, the angel would not be a simple form, which flies in the face of everything we have said earlier.

3. Moreover, Augustine says in *Confessions* 12.7 that God made the angelic nature close to himself and prime matter close to nothing, from which it seems that the angel is simpler than prime matter, as closer to God. But prime matter is its potentiality. Much more then should the angel be his intellectual power.

ON THE CONTRARY:
Dionysius says in the *Angelic Hierarchy* 11 that 'angels are divided into

substance, power and operation'. Therefore in them substance is one thing, power another and operation yet another.

RESPONSE:

It should be said that neither in the angel nor in any other creature is the operative power or potency the same as its essence. Which can be seen in this way. For since potentiality is signified with reference to act, it is necessary that the diversity of potentialities follow on the diversity of acts, because of which it is said that the proper act answers to the proper potency. But in every created thing essence differs from its existence, and is compared to it as potentiality to act, as is clear from what has been said above. Moreover, the act to which the operative power is compared is operation. But in the angel understanding and existence are not the same, nor is any other of its operations or that of any other created thing the same as its existence. Hence the essence of the angel is not its intellectual power, nor is the essence of any created thing its operative power.

Ad 1. It should be said that the angel is called intellect and mind because all his knowledge is intellectual. The knowledge of the soul is partly intellectual and partly through the senses.

Ad 2. It should be said that the simple form which is pure act can be the subject of no accident, because subject is to accident as potentiality to act. But this is God alone, and it is of this form that Boethius speaks. The simple form which is not its existence, but relates to it as potentiality to act, can be the subject of an accident, especially of those consequent upon its species, for such accidents pertain to form (the accident in the individual which does not belong to the whole species follows matter, which is the principle of individuation) and the angel is a simple form of this kind.

Ad 3. It should be said that the potentiality of matter is for substantial existence, but the operative potency is for accidental being. Hence they are not the same.

Article 4: Does the angel have agent and possible intellects?

It seems that he does.

1. The Philosopher says in *On the Soul* 3.5 that just as in the whole of nature there is something which makes all things, so too is it in the soul.

But the angel is a certain nature. Therefore, in him there is both agent and possible intellect.

2. Moreover, it is proper to possible intellect to receive, as to illumine is proper to agent intellect, as is clear from *On the Soul* 2.4. But an angel receives illumination from a higher, and illumines a lower, angel. Therefore, in him is both agent and possible intellect.

ON THE CONTRARY:

In us agent and possible intellects are in relation to phantasms, which relate to the possible intellect as colours to sight and to the agent intellect as colours to light, as is clear from *On the Soul* 3.5. But this is not the case with the angel. Therefore agent and possible intellects are not to be found in the angel.

RESPONSE:

It should be said that the need for recognizing the possible intellect in us arises from finding that sometimes we are potentially understanding and sometimes actually, so there must be some power which is potential with respect to intelligible objects before understanding them, but actually becomes them when it comes to know, and further when it exercises its knowledge. This power is called possible intellect. The need to recognize the agent intellect arises from the fact that the natures of material things, which we understand, do not subsist outside the soul as actually immaterial and intelligible, but are intelligible only potentially as they exist outside the soul, and there must be some power which makes such natures actually intelligible.

In us, this power is called the agent intellect. Neither need arises in the case of the angels. Because neither are they sometimes understanding only potentially with respect to the things they naturally know, nor are their intelligibles intelligible potentially, but actually. For they understand immaterial things first and foremost, as will be clear below. Therefore, there cannot be an agent and possible intellect in them except equivocally.

Ad 1. It should be said that the Philosopher understands these two to be in every nature in which to be generated or to become occurs, as the very words suggest. Science is not generated in the angel but is naturally present. So there is no need to posit agent and possible intellects in the angel.

Ad 2. It should be said that it is not proper to agent intellect to illumine another understander, but things potentially intelligible, insofar as by abstraction it makes them actually intelligible. And the possible intellect is potential with respect to the naturally knowable and sometimes becomes actual. Hence, the fact that an angel illumines an angel is not relevant to the notion of agent intellect; nor is it relevant to the notion of possible intellect that it is illumined concerning supernatural mysteries, towards knowing which it was at one time in potency. If one were to call this agent and possible intellect, he would speak equivocally, nor should our discussion be about words.

Article 5: *Whether the intellect is the angel's only knowing power.*

It seems that it is not.

1. Augustine says in the *City of God* 8.6 that in the angels there is the life which understands and senses. Therefore, the sense power is in them.

2. Moreover, Isadore says that the angels know many things through experience. But experience arises from many memories, as is said in *Metaphysics* 1.1. Therefore, the power to remember is in them.

3. Moreover, Dionysius says in *On the Divine Names* 4 that there is an evil fantasy in the demons, but fantasy pertains to the imaginative power. Therefore, in the demons there is an imaginative power. For the same reason, it is in the angels, because they are of the same nature.

ON THE CONTRARY:

Gregory says in his *Homily on the Ascension* that man senses with the beasts and understands with the angels.

RESPONSE:

It should be said that in our soul there are powers whose operations are exercised through bodily organs, and powers of this kind are the acts of certain parts of the body, as sight is in the eye, and hearing in the ear. But there are powers of our soul whose operations are not exercised through bodily organs, such as intellect and will, and their acts are not the acts of parts of the body. Angels do not have bodies naturally united to them, as is clear from what has been said. Hence only intellect and will of the powers of the soul can belong to them. This is what the Commentator says on *Metaphysics* 12, that separated substances are divided into intellect and will. And it befits the order of the universe that the supreme intellectual creature should be completely intellectual, and not just in part, like our soul. Because of this, angels are called intellects and minds, as was said above.

To what is said on behalf of the opposite answer a twofold response can be made. First, that those authorities speak according to the opinion of those who held that angels and demons have bodies naturally united to them. Augustine frequently uses this opinion in his books, although he does not intend to assert it, hence he says in the *City of God* 21 that one ought not to struggle much with this inquiry.

Second, it can be said that those authorities, and others like them, should be understood according to a certain similitude. Because, since sense has a certain grasp of its proper sensible, it becomes a matter of usage for us to say that the certain grasp of intellect is a kind of sensing. Hence it is even called a sense [*sententia*].

Experience can be attributed to the angels through a likeness of the things known, not by a likeness of the knowing power. Experience occurs in us because we know singulars by our senses; angels know singulars, as will be shown below, but not through senses. But memory can be posited in the angels insofar as Augustine locates it in mind, although it cannot belong to them insofar as it is a part of the sensitive soul. Similarly it should be said that evil phantasy is attributed to the demons because they have a false practical estimate of the true good, and deception in us is properly due to phantasms thanks to which we sometimes adhere to the likenesses of things as if they were the things themselves, as is clear in the sleeping and demented.

QUESTION 55
HOW ANGELS KNOW

We must now discuss the means by which angels know, and this involves three questions: (1) whether they know all things in their own substance or through concepts; (2) if through concepts, whether these are connatural or are drawn from things; (3) whether the higher angels know through more universal concepts than the lower ones.

Article 1: Does an angel know all other things in his own substance?

It seems that he does.

1. Dionysius says in *On the Divine Names* 7 that the angels know the things of earth in their mind's own nature. But the nature of the angel is his essence. Therefore the angel knows things through his own essence.

2. Moreover, according to the Philosopher in *Metaphysics* 11.9 and in *On the Soul* 3.4, with regard to things which exist apart from matter, intellect and what is understood are the same. But what is understood is the same as the one understanding by reason of that by which it is understood. Therefore, in things which exist apart from matter, like the angels, that by which something is understood is the very substance of the knower.

3. Moreover, whatever is in another is in it according to the mode of the thing in which it is. But the angel has an intellectual nature. Therefore, whatever is in him is in him in an intelligible mode. But all things are in him, because the lower beings are in the higher essentially, and the higher are in the lower by way of participation. Therefore, Dionysius says in *On the Divine Names* 4 that God gathers the whole in all things, that is, all in all. Therefore the angel knows all things in his own substance.

ON THE CONTRARY:
Dionysius says in the same chapter that angels are illumined by the notions of things. Therefore, they know by means of concepts of things, and not by their own substance.

RESPONSE:
It should be said that that by which the intellect understands is compared to the understanding intellect as its form, because form is that whereby the agent acts. But in order for the potential to be perfectly completed by form, it is necessary that everything be contained in the form to which the potentiality extends. That is why in corruptible things form does not perfectly complete the potentiality of matter, because the potentiality of matter extends to more things than are contained in the form of this or that. But the intellectual potency of the angel is for knowing everything, because universal being and truth are the object of intellect. But the essence of the angel does not include everything in it, since it is an essence determined to a genus and species. It is peculiar to the divine essence, which is infinite, that it perfectly and absolutely includes in itself all

things. Therefore God alone knows all things in his own essence. The angel cannot know all things in its essence, and his intellect must be perfected by concepts in order to know things.

Ad 1. It should be said that when the angel is said to know things by his nature, the word 'by' does not indicate the means of knowing, which is the likeness of the thing known, but the knowing power, which belongs to the angel because of his nature.

Ad 2. It should be said that just as the actualized sense is the actualized sensible, as is said in *On the Soul* 3.8, not that the sense power itself is the sensible likeness that is in the sense, but because from the two something one comes to be, as from act and potency. So too the actualized intellect is said to be what is actually understood, not because the intellectual substance is the likeness through which it understands, but because that likeness is its form. It is the same when it is said that in things which exist apart from matter the intellect and what is understood are the same – as if it were said that actualized intellect is what is actually understood, for something is actually understood because it is immaterial.

Ad 3. It should be said that the things that are below the angel and the things that are above him are in a way in his substance, though not perfectly, nor according to their own nature, since the essence of the angel, being finite, is distinct from other things by its proper nature, but according to some common notion. But all things are in the essence of God perfectly and in their proper nature, as in the first and universal acting power from which proceeds whatever in anything is either proper or common. Therefore, God has in his essence proper knowledge of all things, but the angels have only common knowledge of all things.

Article 2: Do angels understand by means of concepts received from things?

It seems that they do.

1. Whatever is understood is understood by means of a likeness of itself in the knower. But the likeness of a thing existing in another is either by way of exemplar such that the likeness is cause of the thing, or by way of image such that it is caused by the thing. Therefore any knowledge of the knower is either cause of the thing understood or caused by the thing. But the knowledge of the angel is not the cause of things existing in nature: only the divine knowledge is that. Therefore, the concepts by

which the angelic intellect understands must be received from things.

2. Moreover, the angelic light is stronger than the light of the agent intellect in the soul. But the light of the agent intellect abstracts intelligible species from the phantasms. Therefore, the light of the angelic intellect can also abstract species from sensible things. So nothing prevents our saying that the angel understands by species received from things.

3. Moreover, the species in the intellect relates indifferently to the present and to the far off, except as it is received from sensible things. Therefore if an angel does not understand through concepts received from things, his knowledge would relate indifferently to the near and distant, and thus it would make no sense for him to move with reference to place.

ON THE CONTRARY:

Dionysius says in *On the Divine Names* 7 that angels do not gather divine knowledge from divisible or sensible things.

RESPONSE:

It should be said that the species by which the angels understand are not received from things but are connatural to them. The order and distinction of spiritual substances have to be understood as like the distinction and order of bodies. But the potentiality in the nature of the supreme body is totally perfected by its form, but in lower bodies the potentiality of matter is not totally perfected by form, but it receives now one, now another form, from an agent. Similarly the lower intellectual substances, like human souls, have an intellectual potentiality that is not completed naturally, but is completed successively by the reception in them of intelligible species from things. But the intellectual potentiality in the higher spiritual substances, that is, the angels, is naturally completed by intelligible species, insofar as they have connatural intelligible species for understanding everything which they can naturally know.

This is apparent from the mode of existing of such substances. For lower spiritual substances, namely souls, have an affinity with body insofar as they are the forms of bodies, and therefore by their very mode of existing it is fitting that they should attain intelligible perfection by and through bodies. But the higher substances, that is, the angels, are totally apart from bodies, subsisting immaterially and in intelligible existence. Therefore they attain their intelligible perfection from an efflux from God in which they receive the species of things known along with their intellectual nature. Hence Augustine says, in his *Literal Commentary on Genesis* 2.8, that the other things below the angels are so created that they first come to be in the knowledge of a rational creature and then in their own kind.

Ad 1. It should be said that there are likenesses of creatures in the mind of the angel, not as received from these creatures but rather from God, who is the cause of the creatures in whom the likenesses of things first exist. Hence Augustine says, in the same book, that just as the notion by which the creature is made is first in the Word of God, then in the creature that is made, so knowledge of that same notion is first in an intellectual creature and then in the condition of the creature.

Ad 2. It should be said that one does not get from extreme to extreme except through the middle. The form as it exists in imagination, without matter indeed but not without the conditions of matter, is midway between the existence of the form in matter and the existence of the form in intellect abstracted from matter and material conditions. Hence no matter how powerful the angelic intellect, it could not convert material forms to intelligible existence, since as has been said it lacks imagination. Given that it could abstract intelligible species from material things, it would not abstract them, because it does not need them, since it has connatural intelligible species.

Ad 3. It should be said that the knowledge of the angel is related indifferently to the far and near according to place. But its local motion is not for all that idle, since it does not move locally in order to gain knowledge, but to do something somewhere.

Article 3: Do higher angels understand through more universal concepts than the lower angels?

It seems that they do not.

1. The universal seems to be abstracted from particulars, but the angels do not understand through species abstracted from things. Therefore it cannot be said that the species of the angelic intellect are more or less universal.

2. Moreover, what is known specifically is known more perfectly than what is known universally, because to know something universally is a kind of mean between potentiality and act. Therefore, if the higher angels know by more universal forms than the lower, it would follow that the

higher angels have a less perfect knowledge than the lower, which is absurd.

3. Moreover, the same proper notion cannot belong to many things. But if the higher angel knows different things by one universal form which the lower angel knows by many special forms, it follows that the higher angel uses one universal form to know different things. Therefore, he cannot have proper knowledge of both. Which seems absurd.

ON THE CONTRARY:

Dionysius says in *The Angelic Hierarchy* 12 that the higher angels participate in a more universal knowledge than the lower. And in the *Book of Causes* 10 it is said that the higher angels have more universal forms.

RESPONSE:

It should be said that there are some higher things which are closer and more similar to the one First who is God. But in God the fullness of intellectual knowledge is had in one, namely in the divine essence by which God knows all things. This intelligible plenitude is found in created intellects in an inferior and less simple way. Hence, what God knows in one, lower intellects know through many, and more and more to the degree that the intellect is inferior. Therefore, to the degree that an angel is superior, to that degree he can understand the whole intelligible universe through fewer species. Therefore, it is necessary that its forms be more universal, each of them extending to many. A sort of example of this can be found in us. There are some who cannot grasp intelligible truth unless things are explained to them in great detail, but there are others who are of keener intellect and they grasp much from little.

Ad 1. It should be said that it is incidental to the universal that it is abstracted from singulars, insofar as the intellect knowing it receives knowledge from things. But if there is an intellect which does not receive knowledge from things, the universal known by it will not be abstracted from things, but in a way pre-exist things, either in the order of causality, as the universal notions of things are in the Word of God, or at least in the order of nature, as the universal notions of things are in the angelic intellect.

Ad 2. It should be said that to know something universally can be understood in two ways. In one way, on the part of the thing known, when only the universal nature of the thing is known: to know something universally in this way is less perfect since he who knows of a man only that he is animal knows him imperfectly. In another way, on the part of the means of knowing, and to know something universally in this way is more perfect for the intellect which can know proper singulars by one universal means is more perfect than one which cannot.

Ad 3. It should be said that there cannot be one adequate proper notion of many things. If it excels, the same thing can be taken as a proper notion and a likeness of different things. In a man prudence is universal with respect to the acts of all the virtues and can be taken as the proper notion and likeness of particular prudence which is in the lion an act of magnanimity and in the wolf an act of caution, and so with others. Similarly the divine essence is taken because of its excellence as the proper notion of singulars, because in it singulars are likened to him according to their proper notions. In the same way it should be said of the universal notion in the mind of the angel that through it, because of its excellence, many things can be known with proper knowledge.

QUESTION 56
ANGELIC KNOWLEDGE OF IMMATERIAL THINGS

We now ask about the knowledge of the angels with respect to what they know, and first of their knowledge of immaterial things, and then of their knowledge of material things. Three things must be asked about the first: (1) whether the angel knows himself; (2) whether one angel knows another; (3) whether the angel by its natural powers knows God.

Article 1: Does the angel know himself?

It seems that he does not.

1. Dionysius says in *The Angelic Hierarchy* 6 that angels ignore their own virtues. But to know the substance is to know the virtue. Therefore, the angel does not know its own essence.

2. Moreover, the angel is a singular substance, otherwise he would not act, since acts are of single subsistent things. But no singular is intelligible. Therefore, it cannot be understood. And so, since the angel has only intellectual knowledge, he cannot know himself.

3. Moreover, the intellect is moved by the intelligible, because to understand is a kind of receiving, as is said in *On the Soul* 3.4. But nothing

is moved by or receives from itself, as is apparent in bodily things. Therefore the angel cannot understand himself.

ON THE CONTRARY:

Augustine says in the *Literal Commentary on Genesis* 2.8 that the angel in his very conformation, that is, illustration of the truth, knows himself.

RESPONSE:

It should be said that, as is evident from what has been said above, the object of immanent action is different from the object of transitive action towards something exterior, for in transitive action towards something exterior the object or the matter into which the action passes is separate from the agent, as the heated from the heater, and what is built from the builder. But in action immanent to the agent, in order for the action to take place, the object must be united to the agent, as the sensible is united to sense, in order that actual sensation take place. The object united to the power is to this kind of action as the form which is the principle of action in other agents; just as heat is the formal principle of heating in fire, so the species of the thing seen is the formal principle of seeing in the eye. But it should be noted that this kind of species of object sometimes is only potential in the cognitive power, and then it is only potentially knowing, and in order that it know actually the knowing power must be transformed into the act of the species. If it always actually had it, then it could know through it without any mutation or preceding reception. From which it is clear that to be moved by the object is not of the definition of the knower as knower, but only insofar as he is a potential knower. In order for the form to be a principle of action it makes no difference whether it is inherent in another or subsistent in itself, for heat would not heat less if it were subsistent in itself, than it does as inherent. Therefore, if something in the genus of intelligible things is a subsistent intelligible form, it will understand itself. But the angel, since it is immaterial, is a subsistent form, and therefore actually intelligible. Hence it follows that the angel understands himself through his form, which is his substance.

Ad 1. It should be said that that text is an old translation which is corrected by the new in which we read, 'Moreover and the', that is, the angels, 'knew their own virtues.' Although the old translation can be defended in this respect that angels do not perfectly understand their virtue as it proceeds from the order of divine wisdom, which is incomprehensible to the angels.

Ad 2. It should be said that intellect is not of the singulars which are bodily things as far as we are concerned, not because of singularity, but because of matter, which is in them the principle of individuation. So if some singulars are subsistent without matter, as the angels are, nothing prevents them from being actually intelligible.

Ad 3. It should be said that to be moved or to be acted upon belongs to intellect insofar as it is in potency. Hence it has no place in the angelic intellect, especially insofar as they understand themselves. For the action of intellect is not of the same nature as the action found in bodily things, which passes into another matter.

Article 2: Does one angel know another?

It seems that he does not.

1. The Philosopher says in *On the Soul* 3.4 that if the human intellect should have within it one of the natures of sensible things, that nature existing within would prevent what is outside from appearing, as if the pupil were coloured with some colour it would not be able to see every colour. As the human intellect is to knowing bodily things, so the angelic intellect is to knowing immaterial things. Since therefore the angelic intellect has in itself a nature from among the number of determinate natures, it seems that it cannot know other things.

2. Moreover, in the *Book of Causes* 8, it is said that every intelligence is what is above it insofar as it is caused by it, and what is below it insofar as it is its cause. But one angel is not the cause of another. Therefore one angel does not know another.

3. Moreover, one angel cannot know another through the essence of the knowing angel, since all knowledge is by way of a likeness, but the essence of the knowing angel is not like the essence of the known angel except generically. Similarly it cannot be said that one angel knows another through the essence of the angel known, because that by which the intellect understands is intrinsic to intellect; only trinity comes into the mind. No more can it be said that one knows the other through a species or concept, because that species would not differ from the angel understood, since both are immaterial. Therefore, it seems that there is no way in which one angel can know another.

4. Moreover, if one angel understood another, either this would be by means of an innate species, and then it would follow that if God now created some new angel, it could not be known by those which now exist,

or by means of a species acquired from things, and then it would follow that the higher angels cannot know the lower, from which they receive nothing. Therefore, it seems that there is no way that one angel can know another.

ON THE CONTRARY:

The *Book of Causes* 11 says that every intelligence knows things which are not corrupted.

RESPONSE:

It should be replied, as Augustine says in his *Literal Commentary on Genesis* 8, that the things that eternally pre-exist in the Word of God can flow forth in two ways: into the angelic intellect, or in order to subsist in their proper natures. They proceed into the angelic intellect when God impresses the likenesses of things on the angelic mind, which he produced in natural existence. But in the Word of God there existed from all eternity not only the notions of bodily things but also the notions of all spiritual creatures. Therefore, the notions of all things, both corporeal and spiritual, were impressed on every spiritual creature by the Word of God. Thus the notion of its own species in natural and intelligible existence at the same time were impressed on every angel, such that it might subsist in the nature of its species and through it understand itself, but of other natures, both spiritual and corporeal, only notions according to intelligible existence were impressed, in order that, through these impressed species, it might know both corporeal and spiritual creatures.

Ad 1. It should be said that the spiritual natures of the angels are distinguished from one another by a certain ordering, as was said above. Thus the nature of one angel does not prevent it from understanding the natures of other angels, since both the higher and the lower have an affinity with its nature, the difference coming about only according to different levels of perfection.

Ad 2. It should be said that the notions of cause and caused do not bring it about that one angel knows another, except by reason of likeness, insofar as cause and caused are similar. Therefore, if a similarity without causality is posited among angels, there will remain in one the knowledge of the other.

Ad 3. It should be said that one angel knows another through a concept existing in its intellect, which differs from the angel whose likeness it is, not as material and immaterial existence differ, but as natural and intentional existence differ. For the angel itself is a form subsisting in natural existence, but not the concept of it that is in the intellect of another angel: there it has only intelligible existence. Just as the form of colour in the wall has natural existence, but in the medium bearing it it has intentional existence alone.

Ad 4. It should be said that God makes every creature proportionate to the ordered universe he set out to make. Therefore, if God arranged to make more angels or more natures of things, he would have impressed more intelligible species on the angelic minds. Just as if a builder should wish to make a larger house, he would make a larger foundation. Thus it is for the same reason that God would add another creature to the universe and an intelligible species to the angel.

Article 3: Can the angel by his natural powers know God?

It seems not.

1. Dionysius says in *On the Divine Names* 1 that God is placed above all celestial minds by his incomprehensible power. And afterwards he adds that because he is above every substance, he is set apart from all knowledge.

2. Moreover, God is infinitely distant from the intellect of the angel. But something infinitely distant cannot be reached. Therefore, it seems that the angel through his natural powers cannot know God.

3. Moreover, 1 Corinthians 13.12 says, 'We see now through a mirror in an obscure manner, but then face to face.' From which it appears that there are two kinds of knowledge of God, one, whereby he is seen in his essence, insofar as he is said to be seen face to face, and another insofar as he is seen in the mirror of creatures. Angels cannot have the first kind of knowledge of God by their natural powers, as has been shown above. The mirrored knowledge does not belong to the angels, because they do not receive divine knowledge from sensible things, as Dionysius says in *On the Divine Names* 7. Therefore, the angels cannot know God by their natural powers.

ON THE CONTRARY:

Angels are more powerful in knowing than men. But men can know God by means of their natural capacities, according to Romans 1.19: 'What may be known of God is made manifest in them.' Much more so the angel, therefore.

RESPONSE:

It should be said that angels can have some knowledge of God through their natural powers. In evidence of this, consider that something is known in three ways. In one way, by the presence of its essence in the knower, as if light were seen in the eye, and thus it is said that the angel knows himself. In another way, by the presence of its likeness in the knowing power, as the stone is seen by the eye because a likeness of it occurs in the eye. In a third way, when the likeness of the thing known is not received immediately from the thing known, but from another thing, which it affects, as when we see a man in a mirror. The divine knowledge by which he is seen in his essence is like the first. This knowledge of God cannot be present to any creature by its own natural powers, as has been said. To the third kind belongs the knowledge we have of God in this life, by his likeness resulting in creatures; according to Romans 1.20, 'His invisible attributes are clearly seen – his everlasting power also and divinity – being understood through the things that are made.' Thus we are said to see God in a mirror. But the knowledge by which the angel using its natural powers knows God is midway between these two, and is likened to the knowledge whereby a thing is seen in a concept taken from it. Because the likeness of God is in the nature of the angel, impressed in its very essence, the angel knows God insofar as he is a likeness of God. But he does not see the very essence of God, since no created likeness suffices to represent the divine essence. Hence this knowledge is closer to mirrored knowledge, because the very nature of the angel is a kind of mirror representing the divine likeness.

Ad 1. It should be said that Dionysius speaks of the knowledge of comprehension, as his words expressly show, and in that way God is known by no created intellect.

Ad 2. It should be said that because the intellect and essence of the angel are infinitely distant from God, it follows that he cannot comprehend him, nor by his nature see his essence. But it does not follow from this that he can have no knowledge of him, because just as God is infinitely distant from the angel, so is the knowledge that God has of himself infinitely distant from the knowledge that the angel can have of him.

Ad 3. It should be said that the knowledge that the angel naturally has of God is midway between the two, yet has more in common with one extreme, as has been said.

QUESTION 57
ANGELIC KNOWLEDGE OF MATERIAL THINGS

We now inquire into the material things that are known by angels, and raise five questions in this regard: (1) do the angels know the natures of material things? (2) do they know singulars? (3) do they know the future? (4) do they know the secrets of the heart? (5) do they know all the mysteries of grace?

Article 1: Does the angel know material things?

It seems that he does not.

1. The perfection of the intellect is the thing that is understood. But material things cannot be the perfections of angels, since they are below them. Therefore angels do not know material things.

2. Moreover, intellectual vision is of things which are in the soul by their own essence, as is said in the Gloss on 2 Corinthians 12.2. But material things cannot be in man's soul or in the mind of the angel, in their essences. Therefore, they cannot be known by intellectual vision, but only imaginative, by which the likenesses of bodies is grasped; and sensible, which is of bodies themselves. But in the angels there is no imaginative or sensible vision, but only intellectual. Therefore, the angels cannot know material things.

3. Moreover, material things are not actually intelligible, but are knowable by the grasp of sense and imagination, which are not found in angels. Therefore, angels do not know material things.

ON THE CONTRARY:
Whatever the lower power can do, the higher power can do. But the intellect of man, which in the order of nature is below the intellect of the angel, can know material things. Therefore, ever so much more so can the intellect of the angel.

RESPONSE:
It should be said that such is the order of things that higher beings are more perfect than the lower, and what is deficiently and partially and multiply found in the lower, is found eminently and with totality and simplicity in the higher. Therefore in God, as in the highest peak of things,

all things pre-exist supersubstantially according to his simple existence, as Dionysius says in *On the Divine Names* 1. But angels are of all creatures closest to and most like God, hence they participate in many aspects of the divine goodness, and more perfectly, as Dionysius says in the *Celestial Hierarchy* 4. Therefore, all material things pre-exist in the angels more simply and immaterially than in things themselves, but more multiply and imperfectly than in God. Whatever is in another is in it in the mode of that in which it is. But angels are intellectual by their nature. Therefore, just as God knows material things by his essence, so the angels know them because they are in them by their intelligible species.

Ad 1. It should be said that that which is understood is the perfection of the one understanding according to an intelligible species that he has in his intellect. Thus the intelligible species which are in the angel's intellect are the perfections and actuality of the angelic intellect.

Ad 2. It should be said that sense does not grasp the essences of things, but only exterior accidents. No more does the imagination which only apprehends the likenesses of bodies. The intellect alone grasps the essences of things. Hence in *On the Soul* 3.7 the object of intellect is said to be the quiddity concerning which it does not err, just as sense does not err with respect to the proper sensible. Therefore the essences of material things are in the intellect of man or angel as the understood is in the one understanding, and not according to its real existence. There are some things which are in the intellect or soul according to both kinds of existence. And of both there is intellectual vision.

Ad 3. It should be said that if the angel should receive knowledge of material things from material things themselves, he would have to make them actually intelligible by abstracting them. But he does not receive knowledge of them from material things, but has knowledge of them through actually intelligible species of things connatural to him, just as our intellect knows according to the species which it makes intelligible by abstracting.

Article 2: Do angels know singulars?

It seems not.

1. The Philosopher says in *Physics* 1.5 that sense is of singulars but reason (or intellect) of universals. But in the angels the only knowing

power is the intellectual, as is clear from the above.[1] Therefore they do not know singulars.

2. Moreover, all knowledge is by an assimilation of the knower to the known, but it does not seem that there can be any assimilation of the angel to the singular as singular, since the angel is immaterial, as has been said,[2] but the principle of singularity is matter. Therefore the angel cannot know singulars.

3. Moreover, if the angel knows singulars this is either by singular species or universal species. Not by singular, because then he would have to have infinite species, nor universal, because the universal is not a sufficient principle for knowing the singular as singular, since singulars are only potentially known in the universal. Therefore the angel does not know singulars.

ON THE CONTRARY:

No one can guard what he does not know. But the angels guard individual men, according to Psalm 90.11: 'For to his angels he has given thee in trust, to keep thee in all thy ways.' Therefore angels know singulars.

RESPONSE:

It should be said that some completely take away from the angels knowledge of singulars. But this is in conflict with the Catholic faith which teaches that these lower things are administered by angels, according to Hebrews 1.14: 'Are they not all ministering spirits, sent for service, for the sake of those who shall inherit salvation?' If they did not have knowledge of singulars, they could have no foresight about the things which are done in this world, since acts are of singulars. And that is contrary to Ecclesiastes 5.5: 'And say not before the angel: There is no providence.' It is also in conflict with teachings of philosophy according to which angels are made movers of the heavenly orbs, moving them by intellect and will.

Therefore others said that the angels have knowledge of singulars but in their universal causes, to which all particular effects are reduced. Just as if an astronomer judged about future eclipses by the dispositions of the heavenly motions. But this position does not escape the difficulties of the first one, because to know the singular in its universal cause is not to know it as singular, that is, as here and now. The astronomer, knowing

1. q. 54, art. 5.
2. q. 50, art. 2.

the future eclipse by computation of heavenly motions, knows it in universal, and not as it is here and now, unless he receives it by his senses. But the administration and providence and motions are singular, since they are here and now.

Therefore it must be said that just as man knows all the kinds of things with different knowing powers, by intellect the universal and immaterial, by sense singular and corporeal things, so the angel by one intellectual power knows both. It is in the order of things that the higher a thing is the more unified power it has extending to many things, as in man himself it is clear that the common sense, which is higher than the proper sense, although it is a unique power, knows all the things that are known by the five exterior senses, and some other things not known by the exterior senses, namely the difference between white and sweet. And the same can be found in others. Hence, since the angel is in the natural order above man, it is absurd to say that man by any of his powers knows something that the angel does not know by his one cognitive power, his intellect. That is why Aristotle thought it absurd to say that God did not know strife, which we know, as is evident in *On the Soul* 1.5 and *Metaphysics* 2.4.

The way in which the intellect of the angel knows singulars can be gathered from this that things flow from God in order that they might subsist in their proper natures but also that they might be in angelic knowledge. But it is manifest that there flows from God into things not only that which pertains to their universal nature, but also those things which are the principles of individuation: for he is the cause of the whole substance of the thing, both with respect to matter and with respect to form. And as he causes, so does he know, because his knowledge is the cause of the thing, as was shown above.[1] Therefore, just as God through his essence, by which he causes all things, is the likeness of all things, and through it knows all things, not only with respect to their universal natures but also with respect to their singularity, so the angels, by the species put in them by God, know things not only with respect to universal nature but also according to their singularity, insofar as they are multiplied representations of that unique and simple essence.

Ad 1. It should be said that the Philosopher is speaking of our intellect, which understands things only by abstracting; by that abstraction from

---

1. q. 14, art. 8.

material conditions that which is abstracted becomes universal. But this manner of understanding does not belong to the angels, as has been shown,[1] and therefore it is not the same argument.

Ad 2. It should be said that according to their nature angels are not assimilated to material things as something is assimilated to another according to agreement in genus or in species, or in accident, but as the higher has likeness to the lower, as sun to fire, and in this way too there is a likeness of all things in God, with respect to both matter and form, insofar as whatever is found in things pre-existed in him as in a cause. For the same reason, the species of the angel's intellect, which are likenesses derived from the divine essence, are likenesses of things not only with respect to form, but also with respect to matter.

Ad 3. It should be said that angels know singulars through universal forms, which however are likenesses of things both with respect to universal principles and with respect to the principles of individuation. The way in which many things can be known in one species has been explained above.[2]

Article 3: Do angels know the future?

It seems that they do.

1. Angels are more potent in knowing than men, but some men know many future things. Therefore so much more can the angel.

2. Moreover, present and future are tenses of time, but the intellect of the angel is above time, for the intelligence is made equal to eternity, that is, to the *aevum*, as is said in the *Book of Causes* 2. Therefore, for the intellect of the angel, past and future do not differ, but he indifferently knows both.

3. Moreover, the angel does not know by means of concepts taken from things, but by universal innate species. But universal species refer equally to present, past and future. Therefore, it seems that angels know indifferently past, present and future things.

4. Moreover, a thing can be called distant in time as in space, but angels know things in distant places. Therefore they also know things distant as to future time.

1. q. 55, art. 2.
2. q. 55, art. 3, ad 3.

ON THE CONTRARY:

What is a proper sign of divinity does not belong to angels, but to know the future is a proper sign of divinity, according to Isaiah 41.23: 'Shew the things that are to come hereafter, and we shall know that ye are gods.' Therefore angels do not know the future.

RESPONSE:

It should be said that the future can be known in two ways. In one way, in its cause, and thus things which proceed necessarily from their causes are known with certain knowledge, for example, the sun will rise tomorrow. But things that proceed from their causes only for the most part are not known with certitude but by conjecture, as the physician foreknows the health of the sick person. And this mode of knowing the future is present to the angels, and much more so than in us, insofar as they know the causes of things more universally and perfectly, as the physician who sees the causes more acutely, better prognosticates concerning the future condition of the ill. What proceed only rarely from their causes are wholly unknown, such as chance and fortuitous events.

In another way future things are known in themselves, and thus only God knows them, not only what comes about necessarily, or for the most part, but also chance and fortuitous events, because God sees all things in his eternity. Since he is simple, he is present to the whole of time, and contains it. Therefore the one intuition of God bears on all the things done throughout time as if they were present, and he sees all things in themselves, as was said above[1] when we discussed the knowledge of God. But the angelic intellect and every created intellect fall short of the divine eternity. Hence the future cannot be known by any created intellect as it exists.

Ad 1. It should be said that men do not know future events except in their causes, or by the revelation of God. In these ways the angels much more subtly know future events.

Ad 2. It should be said that although the intellect of the angel is above the time by which bodily motions are measured, there is time in the intellect of the angel according to the succession of intelligible concepts, according to what Augustine says in the *Literal Commentary on Genesis* 8.22, that God moves the spiritual creature through time. Thus, since

1. q. 14, art. 13.

there is succession in the intellect of the angel, not everything that is done through the whole of time is present to him.

Ad 3. It should be said that although the species which are in the angel's intellect, as such relate equally to present, past and future, none the less present, past and future are not equally related to the concepts. Because things that are present have a nature by which they are assimilated to the species in the mind of the angel, and thus they can be known through them. But the things that are future, do not yet have a nature through which they might be assimilated to them, hence they cannot be known through them.

Ad 4. It should be said that distance according to place is already in the nature of things, and they participate in some concept whose likeness is in the angel, which is not true of future events, as has been said. So it is not the same.

Article 4: Do angels know the secrets of the heart?

It seems that they do.

1. Gregory says in the *Morals* with respect to Job 27.17: 'And the innocent shall divide the silver,' that then is in the happiness of the risen that one will be known by another as he is by himself, and when the intellect of anyone is heeded, at the same time conscience is penetrated. But the risen are similar to angels, as is said in Matthew 22.30: 'For at the resurrection they will neither marry nor be given in marriage, but will be as angels of God in heaven.' Therefore, one angel can see what is in the conscience of another.

2. Moreover, as shapes are to bodies, so are intelligible species to intellect. But when the body is seen, its shape is seen. Therefore the intellectual substance being seen, the intelligible species in it are seen. Therefore, when an angel sees another angel, or the soul, it seems that he can see the thought of both.

3. Moreover, what is in our intellect is more like the angel than what is in memory, since they are actually understood, but those only potentially understood. But the things that are in memory can be known by the angel, just as bodily things can be, since memory is a power of the body. Therefore, it seems that the angel can know the intellect's thoughts.

ON THE CONTRARY:

What is proper to God, does not belong to the angels. But to know the thoughts of the heart is proper to God, according to Jeremiah 17.9–10: 'The heart is perverse above all things and unsearchable. Who can know it? I am the Lord, who search the heart and prove the reins.' Therefore angels do not know the secrets of the heart.

RESPONSE:

It should be said that thoughts of the heart can be known in two ways. In one way, in their effects. And thus they can be known not only by the angel but by men as well; and the more subtly insofar as such effects are more hidden. For thought is sometimes known not only by the exterior act but also by expressions of the face, and physicians can know some affections of the soul from the pulse. Much more so can the angels and the demons too, insofar as they examine more subtly the hidden bodily changes. Hence Augustine says in *On the Discernment of Demons* 5 that sometimes they learn with ease the dispositions of men, not only spoken words, but even what is conceived in thought, when signs are expressed in the body by the soul, although in the *Retractions* 2.30 he says it should not be asserted how this comes about. Thoughts can be known in another way, insofar as they are in the intellect and affections as they are in the will.

In this way God alone can know the thoughts of hearts and the affections of wills. The reason for this is that the will of the rational creature is subject to God alone, and he alone can act on it, since he is its principal object and ultimate end. This will be made clearer below.[1] Therefore, the things that are in the will or which depend on will alone are known only to God. Manifestly it depends on will alone that someone should actually consider something, because when one has the habit of knowledge, or intelligible species existing in himself, he uses them as he wills. Therefore the Apostle says in 1 Corinthians 2.11: 'For who among men knows the things of a man save the spirit of man which is in him?'

Ad 1. It should be said that now the thought of one man is not known by another because of a twofold impediment, namely, on account of the grossness of the body and the will concealing its secrets. But the first obstacle is removed in the resurrection, nor does it exist in angels. But the second impediment will remain after the resurrection, and exists now in angels. And yet the brightness of the body will represent the quality of the mind, with respect to the amount of grace and glory. And thus one will be able to see the mind of another.

1. q. 105, art. 4.

Ad 2. It should be said that one angel might see the intelligible species of another because the mode of the intelligible species with respect to greater or less universality is proportioned to the nobility of substances. But it does not follow that one knows how the other uses those intelligible species in actually considering them.

Ad 3. It should be said that the brute's appetite is not master of its acts, but follows the impression of another corporeal or spiritual cause. Therefore, because the angels know bodily things and their dispositions, through these they can know what is in the appetite and imaginative grasp of brute animals, and even of men insofar as in them sense appetite sometimes acts following some bodily impression, as always happens with the brutes. It is not necessary, however, that the angels know the motion of sense appetite and the imaginative grasp of man, insofar as they are moved by will and reason, because the lower part of the soul participates somewhat in reason, as obeying a commander, as is said in *Ethics* 1.13. Nor does it follow that if the angel knows what is in the sense appetite and memory of man, that he knows what is in thought or will, because intellect or will are not subject to sense appetite and images, but can use them in different ways.

Article 5: Do the angels know all the mysteries of grace?

It seems that they do.

1. The mystery of the incarnation of Christ would seem to be of all mysteries the most excellent. But the angels knew this from the beginning, for Augustine says in the *Literal Commentary on Genesis* 5.19 that this mystery was hidden from all ages by God, but he made it known to the principalities and powers in heaven. And the Apostle says in 1 Timothy 3.16: '. . . was justified in the spirit, appeared to the angels . . .' Therefore the angels know the mysteries of grace.

2. Moreover, the reasons for all the mysteries of grace are contained in the divine wisdom. But the angels see the very wisdom of God, which is his essence. Therefore the angels know the mysteries of grace.

3. Moreover, the prophets were instructed by the angels, as is clear from Dionysius in the *Angelic Hierarchy* 4. But the prophets knew the mysteries of grace, for it is said in Amos 3.7: 'For the Lord God does nothing without revealing his secret to his servants the prophets.' Therefore the angels know the mysteries of grace.

ON THE CONTRARY:

No one learns what he knows. But even the highest angels ask about the divine mysteries of grace, and learn them, for it is said in *On the Celestial Hierarchy* 7 that Sacred Scripture led the celestial essences to question Jesus and acquire the knowledge of his divine work on our behalf, Jesus teaching them without intermediary. And Isaiah 63.1: 'Who is this that cometh from Edom?' Where it is the angels who ask and Jesus replies, 'I that speak justice.' Therefore the angels do not know the mysteries of grace.

RESPONSE:

It should be said that there is a twofold knowledge in the angels. One natural, according to which they know things both in their own essence and also in innate species; angels cannot know the mysteries of grace by this knowledge. These mysteries depend on the pure will of God. Thus the Apostle argues in 1 Corinthians 2.11: 'For who among men knows the things of a man save the spirit of man which is in him? Even so the things of God, no one knows but the Spirit of God.'

But there is another knowledge of the angels which makes them happy by which they see the Word and things in the Word. And in this vision they know the mysteries of grace, not all and not all equally but as God chooses to reveal to them; according to the Apostle in 1 Corinthians 2.10, 'To us God has revealed them through his Spirit.' With the result that the higher angels, more keenly contemplating the divine wisdom, know many mysteries and deep things in that vision of God, and they manifest them to the lower angels, illumining them. Some of these mysteries they knew from the beginning of creation, some they were taught after a little while as this was needed for their tasks.

Ad 1. It should be said that one can speak of the mystery of the incarnation of Christ in two ways. In one way, in general, and thus it was revealed to all at the beginning of his happiness. The reason is that this is a kind of general principle to which all the offices are ordered. Hebrews 1.14: 'Are they not all ministering spirits, sent for service, for the sake of those who shall inherit salvation?' which comes about through the mystery of the incarnation. Hence it was necessary that all be taught this mystery in a general way from the beginning. There is another way in which we can speak of the mystery of the incarnation, as to its special conditions. And thus not all angels were told about it from the beginning, indeed some, even of the higher angels, learned it only later, as is evident from the authority of Dionysius cited in the 'On the Contrary'.

Ad 2. It should be said that although the blessed angels contemplate the divine wisdom, they do not comprehend it. Therefore it is not necessary that they know everything contained in it.

Ad 3. It should be said that whatever the prophets knew of the mysteries of grace through divine revelation was more excellently revealed to the angels. And although he revealed to the prophets in general terms what he would do with respect to the salvation of the human race, the Apostles knew some special things about it which the prophets did not know, according to Ephesians 3.4–5: 'And so by reading you can perceive how well versed I am in the mystery of Christ, that mystery which in other ages was not known to the sons of men, as now it has been revealed to his holy Apostles.' Among the prophets, the later knew what the earlier did not, according to Psalm 118.100: 'I understood more than the ancients.' And Gregory says in commenting on Ezekiel that as time passes knowledge of the divine increases.

QUESTION 58
ON THE MODE OF ANGELIC KNOWLEDGE

We now take up the mode of angelic knowledge and ask seven questions in its regard: (1) is the intellect of the angel sometimes potential, sometimes actual? (2) can the angels understand many things simultaneously? (3) do they understand discursively? (4) do they understand by composing and dividing? (5) can there be falsehood in the angel's intellect? (6) can the angel's knowledge be called morning and evening knowledge? (7) are morning and evening knowledge the same or different?

Article 1: Is the angelic intellect sometimes potential, sometimes actual?

It seems that it is.

1. Motion is the act of a thing existing potentially, as is said in *Physics* 3.1. But the minds of the angels move when they understand, as Dionysius says in *On the Divine Names* 4. Therefore the angelic minds are sometimes in potency.

2. Moreover, since desire is for something not had but which can be had, whoever desires to understand something is in potency to it. But

1 Peter 1.12: 'Into these things angels desire to look.' Therefore the angel's intellect is sometimes in potency.

3. Moreover, in the *Book of Causes* 8 it is said that the intelligence understands according to the mode of its substance. But the substance of the angel has something of potency mixed in it. Therefore, he sometimes understands only potentially.

ON THE CONTRARY:

Augustine says in the *Literal Commentary on Genesis* 2.8 that the angels from the time they were created enjoyed the holy and pious contemplation of the very eternity of the Word. But the contemplating intellect is not in potency, but in act. Therefore the intellect of the angel is not in potency.

RESPONSE:

It should be said that, as the Philosopher says in *On the Soul* 3.4 and *Physics* 8.8, the intellect can be potential in two ways, in one way, before it learns or discovers, that is, before it has knowledge, and in another way as when it possesses knowledge but is not using it. The angel's intellect is never potential in the first way with respect to the things to which his natural knowledge extends, much as the celestial bodies have no potentiality to exist which is not actually fulfilled. So the celestial intellects, the angels, have no potentiality to understand that is not completely fulfilled by the intelligible species connatural to them.

But with respect to things divinely revealed to them, nothing prevents their intellects from being in potency, because thus the heavenly bodies are sometimes potentially illumined by the sun. In the second way, the intellect of the angel can be in potency to the things it knows naturally, for it is not always considering everything that it naturally knows. With respect to knowledge of the Word, it is never in potency in this way, because it always actually intuits the Word and sees what is in the Word. In this vision their happiness consists and happiness consists in acting, not just having, as the Philosopher says in *Ethics* 1.8.

Ad 1. It should be said that motion is not taken there for the act of the imperfect, that is, of something potentially existing, but as the act of the perfected, that is, of something actually existing. It is thus that understanding and sensing are called motions, as is said in *On the Soul* 3.7.

Ad 2. It should be said that the desire of the angels does not exclude the thing desired, but its dislike. Or they can be said to desire the vision of God with respect to new revelations which they receive from God in order to fulfil their missions.

Ad 3. It should be said that in the substance of the angel there is no potency denuded of act, and similarly in the intellect of the angel there is no potency that is not actualized.

Article 2: Can the angel know many things simultaneously?

It seems that he cannot.

1. The Philosopher says in *Topics* 2.10 that one can know many things but understand only one.

2. Moreover, nothing is understood except insofar as the intellect is formed by an intelligible species, as the body is formed by shape. But one body cannot have different shapes. Therefore, one intellect cannot simultaneously understand different intelligible things.

3. Moreover, understanding is a kind of motion. But no motion terminates in different goals. Therefore, it cannot happen that many things are simultaneously understood.

ON THE CONTRARY:
Augustine says in the *Literal Commentary on Genesis* 4.32 that the spiritual power of the angelic mind most easily comprehends at the same time all that it wants to.

RESPONSE:
It should be said that unity of term is required for the unity of motion, as unity of operation requires unity of object. But it happens sometimes that things are understood as many or as one, like the parts of a continuum. For if each is taken by itself, they are many and they are not simultaneously received by sense and intellect. But they can otherwise be taken as they are in one whole, and then they are known simultaneously by sense as by intellect, when the whole continuum is considered, as is said in *On the Soul* 3.6. Thus our intellect also simultaneously understands subject and predicate, as they are parts of one proposition; and two things are compared insofar as they agree in some comparison. From which it is clear that many things, insofar as they are distinct, cannot be simultaneously understood, but insofar as they are united in one intelligible object they can be simultaneously understood. A thing is actually intelligible insofar as its likeness is in the intellect. Therefore when things can be known by

one intelligible species they are known as one intelligible, and are known simultaneously. But things known by different intelligible species are graded as different intelligible things. Therefore the angels, by the knowledge with which they know things in the Word, know all things by one intelligible species, which is the divine essence. Thus with respect to such knowledge, they know everything simultaneously, just as in heaven our thoughts will not be flighty, going from one thing to another, but we will see the whole of our knowledge simultaneously in one place, as Augustine says in *On the Trinity* 15.16. But by the knowledge with which they know things by innate species, they can know all those things simultaneously which are known by one species, but not the things that are known by different ones.

Ad 1. It should be said that to understand many as one is sometimes to understand one thing.

Ad 2. It should be said that the intellect is formed by the intelligible species which it has in itself. Therefore many things can be simultaneously intuited by one intelligible species, just as a body with one shape can simultaneously be like many bodies.

Ad 3. The response is the same as to the first objection.

Article 3: Does the angel know discursively?

It seems that he does.

1. Intellectual discourse is had when one thing is known by means of another. But the angels know one thing by another, for they know creatures by the Word. Therefore the intellect of the angel knows discursively.

2. Moreover, whatever a lower power can do, a higher power can do. But the human intellect can syllogize and know causes in their effects, which is to know discursively. Therefore, the intellect of the angel, which is higher in the order of nature, can do this even more.

3. Moreover, Isadore says that the demons know many things from experience. But experimental knowledge is discursive, one experience coming about from many memories, and one universal coming to be from many experiences, as is said at the end of the *Posterior Analytics* and the beginning of the *Metaphysics* 1.1. Therefore the knowledge of the angels is discursive.

ON THE CONTRARY:

Dionysius says in *On the Divine Names* 7 that angels do not gather divine knowledge from diffuse remarks nor are they brought to the specific from something general.

RESPONSE:

It should be said that, as has often been remarked, the angels hold that grade among spiritual substances that celestial bodies do among corporeal, for both are called celestial minds by Dionysius.[1] This is the difference between celestial and terrestrial bodies, that the latter achieve their ultimate perfection by change and motion, whereas the former by their very nature have their ultimate perfection immediately. So lower intellects, those of men, by a kind of motion and discourse achieve the perfection of operation in the knowledge of truth, when from one known thing they proceed to another. If at once in the knowledge of known principle they perceived all the conclusions following on it, discourse would have no place with them.

And so it is with the angels, because they immediately see in what they first know naturally all things that can be known in them. That is why they are called intellectual, since even with us the things that are immediately and naturally known are said to be understood [*intelligi*]: that is why the habit of first principles in the human soul is called intellect [*intellectus*]. Those that acquire knowledge of the truth by way of discourse are called rational. This arises from the weakness of the light of intellect in the latter. For if they had the fullness of intellectual light, as the angels do, immediately at first blush they would comprehend their whole power, intuiting whatever can be syllogized from them.

Ad 1. It should be said that discourse means a kind of motion. But every motion is from something prior to something posterior. Hence discursive knowledge is had insofar as from a thing previously known knowledge of another, at first unknown, is arrived at later. But if in one glance the other is simultaneously seen, as the image of the thing is seen in a mirror when it too is seen, this is not discursive knowledge. But that is how angels know things in the Word.

Ad 2. It should be said that angels can syllogize, insofar as they know syllogisms and see effects in their causes and causes in their effects, but not in the sense that they acquire knowledge of an unknown

---

1. *On the Divine Names* 1.

truth by syllogizing from causes to effects or from effects to causes.

Ad 3. It should be said that the term experience is used of angels and demons according to a certain similarity, insofar as they know present sensible things, but they do so without discourse.

Article 4: Does the angel know by composing and dividing?

It seems that he does.

1. Where there is a multitude of things understood, there is composition of them, as is said in *On the Soul* 3.6. But in the intellect of the angel there is a multitude of things understood, since he knows different things by different species, and not all at once. Therefore, there is composition and division in the intellect of the angel.

2. Moreover, negation is more distant from affirmation than any two opposed natures, because the first distinction is by way of affirmation and negation. But some distant natures the angel does not know by one, but by different species, as is clear from what has been said. Therefore he must know affirmation and negation by different species. Therefore the angel seems to understand by composing and dividing.

3. Moreover, speech is a sign of intellect, but in speaking to men, angels express affirmative and negative propositions, which are signs of composition and division in the intellect, as is clear from many places in Sacred Scripture. Therefore, it seems that the angel understands by composing and dividing.

ON THE CONTRARY:

Dionysius says in *On the Divine Names* 7 that the intellectual power of the angels which shines forth is a perspicuous simplicity of divine understandings. But simple understanding is without composition and division, as is said in *On the Soul* 3.6. Therefore, the angel understands without composition and division.

RESPONSE:

It should be said that just as in the reasoning intellect the conclusion is compared to the principle, so in intellect composing and dividing the predicated is compared to the subject. For if the intellect saw the truth of the conclusion immediately in the principle, it would never understand discursively or by way of reasoning. Similarly, if the intellect immediately in its grasp of the quiddity of the subject had knowledge of everything that could be attributed to or denied of the subject, it would understand by composing and dividing, but only by understanding the quiddity.

It is thereby evident that our intellect's discursiveness and need to compose and divide arise from the same fact, namely that it cannot immediately in the first grasp of what is first known see everything contained virtually in it. Which is a result of the weakness of intellectual light in us, as has been said (a. 3). Hence since in the angel there is perfect intellectual light, since he is a pure and bright mirror, as Dionysius says in *On the Divine Names* 4, it follows that the angel understands neither by reasoning nor by composing and dividing.

None the less, he understands the composition and division of propositions and the reasoning in syllogism, for he understands composed things simply and mobile things immobilely and material things immaterially.

Ad 1. It should be said that not just any multitude of things understood causes composition, but a multitude in which one thing understood is attributed to another, or removed from it. But the angel, in understanding the quiddity of anything, simultaneously understands whatever can be attributed or removed from it. Hence by understanding the quiddity, he understands in one simple understanding whatever we can understand by composing and dividing.

Ad 2. It should be said that the different quiddities of things differ less with respect to their formality of existing than affirmation and negation. But with respect to the formality of knowing, affirmation and negation agree more, because when the truth of the affirmation is known, immediately the falsity of the negative opposite is known.

Ad 3. It should be said that what the angels say in affirmative and negative propositions shows that angels know composition and division, but not that they know by composing and dividing. Rather they know by simply knowing the quiddity.

Article 5: Can the angelic intellect be false?

It seems that it can.

1. Impudence pertains to falseness. But in demons there is an impudent fantasy, as Dionysius says in *On the Divine Names* 4. Therefore it seems that there can be falsity in the intellect of angels.

2. Moreover, lack of knowledge can be the cause of a false estimate.

But there can be nescience in angels, as Dionysius says in the *Celestial Hierarchy* 6. Therefore, it seems that there can be falsity in them.

3. Moreover, everyone who falls short of the truth of wisdom, and has a depraved reason, has falsity and error in his intellect. But this is what Dionysius says of the demons in *On the Divine Names* 7. Therefore, it seems that there can be falsity in the intellect of angels.

ON THE CONTRARY:

The Philosopher says in *On the Soul* 3.6 that the intellect is always true. Augustine also says, in the *Eighty-three Questions*, Question 32, that only the true is understood. But angels know only by understanding. Therefore, there cannot be deception and falsity in the knowledge of the angel.

RESPONSE:

It should be said that the truth of this question depends to a degree on the foregoing. For it has been said that the angel does not understand by composing and dividing, but by understanding the quiddity. But the intellect with respect to the *what* is always true, just as sense is with respect to its proper object, as is said in *On the Soul* 3.6. In us there can incidentally be deception and falsity in understanding what a thing is, namely by reason of some composition or when we take the definition of one thing to be the definition of another, or when the parts of the definition do not cohere, as if we should take as the definition of something that it is a four-footed flying thing (no animal is such), and this occurs with composites, whose definition is drawn from different things, one of which is material with respect to the other. But there is no falsity in understanding simple quiddities, as the Philosopher says in *Metaphysics* 9.10, because either they are completely missed and we understand nothing of them, or they are known as they are.

Therefore there can be no falsity or error or deception as such in the intellect of any angel, but it happens incidentally although otherwise than in us, for by composing and dividing we sometimes come to an understanding of quiddity, as when we seek a definition by dividing or demonstrating, and that does not happen with angels, but by means of the quiddity of the thing they know all the assertions pertinent to that thing. But it is manifest that the quiddity of a thing can be a principle of knowing with respect to those things which naturally belong to a thing, or are removed from it, but not of those things which depend on the supernatural ordinance of God. Therefore, the good angels, having a rectified will, through knowledge of a thing's quiddity judge concerning what naturally pertains to a thing saving only the divine ordinance. Hence there cannot be falsity or error in them. But the demons, because of a perverse will, withdrew intellect from the divine wisdom and sometimes absolutely judge of things according to their natural condition, and are not deceived with respect to what naturally pertains to the thing, but they can be deceived with respect to the things which are supernatural, as when considering a dead man, they judge that he will not be resurrected and seeing the man Christ judge him not to be God.

The response to what was objected on both sides is clear from this. For the perversity of the demons is due to their not being subjected to the divine wisdom. Nescience is in the angels, not with respect to the naturally knowable, but with respect to the supernatural. It is evident that their understanding of the quiddity is always true, save incidentally, insofar as it is unfittingly ordered to some composition or division.

Article 6: Can angelic knowledge be called morning and evening knowledge?

It seems not.

1. Morning and evening contain shadows, but there is no darkness in the knowledge of the angel, since there is no error or falsity there. Therefore the angel's knowledge ought not to be called morning and evening.

2. Moreover, between evening and morning comes the night and between morning and evening falls noon. Therefore if there were morning and evening knowledge in the angels, by parity of reasoning there ought to be noonday and nocturnal knowledge in them as well.

3. Moreover, knowledge is distinguished on the basis of a difference in the things known. Hence in *On the Soul* 3.8 the Philosopher says that the sciences are divided in the way that things are. But there is a threefold existence of things, namely in the Word, in their proper nature and in the angelic intelligence, as Augustine says in the *Literal Commentary on Genesis* 2.8. Therefore, if morning and evening knowledge be posited in the angels, because of the existence of things in the Word and in their proper natures, there ought to be a third knowledge in them as well, because of the existence of things in the angelic intelligence.

ON THE CONTRARY:
Augustine in the *Literal Commentary on Genesis* 4.22 and in the *City of*

God 11.7 distinguishes the knowledge of the angels into morning and evening.

RESPONSE:
It should be said that what is said of morning and evening knowledge in the angels was introduced by Augustine, who does not want the six days in which God is said to have made all things in Genesis 1 to be understood as those usual days which are brought about by the circuit of the sun, since we read that the sun was created on the fourth day, but as one day, namely angelic knowledge presented by the six kinds of things. For just as in an ordinary day morning is the beginning of the day, and evening its term, so its primordial knowledge of the existence of things is called morning knowledge, and this is according as things exist in the Word. But the knowledge of the existence of created things, as they exist in their own natures, is called evening knowledge, for the existence of things flows from the Word as from a primordial principle, and this flowing forth is terminated in the existence that things have in their proper nature.

Ad 1. It should be said that evening and morning are not understood in angelic knowledge by similarity with the admixture of darkness but according to a similitude of beginning and term. Or it might be said that nothing prevents something to be called light in comparison to one and shadow in comparison to another, as Augustine says in the *Literal Commentary on Genesis* 4.23. Just as the life of the faithful and just is called light in comparison with the impious, as in Ephesians 5.8: 'For you were once darkness, but now you are light in the Lord,' but the life of the faithful compared to the life of glory is called dark, as in 2 Peter 1.19: 'And we have the word of prophecy, surer still, to which you do well to attend, as to a lamp shining in a dark place.' Thus the knowledge of the angel whereby he knows things in their proper nature is day in comparison with ignorance or error, but obscure in comparison with the vision of the Word.

Ad 2. It should be said that morning and evening knowledge pertain to the day, that is, to the illumined angels, which are distinct from the dark, that is, the bad angels. But the good angels, knowing the creature, are not fixed on it, which would be to become dark and night, but refer it to the praise of God, in which as in a principle they know all things. Therefore, after evening is put not night but morning, because morning is the end of the preceding day and the beginning of the next, insofar as the angels refer the knowledge of the preceding work to the praise of

God. But noonday is included under day, as the mean between two extremes. Or midday can be referred to the knowledge of God himself, who has neither beginning nor end.

Ad 3. It should be said that the angels too are creatures. Hence the existence of things in the angelic intelligence is comprehended in evening knowledge, along with the existence of things in their proper nature.

Article 7: Are morning and evening knowledge the same or different?

It seems that they are the same.

1. It is said in Genesis 1, 'And there was evening and morning one day.' But by day angelic knowledge is understood, as Augustine says. Therefore, one and same knowledge in the angels is called morning and evening.

2. Moreover, it is impossible that the same power simultaneously have two operations. But the angels are always in the act of morning knowledge, because they always see God and things in God, according to Matthew 18.10: 'Their angels in heaven always behold the face of my Father, etc.' Therefore, if evening knowledge were other than morning knowledge, the angel could in no way actually be in the act of evening knowledge.

3. Moreover, the Apostle says in 1 Corinthians 13.10: 'When that which is perfect has come, that which is imperfect will be done away with.' But if evening knowledge is other than morning, it compares to it as imperfect to perfect. Therefore, evening knowledge cannot be simultaneous with morning.

ON THE CONTRARY:
Augustine says in the *Literal Commentary on Genesis* 4.23 that there is a great difference between the knowledge of a thing in the Word of God and knowledge of it in its own nature, that the former rightly pertains to day, and the latter to evening.

RESPONSE:
It should be said that, as has been remarked, evening knowledge is said to be that by which angels know things in their proper nature. This cannot be understood as if they receive knowledge from the proper nature of things, such that the preposition 'in' indicates the relation of principle, because angels do not receive knowledge from things, as was shown

above.[1] It follows that by 'in their proper nature' is taken the notion of what is known, as they come into knowledge, such that evening knowledge in the angels is said according as they know the existence that things have in their proper nature.

Which they know by two means, by innate species and by the notions of things existing in the Word. For in seeing the Word, they do not know only the existence things have in the Word, but the existence they have in their proper nature, just as God by the fact that he sees himself knows the existence that things have in their proper nature. Therefore, if knowledge is called evening insofar as they know the existence things have in their proper nature, in seeing the Word, then evening and morning knowledge are the same in essence, differing only according to what is known. But if knowledge is called evening insofar as angels know the existence that things have in their proper nature, by innate forms, then evening and morning knowledge differ. That is the way Augustine seems to understand them, since he calls one imperfect with respect to the other.

Ad 1. It should be said that just as the number of six days, as Augustine understands it, is taken from the six kinds of things which are known by the angels, so the unity of the day is taken from the unity of the thing known, which, however, can be known by different knowledges.

Ad 2. It should be said that two operations can be simultaneously of the same power if one is referred to the other, as is clear when will simultaneously wills the end and that which is for the sake of the end, and the intellect simultaneously understands principles and conclusions by the principles, when it has once acquired science. Evening knowledge in the angels is referred to morning knowledge, as Augustine says. Hence nothing prevents them being simultaneously in the angels.

Ad 3. It should be said that when the perfect arrives, the imperfect opposed to it is done away with, just as faith, which is of things not seen, is no more when vision comes. But the imperfection of evening knowledge is not opposed to the perfection of morning knowledge. That something is known in itself is not opposed to its being known in its cause. Nor does the fact that something is known by two means, one of which is more perfect than the other, have anything contradictory in it, for we can come to the same conclusion by a demonstrative and dialectical middle. Similarly, the same thing can be known by the angel by the uncreated Word and by an innate species.

1. q. 55, art. 2.

17. Definitions of Soul. On Aristotle's De anima, 2, 1–3 (1268)

It was while he was still teaching at Santa Sabina in Rome that Thomas Aquinas wrote his commentary on Aristotle's On the Soul. *The year was 1268. The following year he would return to Paris and function as one of the two Dominican regent masters for another three-year term. The situation in Paris was such that we can easily find motivation for commenting on Aristotle, but in Rome at Santa Sabina the Parisian turmoil could not have motivated Thomas. Indeed, internal evidence makes it clear that he was not aware of the distortion of Aristotelian doctrine that came to be called Latin Averroism.*

Thomas knew the writings of Aristotle from the very outset of his career. At Naples he would also have become acquainted with the interpretations of Averroes and Avicenna. Later at Cologne, he attended Albert the Great's commentary on the Nicomachean Ethics *and prepared the manuscript for the stationer. Father Chenu[1] finds it the most natural thing in the world that Dominican theologians would teach courses in such philosophical works as the Ethics. In any case, prior to 1268 there is no such work from Thomas Aquinas.*

We can trace through the writings of Thomas a growing confidence in his own reading of Aristotle. Very early on he is taking exception to the Commentator and this is true as well in the Commentary on On the Soul.

Aristotle's definition of the soul, indeed definitions, figure in Thomas's writings early and late. In the passage below we have a close textual reading of the passages in Aristotle Thomas had been relying on.

---

1. Marie-Dominique Chenu, O. P., perhaps best known for his *Introduction à l'étude de Saint Thomas d'Aquin*, Paris, J. Vrin, 1954.

COMMENTARY ON *ON THE SOUL*

Lesson 1

Let the foregoing suffice as our account of the views concerning the soul which have been handed on by our predecessors; let us now dismiss them and make as it were a completely new start, endeavouring to give a precise answer to the question, What is soul? That is, to formulate the most general possible definition of it.

We are in the habit of recognizing, as one determinate kind of what is, substance, and that in several senses, (a) in the sense of matter or that which in itself is not 'a this', and (b) in the sense of form or essence, which is that precisely in virtue of which a thing is called 'a this', and (c) in the sense of that which is compounded of both (a) and (b). Now matter is potentiality, form actuality; of the latter there are two grades, related to one another as for example knowledge to the exercise of knowledge.

Among substances are by general consent reckoned bodies and especially natural bodies; for they are the principles of all other bodies. Of natural bodies some have life in them, others not; by life we mean self-nutrition and growth (with its correlative decay). It follows that every natural body which has life in it is a substance in the sense of a composite.

But since it is also a *body* of such and such a kind, *viz.* having life, the *body* cannot be soul; the body is subject or matter, not what is attributed to it. Hence the soul must be a substance in the sense of the form of a natural body having life potentially within it. But substance is actuality, and thus soul is the actuality of a body as above characterized. Now the word actuality has two senses corresponding respectively to the possession of knowledge and the actual exercise of knowledge. It is obvious that the soul is actuality in the first sense, *viz.* that of knowledge as possessed, for both sleeping and waking presuppose the existence of soul, and of these waking corresponds to actual knowing, sleeping to knowledge possessed but not employed, and in the history of the individual, knowledge comes before its employment or exercise.

That is why the soul is the first grade of actuality of a natural body having life potentially in it. The body so described is a body which is organized. The parts of plants in spite of their extreme simplicity are 'organs', for example the leaf serves to shelter the pericarp, the pericarp to shelter the fruit, while the roots of plants are analogous to the mouth of animals, both serving for the absorption of food. If, then, we have to give a general formula applicable to all kinds of soul, we must describe it as the first grade of actuality of a natural organized body. That is why we can wholly dismiss as unnecessary the question whether the soul and the body are one: it is as meaningless as to ask whether the wax and the shape given to it by the stamp are one, or generally the matter of a thing and that of which it is the matter. Unity has many senses (as many as 'is' has), but the most proper and fundamental sense of both is the relation of an actuality to that of which it is the actuality.   Aristotle, *On the Soul* 2.1

211. After Aristotle has set down in the first book the opinions of others concerning the soul, in this second book he begins to treat of the soul according to his own opinion, and the truth. In this regard he does two things. First, he states his intention, linking it to what has preceded. Second, he pursues his intention, when he says, 'We say that a substance is of one kind . . .' First, then, he says that in the first book the views of our predecessors about soul were treated, but it is now necessary to go back again to the beginning in order to determine the truth. This should be done with a keen sense of the difficulty rather than presume that the truth is easily discovered. Earlier, in the preface, it was asked whether the soul itself or its parts ought to be discussed first. As if in answer to that question, he says that we ought first to say what soul is, making known its essence; its parts or powers will be determined afterwards. And, as if to give the reason for this, he adds, 'to formulate the most general possible definition of it'. For in showing what the soul is one treats what is common. It is when each part and power of it are discussed that what is special with respect to soul is treated. To proceed from the common to the less common is the order of teaching, as the Philosopher shows at the beginning of the *Physics*.

212. Then, when he says, 'We are in the habit of recognizing . . .' he pursues the intention he stated, and this is divided into two parts. In the first he shows what the soul is; in the second, he treats its parts and powers. He subdivides the first point into two: first, he gives a definition of soul which is as the conclusion of a demonstration; second he gives a definition of soul which is as the principle of a demonstration. We should know that, as is said in *Posterior Analytics* 1.16, every definition is the conclusion of a demonstration, like 'Thunder is a continuous sound in the clouds,' or it is the principle of a demonstration, like 'Thunder is the extinction of fire in the clouds,' or it differs only in arrangement from a demonstration, like 'Thunder is a continuous sound in the clouds because of the extinction of fire in the clouds.' This gives both the conclusion and principle of a demonstration, although not in syllogistic order. The first task is divided into two, in the first of which he gives the first definition

of soul, and then goes on to make it manifest.[1] The first is further subdivided: first, he recalls some divisions which open the way to the investigation of the soul's definition; second, he seeks the definition of soul, 'Now given that there are bodies . . .'[2]

213. Recall that, as the Philosopher teaches in *Metaphysics* 7.4, the difference between the definition of substance and of accident lies in this that the former introduces nothing outside the substance of what is defined, since a substance is defined by its material and formal principles, but the definition of accident mentions things outside the essence of what is defined, for example, 'Snubness is the curvature of the nose.' The reason is that definition signifies the quiddity of the thing, and substance is something complete in its existence and species, whereas the accident, not having complete being, depends on substance. Similarly, no form is a thing complete in species: but the perfection of species belongs to the composed substance. The composed substance is so defined that in its definition nothing outside its essence is introduced, but in the definition of form something outside the essence of the form is mentioned, namely its proper subject or matter. Hence, since soul is form, it is necessary that its matter or subject be put into its definition.

214. His first task involves two things: first, he sets down two divisions necessary for investigating what should be put into the definition of soul in order to express its *essence*. Next he asks what should be put in the definition of soul in order to express its *subject*.[3] In the first step, he gives three divisions, the first is the division of being into the ten categories. And this is signalled when he says 'one determinate kind of what is, substance . . .'

215. The second division is that of substance into matter, form and composite. Matter is not in itself a definite thing [*hoc aliquid*] but only a potentiality to become such. The form is that thanks to which the definite thing is actual. The composed substance is the definite thing. Something is called a definite thing if it is a demonstrable thing complete in being and kind, and this is only true of the composite substance in material things. Separated substances, although they are not composed of matter and form, yet are definite things, since they are actually subsistent and complete in their own nature. The rational soul can in a certain respect be called a definite thing, insofar as it can subsist by itself, but

1. Lesson 2.
2. paras. 220 ff.
3. para. 217.

because it does not have a complete species, being rather part of a species, it is not in every way proper to call it a definite thing. The difference between matter and form is this, that matter is being in potentiality, but form is the *entelecheia*, that is act thanks to which matter comes to be actual, and it is the composite that is actual being.

216. The third division is of act into two kinds, one way as knowledge is an act, in another as the exercise of knowledge is an act. The difference between these two acts can be investigated from their corresponding potentialities. For someone is called a grammarian potentially before he has acquired the habit of grammar by learning and discovering, and this potentiality is actualized when he acquires the habit of science. But there is also a potentiality with respect to the exercise of the knowledge, before one is actually considering it, and this potentiality is realized when one actually considers. So both knowledge and the use of it are acts.

217. Then he sets down divisions enabling us to see what should be put in the definition of the soul as to its subject. He mentions three divisions, the first of substance into those which are bodies and those which are not. The most manifest instance of substance is bodily substances, for what incorporeal substances are is unclear, because they are remote from sense and knowable only by reason. That is why he says that 'Among substances are by general consent reckoned bodies . . .'

218. The second division is of bodies into physical, that is, natural bodies, and artificial. A man, wood and stone are natural bodies, but a house and hatchet are artificial. Natural bodies seem to be substance more than artificial things, because natural bodies are principles of the artificial. For art acts on a matter provided by nature, and the form that is introduced by the artisan is an accidental form, shape and the like. Hence artificial bodies are not in the genus of substance because of their form, but only because of their matter, which is natural. They owe it to natural bodies that they are substances. Hence natural bodies are substance more than artificial bodies, for they are substance not only because of their matter, but also because of their form.

219. The third distinction is of natural bodies into those that have life and those that do not. Those are said to have life which take nourishment by themselves, grow and then decay. Note that this explanation is more by way of example than definition, for something is not alive solely because it grows or ages, but also because it senses and understands and can perform other works of life. Separated substances are alive because they have intellect and will, as is clear from *Metaphysics* 12.8, although there is no growth and ageing in them. He chooses as his example of

living things those that take nourishment and grow because the soul of plants, to which nourishment and growth pertain, is the principle of life, as he said at the end of Book 1. The proper notion of life is drawn from this: anything that can move itself – understanding *move* broadly, as when intellectual activity is called a kind of motion. We say that those things are without life which can only be moved by an extrinsic principle.

220. Now, making use of these divisions, he investigates the definition of soul, and he will speak first of the parts of the definition, then give the definition,[1] and thirdly handle a difficulty raised by the definition he gives.[2] As to the parts of the definition, he will first discuss those which pertain to the essence of soul, and then those that pertain to the essence of its subject.[3] First, then, he discusses this part of the definition 'the soul is act'; next he discusses the meaning of 'first act'.[4]

From what has already been said, he concludes that since natural bodies seem especially to be substance, and every body having life is a natural body, we must say that every body having life is a substance. And, since it is an actual being, it must be a composed substance. When I say 'body having life' I say two things, namely, that it is a body and that it is a body of a certain kind, that is, one having life, and it cannot be said that that part of 'body having life' that is body is the soul. For by soul we understand that whereby one having life lives, so it must be understood as existing in a subject, taking subject largely and not simply insofar as subject is an actual being – thus it is that accidents are in a subject – but insofar as prime matter which is potential being can be called a subject. The body, which receives life, is more like subject and matter than it is something existing in a subject.

221. Substance is of three kinds, the composite, matter and form, and soul is not the composite, which is the body having life, nor is it the matter, which is the body as subject of life. By elimination, then, it must be substance as form or as the species of a certain kind of body, namely of a natural body potentially having life.

222. He says 'having life potentially' and not simply 'having life', since the body having life is understood to be the living composite substance and the composite is not put into the definition of its form. It is the matter of the live body that is compared to life as potentiality to act. And that is the soul, the act by which the body lives. It is as if we were to say that

1. para. 233.
2. para. 234.
3. para. 230.
4. para. 227.

the shape is the act, not of the actually shaped body, for this is a composite of shape and body, but of the body which is the subject of shape, which is compared to shape as potentiality to act.

223. Lest anyone should think that soul is act in the manner of an accidental form, he adds that the soul is act as substance is act, that is, as form. And since every form is in a determinate matter, it follows that it is the form of the kind of body just discussed.

224. This is the difference between substantial and accidental form, that the latter does not cause something actually to be simply but actually to be such and such, for example large or white or something like that. Substantial form causes actual existence simply. The accidental form comes to an already actually existing subject, whereas the substantial form does not come to an already actually existing subject but to one that exists only in potentiality, namely prime matter. It is clear from this that a thing cannot have two substantial forms because the first would cause actual being simply, and what then comes to an already actually existing subject does not cause it actually to be simply, but only in a certain respect.

225. This refutes the position of Avicebron in the *Fountain of Life* where he makes the order of many substantial forms in the same thing follow the order of genera and species, such that in the individual there is one form thanks to which it is substance, another by which it is body, a third whereby it is animated body, and so on. On the basis of the foregoing, it must be said that it is by one and the same substantial form that the individual is a definite thing, that is substance, and by which it is body and animate body and all the rest. The more perfect form gives matter everything that the less perfect form does, and more besides. Hence the soul does not only cause substance to be and body, which the form of stone does, but also makes the body animate. We should not understand the statement that soul is the act of body and body is its matter and subject to mean that body is constituted by one form, which makes it actually to be a body, and the soul supervenes to make it be a living body, but rather that it is from the soul that it is and is a living body. But to be a body is less perfect and material with respect to life.

226. So it is that when the soul leaves, the body does not remain specifically the same, for the eye and flesh in a corpse are so called only equivocally, as the Philosopher makes clear in *Metaphysics* 7. When the soul leaves, it is succeeded by a substantial form which causes another specific existence, since the corruption of one thing is the generation of another.

227. He turns now to the second part of the definition [of soul] and says that act means two things, as exemplified by knowledge and the exercise of knowledge, as was discussed above. Clearly soul is act in the way knowledge is, because when soul is in the animal then sleeping and waking are. Waking is like the exercise of knowledge, because just as exercise is the use of knowledge, so waking is the use of the senses, but sleep is like having knowledge, when one no longer acts by himself, for the animal powers are quiescent.

228. Of these two acts, knowledge is prior in generation in the same person. For exercise is compared to knowledge as act to potentiality. But act, as is said in *Metaphysics* 9, is naturally prior to potentiality, for it is the end and completion of potentiality. But in the order of generation and of time, universally speaking, act is prior to potentiality, for that which is in potency is brought into act by something actual. But in one and the same thing, potentiality is prior to act, for a thing is first potential, and afterwards comes to be act. That is why he says that knowledge is prior in generation in the same thing to exercise.

229. Hence he concludes that, since soul is act in the way knowledge is, it is the first act of a natural body potentially having life. The Philosopher calls soul the first act, not simply to distinguish it from the act that is operation, but also to distinguish it from the forms of the elements, which always act unless impeded.

230. Now he turns to the part of the definition which takes into account the subject, and because he said that soul is the act of a natural body potentially having life, he also says that every organic body is such. By organic body he means one that has a diversity of organs. Diverse organs are necessary in the body receiving life because of the different activities of the soul. For soul, since it is the most perfect among the forms of bodily things, is the principle of different activities: thus it requires a diversity of organs in that which is perfectible by it. The forms of inanimate things, because of their imperfection, are principles of fewer activities and do not require a diversity of organs in the things perfected by them.

231. The plant soul is the least perfect of souls, which is why there is less diversity of organs in plants than in animals. Therefore, in order to show that every body receiving life is organic, he bases his argument on plants in which there is the least diversity of organs. So he says, 'The parts of plants in spite of their extreme simplicity are organs.' These are extremely simple in that they do not much differ from one another as do the parts of animals. For the foot of the animal is composed of different

parts, namely flesh, nerves, bones, and the like, but the organic parts of plants are not composed of different parts.

231. He shows that the parts of plants are organic because different parts are for different activities. The leaf shelters the pericarp, the part in which fruit grows, and the pericarp shelters the fruit. The roots of plants are analogous to the mouth in animals, because both take in nourishment, the root in plants, the mouth in animals.

232. From what has been said, he puts together the definition of soul and says that if a general definition had to be given, one that would be true of every soul, it would be this: *the soul is the first act of a natural organic body*. He need not add now 'potentially having life', since organic has been put in place of that, as is clear from what has been said.

234. Now he takes up a difficulty raised by the definition. For many doubted that the soul and body could become one, and some held that there were intermediates by which the soul is united to body and somehow linked together. But this will not do since, as has been shown, soul is the form of the body. 'That is why we can wholly dismiss as unnecessary the question whether the soul and body are one.' We do not ask if the wax and its shape are one, nor generally matter and the form of the matter. For it was shown in *Metaphysics* 8 that form is united to matter *per se*, as its act, and the same is true of matter united to form, thanks to which the matter exists actually. He adds, 'Unity has many senses (as many as "is" has),' since being is said both of potential and of actual being and that which is properly being and one is act. But just as potential being is not being simply, but only in a certain respect, so it is not simply one, but only in a certain respect. So one has as many senses as being. Just as body exists because of soul, as by form, so it is immediately united to the soul, since soul is the form of the body. But insofar as it is a motor, nothing prevents there being something intermediate, insofar as a part is moved by the soul using another as intermediate.

Lesson 2

We have now given an answer to the question, What is soul? – an answer which applies to it in its full extent. It is substance in the sense which corresponds to the definitive formula of a thing's essence. That means that it is 'the essential whatness' of a body of the character just assigned. Suppose that what is literally an 'organ', like an axe, were in a *natural* body, its 'essential whatness' would have been its essence and so its soul; if this disappeared from it, it would have ceased to be an axe, except in name. As it is, it is just an axe; it wants the character which is required to make its whatness or formulable essence a soul; for that, it would have had to be a *natural* body of a particular kind, *viz.* one having *in itself* the power of setting itself in movement and arresting itself. Next, apply this doctrine in the case of the 'parts' of the living body. Suppose that the eye were an animal – sight would have been its soul, for sight is the substance or essence of the eye which corresponds to the formula, the eye being merely the matter of seeing; when seeing is removed the eye is no longer an eye, except in name – it is no more a real eye than the eye of a statue or of a painted figure. We must now extend our consideration from the 'parts' to the whole living body; for what the departmental sense is to the bodily part which is its organ, that the whole faculty of sense is to the whole sensible body as such.

From this it indubitably follows that the soul is inseparable from its body, or at any rate that certain parts of it are (if it has parts) – for the actuality of some of them is nothing but the actualities of their bodily parts. Yet some may be separable because they are not the actualities of any body at all. Further, we have no light on the problem whether the soul may not be the actuality of its body in the sense in which the sailor is the actuality of the ship.

This must suffice as our sketch or outline determination of the nature of soul.

Aristotle, On the Soul 2.1 (contd)

235. Aristotle now clarifies the definition and, that being done, infers a certain truth from it.[1] The clarification involves, first, looking at the part of the definition expressing the essence of soul and, second, looking at the part expressing its subject.[2] As to the first, having manifested the definition of soul by comparison with artefacts, he goes on to discuss the parts of soul.[3]

Since the forms of artificial things are accidents that are more known to us than substantial forms because closer to the senses, he clarifies the definition by comparing soul to accidental forms. So too the parts or powers of the soul are more obvious to us than the soul itself, for in our knowledge of soul we proceed from objects to acts and from acts to powers, through which the soul itself is made known to us; it is thus fitting that he should manifest the definition by appeal to such parts.

236. Having given a universal answer to the question, What is soul?, for the definition given applies to every soul, he adds that soul is substance,

1. para. 242.
2. para. 240.
3. para. 239.

that is the form from which the definition of the thing is taken. The form which is substance and the form which is not differ. Accidental form is not in the genus of substance and does not pertain to the essence or quiddity of its subject. Whiteness is not of the essence of the white body. But the substantial form is of the essence or quiddity of its subject. So soul is called a substantial form because it is of the essence or quiddity of the animate body. So he adds, 'That means, etc.', that the substance that corresponds to the thing's definitive formula is the quiddity of that body, that is, a body constituted in a species by such a form. For the form pertains to the essence of the thing which is signified by the definition expressing what the thing is.

237. Because substantial forms like the forms of natural bodies are hidden, he clarifies this through artificial forms, which are accidents. 'Suppose that what is literally an organ . . .' That is, imagine that an axe is a natural body whose form relates to it in the way discussed, 'its essential whatness would have been its essence', speaking of the form of the axe from which its definition is drawn. He calls it its essential whatness because thanks to it the axe is an axe and this form he calls the substance of the axe. He says this because the forms of natural bodies are in the genus of substance. Further, if the axe were not just a natural body, but a living body, the form of axe would be its soul which, if separated from it, would leave an axe only equivocally such, just as when soul is separated there is flesh and eye only equivocally. Because the axe is not a natural body nor its form the quiddity of such a body, take away the form of the axe and the substance of the axe remains, for the substance of artefacts is their matter, which remains when the artificial form is removed, although the body is not then an actual artefact.

238. When he says, 'As it is, it is just an axe,' and is different from animate natural body, he explains this by saying that this is so because the soul is not the quiddity or formulable essence, that is, the form of this kind of body, the artificial body, but of a natural body of such a kind that it potentially has life. To make clear what he means by a natural body, he adds 'having in itself the power of setting itself in movement and arresting itself'. For natural bodies are those that have in themselves their principle of motion and rest. That principle is called nature, as you will find in *Physics* 2.

239. Now he clarifies the definition of soul by appeal to its parts, saying, 'Next, apply this doctrine in the case of the parts of the living body . . .' Because if an eye were an animal, sight would be its soul, for sight is the substantial form of the eye and the eye is its matter, as organic body is

matter to the soul. When sight goes, the eye remains only equivocally, just as an eye in stone or painted is called an eye equivocally. This is so because things named equivocally have only the name in common and differ in the account of the substance. Therefore, taking away the form from which is drawn the account of the substance of the eye, there remains an eye only equivocally. What is found in a part of the living body can be extrapolated to the whole living body, such that just as sight is the substantial form of the eye, and there remains an eye only equivocally when it is taken away, so the soul is the substantial form of the living body, and when it is taken away there remains a living body only equivocally. As one part of the sensitive soul relates to one part of the sensitive body, so the whole of sense to the whole sensitive body as such.

240. He turns now to clarify the definition of soul with respect to calling it the act of a body potentially having life. But something is said to be potential in two ways: first, when it does not have the principle of operation and, second, when it does but is not using it. The body, whose act the soul is, potentially has life, not in the first way but in the second. That is why he says 'potentially capable of living', that is, that having life potentially whose act is the soul is not said to be potentially alive as 'what has lost the soul it had, but what still retains it'. But it is true that the seed and the fruit in which is preserved the seed of the plant is potentially a living body of such a kind that it has a soul, for the seed does not have a soul. So it is in potency, as deprived of soul.

241. To show how the body whose act is the soul is in potency to life, he adds that as waking is an act of the sensitive soul, so cutting is an act of the knife and seeing is the act of the eye. Each of them is an activity and a use of a principle possessed. But the soul is first act, like the power of sight and the power of a tool, for each of these is a principle of operation. But the body which is perfected by the soul, is a potency having its first act, but sometimes lacking its second act. But just as the eye is something composed of the pupil as matter and sight as form, so the animal is composed of soul as form and body as matter.

242. When he says, 'From this it indubitably follows . . .', he concludes a truth from what has been established. For it has been shown that the soul is the act of the whole body, and its parts are the acts of parts, but act and form are not separated from that whose act and form they are. Manifestly, the soul cannot be separated from body, either the whole, or certain parts of it, if it is so fashioned as to have parts. It is manifest that some parts of the soul are acts of some parts of the body, as sight was called the act of the eye. But with respect to some parts, nothing prevents

the soul from being separated, because some parts of the soul are not the acts of the body, as will be proved below with respect to the intellect.

243. Because Plato held that the soul is the act of the body not as form but as motor, he adds that it is not yet clear whether the soul is the act of the body in the way that the pilot is of the ship, namely as mover alone.

244. By way of epilogue, he summarizes what he has said. He says that he has given a sketchy description of the soul which is extrinsic, superficial and incomplete. It will be completed when he has succeeded in determining the nature of each part of the soul.

Lesson 3

Is each of these a soul or a part of a soul? And if a part, a part in what sense? A part merely distinguishable by definition or a part distinct in local situation as well? In the case of certain of these powers, the answers to these questions are easy, in the case of others we are puzzled what to say. Just as in the case of plants which when divided are observed to continue to live though removed to a distance from one another (thus showing that in *their* case the soul of each individual plant before division was actually one, potentially many), so we notice a similar result in other varieties of soul, that is, in insects which have been cut in two; each of the segments possesses both sensation and local movement; and if sensation, necessarily also imagination and appetition; for, where there is sensation, there is also pleasure and pain, and where these, necessarily also desire.

We have no evidence as yet about mind or the power to think; it seems to be a widely different kind of soul, differing as what is eternal from what is perishable; it alone is capable of existence in isolation from all other psychic powers. All the other parts of the soul, it is evident from what we have said, are, in spite of certain statements to the contrary, incapable of separate existence, though, of course, distinguishable by definition. If opining is distinct from perceiving, to be capable of opining and to be capable of perceiving must be distinct, and so with all the other forms of living above enumerated. Further, some animals possess all these parts of soul, some certain of them only, others one only (this is what enables us to classify animals); the cause must be considered later. A similar arrangement is found also within the field of the senses; some classes of animals have all the senses, some only certain of them, others only one, the most indispensable, touch.

Since the expression 'that whereby we live and perceive' has two meanings, just like the expression 'that whereby we know' – that may mean either (a) knowledge or (b) the soul, for we can speak of knowing *by* or *with* either and similarly that whereby we are in health may be either (a) health or (b) the body or some part of the body; and since of the two terms thus contrasted knowledge or health is the name of a form, essence or ratio, or if we so express it an actuality of a recipient matter – knowledge or what is capable of knowing, health or what is capable of being made healthy (for the operation of that which is capable of originating change terminates and has its seat in what is changed or altered); further, since it is the soul by or with which primarily we live, perceive and think, it follows that the soul must be a ratio or formulable essence, not a matter or subject. For, as we said, the word substance has three meanings – form, matter and the complex of both – and of these three what is called matter is potentiality, what is called form actuality. Since then the complex here is the living thing, the body cannot be the actuality of the soul; it is the soul which is the actuality of a certain kind of body. Hence the rightness of the view that the soul cannot be without a body, while it cannot *be* a body; it is not a body but something relative to a body. That is why it is *in* a body, and a body of a definite kind. It was a mistake, therefore, to do as former thinkers did, merely to fit it into a body without adding a definite specification of the kind or character of that body. Reflection confirms the observed fact; the actuality of any given thing can only be realized in what is already potentially that thing, that is, in a matter of its own appropriate to it. From all this it follows that the soul is an actuality or formulable essence of something that possesses a potentiality of being besouled.   Aristotle, *On the Soul* 2.1 (contd)

245. Having given a definition of the soul, the Philosopher now intends to demonstrate it; his intention once stated, he goes on to pursue it.[1] First he has to show the kind of demonstration he intends to use, and then show how definitions are demonstrable.[2] With respect to the first, it should be known that, since we must come into knowledge of the unknown from things already known, every demonstration is put forward in order to make something else known; every demonstration must proceed from things more known to us by which through demonstration something else becomes known. In some things there is no difference between what is more known to us and more known in its nature, as in mathematicals, which are abstracted from matter; with these demonstration proceeds from the more known simply and according to nature, namely from

1. para. 253.
2. para. 247.

causes to effects, hence it is called demonstration of the reasoned fact [*propter quid*]. But in other things, what is more known simply and for us differ, as in natural things, where for the part sensible effects are more known to us than their causes. Thus with respect to natural things, we proceed by and large from things which are naturally less known but more known to us, as is said in *Physics* 1.

246. This is the kind of demonstration he intends to use here. Thus he says, 'For it is not enough for a definitive formula to express as most now do the mere fact; it must include and exhibit the ground also.' That which is certain according to nature and what is according to reason more known, becomes more certain for us from things which are less certain according to nature, though more certain for us. So he means to 'reconsider our results' from this point of view, by demonstrating the definition already given.

247. When he says, 'For it is not enough . . .' he gives the reason for his intention, showing that some definitions are demonstrable. And when he speaks of reconsidering the results concerning the soul, he means that the definitive formula should not only state what is the case, as many terms or definitions do, but the cause should be touched on in the definition, and by means of a definition stating the reason or ground the definition stating only the fact must be demonstrated. For there are many accounts of terms or definitions that are, as it were, conclusions. And he gives an example from geometry.

248. In order to understand this we should know that of four-sided figures some have all right angles and are called *orthogonia*, that is, a surface bounded by right angles, and some do not have right angles, and are called rhomboids. The first kind of four-sided figure may have all sides equal, and is called a *tetragone* or square, or may not have all sides equal, but opposing sides equal to one another, and it is called an *orthogone* with one side longer, or a rectangle.

249. Again, it should be known that in any surface of right angles, two straight lines concluded by a right angle are said to contain the whole surface, because when the other two sides are equal to them, each to its opposite, it is necessary one of these lines measure the length and the other the width of the rectangular surface. Hence the whole surface emerges from moving the one along the other. So that if we imagine the one line converging in a right angle moving along the other, the surface is produced.

250. It should also be known that since in the rectangle the two lines containing the angle are unequal, if we take a line that is their proportional

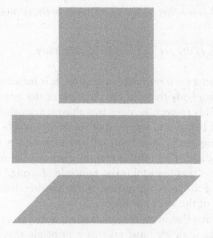

mean and lead it on itself, a square equal to the rectangle will result. Since it would take time to show this by geometrical demonstrations, it will suffice for the present to show it in numbers. Let the long side of the rectangle equal 9 and the short equal 4. Their proportional mean is 6. Because as 6 is to 9, so 4 is to 6. The square of this line will be equal to the rectangle. $4 \times 9 = 36$ and $6 \times 6 = 36$.

251. This then is what he means when he says, 'What is squaring?' and replies that it is the construction of an equilateral rectangle equal to a given oblong rectangle. Such a definition is the reason for the conclusion, that is, for what is concluded by the demonstration. For if someone were to define it as the discovery of a line which is a mean proportional between the two unequal sides of the given rectangle, he would give us the cause of the thing.

252. Note that the example adduced is similar to what he intends concerning the soul in one respect, namely insofar as the definition of soul might be demonstrated, but dissimilar in another, with respect to demonstrating it by a demonstration of the reasoned fact [*propter quid*].

253. Then when he says, 'We resume our inquiry . . .', he begins to demonstrate the definition of soul given above in the foregoing manner, namely, through its effect. And this is his demonstration:

That which is the first principle of living is the act and form of living bodies.

But the soul is the first principle of living in those things which live.

Therefore, it is the act and form of living body.

Clearly this is an *a posteriori* demonstration. It is because the soul is the form of the living body that it is the principle of the acts of life, and not conversely. In this respect, he does two things: first, shows that soul is the principle of living, and second that the first principle of living is the form of the living body, since it is that by which we live and sense. The first task is subdivided into three: first, he distinguishes modes of living; second, he shows that the soul is the principle of living;[1] third he shows how the parts of the souls are related to one another, following which it is the principle of the works of life.[2]

254. He says first that in order to pursue our intention of demonstrating the definition of soul, we must take as a principle that the animate is distinguished from the inanimate in living. The animate live, the inanimate do not. But since there are many ways of living, if one alone is in a thing it is called living and animate.

255. He sets down four modes of living, of which one is by intellect, the second by sense, the third by local motion and rest, the fourth by the motion of taking nourishment, and of growth and decay. He mentions only four modes of living whereas earlier he had set down five kinds of activity of soul, because here he means to distinguish modes of living according to the grades of living thing, which are distinguished according to these four. In some living things there is found only nutrition, growth and decay, namely in plants; in some, along with these is found sense without locomotion, as in imperfect animals, like oysters; in some there is further found locomotion, as in perfect animals, which can move themselves in progressive motion, like the cow and the horse; in some, along with all these, is found intellect, namely in man. The appetitive, which is the fifth beyond these four, does not make a difference in the grades of living thing, since wherever there is sense, there is appetite.

256. Then when he says, 'Hence we think of plants also . . .', he makes clear that soul is the principle of living in all the foregoing modes. He does three things in this regard: first, he shows how the soul is the principle of living in plants; second, in animals;[3] third, he summarizes what has

1. para. 256.
2. Lesson 4.
3. para. 259.

been said and indicates what remains to be said.[1] The first is subdivided into two, the first showing that soul is the principle of living in plants. He says that since it was said that if one of the four modes of living is in something, it is said to live, it follows that all plants live. For all of them have in themselves a power or principle by which they receive the motion of growth and decay.

257. That this principle is the soul and not nature is clear. For nature does not move to contrary places, but the movement of growth and decay is according to contrary places. For all plants grow, not just up and down but both at once. Therefore it is manifest that the principle of these motions is not nature, but soul. And plants not only live while they grow and decrease but they are nourished as long as they live, as long as they are able to take nourishment by which growth comes about.

258. Second, he shows that the principle of living just discussed is first and separable from the others.[2] And he says that the principle of growth and nutrition can be separated from the other principles of living, but they cannot be separated from it in mortal things. He says this because there are immortal things, such as the separated substances and celestial bodies if they are animate, found to be intellectual but not to take nourishment. That this principle is indeed separable from the others is manifest in plants, in which there is no other power of the soul except this. From which it is clear that that on account of which life is first found in mortal things is the principle of growth and nutrition which is called the plant or vegetative soul.

259. Then, when he says, 'The primary form of sense . . .' he shows how soul is the principle of living in animals. First he says that something is primarily called an animal because of sense, although some animals sense and move. We say that things are animals and not only live which though they do not change place, yet have sense. There are many anima' of this kind, which naturally remain in one place and yet have sense, su as the oyster, which is not moved by progressive movement.

260. Second, he shows that touch of all the senses is primary in anir He proves it from this that just as the vegetative can be separated touch and all the senses, so touch can be separated from the other For there are many animals which have only the sense of touch, imperfect animals, but all animals have the sense of touch. We part of the soul the vegetative principle in which plants too p?

1. para. 261.
2. para. 256.

Therefore, three levels of living thing appear against this background. The first is plants, the second is the imperfect immobile animals which have the sense of touch, and there are the perfect animals which move with progressive movement and also have the other senses. Manifestly, on a fourth level are the things which have all these and intellect besides.

261. Finally, he shows what has been said and what remains to be said. Later it will have to be said why both of these occur, namely that the vegetative can be without sense, and that touch can be without the other senses. He will talk about that at the end of the book. Now it is sufficient to say that the soul is the principle of life in the aforementioned modes, and that these four have been distinguished, namely, the vegetative which is in plants and all living things; the sensitive, which is in all animals; and the intellective, which is in all men; and progressive movement, which is in all animals perfected by either sense or intellect.

18. *Platonism and Neoplatonism. Preface to Exposition of* On the Divine Names (1265–8)

Thomas is on record again and again as subscribing to Aristotle's dismissal of the Platonic doctrine of Ideas. None the less, he accepted Augustine's famous interpretation of the Ideas as the divine creative patterns, effectively identical with the Word of God. When Thomas confronted such Neoplatonic works as Dionysius's On the Divine Names *and the* Book of Causes, *that Augustinian influence not only tempered his criticism but, given his acceptance of the quasi-apostolic status of Dionysius, made him a docile and accepting reader.*

During the early part of this century, Thomas's fundamental Aristotelianism obscured for many the other sources of his philosophical thinking. When the tide turned, it did so massively. The work of L.M. Geiger and Cornelio Fabro drew attention to the pervasiveness of the notion of participation in Thomas. Sober studies turned up the fact that Dionysius was the most quoted author in the Summa theologiae. *Some took this to mark an unnoticed shift on Thomas's part from Aristotle to Plato. After all, Aristotle had dismissed participation as an empty metaphor. Others saw the thought of Thomas as eclectic, a hopeless pastiche of incompatible elements.*

Thomas was never a partisan Aristotelian. Indeed, our notion that there are kinds of philosophy, more or less autonomous and unrelated to one another, was foreign to his thinking. Aristotle might not have responded as positively to Plato as he could have, but he was a model of the thinker who sees all his predecessors as engaged more or less in the same enterprise. That is why all make contributions to the emerging understanding of reality.

It would be absurd to think that Thomas opted for Aristotle as against Plato, or vice versa. The prologue to his commentary on Dionysius's On the Divine Names *is a succinct charter for the assimilation of Platonism. The assimilation is guided by his conviction that he has learned many truths from Aristotle. He continues to reject the Ideas as an acceptable account of the species of natural things. But he insists that the Platonic Ideas are of inestimable help in theology and in understanding the divine names. The result is an Aristotelianism that goes beyond the historical Aristotle but is a principled assimilation of truths from whatever source, even those Aristotle had mistakenly failed to recognize.*

PROLOGUE TO THE COMMENTARY ON DIONYSIUS'S
ON THE DIVINE NAMES

In order to understand the books of the blessed Dionysius, consider that he artfully distinguished into four parts what is found in Sacred Scripture about God. For in a book which has not come down to us called the *Divine Hypotyposes*, that is, the *Divine Characters*, he treats what pertains to the unity of the divine essence and the distinction of persons. There is no sufficient similarity to this unity and distinction in creatures since this mystery surpasses the capacity of natural reason.

Where Scripture does says something of God that has a created likeness, a distinction has to be made. For in some this similitude is understood as something that derives from God to creatures, as all goods are from the First Good and all living things from the First Life, and so on with others. Dionysius treats such things in *On the Divine Names*, which we have in our hands.

In some things, however, the similitude is understood according to something carried over from creatures to God, as God is called a lion, a rock, the sun and the like. Dionysius treats such matters in a book that he called *On Symbolic Theology*.

Because every similarity of the creature to God is deficient, and we find that God exceeds anything that is in creatures, whatever we know of creatures is denied of God as it exists in creatures. So it is that after all that our intellect can conceive of God, having been led from creatures, what God is remains hidden and unknown. For not only is God not a stone or the sun, which are grasped by the senses, neither is he the kind of life or essence that can be conceived by our intellect, and thus he remains unknown to us. Concerning these denials whereby God remains unknown and hidden for us, he wrote another book which he called *On Mystical* – that is, hidden – *Theology*.

Note that the blessed Dionysius in all his books uses an obscure style, not because of ineptitude, but intentionally, in order that sacred and divine teachings might be kept from the derision of infidels.

Difficulties in these books arise from many sources. First, because he often uses the style and mode of speaking that the Platonists used, which is not customary nowadays. The Platonists, wanting to reduce all composite and material things to simple and abstract principles, posited separate species of things, saying that there is a man outside matter, and similarly a horse, and so on with the other natural species. Therefore, they said that this singular sensible man is not what man is, but he is called man by participation in that separate man. Hence there is found in this sensible man something that does not pertain to the species of humanity, such as individual matter and the like. But in the separate man there is only what pertains to the species of humanity. So they called the separate man, 'man himself' or 'man as such', insofar as it has nothing that is not of humanity, and 'chiefly man', insofar as humanity is derived to sensible men from the separate man by way of participation. Thus it can also be said that the separate man is above men and is the humanity of all sensible men insofar as human nature belongs purely to the separate man, and is derived from him to sensible men.

The Platonists did not restrict this kind of abstraction to the ultimate species of natural things but applied it as well to the most common, such as good, one and being. For they held that there is a first one that is the very essence of goodness and of unity and of existence, and we call him God, and all other things are called good or one or being by derivation from this first. That is why they named the first good itself or good as such or principal good or supergood or even the goodness of all goods or goodness, essence and substance in the same way that they had spoken of the separate man.

This argument of the Platonists is not in harmony with either the faith or truth with respect to what it says of separate natural species, but it is most true and consonant with the Christian faith with respect to what it says of the first principle of things.

Dionysius, accordingly, sometimes names God good itself or supergood or principal good or the goodness of every good. Similarly, he names him superlife, supersubstance and the thearchic deity, that is, the principal deity, because even some creatures receive the name 'deity' by way of a certain participation.

The second difficulty arises from what he says, because often he uses effective arguments for making a point, by suggesting them with a few words or even only one.

The third source of difficulty is that he often uses many words which may seem superfluous, though to one diligently considering them they are found to contain a great profundity of thought.

PART FOUR
PARIS (1269–72)

When Thomas returned to Paris for an unusual second term as regent master of theology at the Dominican convent on the Rue St Jacques, he was coming into a maelstrom. During his absence in Italy, the academic scene had changed entirely. Before, it was the animosity between the secular masters and the mendicants that had to be contended with. Now Thomas himself and his teachings were being looked at askance. And numbered among his foes were Franciscans.

The bone of contention was Aristotle. The young masters of the Faculty of Arts embraced Aristotle with an enthusiasm that led to heterodoxy. Theologians began to have second thoughts about the growing influence of the Philosopher. After all, Aristotle had taught a number of things that were in real or apparent conflict with revealed truth. Since contradictories cannot be simultaneously true, either Aristotle was wrong or Christianity was. There would of course be little doubt where a Christian's allegiance lay – or so it seemed. But the young masters of arts who came to be called Latin Averroists sought to adopt a mind-boggling *via media*. They appeared to want to accept as philosophical truth what was in conflict with what they as Christians believed.

Aristotle had taught that the world is eternal. Genesis speaks of the beginning of the world's existence. The Latin Averroists seemed to want to assent to both claims. They were called Averroists because they accepted as good money the Commentator's reading of Aristotle. Does every person have an intellect or is there but one intellect existing apart that thinks through each of us? Averroes adopted the latter view. But it was the immaterial activity of the agent intellect that grounded Aristotle's proof of the soul's immortality. On Averroes' reading, personal immortality was not only unproved, but incoherent.

The Aristotelian tenet that each substance has but one constitutive form making it to be and to be what it is was thought to run afoul of the Christian belief that for three days the dead body of Christ awaited resurrection. What made it one body? What made it Christ's? Perhaps we need a substantial form making the body to be the body, before the advent of soul.

These and other issues, involving as they did the religious and cultural underpinnings of the university, were far more than academic questions. Shortly after Thomas's return there was the condemnation of 1270, which expressed the concern about the inroads of pagan philosophy on the understanding of Christian doctrine. An animus against Aristotle, and philosophy itself, was growing. Thomas as we have seen, and as his contemporaries knew, had found little to balk at in the doctrine of Aristotle. His attitude was rather one of grateful amazement at the reach of the human intellect even when unaided by the ambience of grace and revelation. His position was complicated by the fact that he was every bit as appalled by the Latin Averroists as any other theologian. Waffling on the principle of contradiction seemed an odd way for alleged followers of Aristotle to behave. Thomas had to steer a middle course between the Latin Averroists on the one hand and the understandably upset theologians on the other.

He began with two polemical works, On the Eternity of the World and On the Uniqueness of Intellect. The latter is a thorough analysis and rejection of the Averroistic reading of Aristotle's On the Soul. Correctly read, Thomas argued, Aristotle's doctrine on soul re-enforced the Christian belief in immortality. As to the eternity of the world, Thomas attacked those who thought this was an incoherent notion. He argues that it is not. The believer must hold Aristotle mistaken in claiming the world is eternal, but he does so by appeal to Revelation. God could have created an eternal world, however, so Aristotle's position was not incoherent nor was there any philosophical proof that it was false.

Furthermore, the commentary on Aristotle's On the Soul which had occupied Thomas in Rome, became the first in a series of twelve commentaries, close and careful readings clearly meant to show that, correctly understood, Aristotle was one of the greatest assets of the human mind and consequently an invaluable support of Christianity. This did not mean that whatever Aristotle might have meant, we none the less can use his words, according them an irenic sense. Thomas was a serious man. It was the truth he found in Aristotle that won his allegiance in the first place. That allegiance strengthened as he subjected the text to the extended analysis that makes his commentaries a major factor in the history of Aristotelianism.

Everything I have mentioned thus far was on the margin of Thomas's main task as regent master. The polemical writings and the Aristotelian commentaries did not emerge from his teaching. He continued his work on the *Summa theologiae*, he added to the fund of his *Disputed Questions*. But the very manner in which he did theology required the defence of Aristotle contained in polemical writings and effectively in the commentaries. In his remarkable, impressionistic book on Thomas Aquinas, G. K. Chesterton grasped the stakes involved in Thomas's defence of Aristotle. Western civilization had reached a crossroads where obscurantism attracted some and an oddly dissociated conception of the truth of faith attracted others. Thomas was the champion of the compatibility of faith and reason and of their mutual re-enforcing, not as a slogan but as a policy pursued and illustrated in thousands of pages. His victory was not immediate – there was another condemnation in 1277 – nor was it complete. But it has stood as the fullest and most satisfying synthesis of faith and reason produced in the Christian era.

19. *The Range of Natural Philosophy.*
Expositions of Physics, 1, 1, *Preface to*
On the Heavens, *Preface to* On Sense
and the Sensed Object (1269)

The goal of philosophy is such knowledge as men can attain of the divine,
but there is a sense in which God and other separated substances are as
far from the connatural object of our mind as can be. Philosophy begins
with the study of the things known to us through sense experience. Only
on the basis of a science of nature are we in a position to see physical
objects as effects of a cause which is utterly different from them.

In Chapter 2 we read a youthful work of Thomas in which he summar-
ized the main points of Aristotle's teaching about physical objects. How-
ever impressive, and useful, that opusculum might be, it does not
adequately convey how these doctrines are forced upon the inquiring
mind. But it is not typical of Thomas's invocation of the Aristotelian
tenet that the things that come to be as the result of a change are composites
of matter and form. When late in his life he got around to commenting
on the Physics *and other natural writings of Aristotle, Thomas was able*
to speak at length of the trajectory of our knowledge of the natural world.

The fundamental Aristotelian text is Book 1 of the Physics. *A close*
reading of the text shows the progression within the analysis of change
– from incidental change to substantial change – as well as the role that
art, particularly medicine, plays in Aristotle's analysis of the natural
world.

A fundamental methodological insight of Aristotle's is that our know-
ledge progresses from confusion to distinction, from generalities to specific
descriptions. This methodological truth is seen to be the basis for relating
the many natural writings of Aristotle. At the outset of his commentary
on On the Heavens, *Thomas sketches the trajectory of natural philosophy*
and in a prologue to On Sense and the Sensed Object, *he completes the*
map with the inclusion of the life world.

COMMENTARY ON THE *PHYSICS* I.1

When the objects of an inquiry, in any department, have principles, causes, or elements, it is through acquaintance with these that knowledge, that is to say scientific knowledge, is attained. For we do not think that we know a thing until we are acquainted with its primary causes or first principles, and have carried our analysis as far as its simplest elements. Plainly therefore in the science of nature, as in other branches of study, our first task will be to try to determine what relates to its principles.

The natural way of doing this is to start from things which are more knowable and obvious to us and proceed towards those which are clearer and more knowable by nature; for the same things are not 'knowable relatively to us' and 'knowable' without qualification. So in the present inquiry we must follow this method and advance from that which is more obscure by nature, but clearer to us, towards what is more clear and more knowable by nature.

Now what is to us plain and obvious at first is rather confused masses, the elements and principles of which become known to us later by analysis. Thus we must advance from generalities to particulars; for it is a whole that is best known to sense perception, and a generality is a kind of whole, comprehending many things within it, like parts. Much the same thing happens in the relation of the name to the formula. A name, for example 'round', means vaguely a sort of whole; its definition analyses this into its particular senses. Similarly a child begins by calling all men father and all women mother, but later on distinguishes each of them.   Aristotle, *Physics* I.1

1. We intend to comment on the *Physics*, which is the first book of natural science. That is why it was necessary as it begins to assign what the matter and subject of natural science might be. It should be known that since all knowledge is in the intellect, something becomes actually intelligible insofar as it is in some way abstracted from matter. Insofar as things are differently related to matter they pertain to different sciences. And since every science is acquired by means of demonstration, and the middle term of the demonstration is a definition, it is necessary that sciences be distinguished by different modes of definition.

2. It should be known, therefore, that there are some things whose existence depends upon matter nor can they be defined without matter. There are other things which, although they cannot exist except in sensible matter, sensible matter does not enter into their definitions. These two kinds of thing differ as curve and snub do. For the snub is in sensible

matter, and it is necessary to put sensible matter into its definition, for it
is a curved nose; all natural things are like that, such as man and stone.
The curve, however, although it can only exist in sensible matter, sensible
matter is not put into its definition; all mathematicals are like this, such
as numbers, magnitudes, figures. There are some things which depend
on matter neither in order to exist nor to be defined, either because they
never exist in matter, like God and the other separated substances, or
because they are not always in matter, such as substance, potency and
act, and being itself.

3. Metaphysics is concerned with this last sort; mathematics is concerned
with things which, while they depend on matter in order to exist, do not
have matter in their definitions. Natural science, or physics, studies things
which depend on matter not only in order to exist, but also with respect
to their definitions. Because everything that has matter is mobile, mobile
being is the subject of natural philosophy. Natural science is concerned
with natural things and nature is a principle of motion and rest in that
in which it is; therefore, natural science is concerned with things which
have in them a principle of motion.

4. First and foremost we must study what is common, lest it become
necessary to repeat it again and again in treating the parts of it. Thus it
was necessary to put first in natural science a book in which would be
studied what belongs to mobile being in general, just as first philosophy
in which is treated what is common to being as being comes before all
other sciences. This book of the *Physics* is also called *Hearing of the
Natural*, because it was taught to listeners by way of teaching. It subject
is mobile being as such. I do not say mobile body, because that every
mobile thing is a body is proved in this work, and no science proves its
own subject. Therefore at the outset of *On the Heavens*, which follows
on this, he begins to make body known. There follow on this book other
works of natural science in which the species of mobile beings are treated,
as in *On the Heavens*, of being mobile according to local motion, which
is the first species of motion; in *On Generation*, of motion towards form
and of the first mobiles, that is, the elements, with respect to their changes
in general; their specific changes are treated in the *Meteorology*; mixed
inanimate mobile things are treated in *Of Minerals*; and animate things
in *On the Soul* and the books that follow on it.

5. The Philosopher begins with a preface in which he shows the order
of proceeding in natural science. He does two things: first, he shows that
we must begin with a consideration of principles; second, that among
principles, we must begin with the most universal, 'The natural way of

doing this . . .' He gives the following argument on behalf of the first point. In all sciences where there are principles and causes and elements, understanding and knowledge proceed from knowledge of the principles, causes and elements. But the science of nature has principles, elements and causes. Therefore, in it we must begin with a determination of the principles. When he says 'understanding' this refers to definitions, and 'knowledge' refers to demonstration. For both demonstrations and definitions are taken from causes since a complete definition is a demonstration in everything but arrangement, as is said in the *Posterior Analytics*. He does not mean the same thing by principles, causes and elements, for the element is that from which a thing is first composed and which remains within it, as is said in *Metaphysics* 5, as letters are elements of speech, but not syllables. Causes are that on which things depend to be or to become, hence even what is outside a thing or what is in it but is not an element can be called causes. Principle implies the order of some process, so something can be a principle which is not a cause; as that from which motion begins is a principle though not a cause, and the point is the principle of the line but not its cause. Thus by principles he seems to mean moving and agent causes, in which especially the order of any process in found; by causes he seems to mean formal and final causes, on which a thing depends especially with respect to being and becoming; by elements, properly the first material causes. He uses these names disjunctively, not conjunctively, in order to indicate that not every science demonstrates through all the causes. For mathematics demonstrates through formal cause alone, metaphysics chiefly by formal and final cause, but also the agent cause; but natural science demonstrates through all the causes.

He proves the first proposition of his argument from common opinion, just as in the *Posterior Analytics*. Because someone thinks himself to know something, when he knows all its causes from first to last. Nor do we need to take causes and elements and principles differently than above, as the Commentator wishes, but in the same way. He says even to the elements because that which is ultimate in knowledge is matter. Matter is for the sake of form, and form is from the agent for the sake of an end, if it is not itself the end; for example, we say that the saw has teeth in order to cut, and must be iron in order to be apt for cutting.

6. When he says, 'The natural way . . .' he shows that among principles we must first determine the most universal. And first he shows this by an argument, secondly through a sign, 'Now what is plain and obvious . . .' Here is the argument. It is natural to us to proceed in knowing from

things which are more known to us to those which are more known in nature. But the things which are more known to us are confused, as universals are. Therefore, we must proceed from universals to singulars.

7. As clarification of the first proposition, he suggests that what is more known to us and what is more known according to nature are not the same. Because the natural mode or order of learning is to go from what we know to what we do not, we must go from what is more known to us to what is naturally more known, which has more being. A thing is knowable insofar as it is being. A thing is more of a being insofar as it is more actual. Hence the most actual things are what are more known in their natures. But for us the opposite is true, insofar as we proceed in understanding from potentiality to act, and the beginning of our knowledge is from sensible things, which are material, and only potentially intelligible. It is such things that are more known to us than separated substances, which are more known according to nature, as is evident in *Metaphysics* 2. He does not say more known in nature, as if nature knew them, but because they are more known in themselves and according to their own nature. He says more known rather than more certain, because in the sciences it is not just any kind of knowledge that is sought, but the certitude of knowledge.

To understand the second proposition, we must know that confused means here that which contains things in itself potentially and indistinctly. And because to know something indistinctly is midway between pure potentiality and perfect act, since our intellect proceeds from potency to act, it is the confused rather than the distinct that first occurs to it, and science is actually complete when it arrives by analysis at distinct knowledge of principles and elements. This is the reason why the confused rather than the distinct is first known by us. That universals are confused is obvious, because universals contain in themselves their species potentially, and he who knows something in general, knows it indistinctly; and his knowledge will be distinct when each of the things potentially contained in the universal is actually known. For he who knows animal, knows rational only potentially. We first know something potentially and then actually. Therefore, we proceed according to this order of learning from potency to act, and we know animal before we know man.

8. This seems to be contrary to what the Philosopher says in *Posterior Analytics* 1, namely that singulars are more known to us, but universals are more known simply speaking or according to nature. But it should be understood that there he takes singulars to be individual sensible things, which are more known to us because sense knowledge, which is

of singulars, in us precedes intellectual knowledge, which is of universals. Because intellectual knowledge is more perfect, since universals are actually intelligible and singulars, when they are material, are not, simply and according to their nature universals are more known. Here, however, he means by singulars not individuals, but species which are more known in nature, as being more perfect and yielding more distinct knowledge; genera are more known to us as yielding potential and confused knowledge. The Commentator, it should be known, explains it otherwise.

He comments that when he says, 'The natural way . . .', the Philosopher wants to show the mode of demonstration in this science, because he demonstrates through effects and what is posterior in nature, and thus what he says is to be understood of the process of demonstrating and not of determining. And when he says, 'Now what is plain to us . . .' he intends to show, according to the Commentator, what are more known for us and less known in nature, namely, things composed of simples, understanding composed as confused. Finally he concludes that we should proceed from the more to the less universal as a kind of corollary.

His explanation is clearly wrong because it does not bring it all together into one intention. The Philosopher has no intention here of showing the mode of demonstration of this science, since he does this in the second book following the order of determining. What is more, confused ought not to be explained as composite, but as indistinct. Nor would he be able to deduce anything from universals, since genera are not composed of their species.

9. When he says, 'For it is a whole that is best known . . .' he manifests what he has proposed by three signs, the first of which is taken from the sensible integral whole. And he says that the sensible whole is more known to sense; therefore the intelligible whole is more known to intellect. The universal is a kind of intelligible whole which comprises many parts, namely, its inferiors. Therefore the universal is more known to intellect so far as we are concerned. This proof seems ineffective, because he uses whole and part and comprehension equivocally. It should be said that the integral and universal wholes agree in this that both are confused and indistinct. For just as one who apprehends a genus does not apprehend its species distinctly but only potentially, so one who sees a house does not yet distinguish its parts. Since it is by reason of confusion that the whole is known by us before its parts, the same reason applies to both wholes. To be composed is not common to both wholes, so it is clear that he significantly says confused and not composed.

10. When he says, 'Much the same thing . . .' he gives another sign

from the intelligible integral whole. The defined is to the parts of the definition somewhat as an integral whole, insofar as the defining parts are actually in the defined. But one who hears a name, say, man or circle, does not immediately distinguish the defining principles, so the name is a kind or whole and indistinct, but the definition divides into singulars, that is, states distinctly the defining principles. But this seems contrary to what he said above, for the defining principles seem to be more universal, which he said to be more known to us. Again, if the defined were more known to us than the defining principles, the defined would not be made known to us by the definition. It should be said that the defining principles in themselves are more known to us than the defined, but the defined is known to us before we know that these are its defining principles. As we know animal and rational before man, but man is first known to us confusedly, then that animal and rational are his defining principles.

11. Then when he says, 'Similarly a child . . .' he gives a third sign taken from the more universal sensible. For just as the more universal intelligible is first known by us with respect to intellect, as for example animal prior to man, so the more common sensible is first known to us according to sensing, for example this animal before this man. And I say prior to sense both according to place and time. According to place, because when someone is seen at a distance, we first perceive him to be a body and then to be an animal, and that we perceive before perceiving that he is a man, and then that he is this man who is Plato, who is his father. And so he says that a child first calls all men fathers and all women mothers, but later knows each one determinately. This clearly shows that we first know something confusedly rather than distinctly.

PREFACE TO THE COMMENTARY ON *ON THE HEAVENS*

1. As the Philosopher says in *Physics* 1.1, 'When the objects of an inquiry, in any department, have principles, causes or elements, it is through acquaintance with these that knowledge, that is to say, scientific knowledge, is attained.' In these words the Philosopher clearly shows that there is an ordered process in sciences, insofar as we proceed from first causes and principles to proximate causes, which are the elements making up the essence of a thing. This is reasonable, for the procedure in science is a work of reason, whose proper work is ordering. Hence, in every work of reason an order can be seen, insofar as it proceeds from one thing to

the next. This is clear both in practical reason, whose concern is the things that we do, and in speculative reason, which considers things made by another.

2. In the consideration of practical reason one finds a process from the prior to the posterior on the basis of a fourfold order: (1) according to the order of apprehension, insofar as the artisan first grasps the form of the house absolutely, and then produces it in matter; (2) according to the order of intention, insofar as the artisan intends to complete the whole house, and for the sake of that does whatever he does as to the parts of the house; (3) according to the order of composition, insofar as he first dresses stones and afterwards lays them to make a wall; (4) according to the order of maintenance of the work, insofar as the artisan first lays the foundation, on which the other parts of the house are sustained.

Similarly, there is found a fourfold order in the considerations of speculative reason. (1) Insofar as it proceeds from the common to the less common. This answers analogously to the first order, which we called *of apprehension*: for universals are considered according to absolute form, particulars are considered insofar as that form is applied to matter, as the Philosopher says: 'There is a difference, then, between "this universe" and simply "universe"; the second is form and shape, the first form in combination with matter; and any shape or form has, or may have, more than one particular instance.' (2) The second order is that found when we proceed from whole to parts, and this answers analogously to the order we called *of intention*, insofar as the whole is considered prior to the parts, not just any, but the material parts and those of the individual. For example, the semicircle, into whose definition circle is put (the semicircle is half a circle), and the acute angle, into whose definition the right angle is put (the acute angle is less than the right angle). It is incidental to circle and to right angle that they be divided like this, hence these are not parts of the species [of the definitions of circle and right angle]. Parts of the species are prior in consideration to the whole, and are put into the definition of the whole, as flesh and bones are put in the definition of man, as is said in *Metaphysics* 7.10. (3) The third order is seen when we proceed from simples to composites, insofar as the composites are known by means of the simples, as by their principles. This order is compared to the one that was called *of composition*. (4) The fourth order arises because it is necessary to consider the principal parts first, such as heart before arteries and blood. And this is analogous to the practical order, insofar as the foundation must first be laid.

3. This fourfold order is also considered in the procedure of natural

science. For first are determined what is common to nature, in the books of the *Physics* in which the mobile is treated insofar as it is mobile. It remains for the subsequent books of natural science to apply these common features to their proper subjects. The subject of motion is magnitude and body, since nothing is moved unless it is quantified. In bodies three other orders are to be noticed: one, insofar as the whole corporeal universe is prior in consideration to its parts; another, insofar as simple bodies are considered before mixed bodies; a third, insofar as among simple bodies it is necessary first to consider the first, that is, the heavenly body, by which all the others are stabilized. These three are considered in this book, which some Greeks called *On the Heaven*. Things pertaining to the whole universe are treated here, as is clear from the first book; things pertaining to the celestial bodies, as is clear from the second book; things pertaining to the other simple bodies, as is clear from the third and fourth books. This book is reasonably put first after the *Physics*, therefore. On this account immediately at the beginning of the book he treats of body, to which must be applied all the things which were said of motion in the *Physics*.

4. Because this book treats of different things, there was a doubt among the ancient commentators of Aristotle about its subject. Alexander thought that the subject principally treated in this book was the universe itself. Hence, since heaven is said in three ways, sometimes meaning the ultimate sphere, sometimes the whole body which moves in a circle, sometimes the universe itself, he asserts that this book has the title *Of the Heaven*, as if it is 'Of the Universe' or 'Of the World'. In this assertion he assumes that the Philosopher discusses things pertaining to the whole universe in this book, such as that it is finite, that it is only one, and other similar things.

On the contrary, it seemed to others that the subject principally treated in this book is the celestial body that moves in a circle, and for this reason it is titled *On the Heaven*. Other bodies are discussed in the book either by way of consequence, insofar as they are contained by the heaven and receive its influence, as Iamblichus said, or incidentally, insofar as knowledge of the other bodies is assumed to manifest what is said of the heaven, as Syrianus said.

But this seems improbable because after the Philosopher treats of the heaven in the second book, in the third and fourth he adds the consideration of all simple bodies, as if principally interested in them. It is not the Philosopher's practice to assign the principal part of a science to things taken up incidentally.

Therefore it seemed to others, as Simplicius said, that the intention of the Philosopher in this book is to study simple bodies, insofar as they share in the common meaning of simple body. It is because the heaven is the chief among simple bodies, on which others depend, that the whole book is called *On the Heaven*. And, as he says, it precludes that things which pertain to the whole universe might be determined in this book, because such conditions belong to the universe insofar as they belong to heavenly body, namely, to be finite, sempiternal and the like. If the chief intention of the Philosopher were to determine what the universe or world is, Aristotle would have had to extend the consideration to all the parts of the world, down to plants and animals, like Plato in the *Timaeus*.

But for the same reason we can argue against Simplicius because if in this book he intended to treat principally simple bodies, everything pertaining to simple bodies would have to be treated in it, but what it actually treats are the things which pertain to their lightness or heaviness; the others are discussed in *On Generation*.

5. Therefore the opinion of Alexander seems more reasonable: the subject of this book is the universe itself, which is called 'heaven' or 'world'; and he treats simple bodies in this book insofar as they are parts of the universe. The corporeal universe is constituted of its parts according to the order of position. Therefore in this book he treats only those parts of the universe which first and as such have position in the universe, namely, simple bodies. That is why he does not discuss the four elements in this book insofar as they are warm or cold, or anything like that, but only with reference to heaviness and lightness, by which their place in the universe is determined. The place of other parts of the universe, such as rocks, plants and animals, is not determined according to themselves, but according to simple bodies, and that is why they are not discussed in this book. This is consonant with what it is customary among the Latins to say, that this book treats of *body mobile as to position*, or *according to place*, which indeed is a motion common to all the parts of the universe.

PREFACE TO THE COMMENTARY ON *ON SENSE AND THE SENSED OBJECT*

Having now considered the soul, by itself, and its several faculties, we must next make a survey of animals and all living things, in order to ascertain what functions are peculiar, and what functions are common, to them. What has already been determined respecting the soul must be assumed throughout. The remaining parts of our subject must now be dealt with, and we may begin with those that come first.

The most important attributes of animals, whether common to all or peculiar to some, are, manifestly, attributes of soul and body in conjunction, for example sensation, memory, passion, appetite and desire in general, and, in addition, pleasure and pain. For these may, in fact, be said to belong to all animals. But there are, besides these, certain other attributes, of which some are common to living things, while others are peculiar to certain species of animals. The most important of these may be summed up in four pairs, *viz.* waking and sleeping, youth and old age, inhalation and exhalation, life and death. We must examine these, determining their respective natures, and the causes of their occurrence.

But it behoves the natural scientist to obtain also a clear view of the first principles of health and disease, inasmuch as neither health nor disease can exist in lifeless things. Indeed, we may say of most physical inquirers, and of those physicians who study their art more philosophically, that while the former complete their works with a disquisition on medicine, the latter start from a consideration of nature.

That all the attributes above enumerated belong to soul and body in conjunction is obvious; for they all either imply sensation as a concomitant, or have it as their medium. Some are either affections or states of sensation, others, means of defending and safe-guarding it, while others, again, involve its destruction or privation. Now it is clear, alike by reasoning and without reasoning, that sensation is generated in the soul through the medium of the body.

Aristotle, *On Sense and the Sensed Object*

1. As the Philosopher says in *On the Soul* 3, as things are separable from matter so do they relate to intellect. For a thing is intelligible to the degree that it is separable from matter. Hence things which are of their nature separate from matter are in themselves actually intelligible; but things which are abstracted by us from their material conditions become actually intelligible by the light of our agent intellect. And, because the habits of a power are specifically distinguished according to the differences in the object of the power, the habits of the sciences, by which intellect is perfected, are also distinguished according to different separation from matter. That is why the Philosopher in *Metaphysics* 6 distinguishes the kinds of science according to the different mode of separation from matter. For things which are separate from matter as they exist and as they are defined pertain to metaphysics; things which are separate in

definition but not as they exist pertain to mathematics; things which include sensible matter in their definitions pertain to natural science.

2. Just as the different kinds of science are distinguished insofar as things are differently separable from matter, so in each of the sciences, and especially in natural science, the parts of the science are distinguished according to the different mode of separation and concretion. Because universals are more separated from matter, in natural science we advance from the more to the less universal, as the Philosopher teaches at the outset of the *Physics*. Hence he begins natural science with a treatment of what is most common to all natural things, namely motion and the principle of motion. And finally he advances by way of concretion or application of the common principles to certain definite mobile things, some of which are living bodies, with which he proceeds in a similar manner, dividing the consideration into three parts. First, he considers the soul in itself, as it were by a kind of abstraction. Second, he considers what pertains to the soul according to a kind of concretion or application to body, but in general. Third, he introduces an inquiry which applies all these to the single species of animals and plants, determining what is proper to each species. The first inquiry is found in *On the Soul*. The third in the books *On Animals* and *On Plants*. The middle inquiry is contained in books which he wrote about things which pertain commonly, either to all animals or to many kinds of them, or even to all living things, which is the intention of this work.

3. It should be considered that in *On the Soul* 2 four grades of living things were described, the first of which were those which have only the nutritive part of the soul by which they live, such as plants. But some are such that they have also sense but without progressive motion, such as the imperfect animals, like oysters. Some also have progressive local motion, such as the perfect animals, for example the horse and cow. Some have intellect over and above all these, such as men. The appetitive, although it is a fifth kind of power of the soul, does not constitute a fifth grade of living things, because it always follows sense.

4. Of these, intellect is not the act of any part of the body, as is proved in *On the Soul* 3, hence it cannot be considered by way of concretion or application to body or to any bodily organ. Its greatest concretion is in the soul, and its highest abstraction in the separated substances, so Aristotle did not write a book on intellect and the object of intellect after *On the Soul*. If he had written it, it would not have pertained to natural science but to metaphysics which considers separated substances. All the others are acts of some part of the body and therefore there can be a

special consideration of them by application to the body or to bodily organs beyond the consideration they received in *On the Soul*.

5. This mid-consideration should be divided into three parts, of which one contains the things which pertain to the living as living, and this in the book *On Death and Life*, in which he discusses inhaling and exhaling by which things are preserved in life, youth and age, by which the states of life are distinguished. So too in the book called *On Length and Brevity of Life* and in the book *On Health and Sickness*, which pertain to the disposition of life, and in the book *On Food and the Edible*, one we do not have in Latin. Others pertain to the mover, in two works, *The Cause of Movement in Animals* and *On the Progress of Animals*, in which he treats of the parts of animals adapted to movement. The third pertains to the sensitive part, in which what pertains to the acts of the interior and exterior senses can be considered. In this regard, the consideration of the sensitive is contained in this book which is called *On Sense and the Sensed Object*, that is, of the sensitive and the sensible, and the book contains the treatise *On Memory and Reminiscence*. And to the consideration of the sensitive also pertains what makes a difference in the sense in sensing, which is treated in the book *On Sleeping and Waking*.

6. Because one must pass from the more similar to the dissimilar, such seems reasonably to be the order of these books such that after *On the Soul*, in which the soul as such is treated, there immediately follows this book *On Sense and the Sensed Object*, because sensing pertains to soul more than to body, after which should be placed the book *On Sleep and Waking*, which implies the tightening and loosening of sense; then follow the books which pertain to the moving principle, which is closer to sense. In the last place are put the books which pertain to the common consideration of the living, because this largely concerns the disposition of the body.

7. This book, then, which is called *On Sense and the Sensed Object*, is divided into two parts: a preface and the treatise. With respect to the first, he does two things, first states his intention, showing what has to be treated, and second gives the reason why it is necessary to treat of them, 'The most important attributes.' First, he says that of soul itself it has already been determined in *On the Soul*, where he defined soul. Next it must be determined concerning each act and power of it, but I say this on its part. For since powers of the soul, other than intellect, are acts of some parts of the body, they can be considered in two ways. In one way, insofar as they pertain to soul, as its powers and faculties, in another way, on the part of the body. In *On the Soul*, the powers of the soul were

determined on the part of the soul itself, but now we must consider animals and all things having life: which he adds for the sake of determining concerning plants, which operations are proper to each single species of animal and plant, and which are common, as belonging to all living things or to all animals or to many kinds of them, what has been said of soul underlies or is presupposed, that is, we use them in the following as suppositions already made manifest. Of the rest we say, and first the first, that is, first the common and then the proper. For this is the fitting order of natural science, as determined at the outset of the *Physics*.

8. Then when he says, 'The most important attributes . . .' he shows the need for the present consideration, for if both the common and proper activities of animals and plants were proper to the soul itself, the consideration in *On the Soul* would suffice. But because they are common to soul and body there must be after the consideration of soul a consideration of such things in order to know what kind of dispositions are required in bodies for operations and passions of this kind. Therefore the Philosopher here shows all the things common to soul and body, concerning which he does three things. First, he states his intention; second, he enumerates the things he intends to discuss – 'for example sensation, memory, passion . . .' Third, he proves what he has proposed: 'That all the attributes above enumerated . . .' First, then he says that among the things that pertain to animals and plants, those especially and chiefly are common to all animals or to many or are proper to particular species, and even at first glance seem to be common to soul and body. So a consideration beyond that of soul itself is required.

9. Then when he says, 'for example sensation, memory, passion, etc.' he enumerates what falls to his intention. First, he states things pertaining to the sensitive part, namely sense and memory, making no mention of others, such as imagination and the estimative power, because they are not distinguished from sense on the basis of the thing known: they are of things present or quasi-present, but memory is distinct because it is of the past as past.

10. He sets down what pertains to the moving principle. Sensitive appetite is the proximate principle of motion in animals, and is divided into two powers, namely the irascible and concupiscible, as is said in *On the Soul* 3. So he mentions wrath as pertaining to the irascible power and desire as pertaining to the concupiscible, from which two passions as from the most manifest the two powers mentioned are named. For the concupiscible is denominated from desire, the irascible from wrath. But because there are other passions pertaining to the appetitive power, he

adds, 'and desire in general', as it comprises whatever pertains to the appetitive power.

11. Joy or sadness follow on all the passions of the soul, whether of the irascible or concupiscible, as is said in *Ethics* 2, 'in addition, pleasure and pain', as encompassing passions. And he adds that what has been enumerated are found in nearly all kinds of animals, 'nearly' because many of these are found in both perfect and imperfect animals, namely sense, desire, appetite, joy and sorrow. Imperfect animals have only the sense of touch but they have imagination, desire, joy and sorrow, although indeterminately, and they are indeterminately moved, as is said in *On the Soul* 2. Memory and anger are wholly absent from them, but exist only in perfect animals. The reason is that not everything of a lower kind, but only the highest and most perfect, attains to a participation in a likeness of that which is proper to a higher kind. Sense differs from intellect and reason, because the latter are of universals, which are everywhere and always, but sense is of singulars, which are here and now. In its proper nature, therefore, sense is cognoscent only of present things.

12. If there is a power of the sensitive part which extends to other than present things, this is due to a proportional participation in reason or intellect. Thus memory, which is cognoscent of past things, is found only in perfect animals, as something supreme in sense cognition. Similarly sense appetite which properly follows on sense has as its object what is pleasurable to sense, which pertains to the concupiscible power common to animals. But that an animal tends to something arduous, such as a fight or the like, has a similarity to rational appetite which seeks something for the sake of an end which is not pleasant to the senses. Therefore anger, which is a desire for revenge, pertains only to perfect animals because of their propinquity to the genus of rational things.

13. Next he states things which pertain somewhat to the notion of life. And he says that along with the foregoing other things are found in animals, some of which are common to whatever shares life, not only animals, but also plants. Some pertain only to some kinds of animal and the chief of these are listed in a fourfold conjunction: sleep and waking, which are found in all animals but not in plants; youth and old age, which are found in both animals and plants; inhalation and exhalation, which are found in some kinds of animal, namely those with lungs; life and death, which are found in all living things in this lower world. He says that we must ask of each of these what it is and what its cause is. And because he called them the most important, he adds that there are some of less importance, like health and disease, which are not found in

individuals of all these kinds in which they might be. This is not true of the most important, which are natural to all living things, both animals and plants.

14. He says that it is also a task of natural philosophy to discover the first and universal principles of health and disease; it is for the physician to consider their particular principles; he is the artisan who causes health and like any art his must concern itself with the singulars that come under this project, since operations bear on singulars. That this is a task of natural philosophy he proves when he says, 'But it behoves the natural scientist . . .' And this in two ways.

15. First by argument. Health can only be found in living things, from which it is clear that the living body is the proper subject of health and disease. But the principles of a subject are the principles of its proper accident. Hence, since it pertains to natural philosophy to consider the living body and its principles, it must also consider the principles of health and disease.

16. Second, he proves it by a sign or example, which he concludes from the argument just given. For many natural philosophers complete their inquiry with things that belong to medicine, and many physicians, who pursue the art of medicine philosophically, using not only experience but seeking causes, begin the medical inquiry where natural philosophy leaves off. From which it is clear that the study of health and disease is common to philosopher and physician. But since art is not the chief cause of health, but aids nature and assists it, it is necessary that the physician take from natural philosophy the more important principles of his science, as the navigator borrows from the astronomer. This is why physicians practising medicine well begin from natural science. But if there are artefacts which come about only by art, like the house and ship, these in no way belong to natural philosophy any more than things which come about only by nature pertain to the consideration of art, except insofar as art uses natural things.

17. When he says, 'That all the attributes . . .' he proves his thesis, namely that all the foregoing are common to soul and body, and fashions this argument: All the foregoing pertain to sense; but sensing is common to soul and body, for it belongs to soul through the body; therefore all the foregoing are common to soul and body. He manifests the first premiss by induction from what has been said, for some come about with sensation, namely what pertains to sense cognition, like sense, imagination and memory; some come about through the sensation, such as those that pertain to the appetitive power which are moved by the apprehension of

the senses. Of the others, which more manifestly pertain to body, some are states of sensation, like sleep, which is a binding of the sensation, and wakefulness, which loosens it; some are relations of sensation, namely youth and old age, which arise from the fact that sensation is as it should be or is weak; some preserve and guard sensation, such as respiration, life and health; some are destructive of it, like death and infirmity.

The second premiss, namely that sensation is common to soul and body, is manifest, he says, with or without argument. The argument is obvious: because sense is affected by the sensible, as was shown in *On the Soul*, and sensibles are material and corporeal, it is necessary that that which is affected by the sensible be corporeal. It is manifest without argument by experience that a disturbance of the sense organs impedes the activity of sensation, and if they be destroyed, sense is completely taken away.

20. How Words Mean. Exposition
of On Interpretation, 1–5
(1270–71)

The triadic theory of signification taught by Aristotle has often been confused with later theories, notably that of Locke, and has come under a Wittgensteinian critique. If words signify meanings in the mind, questions arise as to how my concepts are like or unlike yours as well as how such concepts relate to things in the world. It has been said that the central problem Descartes bequeathed to philosophy was: How do we get out of our minds? If knowledge bears on mental events, if they are what we first and chiefly know, their relation to things outside the mind becomes problematic. On this view, modern philosophy can look like a suite of unsuccessful ontological proofs – not of the existence of God, but of the existence of something non-mental. It would be ironic indeed if Aristotle, and Thomas following him, were engaged in the problematic of modernism.

As a reading of the following selection will show, neither Aristotle nor Thomas holds that meaningful words arrest our attention at mental events. Rather, concepts or what Aristotle here calls 'passions of the soul' are pure means of knowing, not primary objects of knowledge. The triadic account of significant speech is the product of reflection on how we know. If we did not first know something other than knowing, there would be no knowing to know. The first and direct object of thinking is the nature of sensible reality. Reflection on knowing reveals the extraordinary character of human knowing.

One of the features of human knowing is that it knows sensible singulars in a universal way. Sensing bears on the singular as such, but the mark of intellectual knowledge is that it knows things universally, as to what they are, as to their essences or natures. The Problem of Universals is a logical problem that has a long history stemming from the Neoplatonist Porphyry's Isagoge *or Introduction to the Categories of Aristotle. Before discussing the five universals, genus, species, difference, property and accident, Porphyry mentions three questions which make up the classical problem of universals. Are they real or mere figments of the imagination? If real, are they material or immaterial? If immaterial, are they associated with material things or do they exist apart? Boethius, in commenting on Porphyry, began the long tradition of treating each of these questions.*

In the passage that follows, almost as an aside, Thomas gives his own solution to the problem of universals. For him, as we have seen in Chapter 3, universals like genus and species attach themselves in the manner of accidents to natures as known. They are second intentions. Indeed, the subject matter of logic, for Thomas, is precisely second intentions. The following discussion of significant speech, of noun and verb, conveys well Thomas's understanding of logic.

COMMENTARY ON ARISTOTLE'S *ON INTERPRETATION*

Preface

1. As the Philosopher says in *On the Soul* 3, there is a twofold operation of intellect, one which is called the understanding of indivisibles by which the intellect apprehends the essence itself of a thing, the other the operation of intellect composing and dividing. A third operation, namely, reasoning, is added because reason proceeds from what is known to inquire into the unknown. Of these operations, the first is ordered to the second, because there can be composition and division only of apprehended simple things. The second is ordered to the third, since it is necessary that from a known truth, to which the intellect assents, one goes on to gain certainty about some unknown things.

2. Since logic is called rational science it is necessary that its consideration turn on things which pertain to the three operations of reason. Aristotle treats of the things which pertain to the first operation of intellect, that is, of things which are conceived by simple understanding, in the *Categories*; of those which pertain to the second operation, namely the affirmative and negative speech, the Philosopher treats in the book *On Interpretation*. Of things which pertain to the third operation he treats in the *Prior Analytics* and those which follow on it, in which the simple syllogism is treated, and then of the different kinds of syllogism and argument by which reason proceeds from one thing to another. According to the forgoing order of the three operations, therefore, the *Categories* is ordered to *On Interpretation* which is ordered to *Prior Analytics* and the books that follow.

3. The book that we have in hand is called *Perihermeneias*, that is, *On Interpretation*. According to Boethius, an interpretation is a significant voiced sound which signifies of itself, whether it be complex or incomplex. Hence, conjunctions and prepositions and the like are not called interpretations because they do not of themselves signify anything. Similarly, voiced sounds signifying naturally and not with the intention or imagination of signifying something, such as the sounds of brute animals, cannot be called interpretations. He who interprets intends to expound something. Hence only nouns and verbs and sentences are called interpretations and they are treated in this book. But noun and verb seem to be rather the principles of interpretation than interpretations themselves. For he seems to interpret who expounds something as true or false, therefore only enunciative speech in which the true or false can be found is called an interpretation. Other speeches, such as the optative and imperative, are rather ordered to expressing desire than to interpreting what is in the mind. Therefore this book is entitled *On Interpretation* as one should say 'On Enunciative Speech', in which the true or false is found. The noun and verb are treated here only insofar as they are parts of speech, for it is proper to any science to treat the parts of its subject. It is evident then to which part of philosophy this book pertains, and why it is needed and how it relates to the other books of logic.

Lesson 1

First we must define the terms 'noun' and 'verb', then the terms 'denial' and 'affirmation', then 'proposition' and 'sentence'.

1. The Philosopher provides a preface to this work in which he singly expounds the things which are to be treated in the book. Because all sciences first set forth what pertain to principles and the parts of compound things are their principles, therefore he who would treat of the enunciation must set down its parts. Hence he says that one must first constitute, that is, define, what is a noun and what a verb. In Greek this reads, 'first ought to be posited', but this means the same thing, for because demonstrations presuppose definitions, from which they conclude, fittingly they are called positions. Therefore he sets down definitions only of the things of which he must treat, because from definitions other things are known.

2. Should anyone ask, given the fact that he spoke of simples in the

Categories, what need there is that noun and verb should be discussed again here, it ought to be answered that there is a threefold consideration of things simply said. One, insofar as they simply signify simple under-standings, and thus the consideration of them falls to the *Categories*; two, insofar as they are parts of the enunciation, and thus they are treated in this book under the formality of noun and verb, in whose definitions it is mentioned that they signify something with or without time, and the like, which pertains to the notion of speech insofar as they constitute the enunciation; third, they are considered insofar as the order of syllogism is constituted of them, and thus they are treated under the formality of terms in the *Prior Analytics*.

3. It can also be asked why he puts aside other parts of speech and treats only of noun and verb. The response to this is that because he intends to treat of the simple enunciation, it suffices that he treat only those parts of the enunciation which are needed to form a simple enunciation. For a simple enunciation can be made up of noun and verb alone but not of the other parts of speech without these; therefore, it was sufficient for him to treat these two. For it could be said that only nouns and verbs are principal parts of speech. Under nouns pronouns are included because, though they do not name the nature, none the less they determine the person, and they can be put in the place of nouns: under the verb, participle is included, which consignifies time, although it has things in common with the noun. The others are linkings of the parts of speech, signifying the relation of one to another rather than parts of speech: just as nails and the like are not parts of the ship but join the parts of the ship.

4. These things having been set down as principles, he adds things that also pertain to his principal intention, saying afterwards he will treat what negation and affirmation are. They are parts of the enunciation, not integral parts like the noun and verb (otherwise it would be necessary that every enunciation be composed of affirmation and negation) but subjective parts, that is, species. This is indeed presupposed now but will be made manifest later.

5. But a doubt can arise: since the enunciation is divided into categorical and hypothetical, why does he make no mention of these, as he does of affirmation and negation? And it can be said that the hypothetical enunciation is composed of several categoricals. Hence they differ only as the one and the many.

Or it could be better said that the hypothetical enunciation does not contain absolute truth, knowledge of which is required for demonstration, to which this book is principally ordered, but signifies something true on a supposition, and this does not suffice in demonstrative sciences unless they are confirmed by the absolute truth of the simple enunciation. Therefore Aristotle sets aside the treatment of hypothetical enunciations and syllogisms. But he adds, and enunciation, which is the genus of affirmation and negation, and speech, which is the genus of enunciation.

6. If one asks further why he says nothing more of voiced sound, it should be said that the voiced sound is something natural, hence it pertains to the consideration of natural philosophy, as is clear in *On the Soul* 2 and the final chapter of *On the Generation of Animals*. Hence it is not properly the genus of speech, but is assumed for the constitution of speech, as natural things for the constitution of artefacts.

7. But the order of the enunciation seems preposterous, for affirmation is naturally prior to negation, and enunciation is prior to both as their genus, and consequently speech is prior to enunciation. But it should be said that because he began to enumerate from the parts, he proceeds from parts to whole. He puts negation, which contains division, before affirmation which consists in composition, because division is closer to parts but composition is closer to the whole.

Or it could be said, according to some, that he puts negation first because in things which can be and not be, non-being which negation signifies is before being which affirmation signifies. However, since they are species equally dividing the genus, they are naturally simultaneous, hence it does not matter which of them he puts first.

Lesson 2

Those things which are in speech are the notes of passion of the soul, and what is written are notes of what is spoken.

Just as writing is not the same for all, neither is speech. But that of which these are notes, passions of the soul, are the same in each, and the things of which they are likenesses are also the same. All these things have been discussed in what has been said of the soul and belong to another consideration.

1. Having completed his preface, the Philosopher turns to achieving his project, and because he promised to speak of complex and incomplex significant voiced sounds, he begins with a treatment of the signification of voiced sound. After that, he will turn to the voiced sounds he promised

to define, 'By a noun we mean . . .'[1] Concerning the first, he does two things: first, he discusses what the meaning of voiced sound is; second, he shows the difference between the meaning of complex and incomplex voiced sounds, 'As there are in the mind thoughts . . .'[2] He subdivides the first task into two, the first being to set forth the order of the meaning of voiced sounds, the second, to show of what kind that meaning is, whether natural or conventional, 'Just as all men have not the same writing . . .'

2. Notice that he proposed three things with respect to his first task, from one of which a fourth is suggested. For he mentions writing, speech and the affections of the soul, by which things are understood. For an affection is the effect of some agent, and thus the passions of the soul have their origin in things themselves. If there were some solitary or feral man, the passions of the soul would be sufficient for him; by them he would be conformed to things in order that he might have knowledge of them. But because man is naturally political and social, there is need for one man to make his conceptions known to others, which is done with speech. So significant speech was needed if men were to live together. Which is why those of different tongues do not easily live together. Again, if man employed only sense knowledge, which looks only to the here and now, there would suffice for his living with others the kind of significant sound other animals use, who make their conceptions known to one another by certain voiced sounds. But because man employs intellectual knowledge as well, which abstracts from the here and now, his concern is not only for things present in place and time, but also things distant in place and future in time. Hence in order that a man might manifest his conceptions to those distant in place and who will come to be in future time, the use of writing was necessary.

3. Because logic is ordered to the acquisition of knowledge, the meaning of speech, which is immediate to those conceptions of intellect, belongs to its principal consideration. But the signification of script, as more remote, is not its business but rather grammar's. That is why in explaining the order of signification he does not begin with script but with speech, the meaning of which he first explains when he says, 'Spoken words are the signs . . .', that is, signs of those affections or passions which are in the soul. He speaks therefore as if concluding from the foregoing because he said above that we must define noun and verb and the others, but

1. Lesson 4.
2. Lesson 3.

these are significant speech. Therefore we must explain the signification of speech.

4. He employs this way of speaking, 'the things which are in speech', and not in speeches that he might move smoothly from what he has said before. For he said that we must speak of noun and verb and other like matters. But these have a threefold existence. In one way, in the conception of the intellect; in another, in vocal expression; third, in writing. Therefore he says, 'those things which are in speech', as if to say, nouns and verbs and the others following, which are only in speech, are signs. Or, because not all speech is significant, and of this some is naturally significant, which is far from the notion of noun and verb and the others, in order that he might adjust what he says to the things he intends, he says therefore, 'those things which are in speech', that is, which are included in speech, as parts in a whole. Or, because speech is something natural, but noun and verb signify by human convention which attaches to the natural thing as to matter, as the form of the bed to wood; therefore, to indicate nouns, verbs and the rest, he says, 'those things which are in speech', as he might say of the bed, those things which are in wood.

5. With respect to 'of those things which are passions of the soul', it should be noted that by passions of the soul is commonly meant affections of sense appetite, like anger, joy and such like, as is said in *Ethics* 2.5. And it is true that certain voiced sounds of men naturally signify such passions, as the groan of the sick, as he says in *Politics* 1.1. But his present concern is the voiced sounds significant by human convention, so passions of the soul must mean here conceptions of the intellect, which nouns and verbs and speech immediately signify, according to the opinion of Aristotle. But it is not possible that they should immediately signify the things themselves, as is clear from their mode of signifying. For 'man' signifies human nature in abstraction from singulars, so it cannot immediately signify a particular man. That is why the Platonists held that it signifies some separate idea of man. But because this does not really subsist as abstracted, in Aristotle's view, but is only in the intellect, it was necessary for Aristotle to say that speech signifies the conceptions of the intellect immediately and, by their mediation, things.

6. Because it is not customary for Aristotle to call conceptions of the intellect passions, Andronicus held that this book was not Aristotle's. But it is manifest that all operations of the soul are called passions in *On the Soul* 1.1. Hence the conception of the intellect can be called a passion. Or because our understanding is not without a phantasm, which is not without bodily passion; hence in *On the Soul* 3.4, the Philosopher calls

imagination the passive intellect. Or because by extending the term 'passion' to mean any receiving, the understanding of the possible intellect itself can be called a kind of receiving [*quoddam pati*], as it is in *On the Soul* 3.3. He uses the term 'passions' instead of intellections both because it is due to a passion of the soul, such as love or hate, that a man wishes to signify his inner concept by speech to another, and also because the signification of speech is referred to the conception of the intellect insofar as it arises from things by way of some impression or passion.

7. Second, when he says, 'and written words are the symbols of spoken words', he turns to the signification of writing. According to Alexander he does this to manifest the preceding opinion by way of similitude, so the sense would be: the things which are in speech are the signs of passions of the soul, just as script is the sign of speech. Which he makes clear by what follows, when he says, 'Just as all men . . .', taking this as a sign of the foregoing. That writing signifies speech is clear from this that just as there are different languages among different peoples, so there is different writing. According to this explanation, therefore, he does not say 'and letters of the things that are in speech', but 'those things which are written', because they are called letters as spoken as well as written. although most properly as written; as spoken they are called elements of speech. But because Aristotle does not say, 'just as those things which are written', but gives a continuous narration, it is better to say, as Porphyry explains, that Aristotle proceeds further to complete the order of signification. For afterwards he had said that the nouns and verbs which are written are signs of the nouns and verbs in speech.

8. Then, when he says, 'Just as all men . . .', he shows the differences between the signifying and signified in the foregoing with respect to being natural or not. He does three things in this regard. First, he gives a sign by which it is clear that neither speech nor writing signifies naturally. What naturally signifies is the same with all men, but the signification of writing and speech, with which we are concerned, is not the same with all peoples. No one ever doubted this with respect to writing, of which not only the reason for signifying is conventional but whose very formation is due to art. Speech is formed naturally and for that reason some wondered if it did not signify naturally. But Aristotle here determines by the similitude of writing that just as it is not the same among all, so neither is speech. Clearly, then, neither writing nor speech signifies naturally, but by human institution. Those speech sounds that signify naturally, such as the groan of the sick and the like, are the same with all.

9. Second, when he says 'but the passions of the soul . . .', he shows

that the passions of the soul exist naturally, like things, by this that they are the same with all. Just as the passions of the soul are the same with all (*of which first*, that is, of which first passions speech is a note or sign; for the passions of the soul are referred to speech, as the first to the second, for words are only spoken in order to express the interior passions of the soul), and the things are the same, that is, with everyone, *of which* – that is, of which things – these, namely *passions of the soul are likenesses*. It should be noticed that writing is called the note, that is, the sign of speech, and similarly speech of the passions of the soul, but the passions of the soul are called likenesses of things. And this because things are only known by the soul by a likeness of them existing either in sense or intellect. Writing is a sign of speech and speech of the passions in such a way that there is no reason in likeness, but only in convention, as with many other signs: as the trumpet is the sign of battle. In the passions of the soul there must be recognized likeness as the reason for signifying things, because they designate them naturally, not conventionally.

10. Some wish to object to the claim that the passions of the soul, which speech signifies, are the same with all men. First, because there are different opinions about things and thus the passions of the soul (or thoughts) do not seem the same in everyone. To which Boethius replies that Aristotle here calls passions of soul the conceptions in which intellect is never deceived, and that is why its concepts must be the same in all because if someone disagrees with the truth he does not understand. But because there can be falsity in the intellect as it composes and divides, though not as it knows the quiddity, that is, the essence of the thing, as is said in *On the Soul* 3.5, what is said here has to be referred to the simple conceptions of the intellect (which incomplex speech signifies), which are the same in everyone. Because, if someone truly understands what a man is, whatever else he apprehends he will not understand man. These simple conceptions of the intellect are what speech first signifies. Hence it is said in *Metaphysics* 4 that the account which the word signifies is the definition. And he significantly says, of which first these are the signs, to refer to the first conceptions first signified by speech.

11. But some still object concerning equivocal terms in which there is not the same passion or concept signified by the same word. Porphyry replies to this that one man who utters a word refers it to one conception of intellect, and if someone else to whom he speaks understands something else, the one who speaks, explaining himself, will bring it about that the concept refers to the same thing. But it is better to say that the intention of Aristotle is not to assert the identity of conceptions of the soul by

comparison to speech, such that of one word there will be one conception, since words are different among different peoples; but he intends to assert the identity of the conceptions of the soul with reference to things, which he also says are the same for all.

12. Third, when he says 'This matter . . .', he excuses himself from a further consideration of these matters, because he has already said in *On the Soul* what the passions of the soul are, and how they are likenesses of things. This is not a logical topic but one belonging to natural philosophy.

Lesson 3

As there are in the mind thoughts which do not involve truth or falsity, and also those which must be either true or false, so it is in speech. For truth and falsity imply combination and separation. Nouns and verbs, provided nothing is added, are like thoughts without combination or separation; 'man' and 'white', as isolated terms, are not yet either true or false. In proof of this, consider the word 'goat-stag'. It has significance, but there is no truth or falsity about it, unless 'is' or 'is not' is added, either in the present or some other tense.

1. The Philosopher, having treated the order of signification of speech, turns now to the different significations of speech, some of which signify the true and the false while others do not. He does two things in this regard, first, he states the difference, and, second, he manifests it: 'For truth and falsity . . .' Since conceptions of intellect are in the order of nature preambles to speech, which is spoken in order to express them, therefore, by likeness of a difference according to intellect, he assigns a difference with respect to the meanings of speech, so that this manifestation is not only a simile, but also from the cause which the effect imitates.

2. It should be noted, therefore, as was said at the outset, that there is a twofold operation of intellect, as is taught in *On the Soul* 3.5, in one of which is found the true and false, and in the other not. This is what he means when he says that sometimes in the soul there is understanding without the true and false, and sometimes you necessarily have one or the other. Because significant speech is fashioned to express conceptions of the intellect, in order for the sign to be conformed to the signified, it is necessary that it be as it is with significant speech, some without the true and false, some with it.

3. Then when he says, 'For truth and falsity . . .', he manifests what he said. And first with respect to what he said about intellect, second, with respect to what he said of the assimilation of speech to intellect: 'Nouns and verbs . . .' In order to show that the intellect is sometimes without the true and false and sometimes with one or the other of these, he says first that truth and falsity follow on composition and division. It must be understood that one of the two operations of intellect is the understanding of indivisibles, insofar as the intellect understands absolutely the quiddity or essence of a thing in itself, for example what is man or what is white or the like. The other operation of intellect occurs when it composes and divides such simple concepts. He says, then, that it is in the second operation of intellect, that is, in composing and dividing, that truth and falsity are found, implying that they are not found in the first operation, as indeed is taught in *On the Soul* 3.5.

4. There seems to be a doubt about this first point: since division comes about by resolution to indivisibles or simples, it seems that just as in simples there is neither truth nor falsity, neither is there in division. But it must be said that because conceptions of the intellect are likenesses of things, the things of intellect can be known and named in two ways, in themselves, and according to the notions of the things of which they are likenesses. Just as the image of Hercules taken by itself is said to be and is called bronze, but insofar as it is a likeness of Hercules it is called man. So too, if we should consider things of intellect in themselves, there is always composition where there is truth and falsity, which is never found in intellect unless intellect compares one simple concept with another. But if it is referred to things, sometimes it is said to be composition, sometimes division: composition when the intellect compares one concept to another by seeing a conjunction or identity of the things of which they are likenesses, division when it so compares one concept to another that it apprehends them to be different things. In this way too in speech affirmation is called composition, insofar as it signifies a conjunction on the part of things, and negation is called division insofar as it signifies a separation of things.

5. But it seems that truth does not consist in composition and division alone. First, because things are called true or false, as we speak of true and false gold. And it is also said that being and true are convertible. Hence it seems that the simple concept of intellect, which is the likeness of the thing, does not lack truth and falsity. Moreover, the Philosopher says in *On the Soul* 2.30 that sensation of proper sensibles is always true,

but the senses do not compose or divide; therefore, it is not only in composition and division that truth is found. Again, there is no composition in the divine intellect, as is proved in *Metaphysics* 12, yet the highest and first truth is there; therefore, truth is not only in composition and division.

6. Ad [1] For light on this we should consider that truth is found in something in two ways, in one way, as in that which is true, in another, as in speaking or knowing the true. Truth is found in that which is true both in the case of simples and of composites, but as in the one saying or knowing the true, it is only found according to composition and division. Which is clear from the following.

7. The true is the good of intellect, as the Philosopher says in *Ethics* 6.2. Hence, anything is called true with reference to intellect. Words are referred to the intellect as signs and to things as that of which concepts are likenesses. But we should note that some things are referred to intellect in two ways. In one way, as measure to the measured, and in this way natural things are referred to the human speculative intellect. So the intellect is called true insofar as it is conformed to the thing, and false insofar as it is discordant from the thing. The natural thing is not called true with reference to our intellect, as some ancient natural philosophers held, thinking the truth of things to lie only in this, that they were seen; on that basis contradictories would be simultaneously true, because there are different opinions about contradictories. Some things are called true or false with reference to our intellect, not essentially or formally, but causally, insofar as they are apt to cause a true or false estimate of themselves. In this way gold is called true or false. But things are compared to intellect in another way, as measured to their measure, as is clear in practical intellect, which is the cause of things. Hence the work of the artisan is called true insofar as it attains to the notion of art and false insofar as it fails to.

8. Since all natural things are referred to the divine intellect, as artefacts to art, each thing is called true insofar as it has its proper form, according to which it imitates the divine art. For false gold is true fool's gold. It is in this way that being and true are convertible, because every natural thing is conformed to the divine art because of its form. Hence the Philosopher in *Physics* 1.15 calls form something divine.

9. Ad [2] Just as a thing is called true with reference to its measure, so are both sense and intellect, whose measure is the thing outside the soul. Sensation is said to be true when by its form it is conformed to the thing existing outside the soul. In this way is to be understood the claim that

sensation of the proper sensible is true. In this way, the intellect grasping the quiddity does not compose or divide yet is always true, as is said in *On the Soul* 3.5. But it should be noted that although sensation of the proper object is true, it does not know this to be true, for it cannot know its relation of conformity to the thing, it just grasps the thing. But intellect can know such a relation of conformity, and therefore only intellect can know truth. Hence the Philosopher says in *Metaphysics* 6 that truth is only in the mind, namely in knowing truth. To know this relation of conformity is nothing other than to judge that it is or is not so in things. Which is to compose and divide. Therefore, intellect knows truth only by composing or dividing by its judgement. Which judgement, if it is consonant with things, will be true, for example when the intellect judges the thing to be as it is, or not to be as it is. It is clear, then, that truth and falsity as in the knower and speaker involve composition and division. This is how the Philosopher speaks here. Because speech signifies thought, speech is true when it signifies true thinking, and false when it signifies false thinking, although speech, insofar as it is a certain thing, is called true as other things are. So the statement, 'Man is an ass,' is true speech and a false sign, but because it is a sign of the false, it is called false.

10. Ad [3] It should be kept in mind that the Philosopher speaks of truth here as it pertains to the human intellect, which judges of the conformity of things and intellect by composing and dividing. But the judgement of the divine intellect on this is without composition and division, because, just as our intellect understands material things immaterially, so the divine intellect knows composition and division simply.

11. When he says, 'Nouns and verbs . . .', he manifests what he said of the similarity of speech and intellect. First, he manifests the claim, second he proves it with a sign, 'In proof of this . . .' From what has gone before, he concludes that since truth and falsity in the intellect are linked with composition and division, it follows that nouns and verbs, taken separately, are assimilated to the intellect which is without composition and division, as when 'man' or 'white' is spoken and nothing is added, there is not yet the true or false; but when 'is' or 'is not' is added later, it will become true or false.

12. It is not a counter-example that an answer to a question can be given with a single word, as when to the question, 'What is swimming in the sea?' one answered, 'Fish.' For the verb in the question is understood in the response. And just as the noun taken by itself does not signify the

true or false, neither does the verb. Nor are verbs of the first [*amo*] and second person [*amas*] or impersonal verbs [*pluit*] counter-examples, because their subjects are understood and thus although there is no explicit composition, it is implicit.

13. When he says, 'In proof of this . . .', he gives an example of a compound noun, namely goat-stag, which is made up of goat and stag and is the Greek *tragelaphos*, for *tragos* is goat and *elaphos* stag. Such nouns signify something, namely certain simple concepts, although of composed things. Therefore they are not true or false except when 'is' or 'is not' is added, which express a judgement of intellect. To be or not to be can be added either in the present tense, which is actually to exist or not, and this is existence simply speaking, or according to past or future time, which is not existence simply but in a certain respect, as when we say something was or will be. It is noteworthy that he uses as an example a word signifying what is not to be found in the nature of things, in which falsity immediately appears, but which cannot be true or false without composition and division.

Lesson 4

By a noun we mean a sound significant by convention, which has no reference to time, and of which no part is significant apart from the rest. In the noun 'fairsteed', the part 'steed' has no significance in and by itself, as in the phrase 'fair steed'. Yet there is a difference between simple and composite nouns; for in the former the part is in no way significant, in the latter it contributes to the meaning of the whole, although it has not an independent meaning. Thus in the word 'pirate-boat' the word 'boat' has no meaning except as part of the whole word.

The limitation 'by convention' was introduced because nothing is by nature a noun or name – it is only so when it becomes a sign; inarticulate sounds, such as those which brutes produce, are significant, yet none of them constitutes a noun.

The expression 'not-man' is not a noun. There is indeed no recognized term by which we may denote such an expression, for it is not a sentence or a denial. Let it then be called an infinite noun.

The expressions 'of Philo', 'to Philo', and so on, constitute not nouns, but cases of a noun. The definition of these cases of a noun is in other respects the same as that of the noun proper, but when coupled with 'is', 'was' or 'will be', they do not, as they are, form a proposition either true or false, and this the noun proper always does, under these conditions. Take the words 'of Philo is' or 'of Philo is not'; these words do not, as they stand, form either a true or a false proposition.

1. After the Philosopher determines the order of signification of speech, he turns to a discussion of significant sounds themselves. And because he is chiefly interested in the enunciation which is the subject of this book, and in each science we must have foreknowledge of the principles of the subject, he must accordingly first determine the principles of the enunciation, and second of the enunciation itself.[1] He subdivides the first task into two, for first he determines the principles as the materials of the enunciation, that is, its integral parts, and second he determines the formal principle, that is, speech, which is the genus of the enunciation.[2] Accordingly, he first treats of noun, which signifies the substance of the thing, and then of the verb, which signifies an action or passion proceeding from the thing.[3] As for the noun, he does three things: first, he defines it; second, he explains the definition: 'In the noun "fairsteed" . . .'; third, he excludes certain things which do not save the definition of noun perfectly: 'The expression "non-man" . . .'

2. Notice first that a definition is called a term [*terminus*] because it includes the thing totally, such that nothing of the thing is left outside the definition to which the definition does not apply, nor anything else within the definition, to which the definition belongs.

3. Five things are put into the definition of the noun: first, it is called *significant sound* by way of genus, by which the noun is distinguished from other sounds which are not speech. For speech is a sound from the mouth of the animal, sent forth, with some imagination, as is said in *On the Soul* 2.18. He adds a first difference, *significant*, to differentiate it from non-significant sounds, whether written or articulated, just as *blifty*, whether an unwritten and unarticulated sound, is like *ssssss*, done for nothing. Because he has already dealt with the meaning of speech above, he can conclude that a noun is significant sound.

4. But since sound is a natural thing, and the noun is not something natural but established by human convention, it seems that sound should not be given as the genus, since it is natural, but rather as sign, which is from convention, as who should say: noun is a vocal sign, as a dish is

1. chapter 7.
2. chapter 6.
3. Lesson 5.

more appropriately defined as a wooden vessel, than if one should say that it is wood formed into a vessel.

5. But it should be replied that artificial things are indeed in the genus of substance because of their matter, but in the genus of accident because of their form, for the forms of artificial things are accidents. Therefore, the noun signifies an accidental form concretized in a subject. But since their subject must be put into the definition of accidents, it is necessary that if any names signify an accident abstractly that the accident be put directly into their definition, as a genus and the subject obliquely, as a difference, as when it is said that snubness is the curvature of the nose. But with nouns that signify accidents concretely, the matter or subject is put in their definitions as genus, and the accident as a difference, as when it is said that snub is a curved nose. If then the names of artificial things signify accidental forms as concrete in natural subjects, it is more appropriate that the natural thing be put into their definition as the genus, as we say that the plate is shaped wood, and similarly that the noun is significant sound. It would be otherwise if the names of artificial things were taken as signifying these artificial forms abstractly.

6. Third, he gives the second difference, 'by convention', that is, by human institution proceeding from the agreement of man. In this the noun differs from naturally signifying sounds, like the groan of the sick or the calls of brute animals.

7. Fourth, he gives the third difference – namely, 'which has no reference to time' – by which the noun differs from the verb. But this seems to be false, because the nouns 'day' and 'year' signify time. It should be responded that time can be considered in three ways: first, time itself; second, as a kind of thing, and then it can be signified by a noun like any other thing; in another way, it can be considered as measured by time as such: and since motion is what is principally measured by time, and motion includes action and passion, the verb which signifies action or passion signifies with time. But substance considered in itself, as signified by noun or pronoun, is not as such measured by time, but only insofar as it is in motion, as it is signified by the participle. So verb and participle signify with time, but not the noun and pronoun. Third, the very relation of measuring time can be considered, which is signified by adverbs like 'tomorrow', 'yesterday' and the like.

8. Fifth, he gives the fourth difference, when he adds 'of which no part is significant apart from the rest', that is, from the whole noun, but it is compared to the signification of the noun as it is in the whole. The signification is, as it were, the form of the noun, but no separated part

has the form of the whole, as the hand severed from man does not have the human form. In this the noun is distinguished from speech, whose parts signify separately, as when we say, 'just man'.

9. When he says, 'In the noun "fairsteed" . . .', he manifests the definition, and first with respect to its ultimate particle; second, with respect to its third, 'The limitation by convention . . .'; with respect to the third particle 'which has no reference to time', will be discussed when verb is. On the first point, then, he does two things: he manifests the proposal by composite nouns; then he shows the difference between simple and composite nouns: 'Yet there is a difference . . .'

First he shows that the separate part of a noun signifies nothing, making use of composite nouns in which this is less easily seen. In a noun like 'fairsteed', the part 'steed' does not signify by itself as it does in 'fair steed'. The reason is that one name is imposed to signify one simple understanding, and that from which the name is imposed to signify differs from what the name signifies, as 'stumbling-block' is imposed from stumbling over a block, but that is not what it means, for it signifies the concept of some thing. Hence the part of the composite name is imposed to signify a simple concept not to signify a part of the composite conception from which the name is imposed to signify. But speech signifies the composite conception itself, hence a part of speech signifies part of the composite conception.

10. When he says, 'Yet there is a difference . . .', he shows the difference between simple and composite nouns, and says that it is not with simple nouns as it is with composite, because in simple nouns the part is in no way significant, neither in truth nor in appearance, but in composite nouns it has the appearance of signifying. Yet no part of it signifies, as was said of the noun 'fairsteed'. The reason for the difference is that just as the simple noun is imposed to signify a simple concept, so too it is imposed to signify from some simple concept, but the composite noun is imposed from a composite conception, hence the appearance that its part signifies.

11. When he says, 'The limitation "by convention" . . .', he manifests the third part of the definition, and he says that a noun is said to signify by convention because nothing is naturally a noun: it is a noun because it signifies, but it does not signify naturally, but from convention. That is why he adds, 'it is only so when it becomes a sign', that is, when it is imposed to signify. That which signifies naturally does not come to be, but naturally is a sign. This is what he means when he speaks of 'inarticulate sounds' as of the brutes, which cannot be signified by writing. They can

be called sounds rather than speech, since some animals have no voice because they lack lungs, but by certain sounds naturally signify their own passions, but none of these sounds is a noun. From which it is clear that the noun does not signify naturally.

12. There has been a diversity of opinion about this. For some said that nouns in no way signify naturally, nor does it matter which things are signified by which nouns. Others said that names signify completely naturally, as if nouns were natural likenesses of things. Some said that nouns do not naturally signify in this respect, that their signification is not from nature, as Aristotle holds here, but they naturally signify in this respect that their signification is congruent with the natures of things, as Plato said. Nor does it matter that one thing is signified by many names, because there can be many likenesses of the same thing, and similarly from its different properties many names can be given to one thing. He should not be understood to mean that the sounds of animals do not have names, for they are named by certain nouns, as the roar of the lion and the lowing of cattle, but that the sound itself is not a noun.

13. When he says, 'The expression "not-man" . . .', he excludes some things from the range of the meaning of noun: first, the infinite noun, then the cases of the noun. He says that 'not-man' is not a noun, since every noun signifies some definite nature, like 'man', or a definite person, like the pronoun, or both, like 'Socrates'. But when I say 'not-man', it does not signify a definite nature or person. It is imposed from the negation of man, which can be said equally of non-being. Hence 'not-man' can be said indifferently of that which is not in nature, as if we said, 'The chimera is a not-man,' and of that which is in nature, as when we say, 'The horse is a not-man.' If it were imposed from privation, it would require at least an existing subject, but because it is imposed from a negation, it can be said of being and of not-being, as Boethius and Ammonius say. Because it can signify in the manner of a noun and function as subject and predicate, there is required at least a thought-of subject.

At the time of Aristotle there was no term for such expressions. For it is not speech, because no part of it signifies separately, which excludes composite nouns too; similarly it is not a negation, that is, a negative sentence, because that adds negation to affirmation, which does not happen here. Therefore he coined a term for such expressions, calling them infinite nouns because of the indefiniteness of signification, as was said.

14. When he says, 'of Philo', he excludes the cases of nouns, and says that 'of Philo' or 'to Philo' and others like them are not nouns, but only

the nominative is chiefly called a noun through which the imposition is made to signify something. These oblique forms are called cases of the noun, as if they fall away in a kind of declension from the original nominative, which is called erect because it does not fall. The Stoics said that the nominative is itself a case, and grammarians have adopted this, because it falls or proceeds from the interior conception of the mind. And it is called erect because nothing prevents something from falling and landing on its feet, as the falling knife sticks in wood.

15. When he says, The definition of these cases . . .', he shows how the oblique cases relate to the noun, and he says that the definition which the noun signifies is the same in the cases of the noun, with this difference that the noun joined with 'is' or 'will be' or 'was' always signifies the true or false, which does not happen with the cases. Significantly he employed the example of a substantive verb, since there are impersonal verbs which when conjoined with a case of the noun signify the true or false, as when it is said, 'Poenitet Socratem',[1] because the act of the verb is understood to apply obliquely, as if it were said, 'Regret has Socrates.'

16. On the contrary, if the infinite noun and the cases are not nouns, the definition of noun is inept, because it applies to these. The response to which is that, according to Ammonius, he defined the noun more generally above and now restricts its signification by subtracting these from it. Or the response could be that the definition given does not apply to these, for the infinite noun signifies nothing definite, nor do the cases of the noun according to the first institution, as has been said.

Lesson 5

A verb is that which, in addition to its proper meaning, carries with it the notion of time. No part of it has any independent meaning, and it is a sign of something said of something else.

I will explain what I mean by saying that it carries with it the notion of time. 'Health' is a noun, but 'is healthy' is a verb; for besides its proper meaning it indicates the present existence of the state in question.

Moreover, a verb is always a sign of something said of something else, that is, of something either predicable of or present in some other thing.

Such expressions as 'is not-healthy', 'is not-ill', I do not describe as verbs, for though they carry the additional note of time, and always form a predicate,

1. An impersonal verb with the proper noun in the accusative case.

there is no specified name for this variety; but let them be called infinite verbs, since they apply equally well to that which exists and to that which does not.

Similarly 'he was healthy', 'he will be healthy', are not verbs, but tenses of a verb; the difference lies in the fact that the verb indicates present time, while the tenses of the verb indicate those times which lie outside the present.

Verbs in and by themselves are substantial and have significance, for he who uses such expressions arrests the hearer's mind, and fixes his attention; but they do not, as they stand, express any judgement, either positive or negative. For neither are 'to be' and 'not to be' and the participle 'being' significant of any fact, unless something is added; for they do not themselves indicate anything, but simply a copulation, of which we cannot form a conception apart from the things coupled.

1. Having discussed the noun, Aristotle turns now to the verb, and does three things. First, he defines the verb; second, he excludes certain things from the definition of the verb: 'Such expressions as "is not healthy" . . .' He shows the agreement of verb and noun, 'Verbs in and by themselves . . .' As to the first then, having defined the verb, he then goes on to explain it: 'I will explain . . .'

2. It should be taken into account that Aristotle, seeking to be brief, does not put into the definition of verb the things common to noun and verb, leaving it to the reader to supply those elements. There are three parts of his definition of verb: the first of which distinguishes the verb from the noun; in this he says that it consignifies time. In the definition of noun it was stated that it does not signify with time. The second part is what distinguishes the verb from speech, when he says, 'No part of it has any independent . . .'

3. But since this also occurs in the definition of noun, it seems he should have left it out, just as he does, 'a sound significant by convention'. To this Ammonius replies that this is put into the definition of noun in order to distinguish the noun from speech which is composed of nouns, as when it is said, 'Man is an animal.' Because there are some speeches which are composed of verbs, as when we say, 'To walk is to move,' he repeated the particle to distinguish these from the verb. One could answer otherwise that since the verb implies composition, in which the speech signifying the true or false is perfected, the verb has a greater affinity with speech, as being its formal part, whereas the noun is a material and subjective part of speech. So he had to repeat it.

4. The third particle is what distinguishes the verb not only from the noun but also from the participle which signifies with time. Hence he

says, 'Moreover a verb is always a sign of something said of another.' Nouns and participles can be put in the place of subject and predicate, but the verb is always in the predicate role.

5. But verbs in the infinitive seem counter-examples, for they are sometimes put in the subject position, as when it is said, 'To walk is to move.' The response is that verbs in the infinitive mood, when they are put as subjects, have the force of nouns, hence in Greek and in vulgar Latin they take an article like nouns. The reason is that it is proper to the noun to signify something as existing of itself, and it is proper to the verb that it signify an action or passion. But action can be signified in three ways. In one way, as abstracted by itself, as some thing, and thus it is signified by a noun, for example action, passion, walking, running and the like. In another way, by way of action, namely as emerging from a substance and inhering in it as in a subject, and thus it is signified by verbs of the other modes, which are attributed as predicates. But because the very process or inherence of action can be grasped by intellect and signified as a thing, verbs in the infinitive mode, which signify the inherence of action in the subject, can be taken as verbs, by reason of concretion, and as nouns insofar as they signify certain things.

6. It could be objected that verbs of other modes also seem sometimes to occupy the subject position, as when it is said, 'I run is a verb.' It should be said that in such a locution the verb 'I run' is not taken formally, insofar as its signification refers to the thing, but insofar as it materially signifies that word, which is taken as some thing. Therefore both verbs and other parts of speech when they are used materially, take on the force of nouns.

7. Then when he says, 'I will explain . . .' he explains the definition he has given. First with respect to its consignifying time; second, insofar as he says it is a sign of something said of another. He does not explain the second particle, namely, that no part of it signifies separately, because he has done that already in discussing the noun. He explains what he means by saying that the verb consignifies time with an example, namely 'running' which signifies an action, not in the mode of action but in the manner of an existent thing and does not consignify time, because it is a noun. 'I run', however, since it is a verb signifying action, consignifies time because it is proper to motion to be measured by time; actions are made known to us in time. It was said above that to consignify time is to signify something measured in time. So it is one thing to signify time principally, as some thing, and thus as a noun, and another to signify with time, which does not belong to the noun, but to the verb.

8. When he says, 'Moreover, a verb is always a sign . . .', he explains the other particle. Note that because the subject of the enunciation is signified as that in which something inheres, when the verb signifies action in the manner of action, of whose notion it is to inhere, it is always placed in the role of predicate and never of subject, unless it is taken with the force of a noun, as has been said. The verb is said always to be a sign of something said of another, both because the verb always signifies that which is predicated, and because in every predication there must be a verb, because the verb implies composition, by which the predicate is composed with the subject.

9. But a doubt arises about what he adds: 'something either predicable of or present in some other thing'. For something seems to be said of a subject when it is predicated essentially, as 'Man is animal', but to be present in a subject when accident is predicated of the subject, as 'Man is white'. Therefore, if verbs signify action or passion, which are accidents, the consequence is that they will always signify what is said as in a subject. It is pointless, then, for him to say 'predicable of and present in some other thing'. But because Aristotle uses a disjunction he seems to signify different things by each. Therefore, it can be said that when Aristotle says that the verb is always a sign of something said of something else, this should not be understood as if the things signified by verbs are what is predicated; it is the verbs which are predicated rather than signify predicates. Therefore it is to be understood that the verb is always the sign that some things are predicated, because every predication comes to be through the verb by reason of the implied composition, whether it is predicated essentially or accidentally.

10. Then when he says, 'Such expressions as "is not-healthy" . . .', he excludes certain things from the range of the verb. First, the infinite verb, then verbs of past and future time: 'Similarly, "he was healthy" . . .' He says first that 'not runs' and 'not works' are not properly called verbs. For it is proper to the verb to signify something in the manner of action or passion, which these expressions do not do, for they remove action or passion rather than signify any definite action or passion. But although they cannot properly be called verbs, some of the things put into the definition of the verb belong to them, the first of which is that they signify time, because they signify to act and to be acted upon, which since they are in time, their privations are too. Hence rest is measured by time, as is said in *Physics* 4.20, insofar as it is always put in the predicate place like the verb. And this because negation is reduced to the genus of affirmation. Hence just as the verb signifies action or passion, it signifies

something as existing in another, so the foregoing expressions signify the removal of action or passion.

11. But someone might object, 'If the definition of the verb belongs to those expressions, then they are verbs.' It should be replied that the definition of verb given above is of the verb taken generally, but these expressions are said not to be verbs, because they fall short of the full sense of the term. Nor prior to Aristotle was there a term for this type of expression which differs from verbs, and since they are like verbs in part, but fall short of the definite notion of verb, he calls them infinite verbs. And he gives a reason for the term: each of them can be said indifferently of what is and what is not. For the negative prefix has the force of simple negation, not of privation; privation supposes a definite subject. Verbs of this kind differ from negative verbs because infinite verbs are taken as one expression but negative verbs as having the force of two words.

12. When he says, 'Similarly "he was healthy" . . .', he excludes verbs of the past and present tenses from the verb, and says that just as infinite verbs are not verbs simply, so also 'will run', which is in the future tense, or 'has run', which is in the past, are not verbs, but cases of verb. And they differ from the verb in this that the verb consignifies present time, but these signify then and later. He significantly says present time and not simply present, lest the present be understood as something indivisible, as the instant is. There is no motion in the instant nor action or passion, but it is necessary to present time that it measures action, which begins and is not yet determined by act. Rightly, then, those words which consignify past and future time are not properly called verbs, for the verb properly speaking signifies acting and being acted upon, that is the verb properly signifies actually acting and being acted upon, which is acting and being acted upon simply speaking; acting or being acted upon in the past or future are such only in a certain respect.

13. Verbs of past and future tense are reasonably called cases of the verb, which consignifies present time, because the past or future are said with reference to the present. For the past is what was present and the future what will be present.

14. Declensions of verbs vary in mode, tense, number and person, but the variation which comes about through number and person does not constitute a case of the verb, because such a variation is not on the side of action, but on the side of the subject, whereas the variation by modes and tenses looks to the action itself, and therefore both constitute cases of the verb. Verbs of the imperative and optative moods are called cases,

as are past and future tenses. But verbs of the indicative in the present tense are not called cases, whatever be their person or number.

15. When he says, 'Verbs in and by themselves . . .', he shows the agreement of verbs with nouns, and he does two things: first, he states his intention, second, he manifests it: 'and have significance . . .' First, then, he says that verbs in and by themselves are nouns, which some explain from the verbs which are taken with the force of nouns, as has been said, whether they are of the infinitive mood, as when I say, 'To run is to move,' or some other mood, as when I say, 'I run is a verb.' But that does not seem to be Aristotle's intention, because the sequel does not answer to this intention. So it should be said otherwise that noun is taken here as it commonly signifies any expression, hence it is verbs themselves – insofar as they name, that is, signify, to act or to be acted upon – that are included under nouns or names commonly understood. But the noun, insofar as it is distinguished from the verb, signifies the thing in a definite manner, insofar as it can be understood as existing in itself. Hence nouns can function both as subjects and as predicates.

16. When he says, 'and have significance', he proves what he has proposed. First, by this that verbs signify something, just as nouns do; second, by this that they do not signify the true or false, any more than nouns do. First he proves the claim that insofar as they signify something, verbs are nouns. It was said above that significant speech signifies concepts. Hence it is proper to significant speech that it generate an understanding in the mind of the hearer. Therefore, in order to show that the verb is significant speech, he assumes that the one who speaks a verb brings about an understanding in the mind of his auditor. To show this, he notes that he who hears rests.

17. But this seems false, because only a complete sentence gives the mind repose, but neither noun nor verb, if taken just as such, do this. For if I say 'man', the mind of the listener is in suspense as to what it is I wish to say; if I say 'runs', his mind is in suspense concerning what I am saying. But it should be said that there is a twofold operation of intellect, as was pointed out above, and he who speaks a noun or verb just as such brings about an understanding with respect to the first operation, which is its simple conception, and to this degree, the auditor, who was in suspense before the noun or verb was spoken and the saying of it completed, rests. But noun or verb taken just as such do not bring about an understanding with respect to the second operation, which is of the intellect composing and dividing, nor put the mind of the auditor at rest in this regard.

18. He immediately adds, 'But they do not as they stand yet express any judgement . . .' That is, they do not yet signify by way of composition and division, or express the true or false. This is the second thing he intends to prove. And he does so with those verbs which especially seem to signify truth or falsity, namely that verb which is to be, and the infinite verb which is not to be, neither of which taken by itself is significant of truth or falsity in the thing, hence so much less other verbs.

Or this could be understood as said generally of all verbs. For because he said that the verb does not signify whether the thing is or not, he manifests this, saying that no verb is significant of the existence or the non-existence of the thing, that is, says whether the thing is or is not. For although every finite verb implies existence, because to run is to be running, and every infinite verb implies non-existence, since not to run is not to be running, still no verb signifies this whole, namely that the thing is or is not.

19. Consequently he proves this by the verb which especially seems to do so when he adds, 'For neither are "to be" and "not to be" and the participle "being" significant of any fact.' It should be known that in Greek it is 'Not even if you should say bare being itself, for it is nothing.' To show that verbs do not signify that a thing is or is not, he assumes that which is the fount and origin of existence, namely being, of which he says that it is nothing (as Alexander explains), because being is said equivocally of the ten categories, but every equivocal taken by itself signifies nothing, unless something be added which determines its signification; hence not even 'is' itself taken as such signifies that it is or is not.

But this explanation does not seem to fit, both because being is not properly called equivocal, but rather is according to before and after, so that simply said it is understood of that of which it is primarily said, and also because an equivocal expression does not signify nothing but many things, and is sometimes taken for this, sometimes for that. Furthermore, this explanation is not very relevant to his present intention.

Porphyry explains it otherwise, saying that being itself does not signify the nature of anything, as the names 'man' or 'wise' do, but only designates some conjunction; hence he adds that it consignifies a composition, which cannot be understood without the things composed. But no more does this seem relevant, because if it did not signify some thing, but only a conjunction, it would be neither a noun nor a verb any more than prepositions and conjunctions are.

So it has to be explained differently, as Ammonius says. We are given the reason why 'being itself is nothing', that is, does not signify the true or false, when he adds, 'but it consignifies some composition'. Nor is consignify taken here, as he says, as it was when he said that the verb consignifies time, but it consignifies, that is, signifies with another, namely it signifies a composition joined to another, which cannot be understood without the extremes of the composition. But because this is common to both nouns and verbs, this explanation does not seem to be according to the intention of Aristotle, who takes being to be something special.

20. Therefore, the better to follow the words of Aristotle, consider that he said that the verb does not signify that the thing is or is not, and that being itself does not signify that the thing is or is not. And that is why he says, 'it is nothing', that is, it does not signify that something is. But this especially seemed to be the case with what I call being, because being is nothing other than that which is. Thus it seems to signify both the thing, by this that I say 'that which', and to be, by this that I say 'is'. And if this expression being were to signify existence principally, as it does signify the thing which has existence, without any doubt it would signify that something is. But it does not principally signify the composition that is implied in this that I say 'is', but it consignifies it insofar as it signifies the thing having existence. Hence such a consignification of composition does not suffice for truth or falsity, because the composition in which truth and falsity consists can be understood only as it joins the extremes of the composition.

21. But if it were said 'nor existence itself' as our books have it, the sense is more plain. For that no verb signifies that a thing is or is not, he proves through this verb 'is', which taken by itself does not signify that something is, although it signifies existence. And because this existence itself seems a composition, and thus this verb 'is' that signifies existence could be seen to signify the composition in which the true and false are, to exclude that he adds that that composition, which this verb 'is' signifies, cannot be understood without the components. Because the understanding of it depends on the extremes, which if they are not stated, the understanding of the composition is not complete, so that there might be in it the true or false.

22. Therefore, he says that this verb 'is' consignifies composition, because it does not principally signify it but as a consequence, for it first signifies that which comes into the intellect in the mode of actuality absolutely: for 'is', stated just as such, signifies to be actual, and therefore signifies in the manner of a verb. Because actuality, which this verb 'is' chiefly signifies, is commonly the actuality of every form, either substantial or accidental act, and that is why when we want to signify some form or

act actually to be in some subject, we signify it by this verb 'is', either simply or in a certain respect: simply, in the present tense, in a certain respect, in the other tenses. Therefore, this verb 'is' signifies composition as a consequence.

21. *On the Ultimate End.*
Summa theologiae, *1–2, 1–5*
(1271)

Perhaps nothing generates more surprise than Thomas's acceptance of Aristotle's account of the purpose of human life, the end for the sake of which everything we do is done. The surprise stems from the fact that for Aristotle the human good, happiness, is something achievable in this world by our own efforts. The acquisition of virtues ensures that singular acts will be easily and pleasantly directed to the true ultimate end of human life. A noble ideal and a remarkable achievement for a pagan philosopher. But Thomas Aquinas, as a Christian, held that humans are called to a higher, supernatural end, one to be enjoyed after this life and on the basis of virtues which are infused rather than acquired.

Obviously, of two rival concepts of the ultimate end of human life, one must be wrong. The ultimate end is taken to mean an absolutely sufficient good. If Aristotle taught that the happiness he analysed is man's sufficient good, obviously this would rule out anything like the Christian supernatural end.

Thomas, in the passage below, distinguishes between the notion of the ultimate end and that which is taken to realize the notion. He and Aristotle work with the same notion of ultimate end; their difference lies in what they think realizes it. But there is more. Thomas notes an Aristotelian demur about what is taken to be the realization of the notion of ultimate. The Philosopher seems to be saying that there is a gap between the ideal of happiness and what human beings actually can achieve in this life. It is this demur that enables Thomas to reconcile the philosophical and Christian understanding of human happiness. If Thomas is right, Aristotle is not maintaining that the happiness we can realize satisfies the criteria of ultimate end; rather he maintains that what he describes is the best we can do.

This enables Thomas to say that Aristotle has described an imperfect happiness, a realization of the ultimate end that is admittedly incomplete. Complementing this, Thomas argues, is the perfect realization of the ultimate end that is promised the believer in the next world.

Far from being an incoherent waffling between competing perfect

realizations of the ultimate end, Thomas puts before us two complemen-
tary analyses. Since the supernatural presupposes the natural and does
not destroy it, he sees this as a philosophical basis for the theological
analysis of man's true and supernatural happiness. Just what one would
expect.

Summa theologiae, First Part of the Second Part, Questions 1–5

PROLOGUE

Since man is made to the image of God, insofar as by image is meant having intellect and free will as well as being in possession of oneself, as Damascene explains, after we have spoken of the exemplar, namely God, and of what proceeds from the divine power according to his will, there remains for us to consider his image, that is, man, insofar as he is the principle of his own acts, as having free will and power over his acts.

The first thing to consider is the ultimate end of human life and then how it is that a man can arrive at this end, or deviate from it, for the reason of things which are for the sake of the end is drawn from the end. Because the ultimate end of human life is said to be happiness, we must first speak of the ultimate end in general, and then of happiness. There are eight things to be asked about the first: (1) whether man acts for the sake of an end; (2) whether this is proper to a rational nature; (3) whether a man's acts are specified by the end; (4) whether there is an ultimate end of human life; (5) whether one man can have several ultimate ends; (6) whether a man orders everything to the ultimate end; (7) whether there is the same ultimate end of all men; (8) whether all other creatures have that same ultimate end.

QUESTION I
ON MAN'S ULTIMATE END

Article 1: Does man act for the sake of an end?

It seems that he does not.

1. The cause is naturally prior, but the end has the note of the ultimate, as its very name suggests. Therefore, the end does not have the note of cause. But that for the sake of which a man acts is the cause of his action, since the prepositional phrase 'that for the sake of which', designates the relation of cause. Therefore, man does not act for the sake of an end.

2. Moreover, that which is the ultimate end is not for the sake of the end. But some actions are the ultimate end, as is clear from the Philosopher in *Ethics* 1.1. Therefore, not everything a man does is for the sake of an end.

3. Moreover, a man seems to act for an end when he deliberates, but a man does many things without deliberation, sometimes without any thought at all, as when he moves a hand or foot while intent on other things, or scratches his beard. Therefore, a man does not do everything for the sake of an end.

ON THE CONTRARY:

All the things in a genus depend on the principle of that genus. But the end is the principle in things done by man, as is clear from the Philosopher in *Physics* 2.9. Therefore, it belongs to a man to do everything for the sake of the end.

RESPONSE:

It should be said that of the actions that are done by a man, those alone are properly human which are proper to man insofar as he is a man. A man differs from irrational creatures in this, that he is the master of his acts. Hence only those actions are properly called human of which a man is master. But a man is master of his acts because of reason and will, hence free will is said to be a capacity of will and reason. Those acts are properly called human which proceed from deliberate will. If there are other acts which belong to a man, they can be called actions of a man, but not properly human, since they are not of man insofar as he is man. But it is manifest that all actions which proceed from a power are caused by it under the formality of its object. But the object of will is the end and good. Hence, all human actions must be for the sake of the end.

Ad 1. It should be said that the end, although it is last in execution, is first in the agent's intention, and in this way it has the note of cause.

Ad 2. It should be said that if any human action is the ultimate end it has to be voluntary, otherwise it would not be human, as has been said. But an action can be called voluntary in two ways. In one way, because it is commanded by the will, like walking and talking; in another way, because it is elicited from the will, such as willing. But it is impossible that the elicited act of the will be the ultimate end, for the object of the will is the end, as colour is the object of sight. Hence just as it is impossible that the first thing seen should be seeing itself, because seeing is always of some visible object, so it is impossible that the first desirable, which is the end, should be willing itself. So if any human action is the ultimate end, it must be one commanded by the will. Thus some human action, at least willing itself, is for the sake of the end. Therefore, whatever a man does, it may truly be said that he acts for the sake of the end, even when performing the act which is the ultimate end.

Ad 3. It should be said that such actions are not properly human, because they do not proceed from the deliberation of reason, which is the proper principle of human acts. Therefore, they have some imagined end, but not one set out by reason.

Article 2: Is acting for an end peculiar to rational nature?

It seems that it is.

1. Man, whose nature it is to act for an end, never acts for the sake of an unknown end. But there are many things which do not know the end, or which lack knowledge entirely, such as creatures without senses, or which do not grasp the formality of the end, such as brute animals. Therefore, it seems proper to the rational creature to act for the sake of an end.

2. Moreover, to act for the sake of an end is to order one's action to the end. But this is the work of reason. Therefore, it does belong to those things that lack reason.

3. Moreover, the good and end are the object of will. But the will is in reason, as is said in On the Soul 3.9. Therefore, to act for the sake of an end is proper to rational nature.

ON THE CONTRARY:

The Philosopher proves in *Physics* 2.5 that not only intellect but nature as well act for the sake of an end.

RESPONSE:

It should be said that it is necessary that all agents act for the sake of an end. In causes ordered among themselves, if the first is taken away, it is necessary that the others be taken away. But the first of all causes is the final cause. The reason for this is that matter does not attain form except as moved by an agent, for nothing reduces itself from potency to act. But the agent only moves by intending an end. For if the agent is not determined to some effect, it would not do this rather than that; in order for it to produce a definite effect, it must be determined to something certain, which has the note of end. This determination, which comes about in the rational agent through rational appetite, which is called the will, comes about in other things by natural inclination, which is called the natural appetite. However, it should be noted that a thing tends to the end by its own action or motion in two ways. In one way, as moving itself to the end, as man does; in another way, as moved to the end by another, as the arrow tends to a definite end because it is moved by the archer, who directs its action to the end.

Therefore, things that have reason move themselves to the end because they have dominion over their acts thanks to free will, which is a capacity of will and reason. Things that lack reason, tend to the end by natural inclination, as if moved by another, not themselves, since they do not grasp the notion of end and therefore can order nothing to an end, but are only ordered to an end by another. For the totality of irrational nature relates to God as an instrument relates to an agent principle, as was shown above.[1] Therefore, it is peculiar to rational nature to tend to the end as causing and moving itself to the end, whereas irrational nature tends to the end as caused or led by another, whether to a known end as with brute animals, or an end not known by them in the case of those which lack knowledge entirely.

Ad 1. It should be said that when a man acts by himself for the sake of an end he knows the end, but when he is caused or led by another, as when he acts on another's command or when he is moved forcibly by

1. Part 1, q. 22, art. 2, ad 4.

another, he need not know the end. And that is the way it is with irrational creatures.

Ad 2. It should be said that only the one who himself acts for an end can order to the end, whereas that which is moved to the end by another, is ordered to the end. The irrational creature can do the latter, but only as moved by someone having reason.

Ad 3. It should be said that the object of will is the end and good generally, so will cannot be found in things which lack reason and intellect, since they cannot grasp the universal, but have a natural or sensitive appetite determined to some particular good. But clearly particular causes are moved by a universal cause, much as the ruler of the city, who intends the common good, by his command guides all the particular functions of the city. Therefore, things that lack reason must be moved to their particular ends by some rational will, which extends itself to the universal good, that is, by the divine will.

Article 3: Are human acts specified by the end?

It seems that they are not.

1. The end is an extrinsic cause, but a thing is specified by some intrinsic principle. Therefore, human acts are not specified by the end.

2. Moreover, that which specifies should be prior, but the end is the last to be. Therefore, the human act is not specified by the end.

3. A thing can only be of one species. But numerically the same act can be ordered to different ends. Therefore, the end cannot specify human acts.

ON THE CONTRARY:

Augustine says in *On the Customs of the Church* and in *Against the Manicheans* that our deeds are worthy of praise or blame insofar as their ends are worthy of praise or blame.

RESPONSE:

It should be said that a thing is specified as actual not as potential, hence those things composed of matter and form are placed in their species because of their proper forms. The same thing can be seen in their proper motions. For motion can be distinguished into actions and passions, and both of these are specified by act, the action by the act which is the principle of acting, the passion by the act which is the term of the motion.

Hence, heating is a motion arising from heat and being heated is a movement towards heat. The definition makes clear the motion of the species.

In both ways, whether they be considered in the manner of action or of passion, human acts are specified by the end. Human acts can be considered in both ways because a man moves himself and is moved by himself. It was said above that acts are called human insofar as they proceed from deliberate will, but the object of will is the good and end. It is accordingly clear that the principle of human acts as human is the end. So too it is their term, for that in which the human act terminates is what the will intended as an end, much as in natural agents the form of the thing generated is like the form of the one generating. Ambrose says, in commenting on Luke, morals are properly said to be human. This is because moral acts are properly specified by their ends, for moral acts and human acts are the same.

Ad 1. It should be said that the end is not wholly extrinsic to the act, since it is related to the act as principle or term, and this is of the nature of the act, namely that it should be from something, as action, and to something, as passion.

Ad 2. It should be said that insofar as the end is first in intention, it pertains to the will, and in this way it specifies the human or moral act.

Ad 3. It should be said that numerically one action, once it emerges from the agent, is ordered to only one proximate end which specifies it, but it can be ordered to many remote ends, one of which is the end of the other. It is possible for specifically the same act to be ordered to different ends of the will, as to kill a man, which is of one natural species, can be ordered to the end of the preservation of justice or to the satisfying of anger. Consequently these will be different acts according to their moral species, since one is an act of virtue and the other of vice. A motion is not specified by an incidental term but only by the intended term. Moral ends are incidental to the natural thing; conversely, the natural end is incidental to the moral. Therefore, there is nothing to prevent those acts of the same natural species being in different moral species, and vice versa.

Article 4: Is there an ultimate end of human life?

It seems that there is an infinite regress of ends.

1. The good by reason of its nature is diffusive of itself, as is clear from Dionysius in *On the Divine Names* 4. Thus if that which comes from the good is good, that good must send forth another good, and thus there will be an infinite process of goods. But the good has the note of end. Therefore, there is not an infinite process of goods.

2. Moreover, things that are of reason can be infinitely multiplied, which is why mathematical quantities can be increased to infinity; the species of numbers are infinite too, because, given any number, one can always think of a greater. But the desire for the end follows on the grasp of reason. Therefore it seems that there can be an infinite process in ends as well.

3. Moreover, the good and end are the object of will, but the will can reflect infinitely on itself, for I can will something and will myself to will it and so on infinitely. Therefore, in the ends of the human will there can be a process to infinity, and there is no ultimate end of the human will.

ON THE CONTRARY:
The Philosopher says in *Metaphysics* 2.2 that an infinite process takes away the nature of the good. But the good has the note of end. Therefore, it is contrary to the notion of end that there should be an infinite process, so there must be an ultimate end.

RESPONSE:
It should be said that, speaking *per se*, it is impossible for there to be an infinity of ends on either side. For things which have an essential order to one another are such that take away the first, those ordered to the first must be taken away. In *Physics* 8.5 the Philosopher proves that there cannot be an infinite regress in moving causes since then there would not be a first mover, and take that away, the others cannot move since they only move insofar as they are moved by the prime mover. There is a twofold order in ends, namely the order of intention and the order of execution, and in each there must be a first. That which is first in the order of intention is a principle that moves because desired; hence, take it away and appetite is moved by nothing. That which is a principle in execution is that whence the activity begins; so take it away and nothing would begin to act.

The principle in intention is the ultimate end, the principle of execution is the first of the things which are for the sake of the end. Thus it is impossible on either side to proceed to infinity, because if there were no ultimate end, nothing would be desired, nor would any action terminate, nor would the intention of the agent come to rest; if there is not something first among the things which are for the sake of the end, no one would begin to do anything, nor would deliberation come to an end, but it would go on endlessly.

Nothing prevents things that do not have an essential order but are conjoined only incidentally from proceeding to infinity, for incidental causes are indeterminate. In this way there can be an incidental infinity of ends and of things which are for the sake of the end.

Ad 1. It should be said that it is of the nature of the good that something flow from it but not that it proceed from another. Therefore, since good has the note of end, and the first good is the ultimate end, this argument does not prove that there is no ultimate end but that, supposing a first end, there can be an infinite process downward in things for the sake of the end. And this would work if we took into account only the power of the first good, which is infinite. But because the diffusion of the first good is according to intellect, the mark of which is that it is according to a certain form that the good flows into the caused, a certain mode is attached to the flow of goods from the first good, by which all other goods participate in the diffusive power. Therefore, the diffusion of goods does not proceed to infinity, but as is said in Wisdom 11.21: 'Thou hast ordered all things in measure, and number, and weight.'

Ad 2. It should be said that in things that are *per se*, reason begins from principles naturally known by us and progresses to some term. Hence the Philosopher proves in *Posterior Analytics* 1.3 that there is no infinite regress in demonstrations because demonstrations involve things connected among themselves essentially and not incidentally. In things incidentally connected nothing stops reason from proceeding to infinity. It is incidental to any given number as such that one be added to it, which is why in such matters there is nothing to prevent reason from proceeding to infinity.

Ad 3. It should be said that that multiplying of acts of the will reflecting on itself is incidentally related to the order of ends, which is clear from this that it is one and the same end that is taken once or many times as will reflects on itself.

Article 5: Can a man have several ultimate ends?

It seems that he can.

1. Augustine says in the *City of God* 19.1 that some posited the ultimate end of man in four things: namely in pleasure, in rest, in the first things of nature, and in virtue. These are clearly plural. Therefore, a man can fix the ultimate end of his will in many things.

2. Moreover, things that are not opposed to one another do not exclude one another. But there are many things that are not opposed to one another. Therefore, if one is taken as the ultimate end of the will, other things are not excluded by that fact.

3. Moreover, the will does not set aside its free power by the fact that it takes something for its ultimate end. But before it placed its ultimate end in that, for example in pleasure, it was able to take something else for its ultimate end, for example riches. So too later, when it takes pleasure for its ultimate end, it can at the same time take riches for its ultimate end. Therefore, it is possible for the will of the same man to bear on different ultimate ends at the same time.

ON THE CONTRARY:
That in which one rests as in the ultimate end dominates a man's affections, since the whole rule of his life is taken from it. Hence it is said of gluttons in Philippians 3.19, 'whose god is their belly', because they take the delights of the stomach as their ultimate end. But it is said in Matthew 6.24, 'No one can serve two masters', that is, not ordered to one another. Therefore, it is impossible for there to be many ultimate ends of the same man unless they are ordered to one another.

RESPONSE:
It should be said that it is impossible for the will of one man to relate to different things as to ultimate ends. Three reasons can be given for this. First, since every thing desires its own perfection, it desires as its ultimate end that which it desires as its perfect good, of itself fulfilling. Hence Augustine says in the *City of God* 19.1 we now call the end or good not what is consumed and is no more but that which perfects so that it might be full. Therefore, the ultimate end must so fulfil the whole of man's desire that there is nothing further left to desire outside it. This would be impossible if something extraneous to it were needed for its perfection.

Hence there cannot be two things towards which appetite would tend as if both were the good perfective of it.

The second argument is this. In the process of reason the principle is that which is naturally known, and so too in the process of rational appetite or will there must be a principle that is naturally desired. But this must be one, because nature only tends to one. But the principle in the process of rational appetite is the ultimate end. So that towards which will tends under the formality of ultimate end must be one.

The third argument is this. Since voluntary actions are specified by the end, as has been shown, the ultimate end, which is common, must have the note of a genus, as natural things are placed in a genus according to their common formal notion. Therefore, since all things desirable by will, as such, are of one genus, the ultimate end must be one. Especially because in any genus there is a first principle, and the ultimate end has the note of first principle, as has been said. As the ultimate end of man simply relates to the whole human race, so does the ultimate end of this man relate to him. Hence, just as there must naturally be one ultimate end of all men, so the will of this man must be placed in one ultimate end.

Ad 1. It should be said that all those many things are included in the notion of one perfect good constituted of them, by those who put the ultimate end in these.

Ad 2. It should be said that although many things can be taken which are not opposed to one another, that there be something of perfection outside it is opposed to the perfect good.

Ad 3. It should be said that the power of the will is not such that it might make opposites to be at the same time, which could happen if it tended towards many disparate things as ultimate ends, as is clear from what has been said.

Article 6: Does a man will everything for the sake of the ultimate end?

It seems that he does not.

1. Those things which are ordered to the ultimate end are called serious, because useful. But the frivolous is distinguished from the serious. Therefore, the things that a man frivolously does are not ordered to the ultimate end.

2. Moreover, the Philosopher says at the beginning of the *Metaphysics* 1.2 that speculative sciences are sought for their own sake. But it cannot

be said that each of them is the ultimate end. Therefore not everything that a man desires does he desire for the sake of the ultimate end.

3. Moreover, whoever orders something to an end, thinks about that end. But a man does not always think of the ultimate end in every thing he desires or does. Therefore, a man does not desire or do everything for the sake of the ultimate end.

ON THE CONTRARY:

Augustine says in the *City of God* 19.1 that that for the sake of which other things are loved but is itself loved for its own sake is the end of our good.

RESPONSE:

It ought to be said that it is necessary that whatever a man seeks, he seek for the sake of the ultimate end. Two arguments make this clear. First, because whatever a man desires, he desires under the formality of the good, and if it is not desired as the perfect good, which is the ultimate end, it must be desired as tending to the perfect good, because the beginning of something is always ordered to its fulfilment, which is through the ultimate end. Second, because the ultimate end is to moving the appetite as the first mover is to other motions. It is manifest that secondary moving causes move only insofar as they are moved by the first mover. Hence the secondary desirables do not move appetite except as ordered to the first desirable, which is the ultimate end.

Ad 1. It should be said that playful actions are not ordered to any extrinsic end, but are ordered to the good of the player himself insofar as they delight or afford rest. But the fulfilled good of man is his ultimate end.

Ad 2. It should be said, concerning speculative science which is sought as the good of the knower, that it is comprehended in the complete and perfect good, which is the ultimate end.

Ad 3. It should be said that one need not always think of the ultimate end whenever he desires or does something, but the force of the first intention, which looks to the ultimate end, remains in the desire of anything whatsoever, even if the ultimate end is not actually thought of. No more does one who is on a journey have to think at every step of his destination.

Article 7: Is there the same ultimate end for all men?

It seems that there is not.

1. Man's ultimate end seems to be above all an unchanging good. But some turn away from the unchanging good by sinning. Therefore, there is not the same ultimate end for all men.

2. Moreover, a man's life is regulated with respect to the ultimate end. Therefore, if there were the same ultimate end of all men, it would follow that there would not be different manners of living among men, which is evidently false.

3. Moreover, the end is the term of action, and actions are of singulars. But men, although they share the nature of a species, differ with respect to what pertains to individuals. Therefore, there is not the same ultimate end for all men.

ON THE CONTRARY:
Augustine says in *On the Trinity* 13.3 that all men are alike in seeking the ultimate end, which is happiness.

RESPONSE:
It should be said that we can speak of the ultimate end in two ways. In one way, according to the notion of ultimate end, in another way, according to that in which the notion of ultimate end is realized. With respect to the notion of ultimate end, all agree in the desire of the ultimate end, because every one seeks to fulfil his own perfection, which is the notion of the ultimate end, as has been said. But with respect to that in which this notion is realized, all men do not agree on the ultimate end, for some seek riches as the complete end, others pleasure, and others something else, just as the sweet is delightful to taste, yet for some it is the sweetness of wine that is most delightful, while for others it is the sweetness of honey, or of something else. But that sweet must be simply more delightful in which those of good taste take most delight. Similarly, that good is most complete which those having a well disposed appetite seek as the ultimate end.

Ad 1. It should be said that those who sin turn away from that in which the notion of ultimate end is truly found, but not from the intention of the ultimate end, which they falsely seek in other things.

Ad 2. It should be said that different ways of living come about among men because of the different things in which the notion of ultimate end is sought.

Ad 3. It should be said that, although actions are of singulars, still the first principle of acting in them is nature, which tends to one, as has been said.

Article 8: Do all other things share this same ultimate end?

It seems that they do.

1. The end answers to the beginning. But he who is the principle of men, namely, God, is also the principle of everything else. Therefore, all other things share in man's ultimate end.

2. Moreover, Dionysius says in *On the Divine Names* 4 that God converts all things to himself as to the ultimate end. But he is also the ultimate end of man, because he alone is to be enjoyed, as Augustine says. Therefore, other things share man's ultimate end.

3. Moreover, the ultimate end of man is the object of will, but the object of will is the universal good, which is the end of all. Therefore, it is necessary that all things share in man's ultimate end.

ON THE CONTRARY:
Man's ultimate end is happiness, which we all desire, as Augustine says. But animals devoid of reason cannot be happy, as Augustine says in the *Eighty-three Questions* 5. Therefore, other things do not share in man's ultimate end.

RESPONSE:
It should be said that, as the Philosopher says in *Physics* 2.2 and in *On the Soul* 2.4, the end is understood in two ways, namely *of which* [*cuius*] and *for what* [*quo*], that is, the thing in which the formality of good is found, and the use or attainment of that thing. For just as we say that the end of the motion of the heavy body is either the lower place as the thing, or to be in the lower place, as use, so we say that the end of the miser is either money as the thing or possession of the money as use.

Therefore, if we speak of the ultimate end of man with respect to the thing which is the end, then all other things share in the ultimate end of man, because God is the ultimate end of man and of all other things. But if we speak of the ultimate end of man with respect to the attainment of the end, then irrational creatures do not share that end. For man and ational creatures pursue the ultimate end by knowing and loving ..., and other creatures cannot do this, but they attain the ultimate end insofar as they participate in some similitude of God, insofar as they exist, live or even know.

The responses to the objections are evident from this.

QUESTION 2

Next we must consider happiness, for happiness means the attainment of the ultimate end. First, what it consists of; second, what it is; third, how we can attain it. Eight things are asked about the first: (1) whether happiness consists of riches; (2) whether of honours; (3) whether of fame or glory; (4) whether of power; (5) whether in any good of the body; (6) whether of lust; (7) whether of any good of the soul; (8) whether of any created good.

Article 1: Does man's happiness consist of riches?

It seems that it does.

1. Since happiness is man's ultimate end, it will especially consist of that which dominates man's desire. But such are riches, for it is said in Ecclesiastes 10.19, 'For all things obey money.' Therefore man's happiness consists of riches.

2. Moreover, according to Boethius in the *Consolation of Philosophy* 3.2, happiness is the state perfected by the aggregation of all goods. But it seems that all things can be had for money, because, as the Philosopher says in *Ethics* 10, money was invented so that it might be taken in trust for whatever a man wishes to have. Therefore happiness consists of riches.

3. Moreover, the desire for the highest good, since it never fails, seems to be infinite. But this is found especially in riches, because, as is said in Ecclesiastes 5.9, 'A covetous man shall not be satisfied with money.' Therefore happiness consists of riches.

ON THE CONTRARY:

The good of man consists in retaining happiness rather than in losing it. But, as Boethius says in the *Consolation of Philosophy* 2.5, 'They seek to spend rather than amass money, because avarice always makes men odious while liberality makes them renowned.' Therefore happiness does not consist of riches.

RESPONSE:
It should be said that it is impossible that man's happiness should consist of riches. For there are two kinds of riches, as the Philosopher says in *Politics* 1.3, namely natural and artificial. Natural riches are those that enable a man to bear his natural defects, such as food, drink, clothing, a mount, a house and the like. But artificial riches are those whereby nature is not helped, such as money, but human art fashions them for the facility of exchange, that it might be the measure of things to be sold.

But it is manifest that human happiness does not consist of natural riches, for these are sought for something else, namely to sustain the life of man and so they cannot be the ultimate end of man but are rather ordered to man as their end. Hence in the order of nature all such things are below man and made for man according to Psalm 8.7: 'Thou hast put all things under his feet.'

Artificial riches are sought only for the sake of natural riches, for they are only sought in order that with them things necessary for life can be bought. Hence much less do they have the note of ultimate end and it is impossible that happiness, which is man's ultimate end, should consist of riches.

Ad 1. It should be said, therefore, that all bodily things obey money in the view of the mob of stupid men who recognize only bodily goods that can be got with money. But the judgement of human goods ought not to be taken from the stupid, but from the wise, just as judgement about taste is taken from those whose tongue is well disposed.

Ad 2. It should be said that all buyable things can be had with money, but not spiritual things which are not for sale. Hence it is said in Proverbs 17.16, 'What does it avail a fool to have riches, seeing he cannot buy wisdom?'

Ad 3. It should be said that the appetite for natural riches is not infinite, because they suffice according to a certain measure of nature. But the appetite for artificial riches is infinite, because it serves inordinate concupiscence which is not modified, as is evident from the Philosopher in *Politics* 1.3. The desire for riches is infinite in a different way than the desire for the highest good, for the more perfectly the highest good is possessed the more it is loved and other things contemned because the more it is had, the more it is known. Therefore it is said in Ecclesiasticus 24.29, 'They that eat me shall yet hunger.' But in the appetite for riches and any other temporal goods it is the reverse, for once they are had, they are contemned and other things desired, in keeping with what is said in John 4.13: 'Everyone who drinks of this water [which signifies temporal things] will thirst again.' This is so because their insufficiency is known better when they are had. But this reveals their imperfection and that the highest good does not consist of them.

Article 2: Does man's happiness consist of honours?

It seems that it does.

1. For happiness or felicity is the reward of virtue, as the Philosopher says in *Ethics* 1.9. But honour seems especially to be the reward for virtue, as the Philosopher says in *Ethics* 4.3. Therefore, happiness consists especially of honour.

2. Moreover, that which belongs most excellently to God, would seem especially to be happiness, which is the perfect good. But such is honour, as the Philosopher says in *Ethics* 4.3, and the Apostle too in 1 Timothy 1.17: 'To God alone be honour and glory.' Therefore happiness consists of honour.

3. Moreover, that which is most desired by men is happiness, but nothing seems more desirable to men than honour, because men suffer loss of all other things lest there be some detriment to their honour. Therefore happiness consists of honour.

ON THE CONTRARY:

Happiness is in the happy person. But honour is not in the one who is honoured, but rather in the bestower of it, who shows reverence to the honoured, as the Philosopher says in *Ethics* 1.5. Therefore, happiness does not consist of honour.

RESPONSE:

It should be said that it is impossible for happiness to consist of honour, for honour is shown to someone because of some excellence of his, and thus is a sign and testimony of the excellence that is in the one honoured. But man's excellence is especially looked for in happiness, which is his perfect good, and according to its parts, that is, according to the goods which participate in something of happiness. Therefore, honour can indeed follow on happiness, but it cannot consist of it principally.

Ad 1. It should be said that the Philosopher says the same, for honour is not the reward of virtue for the sake of which the virtuous act; rather they accept honour from men in place of a reward, as from those having nothing better to offer. But happiness itself is the true reward of virtue, for the sake of which the virtuous act. But if they acted for the sake of honour, this would not be virtue but rather ambition.

Ad 2. It should be said that honour is owed to God and to the most excellent as a sign or testimony of a pre-existent excellence, not as if honour made them excellent.

Ad 3. It should be said that out of a natural desire for happiness, on which honour follows, as has been said, it happens that men especially desire honour. Hence men seek to be honoured especially by the wise, by whose judgement they think themselves to be excellent or happy.

Article 3: Does man's happiness consist of fame or glory?

It seems that it does.

1. For happiness seems to consist in what is given the saints because of the tribulations they suffer in this life. But this is glory, for the Apostle says in Romans 8.18, 'For I reckon that the sufferings of the present time are not worthy to be compared with the glory to come that will be revealed in us.' Therefore, happiness consists of glory.

2. Moreover, the good is diffusive of itself, as is clear from Dionysius in *On the Divine Names* 4. But by glory the good of man is especially made known to others, because glory, as Ambrose says, is nothing other than full knowledge with praise. Therefore man's happiness consists of glory.

3. Moreover, happiness is the most stable of goods. But fame and glory seem to be such, because through them men share in eternity in a way. Hence Boethius says in the *Consolation of Philosophy* 2.7, 'But you imagine that you make yourselves immortal when you cast your eyes upon future fame.' Therefore man's happiness consists in fame or glory.

ON THE CONTRARY:

Happiness is man's true good, but fame or glory can be false, as Boethius also says in the *Consolation of Philosophy* 3.6: 'For many have often been much spoken of through the false opinions of the common people. Than which what can be imagined more vile? For those who are falsely commended must needs blush at their own praises.' Therefore man's happiness does not consist of fame or glory.

RESPONSE:
It should be said that it is impossible for man's happiness to consist of fame or glory, for glory is nothing other than full knowledge with praise, as Ambrose says. But the thing known compares in one way to human knowledge and in another to divine, for human knowledge is caused by things, but divine knowledge is the cause of the things known. Hence the perfection of the human good, which is called happiness, cannot be caused by human knowledge, but rather human knowledge proceeds from someone's happiness and is in a way caused by human happiness itself, whether inchoate or perfect. Therefore human happiness cannot consist of fame or glory. But the good of man depends on God's knowledge as on its cause. Therefore man's happiness depends, as on its cause, on the glory that is with God, according to Psalm 90.15–16: 'I will rescue him and honour him. I will fill him with length of days and I will show him my salvation.' Another thing too should be considered, namely that human knowledge is often deceived, especially in singular contingents such as human acts. Therefore, human glory is often deceptive. But because God cannot be deceived, his glory is always true, and for this reason it is said in 2 Corinthians 10.18, 'For he is not approved who commends himself, but he whom the Lord commends.'

Ad 1. It should be said that the Apostle does not speak there of the glory which is from men, but of the glory which is from God before his angels. Hence it is said in Mark 8.38, 'Of him the Son of Man will also be ashamed when he comes with the holy angels in the glory of his Father.'

Ad 2. It should be said that the good of a man which comes from fame or glory is in the knowledge of many. If indeed the knowledge is true, it must derive from the good existing in that man, and thus it presupposes perfect or inchoate happiness; but if it is false it is not in accord with reality and thus good is not found in the one whose fame is celebrated. Hence it is clear that fame in no way can make a man happy.

Ad 3. It should be said that fame has no stability; indeed, by false rumour it is easily lost. And if for a time it remains stable, this is incidental. But happiness has stability of itself and always.

Article 4: Does man's happiness consist of power?

It seems that it does.

1. All things seek to be assimilated to God as to their ultimate end and first principle. But men in positions of power, because power is a similitude, seem most conformed to God. Hence in Scripture they are called gods, as is evident in Exodus 22.28: 'Thou shalt not speak ill of the gods, and the prince of thy people thou shalt not curse.' Therefore, happiness consists in power.

2. Moreover, happiness is the perfect good. But the most perfect man is one who can also govern others, which belongs to those constituted in power. Therefore, happiness consists in power.

3. Moreover, happiness, since it is most desirable, is opposed to that which is most to be fled. But men especially flee servitude, to which power is contraposed. Therefore happiness consists in power.

ON THE CONTRARY:

Happiness is the perfect good. But power is most imperfect. For, as Boethius says in the *Consolation of Philosophy* 3.5, 'What power is this, then, which cannot expel nor avoid biting cares and pricking fears?' And later: 'Thinketh thou him mighty who dareth not go without his guard, who feareth others more than they fear him?'

RESPONSE:

It should be said that it is impossible for happiness to consist of power, for two reasons. First, because power has the note of a beginning, as is evident in *Metaphysics* 5.12. But happiness has the note of the ultimate end. Second, because power is related to good and evil, but happiness is man's perfect and proper good. Hence some happiness might consist of the good use of power, which is through virtue, not in power itself.

Four general reasons can be brought forward to show that human happiness cannot consist in any of the foregoing external goods. Of which the first is that since happiness is man's highest good, no evil is compatible with it. But all the foregoing can be found in goods and evils. The second reason is that since it is of the definition of happiness that it be sufficient unto itself, as is evident in *Ethics* 1.7, it is necessary that, happiness being attained, no good necessary for man is absent from it. But those who achieve any of the foregoing can still lack many goods necessary for man, for example wisdom, health of body, and the like. Third, because since

\ess is a perfect good, through it no evil can come to anyone, and that
\ue true of the foregoing, for it is said in Ecclesiastes 5.12, 'Riches kept
to the hurt of their owner.' And the same is so with the other three. The
fourth reason is that man is ordered to happiness by internal principles and
for the most part by fortune, hence they are called the goods of fortune.
Hence it is evident that happiness can in no way consist in the foregoing.

Ad 1. It should be said that the divine power is his goodness, hence he
can only use his power well. But this is not so with men. Hence it does
not suffice for man's happiness that he be assimilated to God with respect
to power, unless he is also assimilated to him with respect to goodness.

Ad 2. It should be said that, as it is best that one use power well in the
governance of others, so it is worst if he uses it badly. And thus power
is related to both good and evil.

Ad 3. It should be said that servitude is an impediment to the good use
of power, and therefore men naturally flee it, and not as if the highest
good is in the power of man.

Article 5: Does man's happiness consist of some bodily good?

It seems that it does.

1. It seems that man's happiness consists of goods of the body. For it
is said in Ecclesiasticus 30.16, 'There are no riches above the riches of
the health of the body.' But happiness consists in that which is best.
Therefore it consists of the health of the body.

2. Moreover, Dionysius says in *On the Divine Names* 5 that to exist is
better than to live and to live better than the other things which follow
on it. But health of body is required for man's existence and life. Therefore
since happiness is man's highest good, it seems that health of body
especially pertains to happiness.

3. Moreover, the more common a thing is the more it depends on a
higher principle, because the higher a cause the more widely its power
extends. But just as the causality of the efficient cause is considered
according to its influence, so the causality of the end is gauged according
to appetite. Therefore just as the first efficient cause is that which acts
on all things, so the ultimate end is that which is desired by all. But
existence itself is the chief thing desired by all. Therefore man's happiness
is especially to consist in the things that pertain to his existence, such as
health of body.

ON THE CONTRARY:

Man excels all other animals in happiness. But many animals excel him in goods of the body, as the elephant in length of life and the lion in bravery and the stag in running. Therefore man's happiness does not consist of goods of the body.

RESPONSE:

It should be said that it is impossible that man's happiness should consist of goods of the body, for two reasons. First, because it is impossible that the ultimate end be the conservation in existence of something that is ordered to it. Hence the captain does not intend, as his ultimate end, the preservation of the ship assigned to him because the ship is ordered to something else as to its end, namely to navigation. Just as the ship is committed to the captain that navigates it, so man is committed to his will and reason, according to Ecclesiasticus 15.14: 'God made man from the beginning and left him in the hand of his own counsel.' But it is manifest that man is ordered to something as to an end, for man is not the highest good. Hence it is impossible that the ultimate end of human reason and will should be the preservation of human existence. Second, because, even given that the end of human reason and will were the preservation of human existence, the end of man could not be said to be a good of body. For human existence consists of body and soul, and although the existence of body depends on soul, the existence of the human soul does not depend on body, as has been shown above; the body itself is for the sake of soul, as matter is for the sake of form, and the instrument for the sake of the mover, in order that through it it might exercise its actions. Hence all the goods of the body are ordered to the goods of the soul as to their end. Hence it is impossible that happiness, which is the ultimate end, should be found in the goods of the body.

Ad 1. It should be said that, just as body is ordered to soul as to its end, so the external goods are ordered to body. Therefore the good of the body is reasonably preferred to the external goods, which are signified by 'riches', just as the goods of soul are preferred to all the goods of body.

Ad 2. It should be said that existence taken simply insofar as it includes in itself every perfection of existing, is more eminent than life and all subsequent things, for thus existence itself has in it all the subsequent [perfections] and this is how Dionysius speaks. But if existence be considered insofar as it is participated in by this thing or that, which does not receive the full perfection of existing but has imperfect existence – something true of the existence of any creature – then it is manifest that existence with a superadded perfection is more eminent. Hence Dionysius says that the living are better than the existing, and the understanding than the living.

Ad 3. It should be said that because the end answers to the beginning, that argument proves that the ultimate end is the first principle of existing, in which there is every perfection of existing, whose similitude men seek according to their proportion, some according to existence alone, others according to living existence, yet others according to living and understanding and happy existence. And this is of the few.

Article 6: Does man's happiness consist of pleasure?

It seems that it does.

1. Happiness, since it is the ultimate end, is not sought for the sake of something else, but other things are sought for its sake. But this is especially the case with pleasure, for it is ridiculous to ask someone why he wants to feel pleasure, as is said in *Ethics* 10.2. Therefore, happiness consists in delight and pleasure.

2. Moreover, the first cause impresses itself more vehemently than the second, as is said in the *Book of Causes* 1. But the influence of the end is seen in the appetite for it. Therefore that which most moves appetite seems to have the note of ultimate end. And this is pleasure, a sign of which is that pleasure can so absorb a man's reason and will that it causes him to disdain other goods. Therefore it seems that man's ultimate end, which is happiness, consists especially of pleasure.

3. Moreover, since appetite is for the good, that which all things desire seems to be best. But all desire pleasure, both the wise and the foolish, and even things lacking reason. Therefore pleasure is best and happiness which is the highest good consists of pleasure.

ON THE CONTRARY:

Boethius says in the *Consolation of Philosophy* 3.7, 'I know not what sweetness their beginnings have, but whosoever will remember his lusts shall understand that the end of pleasure is sadness. Which if it be able to cause happiness, there is no reason why beasts should not be thought blessed.'

RESPONSE:
It should be said that because bodily pleasures are known by many, the term 'pleasure' is appropriated to them, as is said in *Ethics* 7.13. But there are other stronger pleasures in which happiness does not consist. In each thing what pertains to its essence is other than what belongs to it incidentally, as in man to be a rational mortal animal is one thing, and to be risible another. Therefore it must be recognized that every pleasure is some proper accident that follows on happiness, or on some part of happiness, because one delights in having a good that befits him, whether present, hoped for or remembered. The fitting good, if it is perfect, is the very happiness of man, but if it is imperfect it is a participation in happiness, whether proximate or remote or at least apparent. Hence it is manifest that not even the pleasure that follows on perfect happiness is the very essence of happiness, but is rather a *per se* accident following on it. Bodily pleasure cannot even in that way follow on the perfect good. For it follows on the good grasped by sense, which is a power of soul using the body. But the good that pertains to body, which is grasped by sense, cannot be the perfect good of man. For since the rational soul exceeds the proportion of bodily matter, the part of the soul which is free from any bodily organ has a kind of infinity with respect to body and the parts of soul concretized in body, just as immaterial things are in a certain way infinite with respect to the material because form is, as it were, contracted and limited by matter. Therefore sense, which is a bodily power, knows the singular which is determinate because of matter, whereas intellect, which is a power free of matter, knows the universal which is abstracted from matter and contains under itself an infinity of singulars. Hence it is evident that the good befitting body which, when grasped by sense, causes bodily pleasure, is not the perfect good of man, but is least in comparison to the good of soul. Hence Wisdom 7.9 says that 'all gold in comparison to her is as a little sand'. So bodily pleasure is neither happiness itself nor a property of it.

Ad 1. It should be said that the reason for pursuing the good and for pursuing pleasure is the same, which is nothing other than that the appetite might come to rest in the good. So too it is by the same natural power that the heavy is borne downward and rests there when it arrives. Hence just as the good is sought for its own sake, so too pleasure is not sought for the sake of something else, if 'for the sake of' means final cause. If it means formal cause, or rather efficient, then pleasure is desirable for something else, that is, for the good which is the object of pleasure, and

...sequently the principle that gives it form. Pleasure is desirable because it is repose in the good desired.

Ad 2. It should be said that the vehement desire for sensible pleasure happens because the operations of the senses, which are principles of our knowledge, are more perceptible. And that is why most people desire sense pleasure.

Ad 3. It should be said that things desire pleasure in the same way they desire the good, but they desire pleasure because of the good and not vice versa, as has been said. Hence it does not follow that pleasure is the greatest good as such, but that every pleasure follows on some good, and that some pleasure follows on that which is the greatest good and good of itself.

Article 7: Does man's happiness consist in some good of the soul?

It seems that it does.

1. Happiness is a good of man, but of this there are three kinds: external goods, goods of the body and goods of the soul. But happiness does not consist of external goods, nor in goods of the body, as has been shown above; therefore, it consists of goods of the soul.

2. Moreover, we love the one for the sake of whom we desire some good more than we love that good, just as we love the friend for whom we seek money more than the money. But everyone loves the good for himself. Therefore he loves himself more than all other goods. But happiness is especially loved, which is evident from this that all other things are loved and desired for its sake. Therefore happiness consists of some good of man himself, but not in goods of the body; therefore, in goods of the soul.

3. Moreover, perfection is something of the thing perfected. But happiness is a perfection of man, therefore happiness is something of man. But it is not something of body, as has been shown. Therefore happiness is something of soul and thus consists of goods of the soul.

ON THE CONTRARY:
As Augustine says in *On Christian Doctrine*, that in which the happy life consists ought to be loved for its own sake. But man is not loved for himself, since whatever is in man should be loved for the sake of God. Therefore, happiness does not consist in a good of the soul.

RESPONSE:

It should be replied that, as was said above, by end can be meant two things: either the thing itself that we desire to have, or the use and possession of the thing. Therefore if we speak of the ultimate end of man with respect to the thing itself that we love as the ultimate end, it is impossible that the ultimate end be the soul itself or anything of it. For the soul considered in itself is, as it were, existing in potentiality, for it comes to be actually knowing from potentially knowing, and from being potentially virtuous comes to be actually virtuous. But since potency is for the sake of act as its completion, it is impossible that that which is in itself existing in potency, should have the note of ultimate end. Hence it is impossible that the soul be the ultimate end of itself. Similarly too, nothing of it, whether it be a power or habit or act. For the good that is the ultimate end is the perfect good completing the appetite. The human appetite, which is will, is of the universal good. But any good inhering in the soul is a participated good and consequently particular. Hence it is impossible that one of these should be the ultimate end of man. But if we speak of the ultimate end of man with respect to pursuit or possession, or to any use of the thing that is desired as end, then something of man from the side of soul belongs to ultimate end, because man achieves happiness through his soul. Therefore, what is itself desired as end is that in which happiness consists and that makes one happy, but it is the having of the thing that is called happiness. Hence it should be said that happiness is something of soul although that in which happiness consists is something outside the soul.

Ad 1. It should be said that insofar as all the goods desirable by man are comprehended under this division, the good of the soul is not only called power or habit or act, but also object, which is extrinsic. And in this way, nothing prevents our saying that that of which happiness consists is some good of the soul.

Ad 2. It should be said that so far as the proposition goes, happiness is most loved as the good that is desired, but a friend is loved as the one for whom the good is desired, and thus a man also loves himself. Hence there is not the same reason for love in the two cases. However, whether a man loves something above himself by love of friendship will be considered when we get to charity.

Ad 3. It should be said that happiness itself, since it is a perfection of soul, is some good inhering in the soul, but that in which happiness consists, which makes one happy, is something outside the soul, as has been said.

Article 8: Does man's happiness consist of any created good?

It seems that it does.

1. Dionysius says in *On the Divine Names* 7 that divine wisdom conjoins the end of the first with the beginning of the second, from which we gather that the highest of the lower nature touches the lowest of the higher nature. But happiness is man's highest good. Therefore since in the natural order the angel is above man, as was shown in Part 1, it seems that man's happiness consists in this that he in some way attains the angelic.

2. Moreover, the ultimate end of anything lies in its perfected state, hence the part is for the sake of the whole as for its end. But the whole created universe, which is called the greater world, is compared to man, who in *Physics* 7.2 is called the lesser world, as the perfect to the imperfect. Therefore man's happiness consists in the whole created universe.

3. Moreover, a man is made happy when his natural desire comes to rest. But man's natural desire does not extend to a good greater than he can grasp. Therefore, since man is not capable of a good which exceeds the limits of the whole of creation, it seems that man can be made happy by some created good. So man's happiness consists in some created good.

ON THE CONTRARY:

Augustine says in the *City of God* 19.26 that as soul is the life of the flesh, so God is man's blessed life, of whom in Psalm 143.15 it is said, 'Blessed the people whose Lord is its God.'

RESPONSE:

It should be said that it is impossible that man's happiness should lie in any created good. For happiness is the perfect good which totally assuages the appetite since if there were anything remaining to be desired it would not be the ultimate end. But the object of will, which is the human appetite, is the universal good, as the object of intellect is the universal true. From which it is clear that nothing can quiet the appetite of man except the universal good. This is not found in any created thing but only in God because every creature has a participated goodness. Hence God alone can fulfil the will of man. As is said in Psalm 102.5, 'Who fills thy life with good things: thy youth is renewed like the eagle's.'

Ad 1. It should be said that the highest in man indeed attains what is least in angelic nature by a kind of similitude, but it does not rest there as in its ultimate end, but proceeds beyond to the universal fount of the good, which is the universal object of the happiness of all the blessed, existing as infinite and perfect good.

Ad 2. It should be said that if some whole is not the ultimate end, but is ordered to a further end, the ultimate end of the part is not the whole itself, but something else. The universe of creatures, to which man is compared as part to whole, is not the ultimate end, but is ordered to God as to its ultimate end. Hence the good of the universe is not man's ultimate end, but God himself.

Ad 3. It should be said that created good is not less than the good of which man is capable as of the intrinsic and inherent, but it is less than the good of which he is capable as object, which is infinite. But the good as participated in by the angel, and by the whole universe, is a finite and restricted good.

QUESTION 3
WHAT IS HAPPINESS?

Next we must consider what happiness is and what things are required for it. Eight questions are raised with respect to the first consideration: (1) whether happiness is something uncreated; (2) if created, is it an activity? (3) whether it is an activity of the sensitive part or of the intellectual part alone; (4) if it is an activity of the intellectual part, whether it is an activity of intellect or of will; (5) if it is an activity of intellect, whether it is an activity of speculative or of practical intellect; (6) if it is an activity of speculative intellect, whether it consists of the speculation of the theoretical sciences; (7) whether it consists in speculative knowledge of separate substances, that is, angels; (8) whether it lies only in speculative knowledge of God whereby he is seen in his essence.

Article 1: Is happiness something uncreated?

It seems that it is.

1. Boethius writes in the *Consolation of Philosophy* 3.10 that, 'It must be confessed that God is happiness itself.'

2. Moreover, happiness is the highest good. But to be the highest good is proper to God. Since then there are not several highest goods, it seems that happiness is God himself.

3. Moreover, happiness is the ultimate end towards which the human will naturally tends. But the will ought not to tend towards anything other than God as ultimate end, who alone is to be enjoyed, as Augustine says. Therefore, happiness is the same as God.

ON THE CONTRARY:
Nothing made is uncreated, but human happiness is something made, because according to Augustine in *On Christian Doctrine* 1.3 those things are to be enjoyed that make us happy. Therefore, happiness is not something uncreated.

RESPONSE:
It should be said that, as was pointed out earlier, the end is taken in two ways. In one way, as the thing itself that we wish to attain, as money is the end of the miser. In another way, as the attainment or possession, whether use or enjoyment, of the thing desired; for example, possession of money is said to be the miser's end, and the enjoyment of the coveted one the end of the intemperate. Therefore, in the first sense, the ultimate end of man is an uncreated good, namely God, who alone in his infinite goodness can perfectly fulfil the will of man. But in the second sense, the ultimate end of man is something created and existing in himself, which is nothing other than the attainment or enjoyment of the ultimate end. The ultimate end is called happiness. Therefore, if man's happiness is considered with respect to its cause or object, then it is something uncreated; but if it is considered with respect to the essence of happiness, then it is something created.

Ad 1. It should be said that God is happiness in his essence, for he is not happy by attainment or participation in something else, but by his own essence. But men are happy, as Boethius says in the same place, by participation, just as they are called gods by participation. The participation itself of happiness, thanks to which man is called happy, is something created.

Ad 2. It should be said that happiness is said to be the highest good of man because it is the attainment and enjoyment of the highest good.

Ad 3. It should be said that happiness is called the ultimate end in the sense that the attainment of the end is called the end.

Article 2: Is happiness an activity?

It seems that it is not.

1. The Apostle says in Romans 6.22, 'You have your fruit unto sanctification, and as your end, life everlasting.' But life is not an activity so much as the very existence of living things. Therefore the ultimate end, which is happiness, is not an activity.

2. Moreover, Boethius says in the *Consolation of Philosophy* 3.2, 'Happiness is the state perfected by the aggregation of all goods.' Therefore, happiness is not an activity.

3. Moreover, happiness signifies something existing in the happy person, since it is the ultimate perfection of man. But activity does not signify as something existing in the agent, but rather as proceeding from him. Therefore, happiness is not an activity.

4. Moreover, happiness remains in the happy person. But activity does not endure but passes. Therefore, happiness is not an activity.

5. Moreover, there is the same happiness for each man. But activities are many. Therefore, happiness is not an activity.

6. Moreover, happiness is in the happy person without interruption. But human activity is frequently interrupted, as in sleep, or by some other occupation, or by rest. Therefore, happiness is not an activity.

ON THE CONTRARY:

The Philosopher says in *Ethics* 1.13 that happiness is an activity according to perfect virtue.

RESPONSE:

It should be said that insofar as man's happiness is something existing in him as created, it must be called an activity. For happiness is the ultimate perfection of man. Each thing is perfect insofar as it is actual, for potency without act is imperfect. Therefore happiness must consist in man's ultimate act. But it is manifest that activity is the ultimate act of the agent, hence it is called second act by the Philosopher in *On the Soul* 2.1, for a thing having a form can be an agent in potency, as one with knowledge who is only potentially considering it. So it is that in other things as well each is said to be for the sake of its activity, as we read in *On the Heavens* 2.3. Therefore, man's happiness must be an activity.

Ad 1. It should be said that life is taken in two senses. In one, as the very existence of the living thing, and thus happiness is not life, for it was shown that the existence of a man, of whatever sort it is, is not man's happiness. In God alone is happiness identified with existence. In another sense the activity of the living thing is called life, insofar as the principle of life is rendered actual, and in this sense we speak of the active life or the contemplative life or the life lived for pleasure. It is in this sense eternal life is said to be the ultimate end. This is clear from what is said in John 17.3: 'Now this is everlasting life, that they may know thee, the only true God.'

Ad 2. It should be said that Boethius, in defining happiness, considered the common definition of it, for it is the common notion of happiness that it is a perfect common good. This is what he meant when he said that it is the state perfected by the aggregation of all goods, which comes down to saying that the happy man is in the state of perfect good. But Aristotle expresses the very essence of happiness, showing how a man achieves this state, namely, through some activity. Therefore in *Ethics* 1.7 he also shows that happiness is the perfect good.

Ad 3. It should be said that, as is remarked in *Metaphysics* 8.9, action is of two kinds. One kind passes from the agent into external matter, such as sawing and burning, and happiness cannot be an activity like that because such activity is not the perfection of the agent, but rather of the thing acted on, as is said in the same place. The other kind of action remains in the agent himself, like sensing, understanding and willing: such action is the perfection and act of the agent. Happiness can be called an activity of this kind.

Ad 4. It should be said that since happiness means some ultimate perfection, insofar as different things capable of happiness can attain to different levels of perfection, happiness must mean different things. For happiness is in God through his essence, because his existence is his activity, by which he does not enjoy another but himself. In the blessed angels there is ultimate perfection according to an activity by which they are joined with an uncreated good, and this activity is one and sempiternal in them. But in men, according to the present state of life, it is ultimate perfection according to an activity whereby man is joined with God, and this activity cannot be continuous nor one because an activity is multiplied by interruptions.

And because of this, perfect happiness cannot be had by man in the present state of life. Hence in *Ethics* 1.10, speaking of happiness in this life, the Philosopher calls it imperfect, after which he concludes that we call men happy *as men*. But perfect happiness is promised us by God, when we will be like the angels in heaven, as is said in Matthew 22.30. With respect to that perfect happiness, the object ceases, because by one and continuous and sempiternal activity in that state of happiness man is joined to God. But in the present life, to the degree that we fall short of the unity and continuity of such an activity, to that degree we fall short of happiness. But there is some participation of happiness, and so much the greater, insofar as the activity can be more continuous and one. Therefore, in the active life which is concerned with many things, there is less of the notion of happiness than in the contemplative life, which turns on one thing, that is, the contemplation of truth. And if at times man does not actually engage in this activity, he is always ready to do so, and because even taking time out for sleep or some natural activity is ordered to it, it seems to be a continuous activity.

And the answers to the fifth and sixth are evident from this.

Article 3: Is happiness an activity of the sensitive part or only of the intellectual part?

Happiness seems to consist in the activity of sense as well.

1. For in man only intellectual activity is more noble than the activity of sense. But intellectual activity in us depends on sense activity, because we cannot understand without phantasms, as is said in *On the Soul* 3.7. Therefore happiness consists in sensitive activity as well.

2. Moreover, Boethius says in the *Consolation of Philosophy* 3.2 that happiness is the state perfected by the aggregation of all goods. But some goods are sensible, and are attained by the activities of sense. Therefore, it seems that the activity of sense is required for happiness.

3. Moreover, happiness is perfect good, as is proved in *Ethics* 1.7, which it would not be unless man were perfected in all his parts. But some parts of the soul are perfected by sense activities. Therefore sense activity is required for happiness.

ON THE CONTRARY:

Brute animals share sense activity, but not happiness, with us. Therefore happiness does not consist in sensitive activity.

RESPONSE:

It should be said that something can pertain to happiness in three ways. In one way, essentially; in another, antecedently, in a third, consequently. Essentially, the activity of sense cannot pertain to happiness, for man's happiness consists essentially in his conjunction with an uncreated good, which is the ultimate end, as was shown above. But a man cannot be joined with it by the activity of sense. Also, because, as was shown earlier, man's happiness does not lie in bodily goods, which are all that the activity of sense can attain.

The activities of sense can pertain to happiness antecedently and consequently, however. Antecedently, with respect to the imperfect happiness that can be had in the present life, since intellectual activity presupposes the activity of sense. Consequently, in the perfect happiness that is expected in heaven, because after the resurrection, as Augustine says in the Letter to Dioscorus, happiness flows from the soul itself back into the body and bodily senses, as they are perfected in their activities. This will be clearer below, when the resurrection is discussed. But the activity whereby the human mind then is conjoined to God will not depend on sense.

Ad 1. It should be said that this objection proves that the activity of sense is required antecedently for the imperfect happiness had in this life.

Ad 2. It should be said that perfect happiness, such as the angels have, is the coming together of all goods by being joined to the universal fount of all good; not that it needs each singular good. But in this imperfect happiness there is required the coming together of goods sufficient to the most perfect activity of this life.

Ad 3. It should be said that in perfect happiness the whole man is perfected, but in the lower part by redundancy from the higher. But in the imperfect happiness of the present life, the reverse is true: from the perfection of the lower part we proceed to the perfection of the higher.

Article 4: Is happiness an activity of intellect or will?

It seems to consist of an act of will.

1. For Augustine says in the *City of God* 19.10 that human happiness consists of peace. Hence we read in Psalm 147.3, 'He has made peace in thy borders.' But peace pertains to will. Therefore man's happiness consists in will.

2. Moreover, happiness is the highest good, but good is the object of the will. Therefore, happiness consists in the activity of will.

3. Moreover, the ultimate end responds to the first mover, as the ultimate end of the whole army is victory, which is the end of the leader, who moves all. But will first moves to acting, because it moves the other powers, as will be said below. Therefore, happiness pertains to will.

4. Moreover, if happiness consists in some activity, it must be the most noble activity of man. But love of God which is an act of will is a more noble activity than knowledge, which is the activity of intellect, as is clear from the Apostle in 1 Corinthians 13. Therefore it seems that happiness consists of an act of will.

5. Moreover, Augustine says in *On the Trinity* 13.5 that man is happy who has all he wants, and wants nothing bad. And he adds after a bit that he who wills well whatever he wills approximates the happy man, for goods make him happy and some goods he already has, namely good will itself. Therefore, happiness consists in an act of will.

ON THE CONTRARY:
The Lord says in John 17.3, 'Now this is everlasting life, that they may know thee, the only true God.' But eternal life is the ultimate end. Therefore, man's happiness consists in knowledge of God, which is an act of intellect.

RESPONSE:
It should be said that, as has been established, two things are required for happiness, one that is the essence of happiness, another that is as an accident of it, namely the pleasure joined to it. Therefore, I say that, with respect to what happiness essentially is, it is impossible that it consist in an act of will. For it is manifest from the foregoing that happiness is the achievement of the ultimate end. The attainment of the end does not consist in the act of will itself. For the will is borne towards the end, which is absent when it desires it, present when it rests in and takes

pleasure in it. But it is obvious that the desire for the end is not the achievement of the end but a movement towards the end. But pleasure comes to the will because the end is present, but not conversely: a thing is not made present because the will delights in it.

Therefore it is necessary that there be something other than the act of will by which the end comes to be present to the one willing. And this appears clearly in sensible ends. For if one got money by an act of will, straight off the desirer would get money by willing to have it. But at the beginning it is absent, and he gets it when he grasps it with his hand or some such thing, and then he delights in the money had. So too it happens with the intelligible good, for from the beginning we will to attain the intelligible end and we achieve it by making it present to us by an act of intellect, and then the delighted will rests in the end attained. Therefore the essence of happiness consists in act of intellect, but the pleasure following on happiness pertains to will, as Augustine says in *Confessions* 10.23 that happiness is joy in the truth, because that joy is the consummation of happiness.

Ad 1. It should be said that peace pertains to man's ultimate end, not as if it were happiness essentially, but because it relates to it antecedently and consequently. Antecedently, insofar as all distractions and impediments are removed from the ultimate end. Consequently, insofar as man, the ultimate end being achieved, remains at peace, his is desire at rest.

Ad 2. It should be said that the first object of will is not its own act any more than the first object of sight is vision rather than the visible. Hence from the fact that happiness pertains to will as its first object, it follows that it does not pertain to it as its act.

Ad 3. It should be said that the intellect apprehends the end before the will, but the movement towards the end begins in the will. Therefore what ultimately follows on the achievement of the end, namely pleasure and enjoyment, are due to will.

Ad 4. It should be said that love takes precedence over knowledge in moving, but knowledge comes before love in attaining, nor is a thing loved save as known, as Augustine says in *On the Trinity* 10.1. Therefore, we first attain the intelligible end by an activity of intellect, as we first attain the sensible end by an action of sense.

Ad 5. It should be said that he who has all that he wills is happy because he has what he wants but by an act other than that of the will. But to will nothing badly is required for happiness as a certain fitting disposition for it. But a good will is numbered among the goods which make one happy, insofar as it is a certain inclination towards it, much as motion is categorized by its term, as alteration by quality.

Article 5: Is happiness an activity of speculative or practical intellect?

It seems to lie in the activity of practical intellect.

1. Any creature's ultimate end lies in assimilation to God. But man is assimilated to God more by practical intellect, which is the cause of the things understood, than by speculative intellect, whose knowledge is drawn from things. Therefore man's happiness lies in the activity of practical intellect rather than in that of speculative intellect.

2. Moreover, happiness is the perfect good of man. But practical intellect is ordered to the good more than speculative intellect, which is ordered to the true. Hence we are called good thanks to the perfection of practical intellect, not that of speculative intellect, thanks to which we are called knowing or understanding. Therefore man's happiness lies rather in the act of practical than of speculative intellect.

3. Moreover, happiness is a good of man himself. But speculative intellect is occupied rather with things beyond man, whereas practical intellect is occupied with what pertains to man himself, such as his activities and passions. Therefore man's happiness lies rather in the activity of practical than of speculative intellect.

ON THE CONTRARY:
Augustine says in *On the Trinity* 1.8 that contemplation, which is the end of all activities and the eternal perfection of joys, is promised us.

RESPONSE:
It should be said that happiness lies in the activity of speculative intellect rather than practical intellect. This is clear from three things. First, because if man's happiness is an activity, it should be his best activity, but man's best activity is that of the best power with respect to the best object. But intellect is the best power and its best object is the divine good, which is not indeed an object of practical, but of speculative, intellect. Happiness especially lies, therefore, in such activity, namely in contemplation of the divine. And because each thing seems to be that which is best in it, as is said in *Ethics* 9.8 and 10.7, such an activity is most proper to man and especially delightful.

Second, the same appears from this that contemplation especially is sought for its own sake. But the activity of practical intellect is sought for the sake of action, not for its own sake, and those actions are ordered to an end. Hence it is manifest that the ultimate end cannot lie in the active life, which pertains to practical intellect.

Third, the same appears from this that man shares the contemplative life with higher things, namely with God and the angels, to whom he is assimilated by happiness. But even other animals share with man in those things which pertain to the active life, though imperfectly. Therefore ultimate and perfect happiness, which is expected in the future life, consists wholly of contemplation. But imperfect happiness, of the kind that can be had here, consists first and principally in contemplation, but secondarily in the activity of practical intellect ordering human actions and passions, as is said in *Ethics* 10.7.

Ad 1. It should be said that the aforementioned similarity of practical intellect to God is according to proportionality, because it is to its knowledge as God is to his. But the assimilation of speculative intellect to God is according to union and informing, which is a much greater assimilation. It can also be said with respect to the principal thing known, which is his essence, that God does not have practical knowledge, but speculative only.

Ad 2. It should be said that practical intellect is ordered to a good which is outside itself, but speculative intellect has its good within itself, namely contemplation of truth. And if that good, by which the whole man is perfected and becomes good is perfect good, then indeed practical intellect is ordered to it but does not have it.

Ad 3. It should be said that the argument would work if man himself were his own ultimate end, for then the consideration and ordering of his acts and passions would be his happiness. But because the ultimate end of man is an extrinsic good, namely God, to whom we attain by the activity of the speculative intellect rather than by the activity of practical intellect, happiness consists in the activity of speculative intellect rather than in that of practical intellect.

Article 6: Does happiness lie in the speculative knowledge of the theoretical sciences?

It seems that it does.

1. The Philosopher says in the *Ethics* 1.13 that happiness is an activity in accord with perfect virtue. And in distinguishing the virtues he mentions three speculative ones – knowledge, wisdom and understanding – all of which pertain to considerations of the speculative sciences. Therefore man's ultimate happiness lies in the consideration of the speculative sciences.

2. Moreover, that would seem to be man's ultimate happiness that is naturally desired by all for its own sake. But that is true of the consideration of the speculative sciences because, as is said in *Metaphysics* 1.1, 'All men by nature desire to know,' and he adds a little later that the speculative sciences are sought for their own sake. Therefore, happiness lies in the consideration of the speculative sciences.

3. Moreover, happiness is man's ultimate perfection. But a thing is perfected insofar as it is reduced from potentiality to act. The human intellect is made actual by the consideration of the speculative sciences. Therefore, it seems that man's happiness lies in this kind of consideration.

ON THE CONTRARY:

It is said in Jeremiah 9.23, 'Let not the wise man glory in his wisdom.' And he is speaking of the wisdom of the speculative sciences. Therefore man's ultimate happiness does not lie in the consideration of these.

RESPONSE:

It should be said that, as was shown above, man's happiness is of two kinds, one perfect, the other imperfect. By perfect happiness is understood that which attains to the true definition of happiness, and by imperfect happiness that which does not but has some particular likeness to happiness by way of participation. For just as perfect prudence is found in a man who reasons rightly about things to be done, so there is imperfect prudence in some brute animals who have particular instincts to some acts similar to those of prudence. Therefore perfect happiness cannot lie essentially in the consideration of the speculative sciences.

In evidence of which, notice that the consideration of speculative science does not extend beyond the power of the principles of such science, because the whole science is virtually contained in its principles. But the first principles of the speculative sciences are taken from the senses, as is evident from the Philosopher at the beginning of the *Metaphysics* and the end of the *Posterior Analytics*. Hence the whole consideration of the speculative sciences cannot go beyond what knowledge of sensible things can lead to. But the ultimate happiness of man, which is his ultimate perfection, cannot lie in knowledge of sensible things. For a thing is not perfected by what is below it, save insofar as the lower is some participation of the higher. But it is obvious that the form of a stone or any other sensible thing is inferior to man. Hence the human intellect cannot be perfected by the form of the stone insofar as it is such a form but only insofar as it participates in some likeness of that which is above the human intellect, namely the intelligible light, or something of the like. But whatever is through something else is reduced to that which is of itself. Hence man's ultimate perfection must lie in knowledge of something which is above the human intellect.

But it has been shown that we cannot come to knowledge of separate substances through sensible things, since they are above the human intellect. We are left with this, then, that man's ultimate happiness cannot lie in the consideration of the speculative sciences. But just as sensible forms participate in some likeness of higher substances, so the consideration of the speculative sciences is a participation in true and perfect happiness.

Ad 1. It should be said that the Philosopher is speaking in the *Ethics* of imperfect happiness, such as can be had in this life, as has been pointed out above.

Ad 2. It should be said that not only perfect happiness is naturally desired but also any likeness or participation of it whatsoever.

Ad 3. It should be said that our intellect is reduced somewhat to act by the consideration of the speculative sciences, but not to ultimate and complete actuality.

Article 7: Does happiness consist in knowing the angels?

It seems that it does.

1. Man's happiness seems to lie in knowledge of separate substances, that is, angels, for Gregory says in some homily that nothing contributes to the enjoyments of men that does not partake of the joys of the angels, by which he designates final happiness. But we can take part in the joys

of the angels by contemplation of them. Therefore it seems that man's ultimate happiness lies in contemplation.

2. Moreover, a thing's ultimate perfection consists of its union with its principle, which is why the circle is called the perfect figure since its beginning and end are the same. But the principle of human knowledge is from the angels by whom men are illumined, as Dionysius says in the *Celestial Hierarchy* 4. Therefore, the perfection of the human intellect lies in the contemplation of angels.

3. Moreover, a nature is perfected when it is joined with a higher nature, as the ultimate perfection of body is to be conjoined with a spiritual nature. But in the order of nature, the angels are above the human intellect. Therefore, the ultimate perfection of the human intellect lies in its being conjoined with the angels in contemplation.

ON THE CONTRARY:
It is said in Jeremiah 9.24, 'But let him that glorieth glory in this, that he understandeth and knoweth me.' Therefore the ultimate human glory or happiness lies in nothing else than in knowledge of God.

RESPONSE:
It should be said that, as has been established, man's perfect happiness does not lie in a perfection by way of participation, but in that which is essentially perfection. But it is manifest that a thing is the perfection of a power to the degree that the notion of that power's proper object pertains to it. But the true is the proper object of intellect; therefore the contemplation of that which has participated in truth does not confer its ultimate perfection on intellect. Since the disposition of a thing in being and in truth is one and the same, as is said in *Metaphysics* 2.1, things which are being by participation are true by participation. But angels have participated being, because only in God is existence his essence, as was shown in Part 1. It follows that God alone is truth by his essence, and that contemplation of him makes one perfectly happy. But nothing prevents a kind of imperfect happiness from accompanying contemplation of the angels, which is higher and less imperfect than that had in the consideration of the speculative sciences.

Ad 1. It should be said that we enter into the joys of the angels not only by contemplating them but, along with them, contemplating God.

Ad 2. It should be said that to those who hold that human souls are created by angels it seems fitting enough that man's happiness should lie

...plation of the angels, as if in union with their principle. But ...neous, as was said in Part 1. Hence the ultimate perfection of ...man intellect lies in union with God, who is the principle both of the soul's creation and its illumination. But the angel illumines as a minister, as was shown in Part 1, and by his ministry helps man to arrive at happiness, not as the object of human happiness.

Ad 3. It should be said that the lower nature can attain the higher nature in two ways. In one way according to the level of the participating power, and thus the ultimate perfection of man will lie in this that he comes to contemplate as the angels do. In another way as an object is attained by a power, and in this way the ultimate perfection of any power lies in attaining that in which the notion of its object is fully realized.

Article 8: Can human happiness lie in the vision of the divine essence?

It seems that it cannot.

1. Dionysius says in *On Mystical Theology* 1 that it is through that which is highest in intellect that man is joined to God as to the wholly unknown. But that which is seen in its essence is not wholly unknown. Therefore, the ultimate perfection of intellect, happiness, does not lie in seeing God in his essence.

2. Moreover, the higher nature has a higher perfection. But it is the proper perfection of the divine intellect that he see his own essence. Therefore the ultimate perfection of the human intellect cannot lie in this but in something below it.

ON THE CONTRARY:

In 1 John 3.2 we read, 'When he appears, we shall be like to him, for we shall see him just as he is.'

RESPONSE:

It should be said that ultimate and perfect happiness can lie only in the vision of the divine essence. Two things can be adduced in evidence of this. First, that man is not perfectly happy so long as there remains anything to be desired and sought. Second, the perfection of any power is in terms of its object. But the object of intellect is the quiddity, that is, the essence of the thing, as is said in *On the Soul* 3.6. Hence intellect is more perfect to the degree that it knows the essence of the thing. Therefore, if an intellect knows the essence of some effect by which the essence of the cause cannot be known, so that it knows what the cause is, the intellect is not said to attain the cause simply speaking, although from its effect it can know that the cause exists. Therefore, when a man knows the effect and knows that it has a cause, he naturally has a desire to know of the cause what it is. And that desire is of wonder, and causes inquiry, as is said at the outset of the *Metaphysics*.

For example, if someone, knowing the eclipse of the sun, considers that it is produced by a cause, he wonders about it because he does not know what it is, and wondering inquires. Nor does this inquiry rest until it comes to knowledge of the essence of the cause. Therefore, if the human intellect, knowing the essence of some created effect, knows of God only that he exists, it does not yet perfectly attain the first cause simply speaking, but there remains in it a natural desire to inquire into the cause. Hence he is not yet perfectly happy. For perfect happiness the intellect must attain to the very essence of the first cause and then it will have its perfection by union with God as its object, in whom alone man's happiness lies, as has been said above.

Ad 1. It should be said that Dionysius is speaking of the knowledge of those in this life, who are tending towards happiness.

Ad 2. It should be said that, as was pointed out above, end can be taken in two ways. In one way, as the very thing that is desired, and in this way the end of the higher and lower nature, indeed of all things, is the same, as has been argued. In another way, with respect to the attainment of that thing, and then the end of the lower nature differs from that of the higher because they relate to that thing differently. Therefore the happiness of God contemplating his own essence is higher than that of man or angel who see it but do not comprehend it.

QUESTION 4
WHAT IS NEEDED FOR HAPPINESS?

We must now ask what is needed for happiness, and eight questions arise: (1) whether pleasure is required for happiness; (2) which is first in happiness, pleasure or vision? (3) whether comprehension is required; (4) whether rectitude of will is required; (5) whether the body is required for man's happiness; (6) whether perfection of body is required; (7) whether any external goods are required; (8) whether the society of friends is required for happiness.

Article 1: Is pleasure required for happiness?

It seems that it is not.

1. Augustine says in *On the Trinity* 1.8 that vision is the complete reward of faith. But happiness is the reward or prize of virtue, as is clear from the Philosopher in *Ethics* 1.9. Therefore nothing else is needed for happiness beside vision.

2. Moreover, happiness is of itself the most sufficient good, as the Philosopher says in *Ethics* 1.7. But that which has need of something else is not sufficient unto itself. Therefore since the essence of happiness lies in the vision of God, as has been shown, it seems that pleasure is not required for happiness.

3. Moreover, the activity of happiness or beatitude ought not be impeded, as is said in *Ethics* 7.13. But pleasure impedes the action of intellect, for it corrupts the estimate of prudence, as is said in *Ethics* 6.5. Therefore, pleasure is not required for happiness.

ON THE CONTRARY:
Augustine says in the *Confessions* 10.23 that happiness is rejoicing in the truth.

RESPONSE:
It should be said that something is required for another in four ways. In one way, as a preamble or preparation for it, as learning is required for knowledge. In another way, as perfecting it, as the soul is required for the life of the body. In a third way, as an external aid, as friends are needed in order to do a thing. In a fourth way, as something concomitant, as if we should say that heat is required for fire. And in this way pleasure is required for happiness, for pleasure is caused by appetite's coming to rest in the good attained. Hence, since happiness is nothing other than the attainment of the highest good, there cannot be happiness without concomitant pleasure.

Ad 1. It should be said that the will of one who merits a reward comes to rest when it is given, which is to be delighted. Hence pleasure is included in the very notion of the granted reward.

Ad 2. It should be said that pleasure is caused by the very vision of God. Hence he who sees God is not lacking in pleasure.

Ad 3. It should be said that the pleasure concomitant to the activity of intellect does not impede but rather strengthens it, as is said in *Ethics* 10.4, for we do more attentively and persistently the things we do with pleasure. But extrinsic pleasure impedes an operation, sometimes by distracting attention, since, as has been said, we attend more to the things in which we take pleasure, and when we vehemently attend to one thing attention is necessarily distracted from another. But sometimes out of contrariety, as the pleasure of sense that is contrary to reason impedes the estimate of prudence rather than of speculative intellect.

Article 2: Is vision or pleasure prior in happiness?

It seems that pleasure is.

1. For pleasure, as is said in *Ethics* 10.4, is the perfection of activity; but perfection is more powerful than what is perfectible. Therefore pleasure is more powerful than the activity of intellect, which is vision.

2. Moreover, that for the sake of which something is desirable, is more powerful. But activities are desired for the sake of their pleasures, hence nature added pleasure to the activities necessary for the preservation of the individual and species, lest animals neglect these activities. Therefore pleasure is more powerful in happiness than the activity of intellect, which is vision.

3. Moreover, vision responds to faith, as enjoyment does to charity. But charity is greater than faith, as the Apostle says in 1 Corinthians 13.13. Therefore pleasure, which is enjoyment, is more powerful than vision.

ON THE CONTRARY:

The cause is more powerful than the effect. But vision is the cause of pleasure. Therefore vision is more powerful than pleasure.

RESPONSE:

It should be said that the Philosopher raises this question in *Ethics* 10.4 and leaves it unanswered, but if one thinks about it, the activity of intellect, which is vision, must be more powerful than pleasure, for pleasure consists in the repose of will. But will rests in something because of the goodness of the thing in which it rests. Therefore if the will rests in some activity, the repose of the will would follow from the goodness of that activity. The will does not seek a good for the sake of rest, for then the act of will itself would be the end, which is contrary to what has been established. But it seeks to rest in the activity because the activity is its good. Hence it is manifest that the good that is the activity itself, in which the will rests, takes precedence over the will's resting in it.

Ad 1. It should be replied that, as the Philosopher says in the same place, pleasure perfects activity as beauty, which is consequent on youth, perfects youth. Hence pleasure is a perfection concomitant with vision, not a perfection causing vision to be perfect in its kind.

Ad 2. It should be said that the universal character of goodness is not grasped by the senses, but some particular good which is pleasurable. Therefore, in sense appetite, which is found in animals, activities are sought for pleasure. But the intellect grasps the universal note of the good, which when had gives pleasure. Hence it intends good more than pleasure. So it is that the divine intellect, which is the institutor of nature, adds pleasures for the sake of the activities. But a thing should not be appraised on the basis of sense appetite, but rather on the basis of its relation to intellectual appetite.

Ad 3. It should be said that charity seeks a good desired for the sake of pleasure, but as consequent to it, such that it takes pleasure in the loved good attained. Thus pleasure does not answer to it as its end, but rather vision, by which the end first becomes present to it.

Article 3: Is comprehension required for happiness?

It seems that it is not.

1. Augustine says in *To Paulinus on Seeing God* that to attain God with the mind is a great happiness, but to comprehend him is impossible. Therefore there is happiness without comprehension.

2. Moreover, happiness is man's perfection with respect to the intellective part, in which the only powers are intellect and will, as was said in Part 1. But intellect is sufficiently perfected by the vision of God, but will by delight in him. Therefore comprehension as some third thing is not required.

3. Moreover, happiness consists in activity. But activities are specified by objects and there are two general objects, the true and the good: the true corresponds to vision and good corresponds to pleasure. Therefore comprehension is not required as some third thing.

ON THE CONTRARY:
The Apostle says in 1 Corinthians 9.24, 'So run as to obtain it.' But the

spiritual race has happiness as its goal. Hence he says in 2 Timothy 4.7, 'I have finished the course, I have kept the faith. For there is laid up for me a crown of justice.' Therefore comprehension is required for happiness.

RESPONSE:

It should be said that since happiness lies in the attainment of the ultimate end, the things required for happiness should be considered with reference to man's order to the end. Man is ordered to the intelligible end partly indeed by intellect but partly by will. By intellect, insofar as some imperfect knowledge of the end pre-exists in intellect; by will, through love first of all, which is the will's first movement towards anything, but second by the real relation of lover to beloved, which can be of three kinds: sometimes the beloved is present to the lover, and then is no longer pursued; sometimes it is not present but it is impossible to achieve so it is not sought. Sometimes, however, it is possible to achieve it, but it is elevated above the faculty of the achiever, such that it cannot be had at once, and this is the relation of one hoping to the thing hoped for, a condition which causes pursuit of the end. To each of these three something in happiness corresponds, for perfect knowledge of the end corresponds to the imperfect, the presence of the end corresponds to the relationship of hope, but delight in the end now present follows on love, as has been said above. Therefore these three must come together in happiness, vision, which is perfect knowledge of the intelligible end, comprehension, which implies the presence of the end, and pleasure or enjoyment which implies the repose of the one loving in the thing loved.

Ad 1. It should be said that comprehension has two meanings. One, the inclusion of the comprehended in the comprehender, and thus whatever is comprehended by the finite is finite. God cannot be comprehended in this sense by any created intellect. Two, comprehension names the grasping of some thing now present, as one following another is said to comprehend him when he grasps him. It is in this sense that comprehension is required for happiness.

Ad 2. It should be said that just as hope and love pertain to will, because to love something and to tend towards it when not had are the same, so too comprehension and delight pertain to will, because it belongs to the same thing to have something and to rest in it.

Ad 3. It should be said that comprehension is not some activity outside vision, but is a relation to the end once had. Hence vision itself, or the thing seen insofar as it is present, is the also object of comprehension.

Article 4: Is rectitude of will required for happiness?

It seems that it is not.

1. Happiness consists essentially in the activity of intellect, as has been said, but rectitude of will by which men are called clean is not required for the perfect activity of the intellect, for as Augustine says in the *Retractions*, 'I do not approve what I said in prayer, that God willed that only the clean should know. For it can be objected that many even among the unclean know many truths.' Therefore, rectitude of will is not required for happiness.

2. Moreover, the prior does not depend on the posterior; but the activity of intellect is prior to the act of will. Therefore happiness, which is the perfect activity of intellect, does not depend on rectitude of will.

3. Moreover, what is ordered to another as to an end, is not necessary once the end has been achieved, like the ship once it reaches port. But rectitude of will, the effect of virtue, is ordered to happiness as an end. Therefore, once happiness is achieved, rectitude of will is unnecessary.

ON THE CONTRARY:
It is said in Matthew 5.8, 'Blessed are the pure in heart for they shall see God,' and in Hebrews 12.14, 'Strive for peace with all men, and for that holiness without which no man will see God.'

RESPONSE:
It should be said that rectitude of will is required for happiness both antecedently and concomitantly. Antecedently, because rectitude of will involves the due order to the ultimate end, but the end is compared to that which is ordered to it as form to matter. Hence just as matter can only attain form insofar as it is disposed to it in an appropriate manner, so nothing attains the end without an appropriate order to it. Therefore no one can achieve happiness unless he has rectitude of will. Concomitantly, because, as has been said, ultimate happiness lies in the vision of the divine essence, which is the very essence of goodness. Thus the will of one seeing the essence of God necessarily loves whatever he loves under the common notion of the good which he knows. And this is also what makes the will correct. Hence it is manifest that happiness cannot be had without right will.

*

Ad 1. It should be said that Augustine is speaking of knowledge of the true, which is not of the very essence of happiness.

Ad 2. It should be said that every act of will is preceded by some act of intellect, but a given act of will can be prior to a given act of intellect. For the will tends to the final act of intellect, which is happiness. Therefore, the right inclination of will is presupposed to happiness, as the right movement of the arrow to hitting the target.

Ad 3. It should be said that not everything that is ordered to the end ceases once the end is attained, but only that which has in itself the note of imperfection, like motion. Hence the instruments of motion are not necessary one it has achieved its end, but the right order to the end is necessary.

Article 5: Is the body required for man's happiness?

It seems that it is.

1. The perfections of virtue and grace presuppose the perfection of nature. But happiness is the perfection of virtue and grace. Soul without body does not have the perfection of nature, since it is naturally a part of human nature and every part separated from its soul is imperfect. Therefore soul cannot be happy without the body.

2. Moreover, happiness is a perfect activity, as has been said above, but perfect activity follows on perfect being, because a thing acts only insofar as it is in act. Therefore, since soul does not have perfect existence when it is separated from body, any more than any other part separated from its whole, it seems that soul without body cannot be happy.

3. Moreover, happiness is man's perfection, But soul without body is not man. Therefore happiness cannot be in soul without body.

4. Moreover, according to the Philosopher in *Ethics* 7.13, the activity of happiness, in which blessedness consists, is not impeded. But the activity of the separated soul is impeded because, as Augustine says in the *Literal Commentary on Genesis* 12.35, there is in it a natural desire to govern the body, which distracts it from directing its whole attention on the highest heaven, that is, to the vision of the divine essence. Therefore soul without body cannot be happy.

5. Moreover, happiness is a sufficient good and quiets desire. But this is not the case with the separated soul, which still desires union with body, as Augustine says. Therefore the soul separated from body is not happy.

6. Moreover, man is equal in happiness to the angels. But the soul without body is not equal to the angels, as Augustine says. Therefore it is not happy.

ON THE CONTRARY:
Apocalypse 14.13 says, 'Blessed are the dead who die in the Lord.'

RESPONSE:
It should be said that there are two kinds of happiness, one imperfect, which is had in this life, and the other perfect, which consists in the vision of God. But it is manifest that the body is required for happiness in this life, for the happiness of this life is activity of intellect, speculative or practical. But the activity of intellect in this life cannot take place without the phantasm, which exists only in the bodily organ, as was shown in Part 1. Thus the happiness which can be had in this life depends in a certain way on body.

But with respect to perfect happiness, which lies in vision, some held that it cannot come to the soul existing apart from body, saying that the souls of the saints separated from bodies do not attain to that happiness until the day of judgement, when they will take up their bodies again. But this seems false on the basis of both authority and reason. By authority, because the Apostle says in 2 Corinthians 5.6, 'While we are in the body, we are exiled from the Lord,' and he shows what exile means by adding, 'For we walk by faith and not by sight.' From which it is clear that as long as one walks in faith and not in vision, lacking the vision of the divine essence, he is not yet present to God. But the souls of the saints separated from their bodies are present to God, hence he adds, 'We even have the courage to prefer to be exiled from the body and to be at home with the Lord.' Hence it is manifest that the souls of the saints separated from bodies walk by sight, seeing the essence of God, in which lies true happiness.

This is apparent on the basis of reason as well, for intellect does not need body for its activity except for the sake of phantasms in which it sees intelligible truth, as was said in Part 1. Hence, since man's perfect happiness lies in the vision of the divine essence, the perfect happiness of man does not depend on body. Hence the soul can be happy without the body.

But we should note that something pertains to another's perfection in two ways. In one way, as constituting the essence of the thing, as soul is required for the perfection of man. In another way, what pertains to its well-being pertains to the perfection of a thing, such as bodily beauty and quick wit pertain to man's perfection. Therefore although body does not pertain to the perfection of human happiness in the first way, it does in the second. For since activity depends on the nature of the thing, when soul is more perfect in its nature it is more perfectly capable of its proper activity in which happiness consists. Hence Augustine in the *Literal Commentary on Genesis* 12.35, asking whether that highest happiness can be granted to the spirits of the dead without their bodies, replies that they cannot then see the unchanging substance as the holy angels see it, whether for some more hidden reason or because there is in them a natural desire to govern body.

Ad 1. It should be said that happiness is the soul's perfection of soul on the part of intellect thanks to which soul transcends bodily organs, not insofar as it is the form of a natural body. Therefore, the perfection of its nature remains insofar as happiness is due it, although not insofar as it is the form of body.

Ad 2. It should be said that soul relates to existence differently than the other parts do, for the existence of the soul does not belong to any of its parts; hence when the whole is destroyed the part either wholly ceases to be, like the parts of a destroyed animal, or if they remain they have another actual existence, as the part of the line has an existence other than that of the whole line. But the existence of the composite remains in the human soul after the destruction of the body, and this because the existence of form and matter is the same, namely the existence of the composite. But the soul subsists in its own existence, as was shown in Part 1. Hence after its separation from body it has perfect existence, and thus it can have a perfect activity, although it does not have the perfect nature of its species.

Ad 3. It should be said that man's happiness is due to intellect. Therefore while intellect remains there can be happiness in him, much as the teeth of an Ethiopian, which are a basis for calling him white, remain white even after extraction.

Ad 4. It should be said that a thing can be impeded by another in two ways. First, in the mode of contrariety, as cold impedes warm, and such an impediment is repugnant to the notion of happiness. Second, in the mode of some defect, when the impeded thing does not have something that is required for its full perfection, and such an impediment is not repugnant to the activity of happiness, but to its complete perfection. Thus separation from body is said to retard the soul such that it does not with complete attention tend towards the vision of the divine essence. For the soul seeks so to enjoy God that that enjoyment redounds to the body to the degree this is possible. Therefore as long as it enjoys God without its body, its desire is quieted by what it has, which, however, it still wants its body to have by participation in it.

Ad 5. It should be said that the desire of the separated soul is totally at rest with respect to the desirable, because it has what suffices for its desire. But it is not wholly at rest with respect to the one desiring, who does not possess the good in every way that he wishes to possess it. Therefore, when the body is regained, happiness increases extensively but not intensively.

Ad 6. It should be said that what is found in the same place, namely, that the spirits of the dead do not see God as the angels do, is not to be understood according to quantitative inequality, because even now some blessed souls are taken up to the higher orders of the angels, seeing God more clearly than the lower angels. But it should be understood according to proportional inequality, because angels, even the lowest, have every perfection of happiness they will have, which is not so of the separated souls of the saints.

Article 6: Is perfection of body required for happiness?

It seems that it is not.

1. The perfection of body is a bodily good. But it was shown above that happiness does not consist of bodily goods. Therefore, a perfect disposition of body is not required for man's happiness.

2. Moreover, man's happiness lies in the vision of the divine essence, as has been shown. But body contributes nothing to this activity, as has been said. Therefore, no disposition of body is required for happiness.

3. Moreover, the more abstracted from body intellect is, the more perfectly it understands. But happiness lies in the most perfect activity of intellect. Therefore it is necessary that soul be abstracted in every way from body and there is no way in which a disposition of body is required for happiness.

ON THE CONTRARY:

Happiness is the reward of virtue, hence it is said in John 13.17, 'Blessed shall you be if you do them.' But the reward promised the saints is not only the vision of God and delight, but also a good disposition of body, for it is said in Isaiah 66.14, 'You shall see and your heart shall rejoice, and your bones shall flourish like an herb.' Therefore a good disposition of body is required for happiness.

RESPONSE:

It should be said that if we are speaking of man's happiness in the way it can be had in this life, it is obvious that a good disposition of body is necessarily required for it. For this happiness, as the Philosopher says, lies in the activity of perfect virtue and clearly feebleness of body can impede a man in the exercise of any virtue.

But, speaking of perfect happiness, some held that no disposition of body is needed for it, but rather that the soul be wholly separated from body. Hence Augustine in the *City of God* 22.26 cites Porphyry as saying that the soul in order to be happy must flee from every body. But this is absurd. Since it is natural for soul to be united to body, it cannot be that the soul's perfection excludes its natural perfection.

Therefore, it must be said that a perfect disposition of body is required, both antecedently and consequently for a happiness perfect in every way. Antecedently because, as Augustine says in the *Literal Commentary on Genesis* 12.35, if it be such a body that its governance is difficult and heavy, as the flesh which corrupts and weighs down the soul, the mind is turned from that vision of the highest heaven. Hence he concludes that since the body will no longer be animal but spiritual, it will be equal to the angels, and what was a burden will contribute to its glory. Consequently, because the glory of the soul will redound to the body in order that it might share its perfection. Hence Augustine says, in the Letter to Dioscorus, God made our soul strong so that from the fullness of its happiness it might lend to the lower nature the strength of incorruption.

Ad 1. It should be said that happiness does not lies in a bodily good as in its object, but the bodily good can bring about the adornment and perfection of happiness.

Ad 2. It should be said that although body contributes nothing to the activity of intellect by which the essence of God is seen, still it can impede it. Therefore, the perfection of body is required in order that it not impede the lifting up of mind.

Ad 3. It should be said that abstraction from this corruptible body which weighs down the soul is required for the perfect activity of intellect, but not from spiritual body which will be entirely subject to spirit, of which we will speak in the third part of this work.[1]

Article 7: Are some external goods required for happiness?

It seems that they are.

1. What is promised to the saints as reward pertains to happiness. But external goods are promised to the saints, for example food and drink, wealth and the kingdom, for it is said in Luke 22.30, 'That you may eat and drink at my table in my kingdom'; and in Matthew 6.20, 'Lay up for yourselves treasure in heaven,' and 25.34, 'Come, blessed of my Father, take possession of the kingdom.' Therefore, external goods are required for happiness.

2. Moreover, according to Boethius in the *Consolation of Philosophy* 3.2, happiness is the state perfected by the aggregation of all goods. But some of man's goods are external, though they be the least, as Augustine says.[2] Therefore they are required for happiness.

3. Moreover, in Matthew 5.12, the Lord says, 'Your reward is great in heaven.' But to be in heaven means to be in some place. Therefore, at least external place is required for happiness.

ON THE CONTRARY:

We read in Psalm 72.25, 'Whom have I in heaven but thee? And earth does not delight me if I am with thee.' As if he said that he wished nothing except what follows (verse 28): 'But it is good for me to be near God.' Therefore, nothing else that is external is needed for happiness.

RESPONSE:

It should be said that external goods are required for the imperfect happiness that can be had in this life, not as being of its essence, but as instrumentally serving happiness which consists of the virtuous activity, as is said in *Ethics* 1.13. For in this life man needs the necessities of body for the exercise of both contemplative and active virtue, for which many other things are also required. But for perfect happiness, which consists of vision, such goods are in no way required. The reason for this is that all such external goods are needed either to sustain the animal body or

1. cf. the supplement to the *Summa theologiae*, q. 82 ff.
2. *On Free Will* 1.19.

for those activities that we exercise through the animal body and which are proper to human life. But the perfect happiness, which consists of vision, is either of soul without body or of soul united to a body no longer animal but spiritual. Therefore, such external goods, since they are ordered to animal life, are in no way needed for this happiness. Because in this life contemplative rather than active happiness bears a greater likeness to perfect happiness, and is more like God as well, as is clear from what has been said, it has less need of such goods of the body, as is said in *Ethics* 10.8.

Ad 1. It should be said that all these bodily promises that are found in Sacred Scripture are to be understood metaphorically, insofar as in Scripture spiritual things are usually designated by the bodily, in order that from things that we know we might rise to desire the unknown, as Gregory says in some homily. For just as by food and drink the delight of happiness is understood, by riches is meant that God is sufficient to man and by the kingdom man's being raised up even to union with God.

Ad 2. It should be said that the goods serving animal life do not belong to the spiritual life in which perfect happiness lies. However, there will be in that happiness the coming together of all goods because whatever of good is to be found in these will be had wholly in the highest source of goods.

Ad 3. It should be said that, according to Augustine in *The Lord's Sermon on the Mount* 1.5, the reward of the saints is not said to be in the corporeal heavens, but by heaven is understood the height of spiritual goods. None the less, bodily place, namely the celestial empyrean, will be present to the blessed, not out of any necessity for happiness, but because of a certain congruence and beauty.

Article 8: Is the society of friends required for happiness?

It seems that it is.

1. In Scripture happiness is frequently designated by the word glory. But glory consists of this that man's goodness is brought to the notice of many. Therefore, the society of friends is required for happiness.

2. Moreover, Boethius says that the possession of a good is not enjoyed without companionship. But enjoyment is required for happiness. Therefore the society of friends is also required.

3. Moreover, charity is perfected in happiness. But charity includes the

love of both God and neighbour. It seems, therefore, that the society of friends is required for happiness.

ON THE CONTRARY:
It is said in Wisdom 7.11, 'Now all good things come to me together with her,' namely, divine wisdom, which consists of contemplation of God. Thus for happiness nothing else is needed.

RESPONSE:
It should be said that if we are speaking of the happiness of the present life, as the Philosopher does in *Ethics* 9.9, the happy man has need of friends, not indeed for their usefulness, since he is sufficient unto himself, nor for pleasure, because he has in himself perfect pleasure in the exercise of virtue, but for the sake of good activity, namely that he might benefit them and take pleasure in doing so and also be helped by them in benevolence. A man needs the help of friends in order to act well, the deeds of the active life as well as those of the contemplative.

But if we are speaking of the perfect happiness that will be had in heaven, the society of friends is not needed for the necessity of happiness, because a man has the fullness of his perfection in God. But the society of friends makes for the well-being of happiness. Hence Augustine says in the *Literal Commentary on Genesis* 8.25 that the spiritual creature, in order to be happy, is helped intrinsically by the eternity, truth and charity of the creator. But extrinsically, if it can be called being helped, perhaps they are helped by this alone, that they see one another and rejoice in their community with God.

Ad 1. It should be said that the glory that is essential to happiness is not that which a man has from man, but from God.

Ad 2. It should be said that this remark is to be understood when the full sufficiency in the good that is had is absent, which cannot be said in the case in point, since every man has a sufficiency of good in God.

Ad 3. It should be said that the perfection of charity is essential to happiness with respect to the love of God but not with respect to the love of neighbour. Hence if there were only one soul enjoying God he would be happy even without a neighbour whom he could love. But supposing a neighbour, love of him follows from the perfect love of God. Hence friendship is, as it were, concomitant to perfect happiness.

QUESTION 5
ON THE ATTAINMENT OF HAPPINESS

We must now consider the acquisition of happiness, and eight questions arise: (1) whether man can attain happiness; (2) whether one man can be happier than another; (3) whether anyone can be happy in this life; (4) whether happiness once had can be lost; (5) whether man can acquire happiness by his natural powers; (6) whether man attains happiness by the action of some higher creature; (7) whether some acts are needed for a man to achieve happiness from God; (8) whether every man seeks happiness.

Article 1: Can man attain happiness?

It appears that he cannot.

1. Just as rational nature is above the sensible, so the intellectual nature is above the rational, as is evident from Dionysius in *On the Divine Names*, in many places. But brute animals, which have sensible nature alone, cannot achieve the end of rational nature. Therefore neither can man, who is of a rational nature, achieve the end of the intellectual nature, which is happiness.

2. Moreover, true happiness lies in the vision of God, who is pure truth. But it is connatural to man to intuit the truth of material things, hence he understands intelligible species in images, as is said in *On the Soul* 3.7. Therefore, he cannot attain to happiness.

3. Moreover, happiness lies in the attainment of the highest good. But one can only arrive at the highest by way of the intermediates. Therefore, since the angelic nature is midway between God and human nature and man cannot go beyond it, it seems that he cannot arrive at happiness.

ON THE CONTRARY:
Psalm 93.12 says, 'Blessed the man whom thou teachest, O Lord.'

RESPONSE:
It should be said that happiness means the attainment of the perfect good. Therefore anyone capable of attaining the perfect good can achieve happiness. That man is capable of the perfect good is clear from the fact his intellect can grasp the universal and perfect good and his will can desire it.

Therefore man can attain happiness. The same thing is clear from the fact that man is capable of the vision of the divine essence, as was shown in Part 1, in which vision we said that man's perfect happiness lies.

Ad 1. It should be said that rational nature exceeds sensitive nature differently than the intellectual exceeds the rational. For rational nature exceeds the sensitive with respect to the object of knowledge, because sense can in no wise know the universal, which reason does know. But intellectual nature exceeds the rational with respect to the way of knowing the same intelligible truth, for intellectual nature straightaway grasps the truth to which rational nature comes by the inquiry of reason, as is evident from things said in Part 1. Therefore, what intellect grasps, reason comes to by a kind of motion. Hence rational nature can achieve happiness, which is the perfection of intellectual nature, but in a way different from the angels. For the angels attain it immediately from the beginning of their creation, but men come to it after a time. But sensitive nature can in no way attain this end.

Ad 2. It should be said that the mode of knowing intelligible truths through images is connatural to man in the present life, but after the condition of this life, he will have another connatural mode, as was said in Part 1.

Ad 3. It should be said that man cannot transcend the angels in the grade of nature, such that he might be superior to them in nature. But he can transcend them by the activity of intellect, since he understands something to be higher than the angels which will make him happy and he will be perfectly happy when he perfectly attains it.

Article 2: Can one man be happier than another?

It seems that he cannot.

1. Happiness is the reward of virtue, as the Philosopher says in *Ethics* 1.7, but all are given an equal reward for the works of virtue, for it is said in Matthew 20.10 that all who worked in the vineyard received a single denarius, that is, as Gregory notes, they received the equal reward of eternal life. Therefore, no one will be happier than another.

2. Moreover, happiness is the greatest good. But nothing can be greater than the greatest. Therefore one man's happiness cannot be greater than another's.

3. Moreover, since happiness is a perfect and sufficient good it gives

rest to man's desire. But desire is not at rest if some good that could be added is lacking. But if nothing that could be added is lacking there can be no greater good. Therefore either a man is not happy or if he is happy there cannot be another and greater happiness.

ON THE CONTRARY:

We read in John 14.2, 'In my Father's house there are many mansions,' by which, as Augustine says, the different dignities of merit in eternal life are to be understood. But the dignity of eternal life, which is given for merit, is happiness itself. There are then different levels of happiness and not equal happiness for all.

RESPONSE:

It should be said that, as was argued earlier, two things are included in the definition of happiness: the ultimate end itself, which is the greatest good, and the attainment or enjoyment of that good. With respect to the good itself, which is the object and cause of happiness, one happiness cannot be higher than another because there is only one highest good, namely God, enjoyment of whom makes men happy. But with respect to the attainment or enjoyment of such a good, one can be happier than another since a man is happy to the degree that he enjoys the good. But it happens that one person more perfectly enjoys God than another because he is better disposed or ordered to enjoyment of him. And for this reason one person can be happier than another.

Ad 1. It should be said that one denarius signifies the unity of happiness on the side of the object. But the different mansions signify the diversity of happiness according to different levels of enjoyment.

Ad 2. It should be said that happiness is called the greatest good insofar as it is the perfect possession or enjoyment of the greatest good.

Ad 3. It should be said that there is no good left to be desired by any happy person since he has the infinite good which is the good of all goods, as Augustine says. But one is said to be happier than another because of a different participation in this good. The addition of other goods does not increase happiness and that is why Augustine says in the *Confessions* 8.4, 'He who knows thee and other things, is not happier because of them, but is happy because of thee alone.'

Article 3: Can anyone be happy in this life?

It seems that he can.

1. It is said in Psalm 118.1, 'Blessed are they whose way is undefiled, who walk in the law of the Lord.' But this occurs in this life. Therefore, someone can be happy in this life.

2. Imperfect participation in the highest good does not detract from the notion of happiness, otherwise one would not be happier than another. But in this life men can participate in the greatest good by knowing and loving God, although imperfectly. Therefore a man can be happy in this life.

3. Moreover, what is said by many cannot be wholly false, for what is for the most part seems natural and nature does not wholly fail. But many posit happiness in this life, as is evident from Psalm 143.15: 'Blessed the people that have such things; blessed the people whose God is the Lord.'

ON THE CONTRARY:
It is said in Job 14.1, 'Man, born of a woman, living for a short time, is filled with many miseries.' Therefore, a man cannot be happy in this life.

RESPONSE:
It should be said that some participation in happiness can be had in this life, but perfect and true happiness cannot. And this can be considered in two ways: first, in terms of the common notion of happiness. For happiness, being a perfect and sufficient good, excludes all evil and fulfils every desire. But in this life evil cannot be eliminated, for the present life is subject to many ills that cannot be avoided, for example, ignorance on the part of intellect and inordinate affection on the part of will and many punishments on the part of the body, such as Augustine thoroughly examines in the *City of God* 19.4. So too the desire for the good cannot be satisfied in this life, for man naturally desires the permanence of the good he has, but the goods of the present life are transitory and the life itself, which we naturally desire, passes away, yet we naturally desire it to be perpetual since we naturally shun death. Hence it is impossible that true happiness be had in this life.

Second, if we consider that in which happiness especially consists, namely the vision of the divine essence, which cannot be had by man in this life, as was shown in Part 1, then it is apparent that one cannot attain true and perfect happiness in this life.

*

Ad 1. It should be said that some are called happy in this life, either because of the hope of attaining happiness in the future life, according to Romans 8.24, 'For in hope were we saved,' or because of a participation in happiness, according to some enjoyment of the highest good.

Ad 2. It should be said that participation in happiness can be imperfect in two ways. In one way on the side of the object of happiness itself which is not seen in its own essence. And this imperfection is incompatible with the notion of true happiness. In another way it can be imperfect on the side of the one participating who, though he attains to the object of happiness as such, namely God, does so imperfectly by comparison with the way in which God enjoys himself. This imperfection is not incompatible with the true notion of happiness because, since happiness is a kind of activity, as has been said above, the true notion of happiness is considered from the side of the object that specifies the act, and not from the side of the subject.

Ad 3. It should be said that men are thought to have some happiness in this life because of a similarity to true happiness, and thus in their estimation they do not wholly fall short.

Article 4: Can happiness once had be lost?

It seems that it can.

1. Happiness is a perfection, but every perfection is in the perfectible according to its mode. Therefore, since man is mutable in his nature, it seems that happiness is participated by him in a mutable manner. And thus it seems that man can lose happiness.

2. Happiness lies in an activity of intellect which is subject to will. But the will is related to opposites. Therefore, it seems that it can desist from the activity whereby man is made happy and the man cease to be happy.

3. Moreover, an end corresponds to a beginning. But man's happiness has a beginning, because man was not always happy. Therefore, it seems that it should have an end.

ON THE CONTRARY:

It is said in Matthew 25.46 that they will go into everlasting life which, as has been said, is the blessedness of the saints. But what is eternal does not give out. Therefore, happiness cannot be lost.

RESPONSE:

It should be said that if we are speaking of the imperfect happiness that can be had in this life, then it can be lost. And this is clear in contemplative happiness, which is lost either through forgetfulness, as when knowledge is lost because of illness, or even by other occupations that wholly distract one from contemplation. And the same is clear in active happiness, for a man's will can be changed and degenerate from virtue, in whose act happiness principally consists, into vice. If virtue remains, however, external changes can disturb such happiness by impeding many acts of virtue, although it cannot be wholly taken away since the acts of virtue still remain if a man nobly bears adversities. Because the happiness of this life can be lost, which seems counter to the notion of happiness, the Philosopher says in *Ethics* 1.10 that some are happy in this life, not simply but in the way men can be whose nature is subject to change.

But if we are speaking of the perfect happiness that is expected after this life, it should be noted that Origen held, following the error of some Platonists, that after attaining ultimate happiness a man can become miserable. But this appears manifestly false for two reasons. First, from the common notion of happiness, for since happiness itself is a perfect and sufficient good, it must give rest to man's desire and exclude all evil. But a man naturally desires to retain the good he has and seeks security in the having of it, otherwise the fear of loss or sadness from the certainty of loss would afflict him. Therefore true happiness requires that a man have certain knowledge that he will have it and never lose it. If this opinion is true, the result is that he will never lose happiness, but if it is false, having a false opinion is itself a kind of evil, for falsehood is the evil of intellect, as true is its good, as is said in *Ethics* 6.2. Therefore, he will not be happy now if there is some evil in him.

Second, the same thing is clear when the special notion of happiness is considered. It was shown above that perfect happiness lies in the vision of the divine essence. But it is impossible that anyone seeing the divine essence should wish not to see it, because any good that one wishes to lose is either insufficient and something more sufficient is sought in its place, or it has something inappropriate connected with it which brings on loathing. But the vision of the divine essence fills the soul with all goods since it is then united with the source of all goodness. Hence it is said in Psalm 16.15, 'I shall be satisfied with the sight of thy face,' and in Wisdom 7.11, 'Now all good things come to me together with her,' namely with the contemplation of wisdom. So too the soul does not have anything inappropriate because of the contemplation of wisdom it is said in Wisdom

8.16, 'For her conversation hath no bitterness, nor her company any tediousness.' Thus it is clear that the happy person would not willingly put happiness away. So too he cannot lose it because, since the losing of happiness is a kind of punishment, this could only be justly done by God for some fault into which one seeing the essence of God could not fall, since rectitude of will follows necessarily on this vision, as was shown above.

Nor could any other agent take it away. The mind joined with God is raised up above all other things and no other agent can deprive him of this union. Hence it seems unfitting that a man should pass from happiness to misery by any alterations of time, except in things subject to time and motion.

Ad 1. It should be said that happiness is consummate perfection which excludes any defect in the blessed. Therefore it comes to the one having it without mutability, acting by the divine power, which elevates man to participation in an eternity transcending all change.

Ad 2. It should be said that will is related to opposites with respect to what is ordered to the end, but it is ordered to the ultimate end by natural necessity. This is evident from the fact that he cannot will not to be happy.

Ad 3. It should be said that happiness has a beginning because of the condition of the participant, but it lacks an end because of the condition of the good, participation in which makes one happy. Hence there is a beginning of happiness due to one cause, but it has no end due to another.

Article 5: Can man by his natural powers attain happiness?

It seems that he can.

1. For nature does not fail in what is necessary. But nothing is so necessary for man than that he attain his ultimate end. Therefore this cannot be lacking to human nature and a man can attain happiness by his natural capacities.

2. Moreover, since man is more noble than irrational creatures, he seems to be more sufficient. But irrational creatures can by their natural capacities achieve their ends. Therefore, so much more man can achieve happiness by his natural capacities.

3. Moreover, happiness is perfect activity, according to the Philosopher. But it falls to the same to begin something and to perfect it. Therefore

since imperfect happiness, which is, as it were, the beginning in human activities, is subject to the natural power of man by which he is master of his acts, it seems that by his natural power he can attain to perfect activity, which is happiness.

ON THE CONTRARY:
Man is naturally the principle of his acts by means of intellect and will. But the ultimate happiness prepared for the saints exceeds man's intellect and will, for the Apostle says in 1 Corinthians 2.9, 'Eye hath not seen, nor ear heard, neither hath it entered into the heart of man, what things God hath prepared for them that love him.' Therefore, man cannot achieve happiness by his natural powers.

RESPONSE:
It should be said that the imperfect happiness that can be had in this life is acquired by man with his natural powers as can be the virtue in which this activity consists, of which we will speak below. But man's perfect happiness, as we have noted, lies in the vision of the divine essence and to see God in his essence is not only above man's nature but that of any creature, as was shown in Part 1. For a creature's natural knowledge is in line with its substance; for example, of intelligence it is said in the *Book of Causes* 8, that it knows things above itself and below itself in the mode of its own substance. But all knowledge that is according to the mode of created substance falls short of the vision of divine essence, which infinitely exceeds every created substance. Hence neither man nor any other creature can achieve ultimate happiness by its natural powers.

Ad 1. It should be said that nature does not fail a man in necessary things, although it does not provide him with armour or clothing as it does other animals but gives him reason and a hand, by which he can provide for himself. Thus it does not fail man in what is necessary even thought it did not give him a principle whereby he can achieve happiness, for this was impossible. But it gave him free will whereby he can turn to God who will make him happy. And what we can do through friends, we are in a sense capable of, as is said in *Ethics* 3.3.

Ad 2. It should be said that the nature that can attain the perfect good is of a nobler condition, even though it needs an external help to achieve it, as the Philosopher says in *On the Heavens* 2.12. One who can achieve perfect health, though he needs the help of medicine for this, is better disposed than one who can achieve imperfect health without the aid of medicine. Therefore the rational creature that can achieve the perfect good of happiness but needs divine help in this is more perfect than the irrational creature which is incapable of such a good but attains some imperfect good in virtue of its nature.

Ad 3. It should be said that when the imperfect and perfect are of the same species, they can be caused by the same power; however, this is not necessary if they are of different species, for whatever can cause the disposition of matter can confer the ultimate perfection. But imperfect activity which is subject to man's natural power, is not of the same species as that perfect activity which is man's happiness, since the species of the activity depends on the object. Hence the argument does not work.

Article 6: Does man attain happiness by the action of some higher creature?

It seems that he does.

1. It seems that a man can become happy through the action of some higher creature, namely, an angel. There is a twofold order found in things: one of the parts of the universe to one another, the other of the whole universe to the good which is outside the universe. The first is ordered to the second as to its end, as is said in *Metaphysics* 11.10, in the way that the order of the parts of the army to one another is for the sake of the order of the whole army to the leader. The order of the parts of the universe to one another results from the action of higher creatures on lower, as was said in Part 1. But happiness lies in the order of man to a good that is outside the universe, that is, God. Therefore a man is made happy by the action of a higher creature, namely, an angel.

2. Moreover, that which is potentially such-and-such can be brought to actuality by that which is actually such-and-such, as water that is potentially hot becomes actually hot by that which is actually hot. Therefore man who is potentially happy will become actually happy through the angel who is actually happy.

3. Moreover happiness lies in the activity of intellect, as has been said, but the angel can illumine the intellect of man. Therefore the angel can make man happy.

ON THE CONTRARY:
There is what is said in Psalm 83.12: 'For God loveth mercy and truth.'

RESPONSE:

It should be said that every creature is subject to the laws of nature, as having limited power and action; but that which exceeds created nature cannot come to be by the power of any creature. Therefore if something must come about that is beyond nature it comes immediately from God, such as the raising of the dead, restoring sight to the blind and the like. But it has been shown that happiness is a good exceeding created nature. Hence it is impossible that it come about by the action of any creature, but a man becomes happy solely through the agency of God, if we are talking of perfect happiness. But if we are speaking of imperfect happiness, the same is true of it as of any virtue in whose activity it consists.

Ad 1. It should be said that where active powers are ordered it often happens that achieving the ultimate end pertains to the highest power while the lower powers aid in the attainment of the ultimate end by disposing, as the art of navigation had by the shipbuilder pertains to the use of the ship for the sake of which it is built. So in the order of the universe, man is aided by the angels in the attainment of the ultimate end, with respect to some things that precede and dispose him to achieve it. But he achieves the ultimate end thanks to the first cause, God.

Ad 2. It should be said that when a form actually exists in something according to perfect and natural existence, it can be the principle of an action towards another, as the warm by its heat makes another warm. But if the form exists in a thing imperfectly and not according to natural existence, it cannot be the principle of the thing's communication with another, as the intention of colour which is in the pupil cannot cause a white thing, nor can all illumined and heated things illumine or heat for then illumination and heating would extend to infinity. But the light of glory by which God is seen is in God perfectly according to natural existence and in the creature imperfectly according to a similar or participated existence. Hence no happy creature can communicate his happiness to another.

Ad 3. It should be said that the blessed angel illumines man's intellect, and that of a lower angel, with respect to some reasons of the divine works but not with respect to the vision of the divine essence, as was said in Part 1. For in seeing it, all are immediately illumined by God.

Article 7: Are some good works needed if man is to receive happiness from God?

It seems not.

1. God, since he is an agent of infinite power, does not presuppose any matter when he acts, or disposition of matter, but can immediately produce the whole. But since man's works are not required for his happiness as efficient cause, as has been said, they can only be required for it as dispositions. Therefore, God, who does not presuppose dispositions when he acts, confers happiness without any preceding works.

2. Moreover, God is the immediate author of happiness, so too he institutes nature immediately. But in the first institution of nature he produced creatures without any prior disposition or action of a creature, but immediately made what he made perfect in its species. Therefore it seems that he confers happiness on man without any preceding operations.

3. Moreover, the Apostle says in Romans 4.6, 'Thus David declares the blessedness of the man to whom God credits justice without works: "Blessed are they whose iniquities are forgiven . . ."' Therefore no works of man are required for achieving happiness.

ON THE CONTRARY:

It is said in John 13.17, 'If you know these things, blessed will you be if you do them.' Therefore, happiness is attained through action.

RESPONSE:

Rectitude of will, as was said above, which is nothing other than the fitting order of will to the ultimate end, is required for happiness in the same way that the disposition of matter is needed for the reception of form. But from this it does not follow that some activity of man ought to precede his happiness, for God could at the same time make the will to tend to the end rightly and to attain it, as sometimes at the same time he disposes matter and introduces the form. But the order of divine wisdom requires that this not happen, for as is said in *On the Heavens* 2.12, of things whose nature it is to have a perfect good, one has something of it without motion, another with one motion, and yet another with many motions. But to have perfect good without motion belongs to that which naturally has it, and only God naturally has happiness. Hence it is proper to God alone that he does not come to happiness without a preceding movement. When happiness exceeds the whole of created nature, no pure creature can fittingly attain happiness without an activity by which it tends to it.

But the angel, who is higher than man in the order of nature, by the order of divine wisdom, attains happiness by one motion of meritorious activity, as was explained in Part 1. But men attain it by many activities which are called merits. Hence too, according to the Philosopher, happiness is the reward for virtuous activities.

Ad 1. It should be said that man's activity is not required as a condition for attaining happiness because of any insufficiency of the divine beatifying power, but in order that the order of things might be saved.

Ad 2. It should be said that God made the first creatures perfect, right off, without any preceding disposition or created activity. In this way he established the first members of species, so that by them a nature might be propagated to posterity. Similarly, because from Christ who is God and man happiness was to derive to others, as the Apostle says in Hebrews 2.10, 'Who had brought many sons in to glory,' immediately from the beginning of his conception without any preceding meritorious activity his soul was happy. But this is singular to him, for the merit of Christ helps baptized children to attain happiness, although they lack any merit of their own, because through baptism they are made members of Christ.

Ad 3. It should be said that the Apostle is speaking of the happiness of hope which is had by justifying grace that is not given for preceding deeds. For it does not have the note of the term of motion, like happiness, but instead is the beginning of a motion whereby one tends towards happiness.

Article 8: Does every man seek happiness?

It seems not.

1. No one can want what he does not know since the apprehended good is the object of appetite, as is said in *On the Soul* 3.10. But many do not know what happiness is, something clear, as Augustine says in *On the Trinity* 13.4, from the fact that some held happiness to lie in the delights of the body, others in the virtue of the soul, others in other things. Therefore, all do not seek happiness.

2. Moreover, the essence of happiness is the vision of the divine essence, as has been said. But some think it to be impossible that God should be

seen in his essence by man, hence they do not seek this. Therefore, not all men seek happiness.

3. Moreover, in *On the Trinity* 13.5 Augustine says that a happy man is one who has everything he wants and wants nothing badly. But not all will this, for some seek some things badly and yet will themselves to will them. Therefore, not all seek happiness.

ON THE CONTRARY:

Augustine says in *On the Trinity* 13.3 that if he should say less, namely that you all wish to be happy and do not want to be miserable, he would have said something that no one could fail to know in his own will. Therefore, each person wants to be happy.

RESPONSE:

It should be said that happiness can be considered in two ways. In one way, according to the common notion of happiness, and thus it is necessary that every man wants happiness. But the common notion of happiness is of a perfect good, as has been said. But since good is the object of will, the perfect good of anyone completely satisfies his will. Hence to seek happiness is nothing other than to seek that the will be satisfied. Which everyone wills. In another way we can speak of happiness according to a special notion, with respect to that in which happiness lies, and then not all men know happiness, because they do not know the thing that fulfils the common notion of happiness. Consequently, so considered, not all will it.

Ad 1. The answer is obvious from what has just been said.

Ad 2. It should be said that since will follows the grasp of intellect or reason, just as it can happen that something is the same in reality but diverse according to the consideration of reason, so it happens that something is one in reality and yet is desired in one way and not in another. Happiness can be considered under the notion of final and perfect good, which is the common note of happiness, and then naturally and of necessity the will tends towards it, as has been said. It can also be considered according to other special considerations, either on the part of the activity or on the part of the operative power or on the part of the object, and thus the will does not tend to it of necessity.

Ad 3. It should be said that the definition of happiness that some maintained – the happy man is the one who has all he desires, or the one to whom all that he wanted comes – understood in one way is good and sufficient, but in another way is imperfect. For if it is understood simply of everything that man wills by natural appetite, then it is true that he who has all that he wills is happy, for nothing satisfies man's natural appetite except the perfect good which is happiness. But if it is understood of the things that a man wants following the grasp of reason, then to have everything one wants does not pertain to happiness, but rather to misery, insofar as when such things are had they impede a man from having whatever he naturally desires, just as reason sometimes takes as true what obstructs knowledge of the truth. Considering this, Augustine added that for the perfection of happiness one willed nothing badly. Although the first, namely that the happy man is he who has all he wills, could suffice if it is rightly understood.

22. *On Human Choice.* Disputed Question on Evil, 6 (1266–72)

The will is a rational appetite, that is, a desire consequent upon knowledge. What specifies and individuates will-acts is the cognitive content that gives them direction. This is why reason is called the formal cause of willing; it specifies willing and gives it direction. But will as efficient cause can move mind and other human faculties. We choose to think or not to think about this or that.

Now it might be thought that once mind has specified an object for will, put before it, so to speak, something as good, fulfilling and perfective, the will must necessarily desire that good. What assures the freedom of the will is not that appetite can, as it were, freak out, and opt for something unthought of – a concept of will that has led many to deny that Aristotle had a concept of will. Rather, whatever particular good the mind puts forward as specifying the will falls short of goodness itself. That is, any proposed object of will is a mixed case, comprising negative as well as positive aspects. Because of the inadequacy as good of any object proposed to the will, the will is free in its regard.

Thomas will say that the will cannot not will goodness itself. Moreover, if the mind knew an object that realized perfectly the notion of goodness, the will would necessarily love that object. God is goodness, as we have seen, and thus when we see God as he is, the will will necessarily love him. There is nothing of goodness absent from God, so there would be no reasonable basis for preferring anything else to him.

In this life, we do not see God as he is; consequently God is seen as a good with negative and positive characteristics and we can prefer creatures to God. This is Thomas's definition of sin.

In the text below, Thomas drives the analysis back to this basic act of the will, its desire for goodness as such. The will is precisely an appetite for goodness. When reason proposes an object to will, this orientation to the good as such is presupposed. Everything we choose must be made to fit under the formality of goodness, that is, be presented as something perfective and fulfilling of us. Considered as a nature, it is of the essence *of will to seek goodness itself. The cause of this is the cause of the will's nature, God. Does God's causality negate freedom? The following text is rightly considered to be Thomas's most thorough discussion of this question.*

DISPUTED QUESTION ON EVIL
QUESTION 6

Does a man have free choice in his actions or does he choose necessarily?

It seems that he chooses necessarily, not freely.

1. For it is said in Jeremiah 10.23 'that the way of a man is not his, neither is it in a man to walk and direct his steps'. But that with respect to which a man has freedom is his, as constituted, as it were, within his dominion. Therefore, it seems that a man does not have free choice of his way or of his acts.

2. It might be objected that this does not refer to the execution of choice, which sometimes is not within a man's power. On the contrary, there is what the Apostle says in Romans 9.16: 'So then there is the question not of him who wills or him who runs, but of God showing mercy.' But running pertains to the external execution of acts and willing to the interior choice. Therefore, not even interior choices are in man's power, but are in man from God.

3. But it will be said that a man is moved to choice by an inner instinct, namely by God himself, and immovably and that this is not repugnant to freedom. On the contrary, any animal moves himself through appetite, but animals other than man do not have free choice because their appetite is moved by some external agent, for example the power of a heavenly body or by the action of some other body. Therefore, if man's will is immovably moved by God, it would follow that a man does not have free choice in his actions.

4. Moreover, the cause of the violent is from outside, the thing being acted upon contributing nothing. If then the principle of free choice is from without, namely God, it seems that the will is moved by violence and necessity. Therefore it does not have free choice of its acts.

5. Moreover, it is impossible for man's will to be out of harmony with the will of God because, as Augustine says in the *Enchiridion*, either man does what God wills or God fulfils his will concerning him. But God's

will is immutable. Therefore, man's will is too. Therefore, all human choices proceed from an unchangeable choice.

6. Moreover, the act of any power bears on its own object, as sight bears only on the visible. But the object of will is the good. Therefore, the will can only will the good. Therefore, it necessarily wills the good and does not have free choice of good or evil.

7. Moreover, any power whose object relates to it as mover to moved is a passive power and for it to act is to be acted upon, so sense is a passive power and sensing is a kind of being acted upon because the sensible moves sense. But the object of will relates to it as mover to moved. The Philosopher says in *On the Soul* 3 and in *Metaphysics* 11 that what is desired is a mover not a moved, but appetite is a moved mover. Therefore will is a passive potency and to will a being acted upon. But every passive power is moved necessarily by what activates it, if it is sufficient. It seems, therefore, that the will is necessarily moved by the appetitible. Therefore a man is not free to will or not will.

8. It will be said that there is necessity in the will with respect to the ultimate end, because everyone necessarily wants to be happy, but not with respect to what is for the sake of the end. On the contrary, just as end is the object of will, so too are things which are for the sake of the end, because both have the note of the good. If, therefore, the will is moved necessarily by the end, it would seem to be necessarily moved to those things which are for the sake of the end.

9. Moreover, where there is the same mover and the same moved, there is the same manner of moving. But when one wills the end and the things that are for the sake of the end, the same thing is moved, namely, will, and there is the same mover, because no one wills the things that are for the sake of the end unless he wills the end. Therefore, there is the same manner of moving such that just as one necessarily wills the ultimate end, so he necessarily wills those things that are for the sake of the end.

10. Moreover, just as intellect is a power separated from matter, so too is will. But the intellect is necessarily moved by its object, for man is necessarily moved to assent to a truth by the force of the argument. For the same reason, therefore, will is necessarily moved by its object.

11. Moreover, the disposition of the first mover is felt in those that follow, because all secondary movers move insofar as they are moved by the prime mover. But in the order of voluntary motions, the prime mover is the perceived desirable thing. Since the grasp of what is appetitible comes about with necessity if by a demonstration it is proved to be good,

its necessity should affect all subsequent movement, and thus the will is moved to will necessarily and not freely.

12. Moreover, the thing is more of a mover than is intention. But according to the Philosopher in *Metaphysics* 6, the good is in things, but the true is in the mind, and thus the good is the thing and the true the intention, and thus the good has more the character of mover than does the true. But the true necessarily moves the intellect, as has been said. Therefore, the good necessarily moves the will.

13. Moreover, love, which pertains to will, is a more intense motion than knowledge which pertains to intellect, because knowledge assimilates but love transforms, as Dionysius says in *On the Divine Names* 4. Therefore, will is more movable than is intellect. If then the intellect is necessarily moved, the will should be even more so.

14. But it will be said that the action of intellect is by a way of a movement towards the soul, but the act of will is by way of movement from the soul, and thus intellect has more of the character of the passive and will of the active, hence the latter is not acted on necessarily by its object. On the contrary, assent pertains to intellect and consent to the will. But assent implies a movement towards the thing assented to just as consent does to the thing consented to. Therefore, the movement of will is no more from the soul than is the movement of intellect.

15. Moreover, if there are things which do not necessarily move the will, the will would have to be said to be ordered to opposites: because that which does not exist necessarily, only possibly exists. But whatever is in potency to opposites becomes actual only through something actual, and we call that which makes a thing actual its cause. Therefore, if will wills something determinately, there must be some cause that makes it will it. Given the cause, however, the effect must follow, as Avicenna proves, because if the cause is given and it is still possible that the effect not be, there would be need of yet another to make it actual, and thus the first is not a sufficient cause. Therefore, will is necessarily moved to will a thing.

16. Moreover, no power that relates to contraries is active because every active power can do that of which it is the cause. But given the possible, the impossible does not follow, for it would be possible for two opposites to exist simultaneously, which is impossible. But the will is an active power, therefore it is not ordered to opposites and necessarily terminates in one thing.

17. Moreover, sometimes the will begins to choose what it did not formerly choose; therefore, either its earlier disposition was changed or

it was not. If not, it follows that just as it formerly did not choose, so not now, and thus not choosing it would choose, which is impossible. If however its disposition is changed, it must have been changed by something, because whatever is moved is moved by another. But the mover imposes necessity on the moved, otherwise it would not sufficiently move it. Therefore, the will is necessarily moved.

18. But it will be said that all these arguments move from material potency, which is in matter, and not from the immaterial potency that is in the will. On the contrary, sense is the beginning of all human knowledge, and nothing can be known by man unless it falls under the senses, either itself or its effect. But the very power that is related to opposites does not fall under the senses, for in its effects which do fall under the senses there are not two contrary acts simultaneously existing, but we always find that it proceeds determinately to one act. Therefore, we cannot judge that there is in man any active power relating to opposites.

19. Moreover, since potency is related to act, as act is to act so potency is to potency, but two opposed acts cannot simultaneously exist. Therefore, a potency cannot be related to two opposites.

20. Moreover, according to Augustine in *On the Trinity* 1, nothing can be the cause of its own being. By parity of reasoning, nothing can be the cause of its own being moved. Therefore, the will does not move itself, but is necessarily moved by another; but it starts to act, previously not acting, and everything of this sort is moved. Hence we say of God that he does not begin to will after having not willed, because of his immutability. Therefore, it is necessary that the will be moved by another, but whatever is moved by another, receives necessity from that other. Therefore, the will wills necessarily and not freely.

21. Moreover, the multiform is reduced to the uniform. But human acts are various and of many forms. Therefore, they should be reduced to the uniform movement of the heaven as to their cause. But whatever is caused by the movement of the heaven comes about necessarily, because a natural cause will produce its effect necessarily unless something impedes it. But nothing can impede the movement of a celestial body such that its effect would not be produced, since the act of the impeding cause would itself have to be reduced back to some celestial principle as its cause. Therefore, it seems that human movements come about necessarily, not from free choice.

22. Moreover, he who does what he does not wish to do does not have free choice; but man does what he does not will; Romans 8.16: 'The evil that I hate, I do.' Therefore a man does not have free choice in his actions.

23. Moreover, Augustine says in the *Enchiridion* that a man who uses his free will badly loses both himself and it. But only one having free will chooses freely. Therefore a man has free choice.

24. Moreover, Augustine says in *Confessions* 8 that when custom is not resisted it becomes necessity. Therefore it seems that at least among those accustomed to do a thing, the will is moved with necessity.

ON THE CONTRARY:

1. There is what is said in Ecclesiasticus 15.14: 'God made man from the beginning, and left him in the hand of his own counsel.' This would not be so if he did not have free choice, which is the desire of what has been previously deliberated about, as is said in *Ethics* 3. Therefore, man has free choice in his actions.

2. Moreover, rational powers are ordered to opposites, according to the Philosopher, and will is a rational power, for it resides in reason, as is said in *On the Soul* 3. Therefore, will is related to opposites and is not necessarily moved to one thing.

3. Moreover, according to the Philosopher in *Ethics* 3, a man is lord of his acts and he has it in him to act and not to act. But this would not be if he did not have free choice in his acts.

RESPONSE:

It should be noted that some held that man's will is necessarily moved to choose something, although they did not say that the will was forced. For not every necessary event is violent, but only that whose principle is from without; hence there are some natural motions which are necessary but not violent: the violent is opposed to both the natural and the voluntary, each of which has its principle within, whereas the principle of the violent is from without.

But this is a heretical opinion, for it takes away the very notion of merit and demerit from human acts. For what someone does necessarily and cannot avoid doing, seems to be neither meritorious nor the opposite. Therefore this should be numbered among the opinions alien to philosophy, since not only is it contrary to faith but it subverts all the principles of moral philosophy as well. If there is nothing free in us, but we are moved to will necessarily, deliberation, exhortation, precept and punishment, praise and blame, in which moral philosophy consists, are swept away. Such opinions, which destroy the principles of some part of philosophy, are called alien positions: for example, 'Nothing moves,' which destroys the principles of natural science. Some men were led to adopt such positions partly from stupidity and partly because of sophistic arguments which they were unable to solve, as is said in *Metaphysics* 4.

To get to the truth of this matter we must first consider that just as in other things there is a principle of their proper activity, so too is there in man. In man intellect and will are the proper active and moving principle, as is said in *On the Soul* 3. This principle is in some ways like the active principle of natural things and in some ways unlike.

Alike, indeed, because just as in natural things there is a form that is the principle of action, and an inclination following form, which is called natural appetite, on which action follows, so in man there is an intellective form and the ensuing inclination of will according to the form apprehended, on which the external act follows. But there is this difference, that the form of the natural thing is individuated by matter so that the inclination following it is determined to one, but the understood form is universal and comprises many within it. Hence, since actions are singular and are not equal to a universal power, the inclination of will is indeterminately related to many. Just as when the artisan conceives the general form of house, under which are included different shapes of house, his will can be inclined to make a square house or a round one or one of another shape.

The active principle in brute animals is midway between the two, for the form apprehended by sense is individual like the form of the natural thing and there follows from it therefore an inclination to one as in natural things, but the form received by sense is not always of the same form as exists in natural things, because fire is always hot, but now this fire, now another, and sometimes pleasant and sometimes not, hence sometimes it is sought and at other times avoided and in this it is like the active human principle.

Second, it should be noticed that any power is moved in two ways: in one way, on the part of the subject; in another, on the part of the object. On the part of the subject, as sight sees more or less clearly because of a change in disposition of its organ; on the part of the object, as sight sees now white, now black. The first change pertains to the exercise of the act, namely that one should act or not act, and well or badly; the second change pertains to the specification of the act, for an act is specified by its object.

It should be noted, however, that with natural things the specification of the act is from form and the exercise is from the agent that causes the motion. But the mover moves for the sake of an end. Thus the first principle of motion with respect to the exercise of the act is from the end.

However, if we should consider the objects of will and of intellect we would find that the object of intellect is the first principle in the order of formal cause, for its object is being and the true, and the object of will is the first principle in the order of final cause, for its object is the good, which comprises all ends, just as all apprehended forms are included in the true. That is why the good itself, insofar as it is a certain apprehensible form, is contained in the true as a kind of truth, and the true itself, insofar as it is the end of intellectual activity, is contained in the good as a particular good. Therefore, if we should consider the motion of powers of the soul from the side of the object specifying the act, the first principle of motion is from intellect, for in this way good as understood moves even the will itself.

If, however, we were to consider the motions of the powers of the soul from the side of the exercise of the act, then the principle of motion is from will. For the power to which the principal end pertains always moves to action the power to which the means to the end pertain, for example the military art moves the maker of harnesses to act, and in this way will moves both itself and all other powers. For I understand because I will to, and similarly I use all the powers and habits because I want to. Hence the Commentator defines habit in [his commentary on] *On the Soul* 3 as a habit that one uses when he wishes to.

Well then, in order to show that the will is not moved with necessity, we must consider the movement of will both with respect to the exercise and with respect to the determination of its act, which is from the object. With respect to the exercise of it first, it is first of all manifest that the will is moved by itself, for just as it moves other powers, so does it move itself. Nor does it follow from this that the will is simultaneously potential and actual, for just as a man in understanding moves himself to knowledge in the mode of discovery, insofar as from one actually known thing he goes on to something unknown, which is known only potentially, so by the fact that a man actually wills something, he moves himself actually to will something else; for example, because he wills health, he moves himself to want to take his medicine. From the fact that he wants health, he begins to deliberate about what health requires and having fixed on it by deliberation, he wants to take the medicine. Deliberation, therefore, precedes the will to take medicine, which in turn proceeds from one's will to deliberate. And since the will moves itself to deliberation, and deliberation is a kind of non-demonstrative inquiry, open to opposites, the will does not move itself necessarily. And since the will does not always will to deliberate, it must be moved by something to want to deliberate, and if by itself, it is necessary that deliberation precede that movement of will and that an act of will precede deliberating. Since this cannot be an infinite regress, it must be acknowledged that, with respect to the first movement of the will, the will of anyone not always actually willing is moved by something outside, by whose instigation the will begins to will.

Some held, accordingly, that this instigation is from a celestial body, but this cannot be, for since will is in reason, according to the Philosopher in *On the Soul* 3, and intellect's reason is not a bodily power, it is impossible that the power of a celestial body should move the will directly. It is those who do not distinguish sense from intellect who hold that the wills of men are moved by the impression of a celestial body just as the appetites of brute animals are. The Philosopher refers to them in the same book of *On the Soul*, when he quotes them as saying that the will of men is such as the father of men and gods makes it, that is, the heaven and the sun.

There remains, then, as Aristotle concludes in the chapter on good fortune, that what first moves will and intellect is something above will and intellect, namely God, who since he moves everything in a way appropriate to what is moved, as the light upward and the heavy downward, moves the will too according to its condition, not by necessity, but as relating indeterminately to many. Therefore it is evident that if the movement of will be considered on the side of the exercise of its act, it is not moved necessarily.

However if the movement of will be considered on the side of the object determining the act of will to this or that, it should be noted that the object moving the will is the apprehended suitable good. Hence, if a good should be proposed which is apprehended as good but not as suitable, it will not move the will. But since deliberations and choices are about particulars, with which acts are concerned, that which is good and suitable has to be apprehended as good and suitable in particular and not only in general. Therefore, if something is grasped as a suitable good in every particular that could be considered, it will necessarily move the will, which is why a man necessarily wants happiness which, as Boethius says, is a perfect state of all goods come together. I say from necessity with respect to the determination of the act, because he cannot will the opposite, but not with respect to the exercise of the act, because one can will now not to think about happiness: the acts of intellect and of will are also particular. Something not found to be good with respect to every possible aspect will not move the will necessarily even with respect to the determination of the act, for one can will its opposite even while thinking of it, perhaps because, considered in one particular, it is suitable, such as the good of health, but it is not pleasant and so forth.

That the will is moved towards that which is offered to it according to this particular condition rather than that can come about in three ways. In one way, insofar as one aspect is preponderant, and then the will is moved according to reason; for example, when a man chooses that which is useful to health because it is useful for pleasure.

In another way, insofar as it thinks of one particular circumstance and not another, and this often happens because something occasions the thought either from within or without.

In a third way, it comes about from a man's disposition, because, according to the Philosopher, as a person is, so does the end appear to him. Hence the will of an angry man is differently moved to something than is a calm man's, because the same thing is not suitable to both; so too food is regarded differently by the well and the sick. Therefore, if the disposition because of which something seems good and suitable to someone is natural and not subject to will, the will would choose it by natural necessity, just as all men naturally desire to be, to live and to understand. If however such a disposition is not natural, but subject to will, for example, when someone is disposed by habit or passion in such a way that something seems good or bad to him in this particular, the will is not moved by necessity, because it could remove this disposition so that the thing would not appear as it does; for example, when someone calms his anger so that he does not judge of something as an angry man does. Passion however is more easily removed than habit.

So, then, with respect to some things the will is necessarily moved on the side of the object, but not with respect to everything, but on the side of exercise of its act it is not moved necessarily.

Ad 1. With regard to the first, it ought to be said that such actuality can be understood in two ways. In one way, as the prophet speaks of the execution of choice, for it is not in the power of man that he effectively completes what the mind deliberates. It can be understood in another way insofar as even the interior will is moved by some higher principle, that is, God, and that is what the Apostle means when he says that it is not of the one willing to will or of the runner to run, as a first principle, but from the merciful God.

Ad 2. The solution to the second is thus evident.

Ad 3. It should be said that brute animals are moved by the instigation of a higher agent to something determined in the manner of a particular form on whose conception sense appetite follows. But God moves the will immovably because of the efficacy of a moving power that cannot fail. But because of the nature of the will moved, which relates indifferently to different things, necessity is not induced, but freedom remains. Just as divine providence works infallibly in all things and yet from contingent causes contingent effects are produced, insofar as God moves all things proportionally, each according to its mode.

Ad 4. It should be said that the will contributes something when it is moved by God, for it is will that acts, though moved by God, and therefore although its movement is from outside as from a first principle, it is not violent.

Ad 5. It should be said that man's will is discordant with the will of God insofar as it wills something God does not want it to will, as when it wills to sin; though God does not want the will to will this, if it so wills God brings it about, for whatever it wills the Lord does. And though in this way man's will is discordant with the will of God with respect to the movement of will, it can never be discordant with respect to result or event, for a man's will always chooses that event because God always fulfils his will concerning man. But with respect to the manner of willing it is not necessary that man's will be conformed to God's, because God wills whatever he wills eternally and infinitely, but man does not. Because of this, it is said in Isaiah 55.9, 'For as the heavens are exalted above the earth, so are my ways exalted above your ways.'

Ad 6. It should be said that because good is the object of will, the will can only will under the formality of the good, but because many and diverse things are contained under the formality of the good, it cannot happen that the will is necessarily moved to this or that.

Ad 7. It should be said that the active moves with necessity only when it surpasses the power of what is acted upon. Since will is in potency with respect to the universal good, no good surpasses the power of will as if moving it necessarily unless it be good in every aspect. Only the perfect good is this, namely happiness, which the will cannot not will, by willing its opposite, but it can not actually will, because it can set aside the thought of happiness insofar as it moves the intellect to its act, and in this respect it does not will even happiness necessarily, any more than one is necessarily warmed if he can will to move away from the heat.

Ad 8. It should be said that the end is the reason for willing that which is for the sake of the end. Hence the will does not relate to both in the same way.

Ad 9. It should be said that when there is only one way to reach the end, there is the same reason for willing the end and the means, but that is not the way it is in the example, for one can reach happiness in many ways. Therefore, although a man necessarily wills happiness, he does not necessarily will the things that lead to happiness.

Ad 10. It should be said that there are similarities and dissimilarities between intellect and will. They are dissimilar with respect to the exercise of their acts, for intellect is moved by the will to act, whereas the will is not moved by another power but by itself. On the side of the object there is a similarity between them, for just as will is necessarily moved by an object which is in every aspect good, though not by an object which can be considered good in one respect and bad in another, so too the intellect is necessarily moved by a necessary truth that cannot be taken as false, but not by a contingent truth, which can be taken as false.

Ad 11. It should be said that the disposition of the prime mover remains in the things moved by it insofar as they are moved by it, for thus they receive its likeness, but they do not wholly receive its similitude. Hence though the first principle is immovable, other things are not.

Ad 12. It should be said that because the true is an intention existing in the mind, it has that which is more formal than the good and more causal in the aspect of object, but the good is more causal in the aspect of end, as has been said.

Ad 13. It should be said that love is said to transform the lover into the beloved insofar as the lover is moved by love to the thing loved. Knowledge assimilates insofar as the likeness of the known comes to be in the knower. The former pertains to the imitation, which is from the agent who seeks the end, but the latter pertains to the imitation, which is according to form.

Ad 14. It should be said that assent does not name a movement of the intellect to the thing, but rather to the conception of the thing which is had in the mind, to which the intellect assents, which it judges to be true.

Ad 15. It should be said that not every cause brings about its effect with necessity, even if it is an efficient cause, because a cause can be impeded so that sometimes its effect does not follow. For example, natural causes, which do not produce their effects with necessity but only for the most part, because they can sometimes be impeded. Therefore, the cause that makes the will to will something, need not do this with necessity, because the will can raise an impediment to it, either by putting aside the consideration which induces it to will or by considering the opposite, namely, that that which is proposed as good is in some respects not good.

Ad 16. It should be said that the Philosopher in *Metaphysics* 6 shows by that means not that some active potency does not relate to contraries, but that the active power that relates to contraries does not produce its effect of necessity. If it did, obviously it would follow that contradictories would simultaneously exist. But if it is given that there is an active power relating to contraries, it does not follow that opposites simultaneously exist, because although both of the opposites to which the power relates are possible, one is not compossible with the other.

Ad 17. It should be said that when the will begins to choose again, it is transmuted from its prior disposition in this respect, that before it was potentially choosing and afterwards it has come actually to choose. And this transmutation is indeed due to some agent, insofar as the will moves itself to act, and also insofar as it is moved by some exterior agent, namely God. But it is not necessarily moved, as has been said.

Ad 18. It should be said that although the principle of human knowledge is in the senses, it is not necessary that whatever a man knows is subject to the senses, or is known immediately through its sensible effect, for intellect understands itself through its act, which is not subject to sense. Similarly, it understands the interior act of the will insofar as the will is in a certain way moved by the act of intellect although in another way the act of intellect is caused by the will, as has been said, as the effect is known through its cause and the cause through its effect. Granted, however, that the power of the will as it relates to opposites cannot be known through any sensible effect, still the argument does not work. For just as the universal, which is everywhere and always, is known by us through singulars, which are here and now, and prime matter which is in potentiality to different forms is known by us through the succession of forms, which are not simultaneously in matter, so the power of the will as it relates to opposites is known by us, not indeed because the opposite acts are simultaneous, but because they successively follow one another from the same principle.

Ad 19. It should be said that the proposition, 'As act is to act, so is potency to potency,' is in some ways true and in some ways false. For if act is understood as corresponding equally to potency as its universal object, the proposition is true, for hearing is to seeing as sound is to colour. But if it be understood as something contained under the universal object as a particular act, then the proposition is not true. For the power of seeing is one, but black and white are not the same. Therefore, although the power of will as it relates to opposites is now in man, the opposites to which the will relates are not simultaneous.

Ad 20. It should be said that a thing does not move itself in the same respect that it is moved, but it can move itself according to something else, for thus the intellect, insofar as it actually understands principles, brings itself from potentiality to act with respect to conclusions, and will, insofar as it wills the end, makes itself actual with respect to the things which are for the sake of the end.

Ad 21. It should be said that the movements of will, although they are of many forms, are reduced to some uniform principle, which, however, is not a celestial body, but God, as has been said – if we speak of a principle which directly moves the will. But if we speak of the movement of the will insofar as it is moved occasionally by an exterior sensible object, then the movement of will is reduced to a celestial body. However, the will is not moved with necessity, for it is not necessary that delightful food being presented, the will desires it. Nor is it true that those things which are directly caused by celestial bodies necessarily come about, for as the Philosopher says in *Metaphysics* 6, if every effect proceeds from some cause and every cause necessarily produces its effect, it would follow that all things are necessary. But both these are false, because some causes, even when they are sufficient, do not necessarily produce their effects, because they can be impeded, as is obvious in all natural causes. Nor again is it true that whatever comes to be has a natural cause; for those things which come to be accidentally do not come about from any active natural cause, because what is accidental is not reduced to a celestial body as to its cause, for the celestial body acts in the manner of a natural agent.

Ad 22. It should be said that he who does what he does not will does not have a free action, but he can have free will.

Ad 23. It should be said that a man by sinning loses free will with respect to the freedom from guilt and misery, but not with respect to freedom from force.

Ad 24. It should be said that custom makes necessity not absolutely, but chiefly in unexpected events, because with deliberation the one accustomed can act contrary to his custom.

23. What Makes Actions Good or Bad? Summa theologiae, 1–2, 18–20 (1271)

The following discussion comprises three of the most important – and longest – articles in the Summa theologiae. *It is the culmination of Thomas's discussion of human acts, which are for him synonymous with moral acts. A complete human act is a complicated interaction of mind and will. Thomas emphasizes the will-acts as components of human action, but it is clear that each of them has a cognitive counterpart. He distinguishes three will-acts bearing on the end – will, enjoyment and intention – and three will-acts which bear on means – consent, choice and use.*

This analysis may seem baroque. Perhaps there are major decisions in life which involve these stages, but is a trip to the mall or the selection of a drink as complicated as all that? The criterion for there being such components of the complete human act is that these are points at which an act may be interrupted. Something is thought of as attractive and the will responds; further dwelling on it leads to an enjoyment of the thought of the possible act; this can solidify into an intention, taking the object as an end to be pursued. When there is only one available means to the end, to want the end is to assent to that way of achieving it. But there may be several means to the end, and the will assents to them all. When it chooses a means, it sets in motion the use of our limbs and other faculties to pursue it. Thomas's thought is that at any one of those points, we may simply turn our minds to something else. Most actions move seamlessly through these stages and we are not reflectively aware of them. But they are implicit in any complete human act.

In the questions below, Thomas turns to the point of his analysis of human action. What are the criteria for morally appraising our acts, distinguishing between the good and the bad? Or are some of them neither, morally indifferent? A large part of the drama of human moral life is interior, prior to overt action. Thomas therefore speaks of the morality of the human act in general and then turns to the morality of the interior act, after which he discusses the morality of the exterior act.

Summa theologiae, First Part of the Second Part,
Questions 18–20

QUESTION 18
THE GOODNESS AND BADNESS OF HUMAN
ACTS IN GENERAL

Next we should consider the goodness and badness of human acts. And first, how human action is good or bad; second, things that follow on the goodness or badness of human acts, such as merit and demerit, sin and fault. With respect to the first, there are three things to take up: first, the goodness and badness of human acts in general (Question 18); second, the goodness and badness of interior acts (Question 19); third, the goodness and badness of exterior acts (Question 20). There are eleven things to ask about the goodness and badness of human acts in general: (1) whether every action is good or some are bad; (2) whether man's action is good or bad because of its object; (3) or because of the circumstances; (4) or from its end; (5) whether any action is good or bad because of its kind; (6) whether an act is specifically good or bad from its end; (7) whether the specification taken from the end is contained under that taken from the object as under a genus, or vice versa; (8) whether any act is specifically indifferent; (9) whether any individual act is indifferent; (10) whether any circumstance can make an act specifically good or bad; (11) whether all circumstances which increase its goodness or badness make the moral act specifically good or bad.

Article 1: Is every action of a man good?

It seems so.

1. It seems that every act of a man is good and none evil. For Dionysius says in *On the Divine Names* 4, that evil only acts in virtue of the good. But evil does not come to be in virtue of the good. Therefore no action is evil.

2. Moreover, nothing acts except insofar as it is actual. But a thing is not evil insofar as it is actual, but insofar as it is a potency lacking act, and when a potency is perfected by act it is good, as is said in *Metaphysics* 11. Therefore, since nothing acts insofar as it is evil, but only insofar as it is good, every action is good and none evil.

3. Moreover, evil can only be an incidental cause, as is clear from Dionysius in *On the Divine Names* 4. But every action has a *per se* effect. Therefore, no action is evil, but every action is good.

ON THE CONTRARY:

The Lord says in John 3.20 that everyone who does evil hates the light. Therefore, some actions of man are evil.

RESPONSE:

It should be said that we must speak of good and evil in actions as we speak of good and evil in things, because a thing acts as it does because of the kind of thing it is. But a thing has as much good as it has being, for good and being are convertible, as was said in Part 1. Only God has the complete fullness of his being as something one and simple, but other things have the fullness of being appropriate to them on several grounds. Thus it comes about that some things have being to a degree, yet fall short of the fullness of being that should be theirs. For the fullness of man's being requires the composition of soul and body with all powers and instruments of knowledge and movement. If any of these be lacking in a man, he falls short of the fullness of his being. He has goodness to the degree he has being but insofar as he is deficient in goodness he is said to be evil, as a blind man has goodness insofar as he lives but it is evil that he lacks sight. If he had nothing of being or goodness he could not be said to be either evil or good. Because the fullness of being is of the very meaning of good, if something should lack any of the fullness of being due it, it would be called good in a certain respect, not simply, although it could be called being simply and non-being in a certain respect, as was said in Part 1.

It must be said, therefore, that every action has goodness to the degree that it has being, but insofar as there is lacking in it anything of the fullness of being due a human action, to that degree it is defective in goodness and is called evil; for example, if there should be lacking to it the amount determined by reason or the appropriate place or the like.

Ad 1. It should be said that evil acts in virtue of a defective good, for if there were nothing of good, neither would there be a being that could act. But if it were not defective, it would not be evil. Hence the action brought about is something deficient in good, which is in a certain respect good, but simply speaking evil.

Ad 2. It should be said that nothing stops a thing from being actual in a certain respect, thanks to which it can act, and deprived of actuality in another respect, which explains the deficiency of the action. Just as a blind man actually has the motor ability thanks to which he can walk, yet insofar as he lacks sight to direct his walking a defect occurs and he stumbles.

Ad 3. It should be said that evil action can have a *per se* effect insofar as it has goodness and being, as adultery is the cause of human generation insofar as it is an intercourse of male and female, but not insofar as it lacks the order of reason.

Article 2: Is the goodness or badness of action due to its object?

It seems not.

1. An action does not seem to derive goodness or badness from its object, for the object of an action is a thing, and evil is not in things but in the use of them by sinners, as Augustine says in *On Christian Doctrine* 3. Therefore, human action does not have goodness or badness from its object.

2. Moreover, the object relates to the action as its matter, but the good of a thing is not from matter, but rather from form, which is act. Therefore, good and evil in acts is not from their object.

3. Moreover, the object of an active power relates to the action as effect to cause; but the goodness of the cause is not dependent on the effect, but rather the reverse. Therefore human action is not good or bad because of its object.

ON THE CONTRARY:

It is said in Osee 9.10: 'And [they] became abominable, as those things were, which they loved.' But a man becomes abominable to God because of the evil of his activity. Therefore, the badness of activity is due to the bad objects that a man loves. And the same is true of the goodness of action.

RESPONSE:

As has been said, the good or evil of action, as of other things, is due to the fullness of being or the defect of being. But the first thing that seems to pertain to the fullness of being is what makes the thing to be of a certain kind. For just as natural things are in a species because of their form, so action is specified by its object, much as motion is by its term.

Therefore, just as the first goodness of the natural thing derives from the form that specifies it, so the first goodness of the moral act derives from an appropriate object, which is why it is called generic goodness by some: for example, to use one's own things. And, just as in natural things the first evil is when the thing generated does not attain its specific form, as when something less than a man is generated, so the first evil in moral actions is caused by its object, for example to take what belongs to another. If it is said to be evil in its genus, genus here is equivalent to species, in much the same way that we speak of the whole human species as human kind (genus).

Ad 1. It should be said therefore that although exterior things are good in themselves, they are not always fittingly related to this or that action. Therefore, considered as objects of such actions, they do not have the character of good.

Ad 2. It should be said that the object is not matter in the sense of *that of which*, but matter as *that about which*, and it has in a way the character of form, insofar as it specifies.

Ad 3. It should be said that the object of a human action is not always the object of an active power, for the appetitive power is in a certain way passive, insofar as it is moved by the desirable thing, and yet it is the principle of human acts. Nor are the objects of passive powers always effects, for example when they have already been changed, as digested food is the effect of the nutritive power but as not yet digested it relates to the nutritive power as the matter on which it acts.

Insofar as the object is in some fashion the effect of the active power, it is the term of its action, and consequently gives it species and form, for motion is specified by its term. And though the goodness of an action is not caused by the goodness of its effect, yet an action is called good because it can bring about a good effect. And this very proportion of action to effect is the reason for its goodness.

Article 3: Is action good or bad because of the circumstances?

It seems not.

1. It seems that action is not good or bad from the circumstances, for circumstances 'stand around' the act as existing apart from it, as has

been said. But good and evil are in the things themselves, as is said in *Metaphysics* 6.4. Therefore, action does not have its goodness or badness from circumstances.

2. Moreover, in the teaching of morals the goodness and badness of the act are of especial concern. But the circumstances, since they are accidents of actions, seem to be beyond the consideration of art, since no art concerns itself with the incidental, as is said in *Metaphysics* 6.2. Therefore, the goodness or badness of action is not from the circumstances.

3. Moreover, that which belongs to something because of its substance is not attributed to it because of any accident. But good and evil belong to the very substance of action because, as has been said, action can be good or evil because of its genus. Therefore, an action is not good or evil because of its circumstances.

ON THE CONTRARY:

The Philosopher says in *Ethics* 2.2 that the virtuous man acts as he should, when he should, and according to all the other circumstances. Therefore, human actions are good or bad because of their circumstances.

RESPONSE:

It should be said that in natural things the fullness of perfection due the thing does not come only from the substantial form which specifies it, but also from many things added to it by way of supervenient accidents, such as a man's shape, colour and the like. If any of these be lacking in appropriate amount, evil results. And so it is with action. For the fullness of its goodness does not consist of its species alone, but there are additions from the things which come to it as kinds of accident, for example the fitting circumstances. Hence if anything be lacking in the appropriate circumstances, the action will be bad.

Ad 1. It should be said that circumstances are outside the action insofar as they are not of the essence of the action, but are in the action as its accidents; no more are the accidents of natural substances parts of their essence.

Ad 2. It should be said that all accidents are incidental to their subjects, but some are properties which are studied by the art. In this way the circumstances of acts are considered in moral doctrine.

Ad 3. It should be said that good converts with being, but something is called being either because it is a substance or an accident; so too good is attributed to a thing not only because of its essential being but also because of its accidents, both in natural things and in moral actions.

Article 4: Is an action good or evil because of its end?

It seems not.

1. Dionysius says in *On the Divine Names* 4 that nothing acts with an eye to evil. Therefore, if good or bad activity were due to the end, no action would be bad, which is patently false.

2. Moreover, the goodness of an act is something existing in it. But the end is an extrinsic cause. Therefore, action is not called good or evil because of the end.

3. Moreover, it can happen that a good activity is ordered to a bad end, as when someone gives alms in order to be praised, and conversely a bad activity can be ordered to a good end, as when someone steals in order to give to the poor. Therefore, the action is not good or evil because of the end.

ON THE CONTRARY:

Boethius says in *On Topical Differences* 1.2 that a thing whose end is good is good and one whose end is evil is evil.

RESPONSE:

It should be said that the disposition of things with respect to goodness and to being is the same. For there are things whose existence does not depend on another, and in these it is sufficient to take their being into account absolutely, but in things whose existence depends on another the cause on which they depend must be considered. But just as a thing's existence depends on agent and form, so its goodness depends on the end. Hence in the divine persons, whose goodness does not depend on another, the notion of goodness does not take the end into account. But human actions, and other things whose existence depends on another, have the character of goodness from the end on which they depend, over and above the absolute goodness which exists in them. Therefore a fourfold goodness can be considered in human action. First, because of genus, insofar as it is an action, because to the degree it has action and being it has goodness, as has been said. Second, because of its species, which is taken from the appropriate object. Third, because of circumstances, as certain accidents of it. Fourth, because of the end, as relating to the cause of goodness.

Ad 1. It should be said that the good with an eye to which one acts is not always a true good: sometimes it is only an apparent good, in which case evil action follows because of end.

Ad 2. It should be said that although the end is an extrinsic cause, the fitting proportion and relation to the end inheres in the action.

Ad 3. It should be said that nothing prevents an action from having one type of goodness and lacking another. In this way it can happen that an action is good in its species or according to circumstances but is ordered to an evil end, and conversely. But it is not a good action simply speaking unless all these goodnesses are present, because any single defect causes evil, but the good is due to the integral cause, as Dionysius says in *On the Divine Names* 4.

Article 5: Are moral acts specified by being good or evil?

It seems that they are not.

1. Good and evil are found in acts conformably with things, as has been said. But things are not specified by good and evil, for good and bad men are in the same species. Therefore, neither should the good and evil in acts make them specifically different.

2. Moreover, since evil is a privation it is a kind of non-being, but non-being cannot be a difference, according to the Philosopher in *Metaphysics* 2.3. Therefore, since the difference constitutes the species, it seems that an act is not constituted in some species from the fact that it is evil. So good and evil do not make human acts specifically different.

3. Specifically different acts have different effects. But the specifically same effect can follow on a good and bad act, as a man can be generated by adultery as well as by a conjugal union. Therefore good and bad acts are not specifically different.

4. Moreover, acts are sometimes called good and evil because of circumstances, as has been said. But circumstances, since they are accidents, do not specify the act. Therefore human acts are not specifically different because of goodness and badness.

ON THE CONTRARY:

According to the Philosopher in *Ethics* 2.1, similar habits produce similar acts. But good and bad habits are specifically different, such as liberality and prodigality. Therefore, good and bad acts are specifically different.

RESPONSE:

It should be said that every act is specified by its object, as has been said above. So some differences in the object must cause specific diversity in acts. But it should be noticed that a difference in the object causes a specific difference in acts insofar as they are referred to one active principle which would not make a difference in the acts insofar as they are referred to another active principle. Because only what is *per se* and not what is incidental constitutes a species, a difference in the object can be *per se* with reference to one active principle and incidental with respect to another, as knowing colour and sound differ *per se* with reference to sense but not with reference to intellect. In human acts, good and evil is said with reference to reason, because as Dionysius says in *On the Divine Names* 4, the good is to be in accord with reason and evil to be outside reason. The good of a thing befits its form and its evil is what is outside its form. Clearly then the difference of good and evil considered in the object relates *per se* to reason, insofar namely as the object is fitting or not fitting to it. An act is a human or moral act insofar as it is from reason. Thus it is manifest that good and evil make moral acts specifically different, for differences divide a species *per se*.

Ad 1. It should be said that even in natural things the good and evil which are respectively in accord with or against nature diversify the natural species, for the dead body and the living body are not of the same species. Similarly the good, insofar as it is according to reason, and evil, insofar as it is against reason, diversify moral species.

Ad 2. It should be said that evil does not imply an absolute privation but one following on such a power. For an act is called specifically evil, not because it has no object, but because it has an object inappropriate to reason, such as to take another's property. Insofar as the object is something positive, it can constitute the species of the evil act.

Ad 3. It should be said that the conjugal act and adultery differ specifically as they are referred to reason, and they have specifically different effects, since one merits praise and reward and the other blame and punishment. But insofar as they are referred to the reproductive power they are not specifically different and then they have an effect specifically the same.

Ad 4. It should be said that the circumstance is sometimes an essential difference of the object, as referred to reason, and then it specifies the moral act. This is the case whenever the circumstance changes the act from good to evil, for a circumstance can only make an act evil insofar as it is repugnant to reason.

Article 6: Does a good or bad end make acts specifically different?

It seems that it does not.

1. It seems that the good and evil which are due to the end do not make acts specifically different, for the act is specified by the object and the end is outside the notion of the object. Therefore the good and evil which come from the end do not make acts specifically different.

2. Moreover, that which is incidental does not constitute the species, as has been said. But it is incidental to an act that it be ordered to some end, as when someone gives alms because of vainglory. Therefore, acts are not specifically different because of the good and evil that come from the end.

3. Moreover, specifically different acts can be ordered to the same end, for example, the acts of different virtues, like those of different vices, can be ordered to the end of vainglory. Therefore, the good and evil taken from the end do not make acts specifically different.

ON THE CONTRARY:

It was shown above that human acts are specified by the end. Therefore, the good and evil that derive from the end make acts specifically different.

RESPONSE:

It should be said that acts are called human insofar as they are voluntary, as was indicated earlier. But there are two kinds of voluntary act, the interior and the exterior, and each has its own object. The end is properly the object of the interior voluntary act, but the object of the exterior act is that on which it bears. Thus, the interior act of will is specified by the end, as by its proper object. But that which is due to will is formal with respect to the exterior act, because in acting the will uses the members as instruments; moreover, exterior acts have the character of morality only insofar as they are voluntary. Therefore, the species of human act are drawn formally from the end, and materially from the object of the exterior act. Hence the Philosopher says in *Ethics* 5.2 that he who steals in order to commit adultery is, speaking formally, more an adulterer than a thief.

Ad 1. It should be said, and was said earlier, that the end too has the character of object.

Ad 2. It should be said that to be ordered to such and such an end, although it is incidental to the exterior act, is not incidental to the interior act of will, which is to the exterior as formal to material.

Ad 3. It should be said that when many specifically different acts are ordered to the same end, the exterior acts are specifically different but the interior act is specifically the same.

Article 7: Is the species of goodness which is from the end contained under that which is from the object as species to genus?

It seems to be.

1. It seems that the species of goodness due to the end is contained as a species under the genus of goodness due to the object, as when one wishes to steal in order to give alms. For the act is specified by its object, as has been said, but it is impossible that something be contained in a species not contained in its proper species, since the same thing cannot be in different species which are not subalternated. Therefore, the species due to the end is contained under the species due to the object.

2. Moreover, the ultimate difference is constitutive of the most specific species. But the difference which is from the end seems to be posterior to that taken from the object, because the end has the character of the ultimate. Therefore, the species taken from the end is contained under the species taken from the object, which is the more specific species.

3. Moreover, the more formal a difference, the more specific it is, because difference is to genus as form to matter. But the species which is from the end is more formal than that which is from the object, as has been said. Therefore, the species which is from the end is contained under the species which is from the object, as the most specific species under a subalternating genus.

ON THE CONTRARY:
Every genus has determinate differences. But acts which are of the same

species because of their object can be ordered to an infinity of ends, as theft to an infinity of goods or evils. Therefore, the species which is from the end is not contained under the species which is from the object, as under a genus.

RESPONSE:
It should be said that the object of the exterior act can relate to the end of the will in two ways, one, as essentially ordered to it, as to fight well is essentially ordered to victory; second, incidentally, as to take what belongs to another is incidentally related to giving alms. But the differences that divide any genus and constitute the species of that genus, must, as the Philosopher says in *Metaphysics* 7.12, divide it essentially. If they do so only incidentally, the division has gone awry; for example, if one should say of animals the one is rational, the other irrational, and of irrational animals, one is winged and the other not winged, these differences are not essential determinants of what is irrational. Rather, the division should go thus: some animals have feet, others do not, and of those having feet, some have two, others four, yet others more, for these are essential determinants of the prior difference. Therefore, when the object is not essentially ordered to the end, the specific difference which is from the object is not essentially determinative of that which is from the end, nor conversely. So neither of these species comes under the other and the moral act has two different species. Hence we say that he who steals in order to commit adultery commits two evils in one act. But if the object is essentially ordered to the end, one of the differences mentioned is determinative of the other.

Hence one of these species will be contained under the other.

But the question remains which is under which? To figure this out we must notice first that to the degree that a difference is taken from a more particular form, it is more specific. Second, that a more universal agent brings about a more universal form. Third, that the later end responds to a more universal cause; for example, victory, which is the ultimate end of the army, is the end intended by the supreme commander, but the ordering of this line or that is the end intended by some inferior officer.

From this it follows that the specific difference which is from the end is more general, and the difference drawn from the object essentially ordered to such an end is specific with respect to it. For the will, whose proper object the end is, is the universal mover with respect to the other powers of the soul whose proper objects are objects of particular acts.

Ad 1. It should be said that with respect to its substance a thing cannot be in two species if one is not under the other. But with respect to what is incidental to a thing it can be in different species; for example, this fruit with respect to colour is in one species, namely white, and with respect to smell, in the species of the redolent. So too the act which with respect to its substance is in one natural species can fall under two species because of the supervenient moral conditions, as has been said.

Ad 2. It should be said that the end is last in execution but first in the intention of reason, with reference to which moral acts are specified.

Ad 3. It should be said that difference is to genus as form to matter insofar as it makes the genus actual, but the genus can be considered to be more formal than the species, insofar as it is more absolute and less restricted. Hence the parts of the definition are put in the genus of formal cause, as is said in *Physics* 2.2. According to this, the genus is the formal cause of the species and the more common it is, the more formal it will be.

Article 8: Is there an act indifferent in species?

It seems not.

1. According to Augustine,[1] evil is the privation of the good. But privation and habit are immediate opposites, according to the Philosopher.[2] Therefore, no act is specifically indifferent, as if it lay midway between good and evil.

2. Moreover, human acts take their species from the end or object, as has been said. But every object and every end has the note of good or evil. Therefore, all human acts are good or evil in their species, and there is none that is specifically indifferent.

3. Moreover, as has been said, an act is called good if it has its due perfection of goodness, and evil if something of this is lacking. But every act must have either the complete fullness of its goodness or be lacking something of it. Therefore, every act must be good or evil in its species and none can be indifferent.

ON THE CONTRARY:

Augustine says in *On the Sermon on the Mount* that there are some

1. *Enchiridion* 11.
2. Aristotle, *Categories* 8.

middle deeds which can come about by a good or evil soul, about which it would be bold to judge. So there are some specifically indifferent acts.

RESPONSE:
It should be said, and has been, that every act is specified by the object, and the human act, which is called a moral act, is specified by the object as related to the principle of human acts, namely reason. Hence if the object of the act includes something befitting the order of reason, it will be specifically good, such as to give alms to the needy. But if it includes something repugnant to the order of reason, it will be specifically evil, such as to steal, which is to take what belongs to another. But it can happen that the object of the act involves nothing pertaining to the order of reason, for example to pick up a stick from the ground, to walk in the park, and the like, and such acts are specifically indifferent.

Ad 1. It should be said that there are two kinds of privation. The first consists in having been deprived, and this leaves nothing but takes away everything; for example, blindness totally takes away sight, and shadows the light, and death life. Between such a privation and the corresponding habit there can be nothing halfway with respect to receiving the thing in question. The second kind of privation consists in being deprived, as sickness is the privation of health, not because it removes health entirely, but because it is on the way towards the total removal of health in death. This privation, since it leaves something, is not opposed without middle to the opposite habit. That is how evil is the privation of good, as Simplicius says in his commentary on the *Categories*, since it does not take away all good but leaves something. Hence there can be something halfway between good and evil.

Ad 2. It should be said that every object or end has some goodness or badness, at least natural, but it does not always involve moral goodness or badness, which involve reference to reason, as has been said. And that is what we are speaking of now.

Ad 3. It should be said that not everything of an act pertains to its species. Hence, although not everything that pertains to its fullness of goodness is in the definition of its species, it is not for this reason either good or evil in its species, as a man is neither virtuous nor vicious according to his species.

Article 9: Is any individual act indifferent?

It seems so.

1. There is no species that does not contain or at least could contain within it some individual. But some acts are specifically indifferent, as has been said. Therefore, some individual act can be indifferent.

2. Moreover, habits are caused by individual acts of a similar kind, as was said in *Ethics* 2.1. But some habits are indifferent. For the Philosopher in *Ethics* 5.1, speaking of some, like the mean and prodigal, says that they are not evil, and yet he notes that they are not good, since they recede from virtue and thus are indifferent as to their habits. Therefore, some individual acts are indifferent.

3. Moreover, the moral good is to virtue as moral evil is to vice. But it sometimes happens that a man does not order an act which is specifically indifferent to the end either of virtue or vice. Therefore, it happens that some individual act is indifferent.

ON THE CONTRARY:

Gregory says in a homily that 'an idle word is one that lacks the usefulness of rectitude or the reason of just necessity or of pious utility'. But the idle word is bad, because men will have to give an account of them on the day of judgement, as is said in Matthew 12: if, however, it does not lack the note of just necessity or pious utility, it is good. Therefore, every word is either good or evil. By parity of reasoning, every other act is either good or bad. Therefore, no individual act is indifferent.

RESPONSE:

It should be said that it sometimes happens that an act specifically indifferent is good or evil considered individually. And this because the moral act, as has been remarked, not only has goodness from the object by which it is specified, but also from the circumstances which are, as it were, accidents, much as something belongs to the individual man because of individual accidents which does not belong to man by reason of the species. But every individual act must have some circumstance by which it is made good or evil, at least because of the end intended. For, since it is reason's role to order, if the act proceeding from deliberate reason is not ordered to an appropriate end, it is repugnant to reason by that very fact and has the character of evil. But if it is ordered to a fitting end it is in agreement with the order of reason and has the character of good. But it must either be ordered to a fitting end or not be so ordered. That is why a man's every act proceeding from deliberate reason, considered individually, is either good or evil. If it does not proceed from deliberate reason but from some imagination, as when one scratches his beard or jiggles hand or foot, such an act is not properly speaking moral or human, since the act has this from reason. Thus it will be indifferent as existing outside the domain of moral acts.

Ad 1. It should be said, therefore, that a specifically indifferent act can exist in many ways: in one way such that it is indifferent according to its species, and that is how the argument proceeds. But no act is in this way specifically indifferent, for there is no object of a human act that cannot be ordered to good or evil, because of the end or circumstances. In another way, it can be called specifically indifferent because it does not have from its species that it is either good or evil. Hence it is by something else that it can become good or evil. Just as a man does not have from his species that he is white or black, but whiteness and blackness come to a man from something other than the principles of the species.

Ad 2. It should be said that, according to the Philosopher, it is what is harmful to other men that is properly evil, and on that basis he says that the prodigal is not evil, because he harms no one but himself. And so too with all the other acts that are not harmful to the neighbour. But we are saying here that evil is generally whatever is repugnant to reason, and on this basis every individual act is good or bad, as has been said.

Ad 3. It should be said that every end intended by deliberative reason pertains to the good of some virtue or to the evil of some vice. For that which one does ordinately for the maintaining or rest of his body, is ordered to the good of virtue in him who orders his body to the good of virtue. And the same is true of the others.

Article 10: Are acts specifically good or bad because of circumstances?

It seems that they are not.

1. The species of the act is from the object; but circumstances differ from the object. Therefore, circumstances do not specify an act.

2. Moreover, circumstances are, as it were, accidents of the moral act, as has been said, but the accident does not constitute a species. Therefore, circumstances do not constitute any species of good or evil.

3. Moreover, there are not several species of the same thing, but there

are several circumstances of the same act. Therefore, circumstances do not place the moral act in some species of good or evil.

ON THE CONTRARY:

Place is a circumstance, but place locates the moral act in a certain species of evil, since to steal something from a sacred place is sacrilege. Therefore, circumstances place the moral act in some species of good or evil.

RESPONSE:

It should be said that just as the species of natural things are constituted by natural forms, so the species of moral acts are constituted by forms conceived in reason, as is clear from what was said above. Because nature is determined to one, a natural process cannot go on to infinity but must come to an ultimate form from which the specific difference is taken, after which there cannot be another specific difference.

Hence it is that in natural things that which is accidental cannot provide a difference constituting a species. But the process of reason is not determined to something one, but given anything it can go further. Therefore, what in one act is taken as a circumstance superadded to the object that specifies the act can be taken again by ordering reason as a principal condition of the object specifying the act. For example, to take what is another's is specified by the notion of another, by which it is put in the species of theft, and any note of place or time that would be considered over and above this would be a circumstance. But because reason can order with respect to place or time and other like things too, it happens that a condition of place with regard to an object can be taken as contrary to the order of reason. For example, reason ordered that no one be injured in a sacred place. Hence, to take something belonging to another in a sacred place adds a special repugnance to the order of reason. Therefore place, which was first considered a circumstance, is now considered to be a principal condition of the object repugnant to reason. In this way, whenever a circumstance looks to a special order of reason, pro or con, the circumstance must specify the moral act as good or evil.

Ad 1. It should be said that insofar as circumstances specify the act, they are taken to be conditions of the object, as has been said, and as a specific difference of it.

Ad 2. It should be said that circumstance, if it retains the status of circumstance and has the character of accident, does not specify, but when it is changed into a principal condition of the object, it does specify.

Ad 3. It should be said that not every circumstance puts the moral act in a species of good or evil, since not every circumstance implies agreement or disagreement with reason. Thus, although there are many circumstances of the same act, it is not necessary that a single act be in several species, even though it is not absurd that the same moral act be in several different moral species, as has been said.

Article 11: Do all circumstances relevant to the goodness and badness of acts cause them to differ specifically?

It seems so.

1. Good and evil are specific differences of moral acts. But what makes a difference in the goodness or badness of the moral act makes it differ according to a specific difference, which is to differ specifically. But that which adds to the goodness or badness of the act makes it differ according to goodness and badness. Therefore, it causes it to differ in species.

2. Moreover, the advening circumstance either has some character of goodness or badness in itself or it does not. If not, it cannot add any goodness or badness to the act, because what is not good cannot make something better, and what is not evil cannot make something worse. But if it does have in itself some character of goodness or badness, it will have some species of good or evil from this. Therefore, every circumstance increasing goodness or badness constitutes a new species of good or evil.

3. Moreover, according to Dionysius in *On the Divine Names* 4, evil is caused from single defects. But any circumstance aggravating evil has a special defect. Therefore, any circumstance adds a new species of sin. For the same reason any circumstance that increases goodness seems to add a new species of good, just as a unit added to a number makes a new species of number: for the good consists of number, weight and measure.

ON THE CONTRARY:
More and less do not diversify a species, but more and less are a circumstance adding goodness or badness. Therefore, not every circumstance adding goodness or badness constitutes a moral act in a species of good or evil.

RESPONSE:
It should be said that, as has been remarked, a circumstance gives to the

moral act a species of good or evil insofar as it observes a special order of reason. Sometimes it happens that a circumstance does not look to an order of reason to good or evil unless another circumstance is presupposed, from which the moral act is specified as good or evil. Just as to take something in large or small quantity does not look to the order of reason to good or evil, unless some other condition is presupposed by which the act has badness or goodness, for example that it belongs to someone else, which is repugnant to reason. Hence to take another's in great or small quantity does not diversify the species of sin. But it can aggravate or diminish sin. And it is the same in other evils and goods. Hence not every circumstance adding to goodness or badness alters the species of the moral act.

Ad 1. It should be said that in things which are intensified or eased, the difference of intensification and easing does not diversify the species any more than the more or less white differ in the species of colour. Similarly what causes diversity in good or evil by intension and remission does not cause a difference in the species of the moral act.

Ad 2. It should be said that the circumstance aggravating sin or increasing the goodness of the act, sometimes has no goodness or badness of itself, except by being ordered to another condition of the act, as has been said. Therefore, it does not give a new species, but increases the goodness or badness which is from another condition of the act.

Ad 3. It should be said that not every circumstance brings along a singular defect in itself but only as ordered to something else. Similarly it does not always add a new perfection except by comparison to something else, and to that degree, although it increases goodness or badness, it does not always alter the species of good or evil.

QUESTION 19
THE GOODNESS AND BADNESS OF THE INTERIOR ACT OF THE WILL

Next we must consider the goodness of the interior act of the will, and ten things must be asked: (1) whether the goodness of the will depends on the object; (2) and whether solely on the object; (3) whether it depends on reason; (4) whether it depends on the eternal law; (5) whether an erring reason obliges; (6) whether the will in following an erring reason against the law of God is evil; (7) whether the goodness of the will with respect to things done for the sake of the end depends on the end intended; (8) whether the quantity of goodness or badness in the will follows on the quantity of good or evil in the intention; (9) whether the goodness of the will depends on conformity to the divine will; (10) whether it is necessary that the human will be conformed to the divine will in what it wills in order that it be good.

Article 1: Does the goodness of the will depend on the object?

It seems that it does not.

1. The will can only be of the good, because evil is outside the will, as Dionysius says in *On the Divine Names* 4. Therefore, if the goodness of the will were judged from the object, it would follow that every will is good and none evil.

2. Moreover, the good is found first in the end, hence the goodness of the end, as such, does not depend on anything else. But according to the Philosopher in *Ethics* 6.5, good action is of the end, although doing is never the end, for it is always ordered as to an end to something made. Therefore, the goodness of the act of the will does not depend on some object.

3. Moreover, everything makes something like unto itself, but the object of will is good with the goodness of nature. Therefore, it cannot bestow moral goodness on the will. Therefore, the moral goodness of the will does not depend on the object.

ON THE CONTRARY:
The Philosopher says in *Ethics* 5.1 that justice is that whereby someone wills just things, and, generalizing, virtue is that whereby someone wills good things. But a good will is one which is according to virtue. Therefore the goodness of the will is due to the fact that one wills the good.

RESPONSE:
It should be said that good and evil are essential differences of the act of the will, for good and evil essentially pertain to the will, as true and false do to reason, whose act is essentially distinguished into true and false, as when we say that an opinion is true or false. Hence to will well and badly are specifically different acts. But acts are specifically different because of their objects, as has been said. Therefore, good and bad acts of the will are properly such because of their objects.

*

Ad 1. It should be said that the will is not always of the true good, but sometimes of the apparent good, which indeed has some character of good, but is not absolutely appropriate to desire. Because of this the act of will is not always good, but sometimes evil.

Ad 2. It should be said that although an act can be the ultimate end of man in a certain fashion, such an act is not an act of the will, as has been said above.

Ad 3. It should be said that reason presents the good to the will as its object, and insofar as it falls under the order of reason, it pertains to the moral order and causes moral goodness in the act of the will. For reason is the principle of human and moral acts, as has been said above.

Article 2: Does the goodness of the will depend only upon the object?

It seems that it does not.

1. The end is closer to will than to any other power. But the acts of the other powers derive their goodness from the end as well as from the object, as has been made clear already. Therefore, the act of the will too receives goodness, not only from the object but also from the end.

2. Moreover, the goodness of the act is not only from its object but also from its circumstances, as was said above. But given the diversity of circumstances, there follows a diversity of goodness and badness in the act of the will, because one wills when he ought, where he ought, as much as he ought, and how he ought – or as he ought not. Therefore, the goodness of the will depends not only on the object but also on the circumstances.

3. Moreover, ignorance of the circumstances excuses the badness of the will, as was said above. But this would not be so if the goodness and badness of the will did not depend on circumstances. Therefore, the goodness and badness of the will depend on the circumstances and not on the object alone.

ON THE CONTRARY:
The act is not specified by the circumstances as such, as was said above. But good and evil are specific differences of the act of the will, as has been pointed out. Therefore, the goodness or badness of the will does not depend on the circumstances, but solely on the object.

RESPONSE:

It should be said that the more something is prior in any genus the more simple it is, consisting of fewer things, as the first bodies are simples. Therefore, we find that those things which are first in a genus are in some way simples, and do not have components. But the principle of the goodness and badness of human acts is from the act of the will. Therefore the goodness and badness of the will should be grounded in one thing, whereas the goodness or badness of other acts can be based on several factors. But that which is a principle in any genus is essential, not incidental, because whatever is incidental is reduced to that which is essential as to its principle. Therefore, the goodness of the will depends on one thing alone which makes its act essentially good, namely the object, and not on the circumstances which are accidents of the act.

Ad 1. It should be said that the end is the object of the will, not of the other powers. Hence, with respect to the act of the act, there is no difference between the goodness which is from the object and that which is from the end, as is the case in the acts of the other powers, save perhaps accidentally, insofar as one end depends on another end, and will on will.

Ad 2. It should be said that, given that the will is of the good, no circumstance can make it evil. When it is said that someone wills some good when he ought not and where he ought not, this can be understood in two ways. In one way, such that this circumstance refers to the thing willed, and then the will is not of the good, because to will to do something when it ought not to be done is not to will the good.

In another way, such that it is referred to the act of willing, and then it is impossible that someone will the good when he ought not, because a man ought always to will the good, save perhaps incidentally, insofar as one, by willing this good, is then impeded from willing some obligatory good. But, then, evil does not ensue from the fact that one wills this good, but from this that he does not will the other good. And the same should be said of the other circumstances.

Ad 3. It should be said that ignorance of the circumstances excuses the badness of action when the circumstances are on the side of the thing willed, and one is unaware of the circumstances of the act that he wills.

Article 3: Does the goodness of the will depend on reason?

It seems that it does not.

1. The prior does not depend on the posterior. But good pertains to will before it does to reason, as is clear from the foregoing. Therefore the good of the will does not depend on reason.

2. The Philosopher says in *Ethics* 6.2 that the goodness of the practical intellect is a truth conformed to right appetite. But right appetite is the good will. Therefore, the goodness of practical reason depends on will rather than the reverse.

3. Moreover, the mover does not depend on what is moved, but vice versa. But the will moves reason and the other powers, as was said above. Therefore, the goodness of the will does not depend on reason.

ON THE CONTRARY:
Hilary says in *On the Trinity* 10, 'Every pertinacious undertaking of the will is immoderate, because will is not subject to reason.' But the goodness of the will consists in being moderated. Therefore, the goodness of the will depends on its being subject to reason.

RESPONSE:
It should be said that, as has been argued, the goodness of the will properly depends on the object, but the object of the will is proposed to it by reason. The good as understood is the object proportioned to the will; the sensible good or the imaginary good are not proportioned to will but to sense appetite, because will can tend to the universal good, which reason apprehends, whereas sense appetite tends only to a particular good, as grasped by sense powers. Therefore, the goodness of the will depends on reason in the way in which it depends on the object.

Ad 1. It should be said that the good under the formality of good, that is, as desirable, pertains to will before it pertains to reason, but it pertains to reason under the formality of the true before it pertains to will under the formality of desirable, because the will's desire can only be of a good apprehended by reason.

Ad 2. It should be said that the Philosopher is speaking there of practical intellect insofar as it is deliberative and calculating of the things which are for the sake of the end, for thus it is perfected by prudence. The rectitude of reason with regard to things which are for the sake of the end consists in conformity to the desire for the obligatory end. But this very desire for the obligatory end presupposes a right grasp of the end, which is by reason.

Ad 3. It should be said that the will in a certain manner moves reason and reason in another manner moves the will, namely on the part of the object, as was said above.

Article 4: Does the goodness of will depend on the eternal law?

It seems that it does not.

1. Each thing has but one rule and measure, but the rule of the human will, on which its goodness depends, is right reason. Therefore, the goodness of the will does not depend on the eternal law.

2. The measure is homogeneous with the measured, as is said in *Metaphysics* 10.9. But the eternal law is not homogeneous with the human will. Therefore, eternal law cannot be the measure of the human will such that its goodness depends upon it.

3. Moreover, the measure ought to be most sure. But the eternal law is unknown to us. Therefore, it cannot be the measure of our will, such that the goodness of our will would depend upon it.

ON THE CONTRARY:

Augustine says in *Against Faustus* 22.27 that sin is to do, say or desire anything against the eternal law. But the badness of the will is the root of sin. Therefore, since the badness of the will is the opposite of goodness, the goodness of the will depends on eternal law.

RESPONSE:

It should be said that in all ordered causes, the effect depends more on the first cause than on the second, because the second cause acts only in virtue of the first. That human reason should be the rule of human will is from eternal law, which is the divine reason, hence Psalm 4.6–7: 'Many say, "Who will show us good things?" Lift up the light of thy countenance upon us, O Lord!' As if to say, the light of reason that is in us can show us the good and regulate our will because it is the light of your countenance, that is, derived from your countenance. Hence the goodness of the will depends much more on the eternal law than on human reason, and where human reason fails, we must have recourse to the divine reason.

*

Ad 1. It should be said that there cannot be many proximate measures of one thing, but there can be many measures if one is subordinate to the other.

Ad 2. It should be said that the proximate, but not the remote, measure is homogeneous with the measured.

Ad 3. It should be said that although the eternal law is unknown to us as it is in the divine mind, it is made known to us in a certain way either through natural reason, which comes from it as its proper image, or through some superadded revelation.

Article 5: Is a will that departs from erring reason evil?

It seems that it is not.

1. Reason is the rule of the human will insofar as it derives from eternal law, as has been said. But erring reason does not derive from eternal law. Therefore, erring reason is not the rule of the human will and the will is not evil if it does not accord with erring reason.

2. Moreover, according to Augustine, the command of a lower power does not oblige if it conflicts with a command of a higher power, as when the proconsul permits what the emperor forbids. But erring reason sometimes proposes something contrary to the precept of a superior, namely God whose power is the greatest. Therefore, the dictate of erring reason does not oblige, nor is the will evil if it is not in accord with erring reason.

3. Moreover, every evil will is reduced to some species of badness. But a will in discord with erring reason cannot be reduced to any species of badness; for example, if reason erred in this that it said that fornication ought to be committed, the will of one not wishing to fornicate cannot be reduced to any evil. Therefore, the will in discord with erring reason is not evil.

ON THE CONTRARY:

As was said in Part 1,[1] conscience is nothing other than the application of knowledge to some act. But knowledge is in reason. Therefore, the will in discord with erring reason is against conscience, but every such will is evil, for it is said in Romans 14.23: 'All that is not from faith is sin,' that is, everything that is contrary to conscience. Therefore, the will in discord with erring reason is evil.

---

1. q. 79.

RESPONSE:

It should be said that since conscience is a kind of dictate of reason (for it is the application of knowledge to an act, as was said in Part 1), it is the same thing to ask whether the will in discord with erring reason is evil as to ask whether an erring conscience obliges. On which score, some distinguish three kinds of act: those which are good in their kind, those which are indifferent, those which are evil in their kind. Therefore, they say, if reason or conscience dictates that something is to be done which is good of its kind, there is no error. Similarly, if it dictates that something is not to be done which is evil of its kind, since it prescribes goods for the same reason that it prohibits evils.

But if reason or conscience tells someone that he is held by precept to do things bad in themselves, or that those things of themselves good are prohibited, this will be an erring reason or conscience. Similarly, if reason or conscience tells one that that which is in itself indifferent, such as to pick up a stick from the ground, is prohibited or commanded, reason or conscience is erring. Therefore, they say, an erring reason or conscience which either commands or prohibits indifferent things obliges, and willing in discord with such an erring reason will be evil and a sin. But reason or conscience erring by prescribing what is of itself evil or prohibiting that which is of itself good and necessary for salvation does not oblige, and in such cases to will in discord with erring reason or conscience is not evil.

But this is absurd. For in indifferent matters, the will in discord with erring reason or conscience is evil in some way because of the object on which the goodness or badness of the will depends, not because of the proper nature of the object, but insofar as it happens to be grasped by reason as an evil to be done or to be avoided.

And because the object of the will is what is proposed to it by reason, as has been said, by the fact that something is proposed by reason as evil, the will, in bearing on it, accepts the formality of evil. But this happens not only in indifferent matters but also in things good or evil of their kind. For it is not only that which is indifferent that can happen to take on the character of good or evil, but even that which is good can be thought by reason to be evil and that which is evil to be good. For example, it is good to abstain from fornication, but the will can only bear on this good if it is proposed to it by reason. Therefore, if it should be proposed as evil by mistaken reason, it would bear on it under the formality of evil, hence the will is evil because it wills evil, not indeed that which is evil in itself, but that which is evil incidentally, because of the grasp of reason. Similarly, to believe in Christ is good as such and necessary for salvation, but the will does not bear on it unless it is proposed by reason. Hence, if reason proposed it as an evil, the willing bears on it as evil – not because it is evil in itself, but because it happens to be grasped by reason as evil.

Therefore, the Philosopher in *Ethics* 7.9 says that, speaking *per se*, the incontinent is one who does not follow right reason, but, speaking accidentally, he is one who does not follow false reason. Hence it must be said that, simply speaking, every will in discord with reason, whether it be correct or mistaken, is always evil.

Ad 1. It should be said that although erring reason does not derive from God, none the less it proposes its judgement as true, and consequently as derived from God, from whom all truth comes.

Ad 2. It should be said that what Augustine says holds when it is known that the inferior commands something contrary to the command of the superior. But if someone believes that the command of the proconsul is the command of the emperor, by despising the command of the proconsul, he despises that of the emperor. Similarly, if a man knows that human reason dictates something contrary to God's command, he is not held to follow reason, but then reason is not completely erring. But when erring reason proposes something as the precept of God, then to despise the dictate of reason is to despise the command of God.

Ad 3. It should be said that reason, when it grasps something as evil, always grasps it under some formality of evil, for example that it is in conflict with the divine command, or that it is a scandal, or some other such thing. And then the evil will is reduced to that species of badness.

Article 6: Is the will in accord with erring reason good?

It seems that it is.

1. Just as the will in discord with erring reason tends towards that which reason judges to be evil, so the will agreeing with reason, tends towards that which reason judges to be good. But the will in discord with reason, even if it be erring, is evil. Therefore the will in agreement with reason, even if it be erring, is good.

2. Moreover, the will in accord with the command of God and eternal law is good. But eternal law and the precept of God are proposed to us

by the grasp of reason, even if it be erring. Therefore, the will in accord even with erring reason is good.

3. Moreover, a will in discord with erring reason is evil. If, therefore, a will in accord with erring reason should also be evil, it seems that whatever one having an erring reason wills is evil. And thus such a man is in a quandary and will of necessity sin, which is absurd. Therefore, the will in accord with erring reason is good.

ON THE CONTRARY:
The will of those killing the Apostles was evil, yet it was in accord with their erring reason, according to John 16.2: 'Yes, the hour is coming for everyone who kills you to think that he is offering worship to God.' Therefore, a will in accord with erring reason can be evil.

RESPONSE:
It should be said that just as the previous question is the same as the question whether an erroneous conscience binds, so this question is the same as whether an erroneous conscience excuses. This question depends on what was said earlier about ignorance, for it was said above that ignorance sometimes causes the involuntary and sometimes not. And because moral good and evil consist in the voluntary act, as is clear from the foregoing, it is manifest that the ignorance which causes the involuntary takes away the character of moral good and evil, but not that which does not cause the involuntary. For it was said above that the ignorance which is in some way willed, whether directly or indirectly, does not cause the involuntary. And I call that ignorance directly voluntary on which the act of will bears, and indirectly voluntary that due to negligence, when one does not wish to know what he is held to know, as was said above. Therefore, if reason or conscience errs with a voluntary error, whether directly or because of negligence, and it is an error about something one is held to know, then such an error of reason or conscience does not excuse and the will in accord with reason or conscience so erring is evil. But if the error which causes the involuntary comes from ignorance of some circumstance without any negligence, then such an error of reason or conscience excuses and the will in accord with erring reason is not evil. If erring reason dictates that a man is held to sleep with the wife of another, the will in accord with such erring reason is evil, because this error arises from ignorance of the law of God, which he is held to know. But if reason errs because one believes some yielding woman is his wife and she asks him to do his duty and he wills to have sex with her, his

will is excused and is not evil, because this error comes from ignorance of the circumstances, which excuses and causes the involuntary.

Ad 1. It should be said that, as Dionysius says in *On the Divine Names* 4, the good comes about from the integral cause, but evil from single defects. Therefore, in order for that on which the will bears to be called evil it suffices that it is either evil in itself or that it is apprehended as evil. But in order to be good, it must be good in both ways.

Ad 2. It should be said that the eternal law cannot err, but human reason can. Therefore, the will in accord with human reason is not always right, nor is it always in accord with eternal law.

Ad 3. It should be said that just as in syllogism, given one absurdity another must follow, so in morals given one unfitting thing others necessarily follow. For example, suppose someone seeks vainglory, then whether he does what he is held to do or fails to because of vainglory, he will sin. Nor is he perplexed or in a quandary, because he can get rid of his evil intention. Similarly, supposing the error of reason or conscience which arises from an ignorance which does not excuse, evil in the will necessarily follows. Yet such a man is not in a quandary, because he can draw back from error, since his ignorance is vincible and voluntary.

Article 7: Does the goodness of the will depend on the intention of the end?

It seems that it does not.

1. It was said above that the goodness of the will depends on the object alone, but as to the things which are for the sake of the end, the object of will is one thing and the end intended another. Therefore, in such things the goodness of the will does not depend on the intention of the end.

2. Moreover, to wish to observe God's command pertains to a good will. But this can be referred to a bad end, namely the end of vainglory or cupidity, when one wishes to obey God because of consequent temporal advantages. Therefore, the goodness of the will does not depend on the intention of the end.

3. Moreover, good and evil, as they diversify acts of will, so do they diversify ends. But the badness of the will does not depend on the badness of the end intended, for one who wishes to steal in order to give alms has a bad will although he intends a good end. Therefore, the goodness of the will does not depend on the goodness of the end intended.

ON THE CONTRARY:

Augustine says in the *Confessions* 9.13 that intention is rewarded by God. But something is rewarded by God because it is good. Therefore, the goodness of the will depends on intention.

RESPONSE:

It should be said that intention relates to will in two ways, either as preceding, or as concomitant. Intention precedes the will causally when we will something because we intend some end. Then the order to the end is considered as a reason for the goodness of the thing willed, as when someone wills to fast for the sake of God. Hence, since the goodness of the will depends on the goodness of the thing willed, as was said above, it is necessary that it depend on the intention of the end.

Intention follows will when it attaches to an already existing will, as when someone wills to do something and afterwards refers it to God. Then the goodness of the first will does not depend on the following intention, unless that act of will is repeated along with the following intention.

Ad 1. It should be said that when intention is the cause of willing, the order to the end is taken as a reason for the goodness in the object, as has been said.

Ad 2. It should be said that the will cannot be called good if a bad intention is the cause of willing. For one who wills to give alms out of vainglory, wills what is of itself good under the formality of evil, and therefore, as it is willed by him, it is evil. Hence his will is evil. But if the intention is consequent, then the will can be good and the act of will that preceded cannot be depraved by the following intention, but only the act of will which is repeated.

Ad 3. It should be said that, as has already been remarked, evil comes about from single defects, but the good from the whole and entire cause. Hence, whether will is of that which is of itself evil, even under the formality of good, or of the good under the formality of evil, the will will always be evil. In order for the will to be good, it must be of the good under the formality of the good. That is, it wills the good for the sake of the good.

Article 8: Does the amount of goodness in the will depend on the amount of goodness in the intention?

It seems that it does.

1. Commenting on Matthew 12.35, 'The good man from his good treasure brings forth good things,' the Gloss says that one does as much good as he intends. But intention not only gives goodness to the exterior act but also to the will, as has been said. Therefore, one will have as much good will as he intends.

2. Moreover, if the cause is increased, the effect is increased. But the goodness of intention is the cause of a good will. Therefore, the will is as good as the amount of good intended.

3. Moreover, with respect to evils, one sins in the amount that he intends, for if someone throwing a stone intends to kill a man, he is guilty of homicide. Therefore, by parity of reasoning, in good things, in the amount that one intends the good, to that amount the will is good.

ON THE CONTRARY:

The intention can be good and the will bad. Therefore, with equal reason, the intention can be more, and the will less, good.

RESPONSE:

It should be said that with respect to the act and the intention of the end, amount or quantity can be measured in two ways: on the side of the object, because one wills a greater good, or from the intensity of the act, because one intensely wills or acts, which is greater on the side of the agent.

Therefore, if we speak of the quantity of both according to object, it is manifest that the quantity of the act does not follow the quantity of the intention. With regard to the exterior act, this can come about in two ways. In one way, because the object intended is not proportioned to that end; for example, if someone offered ten pounds for something costing a hundred, his intention to buy could not be realized. In another way, because of the impediments that can arise with regard to the exterior act which are not in our power to remove; for example, someone intends to go as far as Rome and impediments arise which prevent him from doing so.

But unlike the exterior act the interior act of will is in our power and thus this occurs only in one way. The will can desire some object not proportioned to the intended end, and thus the will which bears on the object considered as such is not as good as the intention. But intention too in its way pertains to the act of will, insofar as it is the reason for it, and that is why the amount of the good intention redounds to will, insofar as the will wishes some great good as its end, although that by which it wills to achieve it is not worthy of that good.

But if the quantity of the intention and of the act are considered according to the intension of each, then the intension of the intention redounds to the interior and exterior acts of the will, because the intention relates formally to both, as is clear from what has been said above.[1] Although materially, given an intense existing intention, the interior or exterior acts can be less intense, materially speaking: as when someone does not desire to take his medicine as intensely as he wishes to be well. However, the intense desire of health redounds formally on an intense desire to take medicine.

But it must be considered that the intension of the interior or exterior acts can be referred to the intention as an object, as when someone intends intensely to will or to do something intensely. But not for this reason does he intensely will or act, because the goodness of the interior or exterior act does not follow the quantity of the good intended, as has been said. Hence it is that one does not merit as much as he intends to, because the quantity of merit consists in the intension of the act, as will be said below.[2]

Ad 1. It should be said that the Gloss is speaking of reputation with God, who especially considers the intention of the end. Hence another gloss on the same text says that the treasury of the heart is intention, by which God judges works. For the goodness of intention, as has been said, in a certain manner redounds to the goodness of will which makes the exterior act meritorious before God.

Ad 2. It should be said that the goodness of intention is not the whole cause of a good will. Hence the argument does not work.

Ad 3. It should be said that the badness of intention alone suffices for the badness of the will, and therefore in the amount the intention is bad, in that amount the will is bad. But it is not the same with goodness, as has been said.

1. q. 18, art. 6.
2. q. 20, art. 4.

Article 9: Does the goodness of will depend on conformity with the divine will?

It seems that it does not.

1. It is impossible that the will of man be conformed to the will of God, as is evident from what is said in Isaiah 55.9: 'For as the heavens are exalted above the earth, so are my ways exalted above your ways, and my thoughts above your thoughts.' Therefore, if conformity to the divine will were required for the goodness of will, it would follow that it is impossible for a man's will to be good, which is absurd.

2. Moreover, just as our will is derived from the divine will, so our knowledge derives from the divine knowledge. But it is not required that our knowledge be conformed to the divine knowledge, for God knows many things of which we are ignorant. Therefore, it is not required that our will be conformed to the divine will.

3. Moreover, will is the principle of action. But our action cannot be conformed to the divine action. Therefore, neither can our will.

ON THE CONTRARY:

Matthew 26.39 says, 'Yet not as I will but as thou willest,' which he says because he wants man to be right and to be directed to God, as Augustine explains in the *Enchiridion*. But the rectitude of will is its goodness. Therefore, the goodness of will depends on conformity to the divine will.

RESPONSE:

It should be said that, as was argued, the goodness of the will depends on the intention of the end. But the ultimate end of the human will is the highest good, God, as was said above. Therefore the goodness of the human will requires that it be ordered to the highest good, God. But this good primarily and as such relates to the divine will as its proper object. That which is first in any genus is the measure and reason of all the rest in that genus. A thing is right and good to the degree that it attains its proper measure. Therefore, in order for the will of man to be good, it must be conformed to the divine will.

Ad 1. It should be said that the will of man cannot be conformed to the divine will by equality, but by imitation. Similarly human knowledge is conformed to divine knowledge insofar as it knows the truth, and man's action to the action of God, insofar as it is appropriate to the agent. But this is by imitation, not equality.

The solutions to the second and third arguments are clear from this.

Article 10: Does the human will have to be conformed to the divine will in what is willed?

It seems not.

1. We cannot will what we do not know, for the good apprehended is the object of will. But for the most part we do not know what God wills. Therefore, the human will cannot be conformed to the divine will in what it wills.

2. Moreover, God wills to damn someone whom he foresees will die in mortal sin. Therefore, if a man were held to conform his will to the divine will with respect to what is willed, it would follow that a man would be held to will his own damnation, which is absurd.

3. Moreover, no one is held to will what is contrary to piety. But if a man willed what God wills, this would sometimes be contrary to piety, as when God wills one's father to die. If the son willed this it would be contrary to piety. Therefore man is not held to conform his will to the divine will with respect to what is willed.

ON THE CONTRARY:

1. Commenting on Psalm 32.1, 'Praise becomes the upright,' the Gloss says that he has a right heart who wills what God wills. But everyone is held to have a right heart. Therefore, everyone is held to will what God wills.

2. Moreover, the form of the will, like that of any other act, is from the object. Therefore, if a man is held to conform his will to the divine will, it follows that he is held to do so with respect to the thing willed.

3. Moreover, the conflict of wills consists in the fact that men will different things. But whoever has a will in conflict with the divine will has an evil will. Therefore, whoever does not conform his will to the divine will with respect to what is willed, has an evil will.

RESPONSE:

It should be said that, as is clear from the foregoing, the will bears on an object proposed to it by reason. But it happens that reason considers something in different ways, such that under one aspect it is good, and under another not good. Therefore, the will of one who wills it to be insofar as it has the aspect of good is good, and the will of another, who wills it not to be insofar as it has the note of evil, will also be a good will. Just so the judge has a good will when he wills the execution of the thief, because it is just, yet the will of another, say of the wife or child who does not wish him killed, insofar as killing is a natural evil, is also good.

But when the will follows the apprehension of reason or intellect under a more common formality of the good, then will bears on a more common good. As is clear in the previous example, for the judge has care of the common good, which is justice, and therefore wills the killing of the thief insofar as this has the note of good with respect to the common condition, but the wife of the thief has to consider the private good of the family, and thus she wills that her husband not be killed.

The good of the whole universe is what is apprehended by God, who is the maker and ruler of the universe; hence whatever he wills, he wills under the formality of the common good, that is, of his own goodness which is the good of the whole universe. But the good of the creature, given his nature, is a particular good proportioned to his nature and it can happen that something is good according to a particular formality which is not good according to a universal formality, and vice versa, as has been said. Therefore it happens that a will is good when willing something considered according to a particular formality which God does not will according to the universal formality, and vice versa. That is why different willings of different men concerning opposites can both be good, insofar as they will them to be or not to be under different particular aspects.

The will of a man willing a particular good is only right when it is referred to the common good as to its end, since even the natural appetite of any part is ordered to the common good of the whole. The formal reason for willing that which is ordered to the end is taken from the end. Hence, in order that someone will a particular good with right will it is necessary that the particular good be willed materially, and that the divine common good be willed formally. Therefore, the human will is held to be conformed to the divine will in what is formally willed, for it is held to will the divine and common good, but not materially, for the reason given. But with respect to both, in a certain respect, the human will is conformed to the divine will. Because, insofar as it is conformed to the divine will in the common formality of what is willed, it is conformed to it in the ultimate end. Insofar as it is conformed to it in what is willed materially, it is conformed to it under the formality of efficient cause, because it has from God as from an efficient cause its proper natural inclination or the particular apprehension of this thing. Hence it is customary to say that a man's will is conformed to the divine will when he wills what God wants him to will.

There is another mode of conformity according to the notion of formal cause, namely when man wills something out of charity, just as God wills. And this conformity too is reduced to the formal conformity which is read from the order to the ultimate end, the proper object of charity.

Ad 1. It should be said that we can know what is willed by God under the common formality, for we know that God wills everything under the aspect of the good. Therefore whoever wills something under any aspect of the good has a will conformed to the divine will with respect to the reason for willing. But in particular we do not know what God wills, and in this respect, we are not held to conform our will to the divine will. But in the state of glory all will see in each thing willed its order to that which God wills concerning it. Therefore, not just formally, but materially too, they conform their will to God in everything.

Ad 2. It should be said that God does not will the damnation of anyone under the formality of damnation, nor anyone's death as death, because he wills all men to be saved, but he wills it under the formality of justice. Hence it suffices in such matters that a man wills the justice of God and that the order of nature be served.

Thus is evident the solution to the third.

To what was said on the contrary:

Ad 1. It should be said that a will is more conformed to God's will in the reason for willing a thing than in the thing willed, because will bears principally on the end, rather than on what is for the sake of the end.

Ad 2. It should be said that the species and form of the act are taken from the formality of the object rather than from that which is material in the object.

Ad 3. It should be said that there is no conflict of wills when people will different things for different reasons. But if something is willed for one reason by one person, that another does not will, this brings about a conflict of wills. But that is not what is at issue.

QUESTION 20
THE GOODNESS AND BADNESS OF EXTERIOR ACTS

Next we must consider goodness and badness with respect to exterior acts, and there are six things to be asked: (1) whether goodness and badness are first in the act of the will or in the exterior act; (2) whether the whole goodness or badness of the exterior act depends on the goodness of the will; (3) whether there is the same goodness and badness of the interior and exterior acts; (4) whether the exterior act adds goodness or badness to the interior act; (5) whether the subsequent outcome adds something of goodness or badness to the exterior act; (6) whether the same exterior act can be good and evil.

Article 1: Do good and evil consist in the exterior act before the act of will?

It seems that they do.

1. Will has its goodness from the object, as was said above, but the exterior act is the object of the interior act of the will, for we are said to will theft, or to will to give alms. Therefore, good and evil are in the exterior act first, then in the act of will.

2. Moreover, good belongs to the end first, because the things that are for the sake of the end have the note of good from being ordered to the end. But the act of the will cannot be the end, as has been said above although the act of another power can be the end. Therefore, the good first consists in the act of another power rather than in the act of the will.

3. Moreover, the act of will is formally related to the exterior act, as has been said above; but that which is formal is later, for form comes to matter. Therefore, good and evil are in the exterior act prior to being in the act of will.

ON THE CONTRARY:
Augustine says in the *Retractions* that the will is that whereby one either sins or lives well. Therefore moral good and evil are first in the will.

RESPONSE:
It should be said that exterior acts can be called good or evil in two ways. In one way, according to their genus as well as according to their

circumstances; thus to give alms, in the appropriate circumstances, is said to be good.

In another way it is said to be good or bad from being ordered to the end; thus to give alms for the sake of vainglory is said to be evil. Since the end is the proper object of the will, it is manifest that the note of good or evil that the exterior act has from being ordered to the end is found first of all in the will and is derived from it to the exterior act.

But the goodness or badness that the exterior act has in itself, because of due matter and circumstances, is not derived from the will, but rather from reason. Hence if the goodness of the exterior act is considered insofar as it is in the ordering and apprehension of reason, it is prior to the goodness of the act of will, but if it is considered as it is in the execution of the work, it follows the goodness of the will, which is its principle.

Ad 1. It should be said that the exterior act is an object of will insofar as it is proposed to will by reason as a good apprehended and ordered by reason, and thus it is prior to the good of the act of will. But insofar as it consists in the execution of the work, it is an effect of will and follows will.

Ad 2. It should be said that the end is first in intention, but last in execution.

Ad 3. It should be said that form, as it is received in matter, is after matter in the process of generation, although it is prior in nature, but insofar as it is in the agent cause it is in every way prior. But the will is compared to the exterior act as efficient cause. Hence the goodness of the act of will is the form of the exterior act, as existing in the agent cause.

Article 2: Does the complete goodness and badness of the exterior act depend on will?

It seems that it does.

1. It is said in Matthew 7.18, 'A good tree cannot bear bad fruit, nor can a bad tree bear good fruit.' By tree is meant the will and by fruit the work, according to the Gloss. Therefore the interior will cannot be good and the exterior act evil, or conversely.

2. Augustine says in the *Retractions* that we sin only through will. Therefore, if there is no sin in the will there will be no sin in the exterior

act. Thus the whole of the goodness or badness of the exterior act depends on the will.

3. Moreover, the good and evil of which we now speak are differences of the moral act. But differences divide the genus essentially, according to the Philosopher in *Metaphysics* 7.6. Therefore, since an act is moral insofar as it is voluntary, it seems that the good and evil in the act come solely from the will.

ON THE CONTRARY:

Augustine says in *On Lying* that there are things which cannot be done well because of any good end or good will.

RESPONSE:

As was already noted, it should be said that the exterior act can be considered to have a twofold goodness or badness, one because of due matter and circumstances, the other from being ordered to the end. The latter depends wholly on the will, but that which is from due matter and circumstances depends on reason, and the goodness of the will depends on this, insofar as it bears upon it. But it must be considered that, as was said above, in order for something to be bad a single defect suffices, although a single good is insufficient for it to be simply good. For that, integral goodness is required. Therefore, if the will is good from its proper object, and from the end, the exterior act is good as a consequence, but the goodness of will which is from the intention of the end does not suffice for the exterior act to be good. But if the will is evil from the end intended or from the act willed, as a consequence the exterior act is evil.

Ad 1. It should be said that the good will, insofar as it is meant by the good tree, must be understood as having its goodness from the act willed and from the end intended.

Ad 2. It should be said that not only does one sin through the will by willing an evil end, but also by willing a bad act.

Ad 3. It should be said that not only the interior act of will is called voluntary, but also exterior acts, insofar as they proceed from will and reason. Therefore, there can be a difference of good and evil in both acts.

*Article 3: Is the goodness or badness of the interior act of the will the
same as the goodness and badness of the exterior act?*

It seems not.

1. The principle of the interior act is the interior apprehensive or
appetitive power, but the principle of the exterior act is the power of
executing motion. Where there are different principles of action, there
are diverse acts. But the act is the subject of goodness or badness and the
same accident cannot be in two subjects. Therefore, the goodness of the
interior and of the exterior act cannot be the same.

2. Moreover, virtue is what makes one good and renders his work
good, as is said in *Ethics* 2.6. But the intellectual virtue in the commanding
power and the moral virtue in the commanded power differ, as is clear
from *Ethics* 1.13. Therefore, the goodness of the interior act, which is of
the commanding power, is different from the goodness of the exterior
act, which is of the commanded power.

3. Moreover, the same thing cannot be both cause and effect, since
nothing is cause of itself, but the goodness of the interior act is the cause
of the goodness of the exterior act, or conversely. Therefore, the goodness
of the two cannot be the same.

ON THE CONTRARY:
It was shown above that the act of the will is formal with respect to the
exterior act. But one thing comes to be from the formal and material.
Therefore, there is but one goodness of the interior and exterior acts.

RESPONSE:
It should be said that, as was explained above, the interior act of the will
and the exterior act, insofar as they are in the moral order, are one act.
But it sometimes happens that an act which is one in subject has several
reasons for its goodness or badness, and sometimes only one. Therefore,
it should be said that sometimes the goodness or badness of the interior
and exterior acts is the same, and sometimes different. For as has already
been said, these two, the goodness or badness of the interior and that of
exterior acts, are related to one another.

But it can happen that in things ordered to another, something is good
solely from the fact of being ordered to another, as bitter medicine is
good only because it makes one well. Hence the goodness of health and
that of medicine are one and the same and do not differ. Sometimes,

however, that which is ordered to another has a character of goodness in itself over and above that following on its being ordered to another good, as tasty medicine has the note of a delightful good over and above the fact that it is curative.

Therefore it should be said that when the exterior act is good or bad solely because of its order to the end, then the goodness or badness of the act of the will which looks to the end, and of the exterior act, which looks to the end through the mediation of the act of will, are in every way the same. But when the exterior act has a goodness or badness in itself, because of matter or circumstances, then the goodness of the exterior act differs from the goodness of the will which is from the end, such that both the goodness of the end redounds to the exterior act from the will, and the goodness of matter and circumstances redound to the act of will, as has already been said.

Ad 1. It should be said that the argument proves that the interior and exterior acts differ as to natural genus, but something one in the moral order is constituted from these different things, as was said above.

Ad 2. It should be said that, as is said in the *Ethics* 6.12, the moral virtues are ordered to the acts of the virtues, which are, as it were, ends; but prudence, which is in reason, is concerned with things which are for the sake of the end. On account of this different virtues are required. But right reason with respect to the very end of the virtues does not have another goodness than that of the virtues, insofar as the goodness of reason is participated in by each virtue.

Ad 3. It should be said that when something derives from one thing to another as from a univocal agent cause, what is in each differs; for example, the heat of that which warms and the heat of that which is warmed differ, though they are specifically the same. But when something derives from one to another according to analogy or proportion, then it is only numerically one; for example, from the health that is in the animal body, health derives to medicine and urine, but there is not a health of medicine or of urine different from that of the animal — which medicine causes and urine signifies. In this way the goodness of the exterior act is derived from the goodness of the will, and conversely, according to the order of one to the other.

Article 4: Does the exterior act add to the goodness or badness of the interior act?

It seems that it does not.

1. Chrysostom says in commenting on Matthew that it is the will that is either rewarded for good or condemned for evil. But works are the testimony of the will. Therefore, God does not ask works for themselves, in order to know how he should judge, but for others, that all may understand that God is just. But good and evil should be estimated according to the judgement of God rather than the judgement of men. Therefore, the exterior act adds nothing to the goodness or badness of the interior act.

2. Moreover, there is one and the same goodness in the interior and exterior acts, as has been said. But increase comes about by adding one to another. Therefore, the exterior act adds no goodness or badness to the interior act.

3. Moreover, the whole of created goodness adds nothing to the divine goodness, because the whole is derived from the divine goodness. But the goodness of the exterior act sometimes derives as a whole from the goodness of the interior act, but sometimes conversely, as has been said. Therefore, the one does not add any goodness or badness to the other.

ON THE CONTRARY:
Every agent intends to pursue the good and avoid evil. Therefore, if nothing of goodness or badness is added by the exterior act, it would be idle for one who has a good or bad will either to do a good work or refrain from an evil one. Which is absurd.

RESPONSE:
It should be said that if we are speaking of the goodness that the exterior act has from the will of the end, then the exterior act adds nothing of goodness, unless it should happen that the will itself should become better in good things or worse in evil. It seems that this can come about in three ways.

In one way, numerically. For example, when someone wills to do something for a good or bad end and does not do it then but later wills and does it, the act of will is duplicated and thus there is a twofold good or a twofold evil.

In another way, with respect to extension. For example, when someone wishes to do something for a good or bad end but because of some impediment desists, whereas another continues the movement of will to the point of perfecting the work; manifestly this kind of will is longer lasting in good or evil, and in this is better or worse.

In a third way, with respect to intension. For there are some exterior acts which, insofar as they are painful or pleasurable, are of a nature to be intended or avoided by the will. But it is the case that insofar as the will tends more intensely to good or evil it is better or worse.

But if we are speaking of the goodness that the exterior act has according to matter and due circumstances, then it relates to will as term and end. And in this way it adds goodness or badness to the will, because every inclination or movement is perfected when it achieves its end or attains its term. Hence there is only a perfected will when, given the opportunity, it acts. If the chance is lacking, the will can be perfect in that it would act if it could, and the defect of perfection which is from the exterior act is simply involuntary. But the involuntary does not deserve punishment or merit praise in doing good or evil, if a man quite involuntarily fails to do good or evil.

Ad 1. It should be said that Chrysostom means when the will of man is fulfilled, and not when it stops acting only because it is impotent to act.

Ad 2. It should be said that the argument proceeds from the goodness the exterior act has from the end willed. But the goodness the exterior act has from matter and circumstances is different from the goodness of the will which is from the end, although not from the goodness the will has from the act willed itself; to that it is related as its reason and cause, as was said above.

Ad 3. The solution to the third is clear from this.

Article 5: Does the subsequent outcome add to the goodness or badness of the act?

It seems that it does.

1. The effect pre-exists virtually in the cause. But outcomes follow the act as effects follow causes. Therefore, they pre-exist virtually in the acts. But a thing is judged good or evil according to its own virtue, for virtue is what makes the one having it good, as is said in *Ethics* 2.6. Therefore, the outcome adds to the goodness or badness of the act.

2. Moreover, the good things that listeners do are effects following on the preaching of the teacher, but such goods redound to the merit of the preacher, as is evident from what is said in Philippians 4.1: 'My brethren, beloved and longed for, my joy and my crown.' Therefore, the subsequent outcome adds to the goodness or badness of the act.

3. Moreover, punishment is not added unless guilt increases, hence it is said in Deuteronomy 25.2: 'According to the measure of the sin shall the measure also of the stripes be.' But the subsequent outcome is added to the punishment, as is said in Exodus 21.29: 'But if the ox was wont to push with his horn yesterday, and the day before, and they warned his master, and he did not shut him up, and he shall kill a man or a woman, then the ox shall be stoned, and his owner also shall be put to death.' But he would not have been killed if the ox had not killed a man, even though it had not been shut up. Therefore, the subsequent outcome adds to the goodness or badness of the act.

4. Moreover, if someone brings on the cause of death by stabbing or by passing sentence, and death does not follow, he would not be convicted of law-breaking. But if death does follow, he is convicted. Therefore, the subsequent outcome adds to the goodness or badness of the act.

ON THE CONTRARY:

The subsequent outcome does not make a good act evil nor a bad one good. If someone should give alms to a poor man, who uses it to sin, nothing is taken away from the one who gave alms, and similarly if someone patiently bears an injustice done him, he who commits it is not for that reason excused. Therefore, the subsequent outcome does not add to the goodness or badness of the act.

RESPONSE:

It should be said that the subsequent outcome either is foreknown or it is not. If it is, it is manifest that it adds to the goodness or badness. For when someone who thinks that many evils can follow from his deed does not refrain from it, his will is revealed to be quite disordered. However, if the subsequent outcome is not foreknown, then we must distinguish.

Because if it follows essentially from such an act, and for the most part, then the subsequent outcome adds to the goodness or badness of the act, for it is obvious that an act from which many good things can follow is a better act of its kind, and an act from which many evils follow is a worse one. But if incidentally or rarely, then the subsequent outcome does not add to the goodness or badness of the act, since a judgement is not passed on what belongs to a thing incidentally, but only on that which is essential.

Ad 1. It should be said that the power of a cause is appraised by its essential, not its incidental, effects.

Ad 2. It should be said that the good things that the listeners do follow on the preaching of the teacher as essential effects, so they redound to the reward of the preacher, and especially when they are intended.

Ad 3. It should be said that the outcome for which punishment is commanded to be inflicted on him follows essentially on such a cause, and, moreover, is taken to be foreknown and therefore it is imputed to punishment.

Ad 4. It should be said that the argument would work if irregularity followed the fault. But it follows not the fault but the deed, because of some defect of the sentence.

Article 6: Can the same act be good and bad?

It seems so.

1. A continuous motion is one, as is said in *Physics* 5.9, but one continuous motion can be good and bad; for example, if someone going along to church at first intends vainglory, but afterwards intends to serve God. Therefore, one act can be good and bad.

2. Moreover, according to the Philosopher in *Physics* 3.3, action and passion are the same act. But passion can be good, as that of Christ, and the action evil, as that of the Jews. Therefore the same act can be good and evil.

3. Moreover, since the servant is as an instrument of the master, the action of the servant is the action of the master, just as the act of the tool is the act of the artisan. But it can happen that the act of the servant proceeds from the good will of the master, and thus is good, but from the bad will of the servant, and this is evil. Therefore, the same act can be good and evil.

ON THE CONTRARY:

Contraries cannot be in the same subject. But good and evil are contraries. Therefore the same act cannot be good and evil.

RESPONSE:
There is nothing to prevent a thing's being one insofar as it is in this genus, and many insofar as it is in another genus. Just as a continuous surface is one, considered in the genus of quantity, but many, insofar as it is referred to the genus of colour if it is partly white and partly black. So too nothing prevents an act from being one with respect to the natural genus but not as referred to a moral genus, and vice versa, as has been said. An uninterrupted walk is one act with respect to its natural genus, but it can happen that it is many moral acts, if the will of the walker alters, will being the principle of moral acts.

Therefore, if we take an act which is of one moral kind, it is impossible for it to be both good and bad with moral goodness and badness. But if the unity is of the natural, not the moral, genus, the act can be both good and bad.

Ad 1. It should be said, therefore, that a continuous motion which proceeds from different intentions, although it is one with the unity of nature, is not one with moral unity.

Ad 2. It should be said that action and passion belong to the genus of morals insofar as they have the mark of the voluntary. Therefore, insofar as voluntary acts are due to different willings they are morally two, and the one can be good and the other bad.

Ad 3. It should be said that the act of the servant, insofar as it proceeds from the will of the servant, is not the act of the master, but only when it proceeds from the command of the master. Hence the evil will of the servant does not make the master bad.

24. On Law and Natural Law.
Summa theologiae, 1–2, 90–94
(1271)

The so-called Treatise on Law *has enjoyed an autonomous career in recent years, often being published separately from Part 1 of Part 2 of the* Summa theologiae, *of which it forms a part. An adequate understanding of it must depend on what has preceded it and on what follows it. This is not to say that no understanding of it as a separated unit is possible, but this severed existence has sometimes led to a distorted view of Thomas's moral doctrine. Readers worry about Thomas's legalism in morals and wonder how what he has to say about law comports with the role of virtue.*

The Treatise on Law *is not another moral theory than that found in the questions and articles that preceded it; rather it complements and depends upon them. Moral goodness consists in willing the good that is recognized by the mind. The moral part of the* Summa *begins with what can be called an end/means analysis of action. By seeming contrast, the* Treatise on Law *employs a rule/application model of action.*

The term law is for Thomas an analogous one. When he sets forth in Question 90 the essence of law, it is clear that human positive law is at the forefront of his mind. The other laws to which he draws our attention – eternal law, natural law, divine law – participate more or less perfectly in the definition of law. From a linguistic point of view, human law is law properly speaking. Ontologically, however, it is the eternal law that is the measure of all other laws.

It is the relation between natural and human law that attracts readers, since the derivation of the latter from the former is what legitimates it. The common principles of natural law are prescriptions that the good or end must be pursued. The process of inquiry leading to a proximate rule for action is the search for appropriate means to achieve the end. The complementarity of the two models of action is inescapable.

Summa theologiae, First Part of the Second Part, Questions 90–94 Treatise on Law

QUESTION 90
THE ESSENCE OF LAW

We must now consider the exterior principles of acts. The exterior principle inclining to evil is the devil, of whose temptations we spoke in Part 1. The exterior principle moving towards good is God, who instructs us through the law and helps us with grace. First then, we must speak of law; second, of grace. With respect to law, we must first consider law in general, and, second, its parts. As for law in general, there are three things to be taken up, first, its essence; second, the different kinds of law; third, the effects of law. Four things must be asked about the first: (1) whether law is something of reason; (2) the end of law; (3) its cause; (4) its promulgation.

Article 1: Is law something of reason?

It seems that it is not.

1. The Apostle says in Romans 7.23, 'I see another law in my members . . .' But nothing that is of reason is in the members, because reason does not use a bodily organ. Therefore law is not something of reason.

2. Moreover, in reason there is only power, habit and act. But law is not the power of reason, nor does it seem to be any habit of reason, because the habits of reason are the intellectual virtues, of which we spoke earlier. Nor is it the act of reason, because then law would cease when the activity of reason stopped, as in those sleeping. Therefore law is not something of reason.

3. Law moves those subject to it to act rightly. But to move to action pertains properly to will, as is clear from the foregoing. Therefore law does not pertain to reason, but rather to will, as even the Jurist says: what pleases the prince has the force of law.

ON THE CONTRARY:
It is for law to command and prohibit. But it is reason that commands, as was said above. Therefore law is something of reason.

RESPONSE:

It should be said that the law is a rule and measure of acts, according to which someone is led to act or to refrain from acting: law [*lex*] comes from 'binding' [*ligando*], because it obligates to act. But reason is the rule and measure of human acts, because it is the first principle of human acts, as is clear from the foregoing: it pertains to reason to order to the end, which is the first principle in things to be done, according to the Philosopher. In no matter what genus that which is the principle is the measure and rule of that genus, as unity in the genus of number, and the first motion in the genus of movements. It follows that law is something pertaining to reason.

Ad 1. It should be said that since law is a rule and measure, it is said to be in something in two ways. In one way, as in the measuring and ruling. Since this is proper to reason, in this way law is in reason alone. In another way, as in the ruled or measured, and thus law is in everything which is inclined to something by some law, such that any inclination coming from some law can be called law, not essentially, but by way of participation. And in this way the inclination of the members to concupiscence is called the law of the members.

Ad 2. It should be said that just as in exterior acts we must consider both the activity and the product of the activity, for example, building and the house, so in the works of reason we must consider the very act of reason, which is understanding and reasoning, and something constituted by them, which in speculative reason is, first, the definition, then the enunciation, and finally the syllogism or argument. And because practical reason uses a kind of syllogism in things to be done, as was said above and as the Philosopher teaches in *Ethics* 8.3, we must find in practical reason something that is to operation as, in speculative reason, the proposition is to conclusions. Such universal propositions of practical reason ordered to action have the character of law. These propositions are sometimes actually considered, and sometimes are held in reason habitually.

Ad 3. It should be said that reason has the power to move from the will, as has been said above. From the fact that someone wills the end, reason issues commands about things which are for the sake of the end. But in order for the things commanded to have the character of law, will must be regulated by reason. And thus we should understand that the will of the prince has the force of law, otherwise the will of the prince would be iniquity rather than law.

Article 2: Is law always ordered to the common good?

It seems not.

1. It pertains to law to command and prohibit. But precepts are ordered to quite singular goods. Therefore the common good is not always the end of law.

2. Moreover, law directs man to act; but human acts concern particulars. Therefore law is ordered to a particular good.

3. Moreover, Isidore says in the *Etymologies* 2.10 that if law is established by reason, everything that reason establishes would be law. But reason does not only order to the common good, but also to the private good. Therefore, law is not ordered to the common good alone, but also to the private good of an individual.

ON THE CONTRARY:

Isidore says in the *Etymologies* 5.21 that law is not written for some private advantage but for the common utility of the citizens.

RESPONSE:

It should be said that, as has been mentioned, law pertains to that which is the principle of human acts, because it is a rule and measure. For just as reason is the principle of human acts, so too there is in reason itself something which is a principle with respect to all else, and law pertains to this especially and principally. The first principle in things to be done, with which practical reason is concerned, is the ultimate end. Felicity and happiness are the ultimate end of human life, as was said above. Hence law must especially look to the ordering to happiness. Again, since every part is ordered to its whole as the imperfect to the perfect, and one man is a part of the perfect community, it is necessary that law properly look to the order to the common happiness. Hence the Philosopher, in the cited definition of legal matters, makes mention of happiness and political community. For he says in *Ethics* 5 that we call those things legally just that are creative and conservative of happiness and its particulars by political co-operation; for the city is the perfect community, as is said in *Politics* 1. In whatever genus that which is the most is the principle of the others, and the others are named as ordered to it, as fire, which is the most hot, is the cause of heat in mixed bodies, which are called hot to the degree that they participate in fire. Hence it is necessary that, since law is said to consist especially in its order to the common good, any other precept concerning a particular deed has the character of law only insofar as it is ordered to the common good. Therefore, every law is ordered to the common good.

Ad 1. It should be said that a precept implies an application of law to the things which are regulated by law. But the ordering to the common good, which pertains to law, is applicable to singular ends. And so far forth precepts are given of some particulars.

Ad 2. It should be said that operations are indeed concerned with particulars, but those particulars can be referred to the common good, not by a community of genus or species, but by the community of final cause, insofar as the common good is said to be the common end.

Ad 3. It should be said that just as nothing is firmly established in speculative reason save by resolution to first indemonstrable principles, so nothing is firmly established in practical reason save through ordering to the ultimate end, which is the common good. What relates to [practical] reason in this way has the character of law.

Article 3: Is anyone's reason the cause of law?

The answer seems to be yes.

1. For the Apostle says in Romans 2.14, 'When the Gentiles who have no law do by nature what the Law prescribes, these having no law are a law unto themselves.' He says this universally of all. Therefore anyone can make a law for himself.

2. Moreover, as the Philosopher says in *Ethics* 2.1, it is the intention of the legislator to lead men to virtue. But any man can lead another to virtue. Therefore, the reason of any man is cause of law.

3. Moreover, as the prince of the city is its governor, so any father is governor of the home. But the prince of the city can make law in his city; therefore any father who heads a household can make law in his home.

ON THE CONTRARY:
Isidore says in the *Etymologies* 5.10 – and it is also to be found in the *Decretals*, Distinction 2 – that law is an ordinance of a people insofar as the elders along with the people sanction something. Therefore, it is not for just anyone to make law.

RESPONSE:
It should be said that law properly, first and chiefly, looks to the order to the common good. But to order something to the common good is either the task of the whole multitude or of someone bearing the power of the multitude. Therefore, to fashion law pertains either to the whole multitude or to some public person who has charge of the whole multitude. Because, as in all other cases, ordering to the end is proper to the one whose end it is.

Ad 1. It should be said that, as was explained above, law is not only in the one regulating but also by way of participation in the regulated. In this way, each person is a law unto himself, insofar as he participates in the order of some ruler. Hence in the same place is added, 'They show the work of the Law written in their hearts.'

Ad 2. It should be said that the private person cannot efficaciously lead to virtue. He can admonish, but if his warning is ignored, he does not have any power to coerce, as law does, in order that it might efficaciously lead to virtue, as the Philosopher says in *Ethics* 10.9. The multitude or the public person has this coercive power which pertains to the exacting of punishment, as will be said below. Therefore it pertains to it alone to make laws.

Ad 3. It should be said that just as a man is part of a household, so the household is a part of the city, for the city is a perfect community, as is said in *Politics* 1.1. Therefore, just as the good of one man is not the ultimate end, but is ordered to the common good, so too the good of one household is ordered to the good of one city, which is a perfect community. Hence he who governs a family can indeed make precepts or statutes, but they will not properly have the character of law.

Article 4: Is promulgation of the essence of law?

It seems that it is not.

1. Natural law especially has the character of law, but natural law does not need promulgation. Therefore it is not of the essence of law that it be promulgated.

2. Moreover, it properly belongs to law to oblige that something be done or not done. But not only those before whom the law is promulgated are obliged, but also others. Therefore, promulgation is not of the essence of law.

3. Moreover, the obligation of law extends into the future, because laws impose necessity on future business, as the jurists say. But promulgation is made to the present generation. Therefore, promulgation is not necessary for law.

ON THE CONTRARY:

It is said in Distinction 4 of the *Decretals* that laws are instituted when they are promulgated.

RESPONSE:

It should be said, as has been mentioned, that law is imposed on others by way of rule and measure. But the rule and measure are imposed by being applied to those ruled and measured. Hence, in order for a law to have the power of obliging, which is proper to law, it is necessary that it be applied to those who should be regulated by it. Such application comes about insofar as they come to know of it by its promulgation. Hence promulgation is necessary in order that law have its power.

From the foregoing four parts a definition of law can be constructed: Law is nothing else than a certain promulgated ordinance of reason to the common good by one who has charge of the community.

Ad 1. It should be said that promulgation of the law of nature comes about when God inserts it in the minds of men in order that they might naturally know it.

Ad 2. It should be said that those before whom the law is not promulgated are obliged to keep the law insofar as it comes to their knowledge through others, or can so come, the promulgation having been made.

Ad 3. It should be said that present promulgation extends into the future through the permanence of writing, which in a way promulgates it always. Hence Isidore says in the *Etymologies* 2.10, that law [*lex*] comes from reading [*legendo*], because it is written.

QUESTION 91
THE DIVERSITY OF LAW

Next the diversity of law must be considered, and on this point six things are asked: (1) whether there is an eternal law; (2) whether there is natural law; (3) whether there is human law; (4) whether there is divine law; (5) whether there is one or several divine laws; (6) whether there is a law of sin.

Article 1: Is there an eternal law?

It seems that there is not.

1. Every law is imposed on someone. But there was not from all eternity someone on whom law could be imposed, for only God is from all eternity. Therefore, no law is eternal.

2. Moreover, promulgation is of the essence of law. But promulgation cannot be from all eternity, because there was not from all eternity someone to whom it could be promulgated. Therefore no law can be eternal.

3. Moreover, law implies an ordering to the end. But nothing is from all eternity ordered to an end, since only the ultimate end is eternal. Therefore no law is eternal.

ON THE CONTRARY:
Augustine says in *On Free Will* 1.6, that the law which is called the supreme reason cannot seem to anyone with understanding to be other than changeless and eternal.

RESPONSE:
It should be said that, as was stated above, law is nothing other than a dictate of practical reason in the prince who governs some perfect community. But it is clear, supposing the world to be governed by divine providence, as was proved in Part 1, that the whole community of the universe is governed by divine reason. Then the very idea of the governance of things existing in God as the prince of the universe has the character of law. And because the divine reason conceives nothing temporally but has an eternal concept, as is said in Proverbs 8.23, such a law ought to be called eternal.

*

Ad 1. It should be said that things which do not themselves exist, exist in God, insofar as they are foreknown and foreordained. according to Romans 4.17, '. , . and calls things that are not as though they were'. Thus the eternal concept of the divine law has the character of eternal law, insofar as ordered by God for the governance of things foreknown by him.

Ad 2. It should be said that promulgation comes about by word and writing, and in both these ways the eternal law has promulgation from the promulgating God, because the divine Word is eternal and the writing in the Book of Life is eternal. But on the part of the creature hearing or reading, there cannot be an eternal promulgation.

Ad 3. It should be said that law implies an order to the end actively, insofar as some things are ordered to the end by it, but not passively, that is, that the law itself is ordered to the end, except incidentally in the one governing whose end is outside himself, to which it is necessary that his law too be ordered. But the end of divine governance is God himself, nor is his law other than himself. Hence eternal law is not ordered to another end.

Article 2: Is there some natural law in us?

It seems that there is not.

1. A man is sufficiently governed by eternal law, for Augustine says in *On Free Will* 1.6 that the eternal law is that by which it is just that all things are perfectly ordered. But nature does not abound in superfluities, just as it is not deficient in what is necessary. Therefore there is no natural law in man.

2. Moreover, by law a man's acts are ordered to the end, as was said above, but the ordering of human acts to the end is not by nature, as happens in irrational creatures, which by natural appetite alone act for the sake of the end; man acts for the sake of the end through reason and will. Therefore, there is no natural law in man.

3. To the degree that one is free he is less subject to the law. But man is freer than the other animals, thanks to free will, which he has beyond the other animals. Therefore since other animals are not subject to natural law, neither should man be subject to any natural law.

ON THE CONTRARY:

On Romans 2.14, 'These having no law are a law unto themselves,' the

Gloss says that although they do not have the written law, they have the natural law which each understands and is thereby conscious of what is good and what is evil.

RESPONSE:

It should be said that, as has been urged, law, since it is a rule and measure, can be in something in two ways: in one way, as in the one ruling and measuring, in another way, as in the ruled and measured, since insofar as they participate in something of the rule or measure, they are ruled and measured. Since all things subject to divine providence are ruled and measured by the eternal law, as is clear from what has been said, it is manifest that all things participate in some way in eternal law, insofar as by its impression they have inclinations to their proper acts and ends. Among others, however, the rational creature is subject to divine providence in a more excellent manner, insofar as he comes to be a participant in providence, providing for himself and others. Hence in him the eternal reason is participated in in such a way that he has a natural inclination to the fitting act and end. Such a participation in eternal law in the rational creature is called natural law. Hence when the Psalmist says in Psalm 4.6, 'Offer sacrifices of righteousness, and hope in the Lord,' he adds as if in response to someone asking what the works of justice are, 'Many say: "Who will show us good things?"' Replying to that question, he says, 'Lift up the light of thy countenance upon us, O Lord,' as if the natural light of reason, whereby we discern good and evil, which pertains to natural law, is nothing else than the impression of the divine light in us. Hence it is evident that natural law is nothing other than the participation in eternal law on the part of the rational creature.

Ad 1. It should be said that that argument would work if natural law were something different from eternal law. But it is nothing but a participation in it, as has been said.

Ad 2. It should be said that every act of reason and will in us is derived from that which is according to nature, as was said above, for all reasoning derives from principles naturally known, and every desire for the things which are for the sake of the end derives from the natural desire for the ultimate end. Thus it is necessary that the first direction of our acts to the end should come about through natural law.

Ad 3. It should be said that even the irrational animals participate in the eternal law in their fashion, as does the rational creature. But because the rational creature participates in it intellectually and rationally, the participation in eternal law by the rational creature is properly called law, for law is something of reason, as has been said. But in the irrational creature it is not participated in rationally, hence it can only be called law by way of similitude.

Article 3: Is there a human law?

It seems that there is not.

1. Natural law is a participation in eternal law, as has been said. But all things are perfectly ordered through natural law, as Augustine says in *On Free Will* 1.6. Therefore natural law suffices for ordering all human affairs and there is no need for any human law.

2. Law has the character of measure, as has been said, but human reason is not the measure of things, but rather the reverse, as is said in *Metaphysics* 10.9. Therefore, no law can proceed from human reason.

3. Moreover, a measure ought to be most certain, as is said in *Metaphysics* 10.9. But the dictate of human reason as to what ought to be done is uncertain, in keeping with Wisdom 9.14: 'For the thoughts of mortal men are fearful, and our counsels are uncertain.' Therefore, no law can proceed from human reason.

ON THE CONTRARY:
Augustine in *On Free Will* 1.6 posits two laws, one eternal and the other temporal, which he calls human.

RESPONSE:
It should be said that, as was remarked above, law is a dictate of practical reason. But a similar process is found in practical and speculative reason, for both proceed from principles to conclusions, as we argued earlier. Because of this it should be said that just as in speculative reason conclusions in the various sciences are produced from indemonstrable principles naturally known, knowledge of which is not naturally given to us but which are discovered by human inquiry, so too from the precepts of natural law, as from some common and indemonstrable principles, human reason must proceed to dispose of more particular matters. And these particular dispositions discovered by human reason are called human laws, all the conditions of the essence of law being met, as was said above. Hence Cicero says in his *Rhetoric* 1.2 that the beginning of law is provided by nature, then some things become customary from the usefulness of

reason; afterwards both the things provided by nature and approved by custom sanction the measure and rule of the law.

Ad 1. It should be said that human reason cannot participate fully in the dictate of divine reason, but in its own way and imperfectly. Therefore, just as on the part of speculative reason, by a natural participation in the divine wisdom, we have knowledge of some common principles, but not proper knowledge of every truth, as divine wisdom does, so on the part of practical reason, man naturally participates in eternal law with respect to some common principles, though not with respect to the particular direction of singulars, which, however, is contained in eternal law. So it was necessary that human reason proceed further to the particular sanctions of the laws.

Ad 2. It should be said that human reason as such is not the rule of things, but the principles naturally written in it are general rules and measures of all those things which are to be done by man, of which natural reason is the rule and measure, although not the measure of the things which are by nature.

Ad 3. It should be said that practical reason is concerned with things to be done, which are singular and contingent, and not with necessary things as speculative reason is. Therefore human laws cannot have the infallibility that the conclusions of the demonstrative sciences have. Nor is it necessary that every measure be in every way infallible and certain, but only to the degree possible in its domain.

Article 4: Was some divine law needed?

It seems that it was not.

1. Natural law is a participation in us of the eternal law. But the eternal law is divine law, as has been said. Therefore there is no need beyond natural law and the human laws derived from it for another divine law.

2. Moreover, Ecclesiasticus 15.14 says, 'God made man from the beginning and left him in the hand of his own counsel,' but counsel is an act of reason, as was shown above. Therefore, a man is left in the governance of his own reason. But the dictate of human reason is human law, as has been said. Therefore, it is not necessary that man be governed by another divine law.

3. Moreover, human nature is more sufficient than irrational creatures.

But irrational creatures do not have any divine law beyond the natural inclination inserted in them. So much less, then, ought the rational creature to have any divine law beyond natural law.

ON THE CONTRARY:
David asks that a law be imposed on him by God, saying, in Psalm 118.34, 'Instruct me that I may observe thy law, and may keep it with all my heart.'

RESPONSE:
It should be said that beyond natural and human law a divine law was necessary for the direction of human life. And this for four reasons. First, because a man is directed by law in his proper acts as ordered to the ultimate end. If indeed man were only ordered to an end which does not exceed the proportion of man's natural capacity, man would not need any directive on the part of reason beyond natural law and the human law derived from it. But because man is ordered to the end of eternal happiness, which exceeds the proportion of human natural capacity, as has been said, therefore it was necessary that above natural and human law, he should be directed to his end by a divinely given law.

Second, on account of the uncertainty of human judgement, especially concerning contingent and particular things, from which different and conflicting laws arise. Therefore in order that man might know without doubt what he ought to do and what he ought to avoid, it was necessary that he be directed in his proper acts by a law divinely given, which he would know could not err.

Third, because man can make laws of the things he can judge. Man's judgement cannot bear on internal movements, which are hidden, but only on exterior acts, which are apparent. But for the perfection of virtue it is required that a man be rectified in both acts. Therefore human law cannot sufficiently restrain and order interior acts, but it was necessary that a divine law supervene for this purpose. Fourth, because, as Augustine says in *On Free Will* 1.5, human law cannot punish or prohibit all the evils that are done, because when it tries to remove all evils, many good things are also taken away, and the utility of the common good is impeded, which is necessary for human community. In order that no evil should escape prohibition and punishment, it was necessary for a divine law to supervene by which all sins are forbidden.

These four reasons are touched on in Psalm 18.8, where we read, 'The law of the Lord is perfect,' that is, permitting no baseness of sin, 'quickening the soul' since it directs not only exterior acts, but interior as well; 'the rule of the Lord is steadfast' because of the certainty of truth and rectitude, 'giving wisdom to the lowly', insofar as it orders man to a supernatural and divine end.

Ad 1. It should be said that the eternal law is participated in according to the proportion of human nature's capacity by natural law. But man needs to be directed in a higher way to the supernatural ultimate end. Therefore, a law divinely given was added, by which the eternal law is participated in in a higher mode.

Ad 2. It should be said that counsel is a kind of inquiry, so it must proceed from principles. Nor does it suffice that it proceed from principles naturally inserted, which are the precepts of natural law, because of what has been said, but certain other principles must be added, namely the precepts of divine law.

Ad 3. It should be said that irrational creatures are not ordered to an end higher than the end which is proportionate to their natural power. So the case is not similar.

Article 5: Is there only one divine law?

It seems that there is.

1. There is one law of one king in one realm. But the whole human race is compared to God as to one king, according to Psalm 46.8: 'For God is king of all the earth.' Therefore, there is only one divine law.

2. Moreover, every law is ordered to the end that the legislator intends for those to whom the law applies. But God intends one and the same thing for all men, according to 1 Timothy 2.4: 'Who wishes all men to be saved and to come to knowledge of the truth.' Therefore, there is only one divine law.

3. Moreover, divine law seems to be closer to eternal than natural law is, much as the revelation of grace is higher than the knowledge of nature. But natural law is one for all men. Therefore, this should be even more so with divine law.

ON THE CONTRARY:

The Apostle says, in Hebrews 7.12, 'For when the priesthood is changed, it is necessary that a change of laws be made also.' But the priesthood is of two kinds, as is said in the same text, namely the levitic priesthood and the priesthood of Christ. Therefore divine law is of two kinds, namely the old law and the new law.

RESPONSE:

It should be said that, as was established in Part 1, distinction is the cause of number. But something is distinguished in two ways. In one way, as things which are wholly diverse in species, like horse and cow. In another way, as perfect and imperfect in the same species, like boy and man. It is in this way that the divine law is distinguished into the old law and the new law. Hence the Apostle, in Galatians 3.24–5, compares the state of the old law to that of a boy subject to his teacher. But the perfection and imperfection of both laws are gauged by three things which pertain to law, as has been said above.

First, it pertains to law to be ordered to the common good as to its end, which can happen in two ways. To the sensible and terrestrial good, and the old law orders directly to this; hence immediately in Exodus 3.8–17, at the beginning of the law, the people are invited to the earthly realm of the Canaanites. On the other hand is the intelligible and celestial good, and the new law orders to this, hence Christ right at the beginning of his preaching invites to the kingdom of heaven, in Matthew 4.17 saying, 'Do penance, the kingdom of heaven is nigh.' Therefore, Augustine says in *Against Faustus* 4.2 that promises of temporal things are contained in the Old Testament, which is why it is called old, but the promise of eternal life pertains to the New Testament.

Second, it pertains to law to direct human acts according to the order of justice. In this too the new law excels the old, ordering interior acts of the soul, according to Matthew 5.20: 'For I say to you that unless your justice exceeds that of the Scribes and Pharisees, you shall not enter the kingdom of heaven.' Therefore, it is said that the old law restrains the hand, the new the soul.

Third, it pertains to law to lead men to the observance of the commandments. The old law does this with the fear of punishment, but the new law does it through love, which is infused into our hearts by the grace of Christ, which is conferred in the new law but was only prefigured in the old. Therefore Augustine says in *Against Adimantus, Disciple of Manichee* 17 that 'the difference between the law and the Gospel, put most briefly, is fear and love'.

Ad 1. It should be said that just as the father of a family proposes different commandments to children and adults, so too God the one king gave one law to men who were still imperfect, and another more perfect law to those prepared by the prior law for a greater capacity for the divine.

Ad 2. It should be said that the salvation of men can only come through Christ, according to Acts 4.12: 'For there is no other name under heaven, given to men by which we must be saved.' Therefore, a law perfectly leading men to salvation could only be given after the advent of Christ. Before that a law preparatory to the acceptance of Christ had to be given to the people from which Christ would be born, in which the rudiments of saving justice are contained.

Ad 3. It should be said that natural law directs man by way of common principles which unite both the perfect and the imperfect, and therefore it is one for all. But the divine law also directs man in certain particulars, to which the perfect and imperfect do not relate in the same way. Therefore it was necessary that the divine law be of two kinds, as has already been said.

Article 6: Is there a law of sin?

It seems that there is not.

1. Isidore says in the *Etymologies* 5.3 that law is constituted by reason. But concupiscence was not constituted by reason, indeed it deviates from reason. Therefore, concupiscence does not have the character of law.

2. Moreover, every law is obligatory, such that those who do not keep it are called transgressors. But concupiscence does not make the one not following it a transgressor; rather one who follows it is a transgressor. Therefore concupiscence does not have the character of law.

3. Moreover, law is ordered to the common good, as has been said. But concupiscence does not incline to the common good but rather to the private good. Therefore, concupiscence does not have the character of law.

ON THE CONTRARY:

The Apostle says in Romans 7.23, 'I see another law in my members, warring against the law of my mind.'

RESPONSE:

It should be said that, as was argued earlier, law is found essentially in the one ruling and measuring, but by way of participation in that which is measured and ruled, such that every inclination or ordering which is found in those subject to the law is called law by way of participation, as is clear from the foregoing. But there can be found in those subject to the law a twofold inclination stemming from the lawgiver. In one way, insofar as he directly inclines his subjects to something, and sometimes inclines different ones to different acts. In this way it can be said that the law of soldiers is different from the law of merchants. In another way, indirectly, insofar as the legislator takes away some dignity from one subject to him, with the result that he passes into another order and as if to another law, for example if the soldier is removed from the army he will pass into the ranks of rustics and merchants.

Thus under God the lawgiver different creatures have different natural inclinations, such that something that is according to the law for one, is against the law for another, as if I should say that to be ferocious is in some way the law of the dog, but would be against the law of the sheep or any other mild animal. There is then the law of man, which arises from the divine ordinance according to his proper condition, that he should act according to reason. Which law was so strong in the first state that nothing either outside reason or against reason could come about in man. But when man turned from God, the result was that he was carried by the impetus of sensuality, and to each particular one this happens the more he recedes from reason, such that they become like unto the beasts, which are borne along by the impulse of sensuality, according to Psalm 48: 'Man living in wealth and not understanding is like unto the beasts that perish.'

Therefore, this inclination of sensuality, which is called concupiscence [fames], in other animals simply has the character of law in the way that the law can be in them according to direct inclination.

In men it does not have the character of law in this way, but is rather a deviation from the law of reason. But insofar as by divine justice man was deprived of original justice and the strength of reason, the impetus of sensuality which leads him has the character of law, insofar as it is a punishment following on the divine law, man having abandoned his proper dignity.

Ad 1. It should be said that the argument proceeds from concupiscence taken in itself, insofar as it inclines to evil. Thus it does not have the character of law, as has been said, but only insofar as it follows from the justice of divine law, as if someone should say that it is a law that someone noble, because of his own fault, is permitted to engage in servile works.

Ad 2. It should be said that this objection proceeds from the fact that law is as a rule and measure, for thus those deviating from the law are transgressors. Concupiscence is not law in that way, but by a kind of participation, as was said above.

Ad 3. It should be said that this argument proceeds from concupiscence with respect to its proper inclination, but not with respect to its origin. If we consider the inclination of sensuality as it is found in other animals, it is thus ordered to the common good, that is, to the preservation of nature in the species or in the individual. This is also true of man, insofar as sensuality is subject to reason. But it is called concupiscence insofar as it rejects the order of reason.

QUESTION 92
THE EFFECTS OF LAW

Next we must consider the effects of law, and two things are asked concerning this: (1) whether the effect of law is to make men good; (2) whether the effects of law are to command, forbid, permit and punish, as the Jurist says.

Article 1: Is the effect of law to make men good?

It seems that it is not.

1. Men are good through virtue, but virtue is that which makes the one having it good, as is said in *Ethics* 2.6. But virtue in man is from God alone, for he brings it about in us without us, as was said above in the definition of virtue. Therefore, it is not for law to make men good.

2. Moreover, law does not help man unless he obeys it. But this very obeying of the law is due to goodness. Therefore goodness is needed in man before the law. Therefore, law does not make men good.

3. Moreover, law is ordered to the common good, as has been said. But one can do well with respect to things that pertain to the common good, and none the less not act well in his own affairs. Therefore, it does not pertain to law to make men good.

4. Moreover, some laws are tyrannical, as the Philosopher says in *Politics* 3.6. But the tyrant does not look to the goodness of his subjects, but only for his own gain. Therefore, it is not for law to make men good.

ON THE CONTRARY:

The Philosopher says in *Ethics* 2.1 that the desire of any lawgiver is this, that he might make good citizens.

RESPONSE:

It should be said that, as was explained above, law is nothing other than a dictate of reason in the one presiding, by which the subjects are governed. The virtue of any subject is to be a good subject to the one by whom he is governed, as we see that the virtue of the irascible and concupiscible appetites consists in this that obey reason well. In this way the virtue of any subject is to be a good subject to his prince, as the Philosopher says in *Politics* 1.5. Any law aims at this that it be obeyed by those subject to it. It is manifest then that this is proper to law, to lead subjects to their proper virtue. And since virtue is that which makes the one having it good, it follows that the proper effect of law is to make good those to whom it is given, whether absolutely or in a certain respect. For if the intention of the one making the law bears on the true good, which is the common good regulated according to divine justice, it follows that through the law men become good absolutely. But if the intention of the lawmaker bears on that which is not good absolutely, but only useful or pleasant to him, or even repugnant to divine justice, then the law does not make men good absolutely, but in a certain respect, namely in the order of such a regime. But in this way good is found even in things as such evil, as someone is called a good thief, because he works efficiently towards his end.

Ad 1. It should be said that virtue is twofold, as is clear from the foregoing, namely acquired and infused. For both, that someone become accustomed to the act is important, but differently, for this *causes* acquired virtue, and *disposes* to infused virtue, and preserves and strengthens it once had. Since law is given to direct human acts, insofar as human acts work towards virtue, they make men good. Hence the Philosopher says in *Politics* 2 that lawgivers make men good by accustoming them to certain acts.

Ad 2. It should be said that one does not always obey the law out of perfect virtue, but sometimes because of fear of punishment; sometimes, however, solely because of the dictate of reason, which is the principle of virtue, as was said above.

Ad 3. It should be said that the goodness of any part is considered in proportion to its whole. Hence Augustine says in *Confessions* 3.8 that every part is foul that does not befit its whole. Since any man is a part of the city, it is impossible that a man be good unless he is well proportioned to the common good, nor can the good be made up of anything other than from parts proportioned to it. Hence it is impossible that the common good of the city be had unless the citizens are virtuous, at least those who must govern. But it suffices, with respect to the good of the community, that others are virtuous insofar as they obey the commands of the prince. Therefore the Philosopher says in *Politics* 3.2 that the virtue of the prince and of the good man are the same, but the virtue of just any citizen and of the good man are not the same.

Ad 4. It should be said that tyrannical law, since it is not according to reason, is not law absolutely, but is rather a perversion of law. But insofar as it has something of the character of law, it intends that the citizens be good. All it has of the character of law is that it is a dictate of the one presiding to his subjects, and intends that those subject to the law should obey it well, which is for them to be good, not absolutely, but with respect to that regime.

Article 2: Are the acts of the law properly assigned: to command, to forbid, to permit and to punish?

It seems that they are not.

1. Every law is a universal precept, as the jurist says. But precept and command come to the same thing. Therefore, the other three are superfluous.

2. Moreover, the effect of law is to lead its subjects to the good, as has been said above. But counsel is concerned with a better good than is the precept. Therefore, it pertains to the law rather to counsel than to command.

3. Moreover, just as a man is incited to the good by penalties, so also by rewards. Therefore, if to punish is put among the effects of law, to reward ought to be too.

4. Moreover, the lawgiver's intention is to make men good, as has been said. But one who obeys the law only out of fear of punishment is not good, for although servile fear, which is fear of punishment, might make one act well, it does not cause someone to become good, as Augustine says. Therefore it does not seem proper to law to punish.

ON THE CONTRARY:

Isidore says in the *Etymologies* 5.19 that every law either permits something, as a brave man seeks his reward, or it forbids, by saying it is not licit to seek to marry one of the sacred virgins, or it punishes, as, he who kills loses his head.

RESPONSE:

It should be said that just as the sentence is the dictate of reason by way of enunciating, so is law by way of commanding. It is proper to reason that it leads us from one thing to another. Hence just as in the demonstrative sciences reason leads to assent to the conclusion by way of the principles, so it leads to assent to the precept of law through something. Precepts of the law concern human acts which the law directs, as was said above, and some acts are good in kind, namely the acts of virtue, and relevant to these are those acts of law, to command and order. Other acts are evil in kind, such as vicious acts, and with respect to these the law forbids. Others are indifferent in their kind, and with respect to these the law permits. All those acts which are either of little good or evil can be called indifferent. It is by the fear of punishment that law induces us to obey, and with respect to this punishment is numbered among the effects of law.

Ad 1. It should be said that just as ceasing from evil has the note of good, so too prohibition has something of the precept. On this basis, taking precept broadly, the law is universally said to be a precept.

Ad 2. It should be said that to counsel is not a proper act of law, but it can pertain to the private person, who does not make law. So too the Apostle in 1 Corinthians 7.12, when giving counsel, says 'To others I say, not the Lord.' Therefore, it is not numbered among the effects of the law.

Ad 3. It should be said that to reward can be done by anyone, but only the minister of the law can punish: it is by his authority that punishment is inflicted. Therefore, to reward is not listed among the acts of law, but only to punish.

Ad 4. It should be said that because someone begins to accustom himself to avoid evils and to fulfil goods out of a fear of punishment, he is sometimes led to do it with pleasure and from his own will. Thus the law, even by punishing, leads me to become good.

QUESTION 93
THE ETERNAL LAW

Next we must consider each kind of law. And first eternal law; then, natural law; third, human law; fourth, the old law; fifth, the new law, which is the law of the Gospel. As to the sixth, the law of sensuality, what has been said of Original Sin suffices for that. Six questions arise concerning eternal law: (1) what is eternal law? (2) whether it is known to all; (3) whether every law is derived from it; (4) whether necessary things are subject to eternal law; (5) whether the contingent things of nature are subject to eternal law; (6) whether all human matters are subject to it.

Article 1: Is eternal law the highest idea existing in God?

It seems that it is not.

1. There is only one eternal law. But the notions of things in the divine mind are many, for Augustine says in *Eighty-three Questions* that God makes each thing according to its proper notion. Therefore the eternal law does not seem to be the same as the notion existing in the divine mind.

2. Moreover, it is of the essence of law that it be promulgated by word, as was said above. But Word in divine things is used personally, as was shown in Part 1, and idea is used essentially. Therefore the eternal law and the divine idea are not the same.

3. Moreover, Augustine says in *On True Religion* that the law that is truth seems to be above our minds. But the law which is above our minds is eternal law. Therefore, the notion of truth and of idea are not the same, so eternal law does not seem to be the supreme idea.

ON THE CONTRARY:
Augustine says in *On Free Will* 30 that eternal law is the highest idea, which is always to be complied with.

RESPONSE:
It should be said that just as there pre-exists in any artisan the idea of what is constituted by art, so in every governor there must pre-exist the idea of the order of the things which are to be done by those subject to

his governance. And just as the notion of the things to come about through art is called art or the exemplar of artificial things, so the reason of the one governing the acts of subjects takes on the character of law, saving the other conditions of the essence of law given above. God through his wisdom is the maker of the universe of things, to which he relates as artisan to artefacts, as was said in Part 1. Just as the notion of divine wisdom, insofar as all things are created through it, has the note of art or exemplar or idea, so the notion of divine wisdom moving all things to their fitting end takes on the note of law. By this token, the eternal law is nothing other than the idea of divine wisdom insofar as it is directive of all acts and movements.

Ad 1. It should be said that Augustine is speaking of the ideal reasons, which look to the proper natures of singular things, and therefore distinction and plurality are found in them, according to their different relations to things, as was said in Part 1. Things which are different in themselves are considered to be one insofar as they are ordered to something common. Therefore, the eternal law, which is the reason for this order, is one.

Ad 2. It should be said that the word can be considered in two ways, namely as the word itself and as the things which are expressed by it. For the spoken word is something fashioned by the mouth of man, but this word expresses what is signified by human words. The same is true of man's mental word, which is nothing other than something conceived by the mind whereby man expresses mentally the things of which he thinks. In the divine, the Word itself, which is the conception of the paternal intellect, is said personally, but whatever is in the knowledge of the Father, whether essential or personal, or even the works of God, are expressed by this Word, as is clear from Augustine in *On the Trinity* 15.14. The eternal law is among the other things expressed by this Word. But it does not follow from this that eternal law is said personally in the divine, for it is appropriated to the Son because of the affinity of reason and word.

Ad 3. It should be said that the idea of the divine intellect relates differently to things than does the idea of the human intellect. For the human intellect is measured by things, such that the concept of man is not true on account of itself, but is said to be true because it is in harmony with things; insofar as the thing is or is not, the opinion is true or false. But the divine intellect is the measure of things, because any thing has truth to the degree that it imitates the divine intellect, as was shown in Part 1. Therefore the divine intellect is true of itself and its notion is truth itself.

Article 2: Is the eternal law known to all?

It seems that it is not.

1. As the Apostle says in 1 Corinthians 2.11, 'The things of God no one knows but the Spirit of God.' But the eternal law is a kind of reason existing in the divine mind. Therefore, it is unknown to everybody but God.

2. As Augustine said in *On Free Will* 1.6, the eternal law is that whereby it is just that everything is perfectly ordered. But not everyone knows that all things are perfectly ordered. Therefore, not everyone knows the eternal law.

3. In *On True Religion* 31 Augustine says that the eternal law is that which men cannot judge, and it is said in *Ethics* 1.3 that anyone judges well what he knows. Therefore, eternal law is not known to us.

ON THE CONTRARY:
Augustine says in *On Free Will* that the notion of eternal law is impressed upon us.

RESPONSE:
It should be said that a thing can be known in two ways, in one way, in itself, in another way, in its effect, in which some likeness of it is found, as someone not seeing the sun in its substance knows it in its shining. Therefore, it should be said that no one can know the eternal law as it is in itself, except for the blessed who see God in his essence. But every rational creature knows it according to some irradiation of it, whether greater or less. For every knowledge of the truth is some irradiation or participation in the eternal law, which is unchanging truth, as Augustine says in *On True Religion*. But all know the truth in some degree, at least with respect to the common principles of natural law. In other things some participate more, some less, in knowledge of the truth, and on this basis they know the eternal law more or less.

Ad 1. It should be said that the things that are of God cannot be known in themselves by us, but are made manifest to us in his effects, according to Romans 1.20: 'His invisible attributes are clearly seen, being understood through the things that are made.'

Ad 2. It should be said that although everyone knows the eternal law according to his capacity, in the manner mentioned, no one can comprehend it, nor can it be totally made manifest through its effects. Therefore, it is not necessary that whoever knows eternal law in the manner mentioned should know the whole order of things, whereby they are perfectly ordered.

Ad 3. It should be said that to judge of something can be understood in two ways, in one way, as the cognitive power judges its proper object, according to the text in Job 12.11: 'Doth not the ear discern words, and the palate of him that eateth, the taste.' According to this way of judging, the Philosopher says that anyone judges well the things he knows, that is, judging whether what is proposed is true. In another way, insofar as the superior judges the inferior by a practical judgement, that is, whether it ought to be so or not. And thus no one can judge of the eternal law.

Article 3: Is every law derived from eternal law?

The answer seems to be no.

1. There is a law of sensuality, as was said above, but it is not derived from divine law, which is eternal law, for to it the prudence of the flesh pertains, of which the Apostle says in Romans 8.7, 'For the wisdom of the flesh is hostile to God, for it is not subject to the law of God.' Therefore, not every law proceeds from eternal law.

2. Moreover, nothing unfair can proceed from eternal law, because as has been said, eternal law is that according to which it is just that all things are perfectly ordered. But some laws are unfair, according to Isaiah 10.1: 'Woe to them that maketh wicked laws: and when they write, write injustice.' Therefore, not every law proceeds from the eternal law.

3. Moreover, Augustine says in On Free Will 1.5 that the law which is written for ruling people rightly permits many things which are punished by divine providence. But the notion of divine providence is eternal law, as has been said. Therefore, not all law proceeds from eternal law.

ON THE CONTRARY:

In Proverbs 8.15 divine wisdom says, 'By me kings reign, and lawgivers decree just things.' But the notion of divine wisdom is eternal law, as was said above. Therefore, all laws proceed from eternal law.

RESPONSE:

It should be said that, as was explained above, law involves a reasoned directive of acts to the end. But in all ordered movers the force of the secondary mover must derive from that of the primary mover, because the secondary mover moves only insofar as it is moved by the primary. We see the same thing in all governors, that the notion of governance derives from the first to the secondary governors, as the reason for things to be done in the city derives from the king to inferior administrators by the precept. And in artificial things, the reason for the acts of the artisans is derived from the master builder to inferiors who work with their hands. Since therefore the eternal law is the reason of governance in the supreme governor, it is necessary that all reasons of governance in inferior governors are derived from eternal law. Such reasons of inferior governors are laws beyond eternal law. Hence all laws, insofar as they participate in right reason, derive from eternal law. Because of this Augustine says in *On Free Will* 1.6 that there is nothing just and legitimate in temporal law which men have not derived for themselves from eternal law.

Ad 1. It should be said that sensuality has the note of law in man insofar as it is a punishment of divine justice. According to this it is clear that it is derived from eternal law. Insofar as it inclines to sin, however, it is contrary to the law of God and does not have the character of law, as is clear from the foregoing.

Ad 2. It should be said that human law has the character of law to the degree that it is according to right reason, and thus it is manifest that it is derived from eternal law. Insofar as it departs from reason, it is called unfair law, and thus does not have the character of law, but rather of a violation of it. Yet in that very unfair law, insofar as it retains some similarity to law on account of the power of the one legislating, in that respect it derives from the eternal law, for all power is from the Lord God, as is said in Romans 13.1: 'For there exists no authority except from God.'

Ad 3. It should be said that human law is said to permit some things, not as approving them, but as not being able to direct them. For many things are directed by divine law which cannot be directed by human law, for more things are subject to the superior cause than to the inferior. Hence the fact that human law does not involve itself with things it cannot direct, comes from the order of eternal law. It would be otherwise if it approved things which are forbidden by eternal law. Hence this does not tell against human law's being derived from eternal law, but shows that it cannot perfectly follow it.

Article 4: Are necessary and eternal things subject to eternal law?

They seem to be.

1. Everything that is reasonable is subject to reason, but the divine will is reasonable, since it is just, therefore it is subject to reason. But eternal law is divine reason. Therefore, the will of God is subject to eternal law. But the will of God is something eternal. Therefore, the eternal and necessary are subject to eternal law.

2. Moreover, whatever is subject to the king, is subject to the law of the king. But the Son will be subject to God the Father when he delivers the kingdom to him (1 Corinthians 15.24). Therefore, the Son, who is eternal, is subject to eternal law.

3. Moreover, the eternal law is the reason of divine providence, but many necessary things are subject to divine providence, such as the permanence of incorporeal substances and the celestial bodies. Therefore, necessary things too are subject to eternal law.

ON THE CONTRARY:

It is impossible for necessary things to be otherwise, hence they do not require restraint. But law is imposed on men to restrain them from evils, as is clear from the foregoing. Therefore, necessary things are not subject to law.

RESPONSE:

It should be said that, as has been argued, the eternal law is the reason for divine governance. Therefore, whatever things are subject to divine governance are also subject to eternal law, but eternal things are not subject to divine governance nor to eternal law. Their difference can be grasped from the fact that things are subject to human governance to the degree that they can come to be by men, whereas what pertains to the nature of man is not subject to human governance; for example, that man has a soul, or hands or feet. Therefore everything that is created by God is subject to eternal law, whether it be contingent or necessary, but those things which pertain to the divine nature or essence are not subject to eternal law, but *are* the eternal law.

Ad 1. It should be said that we can speak of the will of God in two ways, in one way, with respect to the will itself, and thus, since the will of God is his very essence, it is not subject to divine governance nor to eternal law, but is the same as eternal law. In another way, we can speak of the divine will with respect to the things that God wills in creatures, which are subject to eternal law, insofar as the reason for them is in the divine wisdom. And by their reasons the divine will is called reasonable. Otherwise, by reason of itself, it would rather be called reason itself.

Ad 2. It should be said that the Son of God is not made by God, but is naturally generated from him. Therefore he is not subject to divine providence or eternal law, but rather he is the eternal law by way of appropriation, as is clear from Augustine in *On True Religion*. He is said to be subject to the Father by reason of his human nature, with reference to which the Father is also said to be greater than he.

Ad 3. We concede the third because it proceeds from created necessary things.

Ad 4. It should be said that, as the Philosopher teaches in *Metaphysics* 5.5, some necessary things have a cause of their necessity, and thus their not being able to be otherwise is something they have from another. This is the most efficacious restraint, for some things are restrained – to the degree that they are said to be restrained – insofar as they can only do what they are fashioned to do.

Article 5: Are the contingent things of nature subject to eternal law?

It seems that they are not.

1. Promulgation is of the essence of law, as was said above, but promulgation cannot come about except with rational creatures to whom something can be announced. Therefore, only rational creatures are subject to eternal law, and not the contingent things in nature.

2. Moreover, things which obey reason, participate somewhat in reason, as is said in *Ethics* 1.13. But eternal law is the highest reason, as was said above. Since natural contingent things do not participate in reason, but are wholly irrational, it seems that they do not come under eternal law.

3. Moreover, eternal law is most efficacious. But defects occur in natural contingent things. Therefore, they are not subject to eternal law.

ON THE CONTRARY:
There is what is said in Proverbs 8.29: 'When he compassed the sea with bounds, and set a law to the waters that they should not pass their limits.'

RESPONSE:

It should be said that we must speak differently of the law of man and of eternal law, which is the law of God. For man's law extends only to rational creatures who are subject to man. The reason is that law is directive of acts which belong to those subject to some governance, hence no one, properly speaking, imposes a law on his own acts. Whatever is done with respect to the use of irrational things subject to man is done by the act of man moving such things, for such irrational creatures do not act of themselves, but are acted on by others, as was said above. Therefore man cannot impose a law on irrational things, even if they are subject to him, but he can impose a law on rational creatures subject to him, insofar as by his command, or whatever pronouncement, he impresses on their minds a rule which is a principle of acting. For just as a man by announcing impresses an interior principle of acts on the man subject to him, so also God impresses on the whole of nature principles of their proper acts. In this way God is said to command the whole of nature, according to Psalm 148.6: 'He gave a decree that shall not pass away.' For this reason all movements and acts of nature as a whole are subject to eternal law. Hence irrational creatures are subject to eternal law in another way, insofar as they are moved by divine providence, but not by understanding the divine precept, as rational creatures do.

Ad 1. It should be said that in this way the impression of the intrinsic active principle in natural things is like the promulgation of the law to men, because by the promulgation of the law there is impressed on men a directive principle of human acts, as has been said.

Ad 2. It should be said that irrational creatures do not participate in human reason nor do they obey it, but they participate by way of obedience in the divine reason. The power of divine reason extends to more things than does human reason. Just as the members of the human body are moved by the command of reason, but do not participate in reason, because they do not have any apprehension ordered to reason, so also irrational creatures are moved by God, but are not for all that rational.

Ad 3. It should be said that the defects that occur in natural things, although they are outside the order of particular causes, are not outside the order of universal causes, and especially of the First Cause, who is God, from whose providence nothing escapes, as was said in Part 1. And, because the eternal law is the reason of divine providence, as has been said, the defects in natural things are subject to eternal law.

Article 6: Are all human affairs subject to eternal law?

It seems not.

1. The Apostle says in Galatians 5.18, 'But if you are led by the Spirit, you are not under the Law.' But just men, who are sons of God by adoption, are led by the Spirit of God, according to Romans 8.14: 'For whoever are led by the Spirit of God, they are the sons of God.' Therefore, not all men are subject to eternal law.

2. Moreover, the Apostle says in Romans 8.7, 'For the wisdom of the flesh is hostile to God, for it is not subject to the law of God.' Therefore not all men are subject to the eternal law, which is the law of God.

3. Moreover, Augustine says in *On Free Will* that eternal law is that whereby 'the evil merit misery and the good a happy life'. But men already blessed or damned are not in a position to merit. Therefore they are not subject to eternal law.

ON THE CONTRARY:
Augustine says in the *City of God* 19.12 that there is no way in which something can be subtracted from the laws of the most high creator and fashioner, by whom the peace of the universe is administered.

RESPONSE:
It should be said that something is subject to eternal law in two ways, as is clear from the foregoing. In one way, insofar as the eternal law is participated in by way of knowledge; in another way, by way of action and passion, insofar as it participated in the manner of moving principle. In the second way irrational creatures are subject to eternal law, as has been said. But because the rational nature, along with what is common to all creatures, has something proper to it as rational, it is subject to eternal law in both ways, because it has the notion of eternal law in a certain way, as was said above, and moreover in each rational creature there is a natural inclination to that which is consonant with eternal law. For we are born to have virtues, as is said in *Ethics* 2.1.

Both ways are imperfect and indeed corrupted in the bad, in whom the natural inclination to virtue is depraved by vicious habits, along with the natural knowledge of the good in them, for it is obscured by passions and the habit of sin. In the good both kinds are found in a more perfect manner, because to their natural knowledge of the good is added the knowledge of faith and wisdom, and to their natural inclination to the good is added an interior impulse of grace and virtue.

Therefore, the good are perfectly subject to the eternal law, as always fulfilling it. The bad are indeed subject to eternal law but imperfectly as to their actions insofar as they imperfectly know and are imperfectly inclined to the good, and the more their acts are defective, the more they are buffeted by passion, such that they suffer what the eternal law decrees concerning them to the degree that they fail to do what is in conformity with eternal law. Hence Augustine says in *On Free Will* 1.15, 'I think the just act under eternal law.' And in *On Catechizing the Simple* 18 he says that God out of the just misery of souls deserting him knows how to adorn with the most fitting laws the lower parts of his creation.

Ad 1. It should be said that that word of the Apostle can be understood in two ways. In one way, that he who is unwilling to accept the obligation of the law is under it as under a weight. Hence the Gloss says at that place that he who is under the law because of the fear of punishment that the law threatens and not by love of justice abstains from an evil act. Spiritual men are not under the law in this way, because through charity, which the Holy Spirit infuses into their hearts, they voluntarily fulfil what is of the law. In another way it can be understood insofar as the works of man which are done by the Holy Spirit are rather called works of the Holy Spirit than of man himself. Hence, since the Holy Spirit is not under the law, no more than is the Son, as was said earlier, it follows that such works, insofar as they are of the Holy Spirit, are not under the law. The Apostle attests to this in 2 Corinthians 3.17: 'Where the spirit of the Lord is, there is liberty.'

Ad 2. It should be said that the prudence of the flesh cannot be subject to the law of God on the side of action, because it inclines to actions contrary to the law of God. But it is subject to the law of God on the side of passion, because it merits to suffer punishment according to the law of divine justice. Nevertheless, the prudence of the flesh does not so dominate in any man that it completely destroys the good of nature. Therefore there remains in a man the inclination to do the things of eternal law, for it was proved above that sin does not remove the whole good of nature.

Ad 3. It should be said that it is the same thing by which something is preserved in its end and is moved towards it, as the heavy body comes to rest in a lower place because of gravity, by which it is also moved to that place. So it should be said that just as through eternal law some merit misery and some beatitude, so by the same law they are preserved in either beatitude or misery. On this basis, the blessed and the damned are both subject to eternal law.

QUESTION 94
NATURAL LAW

Next natural law must be considered, and six questions are asked in its regard: (1) what is natural law? (2) what are the precepts of natural law? (3) whether all acts of virtue are of natural law; (4) whether natural law is the same for all; (5) whether it is changeable; (6) whether it can be erased from the mind of man.

Article 1: Is natural law a habit?

It seems that it is.

1. As the Philosopher says in *Ethics* 2.5, there are three things in the soul: power, habit and passion. But natural law is not one of the powers of the soul, nor is it any of its passions, as is clear from an enumeration of each. Therefore, natural law is a habit.

2. Moreover, Basil says that conscience, or synderesis, is the law of our intellect, which can only mean natural law. But synderesis is a habit, as was shown in Part 1. Therefore, natural law is a habit.

3. Moreover, natural law remains in man always, as will become clear below. But man's reason, to which natural law pertains, does not always think about natural law. Therefore, natural law is not an act, but a habit.

ON THE CONTRARY:
Augustine says in *On the Conjugal Good* that a habit is that with which one acts when there is need. But natural law is not like that, for it is also in the young and the damned, who cannot act by it. Therefore, natural law is not a habit.

RESPONSE:
It should be said that something can be called a habit in two ways. In one way, properly and essentially, and thus natural law is not a habit. For it was said earlier that natural law is something constituted by reason, much as a proposition is a work of reason. What one does and that

whereby he does it are not the same, for someone by the habit of grammar forms felicitous phrases. Since a habit is that whereby one acts, no law could be a habit properly and essentially. In another way that which is held by the habit can be called habit, as that which is held by faith is called faith. And in this way, because the precepts of natural law are sometimes actually considered by reason and sometimes are in it only habitually, natural law can be called a habit. So too, in the speculative order, the indemonstrable principles are not the habit of principles, but are the principles held by the habit.

Ad 1. It should be said that the Philosopher intends to investigate the genus of virtue, and since virtue is manifestly a principle of action he sets down only the principles of human acts, namely powers, habits and passions. There are other things besides these three in the soul, such as acts – as willing is in the will and known things are in the knower – and the natural properties of the soul, such as immortality and the like.

Ad 2. It should be said that synderesis is called the law of our intellect insofar as it is a habit containing the precepts of natural law, which are the first principles of human acts.

Ad 3. It should be said that this argument concludes that natural law is held habitually, and this we concede.

To what is said in 'On the Contrary', it should be said that sometimes one cannot make use of what is in him habitually because of some impediment, as a man cannot use the habit of science when he is asleep. Similarly, a child cannot use the habit of principles or even of natural law which are in him habitually because of the defect of age.

Article 2: Is there more than one natural law precept?

It seems that there is not.

1. Law falls under the genus of precept, as was said above. Therefore, if there were many precepts of natural law, it would follow that there were also many natural laws.

2. Moreover, natural law follows on human nature. But human nature is one whole, although it is multiple with respect to its parts. Therefore, either there is only one precept of the law of nature, because of the unity of the whole, or there are many, because of the multiplicity of the parts of human nature. But then it would be necessary that even those things

which are from the inclination of the concupiscible would pertain to natural law.

3. Moreover, law is something pertaining to reason, as was said earlier. But there is only one reason in man. Therefore, there is only one precept of natural law.

ON THE CONTRARY:

In man the precepts of natural law are to things to be done as the first principles are to demonstrative sciences. But there are many first indemonstrable principles. Therefore, there are also many precepts of the law of nature.

RESPONSE:

It should be said that, as was just mentioned, the precepts of the law of nature are to practical reason as the first principles of demonstration are to speculative reason, for both are self-evident principles. Something is called self-evident in two ways: in one way, in itself, in another, with respect to us. A proposition is called self-evident in itself whose predicate is of the definition of its subject, though it can happen that to one not knowing the definition of the subject such a proposition will not be self-evident. For example, 'Man is rational,' is self-evident in its nature, because he who says man, says rational: and yet to someone ignorant of what man is, this proposition is not self-evident. Hence it is that, as Boethius says in *On the Hebdomads*, some are axioms or propositions self-evident to all, and these are those whose terms are known to everyone, for example, 'Every whole is greater than its part,' and 'Equals taken from equals leave equals.' But some propositions are self-evident only to the wise who understand what the terms of the propositions mean. For example, to those who understand that an angel is not a body, it is self-evident that it is not circumscriptively in place, which would not be obvious to the unlearned who do not grasp this.

There is a certain order found among things which are understood by everybody, for that which is first grasped is being, an understanding of which is included in whatever else one grasps. Therefore the first indemonstrable principle is that you cannot simultaneously affirm and deny something, which is founded on the notion of being and not being, and all other principles are grounded in this one, as is said in *Metaphysics* 4.3. Just as being is the first thing grasped simply speaking, so the good is the first thing grasped by practical reason which is ordered to action, for every agent acts for the sake of an end, which has the character of good. Therefore, the first principle of practical reason is grounded in the notion of good: the good is that which all things desire. This, then, is the first precept of the law: good should be done and pursued and evil avoided. All other precepts of the law of nature are grounded in this one, such that all those things that are to be done or avoided pertain to precepts of natural law which practical reason naturally grasps as human goods.

Because good has the note of end and evil has the contrary note, reason naturally grasps as goods all those things to which man has a natural inclination, and consequently as to be pursued in action, and the contrary of these are grasped as evils to be avoided. Therefore, there is an order of the precepts of the law of nature that follows the order of the natural inclinations. For there is in man a first inclination to a good of the nature he shares with all substances, insofar as each substance seeks the preservation of the existence it has according to its own nature, and following this inclination the things by which the life of man is preserved and the contrary prevented pertain to natural law. Second there is in man an inclination to more special things, according to the nature he shares with other animals. Following on this, what nature teaches all animals are said to be of natural law, such as the joining of male and female, and the raising of young, and the like. In a third way there is an inclination in man to the good according to the nature of reason, which is proper to him: man has a natural inclination to know the truth about God and to live in society. Accordingly those things which look to this inclination pertain to natural law, for example, that a man should avoid ignorance, that he should not offend others with whom he must live, and other such things which are relevant to this.

Ad 1. It should be said that all these precepts of the law of nature, insofar as they refer to one first precept, have the note of one natural law.

Ad 2. It should be said that all inclinations of whatever parts of human nature, for example the concupiscible and irascible, pertain to natural law insofar as they are regulated by reason, and are reduced to one first precept, as has been said. Thus, there are many precepts of the law of nature in themselves, which, however, share the same root.

Ad 3. It should be said that although reason is one, it orders everything that pertains to men. Thus, under the law of reason are contained all those things which can be regulated by reason.

Article 3: Are all acts of virtue of natural law?

It seems that they are not.

1. As was said above, it is of the essence of the law to be ordered to the common good. But some virtues are ordered to someone's private good, as is especially obvious in the case of temperance. Therefore, not all acts of virtue are subject to natural law.

2. Moreover, every sin is opposed to some virtuous act. Therefore, if all acts of virtue are of the law of nature, it would seem to follow that all sins are against nature, but this is reserved to some special sins.

3. Moreover, all concur in things which are according to nature. But not everyone agrees about the acts of virtue, for something is virtuous to one, but vicious to another. Therefore, not all acts of virtue are of the law of nature.

ON THE CONTRARY:
Damascene says in *On Orthodox Faith* 3.14 that the virtues are natural. Therefore, virtuous acts are subject to the law of nature.

RESPONSE:
It should be said that we can speak of virtuous acts in two ways, in one way, insofar as they are virtuous, in another, insofar as they are such and such acts considered in their proper species. If then we are speaking of virtuous acts as virtuous, then all virtuous acts pertain to natural law. For it has been said that everything to which a man is inclined according to his nature pertains to the law of nature. But each thing is naturally inclined to the activity that befits its own form, as fire to heating. Hence since the rational soul is the proper form of man, there is a natural inclination in man to act according to reason. And this is to act according to virtue. On this basis, all acts of virtue are of natural law, for everyone's own reason dictates this, that he should act virtuously. But if we are speaking of virtuous acts in themselves, that is, considered in their proper species, then not all virtuous acts are of the law of nature. For many things are done according to virtue to which nature does not first incline, but by the inquiry of reason men discover them as useful to living well.

Ad 1. It should be said that temperance is concerned with the natural concupiscence of food, drink and sex, which indeed are ordered to the common good of nature, just as all legal matters are ordered to the moral common good.

Ad 2. It should be said that the nature of man can mean either that which is proper to man, and then all sins, insofar as they are against reason, are also against nature, as is clear from Damascene in *On Orthodox Faith* 2.30. Or it can mean that which is common to man and the other animals, and then certain special sins are said to be against nature, as it is against the union of male and female, which is natural to all animals, that two men should seek sexual union, which especially is called a vice against nature.

Ad 3. It should be said that this argument proceeds from acts considered in themselves, and thus, because of the different conditions of men, it happens that some acts are virtuous for some, as proportionate and befitting them, which, however, are vicious for others, as not proportioned to them.

Article 4: Is natural law the same for all?

It seems that it is not.

1. In the *Decretals* it is said that natural right is what is contained in the law and in the Gospel. But this is not common to all, because, as is said in Romans 10.16, 'But all did not obey the Gospel.' Therefore, natural law is not the same for all.

2. Moreover, what is according to the law is said to be just, as is said in *Ethics* 5.1. But in the same book it is said that nothing is so just for all that it is not different with some. Therefore, natural law is not the same for all.

3. Moreover, that to which man is inclined according to his own nature pertains to the law of nature, as was said above. But different men are naturally inclined to different things, some to the concupiscence of pleasure, others to the desire for honour, and others to other things. Therefore, there is not the same natural law for all.

ON THE CONTRARY:

Isidore says in the *Etymologies* 5.4 that natural right is common to all nations.

RESPONSE:

It should be said, as was argued earlier, that all those things to which a man is naturally inclined pertain to the law of nature, among them that it is proper for man to be inclined to act according to reason. But it is a mark of reason that it proceeds from the common to the proper, as is clear in *Physics* 1.1. But speculative reason does this differently than practical reason. Speculative reason deals with the necessary, which cannot be otherwise, and truth is found without diminishment in the proper conclusions just as it was in the common principles. But practical reason deals with contingent matters, among which human activities are numbered, and therefore, although there is some necessity in the common principles, the more one descends to the proper, the more defects are found. Therefore, in speculative matters there is the same truth for everyone in principles as well as conclusions, although the truth of the conclusions is not known by everybody, but only the principles which are called common conceptions. In things to be done, however, there is not the same truth or practical rectitude for all with respect to the proper, but only with respect to the common, and with those for whom there is the same rectitude in proper matters, it is not equally known by all.

Therefore, it is clear that with respect to the common principles of reason, whether speculative or practical, there is the same truth or rectitude for all, and equally known. As for proper conclusions of speculative reason, there is the same truth for all, but not equally known to all: it is true for everyone that a triangle has three angles equal to two right angles, although this is not known by everybody. But with respect to the proper conclusions of practical reason, there is not the same truth or rectitude for all, nor even with those for whom it is the same is it equally known. It is true for everyone that this right thing is true, that one should act according to reason. From this principle there follows as a proper conclusion that borrowed items ought to be returned, and this is by and large true, but it can happen in some cases to be harmful and consequently irrational if borrowed items are returned: for example if someone requested them in order to fight against his country. And this would be found to be more and more defective the more one descends into particulars, for example, if one said that borrowed items ought to be returned with such and such caution, or in such a manner. The more conditions are added the more ways it can fail to apply such that it is not right either to return or not to return.

Therefore, it should be said that the law of nature, with respect to first common principles, is the same for all, both as to rectitude and to knowledge. But with respect to the proper, which are, as it were, conclusions from the common principles, it is the same for all for the most part as to both rectitude and knowledge, but in the rare case it can fail as to both rectitude – on account of particular impediments (just as things generable and corruptible by nature fail rarely, on account of impediments) – and knowledge, and this because some have a reason depraved by passion or by evil custom or from a bad cast of nature, as theft was once thought by the Germans not to be wrong, although it is expressly against the law of nature, as Julius Caesar recounts in *On the Gallic Wars*.

Ad 1. It should be said that this word is not to be understood as meaning that everything contained in the law and the Gospel is of the law of nature, since many things are treated there which are above nature, but because the things which are of the law of nature are taught more fully there. Hence when Gratian said that natural right is contained in the law and Gospel, he immediately added by way of example, that each one is admonished to do to others what he would wish to be done to himself.

Ad 2. It should be said that the Philosopher's remark is to be understood of those things which are naturally just, not as common principles, but as conclusions derived from them, which by and large have rectitude, but fail rarely.

Ad 3. It should be said that reason in man rules over and commands the other powers, and thus it is necessary that the natural inclinations of the other powers be ordered by reason. Hence this is universally right for all, that all man's inclinations should be directed by reason.

Article 5: Can natural law be changed?

It seems that it can be.

1. With respect to Ecclesiasticus 17.9, 'Moreover, he gave them instructions, and the law of life for an inheritance,' the Gloss says that the scribes meant the written law, as a correction of natural law. But that which is corrected is changed. Therefore, natural law can be changed.

2. Moreover, the killing of the innocent is against natural law, and so too adultery and theft. But we find these to have been changed by God, as for example when God commanded Abraham to kill his innocent son, as is told in Genesis 22.2, and when he commanded the Jews to borrow and steal the jars of the Egyptians, as is told in Exodus 12.35; and when he commanded Osee that he should take a prostitute for wife, as can be found in Osee 1.2. Therefore natural law can be changed.

3. Moreover, Isidore says in the *Etymologies* 5.4 that the common

possession of all things and one and the same freedom is of natural law. But we see these changed by human laws. Therefore, it seems that natural law is mutable.

ON THE CONTRARY:

It is said in the *Decretals* that natural right which takes its rise from the rational creature does not vary with time, but remains immutable.

RESPONSE:

It should be said that natural law can be understood to change in two ways. In one way, because something is added to it, and nothing prevents natural law from changing in this way, for many things useful for human life are added to natural law both by divine law and by human law. In another way the change of natural law is understood by way of subtraction, such that something ceases to be of natural law which before was of natural law. In this sense, with respect to its first principles, the law of nature is completely immutable. But with respect to secondary precepts, which we have called proper conclusions, proximate to the first principles, the natural law is not changed as if what it contains is not for the most part right. But it can be changed in some particular, and rarely, because of some cause impeding the observance of such precepts, as was said above.

Ad 1. It should be said that the written law is said to be given for the correction of the law of nature either because something lacking in the law of nature is supplied by the written law, or because the law of nature, in some hearts, with respect to some things, was so corrupted that they thought what is naturally evil to be good, and such corruption needs correction.

Ad 2. It should be said that it is universally true and natural that everyone will die, both the guilty and the innocent, which natural death was brought about by the divine power on account of original sin, according to 1 Kings 2.6: 'The Lord killeth and he maketh alive.' Therefore, without any injustice, according to the mandate of God, death can be inflicted on any man, guilty or innocent. Similarly, adultery is sleeping with another's wife, who is given to him according to the law divinely handed down. Hence if someone goes to whatever woman by the divine mandate, it is neither adultery nor fornication. And the same applies to theft, which is taking the goods of another. But whatever one takes by the command of God who is Lord of the universe, he does not take without the will of the Lord – which is what theft is. Not only in human affairs is whatever God commands fitting, but also whatever comes to be from God in the natural world is in some way natural, as was said in Part 1.

Ad 3. It should be said that something is said to be of natural law in two ways. In one way, because nature inclines to it, such as that no injury ought to be done to another. In another way, because nature does not lead to the contrary, as we might say that for man to be naked is of natural law because nature did not provide him with clothing, which is fashioned by art. In this way the common possession of all things and one and the same liberty for all can be said to be of natural law, because the distinction of ownership and servitude are not brought about by nature, but by the reason of men for the usefulness of human life. And thus natural law is not changed by addition.

Article 6: Can natural law be erased from a man's heart?

It seems that it can be.

1. The Gloss says about Romans 2.14, 'The gentiles, who have not the law . . .', that in the inner man renewed by grace the law of justice is inscribed, which guilt bears off. But the law of justice is the law of nature. Therefore, the law of nature can be erased.

2. Moreover, the law of grace is more efficacious than the law of nature. But the law of grace is deleted by guilt. So much the more, then, can the law of nature be erased.

3. That which is established by law is put forth as just. But many things are instituted by men against the law of nature. Therefore, the law of nature can be abolished from the hearts of men.

ON THE CONTRARY:
Augustine says in the *Confessions* 2.4, 'Your law is written in the hearts of men, and no iniquity can erase it,' but the law written in the hearts of men is the natural law. Therefore natural law cannot be erased.

RESPONSE:
It should be said that, as was stated above, to natural law first pertains certain most common principles, known to all, and certain secondary precepts, more proper, which are, as it were, conclusions close to the principles. With respect to those common principles, natural law in

general can in no way be erased from the hearts of men, but it can be in the particular thing to be done, insofar as reason is prevented from applying the common principle to the particular things to be done because of concupiscence or some other passion, as was said above. With respect to the other, secondary principles, natural law can be erased from the hearts of men, either because of bad persuasion, in the way in which errors occur in speculative matters with respect to necessary conclusions, or because of depraved customs and corrupt habits, as with those who do not think theft or even sins against nature to be sin, as the Apostle says in Romans 1.24 ff.

Ad 1. It should be said that guilt removes the law of nature in particular, but not universally, unless except for secondary precepts of the law of nature, in the way that has been discussed.

Ad 2. It should be said that although grace is more efficacious than nature, yet nature is more essential to man, and therefore more permanent.

Ad 3. It should be said that this argument proceeds from the secondary precepts of the law of nature, against which some legislators frame statutes, which are evil.

25. *The Virtues.* Summa theologiae 1–2, 55–7 (1271–2)

Thinking about how to act well is a far cry from acting well, at least when the thinking is on the level of generality. There is, however, another kind of thinking, that embedded in the singular action. From the beginning philosophers, like the rest of us, pondered the transition from general reflections about good actions to the actual performance of them, and discursive transitions in thought seemed relatively simple compared to the transition from thought to action.

To act is to choose and all choices are singular. Choice does not seem to be adequately described merely as a mindless leap; rather, it is minded, conscious, an opting for what we think best. Like Aristotle, Thomas wavered between calling human action a choosing knowing or a knowing choosing; in either case, there are two components, mind and appetite. But actions have their antecedents, they are performed against the background of earlier performances; the agent acquires a history and with it a bent or inclination to act as he has before. Thus mind and will, powers that at the outset might go this way or that, acquire a character of stability. Habits are acquired. Habits, however, are good or bad, depending on whether they incline us to what is fulfilling of us or not. Thus is the subject of virtue – of good habits – introduced. In the following key questions of the Prima Secundae *of the* Summa theologiae, *Thomas defines virtue and begins to look into the many kinds of virtue.*

Summa theologiae, First Part of the Second Part, Questions 55–7

QUESTION 55
ON THE VIRTUES

Next we must consider habits in a special way and since, as was said, habits are good or bad, we must first speak of good habits, that is, the virtues, and of other things linked to them, namely the gifts, beatitudes and fruits. Then we will take up bad habits, namely vices and sins. With respect to virtues, there are five things to be considered: first, the essence of virtue; second, its subject; third, the kinds of virtue; fourth, the cause of virtue and, fifth, certain properties of virtue. With respect to the essence of virtue, there are four issues: (1) whether human virtue is a habit; (2) whether it is an operative habit; (3) whether it is a good habit; (4) the definition of virtue.

Article 1: Is virtue a habit?

It seems that it is not.

1. Virtue is the 'utmost of a power', as is said in *On the Heavens* 1.11. But an utmost is reduced to the genus of which it is the utmost, as point to the genus of line. Therefore virtue is reduced to the genus of power, not habit.

2. Moreover, Augustine says in *On Free Will* 2.19 that 'virtue is the good use of free will'. But the good use of free will is an act. Therefore, virtue is not a habit, but an act.

3. Moreover, we do not earn merit because of habits but because of acts, otherwise a man would be earning merit continuously, even while sleeping. But we gain merit by the virtues. Therefore the virtues are not habits but acts.

4. Moreover, Augustine says in *On the Morals of the Church* 15 that 'virtue is the order of love', and in the *Eighty-three Questions* 39 he says that 'the order that is called a virtue is enjoying what ought to be enjoyed and using what ought to be used'. But order or ordering signifies an act or relation. Therefore, virtue is not a habit but an act or relation.

5. Moreover, human virtues are like natural virtues. But natural virtues are powers, not habits. So the same should be true of human virtues.

ON THE CONTRARY:
The Philosopher in the *Categories* says that knowledge and virtue are habits.

RESPONSE:
It should be said that virtue signifies the perfection of a power, but a thing's perfection is read chiefly in terms of its end. But to act is the end of a power. Hence a power can be said to be perfected insofar as it is

determined to its act. Now some powers are such that they are of themselves determined to their acts, such as the natural active powers, and these powers are themselves called virtues. But rational powers, which are proper to man, are not determined to one thing but are indifferently related to many; they are determined to acts by habits, as is clear from the foregoing.[1] Therefore, human virtues are habits.

Ad 1. It should be said that sometimes virtue means that which is of the virtue, namely its object or its act, as faith sometimes means that which is believed, sometimes believing itself, and sometimes the habit whereby it is believed. Hence when virtue is said to be the utmost of a power, virtue is taken for the object of virtue. That of which a power is ultimately capable is that to which the power is said to extend, as when one can carry one hundred pounds and no more, his capacity is one hundred pounds, not sixty. The objection assumes that virtue is in essence the utmost of a power.

Ad 2. It should be said that the good use of free will is called virtue in the same sense, because it is that to which virtue is ordered as to its proper act. For the act of virtue is nothing else but the good use of free will.

Ad 3. We are said to merit because of something in two ways. In one way, as we are said to run because of running, and in this way we merit by acts. In another way we are said to merit by that which is the principle of meriting, as we are said to run because of the motive power. It is in this way that we are said to merit by virtues and habits.

Ad 4. It should be said that virtue is called the order or ordering of love because of what virtue is for, since love is ordered in us by virtue.

Ad 5. It should be said that natural powers are of themselves determined to one, but rational powers are not. Therefore, the analogy limps, as has been said.

Article 2: Is human virtue an operative habit?

It seems not.

1. Cicero says in the *Tusculan Questions* 13 that virtue is to the soul as health and beauty are to the body. But health and beauty are not operative habits, so neither is virtue.

2. Moreover, in natural things there is not only a capacity (virtue) for

acting, but also for being, as is clear from the Philosopher in *On the Heavens* 1.12: some things have the capacity to exist always, others for a given time but not always. But human virtue in rational matters is like natural virtue in natural matters. Therefore, human virtue too is not only for acting, but also for existing.

3. Moreover, the Philosopher says in *Physics* 7 that virtue is the disposition of the perfected for the best. But the best to which a man can be disposed by virtue is God himself (as Augustine proves in *On the Morals of the Church* 2.3), to whom the soul is disposed by assimilation to him. Therefore, virtue seems to signify some quality of soul as ordered to God, as making us like him, not in being ordered to operation. Therefore it is not an operative habit.

ON THE CONTRARY:
There is what the Philosopher says in *Ethics* 2.6, namely that the virtue of a thing is that which makes its work good.

RESPONSE:
It should be said that virtue, as the meaning of the word suggests, implies the perfection of a power, as was said above. Hence, since there are two kinds of power, namely that to exist and that to act, the perfection of each is called virtue. But the virtue or capacity to exist arises from matter, which is potential being, whereas the capacity to act arises from form, which is the principle of acting insofar as a thing acts to the degree that it is actual. But in man's make-up, the body is as matter, the soul as form, and with respect to body, man is like other animals. Similarly, with respect to powers common to soul and body; only the powers which are proper to soul, that is, rational powers, belong to man alone. Therefore, human virtue, of which we are speaking, cannot pertain to body, but only to what is proper to soul. Hence human virtue is not ordered to existence, but rather to acting. Thus it is of the definition of human virtue that it be an operative habit.

Ad 1. It should be said that the mode of action follows the disposition of the agent, for a thing acts in the way in which it exists. Therefore, since virtue is the principle of an operation, there must pre-exist in the agent thanks to the virtue some similar disposition. But since virtue makes activity ordered, virtue itself is an ordered disposition in the soul, insofar as the powers of soul are in a certain manner ordered to one another and to that which is outside. Therefore virtue, insofar as it is a fitting disposition of soul, is like health and beauty, which are fitting proportions of body. But this does not prevent virtue from being a principle of operation as well.

Ad 2. It should be said that the virtue which [is a capacity] for existing is not peculiar to man, but only that virtue which is ordered to works of reason which are peculiar to man.

Ad 3. It should be said that since God's substance is his action, the highest assimilation of man to God is by way of some operation. Hence, as was said earlier, happiness or beatitude, by which man is especially conformed to God, who is the end of human life, consists in operation.

Article 3: Is human virtue a good habit?

It seems that it is not.

1. Sin always consists in evil. But there is virtue in sin, according to 1 Corinthians 15.56: 'The power [*virtus*] of sin is the Law.' Therefore virtue is not always a good habit.

2. Moreover, virtue answers to a power, but a power relates to evil as well as good, according to Isaiah 5.22: 'Woe to you that are mighty to drink wine, and stout men at drunkenness.' It seems therefore that virtue is related to both good and evil.

3. Moreover, according to the Apostle in 2 Corinthians 12.9, 'For strength is made perfect in weakness.' But weakness is a kind of evil. Therefore, virtue relates not only to the good, but also to evil.

ON THE CONTRARY:
Augustine says in *On the Morals of the Church* 6 that no one doubts that virtue makes the soul good, and the Philosopher says in *Ethics* 2.6 that virtue is what makes the one having it good and makes his action good.

RESPONSE:
It should be said that, as was pointed out earlier, virtue implies the perfection of a power, which is why a thing's virtue is determined by the utmost of which a thing is capable, as is said in *On the Heavens* 1.11. But the utmost of which a thing is capable must be good, since every evil implies some defect. Hence Dionysius says in *On the Divine Names* 4 that every evil is a weakness. For this reason the power of anything must be ordered to the good. Hence human virtue, which is an operative habit, is a good habit, and operative of the good.

*

Ad 1. It should be said that good like the perfect is said metaphorically of evil things, for we speak of a perfect thief or bandit and a good thief or bandit, as is clear from the Philosopher in *Metaphysics* 4.16. In this way virtue too is spoken of metaphorically in evil things, and thus law is called the virtue or power of sin insofar as it is the occasion for the increase of sin and brings it, as it were, to its maximum.

Ad 2. It should be said that the evil of drunkenness and excess in drink consists in a defect of the order of reason. But it can happen that, along with the defect of reason, some lesser power is perfected with respect to that which is proper to it, although with a repugnance to or defect of reason. But the perfection of such a power, when it is accompanied by a defect of reason, cannot be called a human virtue.

Ad 3. It should be said that reason is more perfect to the degree that it is more capable of subduing or bearing the weaknesses of the body and the lower parts. Therefore human virtue, which is attributed to reason, is said to be made perfect, not in the weakness of reason, but in that of body and the lower parts.

Article 4: Is virtue defined properly?

It seems that it is not.

1. The definition of virtue as 'a good quality of mind whereby one lives rightly and uses no one badly and which God without our help works in us' is not a good definition. Virtue is man's goodness, for it makes the one having it good, but goodness is not called good any more than whiteness is called white. Therefore it is improper to say that virtue is a good quality.

2. Moreover, no difference is more common than its genus, since it divides the genus, but good is more common than quality, for it is convertible with being. Therefore good ought not to be put in the definition of virtue as the difference of quality.

3. Moreover, as Augustine says in *On the Trinity* 12.8, that pertains to mind which is in us and is not common to us and the beasts; but there are virtues of the irrational parts, as the Philosopher says in *Ethics* 3.10. Therefore not every virtue is a good quality of mind.

4. Moreover, rectitude seems to pertain to justice, which is why the right and just are said to be the same, but justice is a species of virtue. Therefore, it is improperly introduced into the definition of virtue when it is called that whereby one lives rightly.

5. Moreover, those who take pride in something use it badly, but many take pride in virtue, for Augustine says that pride undermines good works so that they perish. Therefore it is false that no one uses virtue badly.

6. Moreover, man is justified by virtue, but Augustine says, in commenting on John 14.12, 'He who believes in me, the works that I do he shall do, and greater than these he shall do,' that he who created you without your help, will not justify you without your help. Therefore, it is improper to say that God works virtue in us without our doing anything.

ON THE CONTRARY:
There is the authority of Augustine, from whose words the foregoing definition is taken, especially from *On Free Will* 2.

RESPONSE:
It should be said that this definition perfectly expresses the complete notion of virtue. The perfect account of anything is drawn from all its causes. The foregoing definition includes all the causes of virtue. For the formal cause of virtue, as of anything else, is drawn from its genus and difference, when it is called a good quality, for the genus of virtue is quality, and its difference is good. It would be an even more fitting definition if habit replaced quality, since it is the proximate genus.

Virtue does not have a matter *of which* any more than the other accidents do, but it has a matter *about which*, that is, the object of the virtue, which could not be put in the foregoing definition because the virtue is determined to its species by the object, whereas here a common definition of virtue is offered, so that the subject is put in the place of the material cause, and so it is called a good quality of mind.

The end of virtue, since it is an operative habit, is action itself. But note that some operative habits are always inclined towards evil, such as vicious habits, and others incline sometimes to good and sometimes to evil, much as opinion relates to the true and false. But virtue is a habit which is always related to the good. Therefore, to distinguish virtue from habits which always relate to evil it is said to be that whereby one lives rightly, and to distinguish it from things which sometimes relate to good and sometimes to evil, it is said to be that which no one can use badly.

The efficient cause of infused virtue, whose definition is being given, is God, which is why it is called that which God works in us without us. If this particle were removed, the remaining definition would be common to all the virtues, both acquired and infused.

*

Ad 1. It should be said that being is what intellect first grasps, which is why we can attribute being to anything we grasp as well as one and good which are convertible with being. Hence we say that essence is being and one and good, and that unity is being and one and good, and similarly with goodness. This does not obtain in more particular forms, however, such as whiteness and health, for not everything that we grasp falls under the notions of white and healthy. But it should be realized that just as non-subsistent accidents and forms are called beings, not because they have existence but rather because by them something is, so too they are called being and one, not indeed by any other goodness or unity, but because by them something is good or one. It is in this way that virtue is called good, namely, because by it something is good.

Ad 2. It should be said that the good put into the definition of virtue is not the universal good that is convertible with being and thus in more than quality, but it is the good of reason; according to Dionysius, *On the Divine Names* 4, the soul's good is to exist according to reason.

Ad 3. It should be said that virtue cannot be in the irrational part of the soul save insofar as it participates in reason, as is said in *Ethics* 1.13. Therefore, reason or mind is the proper subject of human virtue.

Ad 4. It should be said that to justice belongs the proper rectitude which concerns the external things that men use and that are the proper matter of virtue, as will be made clear below.[1] But the rectitude that implies an ordering to the fitting end and to divine law, which is the rule of the human will, as has been said above, is common to every virtue.

Ad 5. It should be said that someone can use virtue badly as an object, as when he thinks badly of virtue or hates it or takes pride in it, but not as a principle of use, such that the act of virtue is evil.

Ad 6. It should be said that infused virtue is caused in us by God without our acting but not without our consent. That is how 'God works in us without us' must be understood. God indeed causes the things we do but not without our acting, for he works in every will and nature.

---

1. q. 60, art. 2.

QUESTION 56
THE SUBJECT OF VIRTUE

With respect to the subject of virtue, there are six things to be asked: (1) whether virtue is in a power of the soul as in its subject; (2) whether one virtue can be in several powers; (3) whether intellect can be the subject of virtue; (4) whether the irascible and concupiscible appetites can be the subject of virtue; (5) whether the sensory apprehensive powers can be; and (6) whether will can be the subject of virtue.

Article 1: Is virtue in a power of the soul as in its subject?

It seems that it is not.

1. Augustine says in *On Free Will* 19 that virtue is that whereby we live rightly. But living is due, not to a power of the soul, but to its essence. Therefore, virtue is not in a power of the soul, but in its essence.

2. Moreover, the Philosopher says in *Ethics* 2.6 that virtue is that which makes the one having it good and renders his action good. But just as action comes about through a power, so having virtue comes about through the essence of soul. Therefore, virtue pertains rather to the essence of soul than to its power.

3. Moreover, a power is in the second species of quality. But virtue is a kind of quality, as has been said, but there is no quality of quality. Therefore, virtue is not in a power of soul as in its subject.

ON THE CONTRARY:

Virtue is the utmost of a power, as is said in *On the Heavens* 1.11. But the utmost is in that whose utmost it is; therefore, virtue is in a power of the soul.

RESPONSE:

It should be said that there are three ways in which it can be shown that virtue belongs to a power of the soul. First, from the very definition of virtue, which implies the perfection of a power; perfection is in that of which it is in the perfection. Second, from the fact that virtue is an operative habit, as it is said to be. But every activity is from the soul by way of some power. Third, from that which disposes for the best, the best being the end, which is either the activity of the thing or something achieved by an activity arising from a power. Hence human virtue is in a power of the soul as in its subject.

Ad 1. It should be replied that something is said to live in two ways. For sometimes to live means the existence of the living thing and pertains to the essence of soul; at other times to live means the activity of the living thing, and thus one lives rightly by virtue insofar as one acts rightly by means of it.

Ad 2. It should be said that what is called good is either the end or is ordered to the end. Therefore, since the good of the agent consists in action, by the very fact that virtue makes the agent good it is referred to action and consequently to power.

Ad 3. It should be said that one accident is said to be in another as in a subject because it inheres in substance by the mediation of the other accident, not because one accident can sustain another. Colour inheres in body by the mediation of surface, so surface can be called the subject of colour, and only in that sense can the power of the soul be called the subject of virtue.

Article 2: Can a virtue be in several powers?

It seems that it can.

1. Habits are made known through acts, but one act arises differently from different powers, as walking arises from reason as directing it and from will as mover and from the motive power as executing it. Thus one habit of virtue can be in several powers.

2. Moreover, the Philosopher says in *Ethics* 2.4 that three things are required for virtue: knowing, willing and changeless acting, but knowing pertains to intellect, willing to will. Therefore, virtue can be in several powers.

3. Moreover, prudence is in reason since it is right reason about things to be done, as is said in *Ethics* 6.5. But it is also in will, since it cannot be if the will is perverse, as is said in the same place. Therefore, one virtue can be in two powers.

ON THE CONTRARY:
Virtue is in a power of the soul as in its subject. But the same accident cannot be in several subjects. Therefore the same virtue cannot be in several powers of the soul.

RESPONSE:

It should be said that something can be in two things in two ways. First, such that it is equally in both, and in this way it is impossible for the same virtue to be in two powers, because the diversity of powers is taken from the general conditions of objects and the diversity of habits from special conditions, hence wherever there is diversity of powers, there is diversity of habits, but not conversely. Second, something can be in two or several things, not equally, but in an ordered way. In this way one virtue can pertain to several powers such that it is in one principally and extends to others by way of diffusion or by way of disposition, insofar as one power is moved by another, and insofar as one power receives from another.

Ad 1. It should be said that the same action cannot pertain to different powers equally and in the same order, but according to different notions and a different order.

Ad 2. It should be said that knowing is a prerequisite of moral virtue insofar as moral virtue acts according to right reason. But moral virtue consists essentially in desiring.

Ad 3. It should be said that prudence is really in reason as in a subject, but presupposes the rectitude of will as a principle, as will be said below.

Article 3: Can intellect be the subject of virtue?

It seems that it cannot.

1. Augustine said, in *On the Morals of the Church* 15, that every virtue is love. The subject of love is not intellect, however, but only the appetitive power. Therefore, no virtue is in intellect.

2. Moreover, virtue is ordered to the good, as is clear from the foregoing. But good is the object of the appetitive power, not of intellect. Therefore the subject of virtue is the appetitive power, not intellect.

3. Moreover, virtue is that which makes the one having it good, as the Philosopher says. But the habit perfecting intellect does not make the one having it good, since it is not because of knowledge or art that a man is called good. Therefore, intellect is not the subject of virtue.

ON THE CONTRARY:

The mind is called intellect most of all, but the subject of virtue is mind, as is clear from the definition of virtue discussed earlier. Therefore intellect is the subject of virtue.

RESPONSE:

It should be said that, as has been pointed out, virtue is the habit whereby one acts well, but a habit is ordered to a good act in two ways. In one way, insofar as through such a habit a man acquires the capacity for the good act, as a man has the capacity to speak well thanks to the habit of grammar. But grammar does not bring it about that a man always speaks well, for the grammarian can speak infelicities or solecisms. And it is the same in the other sciences and arts. In another way, a habit can give not only the capacity of acting but also bring it about that one uses the capacity rightly, as justice not only brings it about that a man has a will prompt to do just things, but also brings it about that he acts justly.

Because something is called good or being simply speaking insofar as it is actual, not insofar as it is potential, a man is said to do good and to be good simply speaking because of such habits, that is, to be just or temperate, and similarly with the others. And because virtue is what makes the one having it good and makes his action good, only such habits are called virtues simply speaking, for they bring about an actual good work and make the one having it good simply speaking.

The first kind of habits are not called virtues simply speaking, because they do not make a good work except by way of a capacity for it, nor do they make one having them good simply, for a man is not called a good man simply because he knows or is an artisan, but good only in a certain respect, namely, a good grammarian or a good maker, which is why sometimes science and art are distinguished from virtue and sometimes are called virtues, as is clear from *Ethics* 6.2.

Intellect can be the subject of habits which are virtues only in a sense, and not only practical but also speculative intellect, without any order to will, and that is why the Philosopher in *Ethics* 6.2 mentions science, wisdom, understanding and also art as intellectual virtues.

The subject of the habits which are called virtues simply speaking can only be the will or some power moved by the will. The reason for this is that the will moves all the other powers which are in any way rational to their acts, as was said above, therefore a man acts well insofar as he has a good will. Hence the virtue that makes one actually act well and not only gives the capacity is either in the will or in some power insofar as it is moved by will.

The intellect is moved by will, as are the other powers, for one actually considers something because he wills it and thus intellect, insofar as it has an order to will, can be the subject of virtue simply speaking. And in this way speculative intellect or reason is the subject of faith, for intellect is moved to assent to the things of faith by the command of will, for no one believes unless he wills to. The practical intellect is the subject of prudence. Since prudence is right reason about things to be done, prudence requires that a man be well disposed to the rational principles for so acting, and these are ends to which one is well disposed by the rectitude of will, just as one is well disposed to the principles of speculative objects by the natural light of the agent intellect. Just as the subject of science, which is right reason about objects of speculation, is speculative intellect as ordered to agent intellect, so the subject of prudence is practical intellect as ordered to right will.

Ad 1. It should be said that Augustine's statement should be understood of virtue simply speaking, and not taken to mean that every such virtue is simply love, but depends somehow on love insofar as it depends on will whose first affection is love, as has been said.

Ad 2. It should be said that the good of anything is its end; therefore, since the true is the end of intellect, to know the true is the good act of intellect. Hence the habit perfecting intellect with respect to knowing the truth, whether in the speculative or practical matters, is called virtue.

Ad 3. It should be said that this argument proceeds from virtue simply speaking.

Article 4: Are the irascible and concupiscible subjects of virtue?

It seems that they cannot be.

1. These powers are common to us and the brutes, but we are now speaking of virtue as proper to man, which is why it is called human virtue. Therefore the irascible and concupiscible cannot be subjects of human virtues, because they are parts of sense appetite, as has been said.

2. Moreover, sense appetite is a power that uses a bodily organ; but the good of virtue cannot be in man's body. The Apostle says in Romans 7.18, 'For I know that in me, that is, in my flesh, no good dwells.' Therefore, sense appetite cannot be the subject of virtue.

3. Moreover, Augustine proves in *On the Morals of the Church* 5 that virtue is not in the body, but in the soul, because body is ruled by soul, hence one's good use of body is referred entirely to soul, just as if I rightly

steer horses by means of reins, the whole is due to me. But just as the soul rules the body, so does reason rule sense appetite. Therefore, it is due to the rational part that the irascible and concupiscible are rightly ruled. But virtue is that whereby one lives rightly, as has been said; therefore, virtue is not in the concupiscible and irascible, but in the rational part alone.

4. Moreover, choice is the chief act of moral virtue, as is said in *Ethics* 8.13, but choice is an act of reason, not of the irascible or concupiscible, as was said above. Therefore, moral virtue is not in the irascible or concupiscible, but in reason.

ON THE CONTRARY:

Courage is located in the irascible and temperance in the concupiscible. Hence the Philosopher says in *Ethics* 3.10 that these are virtues of the irrational parts.

RESPONSE:

It should be said that the irascible and concupiscible can be considered in two ways. In one way, in themselves, insofar as they are parts of sense appetite, and in this way they are not the subject of virtue. In another way they can be considered as they participate in reason insofar as they are fashioned to obey reason. Thus the irascible and concupiscible can be the subject of human virtue, for they are the principle of human acts insofar as they participate in reason. There must then be virtues in these powers.

That there are virtues in the irascible and concupiscible is clear. For an act which arises from a power insofar as it is moved by another can be perfect only if both powers are disposed to act well, as the act of the artisan can go well only insofar as the artisan and his instrument are disposed to act well. In those things with which the irascible and concupiscible are concerned insofar as they are moved by reason, there must be a perfecting habit for acting well, not only in reason but also in the irascible and concupiscible. And because the good disposition of the power that moves insofar as it is moved lies in its conformity to the moving power, virtue in the irascible and concupiscible is nothing other than the habitual conformity of these powers to reason.

Ad 1. It should be said that the irascible and concupiscible taken in themselves, as parts of sense appetite, are common to us and to the brutes. But insofar as they are rational by participation, as obeying reason, they are peculiar to man. And in this way they can be the subject of human virtue.

Ad 2. It should be said that just as man's flesh does not of itself have the good of virtue but becomes the instrument of the virtuous act insofar as, moved by reason, we employ our members to serve justice, so too the irascible and concupiscible do not of themselves have the good of virtue but rather the infection of lust, yet insofar as they are conformed to reason the good of moral virtue comes to be in them.

Ad 3. It should be said that body is not ruled by soul in the same way that the irascible and concupiscible are ruled by reason, for body obeys soul on command without contradiction with respect to the things in which it is fashioned to be moved by the soul. That is why the Philosopher says in *Politics* 1.2 that soul rules body with a despotic rule, that is, as a master rules his slave, and the complete motion of body is referred to soul. Because of this there is no virtue in the body, but only in the soul. But the irascible and concupiscible do not obey reason on command, but have proper motions of their own which sometimes are opposed to reason, hence in the same book the Philosopher says that reason rules the irascible and concupiscible with a political rule, in the way free men who have a will of their own are ruled. Because of this there must be in the irascible and concupiscible virtues whereby they are disposed to act well.

Ad 4. It should be said that there are two things in choice, namely the intention of the end, which pertains to moral virtue, and the preconception of that which is for the sake of the end, which pertains to prudence, as is said in *Ethics* 6.12. That there is a right intention of the end in the passions of the soul is brought about by the good disposition of the irascible and concupiscible appetites. Therefore, moral virtues which concern the passions are in the irascible and concupiscible, but prudence is in reason.

Article 5: Are the apprehensive powers of sense subjects of virtue?

It seems they are.

1. Sense appetite can be the subject of virtue insofar as it obeys reason; but the interior apprehensive powers of sense obey reason, for at the command of reason, imagination, the cogitative and memory act. There can therefore be virtue in these powers.

2. Moreover, just as rational appetite, that is, will, can be impeded in its act or indeed helped by sense appetite, so too intellect or reason can

be impeded or even aided by the foregoing powers. Therefore, just as there can be virtue in the appetitive powers of sense, so too in its apprehensive powers.

3. Moreover, prudence is a virtue that has memory for a part, as Cicero says in his *Rhetoric* 2.53. Therefore, there can be a virtue in the remembering power as well, and by the same reasoning in the other interior apprehensive powers.

ON THE CONTRARY:
Virtues are either intellectual or moral, as is said in *Ethics* 2.1. But all the moral virtues are in the appetitive part and all the intellectual virtues in intellect or reason, as is clear from *Ethics* 6.1. Therefore, there is no virtue in the interior apprehensive powers of sense.

RESPONSE:
It should be said that there are habits in the interior apprehensive powers of sense; the Philosopher gives the chief reason in *On Memory*, saying that in remembering one thing after another custom is at work, which is a kind of nature, but a customary habit is nothing else than a habit acquired by custom, which acts as nature does. Hence Cicero in his *Rhetoric* 2.53 says that habit acts in the manner of nature, in agreement with reason. But in man what is acquired in memory, and in the other apprehensive powers of sense, by custom is not a habit as such, but something annexed to the habits of the intellective part, as was said above.[1]

If there are habits in such powers, they cannot be called virtues. For since virtue is a perfect habit by which one does only the good, virtue must be in a power which is completive of the good work. But knowledge of the true is not completed in the apprehensive powers of sense: such powers are preparatory to intellectual knowledge. So in such powers there are no virtues whereby the truth is known, but only in intellect or reason.

Ad 1. It should be said that sense appetite is to will, the appetite of reason, as something moved by it. Therefore the act of the appetitive power is consummated in sense appetite. Because of this, sense appetite is the subject of virtue. But the apprehensive powers of sense relate to intellect rather as movers, insofar as phantasms are to the intellective soul, as

1. q. 50, art. 4, ad 3.

colours are to sight, as is said in *On the Soul* 3.7. Therefore, the work of knowledge terminates in intellect, which is why cognitive virtues are in intellect or reason itself.

Ad 2. From this the solution to the second is clear.

Ad 3. It should be said that memory is not said to be a part of prudence in the way that a species is a part of genus, as if memory were of itself some virtue, but because one of the things required for prudence is good memory, and thus in a way it is an integral part.

Article 6: Can will be the subject of virtue?

It seems that it is not.

1. A power does not need a habit with respect to what belongs to it as such. Since it is in reason, according to the Philosopher in *On the Soul* 3.9, it belongs to will as such to tend to the good grasped by reason. Every virtue is ordered to that, since everything naturally seeks its proper good, for virtue is a habit in the mode of nature, agreeing with reason, as Cicero says. Therefore, will is not the subject of virtue.

2. Moreover, a virtue is either intellectual or moral, as is said in *Ethics* 2.1. But an intellectual virtue is in intellect or reason as in a subject, not in will, but moral virtue is in the irascible or concupiscible as in a subject. Therefore, no virtue is in will as in a subject.

3. Moreover, all human acts, to which virtues are ordered, are voluntary. Therefore, if there were some virtue in the will with respect to some human acts, by parity of reason there would be a virtue in will with respect to all human acts. Therefore, either there will be virtue in no other power, or several virtues will be ordered to the same act, which seems absurd. Therefore, will cannot be the subject of virtue.

ON THE CONTRARY:
More perfection is required of the mover than of the moved. But will moves the irascible and concupiscible. Therefore, there is much more reason for there to be virtue in will than in the irascible and concupiscible.

RESPONSE:
It should be said that since a power to act is perfected by a habit, where a power does not suffice of itself it needs a habit perfecting it to act well, which habit is a virtue. But the proper notion of any power is taken from

its object. Thus, since the object of will is the good of reason proportioned to will, as was said, the will needs no perfecting virtue for this.

But if there should be a good to be willed that exceeds the proportion of man's will, whether with respect to the whole human species, such as the divine good, or with respect to the individual, such as the good of the neighbour, the will needs a virtue. Therefore the virtues that order man's will to God or to neighbour are in the will as in their subject, such as charity, justice and the like.

Ad 1. It should be said that this argument applies to the virtues ordered to the proper good of the one willing, such as temperance and courage, which deal with human passions and the like, as is clear from what has been said.

Ad 2. It should be said that the rational through participation is not exhausted by the irascible and concupiscible but is true of the appetitive generally, as is said in *Ethics* 1.13, and will is included in the appetitive. Therefore any virtue of will will be a moral virtue, unless it is theological, as will be clear below.

Ad 3. It should be said that some virtues are ordered to the good of moderated passion, which is proper to this or that man, and there need be no virtue in the will for such things, since the nature of the power is sufficient here, as has been said. This is necessary only in those virtues which are ordered to some extrinsic good.

QUESTION 57
DISTINGUISHING THE INTELLECTUAL VIRTUES

Next we must consider how virtues are distinguished from one another. First, with respect to the intellectual virtues; then, the moral virtues, and third, the theological. Six things must be asked about intellectual virtues. (1) whether the habits of speculative intellect are virtues; (2) whether there are three of them, namely, wisdom, knowledge and understanding; (3) whether the intellectual habit of art is a virtue; (4) whether prudence is a virtue distinct from art; (5) whether prudence is a necessary virtue for man; (6) whether *eubulia*, *synesis* and *gnome* are virtues linked to prudence.

Article 1: Are the habits of speculative intellect virtues?

It seems not.

1. Virtue is an operative habit, as has been said above. But speculative habits are not operative, for the speculative is distinguished from the practical, that is, the operative. Therefore the intellectual habits of the speculative are not virtues.

2. Moreover, virtue is concerned with the things by which a man is made happy or blessed, as is said in *Ethics* 1.9. But intellectual habits do not consider human acts or other human goods by which a man might acquire happiness, but rather natural and divine things. Therefore, such habits cannot be called virtues.

3. Moreover, science is a speculative habit, but science and virtue are distinguished as different genera, one of which is not put under the other, as is clear from the Philosopher in *Topics* 4.2. Therefore, speculative habits are not virtues.

ON THE CONTRARY:

Only speculative habits consider the necessary things that cannot be otherwise. But the Philosopher, in *Ethics* 6.1, posits intellectual virtues in the part of the soul which considers necessary things that cannot be otherwise. Therefore, speculative intellectual habits are virtues.

RESPONSE:

It should be said that since virtue is ordered to the good, as was said above, there are two ways in which a habit can be called a virtue, as was also said earlier,[1] in one way, because it causes the capacity to act well, in another way, because it causes good use as well as the capacity. But the latter, we have seen, pertains only to those habits which look to the appetitive part, because it is the appetitive power of soul that causes the use of all powers and habits.

Therefore, since the intellectual habits of the speculative do not perfect the appetitive part nor involve it in any way but only the intellective part, they can indeed be called virtues insofar as they cause the capacity for good operation, which is the consideration of the true (for this is the good work of intellect). But they are not called virtues in the second sense, as causing the good use of the power or habit. Just because one has the

1. q. 55, art. 3.

habit of speculative science, he is not inclined to use it, but he is made capable of grasping the truth of the things of which he has knowledge, but that he use the knowledge had is due to the moving will. Therefore the virtues which perfect will, like charity or justice, cause one to use well such speculative habits. In this way there can be merit in the acts of such habits, if they are done out of charity. So Gregory in the *Morals* 6.37 says that the contemplative is of greater merit than the active.

Ad 1. It should be said that there are two kinds of work, the external and the internal. The practical or operative which is distinguished from the speculative is drawn from the external work, to which the speculative habit is not ordered. But it is ordered to the interior work of intellect, which is to think the truth and in this respect it is an operative habit.

Ad 2. It should be said that virtue is concerned with something in two ways. In one way, as with objects, and in this sense speculative virtues are not concerned with the things whereby a man is made happy, except perhaps insofar as the word 'whereby' means the efficient cause or the object of complete happiness, which is God, who is the highest speculable object. In another way a virtue is concerned with things as its acts. And in this way the intellectual virtues are concerned with things whereby a man is made happy, both because the acts of such virtues can be meritorious, as was said, and also because they are a kind of beginning of perfect happiness, which consists in contemplation of the true, as was said earlier.

Ad 3. It should be said that science is distinguished from virtue taken in the second sense, which pertains to the appetitive power.

Article 2: Are the only habits of speculative intellect wisdom, science and understanding?

It seems not.

1. Species ought not to be distinguished from their genus, but wisdom is a kind of knowledge, as is said in *Ethics* 6.7. Therefore, wisdom ought not to be distinguished from knowledge in enumerating the intellectual virtues.

2. Moreover, in distinguishing powers, habits and acts, which is done from objects, the distinction that is based on the formal nature of the objects takes precedence, as is clear from what was said above. Therefore different habits should not be distinguished according to their material object, but according to the formal notion of the object. But the principle

of demonstration is the reason for knowing conclusions. Therefore, the understanding of principles ought not to be said to be another habit or virtue from the science of conclusions.

3. Moreover, an intellectual virtue is in what is rational essentially, but reason, even speculative reason, by syllogizing reasons both demonstratively and dialectically. Therefore, just as science, which is caused by a demonstrative syllogism, is called a speculative intellectual virtue, so should opinion be.

ON THE CONTRARY:
The Philosopher in *Ethics* 6.3 gives only these three speculative intellectual virtues, namely wisdom, science and understanding.

RESPONSE:
It should be said that speculative intellectual virtue is that by which the speculative intellect is perfected in considering the true, for this is its work. But the true can be considered in two ways. In one way, as known of itself [*per se notum*]; in another way, as known through another. That which is known of itself is as a principle, and is immediately perceived by intellect and therefore the habit perfecting intellect in this consideration of the true is called understanding, which is the habit of principles.

The true which is known through something else is not grasped immediately by intellect but by the inquiry of reason and has the note of a term. But this can come about in two ways. In one way, such that it is the ultimate in some genus; in another way, such that it is ultimate with respect to the whole of human knowledge, and because those things which are known later by us are in their nature the most known, as is said in *Physics* 1.1, that which is ultimate with respect to the whole of human knowledge is that which is first and most knowable according to nature.

Wisdom is concerned with such things, since it considers the highest causes, as is said in *Metaphysics* 1.1. Hence it properly judges and orders all things because a perfect and universal judgement can only be had by a resolution to first causes. Science on the other hand perfects intellect with respect to that which is ultimate in this or that genus of knowable things. That is why there are different habits of science insofar as there are different kinds of knowable thing, whereas wisdom is one.

Ad 1. It should be said that wisdom is a kind of science, insofar as it has that which is common to all sciences, namely, that it demonstrates conclusions from principles, but because it has something proper to it beyond the other sciences – it judges all things, not only with respect to conclusions but also with respect to first principles – it is a more perfect virtue than science.

Ad 2. It should be said that habits and powers are not distinguished on the basis of object or material object when the notion of the object is referred to the power or habit under one act, as seeing colour and light pertains to the same seeing power, since light is the reason for seeing colour and is seen at the same time as it. But the principles of demonstration can be considered apart from conclusions, or they can be considered along with conclusions, as the principles from which conclusions are deduced. To consider principles in this second way pertains to science, which considers conclusions as well, but to consider principles in themselves pertains to understanding.

Hence if one thinks about it correctly, these three virtues are not distinguished from one another on an equal basis, but in a hierarchical way, as happens with potential wholes, one part of which is more perfect than another, as the rational soul is more perfect than the sensible, and the sensible than the vegetative. In this way science depends on understanding as on the prior, and both depend on wisdom as on the very first, which contains within itself both understanding and science, as judging the conclusions of the sciences and their principles.

Ad 3. It should be said, as was noted above, that the habit of virtue is determined to the good and in no way to evil. But the true is the good of intellect and the false is its evil. Hence only those habits are called intellectual virtues which always express the true and never the false. Opinion and conjecture can be of either the true or false, and therefore they are not intellectual virtues, as is said in *Ethics* 6.3.

Article 3: Is the intellectual habit art a virtue?

It seems not.

1. Augustine says in *On Free Will* 2.18 that no one uses virtue badly. But one can use art badly, for a given artisan can, thanks to knowledge of his craft, work badly. Therefore, art is not a virtue.

2. Moreover, there is no virtue of virtue. But there is a virtue of art, as is said in *Ethics* 6.5. Therefore, art is not a virtue.

3. Moreover, the liberal arts are more excellent than the mechanical arts. But just as the mechanical arts are practical, so the liberal arts are

speculative. Therefore if art were an intellectual virtue, it would have to be numbered among the speculative virtues.

ON THE CONTRARY:

The Philosopher says in *Ethics* 6.3 that art is a virtue, but he does not include it among the speculative virtues whose subject he says is the scientific part of the soul.

RESPONSE:

It should be said that art is nothing other than right reason with respect to works to be made, the good of which does not consist in the human appetite being in a certain condition, but in this that the work that comes to be is good in itself. An artisan is not praised for the will with which he works but for the quality of what he makes.

Therefore art, properly speaking, is an operative habit, yet it is like speculative habits in this that in their case too what counts is the things considered, not the relation of human appetite to them. As long as the geometer demonstrates truths, the state of his appetite does not matter, whether he is happy or angry, any more than this matters in the case of the artisan, as was said. So art is a virtue in the way speculative habits are, since neither art nor a speculative habit causes a good work with respect to use, which is proper to the virtue perfecting appetite, but only with respect to the capacity to act well.

Ad 1. It should be said that when someone who possesses art makes a bad artefact, this is not a work of art, indeed it is against art, just as when someone who knows the truth lies when what he says is not according to knowledge but against it. Hence just as knowledge always relates to good, as was said, so too does art, and in this way it is called a virtue. But it falls short of the full sense of virtue because it does not cause good use: something else is required for that, though there cannot be good use without art.

Ad 2. It should be said that in order for a man to use well the art he has a good will is needed, which is perfected by moral virtue. Therefore, the Philosopher says that there is a virtue of art, namely moral virtue, insofar as some moral virtue is needed for its good use. It is obvious that the artisan is inclined by justice, which causes rectitude of will, to make a faithful work.

Ad 3. It should be said that there is some work even in the objects of speculation, such as the construction of syllogisms or of congruous speech or numbering and measuring. Therefore, the speculative habits ordered to such works of reason are called arts by a kind of similitude, but liberal, to distinguish them from those arts which are ordered to their work by the exercise of body. The latter are in some way servile, insofar as the body is as servant to the soul and a man is free thanks to his soul. Sciences which are not ordered to any work are called simply sciences and not arts. The fact that liberal arts are more noble does not mean that they are more properly called arts.

Article 4: Is prudence a virtue distinct from art?

It seems that it is not.

1. Art is right reason with respect to certain works, but different kinds of work do not cause a thing to lose the note of art, for there are different arts concerned with very different works. Therefore, since prudence too is a kind of right reason about deeds, it seems that it too ought to be called an art.

2. Moreover, prudence is closer to art than to the speculative habits, for both are concerned with contingent things that can be otherwise, as is said in *Ethics* 6.6. But some speculative habits are called arts. So much the more should prudence be called an art.

3. Moreover, taking counsel well pertains to prudence, as is said in *Ethics* 6.5. But in some arts too there is deliberation, as is said in *Ethics* 3.3, for example, the military, navigation and medicine. Therefore, prudence is not distinct from art.

ON THE CONTRARY:

The Philosopher distinguishes prudence from art in *Ethics* 6.5.

RESPONSE:

It should be said that where a different notion of virtue is found, there different virtues must be distinguished. But it was said earlier that some habits have the note of virtue solely from the fact that they give the capacity to do well, whereas others give not only the capacity but also the use. Art gives the capacity only for a good work because it does not engage appetite, but prudence not only gives the capacity for doing well, but also use, for it looks to appetite, since it presupposes the rectitude of appetite.

The reason for the difference is that art is right reason with regard to things to be made, whereas prudence is right reason with respect to things to be done. Making and doing differ, we are told in *Metaphysics* 9.8, because making passes into external matter, as in building, sawing, and the like, whereas doing is an act which remains in the agent, as in seeing, willing, and the like.

Therefore, prudence is to human acts of this kind, which are the use of the powers and habits, as art is to external makings, because both are right reason with respect to the things to which they are related. The perfection and rectitude of reason in speculative matters depends on principles from which reason syllogizes, as we said that science depends on understanding, which is the habit of principles, and presupposes it. In human acts, ends function as principles do in speculative matters, as is said in *Ethics* 7.8. That is why a man must be well disposed with respect to ends, something due to right appetite, if he is to have prudence which is right reason concerning things to be done.

Therefore, moral virtue, which rectifies appetite, is required for prudence. The good of artefacts is not the good of the human will but of the artefacts, so art does not presuppose right appetite. That is why the artisan who errs willingly is praised more than one who does so unwillingly, whereas it is more contrary to prudence to sin willingly than unwillingly, for rectitude of appetite is part of the notion of prudence, though not of the notion of art. It is clear, then, that prudence is a virtue distinct from art.

Ad 1. It should be said that all the different kinds of artefacts are outside man and therefore the notion of virtue is not altered. But prudence is right reason about human acts themselves, and this alters the notion of virtue, as was said.

Ad 2. It should be said that prudence is more like art than speculative habits with respect to subject and matter, for both are in the opining part of the soul and deal with what can be otherwise, but art is more like speculative habits than like prudence with respect to the notion of virtue, as has been said.

Ad 3. It should be said that prudence deliberates well concerning things that pertain to the whole life of man and to the ultimate end of human life. In the arts there is deliberation about things that pertain to the proper ends of those arts. Hence some, insofar as they deliberate well in the affairs of war or of the sea, are called prudent generals or captains, but they are not prudent simply speaking – only those who deliberate well concerning the things important for life as a whole are that.

Article 5: Is the virtue of prudence necessary if a man is to live well?

It seems that it is not.

1. As art, which is right reason, is to makable things, so is prudence to things to be done with respect to human life, since prudence is right reason in their regard, as is said in *Ethics* 6.5. But art is necessary only in order that makable things come to be, but not afterwards. Therefore, neither is prudence necessary in order for a man to live well after he is virtuous, but perhaps only in order that he might become virtuous.

2. Moreover, prudence is that thanks to which we deliberate correctly, as is said in *Ethics* 6.5. But a man can deliberate well both for himself and for others. Therefore a man need not have prudence in order to live well, but it is sufficient that he follow the advice of the prudent.

3. Moreover, thanks to intellectual virtue one always says what is true, never what is false. But this does not seem to be the case with prudence, for it is not human that one should never err in deliberating about what is to be done, since the things humans do are contingent and can be otherwise. Hence in Wisdom 9.14 we read, 'For the thoughts of mortal men are fearful, and our counsels uncertain.' Therefore, it seems that prudence should not be called an intellectual virtue.

ON THE CONTRARY:
Wisdom 8.7 enumerates the other virtues necessary for human life, when of the divine wisdom it is said, 'And if a man love justice, her labours have great virtues. For she teacheth temperance and prudence and justice and fortitude, which are such things as men can have nothing more profitable in life.'

RESPONSE:
It should be said that prudence is a virtue most necessary for human life, for to live well consists of acting well, and this involves not only what one does but how one does it, acting according to right choice and not only from impulse or passion. Since choice is of means to the end, rectitude of choice requires two things, namely, a fitting end and that it be fittingly ordered to that end. A man is fittingly disposed to the fitting end by a virtue which perfects the appetitive part of the soul, whose object is the good and end. In order that he be fittingly ordered to the fitting end a man must be directly disposed by a habit of reason because deliberation and choice, which bear on means, are acts of reason. Therefore, it is

necessary that there be an intellectual virtue in reason by which reason is perfected in order that it be fittingly related to the things that are for the sake of the end. And this virtue is prudence. Hence prudence is a virtue necessary for living well.

Ad 1. It should be said that the good of art is not in the artisan but in the artefact since art is right reason about things to be made, and making, since it passes into exterior matter, is not the perfection of the maker but of the made, just as motion is the act of the movable. Art deals with the makable. But the good of prudence is in the agent himself whose perfection action is, for prudence is right reason about things to be done, as has been said.

Art requires not that the artisan act well, but that he produce a good work; it would rather be required that the artefacts act well – for example, that the knife cut well or the saw saw well – if acting rather than being acted upon were proper to them; but, after all, they do not have dominion over their acts. Therefore, art is not necessary in order for the artisan to live well but only for making a good artefact and preserving it. But prudence is necessary if a man is to live well, not only in order that he might become good.

Ad 2. It should be said that the action of a man who does something good not by following his own reason but moved by the advice of another is not in every way a perfect action of his with respect to reason directing and appetite moving. So if he does do something well it will not be well simply, which is to live well.

Ad 3. It should be said that the truth of practical intellect differs from that of speculative intellect, as is said in *Ethics* 6.2. The truth of speculative intellect consists of the intellect's conformity with reality. But since the intellect cannot be infallibly conformed with things in contingent matters, but only in necessary matters, no speculative habit of contingent things is an intellectual virtue, but only of necessary things. The truth of practical intellect consists in conformity with right appetite, a conformity which has no place in necessary matters which do not come about by the human will, but only in the contingent things that can come to be by us, whether internal doable things or external makable things. That is why the virtue of practical intellect is solely about contingent matters, art in the case of the makable, prudence in the case of the doable.

Article 6: Are eubulia, synesis *and* gnome *virtues linked to prudence?*

It seems not.

1. *Eubulia* is the habit thanks to which we deliberate well, as is said in *Ethics* 6.9. But to deliberate well pertains to prudence, as is said in the same book. Therefore *eubulia* is not a virtue linked to prudence, but prudence itself.

2. Moreover, it falls to the superior to judge the inferior. Therefore, that virtue seems supreme whose act is judgement. But *synesis* is good judging. Therefore *synesis* is not a virtue linked to prudence, but is superior to it.

3. Moreover, just as there are different things to be judged, so there are different things to be deliberated. But there is a single virtue with respect to all things that must be deliberated about, namely *eubulia*. Therefore, in order to judge well concerning what is to be done there is no need to have another virtue besides *synesis*, namely *gnome*.

4. Moreover, in his *Rhetoric* 2.53 Cicero sets down three parts of prudence, namely memory of the past, understanding of the present and looking forward to the future. And Macrobius, in the *Dream of Scipio*, mentions other parts of prudence, namely caution, docility, and other similar things. Therefore, these do not seem to be the only virtues linked to prudence.

ON THE CONTRARY:
There is the authority of the Philosopher who mentions these three virtues as linked to prudence.

RESPONSE:
It should be said that in all ordered powers that is primary which is ordered to the primary act. Three acts of reason are involved in human acts, of which the first is to deliberate, the second to judge and the third to command. The first two answer to the acts of speculative intellect, inquiry and judgement, for deliberation is a kind of inquiry. But the third act is proper to practical intellect as operative, for there is no cause for reason to command about things that a man cannot do. It is clear that in things men do, commanding is the chief act to which the others are ordered. Therefore, to the virtue that commands well, namely prudence, as to what is principal, certain secondary ones are joined, *eubulia*, which

counsels well, and *synesis* and *gnome*, which are parts of the judi
a distinction that will be clarified.

Ad 1. It should be said that prudence is deliberating well not as if to
deliberate well were its immediate act but because it perfects this act by
the mediation of a virtue subject to it, namely *eubulia*.

Ad 2. It should be said that judgement about things to be done is
ordered to something further, for it can happen that one judges well of
something to be done and yet does not bring it off correctly. The ultimate
completion is had when reason commands well concerning what is to be
done.

Ad 3. It should be said that a thing is judged by principles proper to
it. Inquiry is not yet through proper principles because once these are
had there is no need for inquiry, since the thing has already been found.
So only one virtue is ordered to deliberating well, but two virtues are
ordered to judging well, because the distinction lies in proper, not in
common principles. In speculative matters there is one dialectic to inquire
into everything, whereas demonstrative sciences, which judge, are diverse
in diverse matters. *Synesis* and *gnome* are distinguished according to the
different rules with which they judge, for *synesis* judges of things to done
by appeal to common law, but *gnome* appeals to natural reason in those
cases where the common law fails, as will be more fully explained later.[1]

Ad 4. It should be said that memory, understanding and foresight, as
well as caution, docility and the like, are not virtues different from
prudence, but relate to it in the manner of integral parts insofar as all are
required for the perfection of prudence. There are also subjective parts
or species of prudence, such as economic, ruling and the like, but the
foregoing three are as it were potential parts of prudence because they
are ordered as the secondary is ordered to the principal. And of this more
will be said below.[2]

1. q. 51, art. 4.
2. q. 48 ff.

26. *The Active and Contemplative Lives.*
Summa theologiae, 2–2, 179–81 (1271–2)

The mission of the Order of Preachers, as the name of the order suggests, is a practical one. St Dominic formed his band of friars to combat the Albigensian heresy by bringing to the people the authentic message of Christianity. It was Dominic's genius to realize that this practical task required a thorough intellectual and spiritual training. As if by instinct, he was drawn to the University of Paris and he wanted his friars to become proficient in theology so that the truth they popularized in sermons and in pastoral care would be solidly anchored in reflective thought.

One of the mottoes of the Dominicans is contemplata tradere – *to pass on to others truths arrived at by contemplation. In the following treatise, Thomas examines the contrast between the contemplative and practical lives and, like Aristotle, allows that a human being might lead a contemplative life not because all he did was think and meditate, but because that was the dominant note of his life.*

One of the misgivings often expressed about Aristotle's account of human happiness in Book 10 of the Nicomachean Ethics *is that the contemplation he speaks of there would seem to be impossibly recherché and to propose it as the nature of human happiness has a somewhat Pickwickian air about it. This is a hasty criticism, however frequently heard. One well versed in that culminating book of Aristotle's* Ethics *will be prepared for the discussion below.*

It is particularly interesting to compare this chapter with Chapter 9. Thomas was a master of theology, his whole adult life was spent in teaching. Was this activity one of the practical or of the contemplative life? He insists that it is practical. But, in keeping with the Dominican motto cited above, he also insists that teaching reposes on a contemplative foundation.

The treatise below is taken from the Summa theologiae *and is a typical theological inquiry, taking off from a philosophical base and bringing the results of natural inquiry under the light of faith. Aristotle's insight that contemplation fulfils maximally the human desire for happiness is complemented by the Christian hope that our ultimate happiness will*

consist in the beatifying vision of God, face to face. Here is contemplation
par excellence.

Summa theologiae, First Part of the Second Part, Questions 179–81

QUESTION 179
THE DISTINCTION BETWEEN THE ACTIVE AND CONTEMPLATIVE LIVES

We must now consider the active and contemplative lives and there are
four things to be taken up, of which the first is the division of life into
active and contemplative; second, on the contemplative life; third, on the
active life; fourth, a comparison of the active and the contemplative life.
The first involves two questions: (1) whether life is fittingly divided by
the active and contemplative, and (2) whether the division is sufficient.

Article 1: Is life fittingly divided into the contemplative and active?

It seems that it is not.

1. The soul is by its essence the principle of life, for the Philosopher
says in *On the Soul* 2 that for living things to exist is to live. But the
principle of action and of contemplation is the soul through its powers.
Therefore, it seems that life is not fittingly divided into the active and
contemplative.

2. Moreover, the prior is unfittingly divided by the differences of the
posterior, but active and contemplative, or speculative and practical, are
differences of intellect, as is clear in *On the Soul* 3. But to live is prior to
understanding, for living is in living things first because of the vegetable
soul, as is clear from the Philosopher in *On the Soul* 2. Therefore, life is
unfittingly divided into active and contemplative.

3. Moreover, the word life implies motion, as is evident from Dionysius
in *On the Divine Names* 6. But contemplation consists rather of rest,
according to Wisdom 8, 'Entering into my home, I will rest with her.'
Therefore, it seems that life is not fittingly divided into active and contemplative.

ON THE CONTRARY:
Gregory says on Ezekiel that there are two lives about which the almighty God teaches us through sacred eloquence, namely the active and contemplative.

RESPONSE:
It should be said that those things are properly called living that move themselves or act. That especially belongs to a thing in itself which is proper to it and to which it is especially inclined. Therefore, every living thing shows itself to be alive by the activity most proper to it, to which it is most inclined, as the life of plants is said to consist in this that they are nourished and generate, that of animals in this that they sense and move, that of men in this that they understand and act according to reason. Hence too among men the life of each man seems to be that in which he takes most delight, and thus a man takes special delight in being with friends, as is said in *Ethics* 9.12. Therefore, because some men tend chiefly to contemplation of truth, and others to exterior actions, the life of man is fittingly distinguished into active and contemplative.

Ad 1. It should be said that the proper form of a thing which makes it actually to be is the principle of its proper operation. Thus it is said that for living things to be is to live, because as living things have existence from their form, they act in such and such a manner.

Ad 2. It should be said that life taken universally is not distinguished into active and contemplative, but the life of man, which is specified from the fact that he has an intellect. Therefore, the division of intellect and of human life is the same.

Ad 3. It should be said that contemplation is indeed rest from exterior movement, none the less to contemplate is itself a motion of intellect, insofar as any activity can be called motion, as the Philosopher says in *On the Soul* 3.7, that to sense and to understand are kinds of motion, where motion means the act of the perfected; and this is the way Dionysius in *On the Divine Names* 4 mentions three motions of the contemplating soul, namely straight, circular and oblique.

Article 2: Is life sufficiently divided into the active and contemplative?

It seems that it is not.

1. In *Ethics* 1 the Philosopher says that there are three especially excellent lives, namely the life lived for pleasure, the civil life, which seems to be the active, and the contemplative. The division of life into the active and contemplative, therefore, is not a sufficient one.

2. Augustine, in the *City of God* 19, sets down three kinds of life: the life of leisure, which pertains to contemplation, the active, which pertains to the active live, and he adds a third which is a compound of the two. Therefore, it seems that life is insufficiently divided into the active and contemplative.

3. Moreover, the life of man is differentiated insofar as men devote themselves to different activities. But the activities pursued are many more than two. Therefore, it seems that life ought to be divided into more types than the active and contemplative.

ON THE CONTRARY:

The two wives of Jacob symbolize these two lives, Leah the active, Rachel the contemplative, and they are also symbolized by the two women who received the Lord into their home, the contemplative by Mary, the active by Martha, as Gregory says in the *Morals* 6. But this would not be a fitting symbolization if there were more than two lives. Therefore, life is sufficiently divided into the active and contemplative.

RESPONSE:

It should be said that this division is one of human life, as was pointed out, and this is read from intellect. But the intellect is distinguished into the active and contemplative, because the end of intellectual knowledge is either the very knowledge of the truth, which pertains to contemplative intellect, or it is some exterior action, which pertains to the practical or active life. Therefore, life seems sufficiently divided into the active and the contemplative.

Ad 1. It should be said that the life lived for pleasure makes bodily pleasure its end, but this is common to us and the brutes. Hence, as the Philosopher says in the same place, it is a bestial life. That is why it is not put into the present division when human life is distinguished into active and contemplative.

Ad 2. It should be said that the middle is made up of the extremes and therefore virtue is contained within them, as the lukewarm in the hot and cold, and the pale in the white and black. Similarly that which is composed of both is contained in the contemplative and active. However, as in any mixture, one of the components predominates, so in the middle type of life sometimes the contemplative dominates, sometimes the active.

Ad 3. It should be said that the aims of all human actions, if they are ordered to the necessity of the present life according to right reason, pertain to the active life, which by ordered action looks to the needs of the present life. But if they serve one's concupiscence, then they pertain to the life of pleasure, which is not contained within the active life. Human pursuits which are ordered to the consideration of truth pertain to the contemplative life.

QUESTION 180
ON THE CONTEMPLATIVE LIFE

Next the contemplative life must be considered and eight questions are asked in its regard: (1) is the contemplative life in the affections or only in the intellect? (2) whether the moral virtues pertain to the contemplative life; (3) whether the contemplative life consists of one act or several; (4) whether the consideration of every truth pertains to the contemplative life; (5) whether man's contemplative life can in this world rises to the vision of God; (6) concerning the movements of the contemplative life mentioned by Dionysius in *On the Divine Names* 4; (7) on the delights of contemplation; (8) on the duration of contemplation.

Article 1: Does the contemplative life involve affection as well as intellect?

The answer seems to be no.

1. The Philosopher says in *Metaphysics* 2 that truth is the end of contemplation, but truth pertains wholly to intellect. Therefore, it seems that the contemplative life consists totally in the intellect.

2. Moreover, Gregory says in the *Morals* on Job 6 that Rachel – her name means the principle beheld – signifies the contemplative life. But the beholding of the principle pertains properly to intellect. Therefore, the contemplative life properly pertains to intellect.

3. Gregory says in *On Ezekiel* 2.2 that refraining from exterior action pertains to the contemplative life. But the affective or appetitive power inclines to exterior actions. Therefore, it seems that the contemplative life in no way pertains to the appetitive power.

ON THE CONTRARY:
Gregory says in the same place that the contemplative life is to hold with the whole mind the love of God and neighbour, with the sole desire of adhering to the maker. But desire and love pertain to the affective or appetitive power, as was said above. Therefore, the contemplative has something in the affective or appetitive power too.

RESPONSE:
It should be said, as has been remarked, that the life of those who chiefly intend the contemplation of truth is called contemplative. But intention is an act of will, as has been shown, because intention is of the end, which is the object of the will. Therefore, the contemplative life, as to the essence of its activity, pertains to intellect, but with respect to that which moves such an operation to exercise, it pertains to the will, which moves all the other powers, even intellect, to their acts, as was said above.

The appetitive power moves to inspecting something either sensibly or intellectually, sometimes out of love of the thing seen, because, as is said in Matthew 6.21: 'For where thy treasure is, there also will thy heart be.' Sometimes out of love of the knowledge which follows on inspection. Because of this Gregory constitutes the contemplative life in the charity of God, insofar as someone out of love of God burns to see his beauty. And because one takes delight in attaining what he loves, the contemplative life terminates in delight, which is in the affection, from which love too is intended.

Ad 1. It should be said that because truth is the end of contemplation it has the note of the desirable and lovable and delighting. And thus it pertains to the appetitive power.

Ad 2. It should be said that love of him incites to the vision of the first principle, namely God. Hence Gregory says, in *On Ezekiel*, that one living the contemplative life, having conquered all care, burns to see the face of his creator.

Ad 3. It should be said that the appetitive power not only moves the bodily members to exercise exterior actions but also intellect to exercise the activity of contemplation, as has been said.

Article 2: Do the moral virtues pertain to the contemplative life?

It seems that they do.

1. Gregory says in *On Ezekiel* that the contemplative life is to hold the love of God and neighbour with the whole mind. But all the moral virtues, with respect to whose acts precepts of the law are given, are reduced to the love of God and neighbour, because love is the fulfilment of the law, as is said in Romans 13.10: 'Love therefore is the fulfilment of the law.' Therefore, the moral virtues seem to pertain to the contemplative life.

2. Moreover, the contemplative life is chiefly ordered to the contemplation of God, for Gregory says, in *On Ezekiel*, that, having conquered all cares, it burns to see the face of its creator. But no one can come to this without the cleanness that moral virtue causes, for as is said in Matthew 5.8, 'Blessed are the clean of heart, for they shall see God,' and in Hebrews 12.14, 'Strive for peace with all men, and for that holiness without which no man will see God.' Therefore, the moral virtues seem to pertain to the contemplative life.

3. Moreover, Gregory in *On Ezekiel* says that the contemplative life is comely in the soul, hence it is signified by Rachel, of whom it is said in Genesis 29.17: 'Rachel was well favoured and of a beautiful countenance.' But beauty of the soul comes from moral virtue, and chiefly temperance, as Ambrose says, in *On Offices* 1.4. Therefore, moral virtues seem to pertain to the contemplative life.

ON THE CONTRARY:
The moral virtues are ordered to exterior actions, but Gregory says in the *Morals* on Job 6 that the contemplative life puts exterior action to rest. Therefore, moral virtues do not pertain to the contemplative life.

RESPONSE:
It should be said that something can belong to the contemplative life in two ways, essentially, and dispositively. The moral virtues do not belong essentially to the contemplative life, because the end of the contemplative life is the consideration of truth. But to know, which pertains to the consideration of truth, carries little weight with the moral virtues, as the Philosopher says in *Ethics* 2.4. Hence, in *Ethics* 10.4 he says that the moral virtues belong to the active life, not the contemplative. However, moral virtues belong to the contemplative life dispositively. For the act of contemplation, in which the contemplative life essentially consists, is

impeded both by the vehemence of the passions which deflect the soul's attention from intelligible to sensible things, and by exterior disturbance. The moral virtues both impede the vehemence of the passions and make exterior disturbances subside. Therefore, the moral virtues belong dispositively to the contemplative life.

Ad 1. It should be said that, as has been remarked, the contemplative life has its mover in the affective part, and in this respect the love of God and neighbour is needed for the contemplative life. But moving causes do not enter into the essence of the thing, but dispose and bring it about. So it does not follow that moral virtues belong essentially to the contemplative life.

Ad 2. It should be said that purity or cleanliness is caused by the virtues which deal with the passions that impede the purity of reason. But peace is caused by justice, which is concerned with activities, according to Isaiah 32.17: 'Peace is the work of justice.' He who abstains from injuring others takes away occasions for litigation and disturbances. Thus the moral virtues dispose for the contemplative life, insofar as they cause peace and purity.

Ad 3. It should be said that beauty, as has been remarked, consists in a certain clarity and fitting proportion. Both of these are found radically in reason, to which pertains the clarifying light as well as to bring about a fitting proportion in the things it orders. Therefore, beauty is found essentially and *per se* in the contemplative life, which consists in an act of reason. Hence Wisdom 8.2, speaking of the contemplation of wisdom, says, 'And I became a lover of her beauty.' Beauty is found by way of participation in the moral virtues, insofar as they participate in the order of reason, especially temperance, which represses the desires which especially obscure the light of reason. Hence it is that the virtue of chastity especially makes a man apt for contemplation, insofar as venereal pleasures especially turn the mind to sensible things, as Augustine says in the *Soliloquies* 1.10.

Article 3: Are there different acts of the contemplative life?

It seems that there are.

1. Richard of St Victor distinguishes between contemplation, meditation and reflection. But all these seem to pertain to the contemplative life. Therefore, there seem to be different acts of the contemplative life.

2. Moreover, the Apostle says in 2 Corinthians 3.18: 'But we all, with faces unveiled, reflecting as in a mirror the glory of the Lord, are being transformed into his very image.' But this belongs to the contemplative life. Therefore, besides the three just mentioned, speculation too belongs to the contemplative life.

3. Moreover, Bernard says in *On Consideration* that the first and highest contemplation is the admiration of majesty. But admiration, according to Damascene, in *On Orthodox Faith* 2.15, is a species of fear. Therefore, it seems that several acts are required for the contemplative life.

4. Moreover, prayer, reading and meditation are said to pertain to the contemplative life. But listening too pertains to it, for in Luke 10.39 it is said of Mary, by whom the contemplative life is signified, 'who also seated herself at the Lord's feet, and listened to his word'. Therefore, it seems that several acts are required for the contemplative life.

ON THE CONTRARY:

Life here means the activity that a man principally intends. Therefore, if there are several activities of the contemplative life, it will not be one contemplative life, but several.

RESPONSE:

It should be said that we speak of the contemplative life now as it pertains to man, for this is the difference between man and angel; it is clear from Dionysius in *On the Divine Names* 7 that angels intuit the truth in simple apprehension, but man by a certain process attains insight into simple truth from many things. Therefore, the contemplative life has one act in which it is finally perfected, namely contemplation of truth, from which it has unity, but there are many acts by which it comes to this final act. Some of them pertain to the grasp of principles, from which one proceeds to the contemplation of the truth, others to deducing from the principles the truth whose knowledge is sought, and the ultimate contemplative act which is contemplation of the truth.

Ad 1. It should be said that reflection [*cogitatio*], according to Richard of St Victor, seems to pertain to the inspection of many things, from which it intends to gather one simple truth. Hence under reflection can be included both the perception of the senses, for knowing certain effects, and imagination, the discourse of reason with respect to certain signs or whatever leads to the knowledge of the truth intended. According to

Augustine, in *On the Trinity* 14, every actual operation of intellect can be called reflection. Meditation however seems to pertain to the process of reasoning from certain principles and attaining to the contemplation of some truth. And consideration pertains to the same, according to Bernard. Although according to Aristotle, in *On the Soul* 2, every operation of intellect can be called consideration. But contemplation pertains to the simple intuiting of truth. Hence the same Richard says that contemplation is the perspicacious and free intuition of the soul into things to be grasped; meditation is the insight of soul occupied in the inquiry into truth, and reflection is the soul's looking around that is prone to wandering.

Ad 2. It should be said that, as the Gloss of Augustine says in the same place, those are denominated speculating [*speculantes*] from mirror [*speculo*], not from tower [*specula*]. To see something in a mirror is to see the cause through its effect, in which its likeness shines. Hence, speculation seems to be reduced to meditation.

Ad 3. It should be said that admiration is a species of fear following on the knowledge of something exceeding our capacity. Admiration, then, is an act following on contemplation of the sublime truth. For it was said that contemplation terminates in the affections.

Ad 4. It should be said that man comes to knowledge of the truth in two ways, in one way, through what he learns from another, and thus, with respect to the things man accepts from God, prayer is necessary, according to Wisdom 7.7: 'I called upon God, and the spirit of wisdom came upon me.' With respect to what he accepts from man, listening is necessary, insofar as he learns from the voice of the speaker, and reading, insofar as he accepts what has been passed on in writing. In another way, it is necessary that he apply himself to his own inquiry. And for this meditation is required.

Article 4: Does the contemplative life consist only in the contemplation of God or of other truths as well?

It seems that the latter is true.

1. It is said in Psalm 138.14: 'I praise thee, because I am so wonderfully made, because thy works are wonderful.' But knowledge of the divine works comes about through a kind of contemplation of truth. Therefore, it seems that not only divine truth but also other kinds pertain to the contemplative life.

2. Moreover, Bernard, in *On Consideration*, says that the first contem-

plation is admiration of majesty; the second of God's judgements; the third, of his blessings, the fourth of his promises. But only the first of these four pertains to divine truth; the other three pertain to his effects. Therefore, the contemplative life does not consist in the consideration of divine truth alone, but also in the consideration of the truth concerning the divine effects.

3. Moreover, Richard of St Victor distinguishes six species of contemplation, the first of which is according to imagination alone, when we attend to bodily things; the second, in imagination according to reason, insofar as we consider the order and disposition of sensible things; the third is in reason according to imagination, namely when through the inspection of visible things we rise to the invisible; the fourth is in reason according to reason, when the soul turns to invisible things, which imagination does not know; the fifth is above reason, when we know through divine revelation what cannot be comprehended by human reason; the sixth is above and beyond reason, when by a divine illumination we know things which seem repugnant to human reason, as what is said of the mystery of the Trinity. But only the last seems to pertain to divine truth. Therefore, contemplation does not involve divine truth alone, but also that which is considered in creatures.

4. Moreover, in the contemplative life the contemplation of truth is sought insofar as it is the perfection of man. But every truth is a perfection of the human intellect. Therefore, the contemplative life consists in any contemplation of truth.

ON THE CONTRARY:
Gregory says in *Morals* on Job 6.37 that it is the principle who is God that is sought in contemplation.

RESPONSE:
It should be said that, as has already been remarked, something can belong to the contemplative life in two ways, principally and secondarily or dispositively. The contemplation of divine truth belongs principally to the contemplative life, because this kind of contemplation is the end of the whole of human life. Hence Augustine says in *On the Trinity* 1.8 that the contemplation of God is promised to us as the end of all actions, and the eternal perfection of the blessed. In the future life this will be perfect, when we will see him face to face, whence he makes us perfectly happy. Now, however, the contemplation of divine truth is had only imperfectly by us, namely through a glass darkly; hence through it a kind

of commencement of happiness comes to be in us, which starts here and will come to term in the future. Hence the Philosopher in *Ethics* 10.7 places man's ultimate happiness in the contemplation of the best intelligible object. But we are led by the divine effects to the contemplation of God, according to Romans 1.20: 'For since the creation of the world his invisible attributes are clearly seen – his everlasting power also and divinity – being understood through the things that are made.' Thus it is that the contemplation of divine effects belongs secondarily to the contemplative life, insofar as man is led from them to knowledge of God. Hence Augustine says in *On True Religion* 29 that a vain and perishing curiosity ought not to be exercised in the consideration of creatures, but it should be a step towards the immortal and everlasting. Therefore, it is clear from the foregoing that four things pertain to contemplation in an orderly fashion: first, the moral virtues; second, the other acts besides contemplation; third, contemplation of divine effects; fourth, the fulfilling contemplation of the divine truth.

Ad 1. It should be said that David sought knowledge of the works of God in order that by this he might be led to God. Hence he says elsewhere,[1] 'I muse on all thy works, I consider the deeds of thy hands. I stretch forth my hands to thee.'

Ad 2. It should be said that from a consideration of the divine judgements man is led to contemplation of the divine justice; from the consideration of the divine blessings and promises, man is led to knowledge of the divine mercy or goodness, as shown or to be shown through his effects.

Ad 3. It should be said that by those six the levels that rise through creatures to the contemplation of God are designated. For on the first level is found the perception of sensible things themselves; on the second, the progress from sensible to intelligible things; on the third, the assessment of sensibles through the intelligibles; on the fourth level is found the absolute consideration of the intelligibles to which one has come by way of sensible things; on the fifth level is placed the contemplation of intelligibles to which we cannot come through sensible things but which can be grasped by reason; on the sixth level is the consideration of the intelligibles that reason can neither discover nor grasp, namely those which pertain to the contemplation of divine truth, in which contemplation is finally perfected.

Ad 4. It should be said that the ultimate perfection of the human

1. Psalm 142.5–6.

intellect is divine truth; other truths perfect intellect as ordered to the divine truth.

Article 5: Can contemplation in this life attain the vision of God?

It seems that it can.

1. As Jacob said in Genesis 32.30, 'I have seen God face to face, and my soul has been saved.' But vision of the face is vision of the divine essence. Therefore, it seems that one can through contemplation in the present life come to see God in his essence.

2. Moreover, Gregory says in the *Morals* on Job 6 that contemplative men return within themselves because they cleave to spiritual things and do not draw to themselves the shadows of bodily things, or perhaps they drive off temptations with the hand of discretion, wishing to look on the boundless light, suppressing all images which would bind it, and because they seek what is above them they conquer themselves. But a man is only impeded with respect to the vision of the divine essence, which is boundless light, by the fact that he necessarily must tend towards it by way of bodily images. Therefore, it seems that contemplation in the present life can extend to seeing the boundless light in its essence.

3. Moreover, Gregory in the *Dialogues* 2.35 says that to the soul seeing the creator every creature is obscure. Therefore, the man of God, namely the blessed Benedict, who saw in the tower a fiery globe and angels going up to heaven, was without a doubt only able to see them in the light of God. But blessed Benedict was still living the present life. Therefore, in the present life contemplation can extend to seeing the vision of God.

ON THE CONTRARY:

Gregory says in commenting on Ezekiel that as long as he lives in this mortal flesh no one so progresses in the power of contemplation as to fix the eyes of the mind in the very ray of the boundless light.

RESPONSE:

It should be said that, as Augustine says in the *Literal Commentary on Genesis* 12.27, no one seeing God lives in that mortal life of the senses, and, unless he in some way dies to this life or wholly leaves the body or is alienated from the carnal senses, he does not come into that vision. This was gone into in depth earlier where we spoke of rapture,[1] and in

---

1. q. 175, arts. 4–5.

Part 1, where we discussed the vision of God.[1] It must be said that someone can exist in this life in two ways, in one way, actually, insofar as he actually uses the senses of the body, and contemplation in the present life can in no way attain to seeing the essence of God. In another way someone can exist potentially though not actually in this life, insofar as the soul is conjoined to its mortal body as its form, but such that it does not use the senses of the body or even imagination, such as happens in rapture. In this way contemplation can in this life attain to the vision of the divine essence. Hence the highest level of contemplation in the present life is that Paul had in rapture, insofar as he was midway between the present life and the future.

Ad 1. It should be replied therefore that, as Dionysius says in his *Letter to Caius the Monk*, if someone seeing God understands what he sees, he does not see him, but something belonging to him. And Gregory says in commenting on Ezekiel that almighty God is not now seen in his brightness, but the soul speculates on something below him, hence it proceeds straight ahead and afterwards comes to the vision of his glory. When Jacob says, 'I saw God face to face,' this should not be understood to mean that he saw the essence of God, but that he saw an imaginary form in which God spoke to him. Or, because we know someone by his face, he calls knowledge of God his face, as Gregory's gloss says on this text.

Ad 2. It should be said that human contemplation in the present state of life cannot exist without images, because it is connatural to man that he see intelligible species in images, as the Philosopher says in *On the Soul* 3.7. But intellectual knowledge does not remain in these images, but contemplates in them the purity of intelligible truth. And this not only in natural knowledge, but also in the things we know through revelation, for as Dionysius says in *On the Celestial Hierarchy* 1.2 the divine clarity manifests the hierarchies of angels to us in figured symbols by the power of which we are restored in the simple ray, that is, in the simple knowledge of intelligible truth. That is how what Gregory says should be understood, namely that those contemplating do not take along with them the shadows of bodily things; that is to say their contemplation does not remain in them, but rather in the consideration of intelligible truth.

Ad 3. It should be said that we are not given to understand by those words of Gregory that the blessed Benedict in that vision saw God in his essence, but he means to show that, because to one seeing the creator all creatures are obscure, as a consequence by the illustration of the divine light everything is seen more easily. Hence he adds that no matter how little of the light of the creator you might see, everything that is created comes to be shallow.

Article 6: Is contemplative activity fittingly divided into three motions?

It seems that it is not.

1. It seems that the activity of contemplation is unfittingly divided into three motions, the circular, straight and oblique by Dionysius in *On the Divine Names* 4. For contemplation pertains to rest according to Wisdom 8.16: 'When I go into my house, I shall repose myself with her.' But motion is the opposite of rest. Therefore, contemplative activities ought not to be designated as motions.

2. The action of the contemplative life pertains to intellect, which men share with the angels. But Dionysius describes these motions differently in the angels than in the soul. For he says that the circular motion of the angel is according to the illuminations of beauty and the good. But he defines the circular motion of the soul in several ways, the first of which is the retreat of the soul into itself from exterior things; second is a certain convolution of its virtues by which the soul is freed from error and exterior occupations; the third is union with what is above it. So too he describes the straight motion of each differently. For he says that the straight motion of the angel is insofar as it proceeds to provide for subjects, but he places the straight motion of the soul in two things: first, as it proceeds to the things around it; second, in that it is raised by exterior things to contemplation of simples. And he describes oblique motion differently in the two, for in the angels oblique motion is when, providing for those having less, they remain identical with respect to God. But he speaks of the oblique motion of the soul when the soul is illumined rationally and diffusely by divine thoughts. Therefore, it does not seem fitting that the activities of contemplation should be signified by these three motions.

3. Moreover, Richard of St Victor in *On Contemplation* sets forth many other differences between the motions, likening them to the birds of the air, some of which are now borne up to higher things and then descend to inferior, and are seen to do this over and over, while others dart to left and right repeatedly, and yet others back and forth frequently, and others wheel in large and small circles, and some remain suspended

in one place. So it seems that there are not just three motions of contemplation.

ON THE CONTRARY:
There is the authority of Dionysius.

RESPONSE:
It should be said that, as has been stated, the activity of intellect in which contemplation essentially consists is called motion insofar as motion is the act of the perfect, as the Philosopher says in *On the Soul* 3.7. For because we come to knowledge of intelligible things through sensibles, and sensible activities are not without motion, so it is that intelligible activities too are described as if they were kinds of motion and their differences are assigned according to likeness to different motions. But in bodily motions, the first and more perfect are local, as is proved in *Physics* 8.7, which is why intelligible activities are more powerfully described by likeness to them. But there are three differences between them: some are circular, as something is moved uniformly around a centre; another straight, as something proceeds from A to B; a third is oblique, as composed of the first two. So in intelligible activities that which has uniformity simply is attributed to circular motion, but the intelligible activity by which we proceed from one thing to another is attributed to straight motion, but the intelligible activity having some uniformity along with variation is attributed to oblique motion.

Ad 1. It should be said that exterior bodily motions are opposed to the repose of contemplation, which is understood to be free of exterior occupations. But the motions of intelligible activities pertain to the repose of contemplation.

Ad 2. It should be said that man shares intellect with the angels generically, but the intellectual power is much higher in the angel than in man. Therefore these motions must be described differently in souls and in angels, insofar as they relate differently to uniformity. For the intellect of the angel has uniform knowledge in two respects: first, because he does not acquire intelligible truth from the variety of composed things; second, because he does not understand intelligible truth discursively, but by a simple intuition. But the intellect of the soul receives intelligible truth from sensible things, and understands it by a kind of discourse. Therefore Dionysius assigns the circular motion to angels insofar as without beginning or end they uniformly and unceasingly intuit God, like circular motion which lacks beginning or end and turns uniformly around a centre. But in the soul, before such uniformity is attained, a twofold deformity must be removed. First, that which is from the diversity of exterior things, insofar as it leaves them behind. This is why he puts first in the circular motion of the soul its retreat into itself from things exterior to it. Second, another deformity must be removed, which is from the discourse of reason. The same thing comes about insofar as all the activities of soul are reduced to simple contemplation of intelligible truth. That is why he says that the uniform convolution of its intellectual virtues is necessary, so that, discourse ceasing, its insight is fixed on the contemplation of one simple truth. And in this activity of the soul there is no error, as is clear in that the intellect does not err in the understanding of first principles, because we know them by simple intuition. Then, these two being accomplished, a uniformity similar to the angel's is established, insofar as, setting aside everything else, it remains in the contemplation of God alone. That is what he means when he says that as made uniform, in unity – that is, conformity – with the united virtues, it is led to beauty and good. But the straight motion in angels can be understood insofar as in reflection he proceeds from one to another, but only according to the order of his providence, namely, insofar as the higher angel illumines the lower through intermediates. So it is said that angels are moved directly when they proceed to providing for subjects, passing right through, that is, insofar as they are disposed according to right order. But the straight motion is assigned to soul insofar as it proceeds from exterior sensible things to knowledge of intelligibles. Oblique motion in the angel, composed of straight and circular, is had when he provides for inferiors with respect to the contemplation of God. But oblique motion is posited in the soul, similarly composed of straight and circular, insofar as it uses the divine illuminations in ratiocination.

Ad 3. It should be said that the other kinds of motion are taken according to the differences of up and down, right and left, back and forth, and, according to different circuits, all are contained under straight and oblique motion. For it is the discourse of reason that is signified by all of them. Which, if it is from genus to species, or from whole to part, it will be, as he explains, according to up and down. But if it is from one opposite to the other, it will be according to right and left. But if from causes to effects, it will be before and after. If according to the accidents surrounding the thing, near and far, it will be circuitous. But the discourse of reason, when it is from sensible to intelligible things according to the order of natural reason, pertains to straight motion; but when it is according to divine illuminations, it pertains to oblique motion, as is clear from what has been said. The only immobility he mentions pertains to circular motion. Hence it is evident that Dionysius describes the motions of contemplation much more sufficiently and subtly.

Article 7: Is contemplation pleasurable?

It seems that it is not.

1. Delight pertains to the appetitive power, but contemplation consists principally in intellect. Therefore, it seems that delight does not pertain to contemplation.

2. Moreover, only contention and contest impede delight, but there is contention and contest in contemplation, for Gregory says in commenting on Ezekiel that the soul, when it strives to contemplate God, is put into a kind of contest: sometimes it rises up, because by understanding and sensing, it tastes something of the boundless light; sometimes it falls and fails to taste again. Therefore, the contemplative life has no delight.

3. Moreover, delight accompanies perfect operation, as is said in *Ethics* 10.2, but contemplation here below is imperfect, according to 1 Corinthians 13.12: 'We see now through a mirror in an obscure manner.' Therefore, it seems that the contemplative life has no pleasure.

4. Moreover, bodily wounds impede pleasure, but contemplation brings on bodily wounds, hence Genesis 32.30 tells us that Jacob, after he said I have seen God face to face, adds 'because he touched the sinew of his thigh and it shrank'. Therefore, there is no pleasure in the contemplative life.

ON THE CONTRARY:
Of contemplation it is said in Wisdom 8.16: 'For her conversation hath no bitterness, nor her company any tediousness, but joy and gladness.' And Gregory says in his commentary on Ezekiel that the sweetness of the contemplative life is most lovable.

RESPONSE:
It should be said that contemplation can be delightful in two ways. In one way, by reason of its activity, since everything finds delightful the activity belonging to it because of its proper nature or habit. But contemplation of truth belongs to a man because of his nature, because he is a rational animal. So it is that all men by nature desire to know,

and as a consequence take delight in knowledge of the truth. This becomes yet more delightful to one having the habits of wisdom and knowledge, which enable him to contemplate without difficulty. In another way, contemplation is made delightful by its object, insofar as one contemplates the beloved, just as it happens in corporeal vision which is delightful not only because seeing is delightful but also because one sees the beloved person.

Therefore, because the contemplative life chiefly consists in contemplation of God, it is not only delightful by reason of contemplation itself, but by reason of divine love. In both respects its delight exceeds all human delight, for spiritual delight is more powerful than carnal, as was said above,[1] when we discussed the passions, and the love with which God is loved out of charity exceeds all other love. Thus it is said in Psalm 33.9: 'Taste and see how good is the Lord.'

Ad 1. It should be said that the contemplative life, although it consists essentially in intellect, has its principle in the affective part, insofar as one is incited by charity to the contemplation of God. And because the end answers to the beginning, the term and end of the contemplative life is found in the affections, namely when one delights in the vision of the beloved, and this delight in the thing seen further excites love. Hence Gregory says in commenting on Ezekiel that when anyone sees the one he loves, further love for her is ignited. And this is the ultimate perfection of the contemplative life, that the divine truth is not only seen, but also loved.

Ad 2. It should be said that contention and contest that arise from the contrariety of external reality impede delight in the thing, for one does not delight in something against which he fights. But in the thing for which he fights, when a man has attained it, all else being equal, he delights all the more, as Augustine says in the Confessions 8.3; the greater the peril in battle the greater the joy in victory. But there is no contention and contest because of any contrariety in the truth we contemplate, but from the defect of our intellect and from our corruptible body which draws us to lower things, according to Wisdom 9.15: 'For the corruptible body is a load upon the soul; and the earthly habitation presseth down the mind that museth upon many things.' Hence it is that when man attains the contemplation of truth, he loves it more ardently, and hates more his own defect due to the weight of the corruptible body, and says

1. q. 31, art. 5.

with the Apostle, 'Unhappy man that I am, who will free me from the body of this death?' Hence as Gregory says in commenting on Ezekiel, once God is known through desire and intellect, all fleshly pleasures become arid.

Ad 3. It should be said that contemplation of God in this life is imperfect compared with contemplation in heaven, and so too the delight of contemplation on the way is imperfect compared to the delight of contemplation in the fatherland, of which Psalm 35.9 says, 'Thou givest them to drink of the torrent of thy delights.' But the contemplation of divine things had in this life, although imperfect, is more delightful than all other contemplation, no matter how perfect, because of the excellence of the thing contemplated. Hence the Philosopher says in *On the Parts of Animals* 1.5: 'The scanty conceptions to which we can attain of celestial things give us, from their excellence, more pleasure than all our knowledge of the world in which we live.' And this is what Gregory says on Ezekiel: the contemplative life is most lovable, which takes the soul above itself, opens celestial things, and lays open spiritual things to the eyes of the mind.

Ad 4. It should be said that Jacob was lamed in one foot after contemplation because it is necessary that, when the love of the world weakens, one grows well in the love of God, as Gregory says on Ezekiel, and therefore, after knowledge of the sweetness of God, one of our feet remains healthy, but the other is made lame. For a person lamed in one foot supports himself on the healthy one alone.

Article 8: Is the contemplative life lasting?

It seems that it is not.

1. The contemplative essentially consists in things pertaining to intellect. But all intellectual perfections of this life pass away, according to 1 Corinthians 13.8: 'Prophecies will disappear, and tongues will cease, and knowledge will be destroyed.' Therefore, the contemplative life will pass away.

2. Moreover, man tastes the sweetness of contemplation hastily and transitively. Hence Augustine says in *Confessions* 10.40: 'And sometimes you allow me to experience a feeling quite unlike my normal state, an inward sense of delight, which, if it were to reach perfection in me, would be something not encountered in this life, though what it is I cannot tell. But my heavy burden of distress drags me down again to earth.' And

Gregory, in the *Morals* 5, explaining Job 4.15, 'And when a spirit passed before me,' says that the mind is not long fixed on interior contemplation, because it is recalled to itself, the immensity of the light being driven back. Therefore the contemplative life is not lasting.

3. Moreover, that which is not connatural to man cannot be lasting. But the contemplative life is higher than man, as the Philosopher says in *Ethics* 10.7. Therefore, the contemplative life does not seem to be lasting.

ON THE CONTRARY:
The Lord says in Luke 10.24: 'Mary has chosen the better part and it shall not be taken from her,' because, as Gregory says on Ezekiel, the contemplative begins here, but is perfected in the heavenly fatherland.

RESPONSE:
It should be said that something can be called lasting in two ways, in one way, according to its nature, in another, with respect to us. It is obvious that the contemplative life is in itself lasting, and in two ways. First, because it is concerned with the incorruptible and immobile. Second, because it has no contrariety, for nothing is contrary to the pleasure had in thinking, as is said in *Topics* 2.13. But with respect to us as well the contemplative life is lasting, both because it belongs to us according to the action of the incorruptible part of the soul, namely, intellect, hence it can endure after this life, and because in the works of the contemplative we do not labour physically, hence in such works we can persist continuously, as the Philosopher says in *Ethics* 10.7.

Ad 1. It should be said that the mode of contemplating is not the same in heaven as here, but the contemplative life is said to remain by reason of charity, in which it has its beginning and its end. This is what Gregory says on Ezekiel, the contemplative life begins here and is perfected in the heavenly fatherland, because the fire of love, which begins to burn here, will burn even more with love of him when he who is loved is seen.

Ad 2. It should be said that no action can endure long at its peak. The peak of contemplation is to attain to the uniformity of divine contemplation, as Dionysius says, as was pointed out earlier. Hence although in this respect contemplation cannot long endure, with respect to the other acts of contemplation it can endure lastingly.

Ad 3. It should be said that the Philosopher says that the contemplative life is above man, because it belongs to us according to that which is divine in us, namely intellect, which in itself is incorruptible and impassible, therefore its action can be more lasting.

QUESTION 181
ON THE ACTIVE LIFE

Article 1: Do the acts of all the moral virtues pertain to the active life?

It seems that they do not.

1. The active life seems to consist only of things that relate to others, for Gregory says on Ezekiel that the practical life is giving bread to the hungry, and, at the end, having enumerated many things which pertain to the other, he adds, and which it is expedient to dispense to individuals. But we are not ordered to others by the acts of all the virtues but only by justice and its parts, as is clear from what has been said.[1] Therefore, not all of the moral virtues belong to the active life.

2. Moreover, Gregory says on Ezekiel that by Leah who was bleary-eyed but fecund the active life is symbolized: when she was occupied in work she saw little, but when sometimes by word, sometimes kindling her neighbours to imitate her example, she brought forth many children in good works. This seems to pertain rather to charity, through which we love the neighbour, than to moral virtues. Therefore, it seems that the acts of the moral virtues do not pertain to the active life.

3. Moreover, as was said above,[2] moral virtues dispose to the contemplative life. But disposition and perfection belong to the same thing. Therefore, it seems that the moral virtues do not belong to the active life.

ON THE CONTRARY:
Isadore says in *On the Highest Good*: 'In the active life all vices must first be rooted out by the exercise of good works, as in the contemplative by the already pure edge of the mind one arrives at contemplating God.' But all vices are rooted out by the acts of the moral virtues. Therefore, the acts of moral virtue pertain to the active life.

1. qq. 58 and 60.
2. q. 180, art. 2.

RESPONSE:
It should be said that, as has been remarked,[1] the active and contemplative lives are distinguished according to the different inclinations of men aiming at different ends, one of which is the consideration of truth, which is the end of the contemplative life, another is exterior activity, to which the active life is ordered. Manifestly in the moral virtues it is not the contemplation of truth that is principally sought; they are ordered to acting. Hence the Philosopher says in *Ethics* 2.4 that knowledge counts for little or nothing in the acquisition of virtue. Hence it is manifest that moral virtues essentially pertain to the active life. Hence the Philosopher in the *Ethics* 10.8 says moral virtues aim at active happiness.

Ad 1. It should be said that justice is the principal moral virtue, which orders a person to another, as the Philosopher proves in *Ethics* 5.1. Hence the active life is described by things which are ordered to another, not in these alone, but because it more chiefly consists in this.

Ad 2. It should be said that by the acts of all the moral virtues one can direct his neighbour to the good by example, which Gregory in the same place attributes to active life.

Ad 3. It should be said that just as a virtue which is ordered to the end of another virtue in a way changes into its species, so too when one uses the things which are of the active life only insofar as they dispose to contemplation, they are comprehended under the contemplative life. For those who intend the works of moral virtue as good in themselves, not as disposing to the contemplative life, the moral virtues pertain to the active life – although it can also be said that active life is a disposition for the contemplative.

Article 2: Does prudence pertain to the active life?

It seems that it does not.

1. Just as the contemplative life pertains to the cognitive power, the active life pertains to the appetitive power. But prudence does not pertain to the appetitive power, but rather to the cognitive. Therefore, prudence does not pertain to the active life.

2. Moreover, Gregory says on Ezekiel that the active life, when it is occupied in works, sees less, hence it is symbolized by Leah, who had

---

1. q. 179, art. 1.

bleary eyes. But prudence requires clear eyes, in order that a man might judge rightly about things to be done. Therefore, it seems that prudence does not pertain to the active life.

3. Moreover, prudence is midway between the moral and intellectual virtues. But just as moral virtues pertain to the active life, as has been said,[1] so the intellectual virtues pertain to the contemplative life. Therefore prudence seems to pertain neither to active life nor to the contemplative life, but to the middle kind of living that Augustine mentions in the *City of God* 20.2.

ON THE CONTRARY:

The Philosopher in *Ethics* 10.8 says that prudence pertains to active happiness, to which the moral virtues pertain.

RESPONSE:

It should be said that, as was stated earlier,[2] that which is ordered to something as to an end, especially in moral matters, is specified by that to which it is ordered, 'just as he who commits adultery in order to steal is more a thief than adulterer', according to the Philosopher in *Ethics* 5.2. Manifestly the knowledge of prudence is ordered to the activities of the moral virtues as to an end, for it is 'right reason with respect to what is to be done', as is said in *Ethics* 6.5. Hence the ends of the moral virtues are the 'principles of prudence', as the Philosopher says in the same book. Therefore, as has been said, in one who orders them to the repose of contemplation, the moral virtues belong to the contemplative life, so the knowledge of prudence, which is as such ordered to the activities of the moral virtues, directly pertains to the active life – understanding prudence properly, as the Philosopher speaks of it. But understanding it more commonly, as comprehending any kind of human cognition, then prudence in one of its senses would pertain to the contemplative life. As Cicero says in *On Offices* 1.5, 'He who can quickly and acutely see the truth and explain the reason for it, is rightly held to be most prudent and wise.'

Ad 1. It should be said that moral activities are specified by the end, as was argued earlier.[3] Therefore the knowledge that has knowledge of the truth as its end pertains to the contemplative life, but the knowledge of

1. art. 1.
2. art. 1, ad 3.
3. q. 18, arts. 4–6.

prudence, whose end is rather in the act of appetitive virtue, pertains to the active life.

Ad 2. It should be said that an exterior occupation makes a man see less in intelligible matters, which are separate from sensible things with which the activities of the practical life are concerned. However, the exterior occupation of the active life helps a man see more clearly in judging what ought to be done, which pertains to prudence, both because of experience and because of the mind's attention, since as Sallust says, your wit thrives where its attention lies.

Ad 3. It should be said that prudence is described as midway between the intellectual and moral virtues with respect to this, that it agrees in subject with the intellectual virtues, but in matter it agrees wholly with the moral virtues. That third kind of living is midway between the active and contemplative with respect to the things with which it is occupied, since sometimes it is occupied in the contemplation of truth, sometimes with exterior things.

Article 3: Does teaching belong to the active or contemplative life?

It seems to belong to the contemplative.

1. Gregory says on Ezekiel, 'Perfect men tell their brothers of the celestial goods they are able to contemplate, setting their souls on fire with the love of its inner brightness.' But this pertains to teaching. Therefore, to teach is an act of the contemplative life.

2. Moreover, act and habit seem to be reduced to the same genus. But teaching is an act of wisdom, for the Philosopher says at the outset of the *Metaphysics* 1.1 that being able to teach is a sign that one knows. Therefore, since wisdom or knowledge pertains to the contemplative life, it seems that teaching too belongs to the contemplative life.

3. Moreover, as contemplation is the act of the contemplative life, so too is prayer. But the prayer by which one prays for another nevertheless pertains to the contemplative life. Therefore, when someone brings a truth meditated on to the knowledge of another through teaching, this seems to pertain to the contemplative life.

ON THE CONTRARY:
Gregory says on Ezekiel, 'The active life is to give bread to the hungry, to teach by the word of wisdom the one who does not know.'

RESPONSE:

It should be said that the act of teaching has a twofold object: teaching comes about through speech; speaking is an audible sign of a concept of intellect. Therefore, one object of teaching is the matter or object of the interior concept. With respect to this object, sometimes teaching pertains to the active life, sometimes to the contemplative: to the active when a man conceives within himself some truth such that by means of it he can be directed in exterior action; to the contemplative when a man conceives within some intelligible truth in the consideration and love of which he delights. Hence Augustine says in *On the Words of the Lord*, 'They have chosen the better part,' namely the contemplative life, 'they leave off speech, they taste the sweetness of doctrine, they occupy themselves with saving knowledge,' where manifestly he means that doctrine pertains to the contemplative life.

Ad 1. It should be said that that authority expressly speaks of teaching with respect to its matter, as it turns on the consideration and love of truth.

Ad 2. It should be said that habit and act agree in object, so the argument manifestly proceeds in terms of the matter of the interior concept. To teach can pertain to wisdom or knowledge insofar as it can express the interior concept of the word, in order to lead another to understanding of the truth.

Ad 3. It should be said that he who prays for another, does nothing towards him for whom he prays, but only towards God, who is intelligible truth.

Article 4: Does the active life remain after this life?

It seems that it does.

1. The moral virtues pertain to the active life, as has been pointed out, but moral virtues remain after this life, as Augustine says in *On the Trinity* 14.9. Therefore, the active life remains after this life.

2. Moreover, to teach others pertains to the active life, as has been said. But in the future life, in which 'we will be like the angels' (Matthew 22.30), there can be teaching, as there seems to be in the angels, one of whom 'illumines, cleanses and perfects' the other, which refers to the taking on of knowledge, as is clear from Dionysius in *On the Celestial Hierarchy* 7. Therefore, it seems that the active life remains after this life.

3. Moreover, that which is of itself more durable seems rather to remain after this life. But the active life seems to be more durable in itself, for as Gregory says on Ezekiel, 'We can remain fixed in the active life, but in the contemplative we are not able in any way to remain with an attentive mind.' Therefore, the active life is more able to remain after this life than the contemplative.

ON THE CONTRARY:
Gregory says on Ezekiel: 'The active life will be taken away with the present age, but the contemplative begins here in order to be perfected in the heavenly fatherland.'

RESPONSE:
It should be said, as has been pointed out, that the active life has its end in exterior acts, which if they are referred to the repose of contemplation, pertain to the contemplative life. In the future life of the blessed the occupation with exterior acts will cease, and if there are exterior acts they will be referred to the end of contemplation. For as Augustine says at the end of the *City of God* 22.30, 'We will have leisure there and we will see, we will see and we will love, we will love and we will praise.' And in the same book he says that there God 'will be seen without end, will be loved without distaste, will be praised without let. His gift, this love, this act will be in all.'

Ad 1. It should be said that, as was pointed out above,[1] moral virtues will remain, not with respect to their acts which bear on what is for the sake of the end, but with respect to those bearing on the end. Such acts are what constitute the repose of contemplation, what Augustine signified by the word leisure, which ought to be understood not only with regard to exterior tumult but also from the interior disturbance of the passions.
   Ad 2. It should be said that the contemplative life, as has been pointed out, chiefly consists in the contemplation of God. In this regard, one angel does not teach another because, as is said in Matthew 18.10 of the lesser angels of a lower order, they always see the face of God. So too in the future life no man will teach another about God, but all 'will see even as they are seen', as is said in John 3.2. That is what is meant in Jeremiah 31.34: 'And they shall teach no more every man his neighbour, and every

1. q. 136, art. 1, ad 1.

man his brother, saying: "Know the Lord. For all shall know me from the least of them even to the greatest." '

But with respect to the things pertaining to the dispensations of the ministries of God, one angel can teach another, by purging, illumining and perfecting. In this regard, they have something of the active life so long as the world endures insofar as they attend to administration of the lower creatures. This is signified when Jacob saw the angels going up the ladder, which pertains to contemplation, and going down the ladder, which pertains to action. But as Gregory says in the *Morals* on Job 2.3: 'They will thus go out from the divine vision that they might be deprived of the joys of interior contemplation.' Therefore, the active and contemplative lives are not distinguished in them, as in us, who are impeded from contemplation by exterior works.

Similarity with the angels as to the administration of inferiors is not promised to us, because it does not belong to us, given the order of our nature, as it does belong to the angels, but [similarity] with respect to the vision of God.

Ad 3. It should be said that the durability of the active life in the present life exceeds that of the contemplative not because of what is proper to each considered as such, but because of our defect, because we are pulled down from the height of contemplation by the weight of the body. Hence Gregory in the same place adds that 'by its own infirmity the soul is put off by such immensity and falls back on itself'.

27. On the Eternity of the World
(1271)

Prominent among the 'errors of Aristotle' was the Philosopher's teaching that the world has always existed. In the following opusculum, Thomas defends the Aristotelian teaching from the charge that it makes no sense, denying that there is a contradiction in terms involved in saying that the world was created and that it has always existed.

Thomas, as a Christian believer, had no doubt that the claim that the world had always existed is false. It is false because it contradicts the true statement in Genesis that 'In the beginning God created heaven and earth.' But Thomas is not sure that the claim could be proven false by any philosophical argument.

In reading this short work, we can perhaps understand why many grew impatient with the Aristotelianism of Thomas Aquinas. He spends a good deal of time showing that there is nothing internally inconsistent in talking of a created eternal world. Not only that, he invokes the authority of Augustine and Anselm to the same effect, and denies that the other Christian thinkers invoked by his opponents provide much support for their view.

Who were these 'murmurers' who were unwilling to make their case in public disputation? It is no secret that it was the Franciscans who led the charge against the influence of Aristotle at Paris. They were provoked by the Latin Averroists, no doubt of that, young men who seemed blissfully unconcerned that a philosophical position might conflict with a truth of the faith. But clearly Thomas was anything but a Latin Averroist. He occupied a position between what Canon Van Steenberghen called the 'heterodox Aristotelians,' on the one hand, and the Franciscans, on the other. The latter are often referred to as the Augustinian school, but Thomas's opusculum makes clear that he will not concede that Augustine is on their side.

St Bonaventure, in his commentary on the Sentences, *developed a number of arguments meant to show that it simply makes no sense to say that a created world has always existed. One of the arguments is like that alluded to by Thomas, that there would be an actual infinity of souls if the world had always existed. Still, it seems doubtful that it was Bonaventure himself that Thomas had in mind. The ironic digs at his opponents would have been inappropriate if used against the esteemed Bonaventure. But the Franciscans who rose up against Aristotle saw Bonaventure as their leader and doubtless employed some of his arguments.*

In the short term, the anti-Aristotelians prevailed, at least locally. In 1270 and again in 1277, three years after the death of Thomas, there were Parisian condemnations of questionable propositions, some of them, in the case of the condemnation of 1277, teachings of Thomas Aquinas. It is frightening to think what the history of the west would have been like if the obscurantists had won. But it is equally frightening to imagine the triumph of the Latin Averroists. In the long run, it was the principled Aristotelianism of Thomas Aquinas that prevailed.

ON THE ETERNITY OF THE WORLD AGAINST MURMURERS

If we suppose, in agreement with the Catholic faith and contrary to what some philosophers mistakenly have thought, that the world has not existed eternally, and that its duration has a beginning, as Holy Scripture which cannot deceive attests, a doubt arises as to whether it could always have been.

In order to get to the truth of the matter, we should first set down wherein we agree and wherein we disagree with our opponents.

Were it to be supposed that the world could always have been independently of God, as if something apart from him could be eternal and unmade by him, this would be an abominable error, not only in the eyes of faith, but also among the philosophers who maintain and prove that whatever in any way exists must be caused by him who fully and most truly has existence. However, we must ask if it could be maintained that something always existed and yet is wholly caused by God.

Were this to be judged impossible, this would either be because God could not make something that always was or that it could not come to be even if God could make it. All would agree on the first point, namely, that given his infinite power, God can make something that always was. But it remains to be seen whether it is possible for something to come to be that always was.

The claim that it is not possible can be understood in two ways, that is, as being true for one of two reasons, either on account of the removal of passive potency or because it is conceptually incoherent.

In the first way, it could be said that before an angel was made, the angel was not able to come to be, because no passive potency preceded its existence, since it was not made from any underlying matter. Nevertheless, God was able to make the angel and was able to bring it about that the angel came to be, because he did it and it is. So understood, it must simply be granted that according to the faith something caused by God could not always be, if this is tantamount to holding that a passive potency always existed, for that is heretical. But it does not follow from this that God cannot bring it about that some being should always be.

In the second understanding, something is said not to have happened because it involves conceptual incoherence, on the order of an affirmation and its denial not being able to be simultaneously true, although there are some who claimed God could bring this about. Others say that he cannot because it is a nullity. It is, of course, clear that he could not effect *this*, because if he could he could not. Should someone say that God can do this, the view may not be heretical but it is in my opinion false, in the way that the claim that the past was not involves a contradiction. Thus Augustine, in *Against Faustus*, writes, 'Whoever says, "If God is omnipotent he can make the things that were such that they were not," does not see that he is in effect saying, "If he is omnipotent he can make what is true, as true, be false." ' None the less there have been those who with great piety said that God can make the past not to have been past and it was not judged heretical.

Is there then some conceptual incoherence, an incompatibility, between something's being caused by God and always having been? However this comes out, it is not heretical to say that something caused by God has always been. I none the less believe that if there is incoherence (self-contradiction) in the claim, it is false. If there is no incoherence, not only is it not false, it could not be otherwise, and to say so is erroneous. Since it pertains to God's omnipotence to exceed all understanding and power, one who said that something that could come about in creatures cannot be brought about by God would derogate from God's omnipotence. (Sins are not a counter-example, since as such they are nullities.)

The whole question then comes down to this: whether or not to be created by God in its complete substance is incompatible with not having a beginning of its duration. That they are not can be shown in this way. There could be only two reasons for their incompatibility, whether the one or the other, or the two together: either because the efficient cause must precede its effect in duration, or because non-existence must precede existence in duration, which is why it is said to be created from God from nothing [*ex nihilo*].

The first thing to show is that it is not necessary that the efficient cause, namely God, precede his effect in duration, should he so will.

The first, then. No cause which produces its effect immediately [*subito*] need precede its effect in existence. But God produces his effect immediately, not through motion. Therefore, it is not necessary that he precede his effect in duration.

The first premiss is inductively evident from all immediate changes, such as illumination and the like. None the less, it can be proved as follows.

In any instant in which a thing exists, the principle of its action can be posited, as is clear in all generable things since in that instant in which fire begins to be, heating begins. But in immediate activity, its beginning and end are the same, as is the case with all indivisibles. Therefore, in any instant in which an agent producing its effect immediately is given, the term of its action can also be posited. But the term of its action is simultaneous with the things having been made. Therefore, it is not incoherent to posit a cause producing its effect immediately and not preceding it in duration.

It would be incoherent to say this of causes which produce their effects through motion, because the beginning of motion must precede its end. Because we are accustomed to makings that involve motion, the claim that an efficient cause need not precede its effect in duration is not easily grasped. So it is that many unlearned men, taking into account only a few things, arrive at easy answers.

The fact that God is a voluntary cause presents no difficulty, because it is not necessary that the will precede its effect in duration, nor the voluntary agent, unless because he acts on deliberation, something we should not attribute to God.

Furthermore, the cause producing the whole substance of the thing is no more restricted than the cause producing the form in the production of the form, indeed much less so, because it does not produce by educing it from the potentiality of matter, in the way the one producing form does. But an agent which produces form alone can so act that its effect exists whenever it does, as is the case with the sun shining. Much more, then, can God, who produces the complete substance of the thing, bring it about that his effect exists whenever he exists.

Moreover, if there should be a cause whose effect does not immediately proceed from it in any instant in which the cause exists, this can only be because the cause lacks something of its perfection: a perfect cause and its effect exist simultaneously. But God is lacking in nothing. Therefore his effect can always exist when he exists and he need not precede it in duration.

Moreover, the will of one willing does not lose its power, particularly in God. But all those attempting to refute the arguments of Aristotle by which he proves that something always was from God because a thing always produces its like, say that this would follow if he were not a voluntary agent. But even given that he acts through will, it none the less follows that he can make something be caused by him that might always be.

It is clear, then, that it is not incoherent to say that an efficient cause need not precede its effect in duration; if it were conceptually incoherent, God could not of course bring it about.

It remains to be seen whether it is repugnant to reason that something made should always exist because as a thing made from nothing it is necessary that non-existence precede its duration.

That it is not repugnant is shown by the remark of Anselm in the *Monologion* 8, where he is discussing how the creature is said to be made from nothing. He writes, 'The third interpretation of what is meant by saying something is made from nothing is when we understand it to be made and yet there is nothing from which it was made. Something similar in meaning seems involved when a man grows sad without cause and it is said that nothing saddens him. On this understanding, remembering what was said above, apart from the highest essence, all the things that are from him are made from nothing, that is, not from something else. There is nothing absurd in that.' On this exposition what is made is not ordered to nothing as if, prior to its being, nothing existed and only afterwards something exists.

Furthermore, let it be supposed that the relation to nothing implied in the preposition is positive, in this sense that for the creature to be made from nothing means to be made after nothing, the preposition 'after' implying an order absolutely. But there is order and order, namely that of duration and that of nature. If then the proper and particular does not follow from the common and universal, it would not be necessary that from the fact that the creature is said to exist after nothing that *nothing* should have been prior in duration and afterwards there was something. It suffices that nothing is prior to being in nature. That in a thing which belongs to it of itself is prior to that which it owes to another. But existence is something the creature has only from another; considered as left to itself it is nothing. Thus in the creature nothing is naturally prior to existence.

It doesn't follow from the fact that there is no priority in duration that nothing and being are simultaneous, for it is not maintained that, if the creature always was, at some time it was nothing, but rather that its nature is such that it would be nothing if left to itself. For if we were to say that the air is always illumined by the sun, we must say that air has been made lucid by the sun. And because whatever comes to be comes to be from the non-contingent, that is comes to be from that which does not exist simultaneously with what is said to come to be, it must be said that if it was made lucid from the non-lucid, or shady, not in the sense that it ever was non-lucid or shaded, but rather because it would be if the sun deserted it. This is crystal-clear in the stars and planets, which are always illumined by the sun.

It is clear, then, that when something is said to have been made by God and to have always existed, there is no incoherence. If there were, it is marvellous that it was not seen by Augustine, since this would be a quick way to disprove the eternity of the world. But he fashioned, in the eleventh and twelfth books of the *City of God*, many arguments to disprove the eternity of the world. Why would he have omitted this one [that is, that it is incoherent to say that the world is eternal]?

Indeed, he seems to imply that there is no such incoherence, for speaking of the Platonists in 10.31, he writes, 'Their understanding of this does not seem to involve time but a principle of subordination. For they say, just as if a foot were eternally in the dust, its imprint would always be there, yet no one would doubt that it had been made by the foot, yet the one would not be prior to the other even though the one is caused by the other. So too, they say, the world and the gods created in it always were, since the one making them always exists, yet they are made.' He never says that this cannot be understood, but proceeds otherwise against the position.

So too, in 11.4, he says, 'One confessing that the world was made by God but wanting for there to be no beginning in time of its creation, such that in a manner scarcely intelligible it was always made, says something indeed (and wishes to defend God, as it were, from fortuitous rashness).' The reason why it is scarcely intelligible was touched on in our first argument.

It is cause for wonder, then, why the greatest philosophers seem unaware of the supposed incoherence. For Augustine says in 11.5, referring to those mentioned in the previous text, 'We now discourse with those who agree with us in saying that there are no bodies or natures of which God is not the creator,' and later adds, 'These philosophers surpass all others in nobility and authority.'

Anyone thinking seriously about it, then, must conclude that those who held that the world has always existed, but at the same time said that it was caused by God, are guilty of no conceptual incoherence. Those who detect this incoherence, therefore, must alone be men and wisdom must first have arisen with them!

Since some authorities seem to support them, however, we must show how weak that support is. St John Damascene, in *On Orthodox Faith* 1.8, says, 'It is not in the nature of things that what is brought from non-being to being should be coeternal with him who is without beginning and always is.'

And Hugh of St Victor, at the beginning of *On the Sacraments*, writes, 'The power of the ineffable omnipotence cannot have something beside itself and coeternal that it uses in making.'

But these and similar authorities can be understood by means of what Boethius says in the *Consolation of Philosophy* 5.6: 'They are incorrect who, when they hear that Plato held that this world neither had a beginning in time nor will have an end, understand him to mean that this made world becomes coeternal with its maker. For it is one thing to endure through an unending life, which is what Plato says of the world, and another to be unending life whole and presently complete, which is clearly proper to the divine mind.'

So it is clear that what some maintain does not follow, namely, that creatures would be equal to God in duration. So understood, nothing can be coeternal with God because only God is immutable. This is clear from Augustine, *City of God* 12.15: 'Time which runs on mutably cannot be coeternal with immutable eternity. Thus if the immortality of the angels does not traverse time nor have a past which no longer is nor a future which is not yet, their movements go through successive times and change from future to past. They cannot, then, be coeternal with the creator, of whom we cannot say that there is any movement which no longer is nor future that is not yet.' So too in the *Literal Commentary on Genesis* 8.23, 'The nature of the Trinity is wholly immutable and for this reason is eternal in such a way that nothing can be coeternal with it.' And much the same can be found in the *Confessions* 11.30.

They [the murmurers] also adopt arguments from Aristotle, among which the most difficult has to do with the infinity of souls, because if the world has always been it would be necessary that there are now souls infinite in number. But this argument is not relevant, because God could make the world without animals and souls and make man when he did, the rest of the world being eternal, and thus an infinity of souls would not arise. Besides, it has not been proven that God could not create an actual infinite.

There are other arguments, but I will not refute them now, either because they have been dealt with elsewhere or because they are so weak that of themselves they render the opposite position unlikely.

28. The Love of Wisdom. Exposition of Metaphysics, Preface and 1, 1-3 (1271)

This chapter presents Thomas's preface to his commentary on the Metaphysics *of Aristotle and then his close analysis of the opening panorama in which Aristotle eloquently conveys his conception of the theology that is the culmination of the philosopher's quest.*

Anyone acquainted with the philological discussions that flourished in the wake of Werner Jaeger's 1912 argument that the Metaphysics *of Aristotle is a pastiche of lecture notes dating from different times in the author's life and thus conveying conflicting views of what the nature of the science he is seeking is, will find Thomas's prologue a delightful surprise. For Jaeger, in the* Metaphysics *there is a Platonic layer, there are Aristotelian layers, but what there is not is literary unity.*

This suggestion is all the more surprising since Neoplatonic, medieval and Renaissance commentators had all assumed that the Metaphysics *was a unified book and produced readings of it to bear out this assumption. On Jaeger's hypothesis, they were all slightly mad, finding what is in no wise in the text.*

Of course it was Jaeger and his eager rivals and followers who exhibited that peculiar dementia that seems somehow endemic to philology. Jaeger held that there were two competing and incompatible notions of First Philosophy in the Metaphysics. *The one has God as its subject matter and is a theology. The other has everything that is as its subject matter, and is an ontology. Aristotle's inability to reconcile these views makes his effort a tragic failure.*

Thomas's prologue can almost be read as anticipating the Jaegerian problem and providing its solution. The prologue is by way of being a promissory note which is redeemed in detail in the commentary to follow.

The opening chapters of Book 1 of the Metaphysics *convey an Aristotelian vision of philosophy that Thomas embraced enthusiastically. From the seemingly arguable generalization that all men by nature desire to know, Aristotle takes us on a tour of the external and internal senses, of the difference between experience and art, the distinction between the practical and theoretical, and pursues the spoor of wonder to the point where the only thing that can assuage the human thirst for knowledge is God himself.*

That so noble a vision came from a pagan intellect stirred Thomas's wonder and admiration. Philosophical theology may not be the whole story of man's desire for wisdom, but it is an essential component of it.

COMMENTARY ON THE *METAPHYSICS*, PREFACE AND LESSONS 1–3

Preface

As the Philosopher teaches in the *Politics*, when several things are ordered to one, it is necessary that one is regulative or ruling and the others regulated or directed. This is clear from the union of soul and body, for the soul naturally commands and the body obeys. Similarly, between the powers of the soul, for the irascible and concupiscible are in the natural order ruled by reason. But all sciences and arts are ordered to one, namely to man's perfection, which is his happiness. Hence it is necessary that one of these be ruler of the others, and it will rightly claim the title of wisdom. For it belongs to the wise man to order.

What this science might be and what might be its concerns can be considered if one thinks carefully about how one is fit to rule. For, as the Philosopher also says in the work mentioned, men strong in intellect are naturally the rulers and lords of others, but men robust in body but of less intellect are naturally servants. So that science which is most intellectual ought to be naturally regulative of the others, and it is such because it considers the most intelligible things.

There are three ways in which things can be called most intelligible.

First, on the basis of the order of understanding. For the things from which the intellect takes certainty seem to be most intelligible. Hence, since the certitude of science is acquired by intellect through causes, it seems that knowledge of causes is especially intellectual. Hence the science which considers the first causes seems especially to be the ruler of the others.

Second, by comparison of intellect to sense. For, since sensation is knowledge of particulars, the intellect seems to differ from the senses in this that it comprehends universals. Hence that science is especially intellectual which is concerned with the most universal principles, such as being, and the things which follow on being, like one and many, potency and act, and the like. Such things ought not to be left wholly undetermined, since without them complete knowledge of what is proper to a genus or species cannot be had. Nor should they be treated in any particular science, because knowledge of each kind of being needs them, and by parity of reasoning they would have to be considered in all the particular sciences. It follows that they should be treated in a common science, which, since it is most intellectual, is regulative of the others.

Third, from the very knowledge of the intellect. Since anything has the intellective power to the degree that it is immune to matter, those things must be most intelligible which are most separate from matter. The intelligible and the understood should be proportional to one another and of the same genus, since intellect and the actually intelligible are one. Those things are most separate from matter which not only abstract from signate matter, like natural forms taken universally, of which natural science treats, but wholly from sensible matter. And not only separate by reason, like mathematicals, but also as they exist, such as God and the Intelligences. Hence the science which considers these things, seems especially to be intellectual, and lord and ruler of the others.

This threefold consideration ought not to be assigned to different sciences, but to one. For the separate substances mentioned are the first and universal causes of being. It falls to the same science to consider the proper causes of a genus and the genus, as the natural philosopher considers the principles of natural body. So it falls to the same science to consider separate substances and common being, which is the genus of which the aforesaid substances are the common and universal causes.

From this it appears that although this science considers the three things mentioned, it does not consider each of them as its subject, but only common being. The subject of a science is that whose causes and properties we seek, not the causes themselves of the genus sought. For knowledge of the causes of any genus is the end towards which the consideration of the science moves. Although the subject of this science is common being, the whole is said to be of things which are separate from matter both as thought of and as they exist. Not only things that never exist in matter, like God and intellectual substances, are said to be separate both in thought and as they exist, but also things which *can be* without matter, like common being: this would not happen if they depended on matter in order to exist.

From these three, on which the perfection of this science depends, come three names. For it is called *divine science* or *theology*, insofar as it considers the substances mentioned. It is called *metaphysics*, insofar as it considers being and the things which follow on it, for these are found to be after the physical in the order of resolution, as the more common after the less common. It is called *First Philosophy*, insofar as it considers the first causes of things. Thus it is evident what the subject of this science is, and how it relates to the other sciences, and the names by which it is called.

Lesson 1

All men by nature desire to know. An indication of this is the delight we take in our senses; for even apart from their usefulness, they are loved for themselves; and above all others the sense of sight. For not only with a view to action, but even when we are not going to do anything, we prefer seeing (one might say) to everything else. The reason is that this, most of all the senses, makes us know and brings to light many differences between things.

By nature animals are born with the faculty of sensation, and from sensation memory is produced in some of them, though not in others. And therefore the former are more intelligent and apt at learning than those which cannot remember; those which are incapable of hearing sounds are intelligent though they cannot be taught, for example the bee, and any other race of animals that may be like it; and those which besides memory have this sense of hearing can be taught.

The animals other than man live by appearances and memories, and have but little of connected experience; but the human race lives also by art and reasonings. Now from memory experience is produced in men; for the several memories of the same thing produce finally the capacity for a single experience. And experience seems pretty much like science and art, but really science and art come to men *through* experience; for 'experience made art,' as Polus says, 'but inexperience luck'. Now art arises when from many notions gained by experience one universal judgement about a class of objects is produced. For to have a judgement that when Callias was ill of this disease this did him good, and similarly in the case of Socrates and in many individual cases, is a matter of experience; but to judge that it has done good to all persons of a certain constitution, marked off in one class, when they were ill of this disease, for example to phlegmatic or bilious people when burning with fever – this is a matter of art.

With a view to action experience seems in no respect inferior to art, and men of experience succeed even better than those who have theory without experience. (The reason is that experience is knowledge of individuals, art of universals, and actions and productions are all concerned with the individual; for the physician does not cure *man*, except in an incidental way, but Callias or Socrates or some other called by some such individual name, who happens to be a man. If, then, a man has the theory without the experience, and recognizes the universal but does not know the individual included in this, he will often fail to cure; for it is the individual that is to be cured.) But yet we think that *knowledge* and *understanding* belong to art rather than to experience, and we suppose artists to be wiser than men of experience (which implies that Wisdom depends in all cases rather on knowledge); and this because the former know the cause, but the latter do not. For men of experience know that the thing is so, but do not know why, while the others know the 'why' and the cause. Hence we think also that the masterworkers of each craft are more honourable and know in a truer sense and are wiser than the manual workers, because they know the causes of the things that are done (we think the manual workers are like certain lifeless things which act indeed, but act without knowing what they do, as fire burns – but while the lifeless things perform each of their functions by a natural tendency, the labourers perform them through habit); thus we view them as being wiser not in virtue of being able to act, but of having the theory for themselves and knowing the causes. And in general it is a sign of the man who knows and of the man who does not know, that the former can teach, and therefore we think art more truly knowledge than experience is; for artists can teach, and men of mere experience cannot.

Again, we do not regard any of the senses as Wisdom; yet surely these give the most authoritative knowledge of particulars. But they do not tell us the 'why' of anything – for example, why fire is hot; they only say *that* it is hot.

At first he who invented any art whatever that went beyond the common perceptions of man was naturally admired by men, not only because there was something useful in the inventions, but because he was thought wise and superior to the rest. But as more arts were invented, and some were directed to the necessities of life, others to recreation, the inventors of the latter were naturally always regarded as wiser than the inventors of the former, because their branches of knowledge did not aim at utility. Hence when all such inventions were already established, the sciences which do not aim at giving pleasure or at the necessities of life were discovered, and first in the palaces where men first began to have leisure. This is why the mathematical arts were founded in Egypt; for there the priestly caste was allowed to be at leisure.

We have said in the *Ethics* what the difference is between art and science and the other kindred faculties; but the point of our present discussion is this, that all men suppose what is called Wisdom to deal with the first causes and the principles of things; so that, as has been said before, the man of experience is thought to be wiser than the possessors of any sense perception whatever, the artists wiser than men of experience, the masterworker than the mechanic, and the theoretical kinds of knowledge to be more of the nature of Wisdom than the productive. Clearly, then, Wisdom is knowledge about certain principles and causes.   Aristotle, *Metaphysics* 1.1

1. Aristotle provides a preface to this science in which he treats two things. First, he shows what this science is concerned with. Second, what kind of science it is.[1] He subdivides the first into two: first, he shows that this science, which is called wisdom, considers causes; second, what kind of causes it considers.[2] With respect to the first point, he sets down some things from which he will argue the point; then he formulates an argument. By way of preliminary, he shows the dignity of science in general, the order of knowledge, beginning with the animals. He shows the dignity of science from this that it is naturally desired by everybody as an end. So he first states his thesis (that all men naturally desire to know) and then sets about proving it: 'A sign of this . . .'

2. There is a threefold reason for this. First, everything naturally desires its own perfection. Hence matter is said to desire form, as the imperfect desires its perfection. Therefore, intellect, by which a man is what he is, considered in itself is potentially all things, and actually becomes them through knowledge, since it is none of them prior to understanding, as is said in *On the Soul* 3: thus everyone naturally desires knowledge as matter desires form.

3. Second, everything has a natural inclination to its proper activity: as heat to heating and the heavy to moving downward. But the proper activity of man, as man, is to understand: it is in this that he differs from all other things. Hence man's desire is naturally inclined to understanding, and consequently to knowing.

4. Third, everything desires to be united with its principle, for in this the perfection of anything consists. That is why circular motion is most perfect, as is proved in *Physics* 8, because it unites the end and the beginning. Only through intellect is man united with separated substances, which are the principles of the human intellect and to which the human intellect compares as imperfect to perfect: man's ultimate happiness consists in this. Therefore a man naturally desires knowledge. It does not count against this that some men do not devote themselves to the pursuit

1. Lesson 3.
2. Lesson 2.

of knowledge, since often those who desire an end are prevented from pursuing it, either because of the difficulty of attaining it, or because of other occupations. Thus although all men desire knowledge, they are deterred either by pleasures or by the necessities of the present life, or out of laziness they avoid the labour of learning. Aristotle asserted this in order that he might show that seeking knowledge, and not for the sake of the useful, as this science does, is not vain, since a natural desire cannot be vain.

the college life

5. Then he manifests through a sign what he has proposed: since the senses serve us in two ways, namely for knowledge of things, and for their usefulness for life, they are loved by us for their own sake insofar as they are cognitive, but also because they are useful for living. This is clear from the fact that that sense is especially loved by everyone which is especially cognitive, that is, sight, which we love not only in order to do something, but also when we have nothing to do. The reason is that the sense of sight of all the senses most makes us know and shows us the many differences among things.

6. From this it is manifest that sight is pre-eminent among the senses with respect to knowing, and in two ways. One, because it knows more perfectly, and this is true of sight, because it is more spiritual than the other senses. A knowing power is more perfect in knowing to the degree that it is immaterial. That sight is more immaterial is clear if we consider how it is changed by its object. The other sensibles change the organ and medium of sense in a material way, as the object of touch by warming and cooling, the object of taste by affecting the organ of taste by way of saliva, the object of hearing by bodily movement, and the object of smell by a smoky evaporation. Only the object of sight changes its organ and medium spiritually, for neither the pupil nor the air is coloured, but they receive the species of colour according to a spiritual existence. Therefore, because actual sensing consists in the actual change of sense by the object, it is manifest that this sense has a more spiritual activity, because it is changed more immaterially and spiritually. Therefore sight judges sensible objects much more certainly and perfectly than the other senses.

7. The second reason for its pre-eminence is that it shows us many things, which is the case because of its object. Touch, taste, smell and hearing are of those accidents which distinguish lower from higher bodies, but sight is of those accidents which the lower bodies share with the higher. For something is actually visible by light, in which lower and

higher bodies share, as is said in *On the Soul* 2. Therefore, the heavenly bodies are sensible only to sight.

8. The other reason is that sight shows many differences among things. We seem to know sensible bodies chiefly through sight and touch, and more so by sight. A reason for this can be found in the fact that the other three senses are cognitive of things which in a certain way flow from sensible bodies and do not exist in them: as sound flows from the sensible body and does not remain in it, so too the evaporation with which and from which odour is diffused. But sight and touch perceive accidents immanent in things, like colour and heat and cold. Hence the judgement of touch and sight extend to the things themselves, but the judgement of hearing and smell to what proceeds from things, not the things themselves. Hence shape and size and the like, which are dispositions of the sensible thing, are perceived by sight and touch rather than the other senses. And much more by sight than touch, both because sight has a greater efficacy in knowing, as has been said, and because quantity and what follows on it, which seem to be common sensibles, are closer to the object of sight than to that of touch. This is clear from the fact that the object of sight includes every body having quantity of any kind, which is not true of the object of touch.

9. Next he takes up the order of knowledge, first in brutes, then in men. With respect to brutes, he first touches on that which all animals have in common, second on that which distinguishes them. All animals have this in common that they naturally have senses, for it is this that makes an animal an animal, and that is the nature of animal because the form proper to anything is its nature. But although all animals naturally have senses, not all animals have all of them, but only perfect animals. They all have the sense of touch, for it is in a way the foundation of all the other senses; but not all have the sense of sight, because the sense of sight is more perfect than the others with respect to knowing, but touch is the most necessary as coming first in the order of generation. Things that are more perfect are generated later with respect to this individual, which moves from being imperfect to perfection.

10. Next he points out the diversity of knowledge in the brutes, and he touches on three levels of knowledge in such animals. For there are some which, although they have sense, do not have memory, which comes to be from sensing. For memory follows the image which is 'the motion made by the actualized sense', as is said in *On the Soul* 2. But in some animals, the phantasm does not come to be from sense, and thus there

can be no memory in them: such animals are imperfect, and are immobile with respect to place, like oysters. But animals in which sense knowledge provides for the necessities of life and its own proper activity have memory, and move to another place by progressive motion; unless they retained in memory the intention which led them to move, the motion could not continue and the end be achieved. The grasp of the present sensible is sufficient for the activities of immobile animals, since they do not move to a place but have an indeterminate motion based only on a confused imagination, as is said in *On the Soul* 3.

11. Because some animals do, and others do not, have memory, it follows that some are prudent and others are not. For since prudence provides for the future on the basis of memory of the past (hence Cicero, in *Rhetoric* 2, gives as its parts memory, understanding and foresight), animals which lack memory cannot have prudence. The animals that do have memory can have something of prudence. Of course 'prudence' does not mean the same thing in brute animals and in men. In men, prudence is that according to which they rationally deliberate about what they ought to do; hence in *Ethics* 6 prudence is called right reason with respect to things to be done. In animals prudence is called the judgement about what is to be done, not from rational deliberation but by a kind of natural instinct. In the animals prudence is a natural estimate of things fitting to pursue and thing harmful to be fled, as the lamb follows its mother and flees the wolf.

12. Among those that have memory, some have hearing and some do not. Those which do not, like the bees and any other such animals, although they can have prudence, are not teachable, such that they can accustom themselves to do or avoid something by the instruction of another: for such instruction takes place chiefly through hearing. Hence it is said in *On Sense and the Sensed Object* that hearing is the sense of discipline. What he says about bees not having hearing does not mean that they cannot be frightened by sounds. For a loud sound can kill an animal and split wood, as is clear with thunder, but this is not as sound but rather because of the vehement motion of air carrying the sound. So animals which lack hearing, although they cannot judge of sounds, can be frightened by the motions of air. Those animals which have both memory and hearing are teachable and can be prudent.

13. Clearly, then, there are three levels of knowledge in the animals. The first is of those which have neither hearing nor memory, and thus are neither teachable nor prudent. The second is of those which have memory but not hearing, hence they are prudent but not teachable. The

third is of those which have both, and are prudent and teachable. There cannot be a fourth level, namely, an animal which has hearing and not memory, for the senses, which grasp their object through an exterior medium, among them hearing, are only in animals which move with progressive movement, who cannot lack memory, as was said.

14. Then he shows the levels of human knowledge, and he does two things. First, he shows how human knowledge surpasses knowledge as discussed thus far; second, he shows how human knowledge is distributed through different levels. On the first point, he says that the life of animals is ruled by imagination and memory: by imagination in the imperfect animals; by memory in perfect animals. Even though the latter have imagination, a thing is ruled by that which is principal in it. To live here is not understood as the existence proper to the living, as in *On the Soul* 2, where it is said that for living things to exist is to live. For an animal to live (in the sense of exist) precedes both memory and imagination. To live here means the action of life, as we are wont to call the interchange among men their life. By determining the knowledge of animals by comparison with a rule of life, we are given to understand that knowledge is in these animals not for the sake of knowledge but for the needs of action.

15. In men, as will be said below, experience is close to memory, in which animals share only minimally. For experience comes from putting together many singulars retained in memory. But this kind of putting together is proper to man, and pertains to the cogitative power, which is called particular reason: it is a bringing together of individual intentions in the way that universal reason does universal intentions. Because from many sensations and from memory animals are accustomed to pursue or avoid something, they have something, though little, of experience. Above experience, men have universal reason, by which they live as by that which is principal in them.

16. As experience is to particular reason, and custom to memory in animals, so is art to universal reason. Just as the perfect rule of life of animals is through memory conjoined with an accustoming that comes from being taught, or in some other way, so the perfect rule for man is through reason perfected by art. Some are ruled by reason without art, but this is an imperfect rule.

17. Next he shows the different levels of human knowledge, and in this regard does two things: first he compares experience and art, second he compares speculative and active arts. He subdivides the first into two: first, he shows how art and experience come about, then he shows the

pre-eminence of the one over the other. As to the way experience comes about, he says it is caused in men by memory, and the way of causing is this, that from many memories of the same thing a man acquires experience of it which enables him to act easily and rightly. Because experience confers the ability to act well and easily, it seems similar to art and science. The similarity lies in this, that both have one 'take' on a thing from many instances. They are dissimilar in that the universal is acquired in art, whereas experience is confined to singulars, as will be discussed.

18. He discusses how art comes about, and says that in men science and art come from experience. And he cites Polus who says that experience causes art and inexperience chance. For when someone inexperienced acts well, it is luck. The way in which art comes to be from experience is like the way experience comes from memory. For from many memories comes one knowledge of the experienced, and from many experiences comes the universal grasp of all similars. But art is more than experience, because experience bears only on singulars, but art on universals.

19. He shows this by way of examples. For when a man comes to know that a certain medicine was effective when Socrates and Plato, and many others, were ailing in a certain way, this is a matter of experience. But when someone grasps that it is effective with those who have a determinate illness, with a certain disposition, and helps both the phlegmatic and choleric who have fevers, this is a matter of art.

20. Next he asks whether art or experience is pre-eminent, and first he compares them on the level of action, second on the level of knowledge. With respect to action, experience seems not to differ from art. For when it comes to action, the difference based on the fact that art is of universals and experience of singulars disappears, because both art and experience deal with singulars. Thus the foregoing difference is on the level of knowledge alone. But although art and experience do not differ in their mode of acting, because both deal with singulars, they differ in the efficaciousness of their acting. For the experienced are more proficient in acting than those who have the universal knowledge of art without experience.

21. The reason for this is that actions deal with singulars and it is singulars that come to be. Universals are neither generated nor moved except incidentally, insofar as singulars are. Man is generated when this man is. Hence a physician does not cure man save incidentally, it is Plato or Socrates he saves as such, or some other singular man who is a man incidentally. For although to be a man belongs as such (*per se*) to Socrates, it is incidental to the cured or medicated. This is *per se*: Socrates is a

THE LOVE OF WISDOM 729

man. If Socrates were defined, man would be put into his definition, as is said in Book 4 below. But this is incidental: the one cured or medicated is a man.

22. Since art is of universals and experience of singulars, if one has the knowledge of the art without experience, he will be perfected insofar as he knows the universal, but because he does not know the singular, since he lacks experience, he will often err in trying to cure; curing bears on the singular, not the universal, since it pertains to the former as such, and to the latter incidentally.

23. Then he compares art and experience on the basis of knowledge, and does two things, first, he states the pre-eminence of art over experience; second, he proves it. He bases the pre-eminence of art over experience on three things: *with respect to knowing*, since we are rather thought to know through art than experience; *with respect to difficulties*, which arise in disputes, for one having the art can respond to what is raised against the art, whereas the man of experience alone cannot; *with respect* to this that those having an art come closer *to the end of wisdom* than the experienced, since wisdom seems to follow on knowing, that is, on the universal. The one having the art is judged wiser than the experienced because he considers universals. Wisdom is thus rather linked to knowledge than to action.

24. He now proves this pre-eminence in three ways. The first proof is this: those who know the cause and the *why* are more knowing and wise than those who do not know the why, but only the *that*. The experienced know *that* something is the case, but they do not know *why*. Those who have art know the cause and the *why* and not only *that*: therefore, those with the art are wiser and more knowledgeable than the experienced.

25. He offers a proof of this. Those who know the cause and the *why* are compared to those knowing only *that*, as the master builder to those who do the manual arts. But the art of the master builder is more noble. Therefore, those who know causes and *why*, are more knowledgeable and wise than those who know only *that*.

26. The premiss of the proof is apparent from this: the master builders know the causes of the things made. The master builder is the principal artisan or architect: *archos* meaning principal and *techne* meaning art. One art is more principal than another which has the principal activity; but the activities of artisans are distinguished in this way: some dispose the matter of the artefact, as carpenters by sawing and planing wood dispose the matter for the form of the ship. There is another activity of inducing the form, as when someone takes the prepared lumber and

constructs a boat. Another activity is the use of the thing once made, and this is the most principal. The first is the least, since the first is ordered to the second, and the second to the third. The shipbuilder is the chief artisan with respect to those who prepare the materials, but the navigator who uses the ship once made exercises an art higher than that of the shipbuilder.

27. Since matter is for the sake of form, and the matter should be such as the form requires, the shipbuilder knows the cause, knows why the wood should be prepared in such a way, which those preparing it do not know; similarly, since the whole ship is for his use, the one who uses the ship knows why it should be of such a form, since it must be of such a form in order to serve such and such a use. So, the form of the artefact is the cause of the activities which dispose the matter, and the use is the cause of the activities which bear on the form of the thing made.

28. Thus it is manifest that master builders know the causes of the things made. Those who work with their hands we think of as like inanimate things, not because they make artefacts, but because in making them they do not know what they are making. They know the *that*, but not the causes, as fire burns without any knowledge. There is then this similarity between those who work with their hands and inanimate things, that just as inanimate things which act without knowledge of the cause are ordered by some higher intellect to their proper end, so too manual workers. But there is this difference, that the inanimate do what they do by nature, but manual workers out of custom, which though it has the force of nature insofar as it inclines determinately to one, still differs from nature in this, that it deals with things which can come about in different ways following human knowledge. Natural things are not habituated, as is said in *Ethics* 2; one does not train things lacking knowledge. What has been said should be understood as following from this, that some are more wise, not because they are practical – that is, engaged in activity which belongs to the experienced – but insofar as some have knowledge of what is to be done, and know the causes of what is to be done, from which reasons can be drawn, which is proper to master builders.

29. He gives another argument, which is this: a sign that one knows is that he can teach. This is so because anything is actually perfect when it can make another like itself, as is said in *Meteorology* 4. Therefore, just as it is a sign of heat that it can warm something, so it is a sign that one knows that he can teach, which is to cause knowledge in another. Those who have the art can teach because they know the causes from which

they can demonstrate: for demonstration is a syllogism that causes one to know, as is said in *Posterior Analytics* 1. But the experienced cannot teach because they cannot lead to knowledge since they do not know the cause. If those who know by experience pass it on to others, it is not received in the mode of knowledge, but of opinion or belief. So it is obvious that those who have the art are wiser and more knowing than the experienced.

30. He gives a third argument, which is this: knowledge of singulars is proper to sense rather than to any other knowledge, for all knowledge of singulars arises from sense; but we do not call any or all senses wise, because though a sense may know *that*, it does not know *why*. Touch judges that fire is hot, but it does not grasp why; therefore, the experienced who have knowledge of singulars and do not know the cause are not called wise.

31. Next he compares active and speculative art. First he shows that the speculative is more wisdom than practical art, and then responds to an objection. Those sciences are more honourable and worthy of the name of wisdom when those knowing them are held in honour and admiration by other men. The discoverer of an art is held in admiration, because he has sense and judgement and discernment of the cause beyond those of others, not because of the usefulness of what he discovers: he is more admired as distinguished from others in wisdom. Wise, with respect to a subtle inquiry into the causes of the thing discovered; distinguished,[1] with respect to the investigation into the difference of one thing from another; or distinguished, in the passive as recognized to be different from others. Thus, some sciences are more admirable and worthy of the name wisdom because of their more eminent knowledge, not their utility.

32. Since there are many arts prized for their utility, some of which are ordered to the necessities of life, like the mechanical arts, but others because they introduce others to the sciences, like the logical sciences, among those having arts those are accounted more wise whose arts are not for the sake of utility, but for the sake of knowledge itself, such as the speculative sciences.

33. That the speculative sciences were not discovered for utility is clear from this sign: while all the other arts had been discovered which are able to introduce to knowledge, or are for the necessities of life, or for pleasure, such as the arts devised for the amusement of men, the speculative were not sought for any of these reasons, but for their own sake. That

1. Thomas has a text reading 'distinguishing'.

they are not for utility is clear from the place where they were discovered, for they were first discovered where men pursued such things. Another reading has: and first in those places where there was leisure, that is, other occupations being set aside, the necessities having been provided for. Hence it was in Egypt that the mathematical arts, which are quite speculative, were first discovered by the priests, who were given leisure for study at the public expense, as we also read of in Genesis.

34. Since he has used the name art indifferently of wisdom and science, lest anyone think these are synonyms in every way meaning the same, he corrects this by referring to his work on morals, that is *Ethics* 6, where is discussed the way science and art and wisdom and prudence and understanding differ. To put it briefly, wisdom and science and understanding are in the speculative part of the soul, which he here calls the scientific part of the soul. They differ in that understanding is the habit of the first principles of demonstration; science is of conclusions about lesser things, whereas wisdom considers the first causes, so in the same place it is called the chief of the sciences. Prudence and art are in the practical part of the soul, which is ratiocinative about contingent things that can be done by us. But they differ, for prudence directs actions which do not pass into exterior matter but are perfections of the agent, hence prudence is called there right reason about things to be done. But art directs in making, which passes into exterior matter, such as building and sawing; hence art is called right reason about things to be made.

35. From what has been said, he now argues for his principal thesis, namely, that wisdom is concerned with causes. For he says that this is the point of this discourse, that is, the foregoing reasoning: the science that is called wisdom seems to be concerned with the first causes and first principles. Which is clear from what has been said. For someone is wiser to the degree that he has knowledge of causes since, relying on the preceding, the experienced is wiser than one who has sense without experience, and the one having the art is wiser than any experienced person, and among those having art, the master builder is wiser than the manual worker, and in both the arts and sciences, the speculative have more knowledge than the active, and all these follow from the foregoing. It remains that the science which is wisdom simply is concerned with causes. And the mode of arguing is as if we should say that that which is hotter is more fiery, hence that which is fire absolutely is heat absolutely.

Lesson 2

Since we are seeking knowledge, we must inquire of what kind are the causes and the principles, the knowledge of which is wisdom. If one were to take the notions we have about the wise man, this might perhaps make the answer more evident. We suppose first, then, that the wise man knows all things, as far as possible, although he has not knowledge of each of them in detail; secondly, that he who can learn things that are difficult, and not easy for man to know, is wise (sense-perception is common to all, and therefore easy and no mark of wisdom); again, that he who is more exact and more capable of teaching the causes is wiser, in every branch of knowledge; and that of the sciences, also, that which is desirable on its own account and for the sake of knowing is more of the nature of wisdom than that which is desirable on account of its results, and the superior science is more of the nature of wisdom than the ancillary; for the wise man must not be ordered but must order, and he must not obey another, but the less wise must obey him.

Such and so many are the notions, then, which we have about wisdom and the wise. Now of these characteristics that of knowing all things must belong to him who has in the highest degree universal knowledge; for he knows in a sense all the instances that fall under the universal. And these things, the most universal, are on the whole the hardest for men to know; for they are farthest from the senses. And the most exact of the sciences are those which deal most with first principles; for those which involve fewer principles are more exact than those which involve additional principles, for example arithmetic than geometry. But the science which investigates causes is also instructive, in a higher degree, for the people who instruct us are those who tell the causes of each thing. And understanding and knowledge pursued for their own sake are found most in the knowledge of that which is most knowable (for he who chooses to know for the sake of knowing will choose most readily that which is most truly knowledge, and such is the knowledge of that which is most knowable); and the first principles and the causes are most knowable; for by reason of these, and from these, all other things come to be known, and not these by means of the things subordinate to them. And the science which knows to what end each thing must be done is the most authoritative of the sciences, and more authoritative than any ancillary science; and this end is the good of that thing, and in general the supreme good in the whole of nature. Judged by all tests we have mentioned, then, the name in question falls to the same science; this must be a science that investigates the first principles and causes; for the good, that is, the end, is one of the causes. Aristotle, *Metaphysics* 1.2

36. After the Philosopher shows that wisdom is a science that bears on causes, here he wishes to show the kind of causes and principles with which it is concerned. He shows that it is concerned with the first and most universal causes, arguing from the definition of wisdom. There are three things that he does: first he gathers a definition of wisdom from the way men speak of the wise man and of wisdom. Second, he shows that all these traits belong to a universal science which considers first and universal causes. Third, he draws his conclusions. There are six common opinions that men hold about wisdom. First, all commonly take the wise man to know all things, in an appropriate way, because he does not have knowledge of all singulars, for this is impossible, singulars being infinite and the infinite being incomprehensible by intellect.

37. Second, we think that man wise who is capable because of the force of his intellect of knowing difficult matters, and not the easy things commonly known by all. Sensing is common to all, that is, to know sensible things, so it is easy and not *sophon*, something pertaining to the wise man. It is obvious that that which properly pertains to the wise man should not be easily known by all.

38. Third, we say that man is wise who has more certainty about the things he knows than others commonly have.

39. Fourth, we think him more wise in any science who can assign the causes of whatever is sought, and in this way teach.

40. Fifth, that among the sciences is wisdom which is most wanted and desired, that is, wanted for the sake of knowledge and for the sake of knowing, than the science which is the cause of whatever contingent things can follow on knowledge, such as the necessities of life, pleasure, and other like things.

41. Sixth, the wisdom we are talking about must be, or we say it is, more ancient, that is, more worthy, than any ancillary science, as can be understood from the foregoing. For in the ancillary mechanical arts there are those that are executed on the command of the superior artisan, whom we called above both architect and wise.

42. He proves that the notion of wisdom belongs to the commanding sciences rather than to the ancillary sciences in two ways. First, because the ancillary sciences are ordered by the superior sciences, for the ancillary arts are ordered to the end of the higher art, as the equestrian art to the end of the military. But it is everyone's opinion that the wise man ought not to be ordered by others, rather it is for him to order them. Again, lesser master builders are persuaded by their superiors, insofar as they believe the superiors with respect to what is to be done or made. For the

shipbuilder believes the navigator teaching how the form of the ship should be. But it is not proper for the wise man to be persuaded by another, rather he should persuade others with his knowledge.

43. These, then, are the opinions that men have of wisdom and the wise man. A description of wisdom can be formed from them: he is called wise who knows all things, even the difficult, with certitude and through causes, seeking such knowledge for its own sake, ordering and persuading others. And this is, as it were, the major of the syllogism. For every wise man ought to be such, and conversely, whoever is such, is a wise man.

44. Next he shows that all the foregoing belong to him who knows the first and universal causes, and he pursues the same order as above. First, he says that one having universal science especially has it in him to know all things, which was the first point. Proof: whoever knows universals, in some way knows the things that fall under the universals. Therefore, he who knows the most universal, in a certain way knows all things.

45. Next he shows that it has the second characteristic, thus: those things which are most remote from the senses, are difficult for men to know, for sense knowledge is common to all, since in it all human knowledge has its beginning. But the most universal is farthest removed from sensible things, because sense is of singulars. Therefore, universals are most difficult for men to know. Evidently then that science is most difficult which is concerned with the most universal.

46. This seems to contradict *Physics* 1, for there it is said that the more universal is more known to us, but things which are known first are easiest. In reply it should be said that the more universal according to simple apprehension is known first, for being comes first into our mind, as Avicenna says, and animal comes to mind before man. Just as in natural being that which proceeds from potency to act is an animal before it is man, so in the generation of science the intellect conceives animal before man. But with respect to the investigation of natural properties and causes, we first know the less common, because by particular causes which are of one genus or species we go on to universal causes. The things which are universal in causing are known later by us, although they are by nature more known, but universals in predication are in a way more known to us than the less universal, though not known before singulars. For in us the knowledge of sense which has the singular for its object precedes intellectual knowledge, which is of universals.

A point should be made of the fact that he does not say that the most universal are the most difficult, but almost. For the things which are wholly separated from matter in existence, like immaterial substances, are more difficult for us to know than even universals, and therefore this science, which is called wisdom, although it is first in dignity, is last to be learned.

47. He now shows that the third characteristic is in this science by this argument: sciences are more certain to the degree that they are naturally prior. Which is clear from this that the sciences which are said to be by addition to others are less certain than the sciences that have fewer things in their consideration, as arithmetic is more certain than geometry, because geometrical things are by way of addition to arithmetical, which is clear when you consider what each science takes as its first principle, namely, one and point. For the point adds position to the unit. To be indivisible constitutes the notion of unity, and this, insofar as it has the note of measure, is the principle of number. But the point adds position to it.

But the particular sciences are naturally posterior to the universal sciences, because their subjects add to the subjects of the universal sciences. As is clear, mobile being with which natural philosophy is concerned, adds to being simply, with which metaphysics is concerned, and to quantified being with which mathematics is concerned. Therefore, the science of being, and the most universal, is most certain. Nor does that conflict with what he said earlier that only a few know all things. For the universal comprises fewer things actually, but many things potentially. A science is more certain to the degree that fewer things need actually be considered with respect to its subject. Hence the operative sciences are most uncertain, since they must consider many circumstances of the singular things to be done.

48. He shows that the fourth characteristic belongs to it, by this argument: that science is more didactic or doctrinal which most considers causes, for only they teach who state the causes of each thing, for knowing is through the cause, and to teach is to cause science in another. But the science which considers universals, considers the first of all causes, hence it is evidently most doctrinal or teaching.

49. That the fifth characteristic of wisdom belongs to this science, he shows thus: the sciences which know for the sake of knowing, that is, for itself and not for the sake of other things, are concerned with the most knowable. The sciences which are of the first causes are of the most knowable. Therefore these sciences especially are desired for their own sake. Proof of the first: he who desires to know for the sake of knowing, desires knowledge most. But the greatest knowledge is of the most knowable. Therefore those sciences are most desired for their own sake which are of the most knowable. Proof of the second: those things from which

and for the sake of which other things are known are more knowable than the things that are known from them. But from causes and principles other things are known, and not conversely. Etc.

50. He shows that the sixth characteristic belongs to this science, by this argument: that science is principal relative to others – as architectonic to the servile or ancillary – which considers the final cause, for the sake of which each thing is done, as is apparent from what has been already said. For the navigator, to whom the use of the ship, which is the end of the ship, pertains, is as architect to the shipbuilder who serves him. But the science mentioned especially considers the final cause of all things. This is clear because that for the sake of which each thing is done is the good of each, that is, of each particular good. The end is the good in any genus. But that which is the end of all, that is, of the universe itself, is that which is best in the whole of nature. This pertains to the consideration of this science. Therefore, it is principal or architectonic with respect to all others.

51. He concludes from the foregoing what he chiefly intends, saying that from all the foregoing it appears that the name wisdom belongs to the science that we are seeking, namely that science which is theoretical, that is, speculates about the first principles and causes. This is manifest from the six conditions which manifestly pertain to one considering universal causes. But, because the sixth condition touched the consideration of the end, which was not clearly seen to be a cause by the ancients, as will be said below, therefore he especially shows that this is a condition of this science that considers first causes, because the end, which is the good, and for the sake of which others come to be, is numbered among the causes. Hence the science which considers the first and universal causes, must also consider the universal end of all, which is the best thing in the whole of nature.

Lesson 3

That it is not a science of production is clear even from the history of the earliest philosophers. For it is owing to their wonder that men both now begin and at first began to philosophize; they wondered originally at the obvious difficulties, then advanced little by little and stated difficulties about the greater matters, for example about the phenomena of the moon and those of the sun and the stars, and about the genesis of the universe. And a man who is puzzled and wonders thinks himself ignorant (whence even the lover of myth is in a sense a lover of wisdom, for the myth is composed of wonders); therefore since they philosophized in order to escape from ignorance, evidently they were pursuing science in order to know, and not for any utilitarian end. And this is confirmed by the facts; for it was when almost all the necessities of life and the things that make for comfort and recreation had been secured, that such knowledge began to be sought. Evidently, then, we do not seek it for the sake of any other advantage; but as the man is free, we say, who exists for his own sake and not for another's, so we pursue this as the only free science, for it alone exists for its own sake.

Hence also the possession of it might be justly regarded as beyond human power; for in many ways human nature is in bondage, so that according to Simonides, 'God alone can have this privilege,' and it is unfitting that man should not be content to seek the knowledge that is suited to him. If, then, there is something in what the poets say, and jealousy is natural to the divine power, it would probably occur in this case above all, and all who excelled in this knowledge would be unfortunate. But the divine power cannot be jealous (nay, according to the proverb, 'Bards tell many a lie'), nor should any other science be thought more honourable than one of this sort. For the most divine science is also most honourable, and this science alone must be, in two ways, most divine. For the science which it would be most meet for God to have is a divine science, and so is any science that deals with divine objects; and this science alone has both these qualities; for (1) God is thought to be among the causes of all things and to be a first principle, and (2) such a science either God alone can have, or God above all others. All the sciences, indeed, are more necessary than this, but none is better.

Yet the acquisition of it must in a sense end in something which is the opposite of our original inquiries. For all men begin, as we said, by wondering that things are as they are, as they do about self-moving marionettes, or about the solstices or the incommensurability of the diagonal of a square with the side; for it seems wonderful to all who have not yet seen the reason, that there is a thing which cannot be measured even by the smallest unit. But we must end in the contrary and, according to the proverb, the better state, as is the case in these instances too when men learn the cause; for there is nothing which would surprise a geometer so much as if the diagonal turned out to be commensurable.

We have stated, then, what is the nature of the science we are searching for, and what is the mark which our search and our whole investigation must reach.

Aristotle, *Metaphysics* 1.2 (contd)

52. Having shown what this science is concerned with, he shows what kind of science it is. First, he shows the dignity of the science and then

the goal it seeks to reach. He makes four points with respect to its dignity: (1) it is a speculative, not an active science; (2) it is most free; (3) it is more than human; (4) it is most honourable. For each of these, he first gives an argument, then a sign.

53. He gives the following argument on behalf of (1). No science which seeks knowledge for its own sake is an active science; it is speculative. But the science that is called wisdom or philosophy is sought for the sake of knowledge; therefore, it is speculative and not active. He manifests the minor premiss in this way: he who seeks as his end to flee from ignorance, intends knowledge for its own sake. But those who philosophize seek as their end to flee ignorance; therefore, their intention is to know for its own sake.

54. That they seek to flee ignorance is clear from this, that those who first philosophized and those who do so now begin to philosophize by wondering about a cause, but differently in the beginning and now. In the beginning they wondered about fewer doubtful things which were ready to hand in order to know their causes, but afterwards, proceeding from knowledge of more obvious things to inquiry into the more obscure, they began to doubt about greater and more hidden things, such lunar events as its eclipse and its phases which vary as it is differently related to the sun, and so too they raised questions about the sun, its eclipse and motion and size, and about the stars, their number and order and the like, and of the coming into being of the whole universe. Which some said came about by chance, some by intellect, some by love.

55. It is clear that doubt and wonder arise from ignorance, since when we see events whose cause is hidden to us, we wonder about their cause, and given that such wonder was the cause that led to philosophy, the philomyth, or lover of tales, which is the mark of the poet, is in his way a philosopher, because those who first dealt with the principles of things by way of myths were called theologizing poets, such as Perseus, and the seven sages were others. The reason the philosopher is compared to the poet is that both are concerned with wonders and the fables of the poets are filled with wonders. The philosophers were moved by wonder to philosophize, and since wonder arises from ignorance, it is clear that they were moved to philosophize in order to flee ignorance. Whence it is clear that they pursued and studiously sought science solely in order to know, and not because of any use or utility.

56. It should be noticed that whereas he first used the name wisdom now he is speaking of philosophy, taking them for the same thing. For since those who first gave themselves to the study of wisdom were called

sophists or the wise, when Pythagoras was asked what he did, he was reluctant to call himself wise, as his predecessors had, since this seemed to him presumptuous, so he called himself a philosopher, that is, a lover of wisdom. So the term wise was changed to the term philosopher, and wisdom to philosophy. The name is relevant to his point. For he seems to be a lover of wisdom who seeks wisdom for its own sake, not for something else, for he who seeks something for a further purpose loves that more than what he immediately seeks.

57. He proves the same point with a sign, saying that what has been said, namely that wisdom or philosophy is not sought for the sake of its utility, but for the sake of knowing itself, is testified to by an event affecting the pursuers of philosophy. For it was when nearly everything needed for the necessity of life and amusement or pleasure, which consists of leisure, and even what was necessary for learning, like the logical sciences, which are not sought for themselves, but as introductory to other arts – it was after all that had been discovered that this prudence or wisdom began to be sought. From this it is clear that it is not sought for any need beyond itself, but for its own sake: no one seeks what he has. Hence, when everything else was had, it was sought and sought for its own sake, not for the sake of anything else.

58. He proves (2) using this argument: a man is properly called free who does not exist for the sake of another, but for his own sake. Slaves belong to their masters and act for the sake of their masters, and receive from them whatever they receive. But free men are for their own sake, acquiring and acting for themselves. But only this science is for itself. Therefore it alone is free among the sciences.

59. Notice that this can be understood in two ways. In one way, that what is said applies to the genus of speculative sciences alone, and then it is true that only this type of science is sought for its own sake, hence only those arts are called liberal which are ordered to knowing, but those which are ordered to having some usefulness for action are called mechanical or servile. In another way, to show something peculiar to philosophy or wisdom which is concerned with the highest causes, among which is the final cause, as was said above. Which is why this science considers the ultimate and universal end of all. Thus all the other sciences are ordered to it as to their end and only it is fully for its own sake.

60. He now proves (3), that it is not quite human: first he will prove it and then exclude an error in its regard. Here is the proof: the science that is most free ought not to be a possession of one who is in many ways a servant and slave; but in many respects human nature is enslaved; therefore

this science is not a human possession. He says that human nature is enslaved insofar as it is bound by many necessities. This brings it about that one sometimes sets aside what should be sought for its own sake because of the necessities of life; in the *Topics* 3 he says that it is better to philosophize than get rich although sometimes gathering wealth is chosen, as by one who is needy. From this it is evident that this wisdom is sought for its own sake in such a way that it does not belong to man as a possession, which he can use at will, since frequently he is impeded from it on account of the necessities of life. Nor is it man's on command since he can never perfectly attain it, but the little bit of it he can have outweighs what is known in all the other sciences.

61. He then excludes the error of Simonides the poet who said that to God alone belongs the honour of desiring this science which is sought for itself alone and not for something else. It is not fitting for a man, who should seek knowledge in keeping with his condition, one that is ordered to the necessities of life, which a man needs.

62. The error of Simonides arises from that error of the poets to the effect that the divine is jealous and out of jealousy God does not want others to have what pertains to his honour. If God were jealous, he would be much more so in this, namely the science sought for its own sake, which is the most honourable of all. According to their opinion it follows that all imperfect things are unfortunate. For men are said to be fortunate by the providence of the gods, who bestow goods on them. Hence out of the jealousy of the gods not wishing to share their goods it follows that men remaining outside the perfection of this science are unfortunate.

63. The root of this opinion is most false, since it is not fitting that anything divine should envy, which is clear from the fact that envy is sadness at someone's prosperity, which can only happen if the one who envies regards the good of the other as a diminution of his own good. But God is not sad, since he is subject to no evil, nor can another's good diminish his good, because from his goodness, which is a ceaseless fount, all goods flow. Plato too said that all envy must be denied of God. Not only in this, but in many other matters, poets lie, as is said in the popular proverb.

64. Here he proves (4), that this science is the most honourable, by this argument: that science is most honourable which is most divine, just as God is more honourable than all other things; but this science is especially divine. Therefore, it is the most honourable. The minor premiss is proved thus: a science is called divine in two ways and only this science is called divine in both; in one way, it is divine because God has it, in another

because it is concerned with divine things. That both belong to this science is clear. Since this science is of first causes and principles, it must be about God, because this is how all understand God, as one of the causes and as the principle of things. Again, the science which is of God and of first causes is either one that God alone has or, if not, that he especially has. Only he has it according to perfect comprehension. And he especially has it because it is by his action that it is had by men in their way, though not as their possession, but as something borrowed.

65. From this he further concludes that all other sciences are more necessary than this in respect of usefulness for life and are little sought for their own sake. But none of the others can be more worthy than it.

66. He then states the goal at which this science aims, and says that its order consists or terminates in the contrary of that which characterized those who first sought this science, as also happens in natural generations and motions. For a motion terminates in the contrary of that from which it began. And, since inquiry is a kind of motion towards knowledge, it should terminate in the contrary of that from which it begins. But the inquiry of this science began with wonder about everything (as has been said), the first wondering about obvious things, subsequent ones about the more obscure. This wonder reacted to things as if they were wonderful automata – that is, which wonderfully seemed merely to happen (automata means what just happens as such). Men most wonder when things come about by chance in this way, as if they were foreseen and determined by some cause. Chance events are not from a determined cause, and wonder is due to ignorance of the cause. Therefore, before men were able to ask after the causes of things, they wondered about everything as if it were from chance. Just as they wondered about the two tropics of the sun, the winter and summer, for in the summer solstice the sun begins to move from north to south, but in the winter it is the reverse. So too with respect to the fact that the diagonal is not commensurate with the side of the square, for since it does not seem measured by the indivisible alone, just as the one is not measured by number but is the measure of all numbers, it seemed marvellous that something which was not indivisible should not be measured, and that what was least was not measured. It is clear that the diagonal of the square and its side are not indivisibles, or least quantities. Hence it seemed a marvel that they were not commensurable.

67. Therefore, since the inquiry of philosophy begins from wonder, it should end in or achieve the contrary, and to achieve that which is more worthy, as the popular proverb agrees which says that what is achieved is always the better. What that contrary and more worthy state might be

is evident from the marvels already mentioned. When men once learn their causes, they no longer marvel. As the geometer does not wonder that the diagonal is incommensurate with the side, for he knows why, namely because the proportion of the square of the diagonal to the square of the side is not the proportion of square number to square number, but like the proportion of two to one. It follows that the proportion of the side to the diagonal is not one of number to number, and then it is obvious that they cannot be commensurate. For only those lines are commensurable whose proportion to one another is that of number to number. Therefore, the end of this science which we should achieve is that by knowing the causes, we no longer wonder at their effects.

68. The nature of this science is evident from what has been said: it is speculative, free, not human, but divine. And what the intention is that guides its questionings, its method and its whole art, is also clear. For it bears on the first and universal causes of all things, concerning which it both inquires and determines. Given knowledge of these things, it achieves the stated term, namely that known causes are not wondered at.

PART FIVE
NAPLES (1272–4)

After a stormy three years in Paris, Thomas returned to Naples to take up the post of regent master in the Dominican convent there and to create a *studium generale*, in effect, a Dominican university. He continued commenting on Aristotle and completed his exposition of the epistles of St Paul, he commented on the psalms, getting halfway through the 150, and of course he continued work on the *Summa theologiae*, turning now to Part 3. It was in this period that he commented on the *Book of Causes*, a work of Arabic origin that was based on the work of the Neoplatonist Proclus. Thomas was clearly at the peak of his powers. He was forty-seven years old. And yet he was in the twilight of his life.

Josef Pieper, in *The Silence of St Thomas*, meditates on the event that suddenly altered Thomas's life. A mystical experience of great intensity left him with the conviction that everything he had written was no better than straw. And he stopped writing. The last year of his life was spent in literary silence. The great *Summa theologiae* was to remain unfinished.

The canonization process gives us a vivid portrait of Thomas, one we would not otherwise have. There was an inquiry at Naples at which many Dominicans who had known him as a confrère at different stages of his life testified. There emerges a portrait of a man whose great intelligence and intellectual labours were the complement of his spiritual life. We learn of miraculous happenings, of the amount of prayer that formed part of his study and writing. Should we be surprised that a theologian who spent his life meditating on the Christian message exhibited it in his life? But it is the depth of his holiness that strikes us as we read these witnesses. Doubtless they were partisan, of course they wanted a member of their order recognized for his holiness, but only a cynic would think this vitiates their testimony. The Thomas who emerges from these accounts is an engaging personality. His charge against Averroes's reading of Aristotle on mind was that the Commentator could not give a meaningful account of the statement, 'This man thinks.' The recollections of his friends acquaint us with the very singular man behind the thinking and writing.

Thomas was asked to attend a Council at Lyons and set off to comply with the request. He did not get far. He fell ill on the way, sought refuge with a sister but then was transferred to the Cistercian abbey at Fossanova. The abbey is still there. One can visit the room in which Thomas died. The distance from Roccasecca where he was born to Fossanova is perhaps fifty kilometres. The journey from beginning to end seems short. But something began on 7 March 1274 that continues to this day. The measured tones of Thomas continue to form part of the great philosophical conversation as friend and foe alike turn to his writings for clarity, precision and a relevance that transcends the thirteenth century.

29. The Logic of the Incarnation.
Summa theologiae, 3, 16
(1273)

A central mystery of the Christian faith is the incarnation, the belief that Jesus was both human and divine. From the time of Anselm at the beginning of the twelfth century, theology was regarded as faith seeking understanding (fides quaerens intellectum). Understanding cannot of course mean coming to hold the incarnation on the basis of arguments whose premisses are known by everyone. If that were possible, the result would be philosophy, not theology. Rather, what the theologian sought was a clarification of the mystery, analogies in creatures, enlightenment from other aspects of Christian revelation.

For Thomas, as we have seen, the theologian came to his task after a previous immersion in philosophy, a philosophy which, thanks to the introduction of Aristotle, was considerably more sophisticated than that available to Christian thinkers prior to the thirteenth century. The following text from Part 3 of the Summa theologiae *exhibits Thomas's use of grammar and logic as well as metaphysics to sort out the propositions which fittingly express the mystery of the incarnation from those that do not. The terminology poses some difficulties – a 'supposit' is the ultimate subject of predication, the individual. In 'Socrates is a man', the subject points to the individual and the predicate expresses his nature. In the case of Christ, the supposit is the Second Person of the Trinity and the incarnation amounts to that person taking on human nature as well as divine. Thus Christ is one person who has two natures.*

The following discussion explores the fittingness of attributing certain predicates to Christ. Brooding over the discussion is the spectre of 'two things equal to a third are equal to one another'. Thomas manoeuvres adroitly between the Scylla and Charybdis of Christological heresies to display, so to speak, the logic of the incarnation.

Summa theologiae, Third Part, Question 16

THE THINGS THAT BELONG TO CHRIST IN HIS BEING AND BECOMING

Now we must consider consequences of the union of the two natures in Christ. First, with respect to things which belong to Christ as such; second, what belongs to him in comparison with God the Father; third, what belongs to him in comparison to us. Under the first heading, we must first take up what belongs to Christ as to his being and his becoming; then, the things that belong to him by reason of unity.

As to the first, twelve questions arise: (1) whether 'God is man' is true; (2) whether 'Man is God' is true; (3) whether Christ can be called a lordly man; (4) whether what belongs to the son of man can be predicated of the son of God, and vice versa; (5) whether what belongs to the son of man can be predicated of the divine nature and what belongs to the son of God can be predicated of human nature; (6) whether 'The Son of God was made man' is true; (7) whether 'Man was made God' is true; (8) whether 'Christ is a creature' is true; (9) whether 'This man' – pointing to Christ – 'began to exist or always was' is true; (10) whether 'Christ insofar as he is a man is a creature' is true; (11) whether 'Christ insofar as he is a man is God' is true; (12) whether 'Christ, insofar as he is a man, is a hypostasis or person' is true.

Article 1: Is 'God is man' true?

It seems that it is false.

1. Every affirmative proposition in remote matter is false. But this proposition, 'God is man', is in remote matter, because the forms signified by the subject and predicate are maximally distant. Since the proposition is affirmative, therefore, it seems to be false.

2. Moreover, the three persons have more in common than do human and divine nature. But in the mystery of the Trinity one person is not predicated of another, for we do not say that the Father is the Son, or conversely. Therefore, it seems that neither can human nature be predicated of God, as when it is said, 'God is man.'

3. Moreover, Athanasius says that just as soul and body are one man,

so God and man are one Christ. But it is false to say that the soul is the body. Therefore, it is false to say that God is man.

4. Moreover, as was said in Part 1, what is predicated of God, not relatively but absolutely, belongs to the whole Trinity and to each person. But the word 'man' is not relative, but absolute. Therefore, if it is predicated of God, it follows that the whole Trinity and each person is man. Which is evidently false.

ON THE CONTRARY:
In Philippians 2.6–7 it is said 'who, though he was by nature God, did not consider being equal to God a thing to be clung to, but emptied himself, taking the nature of a slave and being made like unto men and appearing in the form of man . . .' But he who was by nature God is God. Therefore, God is man.

RESPONSE:
It should be said that this proposition, 'God is man', is conceded by all Christians, but not for the same reason by all. For some accept the proposition but not according to the proper meaning of its terms. For the Manicheans say that the Word of God is man, although not true man, but a similitude, insofar as they say that the Son of God assumed an imaginary body, in order that it might be said that God is man in the way that figured bronze is called man by bearing a likeness to man. Similarly, those who maintain that in Christ soul and body were not united, did not hold that God is true man, but that he is called man figuratively, by reason of his parts. Both these views have been disproved earlier.[1]

Others, on the contrary, put the truth on the side of man, but denied the truth on the part of God. For they say that Christ, who is the God Man, is God not by nature but by way of participation, namely by grace, much as all holy men are said to be gods: Christ was simply more excellent than all others because of more abundant grace. So, when it is said, 'God is man,' the word God does not stand for the true and natural God. This is the heresy of Photinus, which was disproved above.[2]

Others accept the proposition with the truth of both terms, holding Christ to be true God and true man, but they do not save the truth of the predication. For they say that man is predicated of God by a kind of

1. q. 2, art. 5; q. 5, art. 1.
2. q. 2, art. 10.

conjunction, whether of dignity or of authority or even of love and indwelling. This is the way Nestorius held that God is man, such that this would only mean that God is conjoined to man by such a conjunction that God dwells in man and is united to him according to love and participation of the divine authority and honour. Those who held that there were two hypostases or subjects in Christ fell into a similar error. For it is impossible to understand that one of what are distinct in hypostasis or subject can be properly predicated of the other, except by a kind of figurative way of speaking, insofar as they are conjoined in something, as if we were to say that Peter is John because they are linked in some way to one another. These opinions were also refuted above.[1]

Hence, supposing, according to the truth of the Catholic faith, that the true divine nature is united with true human nature, not only in person, but also in subject or hypostasis, we say that this proposition, 'God is man,' is both true and proper, not only because of the truth of the terms, namely because Christ is true God and true man, but also because of the truth of the predication. The word signifying a common nature concretely can stand for any of the things contained in the common nature, as the word 'man' can stand for any singular man. Therefore this word 'God', by its very mode of signifying, can stand for the person of the Son of God, as was shown in Part 1.[2] A word signifying the nature concretely can be truly and properly predicated of any subject of that nature, as man is truly and properly predicated of Socrates and Plato. Therefore because the person of the Son of God, for which the word 'God' stands, is a subject of human nature, the name 'man' can be truly and properly predicated of this name 'God', insofar as it stands for the person of the Son of God.

Ad 1. It should be said that when different forms cannot come together in one subject, it is necessary that the proposition whose subject signifies one of those forms and the predicate the other is in remote matter. But when two forms can come together in one subject, it is not remote matter, but natural or contingent, as when I say, 'The white is musical.' The divine and human natures, although they are maximally distant, none the less come together in one subject through the mystery of the incarnation, neither of which inheres incidentally, but both *per se*. Therefore, this proposition, 'God is man,' is in neither remote nor contingent matter,

1. q. 2, art. 3.
2. q. 39, art. 4.

but in natural matter. And man is predicated of God, not incidentally, but *per se*, as of its own subject, not indeed by reason of the form signified by the term God, but by reason of the subject, which is a hypostasis of human nature.

Ad 2. It should be said that the three divine persons agree in nature, but are distinguished in subject, and therefore they are not predicated of one another. In the mystery of the incarnation, however, the natures, because they are distinct, are not predicated of one another insofar as they are signified abstractly, for the divine nature is not human nature, but because they agree in subject they are predicated of one another concretely.

Ad 3. It should be said that soul and flesh are signified abstractly, like divinity and humanity. Concretely they are called animate and carnal or corporeal, much as, in the case in point, God and man. Hence in neither case is the abstract predicated of the abstract, but only the concrete of the concrete.

Ad 4. It should be said that this word 'man' is predicated of God by reason of union in person, which union implies a relation. Therefore, it does not follow the rule of those words which are predicated absolutely of God from all eternity.

Article 2: Is 'Man is God' true?

It seems that it is false.

1. God is an incommunicable name. But Wisdom 14.21 blames idolaters because they 'gave the incommunicable name to stones and wood'. By parity of reasoning, it seems unfitting that the name God should be predicated of man.

2. Moreover, whatever is predicated of the predicate is predicated of the subject. But 'God is Father' is true, and also 'God is the Trinity.' Therefore, if 'Man is God' is true, 'Man is the Father' and 'Man is the Trinity' are true. Since these are evidently false, so is the first.

3. Moreover, in Psalm 80.10 it is said, 'No new god shall be among thee.' But man is new, for Christ was not always man. Therefore 'Man is God' is false.

ON THE CONTRARY:

It is said in Romans 9.5, 'From whom is Christ according to the flesh, who is over all things, God blessed for ever, amen.' But Christ according to the flesh is man. Therefore, 'Man is God' is true.

RESPONSE:

It should be said that, assuming the truth of both natures, namely of the divine and human, and a union in person and hypostasis, 'Man is God' is true and proper, just as 'God is man' is. For the term 'man' can stand for any hypostasis of human nature, and so it can stand for the person of the Son, which we say is a hypostasis of human nature. For it is manifest that the term God is truly and properly predicated of the person of the son of God, as was shown in Part 1.[1] It follows that 'Man is God' is true.

Ad 1. It should be said that idolaters attribute the name of the divinity to stones and wood considered in their own nature, because they thought there was something numinous in them. But we do not attribute the name of divinity to man according to human nature, but according to an eternal subject, which by union is also a subject of human nature, as has been said.

Ad 2. It should be said that the word 'Father' is predicated of the word 'God' insofar as the word 'God' stands for the person of the Father. But it is not predicated of the person of the Son, because the person of the Son is not the person of the Father. Consequently, it is not necessary that the word 'Father' be predicated of the word 'man', of which the word 'God' is predicated, insofar as 'man' stands for the person of the Son.

Ad 3. It should be said that although human nature in Christ is something new, the subject of human nature is not new but eternal. And because the word 'God' is not predicated of man by reason of human nature, but by reason of the subject, it does not follow that we say something new of God. That would follow if we held that 'man' stands for the created subject, as those must say who hold that there are two subjects in Christ.

Article 3: Is Christ a 'lordly man'?

It seems that he is.

1. Augustine, in *Eighty-three Questions* 36, says they should be warned who expect the goods that were in the lordly man. But he is speaking of Christ. Therefore, it seems that Christ is the lordly man.

1. q. 39, art. 4.

2. Moreover, as dominion belongs to Christ by reason of his divine nature, so humanity pertains to human nature. But God is said to be 'humaned', as is clear from Damascene in *On Orthodox Faith* 3.6, where he says that 'humanation' shows what is joined to man. By parity of reasoning, it can be said demonstratively that this man is lordly.

3. Moreover, as 'lordly' is said denominatively from lord, so 'divine' is said denominatively from God. But Dionysius calls Christ the most divine Jesus. Therefore, by parity of reasoning, Christ can be called the lordly man.

ON THE CONTRARY:

Augustine says in the *Retractions* 1.19, 'I do not see that the man Jesus Christ is rightly called lordly, although he is indeed the lord.'

RESPONSE:

It should be said that, as was remarked above, when Christ Jesus is called man the eternal subject, which is the person of the Son of God, is designated because there is one subject of both natures. 'God' and 'lord' are predicated essentially of the person of the Son of God and therefore ought not to be predicated denominatively because this derogates from the truth of union. Hence, if 'lordly' is said denominatively from lord, it cannot be truly and properly said that that man is lordly, but rather that he is lord.

If when Christ Jesus is called man a created subject were designated, as it is by those who hold there are two subjects in Christ, that man could be called lordly insofar as he is assumed by participation in the divine honour, as the Nestorians held.

In this way human nature is not called essentially God, but deified, not by being converted into the divine nature, but by conjunction with the divine nature in one subject, as is clear from Damascene.

Ad 1. It should be said that Augustine is taking back those and similar words in the *Retractions*. Hence, after the cited words he adds, 'I have said this everywhere, namely, that Christ Jesus is the lordly man and I wish I had not. Afterwards I saw that this should not be said and could not be defended by any argument,' because someone could say that a man is called lordly by reason of human nature which the word 'man' signifies, not by reason of the subject.

Ad 2. It should be said that the one subject of the divine and human nature was indeed first of the divine nature, namely from eternity, and afterwards in time because of the incarnation made the subject of human nature. That is why it is called 'humanatum', not because it assumed a man, but because it assumed human nature. But it cannot be said conversely that the subject of human nature assumed the divine nature, so man cannot be called deified man or lord.

Ad 3. It should be said that the word 'divine' is customarily predicated of those things of which the word 'God' is predicated essentially. For we say that the divine essence is God, by reason of identity; and that the essence is of God or divine, because of the different mode of signifying; and the divine word, since the word is God. Similarly we say the divine person, like the person of Plato, because of a different mode of signifying. But lordly is not said of those of whom lord is predicated, because we are not accustomed to say that some man who is a lord is lordly. But whatever pertains to the lord we called lordly, as the lordly will or lordly hand or lordly possession. Therefore this man Christ, who is lord, cannot be called lordly, but his flesh can be called lordly flesh, and his passion can be called the lordly passion.

Article 4: Can what belongs to human nature be said of God?

It seems that it cannot.

1. It is impossible that opposites be predicated of the same thing. But the things that belong to human nature are contrary to what is proper to God, for God is uncreated, immutable and eternal, whereas human nature is created, temporal and mutable. Therefore, the things that belong to human nature cannot be said of God.

2. Moreover, to attribute to God what pertains to defect seems to derogate from the divine honour and to be blasphemous. But what belongs to human nature involves defect, as to die, to suffer, and the like. Therefore it seems that what belongs to human nature can in no way be said of God.

3. Moreover, to be assumed belongs to human nature. Therefore, it does not belong to God. Therefore the things of human nature cannot be said of God.

ON THE CONTRARY:
Damascene says in *On Orthodox Faith* 3.4 that God takes on what is peculiar to flesh, that is, its properties, since God is called suffering, and the God of glory was crucified.

RESPONSE:

It should be said that there is a difference on this question between Nestorians and Catholics. For the Nestorians want to distinguish the words said of Christ in such a way that those that pertain to human nature are not said of God, nor are those which pertain to divine nature said of man. Hence Nestorius said if anyone tries to attribute to the Word of God any sufferings, let him be anathema. But of any names that can pertain to both natures, they predicate what belongs to both natures, like the name 'Christ' or 'lord'. Hence they conceded that Christ was born of a virgin and was eternal, but not that God was born of a virgin or that man was eternal.

But Catholics held that such things said of Christ, whether according to the divine or human nature, can be said of both God and man. Hence Cyril said, if anyone divides between two persons or substances, that is, hypostases, what is said in the Gospels and Apostolic writings or what is said of Christ by the saints, or by Christ of himself, and thinks that some of these should be applied to the man, others reserved for the Word alone, let him be anathema. The reason is this: since there is the same subject of both natures, the name of each nature stands for the subject. Therefore, whether he is called man or God it is the hypostasis of the divine and human nature that is meant, and the things of human nature can be said of God.

But note that in a proposition in which something is predicated of something else, we pay attention not only to that of which the predicate is said, but also to that which is predicated of it. Therefore, although the things that are predicated of Christ are not divided, they are distinguished with respect to that according to which both are predicated. For those things which are of the divine nature, are predicated of Christ according to the divine nature, and those things which are of human nature are predicated of him according to human nature. Hence Augustine says in *On the Trinity* 1.11, we distinguish what in Scripture sounds to be according to the form of God from that which is according to the form of the servant. And later: what on account of the one and what on account of the other the prudent, diligent and pious reader understands.

Ad 1. It should be said that it is impossible for opposites to be predicated of the same thing in the same sense, but nothing prevents this being done according to different senses. And in this way, opposites are predicated of Christ, not according to the same, but according to different, natures.

Ad 2. It should be said that if things pertaining to defect are attributed to God according to the divine nature, it would be blasphemy, as amounting to the diminution of his divine honour, but it does no injury to God if they are attributed to him according to the assumed nature. Hence in some sermon at the Council of Ephesus it was said: 'God does not think what is an occasion for man's salvation an injury, for none of the deprivations which he chose on our behalf does an injury to that nature which cannot be the subject of injury; he does what is proper to inferiors in order to save our nature. Therefore such deprivations and lowly things do not injure the divine nature, but effect the salvation of men. How can you say that the things which are the cause of our salvation were an occasion of injury to God?'

Ad 3. It should be said that to be assumed belongs to human nature not by reason of the subject, but by reason of itself. Therefore it does not belong to God.

Article 5: Can what is of human nature be said of the divine nature?

It seems that it can.

1. Things which pertain to human nature are predicated of the Son of God and of God. But God is his own nature. Therefore, those things which are of human nature can be predicated of the divine nature.

2. Moreover, flesh pertains to human nature. But, as Damascene says in *On Orthodox Faith* 3.6, we say that the nature of the Word is incarnate, following the blessed Athanasius and Cyril. Therefore, by parity of reasoning, it seems that the things of human nature can be said of the divine nature.

3. Moreover, those things which are of the divine nature belong to human nature in Christ, such as to know the future and to have salvific power. Therefore, it seems that, by parity of reasoning, the things of human nature can be said of the divine nature.

ON THE CONTRARY:
Damascene says in *On Orthodox Faith* 3.4, speaking of the deity, that we do not say of it what is peculiar to humanity, that is, its properties, for we do not call the deity passible or creatable. But the deity is the divine nature. Therefore, those things which are of human nature cannot be said of the divine nature.

RESPONSE:

It should be said that what belongs properly to one thing cannot be predicated of another unless it is the same as the first, as risible does not belong to anything but man. But in the mystery of the incarnation, the divine nature is not the same as the human nature, although there is the same hypostasis of both natures. Therefore, what is of the one nature cannot be predicated of the other insofar as they are abstractly signified. For concrete terms stand for the hypostasis of the nature. Therefore the things that belong to each nature can be indifferently predicated of concrete names whether the word of which they are said makes us understand both natures, like the name 'Christ' in which is understood the anointing divinity and the anointed humanity; or divine nature alone, like the name 'God' or 'Son of God'; or human nature alone, like 'man' or 'Jesus'. Hence Pope Leo says in his Letter to the Palestinians, 'It makes no difference from which substance Christ is named, since the unity of person inseparably remains; the same is both wholly the son of man because of the flesh and wholly the Son of God because of the one divinity with the Father.'

Ad 1. It should be said that in divine things the person and nature are really the same, and by reason of this identity the divine nature is predicated of the Son of God. But the mode of signifying is not the same. Therefore some things are said of the Son of God which are not said of the divine nature, as we say that the Son of God is begotten, but we do not say that the divine nature is begotten, as was shown in Part 1.[1] Similarly, in the mystery of the incarnation we say that the Son of God suffered, but we do not say this of the divine nature.

Ad 2. It should be said that the incarnation implies the union with flesh rather than the property of the flesh. The two natures in Christ are united in one person, by reason of which union the divine nature is said to be incarnate and the human nature deified, as was said earlier.

Ad 3. It should be said that the things of divine nature are said of human nature, not as they belong essentially to the divine nature, but insofar as they are derived to human nature by participation. Hence the things that cannot be participated in by human nature, such as to be uncreated or omnipotent, are in no way said of human nature. But the divine nature receives nothing by way of participation from human nature. Therefore, those things which are of human nature can in no wise be said of the divine.

1. q. 39, art. 5.

Article 6: Is 'God was made man' true?

It seems to be false.

1. Since man signifies substance, to become a man is to come to be simply speaking. But 'God came to be simply speaking' is false. Therefore 'God was made man' is false.

2. Moreover, to become man is to be changed. But God cannot be the subject of change, according to Malachi 3.6: 'For I am the Lord and I change not.' Therefore, 'God became man' seems to be false.

3. Moreover, 'man', as said of Christ, stands for the person of the Son of God. But 'God is made the person of the Son of God' is false. Therefore, 'God was made man' is false.

ON THE CONTRARY:
There is what is said in John 1.14: 'And the Word was made flesh.' And, as Athanasius says in the Letter to Epictetus, 'When it is said, "the Word was made flesh", it is the same as saying, "he was made man".'

RESPONSE:
It should be replied that anything can be said to have become that which begins to be newly predicated of it. But to be man is newly predicated of God, as has been said, in that to be man does not belong to God from all eternity, but in time through the assumption of human nature. Therefore, 'God was made man' is true. But it is differently understood by different people, much as is 'God is man,' as was said above.

Ad 1. It should be said that to become man is to come to be absolutely in all those things in which human nature begins to be in a newly created subject. But God is said to be made man because human nature begins to be in the subject of divine nature which pre-existed it from eternity. Therefore, for God to become man is not for God to come to be absolutely.

Ad 2. It should be said that, as has been mentioned, to become implies that something is newly predicated of another. Hence whenever something is newly predicated of another with a change in it of which we have spoken, then to become is to be changed. And this belongs to everything which is said absolutely, for whiteness or extension cannot newly come to something unless it is newly changed to whiteness or extension. But things said relatively can be newly predicated of something without any change, as a man comes newly to be on the right without any change on his part because of the motion of that which comes to be on his left. In such things it is not necessary that whatever is said to come to be is changed, because this can happen through the change of something else. And in this way we say to God, 'O Lord, thou hast been made a refuge for us.' (Psalm 89.1) To be man belongs to God by reason of the union, which is a kind of relation. Therefore to be man is newly predicated of God without any change on his part, but by a change of human nature, which is assumed by the divine person. Therefore, when it is said, 'God was made man,' no change on the part of God is understood, but solely on the part of human nature.

Ad 3. It should be said that man stands for the person of the Son of God, not *sans phrase*, but as it subsists in human nature. And although 'God was made the person of the Son' is false, 'God was made man' is true, because it is united with human nature.

Article 7: Is 'Man was made God' true?

It seems to be true.

1. Romans 1.2–3 says, 'which he had promised beforehand through his prophets in the holy Scriptures, concerning his Son who was to be born to him according to the flesh of the offspring of David'. But Christ as man is from the seed of David according to the flesh. Therefore, man was made the Son of God.

2. Augustine says in *On the Trinity* that such was the taking up that made God man and man God. By reason of that assumption this is true, 'God became man.' Similarly this is true, 'Man was made God.'

3. Moreover, Gregory Nazianus says in the Letter to Chelidonium, 'God indeed was humanized, and man deified, or however otherwise we might name it.' But God is said to be humanized because he was made man. Therefore, man is said to be deified because he was made God, and 'Man was made God' is true.

4. Moreover, when it is said that 'God was made man', the subject of the making or union is not God, but human nature, which the word man signifies. But that to which the making is attributed seems to be the subject of the making. Therefore 'Man is made God' is truer than 'God was made man.'

ON THE CONTRARY:

Damascene says that we do not say that man was deified but that God was humanized. It is the same thing to become God as to be deified. Therefore, 'Man was made God' is false.

RESPONSE:

It should be said that this proposition, 'Man was made God', can be understood in three ways. In one way, such that the participle 'made' absolutely determines either the subject or the predicate, and in this sense it is false, because neither the man of which it is predicated was made nor was God made, as will be said below. And in the same sense 'God was made man' is false. But this is not the sense in which we are examining these propositions here.

In a second way it can be understood such that 'made' determines the composition, so that the sense is 'Man was made God,' that is, it was brought about that man is God. And in this sense it is true and both 'Man was made God' and 'God was made man' are true. But this is not the proper sense of these locutions, unless perhaps it is understood that 'man' does not have personal, but simple, supposition. For although this man was not made God, because this subject, the person of the Son of God, was God from eternity, but man, universally speaking, was not always God.

In a third way it is understood properly insofar as the participle 'made' expresses a becoming of man with respect to God as the term of the making. And in this sense, supposing that in Christ there is the same person and hypostasis and subject of God and man, as was shown above, this proposition is false. Because when it is said 'Man is made God', the word man has personal supposition; for God is not verified of man by reason of human nature, but by reason of his subject. But the subject of human nature of which it is true that it is God, is the same as the hypostasis or person of the Son of God, which was always God. Hence it cannot be said that this man began to be God or that he becomes God or that he was made God.

But if the person or hypostasis of God and man differ, such that to be God would be predicated of man, and conversely by some conjunction of subjects, either of personal dignity or affection or indwelling, as the Nestorians said, then by parity of reasoning it could be said that man was made God, that is, was conjoined to God, just as that God was made man, that is, was conjoined to man.

Ad 1. It should be said that in those words of the Apostle the relative 'who' which refers to the person of the Son ought not to be understood on the part of the predicate, as if something existing of the seed of David according to the flesh was made the Son of God, in which sense the objection is phrased. It ought to be understood on the part of the subject, such that the sense is that the Son of God was made for this – that is, for the honour of the Father, as the Gloss explains – existing from the seed of David, as if he should say, the Son of God having flesh from the seed of David for the honour of God.

Ad 2. It should be said that the word of Augustine should be understood in the sense that from the very assumption of the incarnation it was brought about that man would be God and God would be man. In this sense both locutions are true, as has been said.

Ad 3. The answer is similar, for to be deified is the same as to become God.

Ad 4. It should be said that the term placed as subject is taken materially, that is, for the subject, whereas the predicate term is taken formally, that is, for the nature signified. Therefore, when it is said that 'Man was made God' the becoming is not attributed to the human nature, but to the subject of human nature, which is God from all eternity, and therefore it does not belong to it to become God. But when it is said, 'God was made man,' the making is understood to terminate in human nature itself. Therefore, properly speaking, this is true, 'God was made man,' and this is false, 'Man was made God.' Just as if Socrates before was man and afterwards became white, this is true, pointing at Socrates, 'Today this man was made white.' But this is false, 'This white today became man.' However if some name signifying human nature abstractly were put in the place of the subject, in this way it could be signified as the subject of the making, for example, if it were said that human nature was made the Son of God.

Article 8: Is 'Christ is a creature' true?

It seems that it is.

1. Pope Leo says, 'By a new and unheard-of convention, God who is and was became a creature.' But it can be predicated of Christ that he was made the Son of God through the incarnation. Therefore, 'Christ is a creature' is true.

2. Moreover, the properties of both natures can be predicated of the hypostasis common to both natures, by whatever name it is signified, as was said above. But it is a property of human nature to be a creature, as it is a property of divine nature to be creator. Therefore both can be said

of Christ, namely that he is a creature and that he is uncreated and creator.

3. Moreover, the soul not the body is the principal part of man. But Christ by reason of the body which he took from the virgin is said, simply speaking, to have been born of the virgin. Therefore, by reason of the soul which is created by God, it ought simply to be said that Christ is a creature.

ON THE CONTRARY:

Ambrose says in *On Faith* 1.16, 'Christ was not made by edict, was he? Or created on command?' As if he should say, no. Hence he asks how can a creature be in God. But the God of nature is simple, not conjoined. Therefore it is not to be conceded that Christ is a creature.

RESPONSE:

It should be said that, as Jerome remarks, from words spoken carelessly, heresy results. Hence we should not have even words in common with heretics lest we seem to approve their error. The Arian heretics said that Christ was a creature and less than the Father, not only by reason of human nature but also by reason of the divine person. Therefore, it ought not to be said absolutely that Christ is a creature or less than the Father, but with an addition, namely according to human nature. Those things which cannot be thought to belong to a divine person in himself can be said absolutely of Christ by reason of human nature, as we say simply that Christ suffered, died and was buried. Just as in bodily and human things, things of which it can be doubted whether they belong to the whole or to a part, if they are in some part, we do not attribute to the whole simply, that is, without addition, for we do not say that an Ethiopian is white, but that he is white as to his teeth. But we say without addition that he is grey because this can only belong to him because of his hair.

Ad 1. It should be said that sometimes the holy doctors for the sake of brevity omit the addition and use the name of the creature of Christ. But this is understood in what they say.

Ad 2. It should be said that all the properties of human nature, like those of the divine, can in some wise be said of Christ. Hence Damascene says that Christ, who is called God and man, is both creatable and uncreatable, and divisible and indivisible. But when there is doubt as to the nature of which they are said, they are not to be said without qualification. Hence afterwards he adds that one hypostasis, namely of Christ, is uncreated as to deity, and created as to humanity. Just so

THE LOGIC OF THE INCARNATION

conversely it ought not to be said without qualification that Christ is incorporeal or impassible, for we should avoid the error of the Manicheans who held that Christ did not have a true body nor did he truly suffer, but it should be said with the qualification that Christ as to deity is incorporeal and impassible.

Ad 3. It should be said that there can be no doubt that being born of the virgin belongs to the person of the Son of God, as it can be of creation. Therefore, the reason is not the same in both cases.

Article 9: Did 'This man' – indicating Christ – 'come to be'?

The answer seems to be yes.

1. Augustine says in his commentary on John that before the world existed, not only did we not exist but neither did that mediator between God and man, the man Jesus Christ. But that which did not always exist, begins to be. Therefore this man – pointing to Christ – began to be.

2. Moreover, Christ began to be man. But to be a man is to be simply speaking. Therefore he began to be simply speaking.

3. Moreover, man implies a subject of human nature. But Christ was not always a subject of human nature. Therefore, that man began to exist.

ON THE CONTRARY:
There is what is said in Hebrews 13.8, 'Jesus Christ is the same, yesterday and today, yes, and for ever.'

RESPONSE:
It should be replied that we ought not to say that this man, indicating Christ, began to be without some qualification. And this for two reasons. First, because the locution is simply false according to the teaching of the Catholic faith whereby we posit in Christ one subject and one hypostasis, just as one person. Given that, when it is said 'this man' (indicating Christ), an eternal subject is designated, and it is repugnant to say that his eternity began to be. Hence 'This man began to be' is false. Nor does it count that beginning to be belongs to human nature, which is signified by the word 'man', because the term in the subject position is not taken formally for the nature, but rather materially for the subject, as has been said.

Second, because, even if it were true, it ought not to be used without qualification in order to avoid the heresy of Arius who, just as he attributed to the Son of God that he was a creature and less than the Father, so he attributed to him that he began to be, saying that there was a time when he was not.

Ad 1. It should be said that this authority must be understood with a qualification, as if we were to say that the man Christ Jesus was not before the world existed – according to his humanity.

Ad 2. It should be said that with this verb 'began' the argument from lower to higher does not follow, for it does not follow from 'This began to be white' that it began to be coloured. And this because to begin implies to be now and not before, but it does not follow from 'This was not white before' that therefore it was not coloured. But to be simply speaking is higher than to be a man. Hence it does not follow from 'Christ began to be man' that therefore he began to be.

Ad 3. It should be said that the word 'man' insofar as it is taken for Christ, although it signifies human nature, which begins to be, stands for the eternal subject which does not begin to be. Therefore, insofar as it is in the subject position, it is taken for the subject, and insofar as it is in the predicate position it refers to the nature. That is why this is false: 'The man Christ began to be' and this is true: 'Christ began to be man.'

Article 10: Is 'Christ insofar as he is man is a creature or began to be' true?

This seems false.

1. Nothing in Christ is created except human nature. But 'Christ, as man, is human nature' is false. Therefore this too is false: 'Christ, as man, is a creature.'

2. Moreover, the predicate is rather predicated of the term in the reduplicative position than of the subject of the proposition itself, just as, if it is said, 'Body, insofar as it is coloured, is visible,' it follows that the coloured is visible. But the following ought not to be absolutely conceded: 'The man Christ is a creature.' Therefore, neither should this be: 'Christ, insofar as he is a man, is a creature.'

3. Moreover, whatever is predicated of whatever man insofar as he is a man is predicated of him as such and simply, for 'as such' is the same as 'insofar as it is', as is said in *Metaphysics* 5. But this is false: 'Christ

as such and simply is a creature.' Therefore this is also false: 'Christ, insofar as he is a man, is a creature.'

ON THE CONTRARY:

Everything that is is either the creator or a creature. But this is false: 'Christ, insofar as he is a man, is creator.' Therefore this is true: 'Christ, insofar as he is a man, is a creature.'

RESPONSE:

It should be said that when we say, 'Christ insofar as he is man', the word 'man' can be taken in reduplication either by reason of the subject or by reason of the nature. If it is taken again by reason of the subject, since the subject of human nature in Christ is eternal and uncreated, this will be false: 'Christ, insofar as he is a man, is a creature.' But if it is taken again by reason of human nature, then it is true, because by reason of human nature, or according to human nature, it belongs to him to be created, as was said above.

But it should be known that a name so taken again in reduplication is more properly understood as the nature than as the subject, for it is taken again with the force of a predicate which is understood formally: it is the same to say 'Christ as man' as to say 'Christ insofar as he is man'. Hence this is rather to be conceded than denied: 'Christ, as man, is a creature.' But if something were added that referred to the subject, the proposition is rather to be denied than conceded, for example if it should be said: 'Christ, as this man, is a creature.'

Ad 1. It should be said that although Christ is not human nature, he is someone having human nature. But the word 'creature' is fashioned to be predicated not only of the abstract, but also of the concrete, for we say that humanity is a creature and that man is a creature.

Ad 2. It should be said that 'man' insofar as it is in the subject position looks rather to the suppositum, but insofar as something is added as reduplication it looks rather to the nature, as has been said. And because the nature is created, and the subject uncreated, therefore, although this ought not to be conceded simply, 'This man is a creature,' this can be conceded, 'Christ, as man, is a creature.'

Ad 3. It should be said that any man who is the subject of human nature alone, has existence only according to human nature. And, therefore, of any such subject it follows: 'If as a man he is a creature, he is a creature simply.' But Christ is not only a subject of human nature, but also of divine nature, thanks to which he has uncreated existence. Therefore it does not follow that, if as man he is a creature, he is simply a creature.

Article 11: Is 'Christ insofar as he is man is God' true?

It seems that it is.

1. For Christ is God by the grace of union. But Christ, as man, has the grace of union. Therefore, Christ, as man, is God.

2. Moreover, to forgive sins is proper to God, according to Isaiah 43.25, 'I am he that blots out thy iniquities for my own sake: and I will not remember your sins,' and according to Matthew 9.6, 'But that you may know that the Son of Man has power on earth to forgive sins . . .' Therefore, Christ, as man, is God.

3. Moreover, Christ is not universal man, but this particular man. But Christ, insofar as he is this man, is God, because in this man the eternal subject is designated which by nature is God. Therefore Christ, as man, is God.

ON THE CONTRARY:
What belongs to Christ as man belongs to any man. Therefore if Christ, as man, is God, it would follow that every man is God, which is patently false.

RESPONSE:
It should be said that the word 'man', put in reduplication, can be taken in two ways. In one way, with respect to nature, and thus it is not true that, as man, he is God, because human nature is distinct from the divine by a distinction of nature. In another way, it can be taken by reason of the subject, and then, since the subject of human nature in Christ is the person of the Son of God, to which it belongs as such to be God, it is true that Christ, as man, is God. However, because a term put in reduplication is more properly taken for nature than for the subject, as has been said above, therefore it is rather to be denied than affirmed that Christ, as man, is God.

Ad 1. It should be said that it does not belong to a thing to be moved to something and to be it in the same sense, for to be moved belongs to something by reason of matter or subject, but actually to be by reason of form. And similarly it does not belong to Christ to be ordered to this that he is God by the grace of union and to be God in the same sense. But it belongs to him first according to human nature, and secondly according to divine nature. Therefore this is true, 'Christ as man has the grace of union,' but not this, 'Christ, as man, is God.'

Ad 2. It should be said that the son of man has on earth the power to forgive sins, not by virtue of human nature, but by the divine, in which divine nature consists the power of forgiving sins by authority; but in human nature it consists instrumentally and ministerially. Hence Chrysostom, on Matthew, explaining this, says that he significantly spoke of forgiving sins on earth in order that he might show that the power of divinity is united to human nature by an indivisible union. Because, although he was made man, he remains the Word of God.

Ad 3. It should be said that when we say 'this man' the demonstrative pronoun pulls the word man towards the subject, and therefore this is true: 'Christ, as this man, is God' rather than this, 'Christ, as man, is God.'

Article 12: Is 'Christ insofar as he is man is a person' true?

It seems to be.

1. That which belongs to any man, belongs to Christ insofar as he is a man, for he is like other men, according to Philippians 2.7, 'being made like other men'. But every man is a person. Therefore Christ, as man, is a person.

2. Moreover, Christ, as man, is a substance of a rational nature and not a universal substance. Therefore, an individual substance. But a person is nothing other than an individual substance of a rational nature, as Boethius says in *On the Two Natures*. Therefore Christ, as man, is a person.

3. Moreover, Christ, as man, is a being of human nature, and a subject and hypostasis of that nature. But every hypostasis and subject and thing of human nature is a person. Therefore, Christ, as man, is a person.

ON THE CONTRARY:
Christ as man is not an eternal person. Therefore, if, as man, he is a person, it would follow that there are two persons in Christ, one temporal and the other eternal. Which is erroneous, as was said above.

RESPONSE:
It should be said, as was argued above, that this word 'man', in the reduplicative position, can be taken either for the subject or for the nature. Therefore, when it is said that Christ, as man, is a person, if it is taken for the subject, it is manifest that Christ, as man, is a person, because the subject of human nature is nothing other than the person of the Son of God.

But if it is taken for the nature, then it can be understood in two ways. In one way, that to exist in human nature belongs in each person. And in this way too it is true that everything that subsists in human nature is a person. In another way, it can be understood as meaning that Christ's proper personality is due to human nature and caused by the principles of human nature. And thus Christ, as man, is not a person, because human nature is not as such existing apart from the divine nature, which requires the notion of person.

Ad 1. It should be said that it belongs to every man to be a person insofar as everything subsisting in human nature is a person. But it is proper to the man Christ that the person subsisting in his human nature is not caused by the principles of human nature, but is eternal. Therefore, in one way he is a person as man, in another way he is not, as has been said.

Ad 2. It should be said that individual substance as put in the definition of person implies a complete substance subsisting of itself separately from others. Otherwise the hand of a man could be called a person since it is a kind of individual substance, but because it is an individual substance existing in another, it cannot be called a person. For the same reason neither can human nature in Christ which, however, can be called something individual or singular.

Ad 3. It should be said that, just as person signifies something complete and subsisting of itself in a rational nature, so hypostasis, subject and thing of nature in general signify substances subsisting of themselves. Hence, just as human nature is not as such apart from the person of the Son, so too it is not of itself hypostasis or subject or thing of nature. Therefore, in the sense in which this is denied, 'Christ, as man, is a person,' all the others must be denied.

30. *What is a Sacrament?* Summa theologiae, 3, 6 (1273)

The charge Christ gave his apostles before he left them was to go forth and baptize all nations. The rite of baptism is a visible sign – the pouring of or immersion in water – that symbolizes the cleansing of the soul from sin. Baptism is a sacrament and one retained by Christians who let all the other sacraments slip into oblivion. It is rightly held to be the sine qua non of the Christian life. Why should one person's pouring water on another and saying the prescribed words have the spiritual effect it is supposed to have?

Taken as such, water and words have no such power. But baptism was instituted by Christ as a means of making available the grace he had won by his suffering and death. The human minister is merely an instrument, a surrogate.

Thomas recognized seven sacraments which differ from one another in important ways. None the less, they share not only the name but an essence or nature, and in the following discussion Thomas sets out to state what that common nature of the sacraments is.

SUMMA THEOLOGIAE, THIRD PART, QUESTION 6

After considering matters pertaining to the Incarnate Word, we must discuss the sacraments of the Church which have their efficacy from that very Incarnate Word. First, we will discuss sacraments in general, then each sacrament in particular. With respect to the first, there are five topics to take up: what is a sacrament; the necessity of the sacraments; the effects of the sacraments; their cause; and their number.

Eight questions arise as to the nature of a sacrament: (1) whether the sacrament is a kind of sign; (2) whether every sign of the sacred is a sacrament; (3) whether a sacrament is the sign of only one thing; (4) whether a sacrament is always a sensible sign; (5) whether a definite sensible thing is needed for sacrament; (6) whether the meaning of a sacrament requires words; (7) whether definite words are required; (8) whether one can add to or subtract from those words.

Article 1: Is a sacrament a kind of sign?

It seems that it is not.

1. Sacrament seems to derive from *sacrando* as medicament from medicating. But this seems to belong to the genus of cause rather than of sign. Therefore, the sacrament belongs in the genus of cause rather than sign.

2. Moreover, a sacrament seems to signify something hidden, according to Tobias 12.7, 'For it is good to hide the sacrament of the king,' and Ephesians 3.19, 'to know Christ's love which surpasses knowledge'. But that which surpasses knowledge seems to be the opposite of a sign, for a sign is that which, besides the form it exhibits to the senses, makes something else come to be known, as is clear from Augustine in *On Christian Doctrine* 2. Therefore, sacrament does not seem to be a kind of sign.

3. Moreover, an oath is sometimes named a sacrament, for it is said in the *Decretals* 22.5 that youngsters not yet of the age of reason are not forced to swear and he who once perjures himself is not again asked to be a witness, nor does he come forward to the sacrament, that is, to the oath. But an oath does not belong to the genus of sign. Therefore the sacrament is not a kind of sign.

ON THE CONTRARY:

There is what Augustine says in the *City of God*, that the visible sacrifice is the sacrament of the invisible sacrifice, namely the sacred sign.

RESPONSE:

It should be said that all things that are ordered to something one, though differently, can be denominated from it, as from the health that is in the animal not only the animal which is the subject of health is denominated healthy, but medicine insofar as it restores health, diet insofar as it preserves it, and urine insofar as it signifies it. Therefore something can be called a sacrament either because it has in itself some hidden holiness, and according to this a sacrament is the same as a sacred secret, or because it has some order to this holiness, whether of cause or of sign or whatever other relation. But we speak now especially of the sacraments insofar as they imply the relation of sign. And on this basis the sacrament is put into the genus of sign.

Ad 1. It should be said that because medicine is the efficient cause of health, all the things denominated from medicine are said with reference to one first agent, and because of this medication implies some causality. But sanctity, from which sacrament is denominated, is not signified by way of an efficient cause, but rather in the manner of a formal or final cause. Therefore it is not necessary that sacrament always imply causality.

Ad 2. It should be said that this argument proceeds insofar as sacrament is the same as a sacred secret. But it is not only a secret of God, but also of the king, that is said to be sacred and a sacrament. According to the ancients, the holy and sacrosanct were whatever it was not licit to violate, such as the walls of the city and persons constituted in dignity. Those secrets, therefore, whether divine or human, which it is not licit to be violated by anyone making them public are called sacred and sacraments.

Ad 3. It should be said that an oath too has some relation to sacred matters, insofar as testifying is done by something sacred. And on this basis it is said to be a sacrament, but not for the same reason that we are now speaking of sacraments. Although 'sacrament' is not taken equivocally, but analogically, that is, according to different relations to something one, which is the sacred thing.

Article 2: Is every sign of the sacred a sacrament?

It seems that it is.

1. All sensible creatures are signs of sacred things, according to Romans 1.19–20, 'his invisible attributes – his everlasting power also and divinity – being understood through the things that are made'. However, not all sensible things can be called sacraments. Therefore, not every sign of a sacred thing is a sacrament.

2. Moreover, all the things that come about in the Old Law prefigure Christ who is the holy of holies, according to 1 Corinthians 10.11, 'Now all these things happened to them as a type,' and Colossians 2.17, 'These are a shadow of things to come, but the substance of Christ.' But not all the deeds of the fathers of the Old Testament or even all the ceremonies of the law are sacraments, but some special ones, as was shown in Part 2. Therefore, it seems that not every sign of the sacred is a sacrament.

3. Moreover, in the New Testament also many things are done as a

sign of sacred things, which, however, are not called sacraments, such as the sprinkling of holy water, the consecration of the altar, and the like. Therefore not every sign of the sacred is a sacrament.

ON THE CONTRARY:

The definition is convertible with the defined. But some define sacrament by the fact that it is a sign of a sacred thing, and this is seen on the authority of Augustine mentioned earlier. Therefore, it seems that every sign of a sacred thing is a sacrament.

RESPONSE:

It should be said that signs are given to men, who naturally go from the known to the unknown. Therefore, that is properly called a sacrament which is a sign of some sacred thing pertaining to men, such that that is properly called a sacrament, as we now speak of sacraments, which is a sign of a sacred thing sanctifying men.

Ad 1. It should be said that sensible creatures signify something sacred, namely the divine wisdom and goodness, insofar as they are in themselves sacred, but not insofar as through them we are sanctified. Therefore, they cannot be called sacraments as we are now using the term.

Ad 2. It should be said that some things belonging to the Old Testament signified the sanctity of Christ insofar as he is holy in himself. Others signified his sanctity insofar as through it we are sanctified, such as the immolation of the paschal lamb signified the immolation of Christ, whereby we are made holy. Such things are properly called the sacraments of the Old Law.

Ad 3. It should be said that a thing is named from its end and perfection. But disposition is not the end, perfection is. Therefore, things which signify a disposition to sanctity are not called sacraments – and it is from these that the objection proceeds – but only those things that signify the perfection of human sanctity.

Article 3: Is a sacrament the sign of only one thing?

It seems that it is not.

1. That by which many things are signified is an ambiguous sign, and consequently an occasion of deception, as is clear from equivocal terms.

But every fallacy ought to be removed by the Christian religion, according to Colossians 2.8: 'See to it that no one deceives you by philosophy and vain deceit.' Therefore, it seems that a sacrament is not a sign of several things.

2. Moreover, as was said, sacrament signifies a sacred thing insofar as it is a cause of human sanctification. But there is only one cause of human sanctification, namely the blood of Christ, according to Hebrews 13.12: 'And so Jesus also, that he might sanctify the people by his blood, suffered outside the gate.' Therefore, it seems that a sacrament does not signify several things.

3. Moreover, it was said that a sacrament properly signifies the end itself of sanctification. But the end of sanctification is eternal life, according to Romans 6.22: 'You have your fruit unto sanctification, and as your end, life everlasting.' Therefore, it seems that sacraments signify only one thing, namely, eternal life.

ON THE CONTRARY:

In the sacrament of the altar two things are signified, namely the true and mystical body of Christ, as Augustine says in the book on the opinions of Prosperus.

RESPONSE:

It should be said that, as was remarked, a sacrament properly so called is ordered to signify our sanctification. In which three things are to be considered, namely the cause itself of our sanctification, which is the passion of Christ; the form of our sanctification, which consists in grace and virtues; and the ultimate end of our sanctification, which is eternal life. All these are signified by sacraments. Hence a sacrament is a commemorative sign of that which preceded, namely the passion of Christ; and demonstrative of that which is effected in us by Christ's passion, namely grace; and prognostic, that is, foretelling, of future glory.

Ad 1. It should be said that a sign is ambiguous and gives occasion for deception, when it signifies many things one of which is not ordered to another. But when it signifies many things insofar as of them some one order is effected, then it is a certain and not an ambiguous sign, just as the term man signifies soul and body insofar as from them human nature is constituted. And in this way a sacrament signifies the three foregoing insofar as they are of one order.

Ad 2. It should be said that the sacrament, insofar as it signifies a sanctifying thing, must signify the effect which is understood in that sanctifying cause insofar as it is a sanctifying cause.

Ad 3. It should be said that it suffices for the definition of sacrament that it signifies the perfection which is form, nor is it necessary that it only signify the perfection which is the end.

Article 4: Is a sacrament always some sensible thing?

It seems that it is not.

1. According to the Philosopher in *Prior Analytics* 1, every effect is a sign of its cause. But just as there are sensible effects, so there are intelligible effects, as science is an effect of demonstration. Therefore, not every sign is sensible. But it suffices for the definition of sacrament that it be a sign of some sacred thing insofar as man is sanctified by it, as was said above. Therefore it is not required that a sacrament be some sensible thing.

2. Moreover, sacraments pertain to the reign and cult of God. But sensible things do not seem to pertain to the cult of God, for it is said in John 4.24, 'God is spirit, and they who worship him must worship in spirit and in truth,' and Romans 14.17, 'For the kingdom of God does not consist in food and drink.' Therefore sensible things are not required for sacraments.

3. Moreover, Augustine says in *On Free Will* that sensible things are least good and a man can live rightly without them. But sacraments are necessary for human salvation, as will be made clear below, and thus without them a man cannot live rightly. Therefore sensible things are not required for the sacraments.

ON THE CONTRARY:
Augustine says in commenting on John that a 'word attains an element and a sacrament comes to be'. And he is speaking there of a sensible element, namely water. Therefore, sensible things are required for the sacraments.

RESPONSE:
It should be said that divine wisdom provides for each thing according to its own manner, and because of this it is said in Wisdom 8.1, 'She reacheth from end to end mightily and ordereth all things sweetly.' So too Matthew 25.15, 'To each according to his particular ability.' But it

is connatural to man that he arrive at knowledge of intelligible things by way of the sensible. But a sign is that by which someone comes into knowledge of something else. Hence, since sacred things which are signified by the sacraments are spiritual and intelligible goods by which man is sanctified, it follows that the signification of the sacrament is fulfilled through sensible things, just as by the likeness of sensible things in divine Scripture spiritual things are described for us. Thence it is that sensible things are required for the sacraments, as Dionysius too proves in *On the Celestial Hierarchy* 1.

Ad 1. It should be said that a thing is chiefly denominated and defined by that which belongs to it first and of itself, not by what belongs to it by another. The sensible effect as such leads to knowledge of something else, as first and as such making things known to man, because all our knowledge takes its rise from the senses. But intelligible effects only lead to knowledge of something else insofar as they are manifested by something else, that is, by some sensible thing. Thence it is that what are first and principally called signs are things offered to the senses. As Augustine says in *On Christian Doctrine* 2, a sign is that which, over and above the species that it impresses on the senses, brings something else to our knowledge. Intelligible effects only have the note of sign insofar as they are made manifest by signs. And in this way some non-sensible things are said to be in a certain way sacraments, insofar as they are signified by sensible things, of which we will treat below.

Ad 2. It should be said that sensible things, considered in themselves, do not pertain to the cult of the kingdom of God, but only insofar as they are signs of spiritual things, in which the kingdom of God consists.

Ad 3. It should be said that Augustine speaks there of sensible things considered in their own natures, not as they are taken up to signify spiritual things, which are the greatest goods.

Article 5: Are determinate things needed for sacraments?

It seems not.

1. Sensible things are required in the sacraments for signification, as has been said. But nothing prevents the same thing from being signified by different sensible things, as in Sacred Scripture God is sometimes metaphorically signified by a stone, sometimes by a lion, sometimes by the sun, or other like things. Therefore it seems that different things can

converge in the same sacrament and definite things are not required in the sacraments.

2. Moreover, the salvation of the soul is more necessary than the health of the body. But in medicines which are ordered to the health of the body, one can be substituted for another if it is defective. Much more then in the sacraments which are spiritual medicines ordered to the health of the soul can one thing be taken for another when it fails.

3. Moreover, it is not fitting that the salvation of men be restricted by divine law, especially the law of Christ, who came to save all men. But in the state of the law of nature definite things were not required in the sacraments, but were assumed at will, as is clear in Genesis 28.20, where Jacob vows to offer to God tithes and peace offerings. Therefore, it seems that man ought not to be constrained, especially in the New Law, to the use of definite things in the sacraments.

ON THE CONTRARY:
The Lord says in John 3.5, 'Unless a man be born again of water and the Spirit, he cannot enter into the kingdom of heaven.'

RESPONSE:
It should be said that in the use of the sacraments two things can be considered, namely the divine cult and the sanctification of man, of which the first pertains to man with reference to God and the second conversely pertains to God with reference to man. It does not pertain to anyone to determine what is in the power of another, but only what is in his own power. Therefore, because the sanctification of man is in the power of the sanctifying God, it does not pertain to man to assume by his own judgement the things by which he will be sanctified, but this ought to be determined by divine institution. Therefore in the sacraments of the New Law, by which men are sanctified, according to 1 Corinthians 6.11, 'You have been washed, you have been sanctified,' it is necessary to use the things determined by divine institution.

Ad 1. It should be said that if the same thing can be signified by different signs, to decide what sign ought to be used for signifying pertains to the one signifying. But God is the one who signifies to us spiritual things by means of sensible things in the sacraments, and by verbal similarities in the Scripture. Therefore, just as what similitudes will signify spiritual things in certain texts of Scripture is determined by the judgement of the

Holy Spirit, so what things are taken to signify in this or that sacrament ought to be determined by divine institution.

Ad 2. It should be said that sensible things naturally have placed in them powers conducive to bodily health, and therefore it does not matter which of two having the same power one uses. But they are not ordered to sanctification by any power naturally in them, but only by divine institution. Therefore it was necessary that it be determined divinely which sensible things ought to be used in the sacraments.

Ad 3. It should be said that, as Augustine wrote in *Against Faustus* 19, different sacraments suit different times, just as different times are signified by different verbs, namely the present, past and future. Therefore, just as in the state of the law of nature men, with no exterior law being given them, were moved by interior instinct alone to worship God, so also by an exterior instinct were determined for them the sensible things that would be used in the cult of God. Afterwards however it was necessary for an exterior law to be given, both because of the obscurity of the law of nature due to the sins of men, and also for the more express signification of the grace of Christ by which the human race is sanctified. Therefore, it was also necessary that the things men would use in the sacraments be determined. The way of salvation is not constrained by this, because the things whose use is necessary in the sacraments are either commonly had or can be had with a slight effort.

Article 6: Are words needed for the meaning of sacraments?

It seems that they are not.

1. Augustine asks in *Against Faustus*, what are certain bodily sacraments if not, as it were, visible words? Thus it would seem that to add words to the sensible things in the sacraments would be to add words to words. But that is superfluous. Therefore words are not needed along with sensible things in the sacraments.

2. Moreover, a sacrament is something one. But it does not seem possible that something one can be made of things of different genera. Therefore, since sensible things and words are of different genera, because sensible things are from nature and words from reason, it seems that words are not needed in the sacraments along with sensible things.

3. Moreover, the sacraments of the New Law replace those of the Old Law because these are instituted when the latter have been taken away,

as Augustine says in *Against Faustus*. But in the sacraments of the Old Law no form of words was required. Therefore, neither are words required in the sacraments of the New Law.

ON THE CONTRARY:

The Apostle says in Ephesians 5.25–6, 'Christ also loved the Church, and delivered himself up for her, that he might sanctify her, cleansing her in the bath of water by means of the word.' And Augustine says in commenting on John, 'The word attained the element and a sacrament came to be.'

RESPONSE:

It should be said that sacraments, as has been pointed out, are offered for the sanctification of men as certain signs. They can be considered in three ways, each of which underscores that words are joined to sensible things. First, they can be considered on the part of the sanctifying cause, which is the Incarnate Word, to whom the sacrament in a certain way conforms, in that the word is added to the sensible thing, just as in the mystery of the incarnation the Word of God was united to sensible flesh.

Second, the sacraments can be considered from the side of man who is sanctified, who is composed of soul and body, to whom the sacramental medicine is proportioned, which touches the body through the visible sign and by the word is believed by the soul. Hence Augustine says on John 15.3, 'You are already clean because of the word that I have spoken . . .'; 'Whence comes this great power of water that it should touch the body and cleanse the heart if not because the word makes it so, not because it is said, but because it is believed?'

Third, they can be considered on the part of the very sacramental signification. But Augustine says in *On Christian Doctrine* 2.3 that among men words take pride of place in signification because words can be differently formed to express different concepts of the mind, and because of this we can more distinctly express in words what we conceive with the mind. Therefore the perfection of sacramental signification required that the signification of sensible things be determined by certain words. For water can signify both cleansing, because of its wetness, and refreshment, because of its coolness, but when it is said, 'I baptize you,' it is made clear that we use water in baptism to signify a spiritual cleansing.

Ad 1. It should be said that the visible things of the sacraments are called words by a kind of similitude, namely insofar as they shared some of the power of signifying which is chiefly in words themselves, as has been said, and therefore it is not a superfluous doubling of words when words are added to visible things in the sacraments, because one of them is determined by the other, as has been said.

Ad 2. It should be said that although words and other sensible things are in different genera so far as the nature of the thing is concerned, they share the note of signifying, which is more perfectly in words than in other things. Therefore from words and things something one comes to be in the sacraments as from form and matter, insofar as by words the signification of things is perfected, as was said. Under things are included sensible acts themselves, such as washing and anointing and the like, because there is the same note of signifying in them as in things.

Ad 3. It should be said that, as Augustine says in *Against Faustus*, sacraments of present and of future things should differ. But the sacraments of the Old Law were announcements of the coming of Christ. Therefore they did not as expressly signify Christ as do the sacraments of the New Law, which flow from Christ himself and have in them some likeness of him, as was said. However in the Old Law they used certain words in the cult of God, both the priests who were ministers of those sacraments, according to Numbers 6.23–4, 'Thus shall you bless the children of Israel, saying: The Lord bless thee and keep thee,' as well as those who used those sacraments, according to Deuteronomy 26.3: 'I profess this day before the Lord thy God . . .'

Article 7: Are definite words needed in sacraments?

It seems that they are not.

1. As the Philosopher says, words are not the same with all. But salvation which is sought through the sacrament is the same for all. Therefore definite words are not required for the sacraments.

2. Moreover, words are required in the sacraments insofar as they are significant *par excellence*, as was said above. But the same thing can be signified by different words. Therefore definite words are not required in the sacraments.

3. Moreover, the corruption of anything changes its species. But some speak words corruptly and this does not impede belief in the effect of the sacraments; otherwise the illiterate and stutterers who confer the sacraments would frequently cause a defect in the sacraments. Therefore, it seems that definite words are not required for the sacraments.

ON THE CONTRARY:

The Lord spoke definite words in the consecration of the sacrament of the eucharist, Matthew 26.26: 'This is my body.' Similarly he commanded his disciples under a definite form of words, saying in Matthew 28.19, 'Go therefore and make disciples of all nations, baptizing them in the name of the Father, and of the Son, and of the Holy Spirit.'

RESPONSE:

It should be said that, as was pointed out, in the sacraments words are as form and sensible things as matter. But in all things composed of matter and form the principle of determination is from the form which is in its way the end and term of matter. Therefore a definite form is more important for the existence of the thing than determinate matter, for determinate matter is sought that it might be proportionate to the determinate form. Therefore, since in the sacraments definite sensible things are required, which are as matter in the sacraments, much more is a definite form of words required.

Ad 1. It should be said that as Augustine wrote on John, the word operates in the sacraments, not because it is said – that is, not according to the exterior sound of the voice – but because it is believed, according to the sense of the words which is held by faith. And here indeed the sense is the same for all, although not the same words with respect to sound. Therefore, in whatever language such a sense is expressed by words, the sacrament is perfected.

Ad 2. It should be said that although in some languages it happens that the same thing is signified by different words, it is always the case that speakers of the language use some of those words chiefly and more commonly to signify it. And such a word should be used in the signification of the sacrament. For just as among sensible things those are taken for the signification of the sacraments whose use is more common to the act through which the effect of the sacrament is signified, as men more commonly use water for bodily cleansing, by which spiritual cleansing is signified. Therefore, water is taken as the matter in baptism.

Ad 3. It should be said that he who defectively pronounces the sacramental words, if he does this purposefully, does not seem to intend to do what the Church does and then the sacrament is not perfected. If, however, he does this by mistake or by a slip of the tongue and it is a mistake that wholly removes the sense of the locution, the sacrament does not seem to be perfected. This is especially so when the defect occurs at the beginning of the formula, for example, if in place of 'in the name of the Father' were said 'in the name of the mother'. But if the sense of the formula is not completely taken away by such a mistake, the sacrament is none the less perfected. This is especially true when the defect is at the end, for example if someone said 'of the fathers and of the sons'.

For although such words defectively said signify nothing from the force of the imposition, they are taken as signifying from the use to which they are put. Therefore, although the sensible sound is changed, there remains the same sense. What is said about a defect at the beginning or end of the expression is caused by the fact that with us the variation of an expression at the beginning changes its meaning, whereas by and large a change at the end does not change the meaning. But in Greek there is variation at the beginning of words as well as in their endings. But the amount of defect in the expression ought to be taken into account. In both cases there can be a little defect that does not take away the sense of the words, and a large that does. But one of these more easily occurs at the beginning and the other at the end.

Article 8: Can anything be added to the words?

It seems not.

1. There is no less necessity in the sacramental words than in those of Sacred Scripture. But no one may add or diminish the words of Sacred Scripture, for it is said in Deuteronomy 4.2, 'You shall not add to the word that I speak to you; neither shall you take away from it.' And the Apocalypse 22.18, 'I testify to everyone who hears the words of the prophecy of this book, if anyone shall add to them, God will add unto the plagues that are written in this book. If anyone shall take away from the words of the book of this prophecy, God will take away his portion from the tree of life.' Therefore, it seems that no one may add or detract anything from the form of the sacraments.

2. Moreover, words are as form in the sacraments, as has been said, but in forms any addition or subtraction changes the species, as it does with numbers, as is said in *Metaphysics* 8.7. Therefore it seems that if someone should add or subtract from the form of the sacrament, it would not be the same sacrament.

3. Moreover, just as a definite number of words is required for the form of the sacrament, so a definite order of the words is required, as well as continuity of speech. Therefore, if addition or subtraction does

not take away the truth of the sacrament, it seems by parity of reasoning that neither would the transposition of words or even altered pronunciation.

ON THE CONTRARY:

In the form of the sacraments some things are put in by some that are not put in by others, as the Latins baptize under this form, 'I baptize you in the name of the Father . . .' but the Greeks under this, 'the servant of Christ is baptized in the name of the Father . . .' Yet both truly confer the sacrament. Therefore, it is licit to add to or subtract something from the forms of the sacraments.

RESPONSE:

It should be said that in all these changes that can happen in the form of the sacraments, two things ought to be considered. One indeed on the side of the speaker, whose intention is required for the sacrament, as will be said below. Therefore, if he intends by such addition or subtraction to introduce another rite which is not received by the Church, the sacrament does not seem to be perfected because he does not seem to intend to do what the Church does. Another consideration is on the side of the signification of the words. For since words operate in the sacraments because of the sense they convey, as has been said above, it is necessary to consider whether by such a change the fitting sense of the words is taken away, because thus it will be clear if the truth of the sacrament has been removed. But it is manifest that if something of the substance of the sacramental form is subtracted, the fitting sense of the words is removed and the sacrament is not perfected.

Hence Didymus said in *On the Holy Spirit* if someone so tries to baptize that one of the foregoing words is omitted, namely 'Of the Father and of the Son and of the Holy Spirit', he will fail to baptize. But if he subtracts something that is not of the substance of the form, such a diminution does not remove the fitting sense of the words, and consequently not the perfection of the sacrament, although it can happen that he who omits it sins out of negligence or contempt. With respect to addition, it also happens that something is added that is not corruptive of the fitting sense as it is if someone says, 'I baptize you in the name of the greater Father and of the lesser Son,' as the Arians baptized. Such an addition takes away the truth of the sacrament and it does not matter whether such an addition comes at the beginning, the middle or the end. If such an addition does not take away the fitting sense, however, it does not take away the truth of the sacrament, as if someone were to say, 'I baptize thee in the name of God the Father omnipotent, and of the only begotten Son, and of the Holy Spirit the Paraclete,' it will be a true baptism.

Similarly if someone were to say, 'I baptize thee in the name of the Father and of the Son and of the Holy Spirit,' it will be a true baptism. But perhaps if he should say, 'I baptize thee in the name of the Father and of the Son and of the Holy Spirit and of the Blessed Virgin Mary,' it would not be a baptism, because as is said in 1 Corinthians 1.13, 'Was Paul crucified for you? Or were you baptized in the name of Paul?' But this is true if it is so understood that one is baptized in the name of the Blessed Virgin as he is in the name of the Trinity by which the baptism is consecrated, such a sense would be contrary to the true faith, and consequently take away the truth of the sacrament. But if someone so understood what is added – 'and in the name of the Blessed Virgin' – not as if the name of the Blessed Virgin operated in the baptism, but as if her intercession is asked for the one baptized to preserve baptismal grace, the perfection of the sacrament would not be taken away.

Ad 1. It should be said that one may not add to the words of Sacred Scripture as to their sense, but with respect to the exposition of Sacred Scripture many words are added to them by doctors. But it is not licit to add to the words of Sacred Scripture as if the additions belong to the integrity of Sacred Scripture, for this would be the vice of falsity. Similarly if someone should say something is necessarily of the form that is not.

Ad 2. It should be said that words pertain to the form of the sacrament by reason of the sense signified. Therefore, any addition or subtraction of words that does not add or subtract from the proper sense does not change the species of the sacrament.

Ad 3. It should be said that if there should be such a corruption of words that the intention of the one speaking is interrupted, the sense of the sacrament is removed and consequently its truth. But a small interruption that does not take away the intention and understanding does not do this, and the same should be said of the transposition of words. Because, if they take away the sense of the locution, the sacrament is not perfected, as is evident in a sign of negation before or after. If however the transposition is such that it does not change the sense of the locution, the truth of the sacrament is not taken away; the Philosopher says that transposed nouns and verbs signify the same.

31. *The Exposition of the* Book
of Causes, *1–5* (1272)

This commentary was written in 1272. In the Disputed Question on
Truth, *Thomas attributes this work to Aristotle, but now in his Prologue
he off-handedly mentions a discovery that he was the first to make. The*
Book of Causes *was not written by Aristotle. Rather it consists of excerpts
from the* Elements of Theology *of Proclus, a Neoplatonist who flourished
around AD 500, making him a contemporary of Dionysius. Thomas's
discovery explains the character of his commentary.*

There is a constant referring of the propositions of the Book of Causes
*to the corresponding propositions in Proclus. Moreover, there is a regular
appeal to Dionysius, not only a Catholic but, in Thomas's estimation, an
author of almost apostolic authority. But there is more than this trinity
of authorities involved in Thomas's effort to understand this dense and
difficult book. Aristotle plays a key role in Thomas's appraisal of the
contents of the* Book of Causes.

*It is difficult to think of a book less congenial to Thomas's customary
mode of thinking. Were it not for the fact that Dionysius employed
a Platonic framework and Thomas was doggedly docile in trying to
understand him, he would have been ill-equipped to find his way through
the thicket of these excerpts. His prologue, setting forth the order of
learning the philosophical sciences, emphasizes the Aristotelian view that
was Thomas's own. The human mind is not capable of beginning with
what is ontologically first. We must rise slowly and cautiously from the
things of this world to defensible statements about immaterial things.
Epistemologically and linguistically, metaphysics is dependent on our
knowledge of material things and it is possible only after all the other
philosophical sciences have been learned.*

*The Neoplatonist proceeds as if what is first in reality is what we first
know. He sees human knowledge as following the declension of beings
from the First Being. The physical world is for him remote and foreign,
a far cry from the ineffable one.*

*The only way Thomas can find such a book as this philosophically
acceptable is by regarding it as the via* descensus *which complements and*

is made possible by the arduous via ascensus *which strives tow.
metaphysics as its goal. Thomas draws attention to the fact that sometim.
in the commentary he clarifies positions that he would not accept. But
this is not a disengaged reading. The frequent appeals to Aristotle indicate
that truth for Thomas was not Aristotelian or Platonic. If Neoplatonism
had truths to teach him, they must be compatible with those he had
already learned from Aristotle.*

Here is Thomas's explanation of the first five propositions.

EXPOSITION OF THE *BOOK OF CAUSES*

Prologue

As the Philosopher says in *Ethics* 10.7, man's ultimate happiness consists
in man's best activity which is of his highest faculty, namely intellect,
with respect to the most intelligible thing. Because the effect is known by
its cause, it is clear that the cause is in its nature more intelligible than
the effect, although sometimes effects are more known to us than causes
because we acquire knowledge of universal and intelligible causes from
particulars that fall under the senses. Therefore, it is necessary that,
simply speaking, the first causes of things should be in themselves the
highest and most intelligible. This is so because they are maximal beings
and maximal truths and thus the cause of essence and truth in others, as
is evident from the Philosopher in *Metaphysics* 2.1, although such causes
are less and later known for us.

Our intellect relates to them as the eye of a nightbird to the light of
the sun which because of its exceeding brightness it cannot perfectly
perceive. Therefore, it is necessary that the ultimate happiness of man
which is attainable in this life consist in the consideration of the first
causes, because the little that can be known of them is more desirable
and noble than all that can be known of lesser things, as is clear from
the Philosopher in *On the Parts of Animals* 1.5. But when this knowledge
is perfected in us, after this life, man becomes perfectly happy, according
to the Gospel (John 17.3): 'This is life eternal that they might know thee
the one true God.'

Hence the chief aim of philosophers was to consider all things in order
to arrive at knowledge of first causes. That is why they placed knowledge
of first causes last, in the final stage of life, and began first with logic
which treats the mode of the sciences, went on second to mathematics,

of which even children are capable, third, to natural philosophy which requires time for experience, fourth to moral philosophy of which the young are not suitable students, and finally they turned to divine science which considers the first causes of beings.

The intent of this book which is called 'Of Causes' is to determine the first causes of things. And because the word 'cause' implies a certain order and there is an order among causes themselves, he first formulates a proposition pertaining to the order of causes as a kind of principle of the whole work:

I.

Every primary cause is more influential on its effect than the secondary universal cause.

In manifestation of this he introduces a corollary that casts light on it by way of a sign; adding: when the secondary universal cause removes its power from the thing, the first universal cause does not. He makes a third remark in proof of this, saying: this is because the first universal cause produces the effect of the secondary cause more than the second universal does. From this he concludes what was fittingly put second. It is necessary that what comes first be the last to withdraw; for we see that what is first in composition is the ultimate in resolution. Thus the meaning of this proposition involves three things: first, that the first cause influences the effect more than the secondary does; second, the impression of the first cause recedes from the effect later; third, that it first advenes to it.

Proclus states these three in two propositions, the first in Proposition 56 of his book, to wit: Whatever is produced by secondary causes is also and more eminently produced by prior causes, since these are the causes of the secondary causes. The other he expresses in the following proposition, to wit: Every cause both acts prior to the caused and afterwards sustains many things. Having stated these three he goes on to clarify them, first by an example, second by an argument.

The example seems to pertain to formal causes where a cause is first to the degree that it is more universal. Thus, if we take a man, his specific form is found in this that he is rational, the form of his genus in this that he is alive or an animal, and beyond those is what is common to all, namely, existence. Clearly in the generation of one particular man, he is first seen to be in a material subject, then he is seen to be alive, and afterwards to be a man, for he is animal before he is man, as is said in

THE EXPOSITION OF THE *BOOK OF CAUSES* 789

On the Generation of Animals 2.3. Again in the process of corruption, he first loses reason but remains alive and breathing; second, he loses life although some being remains, because he is not corrupted to nothingness. Thus the example can be understood in terms of the generation and corruption of some individual.

And that is his intention, as is clear from what he says: therefore when the individual is not man, that is, according to the proper act of man, he is animal because there yet remains in him animal activity of motion and sensing, and when he is not an animal, there is existence alone, which remains in a completely inanimate body. This example is verified in the order of things, for existent things are prior to living things and the living to men, and if man be taken away animal which contains him is not removed, although if there is no animal, there is no man. And the same goes for animal and being.

When he says, 'and the first cause . . .' he proves the foregoing three by argument. That the first cause influences more than the second, he proves in this way:

> *Something belongs more eminently to the cause than to the effect.*

> *But the activity whereby the secondary cause causes the effect is caused by the first cause, for the first cause aids the secondary cause, making it operate.*

> *Therefore, the first cause is more the cause of the operation by which the effect is produced by the secondary cause than is the secondary cause itself.*

Proclus proves it more explicitly in this way:

> *Since the secondary cause is an effect of the first cause, it has its substance from the first cause.*

> *But a thing has the power or virtue of operation from that which causes its substance.*

> *Therefore, a secondary cause has its power and virtue of operating from the first cause.*

Since the secondary cause causes the effect through its power and virtue, it has the ability to be the cause of the effect from the primary cause. To be cause of the effect, therefore, is primarily in the first cause and secondarily in the secondary cause. But that which is prior in anything is 'more', because the more perfect is naturally prior. Therefore, the first cause is more the cause of the effect than the secondary cause.

Second, that the impression of the first cause recedes last from the effect, he proves where he says: 'and when the second cause is removed . . .' And he fashions this argument:

> *That which is more intensely in something, inheres it the more.*
>
> *But the first cause more intensely imprints itself on the effect than does the secondary cause, as has been proved.*
>
> *Therefore, its impression inheres more, and recedes later.*

The third point, namely that it advenes first, he proves where he says: 'and what is caused by the second cause . . .' using this argument:

> *The secondary cause does not act on its effect save through the power of the first cause.*
>
> *Therefore, the effect does not proceed from the secondary cause save through the power of the first cause; and thus the power of the first cause grants to the effect that it might be brought about by the power of the second cause.*
>
> *Therefore, it is first brought about by the power of the first cause.*

Proclus proves this by one middle term thus:

> *The first cause is more cause than the second cause and therefore has more perfect power.*
>
> *But insofar as the power of a cause is more perfect, it extends to more things.*
>
> *Therefore, the power of the first cause extends to more things than the power of the second cause.*
>
> *But that which is in more, is the first to advene and the last to recede. Therefore, the impression of the first cause advenes first and recedes last.*

We must ask of what causes this proposition holds true. In fact, when the question is referred to the kinds of cause, it is clear that it holds true of every kind in its own way.

The example given was in the genus of formal cause, but a similar argument can be made concerning material cause, for that which first undergirds as matter causes more proximate matter to 'stand under' materially, for example prime matter with respect to the elements, which are in a way the matter of mixed bodies.

He shows that both of these are true of efficient causes. For clearly, insofar as an efficient cause is prior, its power extends to more and its proper effect must be more common. But the proper effect of the secondary cause is found in fewer things, hence it is also more particular. The first cause itself produces or moves the cause that acts secondarily, which is why the latter comes to be a cause that can act. Indeed, the three things touched upon above are found primordially in efficient causes and are extended from them to formal causes. That is why he uses the word 'influence' and Proclus uses the word 'production' which express the causality of the efficient cause.

That it is extended from efficient to material causes is not yet manifest, due to the fact that the efficient causes we know do not produce matter and form; but if we should consider the universal causes from which the material principles of things proceed, it is necessary that this order be derived from efficient causes to material causes. It is because the efficacity or causality of the first and supreme cause extends to many that it is necessary that what first subsists in everything be from the first cause of all. Then the dispositions whereby matter is fitted to each thing are added by secondary causes. The same thing appears in a way in our activities, for in all artefacts nature provides the prime matter and then by prior arts the natural matter is disposed to accept the more particular effects of the artisan. But the first cause of all is related to nature as nature is to art. Hence what first subsists in the whole of nature is from the first cause of all and is fitted to singular things by the work of secondary causes.

In final causes too all the foregoing are manifestly verified, because all ends are desired for the sake of the ultimate end, which is universal, the desire for them coming after the desire for the ultimate cause and ceasing before it. This ordering too is reduced to the genus of efficient cause, for the end is a cause insofar as it moves the efficient cause to act, and this, insofar as it has the note of mover, belongs in a certain way to the genus of efficient cause.

If it is asked, however, of each genus of cause whether the foregoing are verified in all causes no matter how they are ordered, clearly this is not true. For causes are seen to be ordered in two ways. In one way, as such; in another, incidentally.

As such, when the intention of the first cause aims at the ultimate effect through all the intermediate causes, as the manual art moves the hand, and the hand the hammer which in turn strikes the iron, on which the intention of art bears.

Incidentally, when the intention of the cause extends only to the proximate effect, the fact that something else is then brought about by that effect is outside the intention of the first efficient cause. For example, when someone lights a candle, it is not part of his intention that the lighted candle should light another and that another. What is outside the intention we call incidental.

Therefore, this proposition is true of causes ordered as such, namely, those in which the first cause moves all the intermediate causes to the effect. But in causes incidentally ordered it is the reverse, for the effect which is as such produced by the proximate cause, is produced incidentally by the first cause and is outside his intention. That which is as such is more powerful than that which is incidental, and because of this he significantly says universal cause, which is a cause as such.

2

Having set down the first proposition as a principle of the whole subsequent treatise, here he begins to treat of the first causes of things. And this discussion is divided into two parts: first he treats the distinction of first causes; in the second their co-ordination or dependence of one on another – in Proposition 16 when he says, 'all powers to which there is no end . . .', he subdivides the first into two parts: first, he distinguishes the first causes; second he defines each of them – in Proposition 6, when he says, 'the first cause is superior . . .' The universal causes of things are of three kinds, namely the first cause that is God, then the intelligences and finally souls. On the first point he does three things: first, he distinguishes these three kinds, of which the first is undivided, because the first cause is one alone; second, he distinguishes the intelligences, in Proposition 4: 'the first of created things . . .'; third, he distinguishes souls, in Proposition 5, when he says, 'the higher intelligences . . .' He does two things with regard to the first: first, he distinguishes the three kinds mentioned;

second, he shows how they are united by a certain participation in the ultimate – in Proposition 3, when he says, 'every noble soul . . .'

Concerning the first he sets down this proposition: 'Every higher being is either superior to eternity and before it, or it is with eternity, or it is after eternity and above time.' To understand this proposition we must first see what eternity is, and then if the foregoing proposition is true.

The word 'eternity' implies a certain indeficiency or interminability, for the eternal is said to exist as it were outside limits; but, because, as the Philosopher says in *Physics* 7.3, in every motion there is some corruption and generation insofar as something begins to be and something ceases to be, it is necessary that in any motion there be some deficiency. Hence every motion is repugnant to eternity. True eternity therefore, since it implies indeficiency of being, also implies immobility. And, because the before and after in the duration of time come from motion, as is evident in *Physics* 4.11, therefore and thirdly, eternity must be without any before and after, wholly existing at the same time, as Boethius defines it at the end of the *Consolation* 5.6, saying, 'Eternity is the complete, perfect and simultaneous possession of everlasting life.'

Any thing without deficiency of being has immobility and if it lacks temporal succession can be called eternal, and in this sense the Platonists and Peripatetics called separate immaterial substances eternal, adding to the notion of eternity that the thing always exists, something inconsonant with Christian faith. For eternity belongs to God alone. However, we call other things eternal insofar as when beginning to be they obtain from God perpetual and indeficient existence without motion and temporal succession. Dionysius too, in *On the Divine Names* 10, says that the things which are called eternal in Scripture are not absolutely coeternal with God, hence eternity so understood some called *aevum*, which they distinguish from eternity taken in the first sense. But rightly understand, *aevum* and eternity differ only as *anthropos* and man do. For in Greek *aevon* means eternity just as *anthropos* means man.

These things being understood, then, it should be noted that this proposition is found as Proposition 88 in Proclus, stated thus: every 'be-er' or 'exist-er being' is either before eternity, in eternity, or a participant in eternity.' He says 'be-er being' to contrast it with movable being, as to be standing is opposed to being moved, which makes clear that what in this book is called superior existence is above motion and time. According to the books of both authors, existence of this kind is distinguished into three grades, but not quite the same reason is given by the two writers.

Proclus introduces this proposition on the basis of the presuppositions of the Platonists who, positing the abstraction of universals, maintain that something is prior in being to the degree that it is more abstract and universal. For it is manifest that the word 'eternity' is more abstract than 'eternal'; for by 'eternity' the very essence of eternity is signified, and by 'eternal' that which participates in eternity. Again, to exist as such is more common than eternity, 'for whatever is eternal is a being, but not every being is eternal'. Accordingly, separate existence itself is *before eternity*; that which is *with eternity* is sempiternal being; that which is a participant in eternity is, as it were, *after eternity*.

The author of this book agrees with the foregoing position on the first point. Hence he teaches that the being that is before eternity is the first cause since it is the cause of eternity. To prove this, he says that in it, that is, in eternity, there is an acquired, that is, participated, existence. And his proof is that those things which are less common participate in the things which are more common; but eternity is less common than being. So he adds: 'And I say that every eternity is being but not every being is eternity; therefore, being is more common than eternity.' In this way the author proves that eternity participates in being; but abstract being itself is the first cause whose substance is his existence; it follows that the first cause is the cause from which every always existing thing acquires sempiternal being.

But on the other two points the author of this book departs from the meaning of Proclus and rather advances views that are common to Platonists and Peripatetics. For he explains that the second level, which is being with eternity, is the level of the intelligence. Because eternity, as has been said, implies indeficiency with immobility, that which everyone agrees is indefective and immobile attains eternity totally. However, he points out that, according to the aforementioned philosophers, separate intelligence or intellect has indeficiency and immobility with respect to existence, power and operation. Hence Proposition 169 of Proclus is: 'Every intellect in eternity has substance, power and operation.' And on this basis he proves that intelligence is with eternity because it is in every respect wholly one, is not open to otherness either of power or of operation, nor can its substance be destroyed. Because of this he later says that it is 'made equal' with eternity, 'since it is as extended as eternity and is not altered', because eternity extends itself to every thing that is an intelligence.

He explains the third grade, that of soul, which enjoys a higher existence, above motion and time. A soul of this kind is closer to motion than intelligence is, however, because intelligence is not touched by motion either in substance or in its activity. The soul indeed exceeds time and motion according to substance, and touches eternity, but its activity touches on motion because, as philosophers proved, it is necessary that whatever is moved by another is reduced to something first which moves itself. According to Plato this is the soul that moves itself, according to Aristotle, however, it is an animate body whose principle of motion is the body. In both cases therefore, it is necessary that the first principle is soul and motion the activity of the soul itself. Because motion is in time, time touches the activity of the soul itself; that is what Proclus says in Proposition 91: 'Every participable soul has an eternal substance but an operation according to time.' Therefore, he says here that it is connected with eternity from below, connected to eternity in substance, but inferior because it participates in eternity in a lesser way than intelligence. He proves this through the fact that it is more susceptible to impression than intelligence, for the soul not only receives the impression of the first cause as does intelligence, but also receives the impression of intelligence. The more remote a thing is from the first, which is cause of eternity, the more weakly it participates in eternity. And, although the soul attains the lowest level of eternity, it is above time as the cause is above the effect, for it is the cause of time insofar as it is the cause of motion on which time follows.

He speaks here of the soul that the philosophers attribute to the celestial body and for this reason says that on the horizon of eternity it is below and above time. The horizon is a circle terminating vision and is the lower term of the upper hemisphere, but the principle of the lower. Similarly the soul is the ultimate term of eternity and the principle of time. Dionysius also agrees with this opinion in *On the Divine Names* 10, with this exception that he does not say that the heaven has a soul, since the Catholic faith does not teach this. He says that God is prior to the eternal and that, according to Scripture, some eternal things are also called temporal, but this ought to be understood according to the ways posited in Sacred Scripture. 'Between existent and made or generable things there are some which are in one respect eternal and in another respect participate in time.'

3

Because whatever is in the higher is in the lower according to some participation, after he distinguishes three grades of superior beings, one higher than eternity, which is God, another with eternity, which is the intelligence, and a third that is after eternity, which is the soul, he now intends to show how the third participates in what belongs to the first and to the second, saying: 'Every noble soul has three operations, for among its operations are the animal, intelligible and divine operations.' That he calls the soul noble can be understood from the words of Proclus who offers this as Proposition 201: 'All divine souls have three kinds of operation, some as of the soul; some, however, as receiving the divine intellect; some as conjoined to the gods without.' From which it is clear that by the noble soul he means the divine soul.

In evidence of which it should be remembered that Plato held that the universal forms of things are separate and subsist in themselves. And because, according to him, universal forms of this kind have a kind of universal causality over the particular beings which participate in them, he calls all such subsistent forms gods, for the name 'god' implies a certain universal providence and causality. Among these forms he posited this ordering, because the more universal a form the more simple it is and the more a first cause, for it is participated in by later forms, as if we were to say that animal is participated in by man, and life by animal, and so on. The ultimate in which all participate and which itself participates in nothing, is the separate One and Good, which he calls the highest god and the first cause of all things.

Hence in Proclus we find Proposition 116: 'Every god is participable,' that is, participates, 'except the One.' And because forms of this kind, which they call gods, are intelligible in themselves, but the intellect comes actually to understand through the intelligible species, under the order of the gods, that is, of the foregoing forms, they posited the order of intellects, which participate in the foregoing forms in order that they might be intelligent. The ideal intellect is also among such forms. But the aforesaid intellects participate in the forms in an immobile way, insofar as they understand them.

Therefore, under the order of intellect he places the third level, that of souls, which through the mediating intellects participate in the foregoing forms according to motion, insofar as they are principles of bodily motions by which the superior forms are participated in by bodily matter. The fourth level of things is the order of bodies between the intellects. He calls the higher intellects divine, but the inferior, though intellects, are not divine, because the ideal intellect which is god as such, according to them, is participated in by the higher intellects in both respects, as intellect and as god, but by the inferior intellect only insofar as it is intellect, and therefore the inferior intellects are not divine. The higher intellects issue forth not only as intellects but also as divine.

Similarly, since souls are applied to the gods by mediating intellects as closer, the higher souls are divine on account of the divine intellects to which they are applied or in which they participate, whereas the lower souls, being applied to the non-divine intellects, are not divine. And because bodies have motion through soul, it also follows that the higher bodies are divine, according to them, and the lower bodies not divine.

Hence Proclus says in Proposition 129: 'Every divine body is divine through a deified soul, every soul is divine because of the divine intellect, and every intellect is divine by participation in the divine unity.' And because they called the first separated forms gods insofar as they are in themselves universal, consequently they called intellects and souls and bodies divine insofar as they had some universal influence and causality over subsequent things in their own genus and in lower genera.

Dionysius corrects this position insofar as they posited different ordered separated forms which they called gods, such that goodness itself differs from existence itself and life itself and so on with the others. For it must be said that all these are essentially the first cause of all things itself from which things participate in perfections of this kind, and thus we do not posit many gods but one. This is what he says in *On the Divine Names* 5. 'It, namely Sacred Scripture, says that good is not different from existing or life or wisdom, nor do they produce many causes productive of other deities related as above and below, but all good processes are of one being.' He shows how this can be, by noting that, since God is his existence and the very essence of goodness, whatever pertains to the perfection of goodness and existence, belongs totally and essentially to him, such that he is the very essence of life and of wisdom and of virtue and of the others. Hence a little later he adds: 'God does not exist in a certain manner, but has existence in himself simply and as a boundless whole.'

The author of this book agrees with this. For he is not seen to introduce any multitude of gods, but establishes unity in God and distinction in the orders of intellect, soul and body. In this way it is called the noble soul, that is, the divine soul of the celestial body, according to the philosophers who held that the heaven is animate. For this soul, according to them, has a certain universal influence over things through motion, and thus is called divine in that manner of speaking whereby even men who have the universal care of public affairs are called divine.

Of this most nobly divine soul he says that it has a divine activity, and by way of explanation says that 'its activity is divine' in that 'it prepares nature', because it is the principle of the first motion to which the whole of nature is subject and it has this through a power participated in from the first cause which is the universal cause of all from which there passes to things a universal causality. Therefore, giving a reason for this divine activity proper to the soul, he says that it is the exemplar, that is, image, of the higher power, that is, the divine. The universality of the divine power is exemplified in this soul, such that, just as God is the universal cause of all beings, this soul is the universal cause of all the natural things that move.

As the second operation of the noble or divine soul he names intelligible activity which, as he himself explains, consists in this that it knows things insofar as it participates in the power of intelligence. Why it participates in the power of intelligence, he shows by saying that the soul is created by the first cause through the mediation of intelligence; hence the soul is from God as from first cause, and from intelligence as second cause. Since every effect participates in something of the power of its cause, it follows that the soul, which performs a divine activity insofar as it is from the first cause, performs intelligent activity insofar as it is from intelligence, participating in its power.

Some badly understand what is said here, namely that the first cause created the existence of the soul through the mediation of intelligence, thinking the author of this book holds that the Intelligences are creators of the substance of souls. But this is contrary to Platonic opinions. They posit the causalities of simple beings according to participation; it does not participate in that which participates, but in that which is through its essence primarily such. For example, if whiteness were separate, simple whiteness itself, not something participating in whiteness, would be the cause of all white things being white.

In this way the Platonists held that that which is existence itself is the cause that other things exist, and that which is life itself is the cause that other things live, and what is intelligence itself is the cause of all understanding. Hence Proclus says in Proposition 18 of his book: 'Everything giving existence to others is itself primarily that which it passes on to the recipients.' Aristotle agrees with this view when he says in *Metaphysics* 2.1 that what is first and maximally being is the cause of subsequent beings. It should be understood, therefore, that the very essence of soul, according to the foregoing, is created by the first cause which is its own existence, but it has consequent participation from later principles, such that for it to live it has from the first life and to understand from the first intelligence. Hence in Proposition 18 of this book it is said: 'All things have essence through first being and things are alive through the first life, and intelligible things have knowledge because of the first intelligence.'

This, then, is how he understands that the first cause created the existence of the soul by the mediation of intelligence. The first cause alone created the essence of the soul, but the soul might be intelligible because of the activity of intelligence. This meaning is clearly shown by the words which follow. 'Afterwards then,' he says, 'the first cause created the existence of the soul, placing it under intelligence,' that is, putting it under the activity of intelligence, so that intelligence acts in 'its own activity' to make it intelligible. He concludes that on account of this the intelligible soul engages in intelligible activity.

This is in accord with what was said in Proposition 1 that the effect of the first cause pre-exists the effect of the secondary cause and is more universally diffused. For existence, which is most common, is diffused into everything by the first cause, but understanding is not communicated to everything by intelligence, but only to some, presupposing the existence they have from the first.

This position too, if not wisely understood, is repugnant both to truth and to the view of Aristotle, who argues in *Metaphysics* 3.6 against the Platonists teaching this kind of order of separated causes that follows on what is predicated of individuals. Because it would follow that Socrates is many animals, namely Socrates himself and the separated man and also the separated animal: for the separated man participates in animal and thus is animal, and Socrates participates in both, and thus he is man and he is animal. Socrates would not be truly one if he were animal because of one thing and man because of another. Hence, since being intelligible pertains to the nature of soul as its essential difference, if it had existence from one thing and its intellective nature from another, it would follow that it is not simply speaking one thing. So it must be said that just as it has essence from the first cause, so too does it have intellectuality.

This agrees with the view of Dionysius mentioned above, namely that good itself, being itself, life itself, wisdom itself are not different but one and the same being who is God, who brings it about that things are and live and understand, as he himself shows. Hence Aristotle, in *Metaphysics* 12.7, significantly attributes to God both understanding and life, saying that he is life and intelligence, in order to exclude the aforementioned Platonic positions. This can be true in another way, if it is referred not to the intellectual nature, but to the intelligible forms that the intellective soul receives thanks to the activity of intelligences. Hence Dionysius says in *On the Divine Names* 4 that thanks to the angels souls become participants in illuminations emanating from God.

The third operation of the noble or divine soul is animal activity. And he explains that 'animal activity' consists in this that it 'moves body as such' and consequently 'all natural bodies', for it is the cause of motion in things. He gives the reason for this later. Because soul is lower than intelligence since it receives the impression of intelligence, it follows that it operates on things below it in a way inferior to the way in which intelligence acts on things subject to it, because the primary cause has more influence than the secondary, as is clear from Proposition 1. But the intelligence acts on souls without motion, namely insofar as it causes the soul to know, which is without motion. But the soul acts on bodies by motion, and that below it, namely body, does not receive the impression of soul except as moved by it. Consequently he assigns the cause why it should be said that the motions of natural bodies are from soul. For we see all natural bodies directly arrive at their fitting ends by their own activities and motions, which could only be insofar as they are directed by someone understanding. From this it seems that the motion of bodies is from the soul which impresses its power on bodies by moving them.

That the motion of the heaven is from soul is not supported by the faith. Augustine leaves this in doubt in the *Literal Commentary on Genesis* 2.18, but that it is from God directing the whole of nature and that the bodily is moved by God by the mediation of intelligences or angels, Augustine asserts in *On the Trinity* 3.4, and Gregory in the *Dialogues* 4.6.

Finally he concludes what he proposed, namely that the noble soul has the three operations mentioned. What he said of divine intellect and the divine soul agrees with the opinion of Dionysius in *On the Divine Names* 4 where he calls the higher angels divine minds, that is, intellects, by which deiformed souls also participate in the gift according to their power. But it receives divinity by union with God, not according to his universal influence on created things. That is more divine, because in God himself too that which he himself is is greater than what he causes in others.

4

After the author of this book distinguishes three levels of superior being, and shows how the whole is found participatively in the least of them, he now intends to show a distinction in the second level, namely of that being which is with eternity; for he sets aside the first level, which is of the first cause existing prior to eternity, because as has been said it is undivided.

In this he proceeds differently than he has with the others, for in all the others he set down a proposition and, after an explanation of it, proved it, but here, in the manner of dividing, he first sets out what is common. Second, he divides it, when he says 'And to be created, though it is one . . .' Third, he gives the difference between the parts of the division, when he says 'And everything that follows on it . . .'

That which is common to all the different intelligences is to be created first, concerning which he sets forth this proposition: 'The first of created things is existence and before it nothing else is created.' In his book, Proclus states this as Proposition 138, in these words: 'The supreme being is the first of all participants in the divine property and deiformed things.' The reason for this, according to Platonic opinion, is that, as has been said above, the more common a thing the more they held it to be separate and as participated in first by later things, and thus to be their cause.

They held that the one and good are the most common in the order of those things that are predicated, even more common than being, because good and one are found to be predicated of that of which they say being is not predicated, namely, of prime matter which Plato linked with non-being, not distinguishing matter and privation, as is said in *Physics* 1.9. Yet he attributed unity and goodness to matter insofar as it is ordered to form; for good is not only said of the end but of that which is for the end. That is why the Platonists said that the highest and first principle is the separated one itself and good itself, but after one and good there is nothing more common than being; and, therefore, the separated good itself they held indeed to be created, as participating goodness and unity, but they made it the first among all created things.

Dionysius, however, removes an order among separated things, as has been said above, positing the same order as even the Platonists among the perfections which other things participate in from the one principle, God. Hence in *On the Divine Names* 4 he puts good first among all the divine names and shows that its participation extends even to non-being, understanding prime matter by non-being. For he says: 'And, if it be fitting to say it, that good is above all existent things and even the non-existent desires it.' But he puts existence first 'among the perfections of God in which things participate, and that which is exists itself is older than that which is to be life itself, and that which is to be wisdom itself, and that which is to be of itself a divine likeness'. The author of this book seems to think in the same way. For he says that this is so because 'existence is above sense and above soul and above intelligence'. And how it is above these he explains by saying, 'And there is nothing wider', that is, more common, 'after the first cause', and consequently no effect prior to it; but the first cause is wider because it extends even to non-beings, according to what has been said. From what has been said he concludes that 'to be itself is made superior to all created things', because it is more common than the other effects of God and it is also 'more intensely united', that is, more simple, for the things which are less common seem to relate to the more common by way of some addition.

But it seems that it is not his intention to speak of any separated existence, as the Platonists do, nor of the existence commonly participated in by all existing things, as Dionysius does, but of the existence participated in by the first level of created being, which is a higher existence. And although higher being is in both intelligence and soul, yet in intelligence itself the notion of existence itself is considered to be prior to the notion of intelligence, and similarly in soul; on account of this he premisses that it is above soul and intelligence.

He gives as the reason why this existence participated in by intelligence is especially unified, its closeness to the first cause which is 'pure subsistent existence' and is a truly one and non-participated in which there is no plurality of essential differences. What is closer to the one as such is more unified as more participant in unity; hence intelligence which is closest to the first cause has an especially unified existence.

Then when he says: 'And it is not made many . . .' he gives the reason for the distinction that can be found essentially in intelligences. On this matter consider that if some form or nature were wholly separate and simple, manyness could not occur in it, just as, if there were some separated whiteness, it could only be one: now, however, there are many whitenesses which participate in whiteness.

Therefore, if the first created existence were abstract existence, as the Platonists held, such existence could not be multiplied but would be one alone. But because to be created first is to be participated in by the nature of intelligence, it is multipliable according to the diversity of participants.

This is what he says: 'And it indeed,' – namely the first created existence – 'is not made many,' that is, distinct in many intelligences, 'except because, although it itself is simple and there is not in created things anything more simple than it, yet it is composed of the finite and infinite.'

Proclus too mentions this kind of composition, saying in Proposition 86: 'Every be-er being is from the end and infinite.' Which he explains thus: 'Every immobile being is infinite according to the power of being; for if that which can endure longer has greater power of being, that which can endure infinitely is in this respect of infinite power.' Hence he said earlier in Proposition 86: 'Every be-er being is infinite, not in multitude or size but only according to potency,' namely, of existing, as he explains. But if something had the infinite power of existing and did not participate in existence from another it would be infinite alone, and such is God, as is said below in Proposition 16. But, if there should be something that had an infinite power for being with respect to existence participated in from another, the existence it participates in is finite, since what is participated in is not received in the one participating in its full infinity but particularly. Therefore intelligence is composed in its existence of the finite and infinite insofar as the nature of intelligence is called infinite according to its power of being, but the existence itself it receives is finite. It follows from this that the existence of intelligence can be multiplied insofar as it is participated existence: this is what composition of finite and infinite means.

Then when he says: 'And whatever follows on it . . .' he shows the difference between the members of the division, that is, between the many intelligences, and this in three ways: first with respect to their diverse perfections; second, with respect to the influence of some on others, there 'and the first intelligences . . .'; third, with respect to the effects of intelligences on souls and this in the following proposition which in some books is found conjoined with this comment, and begins: 'Higher intelligences . . .'

With respect to the first he does two things: first he shows the difference, second he removes a certain doubt: 'and because they are differentiated . . .' On the first point it should be considered that he assigns a twofold difference to intelligences, one having to do with their nature, the other with the intelligible species through which they understand. With respect to their natures it is necessary that they be placed in a given order. Their difference is formal not material; for they are not composed of matter and form but of nature, which is form, and participated existence, as has been said. In things which differ materially there is nothing to prevent there being many equal individuals, for in substances the individuals of the same species participate equally in the notion of the species; and in accidents too it is possible for different subjects to participate equally in whiteness. But in things which differ formally there is always an order. For if one considers carefully, he will find in all species of the same genus that one is more perfect than the others, as in colours whiteness and in animals man. And this because what differ formally differ according to some contrariety. For contrariety is the difference following form, as the Philosopher says in *Metaphysics* 10.9. In contraries one is always more noble and the other more vile, as is said in *Physics* 1.5, and this because the first contrariety is privation and habit, as is said in *Metaphysics* 10.4. That is why in *Metaphysics* 8.3 the Philosopher says that the species of things are like numbers whose species are diversified by adding one to the preceding. Manifestly a thing is more perfect insofar as it is closer to the most perfect one. Hence he gives this difference with respect to the nature of the intelligences, that that intellectual existence, which follows immediately on the first cause, is 'intelligence whose ultimate completion' with respect to created existence 'in power of being and in the other goods' following on it, is the intellectual existence which is lower in the order of intelligences and retains the nature and notion of intelligence but is beneath the higher intelligence in the perfection of nature and power of being and operating and all the goods and perfections.

With respect to the second difference which is taken from intelligible species, he supposes that the intelligences understand through intelligible species and that such intelligible species have greater breadth and universality than in lower intelligences, and he leaves this for now undiscussed, for it will be shown below in Proposition 10 which is concerned solely with this.

Then when he says: 'And because intelligence is differentiated . . .' he removes a certain doubt. Because it might seem false that intelligible species are different in higher and lower intelligences, because the thing understood is the same, he shows how such intelligible species are differentiated. And first he introduces an example; second he shows the difference: when he says: 'but though they are indeed diversified . . .'

On the first point it should be noted that, as was said above, the Platonist posited separated forms of things through participation in which intellects come actually to understand, just as through participation in them corporeal matter is constituted in this or that species. The same follows even if we do not posit many separate forms, but, in place of them all, put one first form from which they all derive, as was said above according to the opinion of Dionysius, which the author of this book seems to follow, placing no distinction in divine existence.

Therefore since intelligences are essentially different, as was said above, it is necessary that participated intelligible forms are diverse and different in different intelligences, just as participated forms in this sensible world are differentiated by the diversity of the individuals participating in the forms. Then when he says: 'Although they are indeed diversified . . .' he shows the diversity in the foregoing example. For the sensible forms participated in different individuals are individuated forms and are disjoined from one another by that disjunction whereby one individual is disjoined from another, such that two forms do not pertain to the existence of one thing but of diverse things. Intelligible forms are not disjoined because they are in diverse intelligences or intellects, because they are not thus made individual forms but retain the power of their universality insofar as each of them causes universal knowledge of the thing understood in the intellect in which it is.

The reason for this is apparent from what has been said. For since the forms of things, whether they stand as such and divided or whether they are united in one first, have the most universal and divine existence, it is manifest that the more they approach this most universal existence of forms the more universal they are. It was on this basis that he said that participated forms in higher intellects are more universal.

That which is least in things is corporeal matter, hence it receives such forms as particular without any universality. This is what he means when he says that although intelligible forms are diversified in diverse intelligences, they are not distinguished from one another as individuals in sensible things differ, because they have at one time one and manyness: one, on the side of universality, manyness, according to the diverse mode of participation in diverse intellects.

This totally excludes the notion of Averroes who wished to prove the unity of intellect by the unity of intelligible form; for he thought that if intelligible forms are diverse in diverse intellects, they are individuated and intelligible potentially not actually. The silliness of this is clear from the foregoing. When he says: 'And the first intelligences . . .' he states a second difference which follows on the first. For we find in every order of things that that which is actual acts on that which is potential; but the more perfect always relates to the less perfect as act to potency; therefore the more perfect of any kind are fashioned to act on the imperfect. Therefore, since the higher intelligences are more perfect in power and in other goods than lesser intelligences, it follows that, just as the first cause flows into the higher intelligences, so the higher intelligences flow into the lower and thus on to the least.

5

After he has shown in the previous proposition the differences among intelligences, the author here treats of the distinction of souls, the source of which he assigns to the differences of the intelligences which in a certain way cause them, according to his position. Therefore, what is here said about the differences of souls can be referred to the distinction of intelligences insofar as the differences among causes are manifested in the differences of effects. Hence in some copies this proposition is not stated as such, but is added to the comment on the previous proposition, which is also apparent from the epilogue he gives here, which is common to both propositions. This is the proposition: 'The first higher intelligences act on secondary subsistent forms, which are not destroyed so it is necessary to go back to them by way of others; second intelligences impress on separable forms, such as the soul is.' Proclus states two propositions corresponding with this one, namely 182: 'Every divine intellect is participated in by divine souls,' and 183: 'Every participated intellect is intellectual alone, and is participated in by souls neither divine nor made in the altering of understanding and ignorance.' In evidence of this proposition, three things are to be considered: first, concerning the impression of the soul; second, the distinction of souls; third, the difference between distinct souls.

Concerning the impression of the soul: first must be considered how it belongs to the soul to be impressed; second, that by which it is impressed. That it belongs to the soul to be impressed, appears manifestly when one considers the meaning of impression, for which two things are required: first that what is impressed should be existent in something; second, that it be in it not superficially according to extrinsic contact alone, but that it be intimate, as penetrating it in depth.

These two belong to the soul according to its proper notion. For it was said above in Proposition 3 that the proper activity of the soul is to move the body, because the activity of soul itself is below the proper activity of intelligence, which knows things without motion; but the principle of motion must be applied to the mobile because, as was proved in *Physics* 7.2, the mover and the moved exist simultaneously; hence to be in a movable body belongs to soul according to its proper notion. But the motion whereby the soul moves the body is the motion of a living body, which is not from an extrinsic agent, like violent motion or the motion of light and heavy bodies from the one generating, but is an intrinsic movement. Hence living things are said to move themselves. Therefore, the soul that moves the body must be in the body, united to it intrinsically, and on account of this it is said to be impressed.

If it be asked by what it is impressed, according to the opinion of the author of this book it is impressed by intelligence. For he says, 'Nor is it,' – namely the inferior soul – 'from the impression of second intelligence,' that is, of the second order of intelligences, 'which,' – that is, the second intelligence – 'follows lower created existence,' that is, in the lower part of the first created existence which is the existence of intelligences. Or, what he says, 'which follow the existence . . .' could be referred to soul, which is below the eternity of intelligence, as was said in Proposition 2. But this opinion has not up until now been ratified.

For we can speak of the impression of the soul in two ways: in one way, on the part of the soul impressed; in another, on the part of the matter on which it is impressed. And this distinction is found in any soul standing by itself, such as any intelligent soul, as will become clear below, because the existence of its substance does not consist totally in its union with corporeal matter, such as the existence of non-subsistent souls, like those of brutes and plants, so that in these the foregoing distinction is not necessary, because the existence of such animals is considered simultaneous on the side of the matter receiving and on the side of the soul itself.

Therefore, if we speak of a soul subsisting of itself, that is, any intellectual, whether celestial if the celestial bodies are said to be animate, as the author of this book supposes, or of the human soul on the side of the soul itself, then according to the roots of the Platonic positions which the author of this book often follows, such a soul is from the impression of intelligence because, as was said above in Proposition 3, Platonists hold that that which is common in a thing is caused by one principle and that which is proper to it by another lower principle. Therefore on this basis the soul subsisting in itself has its existence from the first cause, but that it should be intellectual and a soul it has from the secondary causes, which are intelligences. Hence, since it belongs to the notion of soul that it be impressed in a body, it will follow that this soul has it from intelligence that it should be impressed on such a body.

But because, as we showed above, this position has no truth and is contrary to the opinion of Aristotle, it must be said that such a soul is intellectual and a soul from the first cause from which it receives its existence, and consequently that it be impressed on a body. Therefore, on this basis, the soul is not from the impression of intelligence but from the impression of the first cause. If indeed we should speak of such a soul from the side of the susceptible on which it is impressed, then with respect to the soul of celestial body, if the heaven has a soul, there would be the same argument. For the nature of celestial bodies is in no way caused by intelligences but by the first cause from which it has existence.

But if we should speak of the human soul from the side of what is susceptible to it, then in a way it is from the impression of intelligence, insofar namely as the human body itself is disposed to be receptive of such a soul through the power of the heavenly body acting in the seed, by reason of which it is said that man and the sun generate a man. But celestial bodies, according to the doctors of the Christian faith as well, namely Augustine and Gregory, are said to be moved by spiritual creatures which are called angels or intelligences or separate intellects. It follows from this that intelligences contribute something towards the fact that the human soul is impressed on body from the side of what is susceptible to it. And in this way it can be said that the other souls which are not of themselves subsistent are due to the impression of intelligences and the celestial bodies.

The second remains to be considered, namely, the distinction of souls. And he gives the same reason for the distinction and multiplication of souls as he gave in the case of intelligences: for just as the existence of intelligence is composed of infinite and finite, insofar as its existence is not subsistent but participated in by some nature, by reason of which it can be distinguished as many, so too is it with the existence of soul. That is why he says: 'And souls are not multiplied except in the way in which intelligences are multiplied, which is that the existence of soul has a limit and for that reason is below the infinite.' He calls this nature that participates in existence 'lower', but also calls it 'infinite' because of its power to endure infinitely in existence. He calls participated existence itself finite because it does not participate in it according to the full infinity of its universality but according to the mode of the nature of the participant. But it should be noted that because the nature of intelligence is completely free of body, the distinction of intelligences is based on the level of the proper nature without reference to any body. It is of the essence of soul that it be impressed on body, and therefore the distinction of souls is based on a reference to animated bodies.

Hence, if animate bodies are of different species, the souls impressed on them will be specifically different, just as we would have to say if the celestial bodies were animate. But if animated bodies are of the same species, the souls impressed would be of one species and multiplied numerically alone, as is evident in human souls.

Then the third point is to be considered, namely the differences between distinct souls. He gives three differences, the first of which is taken from the diverse perfections of souls. For he says that souls, that is, the higher ones such as those of celestial bodies, which follow on intelligence, because they are ranked immediately after them, are complete, namely in the perfection of animal nature.

And he gives a sign of perfection, adding: 'of little falling away and separation'. For it was said above in Proposition 2 that the soul, insofar as it falls away from the perfection of intelligence, draws near to motion. Therefore, to the degree that souls are higher and closer to intelligences, the less they have of motion. For lower souls have motion not only insofar as they move body but also insofar as they are always conjoined to their bodies and are always intelligent and have motion because they move celestial bodies. Therefore he says that they are 'of little falling away' because they decline but little from the immobility of intelligence, and 'of little separation' because they are but little separated into diverse ones, such that they are found sometimes in this, sometimes in that – that is, with respect to the local motion alone of the celestial bodies. Lower souls are less than the higher souls because of less perfection and because of that slight falling away or separation.

The second difference is taken from the influence of souls on one another. For just as he said above that the first intelligences dispense to the second goodnesses that they receive from the first cause, so now he says that the higher souls pass on the goodnesses they receive from the intelligence above the lower souls. And the reason is the same in both cases: because that which is less perfect is perfected by the more complete, as potency by act.

The third difference is drawn from the side of effects. For just as he said of intelligences that the higher impress the more noble souls, so now he says of souls that the higher soul receiving power immediately from intelligence has a stronger impression because the higher cause always acts more forcibly, as was said in Proposition 1; therefore that which is impressed in the body by the higher soul is fixed and stands, that is, is firm and immobile, and its motion is equal, that is, uniform, and continuous, as is evident in the celestial body. The lower soul to which the power of intelligence pertains through the mediation of the higher soul makes a weaker impression on its body since it is a lower cause, and therefore that which it impresses on body, like life and the like, 'is weak', because of the passibility of the body with respect to the exterior agent, 'evanescent and destructible', as transmuted by an internal principle, because finally what the soul effects in body completely ceases to be.

Yet the body in a certain fashion participates in eternity, namely according to species, by way of generation. By attributing the corruptibility of human bodies to the weakness of the impression of their souls, the author of this book shows a better understanding than the Platonists who held that even the human soul has some incorruptible body forever joined to it.

It is clear, according to the opinion of our author, that when the human soul was perfected through its conjunction with the first cause, it can impress perpetual life on its body. Because of this the Catholic faith professes a future eternal life not only for souls but also for bodies after the resurrection. He concluded by summarizing what was said in the two propositions. What we ourselves have said of the souls of the heavens we said not as asserting its truth but as giving the opinions of others.

32. Exposition of Paul's Epistle to Philemon (1273)

Thomas commented on all the epistles of St Paul although not at one time or in one place. All of them are thought to have been done in his mature years, just before his return to Paris in 1269, some perhaps later, after his return to Italy. There is no telling just when his commentary on the shortest of those letters, the Epistle to Philemon, was written. I have chosen to include it, not simply because it is short, but because for all its brevity it conveys the style of his commentaries on Paul. Perhaps of most of his biblical commentaries.

As Thomas makes clear towards the end of this commentary, he does not think the sequence of the epistles as they have been handed down to us canonically represents their chronological order. Indeed, he sees the ordering of them as doctrinal, not just in general, but also in such a subset as the letter to Titus and those to Timothy. But the stress is on the internal development of the text, and Thomas proves himself to be a patient and thoughtful interpreter. The appeal to other biblical texts, sometimes surprising invocations from Exodus in the present case, is grounded in the conviction that the Bible as a whole is a coherent set of books. If there is any palpable rule of Thomas's reading, it is that nothing, nothing, in Scripture is idle or for no purpose so far as our instruction goes.

The Epistle to Philemon would doubtless be listed in a rare book catalogue as 'curious'. Paul imprisoned in Rome writes to Philemon about his runaway slave who has become a convert of Paul's in prison. This may seem to give Paul a claim on Onesimus, but the burden of the epistle is that Paul is sending Onesimus back to Philemon, and he pleads for a kind and welcoming reception. Philemon is a Christian, a mainstay of the church at Colossae, also a convert of Paul's and his host when he is in town. It is clear that Paul does not think that Christianity has abolished slavery. But his appeal to Philemon based on the common origin of all men and the fatherhood of God supplies fuel for the eventual argument against one man owning another.

COMMENTARY ON THE EPISTLE OF PAUL TO
PHILEMON

Paul, a prisoner of Christ Jesus, and our brother Timothy, to Philemon, our beloved and fellow worker, and to Appia, the sister, and to Archippus, our fellow soldier, and to the church that is in thy house: grace be to you and peace from God our Father and from the Lord Jesus Christ.

I give thanks to my God, always making remembrance of thee in my prayers, as I hear of thy charity and of the faith that thou hast in our Lord Jesus and towards all the saints. May the sharing of thy faith be made evident in full knowledge of all the good that is in you, in Christ Jesus. For I had great joy and consolation in thy charity, because through thee, brother, the hearts of the saints have found rest.

For this reason, though I am very confident that I might charge thee in Christ Jesus to do what is fitting, yet for the sake of charity I prefer to plead, since thou art such as thou art; as Paul, an old man – and now also a prisoner of Jesus Christ – I plead with thee for my own son, whom I have begotten in prison, for Onesimus. He once was useless to thee, but now is useful both to me and to thee. I am sending him back to thee, and do thou welcome him as though he were my very heart. I had wanted to keep him here with me that in thy stead he might wait on me in my imprisonment for the Gospel; but I did not want to do anything without thy counsel, in order that thy kindness might not be as it were of necessity, but voluntary.

Perhaps, indeed, he departed from thee for a short while so that thou mightest receive him for ever, no longer as a slave, but instead of a slave as a brother most dear, especially to me, and how much more to thee, both in the flesh and in the Lord! If therefore thou does count me as a partner, welcome him as thou wouldst me. And if he did thee any injury or owes anything, charge it to me. I, Paul, write it with my own hand: I will repay it – not to say to thee that thou owest me thy very self. Yes, indeed, brother! May I too make use of thee in the Lord! Console my heart in the Lord!

Trusting in thy compliance, I am writing to thee, knowing that thou wilt do even beyond what I say. At the same time make ready a lodging for me too, for I hope that through your prayers I shall be restored to you. Epaphras, my fellow prisoner in Christ Jesus, Mark, Aristarchus, Demas and Luke, my fellow workers, send thee greetings. The grace of our Lord Jesus Christ be with your spirit. Amen.   Epistle of Paul to Philemon

Preface

'If thou have a faithful servant, let him be to thee as thy own soul' (Ecclesiasticus 33.31). The wise man shows three things concerning master and slave, namely, what is required on the side of the servant; what ought to be the feeling of the master towards the servant; and what is the use of the servant. From the servant fidelity is asked, for in this he is a good servant, because what he is and all that he has he ought to give to the master. Matthew 24.45: 'Who, dost thou think, is the faithful and prudent servant . . .' And he says, 'if he is faithful', because fidelity is found in few. Proverbs 20.6: 'But who shall find a faithful man?' The master ought to feel towards his servant as a friend, hence it is said, 'as his own soul'. For this is proper to friends, that they are of one mind in what they will and what they do not will. Acts 4.32: 'Now the multitude of the believers were of one heart and one soul.' By which we are given to understand that there is a consensus of master and servant, when the faithful servant becomes a friend. As for his use, he should be treated like a brother, for he is a brother, both with respect to generation of nature, because they have the same author – Job 31.13: 'If I have despised to abide judgement with my man-servant'; Malachi 2.10: 'Have we not all one father? Hath not one God created us?' – and with respect to the generation of grace, which is the same for both. Galatians 3.27: 'For all you who have been baptized into Christ, have put on Christ. There is neither Jew nor Greek; there is neither slave nor freeman; there is neither male nor female. For you are all one in Christ Jesus.' Matthew 23.8: 'And all you are brothers.' These words are relevant to the matter of this epistle. For as it was shown above how spiritual prelates should relate to their subjects, so here he shows how temporal masters should relate to their temporal servants, and how the faithful servant to his master.

The occasion of the epistle is this. At Colossae an important Christian had a servant who secretly fled to Rome where he was baptized by the Apostle who now writes on his behalf. First he gives a greeting, followed by the narrative of the epistle. In the greeting he mentions persons who send their greeting and then the recipients and finally the good hoped for.

Therefore he says *Paul*, – a name to be revered by all the faithful who have been taught by him – *a prisoner*. 2 Timothy 2.9: 'in which I suffer even to bonds, as a criminal'. For now he is a prisoner in Rome, but *of Christ Jesus*, to give the reason for his chains. For it is highly praiseworthy to be imprisoned for the sake of Christ; for in this he is blessed. Matthew 5.10: 'Blessed are they who suffer persecution for justice' sake . . .' 1 Peter 4.15: 'Let none of you suffer as a murderer, or a thief, or a slanderer, or as one coveting what belongs to others. But if he suffer, as a Christian, let him not be ashamed, but let him glorify God under this name.' Acts 5.41: 'So they departed from the Sanhedrin, rejoicing that they had been counted worthy to suffer disgrace for the name of Jesus.'

And our brother Timothy . . . They are brothers with regard to perfect faith. Philippians 2.20: 'For I have no one so like-minded who is so genuinely solicitous for you.' He joins Timothy to himself, that he might more easily succeed, because it is impossible that the prayers of many will not be heard.

Then he mentions the persons greeted. And first the principal person greeted, then others, particularly the husband and wife whose house it is, to whom the servant is obliged. *To Philemon, our beloved and fellow worker, and to Appia, beloved sister* . . . Beloved, he says on account of her good works. John 13.34: 'This is my command, that you love one another.' Fellow worker, because he ministers to the saints. Proverbs 18.19: 'A brother that is helped by his brother is like a strong city.' Then he mentions *Archippus our fellow soldier*, who was so powerful at Colossae that all Christians were under his protection.

That is why he brings in the whole Church there, of which he was the bishop, writing in Colossians 4.17, 'And say to Archippus: "Look to the ministry which thou hast received in the Lord, that thou fulfil it."' And he calls Archippus 'fellow soldier' because all prelates are, as it were, spiritual soldiers of the Church. 2 Corinthians 10.4: 'For the weapons of our warfare are not carnal . . .' *And to the church* . . . He adds this in order to move him to hear plainly the expected good that is set forth, as was customary. Then when he says, *I give thanks to my God*, the burden of the letter begins. First, he gives thanks; then he makes his plea, *For this reason* . . .; finally, he concludes, *For I had great joy* . . .

Again, first he expresses thanks; second he gives the reason for his gratitude: *as I hear of thy charity* . . .; third, the reason why he thanks God: *For I had great joy and consolation . . . I give thanks to my God.* Colossians 3.15: 'Show yourself thankful.' Philippians 4.6: 'With thanksgiving let your petitions be made to God.' As if he said: I give thanks for past things in order that I might pray for future things. Therefore he says: *always making remembrance of thee in my prayers* . . . Philippians 1.7: 'Because I have you in my heart, all of you, alike in my chains.' Isaiah 49.15: 'Can a woman forget her infant, so as not to have pity on the son of her womb? And if she should forget, yet will not I forget thee.'

Stating the matter of his giving thanks and of his prayer, he shows what he asks when he prays for them. The matter of this was the needs and goods of Philemon, namely, both charity and faith. For without charity nothing avails and through it all things are had. 1 Corinthians 13.1: 'If I should speak with the tongues of men and of angels, but do not have charity, I have become as sounding brass or a tinkling cymbal.' Again, without faith no one can love God, because he does not truly know God. He makes no mention of hope, because it is midway between and is understood in the others. But in whom should they have faith and charity? *in our Lord Jesus.* 1 Corinthians 16.22: 'If any man does not love the Lord Jesus Christ, let him be anathema.' This is necessary, because from Christ more sweetly comes love for the members; because he who does not love the members, does not love the head. 1 John 4.20: 'For how can he who does not love his brother, whom he sees, love God, whom he does not see?'

And towards all the saints . . . Faith is based on doctrine insofar as it is manifested through Christ, 'because no one has seen God', John 1.18; and, 'You believe in God, believe also in me,' John 14.1. We have Christ, therefore, through faith. *Towards all the saints* can be understood in two ways. In one way, because from the faith they have in Christ proceed the prayers made for the saints. Or, faith consists principally in the divinity as it is announced by Christ, and not only by Christ, but also by the saints. Matthew 28.19: 'Go therefore and make disciples of all nations . . .' Therefore we ought to believe not only what was said by Christ but also what was said by the saints. Hebrews 2.3: 'For it was first announced by the Lord and was confirmed unto us by those who heard him.'

May the sharing of thy faith . . . This is shared in two ways. In one way, that it might be a sign. *Be made evident in full knowledge* . . . That is, so great is your charity, that the sharing of your faith . . . *I give thanks . . . always making remembrance* . . . That he might show what he seeks for him in praying. And the sharing of the faith can be understood in two ways. Either because in faith they share with all the saints, not having any new faith, like heretics. 1 Corinthians 1.10: 'That you all say the same thing.' Or, sharing, whereby you share good things with the saints, proceeding from faith. 1 Timothy 6.17: 'Charge the rich of this world not to be proud, or to trust in the uncertainty of riches, but in God, who provides all things in abundance for our enjoyment.'

Made evident in full knowledge . . . That is, that the good hidden in the heart become evident in good works. *In full knowledge of all the good that is in you* ... And this *in Christ Jesus*. James 2.18: 'Show me thy faith without works, and I from my works will show thee my faith.' Or, there are in the world many works which are good for men, and yet are not good for God, because they do not come about rightly. Proverbs 14.12: 'There is a way which seemeth just to a man: but the ends thereof lead to death.' Ecclesiastes 8.10: 'I saw the wicked buried: who also when they were yet living were in the holy place, and were praised in the city as men of just works.' But this is manifested through correct faith, when reward comes from God, who only rewards the righteous. Therefore he says *made evident in full knowledge*, that is, that this might be made evident, that you might know every good. Or that *all the good that is in you* might become known, which is the fruit of divinity. Exodus 33.19: 'I will show thee all good.' Wisdom 7.11: 'Now all good things come to me together with her.'

The reason he gives thanks is joy. And he says, *For I had great joy and consolation* ... 3 John 4: 'I have no greater joy than to hear that my children are walking in the truth.' For this joy alleviates anxiety. That is why he adds *consolation*. Psalm 93.19: 'When anxieties are increased in my heart, thy comfortings delight my soul.' He explains why, saying *because through thee, brother, the hearts of the saints have found rest*. Colossians 3.12 ... 'Put on, therefore, as God's chosen ones, holy and beloved, a heart of mercy, kindness, humility, meekness, patience.' 3 John 2: 'Beloved I pray that in all things thou mayest prosper and be in health ...'

Then when he says *For this reason*, he makes his plea. And first he states the confidence with which he asks; second, the petition itself, *I plead with thee ...*; third, his reason, *Perhaps, indeed ...* He says, *For this reason*, that is, because you so abound in charity, I have great trust in Christ Jesus, as if to say, not from me, but from the authority of Jesus Christ, in which faith I gave birth to you. Therefore, I could command you as a father both concerning your own and common matters. Otherwise a prelate would not have had the power to command what was for his usefulness, or the Church's, or of the good morals of the Christian religion. *Yet for the sake of charity I prefer to plead* ... Proverbs 18.23: 'The poor will speak with supplications ...' And why? *Since thou art such as thou art.*

There are two things on account of which one ought to plead. Because of old age. 1 Timothy 1: 'Do not reproach an old man, but ask him as a father.' Again, because of the honourableness of virtue, for where we are not deficient, we are equals. Ecclesiasticus 32.1, 'Have they made thee ruler? Be not lifted up: be among them as one of them.' Therefore he says, *since thou art such as thou art*, as *Paul, an old man*, as if to say, if you were a boy, I would demand this of you, but you too are old. You are of the same stage of life as I. Not that they are such and so much simply speaking, but in a way similar, which he says out of his humility. Romans 12.10: 'anticipating one another with honour'. Origen said that it is rare to find a useful teacher in the Church who is not old, thinking of Peter and Paul.

Having expressed his confidence in Philemon's goodness, here he states his request. And first he indicates the person on whose behalf he pleads; second, he concludes the request. The first is subdivided into two, because first by describing the person he shows that he has received him in spiritual birth; second, by a change of status. Therefore he says, *I plead with thee for my own son, whom I have begotten in prison, for Onesimus*, who is his present concern. And acquiring a son in default of time, he loves him more, as an old man loves sons born to him in his old age. Genesis 37.3: 'Now Israel loved Joseph above all his sons, because he had him in his old age.' This one [Onesimus] was given birth in chains. Second, there is the change in status. For if he had persevered in sin, he would not be worthy of leniency. Note that Paul says little and means much. For as Cicero taught, one ought to make little of one's own deed as much as possible. Thus the Apostle speaks lightly of his offence, saying, *He once was useless to thee*, that is, harmful in taking away your possession, but now, converted from evil to the state of virtue, he is useful for the service of God and man. 2 Timothy 2.21: 'If anyone, therefore, has cleansed himself from these, he will be a vessel for honourable use . . .' Proverbs 25.4: 'Take away the rust from silver, and there shall come forth a most pure vessel.'

Then when he says, *I am sending him back to thee*, he makes his request. First, he makes it, then he answers a question: *I had wanted to keep him here*. And so he says, *and do thou welcome him as though he were my very heart*. And this because I have seen him changed, the sign of which is, I send him back to thee. On the contrary, Deuteronomy 23.15: 'Thou shalt not deliver to his master the servant that is fled to thee.' I reply that is true when the master seeks him in order to put him to death. Therefore, he says, 'I did not want to do anything . . .' Philippians 1.7: 'I have the right to feel so about you, because I have you in my heart, all of you, alike in my chains.'

And he responds to a question, because it might be said if he is useful

to you, why do you not keep him unto death? And he gives the reason
for sending him back. First, he considers why he might keep him; second,
why he rejects that idea: *but I did not want to do anything without thy
counsel.* Therefore, he says to Philemon who, although he is a great man,
is accustomed to minister to the Apostle. Matthew 20.26, 'On the contrary,
whoever wishes to become great among you shall be your servant.' Out
of this confidence he proposed to keep him, so that in place of Philemon
he might minister to him. *I had wanted to keep him here with me that in
thy stead he might wait on me in my imprisonment for the Gospel.* This
was something especially needed since he was in chains for the sake of
Christ, for one is provided for when he suffers for his master. The reason
he rejected the idea was that he did not want to use another's property
without the owner's knowledge. Hence, *but I did not want to do
anything* . . . As if he said: if I should keep him, it would please you who
do not wish to resist but it would be a kind of force. But I did not want
that, indeed I wanted it to come about voluntarily. Exodus 25.2: 'Of every
man that offereth of his own accord, you shall take them,' that is, the
first fruits. 2 Corinthians 9.7: 'Let each one give according as he has
determined in his heart, not grudgingly or from compulsion, for "God
loves a cheerful giver."'

Then when he says, *Perhaps, indeed* . . ., he gives the reason why he
ought to receive him kindly, first, on the side of God, second, on the side
of the Apostle: *If therefore thou dost count me as a partner* . . .; third, on
the part of Philemon himself: *Trusting in thy compliance* . . . On the side
of God, because the providence of God often permits what is evil to come
about, in order that good might follow from it, as is clear from the sale
of Joseph, that he might free Egypt and the family of his father. Genesis
45.5: 'For God sent me before you into Egypt for your preservation.'
He says *Perhaps* because the judgements of God are incomprehensible,
Romans 11.33. And he says *instead of a slave*, that is, in place of a slave.
Matthew 23.8: 'For one is your master and all are your brothers.' And
not only yours, but mine in comparison to God, though he is a son to
the ministry.

How much more to thee, both in the flesh and in the Lord. This can
be expounded in two ways. First, as referring to the first origin of the
divine creation, and thus he is a brother. Deuteronomy 32.6: 'Is not he
thy father, that hath possessed thee, and made thee, and created thee?'
Malachi 2.10: 'Have we not all one father? Hath not one God created
us?' Again, by trust in God. Or it might rather be for the good of Philemon,
because he is close to him in the flesh, since that is how he is his slave,

because whatever he is bodily belongs to Philemon. Hence one is moved by charity for two reasons, by love which has its origin in the flesh, or by spiritual love. On the part of the Apostle, he first declares his friendship, under which aegis he wants Philemon to take Onesimus back; second, he offers to pay any damages; third he shows the function of receiving. Second, *If, therefore, thou dost . . .* Third, *Yes, indeed, brother!*

Therefore, he says, *If, therefore, thou dost count me as a partner, welcome him.* 1 John 1.7: 'But if we walk in the light as he also is in the light, we have fellowship with one another.' And he says *as thou wouldst me* because he is linked with me. Matthew 10.40: 'Who receives you, receives me.'

Second, he offers to make good any injury to Philemon, saying, *And if he did thee any injury or owes thee anything,* namely by leaving his service, *charge it to me.* As if to say, I will make satisfaction. Galatians 6.2: 'Bear one another's burdens.' And more, because he first offers to make it good; second, he shows that Philemon is in his debt, not of necessity but of will.

Therefore he says, *I, Paul,* as if to say, that you might be certain of restitution. *I write it with my own hand.* And this not out of necessity, because *thou owest me thy very self,* because I snatched you from eternal death, and thus he should do this for his liberator. Tobias 9.2: 'If I should give myself to be thy servant, I should not make a worthy return for thy care.' And he adds, *Yes, indeed, brother, may I too make use of thee,* as if to say, if you want me for a partner, take him back, and I will so use you, brother, that is, if you do it, you will fill my wishes with joy. For to make use is to use the fruit and thus it is to use for the useful, as I enjoy fruit. It implies the sweetness of the fruit; Song of Songs 2.3: 'And his fruit was sweet to my palate.' And the end, because the ultimate produce of the tree is its fruit. Therefore, to enjoy is properly to have something which is pleasant and final. Hence Augustine says that we enjoy thinking of things in which the will delights because of their sweetness. Again, to enjoy is to adhere to something for its own sake. Sometimes 'enjoy' and 'use' are taken commonly as implying enjoyment without the contrary. Ecclesiasticus 8.10: 'and to serve great men without blame'. Therefore he says, *May I too make use of thee,* because you are against me in nothing. And if in this you please me, there will be nothing in my heart concerning you that saddens me, and thus you will delight me. But if we take enjoyment as something final, then one does not enjoy man, but God alone. Contrary to this seems to be Wisdom 2.6: 'Come therefore, and let us enjoy the good things that are present: and let us speedily use the creatures as in youth.' Hence he adds *in the Lord*, that is, *May I, too, make use of thee* in the delight of God, rejoicing in the divine good that is in you, because his action is love, and the enjoyment of its effect, namely, charity. That is why he adds *console my heart*. A man is consoled spiritually when the desires of his heart are fulfilled. As if he said: fulfil the deepest desires of my heart. And not with respect to evil, but *in the Lord*, and thus the fulfilment of desire is good.

Then when he says *Trusting in thy compliance*, he provides a reason on the side of Philemon, and a commendation of his obedience. First he shows how he is confident in his obeying; second he adds to it something similar. Therefore he says, *Trusting in thy compliance*. 2 Corinthians 7.16: 'I rejoice that in all things I can have confidence in you.' 1 Kings 15.22: 'For obedience is better than sacrifices.' But he writes more cautiously because a man listens more closely to one he expects to see again than if he despairs. Therefore he says, *At the same time make ready a lodging for me too*. For it was his custom when he was in Colossae to stay in his home. Chrysostom asks what we are to make of this remark in which a poor man commands a rich man by letter from across the expanse of the earth to prepare a lodging for him. What would have to be prepared for one content with bread and cheap victuals? It should be said that it was not for the sake of the preparation of lodging that he says this, but to insinuate familiarity and love; in this way he will be prompt to obey. The Apostle therefore does not say this on account of external trappings but out of his devotion. *For I hope that through your prayers I shall be restored to you.*

Against this is the fact that he never returned to them but died in Rome, therefore his hope was dashed. I reply that the hope of the just is of two kinds, the chief of which is for his own good, and this is never dashed; another secondary hope is the proof of others, and this is sometimes dashed, because their merits are contrary, as the just man is sometimes not heeded by others. But was he deceived in his trust? It should be said that God alone knows the future; that is not for human knowledge, except the prophetic. And no prophet knows all the future events that concern himself. Only Christ did, because he did not have the Holy Spirit in a limited way. Thus Isaac the great prophet was deceived in Jacob. So it is not to be wondered at in an apostle if he does not know.

Then he ends his letter with a greeting, and first on the part of others, second on his own. He says, *they send you greetings*, and we read of them at the end of Colossians. But this can be doubted since he mentions Demas. How can this be, since he said in 2 Timothy 3.8, 'For Demas has deserted me, loving this world'? How, then, can he use his name?

It might be said that he returned to him, but this does not seem to be the case, because this letter was written after that to Timothy and here he says, *I hope that through your prayers*, and there he foretells his death, saying, 'The time of my deliverance is at hand.' Therefore it should be said that Paul was in Rome for nearly nine years, and this letter was written at the beginning, whereas the second letter to Timothy was written at the end of his life and then Demas weary of imprisonment deserted him. The letters of Paul are not arranged chronologically, because the letters to the Corinthians were written before the letter to the Romans, and this before the last letter to Timothy. That is placed first because of its matter, which is worthier. His own greeting here is the same one that ends the second letter to Timothy. Thanks be to God, amen.

33. Exposition of the Angelic Salutation
(Ave Maria) (1273)

When Thomas returned to Naples, he preached some Lenten sermons in 1273 in his native tongue. These sermons dealt with the Ten Commandments and with the Lord's Prayer. The sermon on the Hail Mary may very well date from the same period, although some would place it a year or two earlier, in Paris.

The original of these sermons has been lost and it is their Latin version that has come down to us. It will be noticed that the Immaculate Conception of Mary is not maintained by Thomas. This only became dogma, a matter of certain faith, in the nineteenth century. The Franciscans, notably Duns Scotus, were champions of the view that Mary had been spared any taint and effect of Original Sin from the moment of her conception. (Gerard Manley Hopkins in Duns Scotus's Oxford alludes to this.) Thomas's view on the matter provides for a pre-natal removal of the effects of Original Sin from the woman destined to become the mother of God.

The sermon is notable for its simple piety as well as for locating the Blessed Virgin firmly within the economy of salvation. It is an image to be cherished: the most learned man of his time preaching to simple Neapolitans on their shared faith. How many suspected that the portly friar in the pulpit would come to symbolize the age in which he lived, to become the paladin of his order and eventually the veritable icon of philosophy and theology? But then how many today, believers and non-believers, who turn to Thomas for the best presentation of positions with which they agree or disagree, imagine him in the pulpit pondering the import of those passages in Luke which became the Ave Maria?

ON THE ANGELIC SALUTATION

There are three things contained in this salutation. The first is due to the angel, namely, *Hail, full of grace, the Lord is with thee, blessed art thou amongst women*. Elizabeth, the mother of John the Baptist, contributes the second, namely, *blessed is the fruit of thy womb*. The Church adds the third part, namely, *Mary*, for the angel did not say 'Hail, Mary', but only 'Hail, full of grace'. And this name, Mary, according to its meaning fits the words of the angel, as will become evident.

Hail Mary, full of grace, the Lord is with thee.

With respect to the first, it should be known that in ancient times it was an especially great event when an angel appeared to men, so that men might show them reverence, for they deserve the greatest praise. It was written in praise of Abraham that he received angels hospitably and that he showed them reverence. But it was never heard that an angel showed reverence to a man until he saluted the blessed virgin, saying reverently, 'Hail'.

The reason why in antiquity the angel did not reverence man but man the angel is that the angel was greater than man, and this in three respects. First, with respect to dignity, since the angel is of a spiritual nature. Psalm 103.4: 'who makest the angels spirits'. But man is of a corruptible nature, hence Abraham said, in Genesis 18.27, 'I will speak to my Lord, whereas I am dust and ashes.' It was not then fitting that a spiritual and incorruptible creature should show reverence to a corruptible creature, namely, man.

Second, with respect to familiarity with God. For the angel is a familiar of God, as assisting him. Daniel 7.10: 'Thousands of thousands ministered to him, and ten thousand times a hundred thousand stood before him.' But man is like an outsider, put at a distance from God through sin. Psalm 54.8: 'Lo, I have gone far off, flying away.' Thus it was fitting that man should reverence the angel as one close to and familiar with the king.

Third, he was pre-eminent because of the fullness of the splendour of divine grace: for angels partake most fully of the divine light. Job 25.3: 'Is there any numbering of his soldiers, and upon whom shall not his light arise?' Therefore, he always appears with light. But men, although they partake something of the light of grace, it is but little, and with obscurity.

Therefore, it was not fitting that the angel should show reverence to man until someone should be found in human nature who exceeded the angels in those three respects. And this was the Blessed Virgin. In order to signify that she exceeded him in these three things, the angel wished to show reverence to her; hence he said, *Hail*. So the Blessed Virgin exceeded the angels in these three.

First, in fullness of grace, which the Blessed Virgin has more than any angel. It was to indicate this that the angel showed her reverence, saying, *full of grace*, as if to say: I will show you reverence because you excel me in the fullness of grace.

He says that the Blessed Virgin is full of grace with respect to three things. First, with respect to soul, which has every fullness of grace. For the grace of God is given for two reasons, namely, in order to act well, and to avoid evil. And with respect to these two the Blessed Virgin had most perfect grace. For more than any other holy person save Christ alone she avoided all sin. For sin is either original, and of this she was cleansed in the womb; or mortal or venial, and of these she was free. Hence the Song of Songs 4.7: 'Thou art all fair, O my love, and there is not a spot in thee.' Augustine in *On Nature and Grace* writes: 'The Blessed Virgin Mary excepted, if all the holy men and women were here before us and were asked if they were without sin, they would cry out with one voice, "If we should say we have no sin, we would delude ourselves and the truth is not in us."' Except for this holy virgin, I say, of whom for the honour of the Lord, when sin is spoken of, I wish no question at all to be raised. For we know that more grace was brought together in her to conquer sin from every side than she merited in order to conceive and give birth to him in whom there was no sin. Christ excelled the Blessed Virgin in this that he was conceived and born without Original Sin. The Blessed Virgin was conceived in Original Sin, but not born in it. She performed the works of all virtues whereas the saints exhibit particular ones, this one being humble, that one chaste, another merciful. Therefore they are given to us as examples of special virtues, for example, Blessed Nicholas as an example of mercy, and so on. But the Blessed Virgin is an example of all virtues. You can find in her the example of humility. Luke 1.38: 'Behold the handmaid of the Lord,' and later in verse 48, 'he has looked on the humility of his servant'; and of chastity, 'since I know not man', verse 34, and of all the virtues, as is fully obvious. The Blessed Virgin is thus full of grace both with respect to acting and with respect to the avoidance of evil.

Second, she was full of grace with respect to the overflow from soul to flesh or body. For it is a great thing for the saints to have enough grace to sanctify their soul; but the soul of the Blessed Virgin was so full that from it grace flowed into her body, in order that with it she might conceive the son of God. Thus Hugh of St Victor says, 'Because the love of the Holy Spirit burned so ardently in her heart, she was able to do wonders in the flesh, so that from it might be born God and man.' Luke 1.35: 'The holy child which shall be born of thee shall be called the Son of God.'

Third, with respect to its distribution to all men. For it is a great thing in any saint that he has so much grace that it suffices for the salvation of many, but when enough is had for the salvation of all the men in the world, this is the greatest, and so it is with Christ and with the Blessed Virgin. For in any peril you can obtain salvation from this glorious Virgin. Hence the Song of Songs 4.4: 'a thousand bucklers' – that is, protection against dangers – 'hang upon it'. Again, in every work of virtue you will find her ready to help. Therefore, she herself says in Ecclesiasticus 24.25: 'In me is all the grace of the way, in me is all hope of life, and of virtue.'

She is full of grace, therefore, and exceeds the angels in fullness of grace, and because of this she is fittingly called Mary, which means illumined in herself, hence Isaiah 58.11: 'and will fill the soul with brightness; and she will be a light for others,' meaning the whole world; and therefore she is likened to the sun and moon.

Second, she excels the angels in divine familiarity. As an indication of this, the angel said, *the Lord is with thee*, as if he said, therefore I show reverence to you because you are more familiar with God than I, for the Lord is with thee. Lord, he says, both Father and the same Son, something no angel nor creature has. Luke 1.35: 'And therefore the Holy which shall be born of thee shall be called the Son of God.' Isaiah 12.6: 'Rejoice and praise, O thou habitation of Sion: for great is he that is in the midst of thee, the Holy One of Israel.'

The Lord is with the Blessed Virgin differently than he is with the angel; he is with her as her son, but with the angel as Lord: the Lord the Holy Spirit, as in the temple, hence she is called the temple of the Lord, the sacred place of the Holy Spirit, 'who conceived of the Holy Spirit', Luke 1.35: 'the spirit of the Most High shall come upon you'. So it is that the Blessed Virgin is more familiar with God than the angel, because with her is the Lord Father, the Lord Son and the Lord Holy Spirit, that is, the whole Trinity is with her. Thus it is sung of her: noble resting place of the whole Trinity. To have said of her, *the Lord is with thee*, is the most noble thing that could be said of her. Rightly then does the angel revere the Blessed Virgin, because she is the mother of the Lord, and therefore mistress herself. The name Mary thus becomes her and in the Syrian tongue it means mistress.

Third, she exceeds the angels in her purity, for the Blessed Virgin was not only pure in herself, but she also obtained purity for others. For she was most pure with respect to guilt, because neither mortal nor venial sin could be imputed to this virgin, and she was equally pure with respect to punishment.

Three curses come to men because of sin: the first to woman, who will conceive with stain, bear with heaviness and give birth in sorrow. But the Blessed Virgin was immune to this, because she conceived without sin, bore in comfort and joyfully gave birth to the Saviour. Isaiah 35.2: 'It shall bud forth and blossom, and shall rejoice with joy and praise.' The second curse is the man's, who must earn his bread with the sweat of his brow. The Blessed Virgin was immune to this, because as the Apostle says in 1 Corinthians 7.32: 'He who is unmarried is concerned about the things of the Lord.' The third is common to men and women, namely that into dust they shall return. The Blessed Virgin was free of this, because she was assumed in the body into heaven. For we believe that after death she was raised up and borne to heaven. Psalm 131.8: 'Arise, O Lord, into thy resting place, thou and the ark of thy majesty.'

Blessed art thou amongst women.

Therefore she was immune to every curse, and thereby blessed amongst women, for she alone put away the curse and carried the blessing, and the door of paradise opened; therefore the name Mary becomes her, which is interpreted Star of the Sea, because just as sailors are directed to port by the star of the sea, so Christians are directed by Mary to glory.

Blessed is the fruit of thy womb.

The sinner sometimes seeks in a thing what cannot be attained there, but the just man attains it. Proverbs 13.22: 'The substance of the sinner is kept for the just.' Thus Eve sought in the fruit and did not find there all the things that she desired, but the Blessed Virgin finds in her fruit everything that Eve desired. For Eve desired three things from the fruit. The first what the devil falsely promised her, that they would be as gods, knowing good and evil. You will be, that liar said, like gods, as is read in Genesis 3.5. 'And he lies because he is a liar, and the father of lies.' Eve was not made like God when she ate the fruit, but unlike, because by sinning she receded from God her salvation and was expelled from paradise. But this is what the Blessed Virgin and all Christians find in the fruit of her womb, because by Christ they are united with and made like unto God. 1 John 3.2: 'When he appears, we shall be like him, for we shall see him just as he is.'

The second thing that Eve desired in the fruit was pleasure, because it is good to eat; but she did not find it and immediately knew that she was naked, and felt sorrow. But in the fruit of the Virgin we find sweetness and salvation. John 6.55: 'He who eats my flesh has life eternal.'

Third, the fruit of Eve was beautiful in appearance; but more beautiful is the fruit of the Virgin on whom the angels desire to gaze. Psalm 44.3: 'Thou art beautiful above the sons of men'; this is because he is the splendour of his father's glory.

Eve could not find in her fruit what no sinner can find in his sin. Therefore, what we desire, we should seek in the fruit of the Virgin. Here is a fruit blessed by God, because he has so filled Him with every grace that it comes to us by showing him reverence. Ephesians 1.3: 'Blessed be the God and Father of our Lord Jesus Christ, who has blessed us with every spiritual blessing on high in Christ.' By the angels, Apocalypse 7.12: 'Blessing and glory and wisdom and thanksgiving and honour and power and strength to our God.' The Apostle, Philippians 2.11: 'And every tongue should confess that the Lord Jesus Christ is in the glory of God the Father.' Psalm 117.26: 'Blessed is he that comes in the name of the Lord.'

So therefore is the Virgin blessed, but far more blessed is the fruit of her womb.

Glossary

ABELARD, PETER (c. 1079–c. 1142) The stormy petrel of the twelfth century, Peter was born at Le Pallet near Nantes of minor nobility. He was introduced to nominalism by its celebrated exponent Roscelin, went on to Paris where his arrogance and indocility led to his challenging his realist teacher William of Champeaux. After a distinguished career as a logician, Peter went on to study theology at Laon and again quarrelled with and challenged his professors. He was forty when the fateful affair with Heloise took place. *The Story of My Calamities* tells it all, but must be supplemented by the amazing letters Heloise wrote to her lover. His brief career as abbot of St Gildas in Brittany was troubled. He served briefly as master at Le Paraclet, where Heloise had become abbess. But his life was a wandering one and his theological writings earned him the enmity of the formidable Bernard of Clairvaux. Peter ended as a monk at Cluny.

ALBERT THE GREAT (c. 1200–1280) Born in Lauingen, Germany, died in Cologne, where he is buried. He was a Dominican, a bishop, patron of natural scientists, philosopher, and teacher of Thomas Aquinas. He has been canonized and named a Doctor of the Church. A dominant figure throughout the thirteenth century, he is known for his receptive attitude towards Aristotle, of whose works he wrote an extended Latin paraphrase.

ALBIGENSIANS Medieval heretics named after the town of Albi in Languedoc, a principal centre of the movement. They were also prominent in Toulouse. A species of the Cathar heresy, Albigensianism was at once an ascetic movement, for the élite, and permissive for everyone else, and this gave rise to a kind of sanctioned immorality. Dominic first encountered the heresy in the person of an innkeeper in Toulouse. After an all-night conversation, he brought the innkeeper back to orthodoxy. Countering this heresy was a spur to the Dominican Order at its outset.

AMBROSE, SAINT (c. 340–97) Born perhaps at Trier of an aristocratic and Christian Roman family. Educated at Rome, practised law, appointed governor of a northern province with headquarters at Milan around 370. Succeeded the Arian bishop of the city in 374, elected by acclamation. He was ordained and given a crash course in theology. As bishop he defended the faith against Arianism and the independence of the Church against the power of the emperor. The account that Augustine gives of Ambrose in the *Confessions* is the most widely known. Ambrose baptized Augustine in 387.

ANAXAGORAS (c. 500–428 BC) Pre-Socratic philosopher who first introduced mind as the chief explanation of natural occurrences. He came to Athens, was associated with Pericles and influenced Euripides. Later Aristotle described him as the one sober man in a party of drunks, because of the invocation of *nous* as a cause. In an apparent attempt to deny that change brought about real novelty, Anaxagoras held that there was an infinite amount of numberless kinds of things in each object. Thus any later state could be explained by the emergence of what was already there.

ANSELM OF CANTERBURY (1033–1109) Born in Aosta, Italy, Anselm died at Canterbury whose archbishop he had been since 1093. In 1060 he became a monk at Bec in Normandy, where he had gone to study with Lanfranc. He was elected prior in 1063 and abbot in 1078. His *Monologion* and *Proslogion* and a series of dialogues, *On the Grammarian*, *On Truth*, *On Free Will* and *The Sin of the Devil*, are the most impressive philosophical cum theological works of the early Middle Age. It is a shame that Anselm is known almost exclusively for the formulation of the argument for God's existence later dubbed the 'Ontological Argument'. Anselm succeeded Lanfranc at Canterbury.

ARISTOTLE (384–322 BC) Dante called him 'the master of those who know'. Cardinal Newman said that he 'has told us the meaning of our own words and ideas before we were born'. One of the two greatest philosophers of all time, Aristotle came from Macedonia to Athens, where he studied with Plato and nearly two decades later, after Plato's death, founded the Lyceum. His direct and indirect influence on western thought is incalculable. The editing of his works by Andronicus of Rhodes in the first century BC made possible the tradition of commentary in the Hellenistic period, the Middle Ages, the Renaissance, down to our own time. For the medievals Aristotle was simply the Philosopher.

ATHANASIUS (c. 300–373) Dominant theological figure of his time; the champion of orthodoxy during some forty-five years as bishop of Alexandria. He was the redoubtable foe of the Arian heresy, author of the *Contra Arianos*. His name will be linked for ever to the so-called Athanasian creed.

AUGUSTINE, SAINT (354–430) Born in Tagaste in what is now Algeria, he died as bishop of Hippo in the same province. Between those two events occurred the great drama of his conversion, narrated in the *Confessions*, and his voluminous writing on behalf of the faith and in opposition to heretical deviations such as Arianism and Pelagianism. The authority of Augustine exceeds that of any other Father, Greek or Latin, and he is claimed equally by Protestant and Catholic. The stamp of Augustine's influence is on every medieval master.

AVEMPACE (died in 1138) A Latinization of Ibn Bajja. Born in Saragossa at the end of the eleventh century, he died in Morocco, Andalusia having been reconquered by Christians. He wrote some commentaries on Aristotle and was learned in medicine, mathematics and astronomy. His reputation was largely based on *The Rule of the Solitary*.

AVERROES (c. 1126–c. 1198) A Latinization of Ibn-Rushd. The foremost figure in Islamic philosophy, he was known as the Commentator. Born in Cordoba, the details of his life are obscure. He flourished in Marrakesh and then in Seville; he died in Marrakesh. Averroes's interests were as wide as Aristotle's had been – he was physician, scientist, philosopher. He wrote a medical encyclopedia, commented on Greek medical writers and on Avicenna, but his great influence in Latin Europe was through his commentaries on Aristotle.

AVICEBRON (IBN-GABIROL, SOLOMON BEN JUDAH; c. 1021–58) Author of gloomy songs, he was reputed the greatest Jewish poet of his time. His philosophical work *The Fountain of Life* exercised the most influence on Latin thinkers.

AVICENNA (IBN SINA; 980–1037) Born in Persia, into a sect influenced by Neoplatonism, which he came to find unsatisfying. He seems to have been an autodidact and wrote in both Persian and Arabic. His greatest philosophical work is *The Healing*, of which *The Deliverance* is a digest.

BERNARD OF CLAIRVAUX (1090–1153) One of the most imposing church-men of the twelfth century. He founded the monastery at Clairvaux and served as its abbot. Great champion of Pope Innocent II, foe of Abelard and Gilbert de la Porre. His influence increased when his protégé became Pope Eugene II in 1145. He wrote *On Grace and Free Will, On Loving God, The Grades of Humility*. His sermons on the Song of Songs exhibit his Marian devotion. His writings provide an alternative to 'school' theology.

BOETHIUS (480–524) A member of an aristocratic Roman family, Boethius lived when Italy was under the rule of Theodoric the Ostrogoth. Perhaps educated in Alexandria, Boethius undertook the task of translating into Latin the whole of Aristotle and Plato. The few logical writings of Aristotle that were the fruit of this ambitious plan, along with Boethius's commentaries on them, and on works of Cicero, enjoyed great authority in later medieval education. His *Consolation of Philosophy*, written while he awaited execution in Pavia for what he insisted was a false charge of conspiring against Theodoric, was the most copied book after the Bible in the Middle Ages. His theological treatises – among them *On the Trinity, On the Hebdomads* – attracted commentators well into the thirteenth century.

BONAVENTURE (1217–74) Born near Viterbo, the foremost Franciscan theologian of the Middle Ages, he studied under Alexander of Hales in Paris, completing his studies at the same time as Thomas Aquinas. The secular masters unsuccessfully sought to prevent the two men from joining the professoriate in 1256. Bonaventure was elected master general of the Franciscan Order in 1257. As a result many of his writings are collections of sermons (though we have his earlier commentary on the *Sentences* of Peter Lombard as well as some *Disputed Questions*). Bonaventure became wary of the use some were making of Aristotle, and this affected the Franciscan appraisal of Thomas Aquinas. His *Breviloquium* and *Reduction of the Arts to Theology* convey the flavour of his thought. He arrived at the Council of Lyons, on the way to which Thomas had died, but died himself that same year, 1274.

CASSICIACUM The retreat outside Milan to which Augustine and his entourage repaired as he readied himself for baptism. It was during this period that *On the Teacher*, a dialogue with his natural son Adeodatus, was composed, as well as other short works illustrative of Augustine as professor of rhetoric.

CICERO, MARCUS TULLIUS (106–43 BC) Orator, politician, philosopher of an eclectic sort. He studied at Athens and came under many influences. His philosophical writings are largely moral, betraying Aristotelian, Platonic and Stoic influences. He opposed Epicureanism. He wrote a work *De republica* and, after the triumph of Julius Caesar, spent his last years in exile devoting himself to his philosophical writing. He wrote on law, good and evil, fate, social roles, the nature of the gods, on friendship and old age.

COMMENTATOR, THE (see Averroes)

CONDEMNATION OF 1270 Stephen Tempier, bishop of Paris, condemned thirteen propositions containing errors that exhibited the distorted influence of Aristotle. Among the condemned propositions: there is only one intellect shared by all men; man cannot be said to understand; the human will is not free; the world is eternal; God knows only himself.

CONDEMNATION OF 1277 The condemnation of 1270 having proved ineffective, the bishop of Paris at the urging of Pope John XXI, appointed a commission of theologians who drew up a list of 219 propositions which the bishop condemned on 7 March. These included the thirteen condemned in 1270. The list is particularly notable because it seems to include teachings of Thomas Aquinas, who had died in 1274. For example, that matter is the principle of individuation and that each angel constitutes a species.

DAMASCENE, ST JOHN (eighth century) His dates are unknown but he became a monk in the monastery of St Saba in Jerusalem after 730, was ordained priest and probably died there. He wrote *The Source of Knowledge*, the third part of which was called *De fide orthodoxa* by the Scholastics and exercised a great influence.

DANTE ALIGHIERI (1265–1321) Native of Florence, whose love for Beatrice defined his imaginative life, lived most of his life in exile after the Florentine embassy to the Holy See of which he was a member failed and his city was taken over by a rival faction. Dante had the knack of transposing misfortune into an eternal key. *La vita nuova* narrates the lasting impact on him of his love for Beatrice, and she continues to play a role in what is perhaps the greatest poem ever written, *The Divine Comedy*. Through Hell and Purgatory to Heaven is the itinerary of the poem, each of whose one hundred cantos is a work of perfection. The poem is set in the year 1300 and conveys the intellectual and spiritual culture of the Middle Ages.

DECRETALS (DECRETUM GRATIANI) A collection of papal rulings made by Gratian around 1140 under the title *Concordantia discordantium canonum*. In short it was an effort to introduce order and consistency into the decretals. From the twelfth century onward, the work was much commented on. It constitutes the first part of *Corpus iuris canonici*.

DIONYSIUS (PSEUDO-DIONYSIUS) Perhaps a fifth-century figure Peter the Iberian, he was the author of works that were long thought to be those of Dionysius the Areopagite, a convert of St Paul who became bishop of Athens. Translated by Erigena, these writings enjoyed quasi-apostolic authority and were commented on by Hugh of St Victor, Albert the Great, Thomas Aquinas and Bonaventure and greatly influenced mystical writers. The chief titles are *On the Names of God*, *On the Celestial Hierarchy*, *On the Ecclesiastical Hierarchy*, *On Mystical Theology*.

DISPUTED QUESTIONS The master of theology conducted public disputations on posted topics which often formed a connected suite of questions. A thesis was maintained against the background of objections to it so that an intellectual drama resulted. The master, confronted by these objections, first countered with an authoritative citation favouring his thesis and then defended it with arguments, after which he responded to each of the contrary positions. The written *Disputed Question* arose out of the public occasion and was available from the university stationer shortly after the disputation had taken place.

DOMINIC, SAINT (DOMINGO DE GUZMAN; 1170–1221) Founder of the Order of Preachers. He was born near Burgos in Spain and studied theology at Palencia. In 1199 he became a canon of the cathedral of Osma. It was while accompanying his bishop on a trip that Dominic became aware of the Albigensian heresy. In order to preach against the Albigensians, he thought poverty a necessity and thus the order he founded was a mendicant or begging one like the Franciscans. The founding of the order took place in Toulouse in 1215.

DOMINICANS The name for the Order of Preachers founded by St Dominic. The Latin word is *dominicanes*, which was sometimes broken into *domini canes*, dogs of the Lord.

FREDERICK II (1194–1250) Called *stupor mundi*, wonder of the world, Frederick served as Holy Roman emperor from 1212; he was king of Sicily (1197–1250) as well as of Jerusalem (1226–50). He was born in Sicily, the grandson of Frederick I, Barbarossa. Succeeding his father when he was but three, Frederick at first ruled under the guardianship of Innocent III and various counsellors. Educated at Palermo, he thought of himself as Italian despite belonging to the Hohenstaufen dynasty. He was a patron of learning. At first an ally of the Pope, he became independent and in defence of the papacy encouraged Guelph elements. The resulting political chaos obsessed Dante, who was a victim of it. Frederick was excommunicated a number of times. He is buried in the cathedral of Palermo.

GLOSSA ORDINARIA Product of the school of Anselm of Laon in the twelfth century, a compilation of the comments of the Fathers of the Church, which had been written in the margins of copies of the Bible. The concentration of masters at Paris led to standardization and a gloss on the whole Bible that became an obligatory reference work for scriptural study.

GREGORY THE GREAT, SAINT (540–604) The fourth and last Doctor of the Latin Church. Born to wealth and power in Rome, he forsook it all for the monastic life. By 570 he had founded monasteries in Sicily and Rome. At papal command, he left the monastery in 577 to become one of the seven deacons of Rome. He served as papal envoy to Constantinople. He was elected pope in 590 and founded a papal state the better to deal with the poverty and anarchy of the time. While recognizing civil authority, he insisted on the independence of the Church in spiritual matters as well as on the primacy of the Roman See. This insistence brought about a separation between Orthodox and Catholic bishops. He wrote on pastoral care, on the miracles and lives of the saints; his famous *Morals* is a commentary on the Book of Job. The Gregorian calendar, the Gregorian sacramentary and the Gregorian chant are among his legacies.

HEXAMERON The Work of the Six Days of Creation. Augustine's various commentaries on Genesis and his interpretation of the meaning of 'day' in the Scriptural account of creation had a great influence on medieval exegesis.

HILARY, SAINT (c. 315–66) Like Athanasius, an implacable foe of the Arian heresy. Bishop of Poitiers, where he was born and where he died. Friend of St Martin of Tours. Author of *On the Faith against the Arians*, also known as *On the Trinity*.

HUGH OF ST VICTOR (1096–1141) Born in Flanders, educated in Germany. In 1118 he joined the monastery of St Victor in Paris. Under his leadership, the School of St Victor flourished and exercised great influence. He classified knowledge in his *Didascalicon* and was a notable commentator on Scripture.

ISADORE OF SEVILLE (c. 560–636) Of noble family, he became a monk and acquired encyclopedic learning in order to defend the faith against the Arians. He became bishop of Seville in 600 and sought to convert the Jews of Spain. The most important and influential of his works is the so-called *Etymologies*, actually an encyclopedia.

JAEGER, WERNER Author of two seminal works, one on the evolution of Aristotle's *Metaphysics* (1912) and another applying a developmental interpretation to the whole of Aristotle (1921). This approach dissolved the treatises into fragments and called into question their literary wholeness. If true, this would make the history of Aristotelian interpretation by Hellenistic, Medieval and Renaissance commentators exercises in delusion.

JOACHIM OF FIORE (c. 1132–1202) Little is known of his origins. He became a Cistercian in 1177 and abbot of the monastery at Corazzo, a post from which he resigned to devote himself to writings of an apocalyptic bent. He divided history into three periods, the age of the Father (the Old Testament); the age of the Son (the New Testament), and the age of the Holy Spirit which would synthesize the first two. He thought the third would begin in 1260 and a new spiritual order would convert the whole world.

LATIN AVERROISM Also called Heterodox Aristotelianism. An enthusiastic acceptance of the Aristotle of Averroes and of tenets incompatible with Christianity. Siger of Brabant was its most notable exponent. It was opposed by Thomas Aquinas and Bonaventure and was subject to condemnation in 1270 and again in 1277. The best defence against it, Thomas Aquinas thought, was a more accurate reading of Aristotle and a saner conception of the relationship between faith and reason.

LEUCIPPUS Along with Democritus, a Greek atomist of the fifth century BC. The theory held that atoms – literally, indivisibles – of different shapes came together to make the macrocosmic bodies of our experience. The arrangements were by chance and all things thereby were the same so far as their elements went.

MAIMONIDES, MOSES (1135–1204) Jewish philosopher and physician. He was born in Cordoba and fled to Morocco when Jews were persecuted by the Almohades, a Muslim dynasty. He went on to Palestine and then Cairo. He first engaged in biblical exegesis and then wrote the *Guide for the Perplexed*, his major work. It was composed in Arabic and only later translated into Hebrew and Latin. The work made him the leading Jewish philosopher of the Middle Ages. He sought to achieve a synthesis of faith and reason; his efforts were condemned in the Jewish world and young men were forbidden to read his *Guide*.

MANICHEANS Followers of the third-century heretic Manes, who introduced into Christian belief the Persian notion that good and evil are coequal principles. His teaching was condemned but spread and was the target of refutations of Augustine.

MARITAIN, JACQUES (1882–1973) French philosopher, major interpreter of the thought of Thomas Aquinas. He converted to Catholicism in his twenties and became associated with *L'Action française*, a monarchist anti-democratic movement. When it was condemned by the Church, he accepted the verdict and then moved in a liberal direction, condemning the tendency of Catholics to champion the cause of Franco in Spain. He spent the years of the Second World War in the United States, where he had always enjoyed great popularity. He served as French ambassador to the Holy See in the post-war years and then took a post at Princeton. After the death of his beloved Raissa, he returned to France. He and his wife are buried at Kolbsheim in Alsace. His voluminous writings are appearing in a collected edition of twenty volumes from the University of Notre Dame Press.

MICHAEL SCOT (died 1235) Born in Scotland, educated in England, he went to Spain to study Arabic and became acquainted with Aristotelian treatises. He was one of the translators who made Greek learning available in Latin. He studied mathematics in Pisa, and became the court astrologer of Frederick II.

MONTE CASSINO Benedictine monastery south of Rome founded in 529 by St Benedict and built on the ruins of a Roman temple. It became the flagship of Benedictine monasticism. It was there that the Rule was composed. Its library contained classical manuscripts cared for and copied by the monks in an effort that provided a bridge between antiquity and later times. The monastery was rebuilt after World War II when the Allies demolished it in order to dislodge the German forces that were impeding their drive to Rome.

NEOPLATONISM In the third century, at Alexandria, Plato as interpreted by Hellenistic scholars was studied by such Fathers of the Church as Clement of Alexandria and Origen. The *Enneads* of Plotinus, which had been put together by his anti-Christian disciple Porphyry, exercised indirect influence on Augustine. The original aim of Neoplatonism was to show the underlying agreement between Plato and Aristotle, an aim that led to commentaries on writings of Aristotle. Pseudo-Dionysius, Boethius and the *Book of Causes* were the chief ways in which Neo-platonism entered the intellectual world of Thomas Aquinas.

NESTORIUS (d. 451) Heretic. He held that there were two separate persons in Christ. He was Patriarch of Constantinople, a post from which he was deposed by the Council of Ephesus in 431. The Nestorians persisted and enjoyed religious freedom under Muslim rule. The invasion of the Mongols in the thirteenth century dealt the sect a serious blow.

ORIGEN (185–253) Religious enthusiast who, in his youth, castrated himself when he read of those who have become 'eunuchs for the kingdom of heaven's sake'. He later recognized his exegetical error. He was a prolific writer, always controversial and died a martyr's death.

PARMENIDES Parmenides flourished in the second half of the fifth century BC. One of the great enigmatic figures of Greek philosophy, whose teaching proved to be a great obstacle to the natural science that had been engaged in up to his time. His work is contained in a poem, with a prologue and then two parts, one, the way of truth, and the other, the way of seeming. The truth is that being is one, unique, changeless, homogenous throughout. Plurality is as impossible as change. On the other hand, the world seems otherwise to us and the second part of the poem contains a cosmology like those that had preceded it. Parmenides introduces into philosophy the split between being and appearance and exercised a mesmerizing influence over Plato who devoted a dialogue to him. Aristotle in the *Physics* pointed out the fallaciousness of the central Parmenidian denial of plurality and change.

PETER OF IRELAND (*floruit* 1230–65) One of Thomas Aquinas's teachers at Naples when he went there from Monte Cassino in his late teens. We are told that Thomas studied grammar and logic with Master Martin and natural science with Master Peter of Ireland. But elsewhere Thomas is said to have studied logic and natural science with Peter.

PHILOSOPHER, THE (see ARISTOTLE)

PHOTINUS (810–95) Patriarch of Constantinople. Of noble birth, he entered the imperial service and was named patriarch by Emperor Michael III. He sought papal recognition of his appointment, which was not forthcoming. Instead, the Pope excommunicated Photinus and reinstated his predecessor Ignatius. Photinus protested the *filioque* clause in the Latin creed which states that the Holy Spirit proceeds from the Father *and from the Son*. A new emperor agreed that Ignatius was patriarch and sent Photinus to a monastery, but the *filioque* dispute led to the excommunication of Ignatius and Photinus was once more appointed patriarch by the emperor. This led to schism with Rome. Deposed by the emperor, Photinus ended his life in a monastery, but the schism persisted.

PLATO (427–347 BC) The most accessible of the great philosophers, whose version of Socrates in the dialogues has swamped any historical or rival literary presentation of the witty genius, who, with Plato and Aristotle, forms the most remarkable succession of philosophers in history. While some of Plato's dialogues represent very difficult philosophical literature, others still function as the best introduction to philosophy. In the Middle Ages, Plato was little more than a name and direct accessibility was limited to a partial translation of the *Timaeus*. Indirectly and via Neo-platonism, his influence was great.

PORPHYRY (233/4–305) Porphyry was born in Tyre, studied in Athens and came to Rome in 263 where he entered the school of Plotinus. He edited the works of the master, producing the elegantly arranged *Enneads*, as well as a life of Plotinus. He wrote against the Christians. A little work of his, *Introduction to the Categories of Aristotle*, or *Isagoge*, had a vast influence on the Middle Ages, thanks to Boethius's translation of it and his two commentaries on it in which the so-called Problem of Universals was stated and became a set problem for the logician.

PROCLUS (410–85) Born in Constantinople, Proclus began his studies in Alexandria but then went to Athens where he studied with Plutarch and Syrianus. He is credited with the scholastic systematization of Neoplatonism. He commented on dialogues of Plato and wrote the *Elements of Theology*, from which, as Aquinas discerned, the *Book of Causes* had been excerpted.

PSEUDO-DIONYSIUS see DIONYSIUS

PYTHAGORAS (570–490 BC) It is difficult to distinguish between what Pythagoras himself taught and the tenets of his highly influential school. The medievals knew him largely through Aristotle's presentation of him. His characteristic insight was that number provides a lens through which to read the world. Perhaps things in the world are just numbers.

QUODLIBETAL QUESTIONS A more free-wheeling event than the Disputed Questions, the Quodlibetal (what-you-will) Questions were held at Christmas and Easter and began early in the morning since they were likely to go on and on. Anything could be proposed to the master and he was expected to respond impromptu. The assistants of the master were involved in the response as well. At Paris, after only a few decades, the Quodlibetal Questions became an activity of neophytes rather than masters. While such occasions might hone dialectical skills and perhaps turn up a truth or two, they tended to become capricious and there was the temptation of winning an argument rather than finding out the truth.

REGINALD OF PIPERNO, O.P. One of the 'secretaries' assigned to Thomas Aquinas during his second Parisian regency. Thomas's own hand gave new meaning to the term 'cursive'. It has been dubbed the *litera inintelligibilis*, the unreadable hand. Thomas dictated a significant number of his later works, keeping two to three secretaries busy. Weisheipl says that Reginald was slightly younger than Thomas and served him from 1259 until Thomas's death.

RICHARD OF ST VICTOR (d. 1173) A member of the school of St Victor at Paris, he was a notable biblical exegete and author of a work on the Trinity.

SENTENCES The masterpiece of Peter Lombard (1100–1160), eventual bishop of Paris. A summary of Christian doctrine, the four books of the work treat of the Trinity, the Creation, Original Sin, Incarnation, the Virtues and the Sacraments. The *Sentences* beat several rivals to become the standard textbook of Catholic theology during the Middle Ages.

ST JACQUES, CONVENT OF In 1218, the first Dominicans in Paris were given a hospice with a chapel that had served as a staging point for pilgrims setting off for St James of Compostella. It came into the possession of the university, and was situated on the Left Bank, just above the present Sorbonne. It soon became the centre of Dominican intellectual history in Paris. It was here that Albert and Thomas lived and taught, and a host of great Dominican masters before and after them.

THEMISTIUS (c. 315–88) He wrote many paraphrases of, as well as commentaries on, Aristotle. He also commented on Plato. He was doubtful about Neoplatonism, which he considered to deviate from both Plato and Aristotle.

THEOPHRASTUS (c. 373–c. 287 BC) Studied at the Platonic Academy, and after the death of Plato followed Aristotle to the Lyceum, succeeding him as head of the school. His work on different characters is of great interest; he wrote a *Metaphysics* in which he appears to have rejected the Prime Mover as well as the universal teleology taught by Aristotle.

TRANSCENDENTALS Characteristics which are said to be 'convertible' with being, such as unity, goodness, truth. This means that whatever is is true, is one, is good. The categories – substance and the accidents – are only disjunctively convertible with being. That is, whatever is is either substance or accident. Thomas suggested beauty as another transcendental property of being.

WILLIAM OF ST AMOUR A secular master at the University of Paris who was adamantly opposed to mendicants holding chairs in the faculties. Roger Bacon thought the mendicants were a reproach to the seculars, and that this explained their animosity. Whatever the cause, it was not a fleeting thing. Thomas Aquinas wrote several polemical pieces during his first Parisian regency to counter the accusations of the foes of the Franciscans and Dominicans.

THE STORY OF PENGUIN CLASSICS

Before 1946 ...'Classics' are mainly the domain of academics and students, without readable editions for everyone else. This all changes when a little-known classicist, E. V. Rieu, presents Penguin founder Allen Lane with the translation of Homer's *Odyssey* that he has been working on and reading to his wife Nelly in his spare time.

1946 *The Odyssey* becomes the first Penguin Classic published, and promptly sells three million copies. Suddenly, classic books are no longer for the privileged few.

1950s Rieu, now series editor, turns to professional writers for the best modern, readable translations, including Dorothy L. Sayers's *Inferno* and Robert Graves's *The Twelve Caesars*, which revives the salacious original.

1960s The Classics are given the distinctive black jackets that have remained a constant throughout the series's various looks. Rieu retires in 1964, hailing the Penguin Classics list as 'the greatest educative force of the 20th century'.

1970s A new generation of translators arrives to swell the Penguin Classics ranks, and the list grows to encompass more philosophy, religion, science, history and politics.

1980s The Penguin American Library joins the Classics stable, with titles such as *The Last of the Mohicans* safeguarded. Penguin Classics now offers the most comprehensive library of world literature available.

1990s The launch of Penguin Audiobooks brings the classics to a listening audience for the first time, and in 1999 the launch of the Penguin Classics website takes them online to a larger global readership than ever before.

The 21st Century Penguin Classics are rejacketed for the first time in nearly twenty years. This world famous series now consists of more than 1300 titles, making the widest range of the best books ever written available to millions – and constantly redefining the meaning of what makes a 'classic'.

The Odyssey continues ...

The best books ever written

PENGUIN 🐧 CLASSICS

SINCE 1946